RESOURCE METHODS FOR MANAGING K–12 INSTRUCTION

A Case Study Approach

RICHARD T. SCARPACI

St. John's University

Boston • New York • San Francisco
Mexico City • Montreal • Toronto • London • Madrid • Munich • Paris
Hong Kong • Singapore • Tokyo • Cape Town • Sydney

Acquisitions Editor: *Kelly Villella*
Series Editorial Assistant: *Annalea Manalili*
Marketing Manager: *Darcy Betts Prybella*
Production Editor: *Annette Joseph*
Editorial Production Service: *Publishers' Design and Production Services, Inc.*
Composition Buyer: *Linda Cox*
Manufacturing Buyer: *Megan Cochran*
Electronic Composition: *Publishers' Design and Production Services, Inc.*
Interior Design: *Publishers' Design and Production Services, Inc.*
Cover Administrator: *Elena Sidorova*

For related titles and support materials, visit our online catalog at www.pearsonhighered.com.

Copyright © 2009 Pearson Education, Inc.

All rights reserved. No part of the material protected by this copyright notice may be reproduced or utilized in any form or by any means, electronic or mechanical, including photocopying, recording, or by any information storage and retrieval system, without written permission from the copyright owner.

To obtain permission(s) to use material from this work, please submit a written request to Allyn and Bacon, Permissions Department, 501 Boylston Street, Suite 900, Boston, MA 02116 or fax your request to 617-671-2290.

Between the time website information is gathered and then published, it is not unusual for some sites to have closed. Also, the transcription of URLs can result in typographical errors. The publisher would appreciate notification where these errors occur

Library of Congress Cataloging-in-Publication Data

Scarpaci, Richard T.
   Resource methods for managing K-12 instruction : a case study approach / Richard T. Scarpaci.
    p. cm.
   Includes bibliographical references and index.
   ISBN-13: 978-0-205-52218-7 (alk. paper)
   ISBN-10: 0-205-52218-1 (alk. paper)
   1. Effective teaching—Case studies. 2. Learning—Case studies. I. Title.
LB1025.3.S295 2009
371.102—dc22
                                                                      2008018459

Printed in the United States of America

10 9 8 7 6 5 4 3 2 1 BR 12 11 10 09 08

Allyn & Bacon
is an imprint of

www.pearsonhighered.com

ISBN-10: 0-205-52218-1
ISBN-13: 978-0-205-52218-7

BRIEF CONTENTS

1 Keys to Effective Teaching   1

2 Understanding How We Learn   21

3 Planning to Learn   47

4 Methods for the Mainstream   71

5 Methods for the Special Learner   97

6 Planning for Classroom Management   119

7 Teaching for Literacy   147

8 Thinking for Understanding   171

9 The Standards' Impact   191

10 Assessment Practices for Achievement   213

11 Becoming an Effective Teacher   233

CONTENTS

Preface   *xi*

Case Studies Cast of Characters   *xiv*

1   Keys to Effective Teaching   1

FOCUS POINTS   1

CHAPTER OVERVIEW   1

KEYS TO EFFECTIVE TEACHING   2
- The Learning Paradigm   2
- Effective Teaching   4
- Mini Case from the Field: Core Characteristics for Effective Teaching   6

APPROACHES TO EFFECTIVE TEACHING   8
- Expository Approach   8
- Discovery Approach   8
- Inquiry Approach   9
- Discussion Approach   10

INSTRUCTIONAL PRACTICES FOR EFFECTIVE TEACHING   10
- Direct and Indirect Instructional Practices   10

DIRECT TEACHING   12
- Lecture   12
- Lecture and Discussion   12
- Discussion   12
- Small-Group Discussion   13
- Guest Speakers   13

INDIRECT TEACHING   13
- Cooperative Learning   13
- Group Brainstorming   14
- Multimedia and Technology   14
- Case Studies   14
- Role Playing   14
- Research Surveys   15
- Values and Character Education   15
- Mini Case from the Field: Basic Methods of Instruction for the Effective Teacher   15

CHAPTER SUMMARY   17

CASES FROM THE FIELD   17

TERMS TO REMEMBER   19

DISCUSSION QUESTIONS   19

FIELD EXPERIENCE ACTIVITIES   19

FOR FURTHER READING   19

2   Understanding How We Learn   21

FOCUS POINTS   21

CHAPTER OVERVIEW   21

APPROACHES TO LEARNING   22
- Behaviorist Approach to Learning   22
- Constructivist Approach to Learning   25
- An Eclectic Approach to Learning   29
- Mini Case from the Field: Understanding How Students Learn   30

ALTERNATIVE APPROACHES TO UNDERSTANDING   31
- Maslow's Hierarchy of Needs   31
- Kohlberg's Theory of Moral Development   31
- Erikson's Stages of Psychosocial Development   32

THE BRAIN AND LEARNING 33
   Triune Brain Theory 33
   Theories and Practices 35
   Contradictory Views on Brain Theory 35

INTELLIGENCE AND LEARNING 37
   Theory of Multiple Intelligences 38
   Contrasting Models of Intelligence 39
   Implications for Classroom Instruction 41
   Mini Case from the Field: Are Brain and Intelligence Theories Relevant? 42

CHAPTER SUMMARY 42
CASES FROM THE FIELD 43
TERMS TO REMEMBER 43
DISCUSSION QUESTIONS 44
FIELD EXPERIENCE ACTIVITIES 44
FOR FURTHER READING 44

3 *Planning to Learn* 47

FOCUS POINTS 47
CHAPTER OVERVIEW 47
CURRICULUM 48
   Decision Making 49
   Topic Aims, Goals, and Objectives Defined 49
   Objectives in Planning 51

WRITING A LESSON PLAN 51
   AMCASH 52
   Lesson Presentation Skills 53
   Lesson Design 53
   Mini Case from the Field: Why Write a Lesson Plan? 59
   Lesson Plan Variety 61
   Reflective Lesson Planning 61

SUPERVISORS AND TEACHER OBSERVATION 64
   Supervisor's Observation Forms 65
   Mini Case from the Field: The Formal Lesson Observation 66

CHAPTER SUMMARY 67
CASES FROM THE FIELD 67
TERMS TO REMEMBER 68
DISCUSSION QUESTIONS 68
FIELD EXPERIENCE ACTIVITIES 69

4 *Methods for the Mainstream* 71

FOCUS POINTS 71
CHAPTER OVERVIEW 71
METHODS FOR LEARNING 72
   Discovery Learning 72
   Guided Discovery Learning 72
   Mastery Learning 73
   Bloom's Taxonomy of Educational Objectives 73
   Questioning for Learning 75
   Mini Case from the Field: Methodology Counts 76
   Grouping for Instruction 77
   Cooperative Learning 79
   Multiple Intelligences Approach to Learning 81
   Differentiated Instruction 81
   School Enrichment Model 86
   Outcome-Based Education 86
   Montessori Method 88
   Paideia Program 90
   Waldorf School Method 90
   Mini Case from the Field: Are All Approaches to Learning the Same? 92

CHAPTER SUMMARY 93
CASES FROM THE FIELD 94
TERMS TO REMEMBER 95
DISCUSSION QUESTIONS 95
FIELD EXPERIENCE ACTIVITIES 95
FOR FURTHER READING 95

5 *Methods for the Special Learner* 97

FOCUS POINTS 97
CHAPTER OVERVIEW 97
BRIEF HISTORY OF SPECIAL EDUCATION 98
   The Special Education Referral Process 98

INDIVIDUALS WITH DISABILITIES IN EDUCATION ACT (IDEA) 100
   Principles of IDEA 100

Strategy for IDEA 100
Key Sections of the IDEA 100
INCLUSION 101
Research on Inclusion 102
Strategies for Inclusion 102
Mini Case from the Field: A Problem of Inclusion in a Multicultural Classroom 104
LEARNING DISABILITIES 105
Definitions of a Learning Disability 106
How to Teach Children with Learning Disabilities 107
Emotional Conflict of the Special LD Child 108
Mini Case from the Field: How Do I Teach an LD Child? 108
ATTENTION DEFICIT DISORDER AND ATTENTION DEFICIT HYPERACTIVITY DISORDER 109
Defining ADD 109
Feelings of a Child with ADD 110
Defining ADHD 110
Alternative Strategies for ADD/ADHD 110
Dyslexia 112
Mini Case from the Field: Teaching the Special Child in a Mainstream Class 113
CHAPTER SUMMARY 115
CASES FROM THE FIELD 115
TERMS TO REMEMBER 116
DISCUSSION QUESTIONS 116
FIELD EXPERIENCE ACTIVITIES 116
FOR FURTHER READING 117

6 *Planning for Classroom Management* 119

FOCUS POINTS 119
CHAPTER OVERVIEW 119
CREATING A MANAGEMENT STRATEGY 120
The Basics of Behavior 122
Types and Causes of Misbehavior 122
Analyzing Behavioral Problems: An Overview of the IOSIE Method 122

Sample Case Studies and IOSIE Analysis 124
Twelve Beliefs That Lead to Effective Management Strategies 127
MANAGEMENT STRATEGIES THAT FACILITATE INSTRUCTION 129
Mini Case from the Field: Cheating 129
MANAGEMENT MODELS 130
Consequence Models 130
Group Guidance Control Models 134
Guidance Models 136
MANAGING STUDENTS WITH EMOTIONAL PROBLEMS AND PREVENTING BULLYING 140
Early Warning Signs 140
Strategies for Overcoming Emotional Problems 140
CHAPTER SUMMARY 145
CASES FROM THE FIELD 145
TERMS TO REMEMBER 146
DISCUSSION QUESTIONS 146
FIELD EXPERIENCE ACTIVITIES 146
FOR FURTHER READING 146

7 *Teaching for Literacy* 147

FOCUS POINTS 147
CHAPTER OVERVIEW 147
TO TEACH FOR LITERACY 148
Fluency, Vocabulary, and Domain Knowledge 149
RESEARCH-BASED FINDINGS 149
APPROACHES TO TEACHING FOR LITERACY 152
Traditional Approaches 152
Phonics Approach 154
Whole Language Approach 156
Literacy and Gender: Gender-Specific Teaching 160
Mini Case from the Field: Why Are Boys Failing? 163
PROGRAMS TO IMPROVE LITERACY 165
Mini Case from the Field: What Exactly Does Teaching for Literacy Mean? 167

CHAPTER SUMMARY   168
CASES FROM THE FIELD   168
TERMS TO REMEMBER   169
DISCUSSION QUESTIONS   169
FIELD EXPERIENCE ACTIVITIES   170
FOR FURTHER READING   170

8 Thinking for Understanding   171

FOCUS POINTS   171
CHAPTER OVERVIEW   171
CRITICAL THINKING   172
- Definitions   172
- Literate Critical Thinking   172
- Thinking for Literacy   173
- Mini Case from the Field: A Critical Thinking Program   175

THINKING STRATEGIES FOR UNDERSTANDING   175
- IOSIE Method   175
- Functional Behavioral Assessment   176
- Reasoning Strategies   176

CRITICAL THINKING AND PHILOSOPHY   179
- Mini Case from the Field: Combining an Ethical Philosophy with Critical Thinking   179
- Developing a Critical Thinking Educational Philosophy   181
- Philosophies of Education   181
- Mini Case from the Field: The Effect of Critical Thinking on Student Learning   184

CHAPTER SUMMARY   187
CASES FROM THE FIELD   187
TERMS TO REMEMBER   188
DISCUSSION QUESTIONS   189
FIELD EXPERIENCE ACTIVITIES   189
FOR FURTHER READING   189

9 The Standards' Impact   191

FOCUS POINTS   191

CHAPTER OVERVIEW   191
STANDARDS AND ASSESSMENT   192
- History of Performance Standards and Assessment   192
- Standards in Traditional and Progressive Schools   193

DEFINING STANDARDS   194
- Goals 2000   194
- Compact for Learning   195
- *Curriculum Frameworks*   196
- Standards and Daily Practice   196

NATIONAL STANDARDS FOR TEACHERS   198
- Mini Case from the Field: Are Standards Good for Education?   200

STUDENT PERFORMANCE STANDARDS   204
- New Standards and National Performance Standards   204

STANDARDS-BASED LESSON PLANNING   204
- The Standards Achievement Planning Cycle   205
- Skills for Effective Lessons   207
- Best Practices for Planning   207
- Mini Case from the Field: When Can We Consider Standards High Enough?   208

CHAPTER SUMMARY   210
CASES FROM THE FIELD   210
TERMS TO REMEMBER   211
DISCUSSION QUESTIONS   212
FIELD EXPERIENCE ACTIVITIES   212
FOR FURTHER READING   212

10 Assessment Practices for Achievement   213

FOCUS POINTS   213
CHAPTER OVERVIEW   213
BRIEF HISTORY OF ASSESSMENT IN AMERICA   214
- The Backward Design Process   215

BASIC ASSESSMENT PRACTICES   217
- Understanding Assessment   217
- Improving Assessment   217

TESTING PRACTICES 218
- Forms of Testing: Subjective, Objective, and Authentic 218
- Short-Answer Test Constructions 219
- Mini Case from the Field: Design and Assessment 223

REFLECTING ON EFFECTIVENESS 225
- Reflection and Self-Evaluation 226
- Reasons for Reflection 226
- Reflecting on Effective Instruction 226
- Reflecting on Effective Management 227
- Mini Case from the Field: Aligning Assessments to Standards 228

CHAPTER SUMMARY 229
CASES FROM THE FIELD 229
TERMS TO REMEMBER 230
DISCUSSION QUESTIONS 230
FIELD EXPERIENCE ACTIVITIES 230
FOR FURTHER READING 231

11 Becoming an Effective Teacher 233

FOCUS POINTS 233
CHAPTER OVERVIEW 233

BECOMING A VALIDATED CHANGE AGENT 234
- Mini Case from the Field: Systemic or Individual Change: A New Look at an Old Alternative, K–8 235
- Problems with School Change 236

TEACHER EMPOWERMENT MODEL 238
- Studies of Teacher Empowerment Leading to Student Improvement 240
- Improving Classroom Performance through Action Research: A Strategy for Instructional Improvement 242
- Mini Case from the Field: The Proposal: An Action Research Model to Save Effective Teachers 243

BECOMING AND EFFECTIVE TEACHER 245
- Behaviors of Effective Teachers 245
- Assessing Teacher Competence 246
- Characteristics of the Professional Educator 246
- Design Principles for Professional Development 247
- Professional Development Models 248
- Mini Case from the Field: A Professional Student Teaching Model 249

PREPARATION FOR A JOB INTERVIEW 250
- Typical Interview Format 250
- Preparation Guide 251
- Common Questions 251
- Interview Assessment 253

CHAPTER SUMMARY 253
CASES FROM THE FIELD 254
TERMS TO REMEMBER 255
DISCUSSION QUESTIONS 255
FIELD EXPERIENCE ACTIVITIES 255
FOR FURTHER READING 255

Glossary 256

References 259

Index 268

PREFACE

This book was written because there is a need for a text that is both practical and theoretical, a text whose level of presentation is such that it appeals to the student of education as well as the practitioner. The text strives to define what makes for effective teaching. Effective teaching is an art that can be learned. It consists of being able to ask the right question, in the right way, at the right time. An artist has a vision to share with others. To do this he must choose the right brush, color, and stroke. For a teacher, the vision lies in the personality of the individual. The type of teacher we become, and the methods we use as our brushstrokes, may be as individual as our personalities. We can recognize the work of a particular artist instantly by his style, because it expresses inner self; the same holds true for a master teacher.

The text provides a primer for the student of education that undergraduates, graduates, and career changers can use to make the transition from students to effective teachers. Both the preservice as well as the practicing teacher can use this text by adapting the methods presented to their unique personalities. Its scope is broad and addresses the practical and theoretical knowledge that educators need to know:

1. The keys to effective teaching and the ways we learn
2. How a lesson plan is written
3. Various instructional methods for both the mainstream and special learner in the mainstream, and thinking for understanding
4. Classroom management
5. Teaching for literacy
6. Assessment and the impact of the standards movement
7. Becoming an effective teacher

The text is organized around the five keys to effective teaching: *management, mastery, method, expectation, and personality.* Each key is considered holistically as a component for effective teaching with the prime component being the "teaching personality," which is the unifying thread that weaves its way throughout the book. ***Teaching personality*** is the combination of one's character, values, and thinking skills. ***Expectations*** are seen in the form of our understanding of learning, and the keys we expect to use to achieve our goals. ***Methods*** are clearly expressed through our discussion of the approaches to learning for mainstream and special students and the use of lesson planning and literacy strategies. ***Mastery*** is viewed as multifaceted focusing on standards, assessment, and becoming an effective teacher. ***Management*** is considered essential for all effective teaching. The teacher's role is discussed as a manager and purveyor of procedures.

The text explores the traditional instructional paradigms of knowledge transmission, with the learning paradigm, concluding that the learner, because of the instructor's effective teaching personality, constructs knowledge. Without this step, there would never be effective teaching. This effective teaching personality stems from the emotional commitment one has toward teaching, and it accounts for the enthusiasm that engages students in the learning process.

KEYS TO EFFECTIVE TEACHING: METHODS, MANAGEMENT, MASTERY, EXPECTATIONS, AND PERSONALITY

Chapter Content

1. Keys to Effective Teaching
2. Understanding How We Learn
3. Planning to Learn
4. Methods for the Mainstream
5. Methods for the Special Learner
6. Planning for Classroom Management
7. Teaching for Literacy
8. Thinking for Understanding
9. The Standards' Impact
10. Assessment Practices for Achievement
11. Becoming an Effective Teacher

The content and organization of this book benefits the student in that it presents materials in a clear, factual, and concrete manner. The interpretation of the theories and facts is left up to the reader to synthesize. The reader is encouraged to evaluate and put into practice the theories presented. This supports a basic theme of the text that it is not what is taught that matters, but what is learned.

UNIQUE FEATURES

The text is practical and easy to follow. The organization follows a logical sequence of general topics for both practicing and novice educators. All materials have been class tested and presented in a clear and concise fashion. Chapters begin with focus points and easy to read overviews that provide direction for student thought and reflection and conclude with summaries that emphasize essential concepts. **Mini Cases from the Field, Terms to Remember, Discussion Questions, and Field Experience Activities** assist students in reviewing the key thoughts contained in chapters.

The **Case Studies** are unique in that we follow a cast of characters, each with individual teaching personalities, who interact throughout all of the major case studies.

The difference between just teaching and effective teaching are discussed throughout. The text draws upon a growing body of literature that demonstrates teachers do make a difference in the achievement of students. An operational plan for success in the classroom evolves from understanding that teaching process when combined with effective methods leads to learning. Learning is self-actualization achieved by mastering tools and strategies necessary to construct meaning and produce appropriate end-products. The goal of teaching is to facilitate in the development of a child's ability to become an independent learner.

SPECIAL FEATURES OF THIS TEXT

Chapter 1. Keys to Effective Teaching. This chapter explores the keys and approaches to effective teaching in depth. The importance of teaching personality to effective teaching is seen as an essential element for success. The learning paradigm is spoken of to comprehend the difference between instruction and learning. Explored are effective behaviors and creating smart classrooms where they can be employed. Vignettes of instructional methods are provided to assist the reader in understanding direct and indirect approaches to learning. Two mini case studies are presented to help students learn the keys and basic instructional methods. The case study characters will have a continuing dialogue throughout the text.

Chapter 2. Understanding How We Learn. In this chapter, we attempt to understand how we learn. We look at and explain two basic approaches to learning—behaviorist and constructivist. We briefly explore major theories of human development, expounded by Freud, Erikson, Vygotsky, and Piaget. We question the role the brain plays in the learning process. We describe the difference between instruction and learning, while exploring the various concepts of intelligence.

Chapter 3. Planning to Learn. The chapter is devoted to understanding how to write effective lesson plans. Planning is seen as an integral part of the teaching process. Preparation is discussed in relation to curriculum and decision-making models. A simple procedure for the beginning teacher is discussed as it contrasts the various traditional planning approaches. An attempt is made to answer basic questions such as Why should I plan lessons? and How can direct and indirect instruction be used effectively? to Why must an effective teacher have command of the curriculum? The role of the supervisor in planning and preparing is also discussed.

Chapter 4. Methods for the Mainstream. In this chapter, we discuss various approaches and instructional methods necessary for the effective teacher. Classic approaches to learning are discussed along with specific methods that can bring these approaches to life within the classroom. Mastery learning, grouping for instruction, cooperative learning, and multiple intelligences approach to outcome-based education are reviewed with an eye to implementation in the classroom. Examples of each are provided through case studies for practice and understanding.

Chapter 5. Methods for the Special Learner. This chapter is concerned with the special learner and placement in mainstream situations. We explain what special education is and is not. The Individuals with Disabilities in Education Act is discussed as well as topics that the classroom teacher will face: inclusion, dealing with learning disabilities, attention deficit disorder, hyperactivity, and dyslexia. Much of the material can be used as a ready reference for the teacher.

Chapter 6. Planning for Classroom Management. This chapter assists students in developing an approach to classroom management, while providing an overview of specific strategies. Students are encouraged to understand the goal of discipline, and the differences among procedures, consequences, and punishments as well as the types, categories, and causes of misbehavior as they relate to performance. A method for analyzing student behavioral problems, termed IOSIE, is used to resolve sample management problems through case analysis. Misconduct is explored from the perspective of three basic management tools: consequence, group guidance, and individual guidance approaches. Specific strategies—Assertive Discipline, Judicial Discipline, and Choice Theory and Reality Therapy—are presented as examples for each approach. The chapter ends with a discussion about discipline and the effective teaching personality.

Chapter 7. Teaching for Literacy. In this chapter, we review the basic approaches to reading instruction by comparing phonics and whole language. We explain that there are many ways to teach reading but not all of them are right for everyone. What is a good technique for one student may represent a serious problem for another. We explore sight and phonetic approaches to reading, while discussing the need for a balanced literacy program. Six specific classroom-reading programs are reviewed as well as a concise chart describing contrasting models for literacy.

Chapter 8. Thinking for Understanding. This chapter explores skills for critical thinking as keys for understanding and learning. Skills such as raising questions about content, and gathering data for analysis and conclusions are explained. Discussed also is how to adapt the view of the discipline being studied, in order to communicate that view and relate what has been learned to real life. Examples are given throughout the chapter. Classical philosophies and educational philosophies are reviewed to assist in the development of a personal philosophy of education for the student. The Pantheon Program, which is an original model for classroom educational change that emphasizes critical-thinking strategies, is looked at. The chapter concludes by stating that the purpose of effective teaching is to assist students as independent learners in constructing knowledge related to their lives.

Chapter 9. The Standards' Impact. This chapter explores the meaning and impact that the standards movement will have on student achievement for the immediate future. Standards are viewed from the perspective of the teacher's role, lesson planning, and assessments. Examples are reviewed and compared with emphasis on possible positive and negative outcomes.

Chapter 10. Assessment Practices for Achievement. Classic evaluation and assessment strategies are explained. The argument is made that an effective teacher not only assesses students but also their own effectiveness. Students come to understand that what is considered an appropriate measurement in one situation is not necessarily so in another. The chapter attempts to provide answers for (1) how to evaluate student performance, (2) how to assess your own performance, and (3) the assessment tools available.

Chapter 11. Becoming an Effective Teacher. The final chapter discusses what it means to choose teaching as a life's vocation. It proposes the hypothesis that learning outcomes can be improved because of teacher empowerment and professional development. The cases are presented in brief to support this argument. The chapter reviews the keys to effective teaching, stressing the importance of the individual teacher in student learning. The text concludes with the final step—preparing for a job interview.

The text's purpose is to facilitate the development of methods and practices that will enable preservice and novice teachers becoming effective educators. There are no simple answers to the complex problems facing schools and teachers today. Only quick-fix solutions are being offered, which could never replace the effective teacher. Conservatives equate solutions with the marketplace and accountability, teachers with higher pay, and parents with more control over school policies. There has been a plethora of methods and solutions, each claiming to offer salvation. Charter schools, vouchers, smaller classes, school-based management, whole language, phonics, and higher standards are but a few of the solutions being offered. The key is not to rely on any one solution but to use each as a method for a specific problem at a particular time and place. In short, be eclectic in the use of cure-alls for educational problems in school and in individual classes. This is one of the primary messages contained in this book. There is no one answer to all problems.

The text concludes with what it means to choose teaching as a life's vocation. It explores the responsibility one accepts if one embraces the belief that student achievement is directly related to teacher empowerment and professional development. Cases are presented in brief to support this argument. Two models are offered to demonstrate how a teacher can improve student achievement. The first model focuses on the practices necessary to support curriculum innovations, necessary methods, and retrieval of information and learning products. The second model presents a case for the improvement of learning because of teacher empowerment. The models are based on research that claims that structural classroom change requires classroom cultural change. Rules, roles, and relationships, as well as students, values, and knowledge, must be viewed as a part of a classroom culture, a culture in which all understand the interplay of the prevailing factors necessary for academic success. To create an environment for academic and social success you need personal integrity, an articulated vision, and the ability to inspire children and parents to share that vision. *To expect teachers to educate is to expect what is reasonable.*

ACKNOWLEDGMENTS

My first and most important acknowledgment is to my friend, partner, and wife Lucille Scarpaci. Without a happy home, nothing creative is possible for me. My wife's strength and joy in life makes her the love of my life. Without her help and understanding, this text might never have been completed.

I would like to thank the reviewers for their helpful feedback and suggestions: Deborah Childs, University of Missouri, St. Louis; Emily Lin, University of Nevada, Las Vegas; Joan Pedro, University of Hartford; Jared Stallones, Cal Poly Pomona; and Leslie Zorko, University of Wyoming, Laramie.

Finally, I would like to acknowledge the support staff at Allyn and Bacon who worked with me in shaping the content and structure of this book. I am truly grateful for all their help and support. My editor, Kelly Villella; editorial assistant, Annalea Manalili; marketing manager, Darcy Betts Prybella; production editor, Annette Joseph; composition buyer, Linda Cox; manufacturing buyer, Megan Cochran; cover administrator, Elena Sidorova, all contributed in the development of this text. I extend my sincere appreciation for all the suggestions and encouragement in the production of this book. I especially thank Denise Botelho who through her understanding and fine work made this project a resounding success.

CASE STUDIES
CAST OF CHARACTERS

Margaret Gomez, a novice middle school social studies teacher, is bubbly, bright, and articulate, with a smile that suggests warmth and caring; this assignment is her first teaching job. She was an excellent student in college and quite well liked. Her only apparent drawback is that she has a stubborn streak and at times seems very authoritarian. Her only prior experience was student teaching.

Chandler Thompson is a veteran principal of ten years at McGraw Simpson Elementary and Senior High School. He had made mistakes; as a principal one of his major flaws was that he valued loyalty over experience and competence. He was a small man, just over five foot six, who had learned long ago how to carry himself like a big man.

He is very knowledgeable and dedicated to making his school one of the best in the nation. Unfortunately, he sometimes has difficulty communicating with his staff, which causes a great deal of anxiety among the faculty.

Jane Hemmings is a middle school language arts teacher with five years of experience who has taken Margaret under her wing, acting as both mentor and friend inside and outside of school. Jane is a very competent young woman who knows what she wants and, usually, how to get it. She is very eclectic and appears to have a great deal of wisdom well beyond her years, which she is not shy to expound.

Ed Child teaches mathematics at the high school level with two years' experience. He is a career changer who decided to become a teacher to help students have a better life. His physical presence at times can be overwhelming because he is six foot six and weighs well over 250 pounds. He appears at first sight slovenly, lazy, and bull headed. In actuality, he is quite bright and has a great deal of professional experience that he has acquired outside of school.

Lucille Chan is a veteran childhood teacher of a self-contained fourth-grade class. She has multiple licenses and is both academic and practical. She can be overbearing at times, especially if she believes she is on the right side of a discussion. Her colleagues, though much younger, look to her as a stabilizing influence and as someone they can always go to for help.

Nicholas Saccone is a young man with great potential. Various colleagues, because of his street-smart aggressive attitude that appears in stressful situations, have described him as a diamond in the rough. He is in a unique position being both a high school science teacher and director of the science cluster in the elementary school. He is state qualified in both with a master's degree in biology.

Dr. James Conley is the superintendent of the school district in which the McGraw K–12 Comprehensive School is located. He is an intelligent man who envisions himself as an outstanding educational leader. He is concerned with the loss of teachers occurring in the district.

CHAPTER 1

Keys to Effective Teaching

FOCUS POINTS

1. The "Keys to Effective Teaching" allow access to student learning.
2. Effective teachers share core characteristics.
3. Direct and indirect approaches to instruction are the basic methods used for all instructional strategies.

CHAPTER OVERVIEW

THIS CHAPTER RAISES TWO BASIC QUESTIONS: What are the keys to effective teaching? and What approaches does one need to know in order to implement the keys? The five keys to effective teaching form the model around which the text is organized: management, mastery, methods, expectations, and personality. The keys provide the foundation for effective teaching by encouraging the use of appropriate instructional strategies. An emphasis on learning rather than instruction determines the types of strategies one uses. A paradigm that focuses on student learning rather than teacher instruction is a primary goal for effective teaching. What students learn is much more important than what we teach. A true measure of teacher success is student learning.

To engage student learning we must direct our thinking toward the purpose of instruction. Both mastery and method are essential in assessing teachers' worth. An essential element necessary for success in teaching is one's personality. Mastery of knowledge and understanding of pedagogical methodology does not exist apart from one's character. Personality is the ecology, the milieu, the setting for all one's actions. It is a clear determinant to future success in the classroom. A teacher without an effective teaching personality will not be successful.

There are many types of teaching personalities, from lenient to strict. The funny teacher, the friendly, and the perfectionist are some of the names given to the various teacher personality types. All the classifications are based on typical personality traits. Psychologists have found five broad personality traits through empirical research: neuroticism (a negative emotional state), extraversion (being an extrovert), agreeableness, conscientiousness, and openness. These factors are similar to those found in the Five Factor model: surgency (extraversion), agreeableness, dependability, emotional stability, and culture. Each factor consists of a number of more specific traits (Goldberg, 1993; Costa and McCrae, 1992).

Effective teachers come in many shapes, sizes, and temperaments. Their effectiveness arises from their individual personalities and thinking, the beliefs they have about teaching and learning, how they conceptualize their work, and the ways in which they interact with students. Teachers' personal beliefs and values provide the unconscious foundation for their behavior. Because teachers' mental models are highly individualistic, no two classrooms are, or can be, the same. The tremendous power of teachers' personalities to create both effective and ineffective teaching environments has been largely unexamined (Yero, 2002).

This chapter introduces the keys to effective teaching and discusses the methods and approaches necessary to implement them.

KEYS TO EFFECTIVE TEACHING

The five keys to effective teaching are the foundation upon which can be built the edifice that we call an accomplished teacher. Look at the keys for what they really are—a description of the skills that make up a capable teacher. Management, mastery, methods, expectations, and personality are the gears that turn the wheel for an effective teacher. Teachers adapt each key to their own unique personality type. As a key unlocks a door, the mechanism found in understanding opens the path to efficiency in teaching.

1. Ability to *manage* both instruction and behavior effectively
2. *Mastery* and proficiency in content area and presentation skills
3. Ability to select *methods* related to how children learn
4. *Expectations* that all students will succeed
5. *Personality* suited to positive interaction that engages learning

These five variables make for effective teaching. There is no specific order of importance; each key is important in its own right. No one key could stand alone in defining a teacher; each key must work in concert. The first component, **management**, deals with the practicality of efficient class management and the teacher's role as a manager and purveyor of procedures. Perseverance and ingenuity are personal qualities essential to **mastery** of content. The **methods** we select are expressions of our personalities, as are the instructional practices we implement. Positive **expectations** grow out of our understanding of learning. Our expectations determine the methods we will choose. One's personality, however, acts as a unifying thread. **Teaching personality**, defined as a combination of character and values, is the foundation of effective teaching. Personality plays a major role in choice of management techniques and strategies employed.

The Learning Paradigm

The learning paradigm reflects one of the basic purposes of teaching. We teach in order that students may learn. The learning paradigm is opposite to the traditional teacher instructional model in both mission and purpose. The instructional paradigm measures the efficiency of the teacher's instruction, while the learning paradigm measures the learner's wisdom. Learning is not the transference of knowledge from teacher to student but the construction and discovery of meaning by the learner. An instructor offers courses; a teacher creates environments that leave no students behind. The mission and purposes clearly distinguish learning from instruction. Teachers must improve their instructional practices in order for students to develop skills necessary for the future. To enhance learning, teachers must focus their activities on fostering student understanding. The instructional paradigm highlights formal processes while the learning paradigm emphasizes results or outcomes. The instructional paradigm is teacher centered

> **PRACTICE EXERCISE 1.1**
>
> ### Keys to Effective Teaching
>
> Write a brief explanation for each key and describe its importance for a teacher. Provide an example for each that evidences its importance. The core question is how to run an effective classroom; the answer is to understand and practice using the keys to effective teaching.
>
> **Management of classrooms:**
>
> **Mastery of content:**
>
> **Methods of instruction:**
>
> **Expectations of students:**
>
> **Personality of teacher:**

and attends to lessons. The learning paradigm is child centered and attends to student needs (Tagg and Ewell, 2003).

Throughout the twentieth century, an instructional model based on behaviorist learning theory was the strategy used for all instruction. The teacher was a transmitter of information in this version of teaching. **Behaviorism** regarded teaching as diagnostic prescriptive; the teacher analyzed student deficiencies and provided prescriptions to remedy deficits. This approach led teachers to rely on direct instruction as the primary pedagogical tool (Ornstein, 1998). The focus of instruction became the enhancement and delivery of instruction. Actual learning became a haphazard affair, as evidenced by numerous calls for school reform resulting from poor student standardized test grades.

Teachers have become prisoners of a system, structure, and history not of their own creation. A good many today feel that simply listening, taking notes, reading, and taking examinations is not effective for student learning. Traditional classrooms designed according to behaviorism, to house the transfer of information from teacher to student, are not conducive to authentic learning (Bar and Tagg, 1995).

An alternative view of learning highlights the role of the individual student in the learning process. This position comes from the works of Jean Piaget and Lev Vygotsky who asserted that for students to learn they must be socially engaged in the process. Students must actively create their own knowledge from their beliefs and experiences. This theory, known as **constructivism**, is in direct contrast to the well-developed teaching models based on behaviorism. The theory is descriptive and not prescriptive in nature. It advocates the role of the teacher as a guide who leads students, rather than as a fount of all wisdom who dispenses knowledge. These paradigms set the stage for understanding methods and instructional strategies. When pedagogical beliefs such as behaviorism or constructivism are understood, teacher effectiveness increases. When a teacher has a clear understanding of instructional practices, student learning improves.

The paradigms help us understand the purposes for effective instructional practices by providing an answer for the *why* in teaching. The *what* and the *how* of teaching are readily understood, but we tend to neglect the *who*. It matters as much as what we know and how we teach it. Great teaching is more than just mastery of knowledge and method; it is fashioned out of spirit, personality, and inherent qualities. A teacher's personal characteristics and values are as much if not more important than knowledge and method (Banner, 1997).

Figure 1.1 Paradigms for Teaching

MISSION AND PURPOSES	
Instructional Paradigm	Learning Paradigm
Provide/deliver instruction	Produce learning
Transfer knowledge from teacher to student	Construct knowledge/student discovery
Offer courses and programs	Create powerful learning environments
Improve the quality of instruction	Improve the quality of learning
Achieve access for diverse students	Achieve success for diverse students

Effective Teaching

Effective teaching happens when a teacher brings about intended learning objectives defined in terms of student social and academic achievement. It occurs because a powerful emphasis on what students learn, not on what the instructor teaches, is promoted. Clear lesson objectives facilitate student learning. Effective teaching takes place when the basic psychological needs of all learners are satisfied (Glasser, 1998). A master teacher is one who has developed a philosophical reservoir of knowledge pertaining to methodology, child development, psychological need, subject matter, and brain and intelligence theories. One's core educational philosophy is a synthesis of informational data. The effective teacher combines competency in practice with the understanding of theoretical knowledge about learning and human behavior. Her knowledge of content combined with an understanding of instructional strategies hones presentation skills. Content knowledge and methodology make up the *what* and *how* of teaching; that "mythical ingredient" teaching personality amplifies in the form of the *who*.

Effective teachers have a teaching personality that has developed emotional commitment and enthusiasm that engages students in the learning process. They leave no one behind because they believe all can succeed, and all have the ability to learn to the degree and level of their capabilities. Personality combined with perseverance and ingenuity leads to mastery in teaching. Teaching personality, a primary variable for student success, puts it all in perspective. Great teachers are those who evidence a special type of personality defined and measured by student social and academic achievements.

Children initially come to school wanting to learn. No child enters kindergarten opposed to knowledge. In reality, they are curious, frightened, and excited about a new adventure, school. Wong (1997) in a very simple analysis hit upon the reality of the first day of class as seen by both teachers and students. They are concerned with basic questions such as

1. Am I in the right room?
2. Where do I sit?
3. What are the rules in this class?
4. What will I be doing?
5. How will I be graded? (All students want to know this.)
6. What is my teacher like as a person?
7. Will the teacher treat me as a human being?

Note: The primary concerns of students are related to love, belonging, and personality factors such as fairness and kindness. Sensitivity to student needs is of prime importance.

Somewhere along the line, something goes wrong for many children. Teachers must be aware of how fragile children are and set out at the start to prevent failure. Be aware of opportunities being offered to educate young minds. Take student desires for love and belonging and respond by creating classroom environments that meet this need. Unfortunately, this may be difficult to achieve in the real world. Expectations should be based on reality and not fantasy. By meeting the basic psychological needs of students for love (belonging), fun, freedom, and power, expectations can become reality (Glasser, 1998). Children do the learning, and teachers facilitate learning by meeting needs.

Successful teachers are not applauded when entering a classroom, so why should an inexperienced teacher expect adulation? New teachers do, however, have a honeymoon of sorts before being tested. During this first period of testing, many go into survival mode by keeping students busy with assignments and busywork. This is not meeting student needs, but is a recipe for disaster. No data supports the survival mode as a method for an effective teacher. Selecting a text and designating questions to be answered based on readings may keep some children occupied and quiet, but this is not really teaching. Lecturing and providing an activity (worksheet) for the children to complete followed by a test is not effective teaching for the most part. This approach will only last until teacher or students burn out or are bored out of their minds. This scenario can be avoided by adopting the learning paradigm. It is not what is taught but what is learned that is important. Understand how to develop and implement learning exercises that engage and motivate learning. Model what you want students to understand through trial and error and subtle guidance. Effective teachers establish engaging classrooms where instructional management and discipline are natural outgrowths.

Implementation is the key to success! No matter how well prepared, novice teachers tend to go through four stages of teaching: fantasy, survival, mastery, and impact (Wong, 1997). Teacher mastery facilitates student learning. Impact on students is the final and least recognized stage. The joy of positively influencing a life is only experienced by truly effective teachers. These stages of teaching described by Wong are quite simple to understand, and provide a forecast for expectations as a new teacher.

1. *Fantasy* is when everything is great. The initial rush of teaching is a wonderful experience. Unfortunately, it does not last indefinitely.
2. *Survival* is the stage arrived at when one will do anything to make it through the day. This period is the darkest experience a new teacher can have. It is not teaching; it is an unending feeling of failure.
3. *Mastery* is the light of sunrise. The master teacher is an individual who has the ability to manage a class and knows the methods needed.

4. *Impact* gives purpose to teaching. It happens when a difference occurs in a student's life, as when a young child exclaims, "I can read!"

Behaviors That Affect Teaching Reinhartz and Beach (1997) describe eight behaviors directly related to effective teaching that good teachers employ. These eight effective teaching behaviors can be correlated to the keys to effective teaching. Even though correlation does not necessarily indicate causality, Reinhartz and Beach's eight behaviors bolster intuitive evidence that the keys are a basis for good teaching.

1. Instructional clarity is the result of focused lessons that engage students. This behavior relates to the keys with regard to method and personality. Teaching personality determines the method chosen to facilitate learning. Instructional clarity is difficult to maintain without having an effective teaching personality.
2. Knowledge of content is the result of perseverance and ingenuity, evidenced by the ability to structure and integrate concepts into the curriculum. Linked to this behavior is the effective teaching key for mastery of content knowledge.
3. Establishment of learning expectations is the result of understanding how children learn and creating attainable and measurable objectives. Instructional strategies based on clear objectives become achievable expectations.
4. Variation in teaching is the result of using strategies that promote opportunities for interactive rather than passive learning. Variation in teaching strategy coincides with three keys: *method*, in selection of approaches; *management*, in ability to engage; and *personality*, to communicate.
5. Utilization of resources means using different instructional aids and materials during a lesson. This behavior links to the management key by its use of materials as motivational aids to focus attention, which limits opportunity for misbehavior.
6. Knowledge of learning and development principles involves appropriate learning strategies used to meet student needs. Successful teachers implement effective teaching keys by traditional, progressive, and constructivist strategies.
7. Communication with students on multiple levels includes the practices used to clear the lines of communication with a concentration on higher-order thinking skills. A positive teaching personality enhances communication.
8. Enthusiasm is infectious; a teacher's passion for a subject inspires student participation. Personality is key to creating enthusiastic learners.

PRACTICE EXERCISE 1.2

Keys to Effective Teaching Equal Student Learning

Compare and contrast teacher characteristics and student variables necessary for learning with the five keys to effective teaching. Indicate next to each item if it relates to management, mastery, method, expectation, or personality. Provide an example for each.

Characteristics of the Effective Teacher

The effective teacher

1. Is a good classroom manager.
2. Designs lessons to reach mastery.
3. Believes all can learn.
4. Uses new strategies to meet children's needs.
5. Has positive expectations that students will succeed.

Variables Necessary for Student Learning

1. Classroom management
2. Learning processes taught (how to take notes, read text, work in groups, etc.)
3. Home and parental cooperation
4. Teacher and student interrelationship
5. What teacher does in class

(least important factor is demographic data)

Figure 1.2 Effective Teaching Behaviors

1. Effective teaching occurs when one is able to bring about intended learning outcomes.
2. Intent and achievement are two dimensions of effective teaching.
3. Effective teachers have a philosophy of education, know developmental stages, understand psychological needs and subject matter, and have a theory related to how children learn based on brain and intelligence theories.
4. Effective teachers are equally competent in both theory and practice.

MINI CASE FROM THE FIELD

The following case from the field presents the core characteristics of an accomplished teacher. Read the case and see whether you agree with Margaret Gomez's or with Chandler Thompson's definitions of the five keys to effective teaching.

Core Characteristics for Effective Teaching

Chandler Thompson had been principal of McGraw Simpson Elementary and Senior High School for the past ten years. In all that time, he had not come across a teacher like Margaret Gomez. As a novice teacher, Ms. Gomez evidenced supreme confidence in her abilities. She had many things going for her: She was bright, articulate, cared for children, and spoke well. Unfortunately, her classroom presentations did not live up to expectations. Her initial promise had slowly tarnished. One positive factor had been the lack of major problems or parental complaints. But the fragile balance between expectations and parental complaints began to unravel during March. Parents complained that their children were not learning and that Ms. Gomez's classes were disorderly. Mr. Thompson decided that he would have to speak with Ms. Gomez and see if he could help her finish the year on a positive note.

Margaret Gomez had never been so frightened in her life. This had been her first job out of teachers' college. She had been excited over the opportunity to teach and serve her community. Unfortunately, her good intentions had gone unfulfilled. Being a classroom teacher, left to her own devices, was not like student teaching. There was no one there to tell her what action to take. She was solely responsible for her sixth-grade social studies classes. Her biggest problem had been her students' general lack of motivation and respect for school. Most of her students acted very silly and immature. Some would pretend they forgot where their seat was. Margaret tried to manage the childish behavior by being stern and unbending. She believed that to *manage* a class the teacher had to control every aspect of the learning process. She believed in an authoritarian approach that she felt was the best strategy for her multi-ethnic linguistic classes.

Students came from widely diverse backgrounds sharing the poverty that was rampant for those living in economically depressed communities. Margaret felt that she should set high *expectations* so that the children would be encouraged to achieve the impossible. She tried to be kind and understanding but her sympathy was met with her students' scorn and disobedience. She tried to recall the various methods she had been taught in college, but all she seemed to do was yell at the children to do their work. The less work the children completed the more she hollered and shrieked at them, not an effective method for learning. Margaret decided to use a *method* of instruction based on punishments and rewards even though she really did not like the idea of punishing children. Margaret knew that children learned best by doing so she decided to do as little as possible and let the children obtain *mastery* of the content. This appeared to be a good idea since it allowed her to never lose face before the children or admit she did not know something. Her major achievement was due to her caring *personality*, which allowed her to relate well to children one on one.

When Ms. Gomez entered Mr. Chandler's office she was surprised to see him smiling and apparently in good spirits, but her first impression soon evaporated. Mr. Chandler began the conference by offering her a seat and asking if she would like a glass of water. With the pleasantries over he began by saying, "Margaret, you do realize that your performance with your classes has been less than satisfactory this semester? Do you have any idea why?"

Margaret responded, "That's not really true. The children did learn and they like me most of the time."

"That is not the point," said Mr. Chandler. "Teaching is not a personality contest, even though you will develop a positive teaching personality over time, which is expected. Your problem is that you do not know how to manage sixth-grade classes. Remember, classroom *management* is synonymous with teaching procedures. Children need to be taught how to behave and what is expected of them. Low expectations garner low results.

"You must set *expectations* that are both high and achievable. Your approach to children must be based on your beliefs regarding how children learn. The *methods* you choose to employ should reflect that understanding. Under no circumstance is it appropriate to be unprepared with respect to the material and content you are teaching. Without your understanding and mastery of content, there is no possibility for the transmission of knowledge or encouraging learning. Your personality is your redeeming feature. Because you are bright and articulate and can relate to children, you can develop a true teaching personality. A teaching *personality* is the link to effective teaching that all effective teachers share in common.

"Margaret, you can be a successful teacher. You need to review these five core characteristics of an effective teacher. They are the keys to your future success. Let us meet when you feel ready to discuss how you will implement these five keys in your class."

1. Who had the stronger argument in defining the five keys to effective teaching? Justify your answer.

2. Describe what Margaret missed in her understanding of the five keys.
3. What would you suggest that Margaret do to implement the keys?
4. Give examples of how each key could become a focus of a lesson.
5. Explain your beliefs regarding the core characteristics that effective teachers share in common.

Teacher Effectiveness and Classroom Design Most classrooms today are designed the same way they were fifty years ago. They should instead be organized for success and radiate with the essence of student learning. Rather than focusing on the teacher, look at the ecological and environmental factors evident in the physical organization of a classroom. This approach can be used as an indicator of teacher effectiveness (Kohn, 1999). Kohn uses material components found in classrooms, such as the placement of furniture, decoration, and student materials as indicators of effectiveness. Even though today's classrooms may have more electrical outlets, Internet connections, and computers, they are still, for the most part, "spatially monotonous rooms in which students sit at individual desks and listen to teachers who often are limited to writing on whiteboards" (Day, 2003). Teachers may not have the authority to design a room but they certainly can make suggestions.

A smart classroom design should have computers with presentation software, video projector, document camera, and communication and control capabilities, including links to the Internet as well as space for small-group and problem-based projects. This approach is nontraditionalist and skewed toward a more progressive constructivist approach aimed at encouraging student involvement combined with reliance on technology. There is no best design for all classrooms, but the use of laptop computers with wireless connectivity with ceiling-mounted video projectors appears to be a good starting point.

Environment and the amount of technology are not the only criteria by which to judge effectiveness. Results of tests on the subjects being taught are still used as traditional indicators of effectiveness. When you reflect on the qualities of effective teachers, include academic and cultural needs attainment with environmental and technological factors.

Strauss (2002) takes an alternative view, claiming that we load multimedia equipment into classrooms simply to be able to call them smart classrooms. He does not see how smarter classrooms will produce better learning but believes we must first improve learning and teaching before stressing technology. Most learning does not even occur in classrooms, so why misallocate money to develop smart classrooms? As he sums it up, "We need smart learners, not smart classrooms; and smart classes enough to get us there" (Strauss, 2002).

Teacher Effectiveness and Diversity There is no doubt that good teaching is enhanced by technology, and that smart classrooms will be the wave of the future. Effective teachers also need to demonstrate sensitivity for the cultural backgrounds of students, and be aware of the appropriate instructional strategies that make learning meaningful. Powell (1996) developed a set of questions to use when analyzing effective teacher behaviors with regard to diversity. He was concerned with the personal and professional qualities, strategies, and biographical factors that are inherent in teachers who are effective in diverse settings. He found that these teachers explored students' academic, cultural, and social needs and made them central to the classroom curriculum. These teachers acted as facilitators and guides for student learning; they became cultural anthropologists by creating and implementing alternative curricula relevant to students' cultural backgrounds. A smart classroom used by a culturally aware, effective teacher is an asset.

1. What are the biographical factors that contribute to teachers' successful teaching of diverse learners?
2. What strategies can we use to reach diverse learners academically and personally?
3. What personal and professional qualities do teachers have that enable them to be culturally sensitive?
4. How do culturally sensitive teachers interact with students both inside and outside the classroom?

Effective Teachers Are Culturally Responsive Culturally responsive teaching (CRT) is validating, comprehensive, multidimensional, transformative, and emancipatory (Gay, 2000). CRT may be defined as using the cultural knowledge, prior experiences, and performance styles of diverse students to make learning more appropriate and effective for them; it teaches to and through the strengths of these students. Culturally responsive teaching

1. Acknowledges the legitimacy of the cultural heritages of different ethnic groups, both as legacies that affect students' dispositions, attitudes, and approaches to learning and as worthy content to be taught in the formal curriculum.
2. Builds bridges of meaningfulness between home and school experiences as well as between academic abstractions and lived sociocultural realities.
3. Uses a wide variety of instructional strategies that are connected to different learning styles.
4. Teaches and encourages students to know their own and other cultural heritages.
5. Incorporates multicultural information, resources, and materials in all the subjects and skills routinely taught in schools. (Gay, 2000, p. 29)

>
>
> ### PRACTICE EXERCISE 1.3
>
> **Organizational Design, Diversity, and Cultural Responsiveness as Indicators of Effective Teaching**
>
> Read and analyze the following statement:
>
> "Effective teaching is indicated by appropriate use of technology, classroom design, celebrating diversity, and by cultural responsiveness focused on improved learning."
>
> Upon analyzing, would you agree or disagree with the following declarations? State your reasons.
>
> 1. Diversity is a positive force in a classroom setting.
> 2. You do not have to be culturally responsive to be an effective teacher.
> 3. Technology has little to do with student learning.
> 4. Smart classrooms are not for the future but for today.

APPROACHES TO EFFECTIVE TEACHING

Pedagogy describes how something in education is done; it is the science or art of teaching. It is important to know what to teach as well as how to teach it. Fortunately, to master the *how* of teaching is the comparatively simple process of recognizing four approaches to teaching and varying lesson delivery. Variety will keep lessons eclectic and interesting, cover more ground, and satisfy more needs.

Expository Approach

Expository teaching is a teacher-centered traditional approach to teaching. It is also called direct instruction, deductive or didactic teaching, and is the most common instructional method used by teachers. Expository teaching advances David Ausubel's theory (1962) that we acquire knowledge primarily through reception rather than discovery. The view holds that concepts and ideas are communicated and presented by the teacher more often than discovered by the learner. Ausubel's theory recognizes the difference between meaningful and rote reception of information. *Meaningful reception* is new knowledge connected to existing knowledge. This concept is based on constructivist theory as advocated by Jean Piaget's adaptation process where knowledge is assimilated by fitting new ideas into already existing models of reality. An accommodation is made that changes an already existing model of reality to fit new data by adding information to create new meaning. Ausubel stressed meaningful verbal learning in his expository teaching model and proposed the use of *advanced organizers* to make the association between new material and experiences. The function of the advanced organizer is to provide scaffolding or support for the new information. This is done in most textbooks in a chapter overview section. Organizers aim to (1) focus attention on important information; (2) point out the key relationships in the chapter; and (3) remind the student of what he or she already knows.

An expository lesson usually involves teacher talk in the form of lecturing or leading a discussion. The teacher begins with aims or objectives that focus the lesson, followed by content presented in terms of basic similarities and differences. The teacher uses examples to highlight points and amplify contrasting ideas. Lessons are further enhanced by teacher-student interactions, which usually consist mainly of teacher questions and student answers. The types of questions used in this approach are *recall* (who, what, where, when) and *comprehension* (how, why, compare, describe). Review, practice, and the correction of errors are part of the general procedures followed in this approach. The lesson type that corresponds to the expository format is usually called a developmental lesson, which consists of objectives, motivation, content, application, summary, and homework. This approach has four major features: (1) clear goals; (2) teacher-led instruction; (3) accurate recordkeeping of student learning, and (4) evidence of management skills.

Expository teaching works best when you wish to teach about relationships among several ideas or concepts. Students must have some prior knowledge of the concepts in order to process meaningful reception of information. This approach is developmentally appropriate for students usually above the fifth or sixth grade. The key to this approach is whether students are mature enough to benefit from it.

Discovery Approach

Jerome Bruner viewed discovery teaching as an approach to instruction in which students interact with their environment by exploring and manipulating objects, wrestling with questions and controversies, or performing experiments—the idea being that students retain concepts they discover on their own (Ormrod, 1995).

Discovery teaching may or may not be totally teacher centered, depending on how it is used. If the teacher decides which problems students work on, it is teacher centered and called guided discovery. **Guided discovery** falls in between direct and indirect instruction. Teachers using this approach must prepare by identifying the concepts children need to learn, and the skills needed to lead them in understanding those concepts. They then must prepare a progression of questions that lead to concept discovery. Teaching using this guided discovery approach involves

1. Explaining the purpose of the lesson by stating the objective as a "to discover" or "to understand" question.
2. Presenting the first question to guide students.
3. Student response.
4. Framing the rest of your question to guide students to discover the concept.
5. Summarizing the lesson by asking students what they have discovered.

If the method were used as a non-teacher-centered approach, children would be encouraged to seek information rather than be given it. They would also be allowed to select their own problem. The **discovery method** for learning affords children to develop hypotheses that answer questions they wish to answer. It fosters a broadly divergent level of student thinking. This approach teaches children how to discover solutions to problems that concern them. It can also encourage them to develop a love for learning. Teaching using the discovery method consists of students proposing issues or problems; gathering data and observations to develop hypotheses; and finally explaining or proving hypotheses. In both cases, teacher-centered and student-centered discovery teaching consists of independent learning guided by the teacher in varying degrees. The questioning techniques used are open-ended. There are no single obviously correct answers, and major stress is placed on developing higher order thinking skills. A discovery strategy could include a cooperative learning and a peer-tutoring component when used as a non-teacher-centered problem-solving methodology. An example of a non-teacher-centered problem-solving approach would be to allow the learner to select the problem, explore it, and observe the environment in which it exists. The discovery approach consists of two types: (1) guided discovery in which the teacher presents what is to be learned, and (2) pure discovery in which the students select what they wish to learn. The key is semantic in the use of teacher centered and teacher directed. These terms really are not supposed to be synonymous. One is total while the other is limited, therefore the alternate designation for this approach is guided discovery (Bruner, 1960). It requires thinking and problem-solving skills, and it is student centered as well as being teacher directed.

Inquiry Approach

Defining **inquiry-based education** is difficult since it is a multifaceted educational approach with many interpretations. John Dewey's (1933) vision has been taken to mean constructivism, problem solving, project-based learning, and many other variations. At its core, inquiry is a learner-centered approach to learning that involves a process of exploring the natural or material world. It encourages students to inquire and question in a search for new understandings. Its reliance only on student-centered activities is the essential difference between the inquiry and discovery approaches.

Although Dewey did not coin these terms, progressive education's use of the inquiry approach through use of the scientific method, problem solving, and project-based practices has come to be associated with him. Dewey's work led to the first inquiry-based learning methods in the United States. He advocated for child-centered learning based on real-world experiences. Dewey was a pragmatist who believed in using practical approaches to solving problems. He thought of intelligence as a power to be used for problem solving when people were faced with conflict or challenge. He opposed the traditional method of learning, which focused on the use of memory under the direct authority and supervision of the teacher. In the traditional approach, students learn not to ask too many questions, but instead to listen and repeat the expected answers. To demonstrate his beliefs Dewey established a "Laboratory School" at the University of Chicago that lasted for eight years, from 1896 to 1904. This was his most direct attempt to influence educational practice by becoming a practitioner. He hoped to evidence by his work that education was the same as any other science. His laboratory would be a school that could be used to test his theories. He claimed the difference between his laboratory school and a regular school was that his work could be replicated in a laboratory since its environment was antiseptic. His school was said to have a (a) pure environment, (b) highly qualified staff, (c) reflective environment, (d) risk-taking atmosphere, and (e) high cost. Dewey's school abandoned pedagogical practices such as drill, recitation, rote memorization, lecturing, total-class instruction and chalkboard exercises. It introduced project-based practices, open-ended discussion, trips, and questioning techniques that tended to stress the *how* and *why*.

Dewey wanted to make psychology the scientific basis for educational practice. He viewed education as a science even though its foundation, psychology, was not recognized as a science until 1875. Dewey has been called the most influential writer on education this country has produced, and the least read. His approach is student centered and results in creative thinking and a self-directed seeking of new knowledge by students. It can be summed up in the adage, "Tell me and I forget, show me and I remember, involve me and I understand." The inquiry approach's major features are best described as a self-directed process known as the *scientific method*, which includes

1. Problem identification
2. Hypothesizing

3. Data gathering
4. Data analysis
5. Forming conclusions

Discussion Approach

The discussion approach, also known as the *Socratic method* or *seminar model,* involves a topic being selected and students conversing with each other and the teacher in order to understand. The discussion approach is a self-directed, student-centered method, which results in a complex set of learning outcomes. Those outcomes consist of students constructing their own knowledge through synthesis, analysis, and evaluation. The approach features formats appropriate for large groups and for collective participation. It focuses on questioning techniques and assessments that are usually open-ended and based on checklists, journals, and observations. The usual procedures followed by most teachers in preparing for discussions are to have children prepared before class with the necessary information to partake in the discussion. This is readily achieved by assigning homework before the discussion meeting. The actual setup for a discussion has major features that can be added to or lessened as the situation dictates; These include roundtables and brainstorming; symposia and inquiry-centered discussion; large-group panels and task-directed discussion; debates, role playing, simulation, and tutorials.

The *seminar model* is a collaborative, intellectual discussion propelled by open-ended questions about a text. A text may be a written document or a photograph, a work of art, a map, a graphic math problem, an architectural drawing, or just about anything, as long as it is both rich in ideas and ambiguous. Every seminar should be collaborative, intellectual, and open-ended. Regardless of the chosen text, seminars are carefully planned formal classroom dialogues. Students must be actively engaged with an idea or an exercise that is immediately relevant to them as human beings. This will occur when students become involved in interactive, student-centered seminar dialogues that require reading, thinking, and speaking about and listening to ideas that are important to them. The teacher's role is that of a discussion facilitator, who designs the seminar conditions and then gets out of the way so that students can participate. Both the teacher and student have distinct roles.

Teachers Must

- select an appropriate text and prepare open-ended questions.
- coach students before the seminar so they understand they are expected to speak and listen with regard to the questions.
- model good listening and note-taking skills during a seminar to pose genuine, provocative follow-up questions.
- limit his or her own speaking time.
- develop post-seminar procedures and activities that make the seminar dialogue relevant to the students.

Students Must

- invest the necessary time and energy in reading and studying the text in detail.
- accept responsibility for improving their questioning, speaking, and listening skills during a seminar.
- consciously contribute to the seminar discussion by stating their own ideas and by actively listening to the ideas of others.
- learn to agree and disagree with others in a thoughtful and respectful manner.
- understand that the seminar is a part of the ongoing learning life of their classroom.
- Practice post-seminar writing as a way of articulating their increased understanding of the values and ideas gained from the text and dialogue.

Seminars use Socratic teaching methods in that open-ended questions are the focus of discussions and all discussions attempt to enhance student critical thinking skills. Socratic teaching is teaching by questioning and by conducting discussions (seminars) of the answers elicited with the purpose of understanding, drawing insights, and increasing the student knowledge base. Seminars should occur once or twice a week depending on the book or materials to be read in advance. Seminars should be viewed as conversations with students, conducted by the teacher who acts as leader or moderator. The best seminars occur when issues and questions arise from great books (Adler, 1983). The task of the seminar leader is threefold:

1. to ask questions that define the discussion,
2. to examine, and
3. to engage students in active participation.

INSTRUCTIONAL PRACTICES FOR EFFECTIVE TEACHING

Direct and Indirect Instructional Practices

The basic **direct instruction practice** stems from the expository approach and is a teacher-centered strategy, which uses a lecture and recitation format. It fosters a high level of teacher-student interactions when used effectively. The role of the teacher is to pass on facts and rules, while assisting in modeling how to solve problems. This transmission or direct instructional model features six basic practices (see Figure 1.3).

These practices are those that most teachers would consider best for preparing and presenting lessons.

PRACTICE EXERCISE 1.4

Selecting the Proper Approach

Read each of the following ideas for a lesson, and choose an approach that you feel is appropriate; then justify your selection in a brief paragraph. Following the same process, select an alternative approach and explain how it might also be considered appropriate.

1. Is there such a thing as a justifiable war?
2. Why are there different eye colors?
3. The concept of multiplication is an expression of addition.
4. What is the meaning of respect?
5. Write a cover letter for your resume that will give the reader an accurate picture of your beliefs.
6. Is secondary smoke harmful?
7. Is global warning a factor that should cause us concern?

Unfortunately, they ignore the reality that it is not what you present but what your students learn that matters. The same approaches do not work for all. If they did, there would be no purpose in discussing lesson designs and skills necessary to create effective lessons. The lesson objectives that are most suited to direct instruction relate to three domains—the cognitive, affective, and psychomotor. Your mind, feelings, and physical actions are the determinates of learning. Combining these three domains with understanding the learning paradigm produces the learning process. (See Figure 1.4.)

Indirect Instructional Practices are student centered. They are directed toward problem solving, discovery learning, and the inquiry method. These practices allow for learning within a context of problem solving. The indirect model is best suited for the teaching of concepts and abstractions. The strategies and practices that are usually associated with indirect instruction are seen in Figure 1.5. Instructional and teaching methods mean the same thing. Direct and indirect instruction are the two main categories used for classifying teaching methods. Unfortunately, instruction and teaching are more complicated than just two categories. Each instructional approach used has advantages, disadvantages, and requires some preliminary preparation. On occasion more than one method is appropriate for a lesson. Effective teachers know this and work at developing skills to make the process seamless. The instructional method employed for a specific lesson depends on a number of things. Appropriateness of a lesson depends on age and developmental level of students. You would not teach the philosophical implications of slavery to a kindergarten class. Nor would you teach what is already known, except as a review. The instructional method chosen should fit one's teaching personality and be suited to the lesson's objectives inclusive of time, space and materials, and physical setting. There is no one "right way" for

Figure 1.3 Basic Direct Instructional Practices

1. Daily review
2. Presenting new content
3. Guided practice
4. Feedback and corrections
5. Independent practice
6. Periodic review

Figure 1.4 Lesson Objectives Most Suited to Direct Instruction

Cognitive	Affective	Psychomotor objectives
to recall	to listen	to repeat
to describe	to attend	to follow
to list	to comply	to place
to summarize	to follow	to perform accurately
to paraphrase	to obey	to perform independently
to distinguish	to display	to perform proficiently
to use	to express	to perform with speed
to organize	to prefer	to perform with coordination
to demonstrate		to perform with timing

Figure 1.5 Basic Indirect Instructional Practices

> 1. Cooperative grouping practices are used for focusing on project-based and problem-solving activities.
> 2. Constructivist practices, which encourage learners to use their experiences to construct meanings and knowledge.
> 3. Project-based learning practices that integrate bodies of knowledge by problem solving; encourages student exploration and prediction of problem solutions.
> 4. Scientific problem-centered inquiry practices begin by identifying the problem, stating the research objectives, collecting data, interpreting data, and end by coming to a conclusion.

teaching any individual lesson, but there are guides to assist a teacher in making the best possible decision. Following is a list of instructional methods showing benefits, disadvantages, and the type of teacher homework needed to put them into practice. The instructional methods are divided into brief vignettes describing direct and indirect teaching strategies.

DIRECT TEACHING

Benefits: Direct teaching focuses students on specific learning objectives. The teacher tells the purpose for content and discusses its importance. The teacher lets the students know what they will gain by learning the content: simply, what is in it for them. This practice helps to clarify lesson objectives and maintain task orientation. This method has been a traditional approach for instruction because it is a quick and efficient way to teach facts and skills, and student assessment is relatively easy.

Disadvantages: Direct teaching can stifle creativity and lead to repetitious scripted lessons. To do it effectively requires a great deal of preparation and excellent communication skills. One must become an eloquent lecturer. Lessons must be developmental and require a command of the content area. Direct instruction is not thought to be effective for teaching higher-order thinking skills.

Teacher Homework: All content must be organized in advance, and the teacher should know the level of student readiness for the content to be taught. Teachers should also know if there are any prerequisites for the lesson to be taught effectively.

Lecture

Benefits: Content is presented in a logical and clear manner using a direct instructional methodology. An effective lecturer is eloquent and able to paint verbal pictures that can engage listeners by providing inspirational experiences. It is most beneficial when attempting to convey a great deal of content to large groups within a limited period.

Disadvantages: To be successful the lecturer must have proficient oral skills. Audiences tend to be passive and rarely become engaged in the lesson. It is difficult to evaluate effectiveness, unless a test is used. It fosters a transmission model of education where there is one-way communication. Children below grade 4 have limited attention spans that make this approach inappropriate for young children.

Teacher Homework: Lecturing requires a great deal of content expertise. Ideas and concepts must be clearly presented and developed so that the audience is motivated by the introduction and convinced by the final lesson summary. To be effective the speaker must be able to complete the presentation within the allotted time frame, and completely cover the content. The teacher must prepare for a specific class by knowing both their own and students' strengths and weaknesses. Anecdotes and examples should be used to enliven the lecture.

Lecture and Discussion

Benefits: Lecture combined with discussion attempts to involve students in the lesson by allowing for questions during or after a presentation. Students are permitted to ask questions so that they might clarify points or challenge positions. Lectures that are interspersed with discussions provide a more engaging atmosphere.

Disadvantages: The time it takes to address questions accurately takes away from covering lesson content. Time constraints have to be taken into consideration to provide for suitable discussion opportunities. Questions can come from anywhere, forcing the teacher to change the direction of the lesson. Questioning can become unmanageable. Clarity and focus can be lost.

Teacher Homework: The teacher should attempt to anticipate difficult questions and prepare fitting responses in advance. The teacher should not only allow for questioning but also use the opportunity to question the class to evaluate the effectiveness of the lesson.

Discussion

Benefits: Discussion aids learning by allowing information to be questioned, interpreted, and digested. Discussion affords opportunity for the pooling of ideas and experiences while developing a shared environment. It is effective during or after an oral presentation, video, film, or computer presentation that needs to be clarified and analyzed. A democratic discussion procedure allows everyone to participate.

Disadvantages: Discussion becomes impractical and unwieldy with more than twenty students. The teacher must be careful to avoid allowing a few students to dominate all discussion and others to not participate at all. It can also be time consuming, especially if the teacher is thrown off track by irrelevant questions.

Teacher Homework: Discussion requires careful and skillful planning by teachers to guide the discussion to a fitting conclusion. In most cases, the teacher should prepare a question outline to ensure focus and clarity during the discussion.

Small-Group Discussion

Benefits: Discussion works very well with small groups of up to fifteen because everyone is able to participate. The smaller the group, the more comfortable the students are. In small groups, it is usually easier to reach a consensus on any particular issue, and a greater depth of understanding can be reached.

Disadvantages: The teacher needs to plan and think carefully about how a group should be composed and what its actual purpose should be. Groups can be sidetracked if not balanced properly.

Teacher Homework: The teacher must organize a large class into small effective groups that can work independently on specific topics and questions. The teacher must prepare specific tasks or questions for the group to answer. Problems to resolve can be determined by students with as little teacher guidance as possible.

Guest Speakers

Benefits: Providing for suitable guest experts allows for expansion of thought and inquiry into different opinions and points of view. Having more than one guest speaker can provoke an exchange of ideas and create better discussion episodes. The use of different speakers with controversial views is apt to stop attention from lagging and provide an exciting venue for learning. Individual guest speakers personalize and add character to topics and issues. They also break down an audience's preconceived ideas on specific problems.

Disadvantages: A speaker's personality may be charismatic and overshadow important positions taken by less apt speakers. Not all guest speakers are going to be eloquent; some may even do their cause a disservice. All experts are not effective speakers, and may present accurate material unclearly and illogically. This method is usually not appropriate for elementary students.

Teacher Homework: Students must be prepared before a presentation to know what to listen for. They must be taught how to make unbiased critical judgments. Assembling everyone in the same place at the same time is a tiring experience. The logistics for a good panel presentation may be difficult. The teacher must coordinate panelists and focus, introduce, and summarize positions. Teachers must contact speakers and coordinate programs so that they are relevant to the issues the class is researching.

INDIRECT TEACHING

Benefits: Through indirect teaching students develop understandings that are meaningful and personal. Students develop critical thinking skills that are necessary for life. Indirect teaching encourages creativity and thinking "outside the box," adds to construction of meaning and knowledge, and inspires students to take charge of their own learning.

Disadvantages: Indirect teaching is difficult for teachers to manage and can cause students to lose focus and direction. It is not an efficient way to teach facts and skills. Assessment is difficult since creativity can be relative. Indirect teaching goes against a teacher's natural instinct to direct and instruct students.

Teacher Homework: Teachers must prepare students for higher order thinking skills. They must be guides and facilitators rather than act in their usual role as instructors. Teachers must prepare suggestions that will motivate students to learn independently and in supportive settings.

Cooperative Learning

Benefits: Cooperative learning helps foster mutual responsibility, and it is supported by extensive research as an effective technique. Students develop social skills and learn to be understanding, patient, and how to be team players, acquiring many of the skills necessary for success in future life. Students are social beings and for the most part prefer to work in cooperative settings.

Disadvantages: Some students do not work well in groups, finding it difficult to share work and credit. In many instances, aggressive, bright students tend to take charge, do all the work, and act superior. Cooperative learning is not an effective approach for learning facts and skills because it is difficult to focus students on curriculum objectives.

Teacher Homework: The teacher must determine objectives, skills, and content to be learned, as well as the strategies needed to foster student learning. Instructional time must be used to prepare students to learn how to work in groups. The teacher must also devise an appropriate strategy for evaluating student work.

Group Brainstorming

Benefits: By brainstorming, students learn to listen while developing the skill of creative exploring for new ideas. This process encourages full participation because all ideas are shared and recorded. *Accountable talk* is a practice that goes well with brainstorming. It develops and encourages procedures for children to learn to speak to the topic, based on information they are required to cite, and reference. This process draws on a class's knowledge base and experience while developing a spirit of cooperation.

Disadvantages: Brainstorming can become unwieldy and lose direction if not focused by the teacher. Students have problems in thinking outside their own reality. Negative criticism and personal remarks may be made if students have not been taught to use "accountable talk." This activity has to be monitored with respect to student ages and maturity levels.

Teacher Homework: Planning for brainstorming is difficult. The teacher must select issues that are suitable and motivating for students. Topics brainstormed must be related to the curriculum yet relevant to student interests and experiences. A system must be thought out where the teacher can intervene as an impartial moderator if the brainstorming is stuck on irrelevant positions.

Multimedia and Technology

Benefits: The use of videos, slides, and computer PowerPoint presentations enhance instruction by keeping student attention focused. They can be a novel and charming approach to the introduction of new materials. Today's students live in a multimedia world and expect to be entertained on occasion. The use of technology makes any presentation look professional while stimulating questions and discussion.

Disadvantages: A multimedia approach can be overly stimulating and allow too many issues to be raised, which can cause a loss of clarity and focus in a lesson. Those who are not interested in the topic presented in a multimedia presentation may not participate in the follow-up discussion. Technical glitches are sure to happen whenever multimedia and technology are employed, which can distract from any presentation.

Teacher Homework: The teacher must motivate students before the actual presentation and prepare effective follow-up questions. The teacher must also learn how to use media devices and programs and how to obtain, assemble, and set up equipment. A teacher may have to seek training in the use of new and advanced technology.

Case Studies

Benefits: The use of case studies develops higher order thinking skills to aid in analytic problem solving and for the exploration of solutions for complex issues and topics. It is an excellent way for students to demonstrate, apply, and use newly acquired knowledge and skills. It is an engaging approach that stimulates student participation. Students view studies as stories that are real and meaningful, relating them to their own experiences and creating their own understandings.

Disadvantages: If students do not see the relevance of the case study to their own situation, they tend not to become engaged. If a study provides insufficient information, it can lead to unsuitable results. Students may not possess the abilities necessary to diagnose individual studies. Case studies are not appropriate for elementary school children.

Teacher Homework: Teachers need to spend a great deal of time in preparing clearly written and defined studies or finding case studies that fit their students' needs and correlate with the content being taught.

Role Playing

Benefits: Role playing introduces problems in a dramatic fashion, and offers children a chance to assume the roles of others, helping develop an appreciation for other points of view. It offers a way to solve problems by exploring solutions from different viewpoints. Students can practice their human relation skills in real-life simulation activities.

Disadvantages: Some students may be too shy and self-conscious to participate in role playing. The method is not appropriate for large groups because it allows for limited involvement and participation. Individual students may have negative feelings, and feel threatened by role playing. Students may not grasp the relevance of the role they are expected to portray.

Teacher Homework: The teacher must define each problem situation and the specific roles that children have to play. Instructions must be clearly stated for all to understand. The skills required to role-play take a great deal of time and instruction to be developed. Teachers must have faith that children learn by doing and not solely by instruction.

Figure 1.6 Instructional Practices

Teacher Centered	Student Centered
Direct Instruction	*Indirect Instruction*
Expository teaching	Discovery teaching
Guided discovery	Problem-solving inquiry approach
Scientific method	Seminars
Direct Teaching	*Indirect Teaching*
Lecture	Cooperative learning
Lecture and discussion	Group brainstorming
Discussion	Multimedia technology
Small-group discussion	Case studies
Guest speakers	Role playing
	Research surveys
	Character education

Research Surveys

Benefits: The use of student-prepared research surveys allows students to think for themselves without being influenced by others. Students learn how to analyze data in a scientific fashion and arrive at solutions to predetermined problems. Students also have the opportunity to communicate their findings and share ideas with others. Students are highly motivated when the topics being researched are relevant to their experiences.

Disadvantages: Student research can only be used for specific issues and for limited periods. Students may have difficulty in analyzing data and need teacher guidance. It is not developmentally appropriate for everyone, and may frustrate some. The process is time consuming and requires an inordinate amount of time spent by teachers for student preparation. The products may be subjective and difficult to evaluate.

Teacher Homework: The teacher has to prepare worksheets as handouts to guide and instruct students. Organizing and analyzing data obtained from surveys requires large blocks of instructional time that can slow the pace necessary to cover the curriculum. Some teachers may be uncomfortable acting as facilitators and guides.

Values and Character Education

Benefits: Using an ethical approach to the problems confronting society allows opportunity to explore core values and beliefs that our diverse cultures are founded upon. Students can explain their values in a safe, secure environment, which affords a positive structure for discussion.

Disadvantages: Students may be intimidated and not be completely honest about their values. Some may be too self-conscious or inarticulate and therefore unable to present their values in an effective way. The study of values can become quite controversial due to the complexity of cultures present in our nation. Many may feel that values are best taught at home.

Teacher Homework: The teacher must carefully prepare and plan for any exercise pertaining to values, giving clear instructions and preparing discussion questions in advance. Teachers must be aware of possible controversies that may arise and be prepared to deal with them in a fitting fashion. (See Figure 1.6.)

MINI CASE FROM THE FIELD

The following case from the field presents the basic methods of instruction that must be mastered if one is to become a successful pedagogue. Read the case and compare Margaret's and Mr. Thompson's ideas about what constitutes effective instructional methods.

Basic Methods of Instruction for the Effective Teacher

Chandler Thompson, the principal of McGraw Simpson Elementary and Senior High School, was seated in his second-floor office staring out the window. He had been reflecting on his conversation last week with Margaret Gomez. Where had he gone wrong? He had a distinct feeling that he had not done all he could to help her

PRACTICE EXERCISE 1.5

Direct and Indirect Teaching

Select a teacher-centered and a student-centered practice you could employ for each of the following topics. Justify your choices.

1. Stars in our universe
2. Biodiesel fuel (use of the jatropha plant as a biodiesel fuel source which, unlike corn, is not edible).
3. Presidential elections
4. Holiday play (a class play for Thanksgiving)
5. Ratios (planning a vacation using frequent flyer miles)
6. Honesty
7. Studying for a test
8. Technology and the 21st century
9. Class rules
10. Great musicians

with the difficulties she was experiencing in teaching her classes. He had attempted to explain and clarify the *five keys to effective teaching:* management, mastery, methods, expectations, and personality. What he had not done was to explore the basic methods that every teacher must know.

Margaret was scheduled to meet with Mr. Thompson at 3:30 P.M. to discuss her plans for implementing the keys. She had decided to be concise and take a strong stance for using student-centered *indirect instructional methods.* This complemented her belief that children needed to find their own routes to *mastery.* She was confused about whether punishment, rewards, or both motivated children. The idea, she realized, was more suited to *direct instructional methods* that follow a transmission model in which students learn directly from the teacher. How was she ever going to resolve these problems?

It came to Margaret, like a bolt of lightning, while she was waiting to meet with Mr. Thompson. She would tell him she was a person of conviction, that her approach to teaching was **expository,** and that children acquired knowledge through reception rather than discovery. She would explain that she would work on establishing clear goals using teacher-led instruction in the form of lecture and discussion.

Mr. Thompson looked at Ms. Gomez later, after her brief recital, and said, "You think your plan is for indirect instruction? You seem to have solid ideas but you are confused as to how to achieve your objectives. What you just described to me was a direct instructional teacher-centered approach, which I must say may not be appropriate for your students. You did, however, indicate that you expected to use a *discussion approach,* which expands your methodology. Discussion can take different forms, most of which is student centered and quite apt for your class. *Brainstorming, debates, role playing, simulations, and large and small-group discussions* focused on a specific theme are but a few suitable methods that you could use.

"Do not shy away from *inquiry teaching* where you incorporate *open-ended discussions* with *student research.* Assign or have children select *projects* aimed at developing creative thinking. This method when used properly results in self-motivated children seeking new knowledge. The idea of *discovery learning* is for students to participate in *problem solving* activities of their own choosing. This method can be either direct or indirect depending on your approach.

"I can see by the look in your eyes that we have covered a great deal this afternoon. I would like you to take some time to digest our conversation and reflect on direct and indirect instruction. Try to decide whether you favor teacher- or student-centered instructional methods. I would venture to guess that your thinking is eclectic, and falls somewhere in the middle."

1. List the teacher-centered and student-centered methods discussed by Ms. Gomez and Mr. Thompson. Note the instructional methods that go well with either approach. Be sure to justify your choices.
2. Was Ms. Gomez inconsistent or eclectic in her thinking as Mr. Thompson implied? Defend your reasoning.
3. Compare and contrast Ms. Gomez's views with those of Mr. Thompson.
4. Describe the basic methods for instruction used by effective teachers you have known.
5. How would you determine if the instructional practice you used was appropriate and effective?

Chapter Summary

The importance of understanding the keys to effective teaching was stressed throughout this chapter, with special emphasis on personality as the glue that holds all the others together. Core characteristics and effective teaching behaviors are delineated and reviewed in a case study. The concept that the keys (mastery, method, management, expectations, and effective teaching personality) are essential for an effective teacher is highlighted, as is the purpose for all teaching as learning.

The basic approaches to effective teaching and learning have been explored, as well as the importance of being able to select the proper approach when preparing a lesson. Direct and indirect instructional strategies have been explored from the perspective of benefits, disadvantages, and need for teacher preparation with the aim to determine suitable strategies that teachers can use to create effective classes.

Cases from the Field

CASE ONE

Mary Connors, a kindergarten teacher at Hays Elementary, wasn't sure of the instructional approach she should use when introducing the alphabet to her class. She really didn't understand the difference between the inquiry approach and the discovery method. She knew that Dewey had said something about how the only way to learn was by doing, but she wondered how that would work with five-year-olds. She decided to ask Helen Tamaris, her next-door neighbor, who had been teaching for twenty years, if she could give her some suggestions. Helen responded by asking, "Is there a difference between a person walking with a limp and one walking normally?" Mary replied, "What does that mean?" "What it means is that both can walk and there is a slight difference." Both approaches are at their core child centered, but discovery learning can also be teacher centered.

1. Did Helen's story help in explaining the difference between inquiry and discovery learning?
2. How would you have explained the difference?
3. How could you encourage children to question the different letter shapes?
4. Describe a lesson for kindergarten for introducing the alphabet using a guided discovery approach.
5. Explain how the same lesson would be taught using an expository approach.

CASE TWO

Todd Cummings shouted out, "My dog has fur, he can't be struck by lightning." Mrs. Collins looked at Todd and said, "That certainly is an interesting interpretation on the effects of electricity. You should know, Todd, that lightning is an atmospheric discharge of electricity, which typically occurs during thunderstorms, and sometimes during volcanic eruptions or dust storms. Electricity is a general term used for a variety of observable events such as lightning, electromagnetic fields, and electric currents that result in the flow of electrically charged particles. I hope that satisfies your curiosity about lightning and electricity."

1. Did Mrs. Collins follow the instructional paradigm in her response to Todd's outburst?
2. Explain how you would use the learning paradigm concept in this situation.
3. Describe how a guided discovery approach could have enhanced this learning episode.
4. Did Mrs. Collins miss an opportunity to use an inquiry approach? Explain how this could have been done, and justify your reasoning.
5. Was Mrs. Collins's use of the expository approach reasonable considering the circumstances?

CASE THREE

Mr. Otis had been teaching at Morris High School for the past twenty years. He had seen the school go from one of the city's best to one of the worst. The school was multiculturally diverse and filled with students who spoke languages from all over the world. Mr. Otis was at least ten years away from retirement and a hundred from the joy he first felt as a new teacher. Somewhere along the way his students began to ignore him and to consider him an insensitive teacher to be avoided. Mr. Otis decided he had to do something to change things around if he was going to survive and his students were going to learn. Maybe it wasn't his fault. He tried. His students just didn't understand. What was he to do?

1. Mr. Otis needs to put his teaching life back on track. What strategies are effective in reaching diverse learners, academically and personally?

2. Whose fault was it that students did not relate to Mr. Otis' direct teaching style? Explain your answer.
3. What personal and professional qualities do teachers have that enable them to be culturally sensitive?
4. Describe how culturally sensitive teachers interact with students both inside and outside the classroom.
5. How could Mr. Otis develop partnerships between home and school experiences that create a learning environment?

CASE FOUR

Gail Billow was in her third week of student teaching when she realized that there was something wrong. Since she had first met her cooperating teacher, they had spoken a total of five minutes. She had to make an appointment in writing when she asked for some feedback on her lessons. Gail thought of the concept of "teaching personality" and decided her cooperating teacher had none. Gail decided to call her university supervisor and see if he could change her placement.

1. How would the university supervisor react to Gail's request?
2. Describe how to rectify this situation.
3. Should the principal be informed?
4. What could Gail have done before going to her university advisor?
5. Would changing cooperating teachers solve this problem?

CASE FIVE

Mary Sales was having difficulty adjusting to her student teaching placement. She had always had difficulty with authority figures. She preferred teaching to marking standardized tests, which she considered a menial task. Her problems erupted when her sponsor teacher told her how to dress. She was to dress as a professional and not wear work coveralls. Mary said that violated her right to self-expression. The cooperating teacher called the university supervisor to complain that Mary was not suited to teaching because she was uncooperative and evidenced little collegiality.

1. What do you think will be the reaction of the university supervisor?
2. How would you deal with Mary's personality problem?
3. Describe and address any underlying problems that may be present.
4. How could Mary have avoided this problem?
5. Is it professional to disagree with a cooperating teacher?

CASE SIX

Carrie felt that her cooperating teacher was not being fair to her and never supported her. It seemed that every time Carrie made a suggestion about how she would like to teach a specific topic, Mrs. Blasts would say that was not the way to do it. Carrie could live with that, since Mrs. Blasts was the only teacher who accepted student teachers at the school. The real problem began when Carrie received a note from the teacher committee saying she was not to park in the teachers' lot since it was reserved for veteran teachers. Carrie found this to be untrue, and Mrs. Blasts said she had never heard of such a rule. Carrie asked to speak with the principal to complain that teachers were acting in an unprofessional way toward her.

1. What do you think the principal's response will be to Carrie's inquiry?
2. What should the cooperating teacher do about this situation?
3. How do you explain the actions of the teachers with regard to parking?
4. What options did Carrie have before she went to the principal?
5. What do you think will be the university supervisor's reaction when he or she finds out?

CASE SEVEN

Linda had always wanted to be a special education teacher and looked at her placement as a student teacher at the Bay View School as the start of her teaching career. Her cooperating teacher, Mr. Haddock, was a fine person with years of experience. Linda felt he was the ideal special education teacher. He was a caring educator who knew what methods to use to facilitate learning. He knew what he was doing. On the opposite side of the spectrum was Mrs. Lopez, the class paraprofessional, who acted like a prison warden. Mrs. Lopez also admired Mr. Haddock despite the fact that she believed he was too easy on the children. One day Linda observed Mrs. Lopez screaming, hollering, and pushing one of the children into the back wall of the classroom when Mr. Haddock was not present. Linda told Mr. Haddock when he returned to the room. He told her to forget about it, and he would take care of it.

1. What would you do if you were Linda?
2. Is Mr. Haddock acting in a professional fashion? Explain.
3. What type of advice do you feel Linda's university supervisor would give her?
4. Describe and address any legal issues related to this episode.
5. Is it appropriate for a student teacher to report a colleague?

Terms to Remember

Learning paradigm
Keys to effective teaching
Smart classrooms
Approaches to effective teaching
Discovery (guided discovery)
Discussion approach
Pedagogy

Instructional paradigm
Core characteristics of an effective teacher
Diversity
Expository approach
Inquiry (scientific method)
Direct and indirect instructional methods

Discussion Questions

1. Describe the five keys to effective teaching, and explain how each plays a role in the development of a future teacher.
2. Which of the five keys is most necessary for the effective teacher? Justify your choice.
3. Design a matching list. On one side, list the five keys to effective teaching. Next to each key list one or more effective teaching behaviors.
4. How does a positive classroom environment assist the effective teacher?
5. Why must an effective teacher be aware of the cultural diversity he or she will face in the classroom?
6. Describe strategies to use with diverse learners that meet cultural and academic needs.
7. Select, compare, and contrast the instructional strategies for teaching elementary and high school students.
8. Are instructional strategies interchangeable from grade to grade? Explain.
9. Analyze the "learning paradigm" and compare it to the traditional model for learning.
10. Which, if any, teaching practice helps students learn best? Explain the reasons for your choice.

Field Experience Activities

1. Interview two teachers in any grade level and ask them to describe effective teaching, then compare their responses to those described in this chapter.
2. Visit a classroom and look for different types of diversity (cultural, ability, gender, and language). Note the patterns of interaction with the teacher.
3. Visit a classroom in your area and analyze its instructional appropriateness by describing good signs and possible areas of worry.
4. Draw a diagram of a classroom organized for effective teaching. Explain why you chose to arrange the furniture as you did. Also, discuss the use of decoration, student work centers, and accessibility to supplies.
5. Interview two teachers and ask them to describe their plans for the first day of school. Analyze and compare with your own experiences.

For Further Reading

Adler, M. (1984). *The Paideia program: An educational syllabus.* New York: Collier Books.

Darling-Hammond, L. (1998, February). Standards for assessing teaching effectiveness are key. *Phi Delta Kappan,* 471–472.

CHAPTER 2

Understanding How We Learn

FOCUS POINTS

1. Learning can be defined as an interactive process between learner and content to be learned.
2. Learning is the process of communication that occurs between learner and teacher.
3. Knowledge is a process of individual construction.
4. Instruction and learning play a major role in the learning process.
5. Understanding the five keys leads to good instructional practices.
6. Effective teaching personality develops over time, as does comprehending how learning is achieved.

CHAPTER OVERVIEW

THIS CHAPTER ATTEMPTS TO ESTABLISH AN UNDERSTANDING from among the various philosophies about how we learn. Two philosophies stand out as basic to learning: behaviorist and constructivist. They are essentially both humanistic in that they show a concern for the interests, needs, and welfare of humanity. This is so even though some critics may disagree. Understanding the difference between scholastic instruction and learning is vital to comprehending the roles teachers and students play in the learning process. Understanding these two approaches, combined with a study of brain theory and intelligence, allows us to define how we learn. The psychological foundation upon which this paradigm is based makes this knowledge indispensable. The part our brain plays in understanding is explored in depth, from traditional to fringe alternatives. The meaning of intelligence theory and its relationship to understanding in a diverse multicultural society concludes the chapter. Once the learning process is understood, methods for good instruction will be easy to implement.

APPROACHES TO LEARNING

Two basic approaches to understanding how we learn have been advanced by both behaviorist and constructivist psychologists. An eclectic view of teaching and learning, best expressed in Jerome Bruner's early works (Bruner, 1960), will represent a commonly relied upon third alternative. The path to understanding and learning is not necessarily straight. Bruner indicated that there were different approaches to learning, with distinctive forms of instruction that ranged from imitation to discovery, and included collaboration. These dissimilar eclectic approaches reflect differing beliefs and assumptions about learners. They imply that there might be more than one or two correct ways to understand the learning process. We will focus on two basic approaches defined in Figure 2.1.

Behaviorist Approach to Learning

Burrhus Frederic Skinner (1904–1990), the founder of behavioral psychology, was a psychologist at Harvard University who claimed our choices are determined by environmental conditions under which we live. He found that a student's behavior could be controlled through a program of positive and negative reinforcement. His work led to the science of human behavior known as behavior modification, which allows us to study and analyze human behavior. The controversy that surrounds Skinner developed because he told people they were not as important as they believed they were. He claimed our minds were not our private preserve and felt they could be controlled and shaped by environmental science. His view was as controversial as that of Copernicus who said the earth was not the center of the universe and Darwin who said the human body is not so special because of evolution and natural selection. The historical references that led to behavioral psychology were essentially linear from Aristotle to Watson.

Figure 2.1 Three Basic Approaches to Learning

1. The *behaviorist view* of teaching and learning (also called a *transmission approach*) claims that children are blank slates that respond to stimuli and absorb information in the form in which it is transmitted. This traditional position holds that a teacher tells, shows, or demonstrates facts, knowledge rules of action, and principles, which students then must practice to learn. Learning from this perspective is viewed as measuring attainment of a fixed body of knowledge.

2. The *constructivist view* of teaching and learning (or *cognitive psychologist's approach*) is rooted in an old paradigm that the construction of knowledge occurs in a social-cultural context that embodies an investigative style of learning. It also claims that children are self-regulating and may be influenced by environmental factors, but essentially make their own decisions on how to behave and learn. This is a relativist view of knowledge with an emphasis on assessing higher-order thinking skills.

3. An *eclectic approach* to learning has no specific theoretical rationale: It comprises individual strategies that have been proven effective in the past. The practice has been described as a cookbook approach of do's and don'ts that have been used for ages by teachers. Goodlad (1983) describes an eclectic approach as a composite of strategies such as positive reinforcement, rewards, honor rolls, and special privileges—all taken from other approaches.

The following five historical events led to the founding of behavioral psychology and eventually behavior modification. There is a clear line from the ancient Greeks through the Renaissance and the Victorian period that establishes the thought processes that led to behavioral psychology.

1. Aristotle was the first to classify human behavior into the five categories of sight, smell, hearing, appetite, and fashion.
2. René Descartes (1600s) viewed behavior as mechanical since the body was a machine.
3. In the 1800s Darwin's theory of evolution and natural selection was an explanation of human behavior.
4. Ivan Pavlov demonstrated behavior modification theory by getting dogs to salivate when a bell was rung.
5. John B. Watson formalized previous study into a field called "behavioral psychology."

Skinner's contribution to the field was that he isolated behavior as its own entity separate from all other aspects of life by disregarding the mind, soul, and human spirit. He explained human behaviors as being controlled by consequences and not human will. He claimed all behaviors could be reinforced if a sufficiently strong reward was provided following the behavior. Behaviorists who follow Skinner boast that they can modify behavior by either reinforcement or punishment and thus encourage learning.

Skinner's genius lies in his interpretation of ideas as related to behavior. He claimed, for example, that aggression is not implicit in human nature but taught through culture. He expounded on this idea by claiming that society operated on the principle of self-interest as does humankind. Rewards were what people and society wished to gain as a result of their actions. This led to a theory called "Contingencies of Reinforcement," which Skinner claimed was the result of situations, behavior, and consequences (Skinner, 1948, 1968).

Applying the theoretical principles of behaviorism to learning environments, it is easy to recognize that we have many "behaviorist artifacts" in our learning world. A dissection of the traditional teaching approaches used for years would reveal the powerful influence that behaviorists have had on learning. The concept of direct teaching, in which a teacher is providing the knowledge to the students either directly or through the set-up of "contingencies," is an excellent example of the behaviorist model of learning. The use of exams to measure observable behavior of learning, the use of rewards and punishments in our school systems, and the breaking down of the instruction process into "conditions of learning" are all examples of the behaviorist influence.

With the advent of the computer in school, computer-assisted instruction (CAI) has become a prominent tool for teaching, because from a behaviorist perspective, it is an effective way of learning. CAI uses the drill-and-practice approach to learning new concepts or skills. The question acting as the stimulus elicits a response from the user. Based on the response, a reward may be provided. The "contingencies" of learning are translated into different levels of the program. Rewarding the user with a different level for correct responses follows exactly the approach of operant conditioning. Educators have espoused CAI as an effective teaching approach because it allows for self-paced instruction and it liberates them from the direct instruction of all their students so they can focus on those students with particular needs.

In his book on education entitled *The Technology of Teaching* (1968), Skinner gave practical examples of programmed instruction as part of his philosophy of education. Education was seen as a process in which we arrange the educational environment to expedite learning. His teaching system consisted of lessons and rewards leading to self-control. Skinner claimed that positive reinforcement, not punishment, was the most effective consequence for any human response. This can be readily seen in the so-called correction strategies that behaviorists use to modify behavior (see Figure 2.2).

Skinner wrote, "The application of operant conditioning to education is simple and direct. Teaching is the arrangement of contingencies of reinforcement under which students learn. They learn without teaching in their natural environments, but teachers arrange special contingencies which expedite learning, hastening the appearance of behavior which would otherwise be acquired slowly or making sure of the appearance of behavior which otherwise never occur" (1968, p. 64).

Skinner believed that more complex learning could be achieved by this process of contingencies and reinforcement ". . . through successive stages in the shaping process, the contingencies of reinforcement being changed progressively in the direction of the required behavior" (1968, p. 10).

Remember that behavior modification is the name for the overall process, which derives from Skinner's work. Two key elements are behavior shaping and operant behavior. Behavior shaping is the systematic use of reinforcing stimuli to change one's behavior in a desired direction. Operant behavior, on the other hand, is any voluntary action that an individual performs. This simply means that any (operant) behavior can be reinforced negatively or positively by an outside force—the teacher.

The Neo-Skinnerian Model Skinner's followers applied his principles to create a neo-Skinnerian model for reinforcement in the development of behavior modification. This model is used to shape desired behavior in the classroom. Skinner formulated the principles for behavior shaping while his followers used his principles for disciplining classrooms. The main strength of the neo-Skinnerian model is that behavior modification works, and works well (Ingvorsson and Morris, 2004). It is simple to use and the results are immediate. It accommodates most teachers' desire to maintain control while it allows students to feel successful because they obtain rewards. The standards of behavior are uniform, consistent, and clear to all students. Time does not have to be spent discussing rules and conduct. It can be applied to all ages. It is well researched and works consistently. Without question, it can promote better student behavior and more rapid learning. All teachers use it to some extent, but few systematically. A behavior modification plan consists of three steps, as seen in Figure 2.3.

Unfortunately, there are weaknesses associated with behavior modification. It is too elaborate to be used comfortably throughout the day. Most teachers resist its full application as being either akin to bribing, or overly manipulative, or as subversive to the exercise of free will. Unless punishment is included, behavior modification is ineffective for dealing with blatant misbehavior. The results may not last long because students may not perform as expected when rewards are terminated. It

Figure 2.2 Correction Strategies Used to Modify Behavior

Reinforcement is the term used for the process in which stimuli are used to reinforce behavior. It is the process of supplying reinforcing stimuli. These reinforcers can be used either for negative reinforcement, as in withdrawing stimuli or positive reinforcement, as when stimuli are used for rewards. An example of positive reinforcement would be to give points for good behavior, while an example of negative reinforcement would be taking points away for poor behavior.

Types of Reinforcers

Conditioned reinforcers are reinforcers that are strengthened by association with another reinforcer. An example would be verbal praise for good behavior accompanied by, or associated with, material rewards or special privileges. Catch 'em Being Good: Provide praise for good work.

Edible reinforcers are made up of items such as candy or other goodies, which is not advisable today due to various state laws that prohibit their use.

Material reinforcers consist of items such as physical objects and toys.

Activity reinforcers such as playtime and trips are commonly used. An example would be a token economy in which tokens are used as a system of exchange for any reinforcer the children deem appropriate (edible, material, or activity reinforcers, prizes, or games). Another means would be a contract that formalized agreements signed by a teacher, students, and parents.

Response-cost procedures is the process by which a desirable stimulus is removed as the cost for some inappropriate behavior. The removal of a token each time an infraction occurs would be another example of response-cost procedures. The process of creating rules–rewards and punishments consists of making a rule, rewarding the rule-followers, and punishing the rule-breakers.

Time out is the term used for a strategy in which a student is temporarily removed from the environment in which misbehavior is being reinforced. This usually takes the form of a time-out seat or corner to which a child is sent until he or she is ready to conform.

Punishment should only be used as a last resort when positive approaches have failed. It can be used for behavior deemed as bad behavior that deserves a punishment, an uncontrollable fistfight, or any other violent act.

Extinction is a strategy used to ignore inappropriate behavior until it disappears. It can be very effective when desired behaviors are also reinforced at the same time.

Figure 2.3 Planning for Behavior Modification

1. *Analysis.* Determine your concerns, what is going wrong, and desired behavior.
2. *Develop plan.* Identify desired behavior and rules, reinforcers, and consequences to achieve desired behavior.
3. *Implement plan.*
    a. Correct conditions that may be causing the problem (antecedents).
    b. Review and clarify rules.
    c. Describe consequences.
    d. Tighten up lessons and make as interesting as possible.
    e. Discuss the process with students as often as necessary.

PRACTICE EXERCISE 2.1

Preparing a Behavior Modification Plan

Use the steps outlined in Figure 2.3 to develop a brief plan that you could use to address the following situations.

1. Your class is disruptive as you enter the room.
2. Students claim that you give them too much homework and it interferes with their other class assignments.
3. A student informs you confidentially that members of her class intend to cheat on your midterm.

ignores causes and solutions to problems such as understanding the total ecology in which learning takes place (home and society). Children may not learn how to govern their own behavior, which should be a goal in a democratic society. The rewards undermine intrinsic motivations. It gives no opportunity to clarify emotions, weigh alternatives, decide on solutions, or develop the intellect. Behavior modification is most effective in preventive and supportive aspects of discipline while relatively weak in corrective discipline. It is, however, the key to the traditional views concerning understanding how children learn.

Behaviorist Learning Theory Behaviorism as a teaching approach can be referred to as direct teaching, and as an objectivist theory of learning. The emphasis of behaviorism is that there are observable indicators that evidence learning is taking place, while cognitive psychologists equate learning with mental processes. Behaviorists accept these mental processes but they view them as an unobservable indication of learning.

Behaviorism focuses on conditioning observable human behavior. J. B. Watson, the founder of behaviorism, defined learning as a sequence of stimulus and response actions in observable cause and effect relationships. A classic example of conditioning is Pavlov's experiment with the digestive process in animals. Pavlov noticed that a dog would salivate (response) upon hearing a bell ring. The dog learned to associate unconditional stimuli (normally feeding) with the neutral stimuli of a bell ringing while being fed. Skinner expanded on the foundation of behaviorism by focusing on operant conditioning. According to Skinner, voluntary or automatic behavior is either strengthened or weakened by the immediate presence of a reward or a punishment. The learning principle demonstrated by operant conditioning was that new learning occurs as a result of positive reinforcement, and old patterns are abandoned as a result of negative reinforcement (Belkin and Gray, 1977, p. 59).

Constructivist Approach to Learning

The extremes of learning theory are represented, respectively, by the behaviorist and constructivist theories. These theories represent two alternative attempts to explain the same thing from distinctive perspectives. How knowledge is acquired and the function of the teacher is viewed quite differently by each theory. Behaviorist learning theory is seen as outdated by constructivists. Constructivist learning theory focuses on motivation and ability to construct meaning. Behaviorism is viewed as too teacher centered and directed, emphasizing an educational system as a process of matching skill objectives with test items, and avoiding meaningful learning. Behaviorists imply that knowledge is separate to the human mind and must be transferred to the learner by a teacher. This is fundamentally counter to the constructivist theory of learning that all have the ability to construct knowledge, through a process of discovery and problem solving.

The constructivist approach rests on the belief that a student constructs individual knowledge based on one's schemata of existing beliefs. Constructivism from this perspective is viewed as a philosophical explanation about the nature of knowledge; it is considered by some an instructional approach. It can be easily compared to the *traditional view* of knowledge, which claims that knowledge is fixed and independent of the learner. Knowledge in the traditionalist view is thought to consist of a fixed number of truths that one accumulates. This logically leads to the traditional belief that the more facts one possesses, the more knowledge one has. This view is in direct contrast to the *constructivist view*, which sees knowledge as tentative, subjective, and based on personal beliefs. Constructivists see knowledge as being based on working hypotheses, not on universal truths. Constructivists speculate that knowledge is fostered through interactions and not through the traditional concept of a transmission model.

The basis for constructivist theory is rooted in the works of many prominent educational theorists. Dewey, Montessori, Piaget, Bruner, Vygotsky, Maslow, Erikson, and Kohlberg each added a different dimension to a body of thought that came to be called constructivist. There is no clear line in its development except that it does initially stem from the ancients who believed that one of the ways in which students learned was through a process they called active construction. Constructivist learning has emerged as a prominent approach to teaching. It represents a paradigm shift from education based on behaviorism to education based on cognitive theory. Fosnot (1996) summarized constructivist teaching practices by explaining that its epistemology assumes that learners construct their own knowledge based on interaction with their environment.

Learning is viewed as a personal act in which we create our own approach to how, what, and when we learn. Gardner's theory of multiple intelligences bolsters this view by acknowledging that learning is a holistic experience related to one's learning style. Learning appears to be a simple act, so much so that most of the time we do not question how it occurs. We only seem to question it when it does not occur or we encounter difficulties in learning something, at which point our curiosity is heightened. Learning is taken for granted as a natural process, even though there are many definitions and theories of learning that indicate its complexity. Some see learning as the result of some form of intervention, or as an outcome (Belkin and Gray, 1977). Intervention can imply different things. It can mean the degree of intervention, or the who, what, and how involved in defining a learning theory. Today's learners are not satisfied to be passive recipients, as envisioned in the traditional model of the teaching process; rather, they want to discover for themselves by becoming interactive with the learning (Tapscott, 1998).

Constructivist Learning Design An understanding of learning and its applications are inherent in the work of Gagnon and Collay (1996). They identify four epistemological assumptions consisting of the physical, symbolic, social, and theoretical construction of knowledge as the heart of what they refer to as constructivist learning. This theoretical process can be used as a guide for the constructivist teacher in preparing and reflecting on instructional exercises. (See Figure 2.4.) To be effective, teachers must develop the situations for students to explain. They must build a bridge between what students already know and what the teacher wants them to learn. Teachers have to anticipate questions to ask and be able to answer

Figure 2.4 Steps for Learners to Construct Knowledge

1. Learners who are involved in active learning *physically construct* knowledge.
2. Learners who are making their own representations of action *symbolically construct* knowledge.
3. Knowledge is *socially constructed* by learners who convey their meaning-making to others.
4. Learners who try to explain things they do not completely understand *theoretically construct* knowledge.

without giving away an explanation. Students have to be encouraged to exhibit a record of their thinking and share it with others. The final step for teachers is to solicit students' reflections about learning. The rationale behind this learning design is that teachers are encouraged to think about accomplishing objectives and outcomes rather than writing them. (See Figure 2.5.)

Different Constructivist Theories Swiss psychologist Jean Piaget (1896–1980) observed human development as progressive stages of cognitive development. His four stages, which commence at infancy and progress into adulthood, characterize the cognitive abilities necessary at each stage to construct meaning from one's environment (Piaget, 1952). Constructivist theories break down into two different approaches—the developmental and the environmental.

Figure 2.5 Design for Learning

1. The teacher *designs the situations* in which to place students based on her assessment of students' learning approaches, interests, and needs.
2. The teacher *designs a process for grouping* based on assessment of available materials and a desired mixture of students.
3. A simple assessment of what students already know is used as a *bridge to what teachers expect students to learn.*
4. Questions are designed *to assess student understanding* of concepts, skills, or attitudes to be learned.
5. Teachers arrange opportunities for students to *exhibit* and record what they thought and submit it to others for assessment.
6. Teachers arrange for *reflections* about what students have learned. This is an internal process for self-assessment of individual student learning.

PRACTICE EXERCISE 2.2

Preparing a Constructivist Learning Plan

Use the steps outlined in Figures 2.4 and 2.5 to develop a brief plan that you could use to address the following situations:

1. Your class is unruly when returning from lunch and as a result loses, on average, ten minutes of instructional time each day.
2. Students claim they are not prepared to take your midterm examination because they have difficulty memorizing your notes.
3. A student comes to you and says he is having difficulty working in a cooperative group setting.

Figure 2.6 Piaget's Stages of Cognitive Development

1. *Birth to two years—Sensorimotor stage.* At this stage, infants experience the world through senses and actions such as looking, touching, and mouthing. Infants learn that objects exist even when they are not visible, which is called *object permanence*. They begin to feel distress and anxiety when they see an unfamiliar face that does not fit their schemas.
2. *Two to six years—Preoperational stage.* At this stage, the child is able to represent things with words and images, but cannot reason with logic. They also acquire the ability to pretend and develop egocentrism.
3. *Seven to twelve years—Concrete operational stage.* A child thinks logically about concrete events, can grasp concrete analogies, and perform arithmetical operations at this stage. The concept of conservation is perfected and the child is able to understand mathematical transformations.
4. *Twelve years to adult—Formal operational stage.* During this stage, the teenager develops abstract reasoning and thinks with symbols, as evidenced by the perfection of abstract and scientific reasoning. The potential for mature moral reasoning presents itself during this period.

Developmental Theory of Cognition describes the structures of knowledge as *prelogical, concrete,* and *abstract operations* (see Figure 2.6). Piaget believed children learn to understand concepts through a process of stages. According to *stage theory,* children proceed through a fixed number of cognitive developmental stages before learning occurs and concepts are internalized. *Environmental theory*, on the other hand, states that children learn through an active involvement with their surroundings, called the *Sociocultural Theory of Cognition*.

Piaget felt most teaching methods consisted of direct teaching, or rote force-feeding strategies, and could be loosely termed *transmission models*. His thesis was that humans were different from animals at each stage of development. To be effective, education should be child centered and focused on the learner and on learning, not transmission. The aim of teaching was to teach students to learn, innovate, and produce or verify truth. Concepts are developed when logical understanding overcomes perceptual misunderstanding. The art is in selecting an aim, determining how to verify it, and finding a method to implement it. Learning occurs in three ways as three distinctive processes: developmental, cognitive, and environmental.

1. **Developmental Process** The developmental process deals with the physical growth of children. The development of thinking (cognition) is a process related to the intelligence and maturation of the child. Intelligence is defined as the ability and capacity to learn and acquire knowledge; intelligence is the process of adaptation to the environment. The term *schema* (scheme) refers to any pattern of thought one develops through the process of adaptation to understand the world. The adaptive process consists of two items, assimilation (taking information and incorporating it with what you already know) and accommodation. Piaget defined accommodation as the process of taking in information and adding to our existing knowledge to create new meaning. In effect, Piaget said that the way one understands is to first gather data and combine it with one's experiences, giving data meaning. (See Figure 2.7.)
2. **Cognitive Process** The cognitive process refers to the age at which mental activities such as learning, thinking, and remembering take place. Cognition itself refers to the diverse thinking processes of reflection, conceptualization, problem solving, and decision making.

There are four basic stages in cognitive development: sensorimotor, preoperational, concrete operational, and formal operational. (See Figure 2.6.)
3. **Environmental Process** Piaget has been criticized by *social constructivists* who reject his individualistic approach to learning and lack of stress on environmental factors even though those factors had been acknowledged. Social constructionists believe that knowledge is constructed by interaction within a social milieu, or an environment, which they term a sociocultural theory of cognition. Whether we believe in the social constructivist version or Piaget's developmental version, the theory holds that children are still the constructors of their own knowledge. Both cognitive and social development are necessary in order for one to become a contributing member of society.

There are essentially two opposing views of education—constructivist and traditional behaviorist. Each purports to understand the truth regarding how we learn.

The *traditional view* is that knowledge is fixed and is independent of the learner. Knowledge is the accumulation of truths in a subject area. The more truths you possess, the more knowledge you have. In the transmission model, teachers attempt to convey knowledge to students directly. The teacher lectures and students listen and learn.

The *constructivist view* is that knowledge is not independent; it is a part of the learner and is produced from one's existing beliefs and experiences. Knowledge does not consist of accumulated truths; it is not a set of universal truths, but a set of working hypotheses. All knowledge is understood to be tentative, subjective, and personal. There are two versions of constructivist theory as it applies to cognitive, developmental, and social constructivism.

1. *Developmental constructivism* (the traditional view) claims that one learns by going from the concrete to the abstract, based on Piaget's theory of cognition.

Figure 2.7 Adaptation Process Model

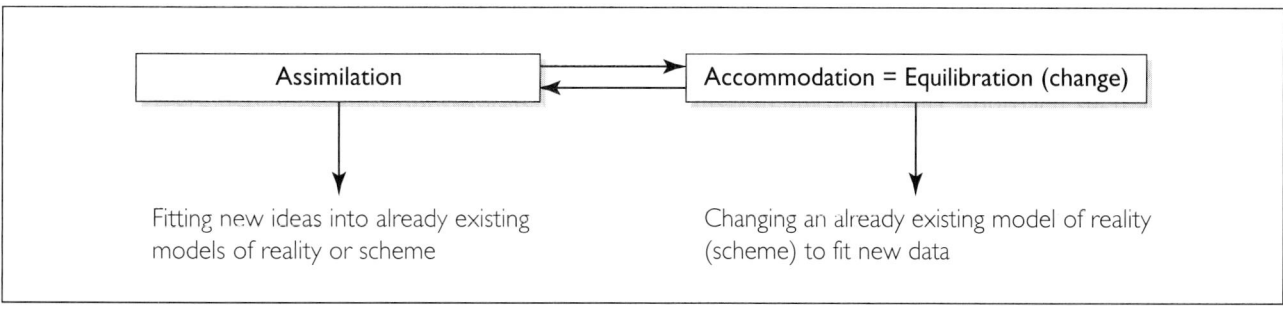

2. *Social constructivism* claims that knowledge is constructed by the individual in a sociocultural context.

The real argument related to appropriate teaching practices can be termed "construction versus instruction." The question is not which form of constructivism is correct, but how constructivism compares to the traditional behaviorist teaching practices.

Constructivist Teaching Practices: The classroom practices advocated by constructivists are focused on non-rote outcomes such as generalizing, analyzing, synthesizing, and evaluation. These higher-order thinking skills are seen as a mantra. Teacher empowerment, cooperative learning, performance assessments, product-oriented activities, and hands-on learning all fit constructivist philosophy. Teachers consider themselves facilitators, not dispensers, of knowledge. They do not tell students what to think; rather, they encourage students to make their own meanings and accept diverse opinions. Two key concepts associated with constructivists are that student construction of meaning is more important than teacher presentation, and secondly, all children can learn because they construct their own knowledge. It should be noted that these progressive concepts are not universally agreed upon. Even Thomas Jefferson, who said, "All men are created equal," was only referring to personal and political equality; he did not advocate social or economic, and certainly not academic, equality. (See Figure 2.8.)

Constructivist practice requires that one look at intelligence in a different way from the traditional ideas concerning intelligence. In addition to Gardner's innovative concepts about multiple intelligence, the works of Daniel Goleman (1998) on emotional intelligence must be considered. Constructivist methodology dictates that teachers become coaches helping others to develop their own understanding. A teacher must become a facilitator who assists a student in constructing solutions to problems. The constructivist approach to classroom practice is based on collaboration rather than the traditionalists' compliance. Traditionalists set goals and require compliance, while constructivists insist on collaboration. Constructivist methodology consists of a four-step process of (1) identifying, (2) solutions, (3) implementation, and (4) evaluation. Constructivists believe that classroom practice needs to be reinvented using a constructivist, collaborative approach. (See Figure 2.9.)

Two questions must be answered before using constructivist practices and assumptions. How do you implement a constructivist program? Moreover, how do you assess students' learning? Implementation of constructivist assumptions and practices are more difficult than just understanding concepts. Assessment cannot be determined by factual objective tests when solutions differ and are not acceptable to all. Use of reflection, self-

Figure 2.8 Ten Constructivist Teaching Practices

1. Encourage and accept student autonomy and initiative.
2. Use raw data and primary sources, along with manipulatives (interactive or physical materials).
3. Use cognitive terminology such as *classify*, *analyze*, *predict*, and *create* when framing tasks.
4. Allow student response to drive lessons, shift instructional strategies, and alter content.
5. Inquire about students' understanding of concepts before sharing understandings.
6. Encourage students to engage in dialogue with the teacher and with others.
7. Promote student inquiry by asking thoughtful, open-ended questions that allow students to question classmates.
8. Engage students in experiences that might engender contradictions to the students' initial hypotheses and discussion.
9. Provide time for students to construct relationships and create metaphors.
10. Nurture curiosity by assisting students to make discoveries, introduce concepts, and apply them.

Figure 2.9 Key Constructivist Assumptions

1. Since we all construct our own knowledge, we all can learn.
2. Philosophy and instructional approach need not be consistent.
3. Teachers are guides, not sages.
4. Teachers create environments for students to obtain meanings.
5. Teachers accept diversity of opinion while not searching for "right" answers.
6. A constructivist class is an open system, not closed and judgmental.
7. Critical thinking is encouraged.
8. Because all construct knowledge, teachers must set criteria and standards, while not compromising the learning process.
9. Teachers address learning in daily activities that generate meaning through assessments.
10. Teachers create opportunities for students to explore big ideas.

evaluation, journals, projects, and other means of authentic assessment are integral to constructivist assumptions and practice. A constructivist approach changes rules we are used to accepting. Teachers are no longer considered sages but guides who facilitate and create situations in which learning can occur. Reductionism, or looking for one right answer or absolute solution to a problem, is no longer the method to follow. A multiplicity of answers and views should be explored and discussed within the framework of established criteria and standards for solutions, without compromising the process. Critics still ask, How can one evaluate answers if all construct their own solutions? While difficult, it can be done through authentic assessment and using big ideas to encourage learning and understanding.

Most teachers say they like the ideas and assumptions behind constructivist theory, but can't use them in class. When asked why not, they inevitably respond, "It's not realistic." What they should be saying is that they think it's too difficult to use. But all good teaching takes effort and has varying degrees of difficulty. When we look at constructivist practices, we recognize many strategies rudimentary to effective teaching. These practices if adopted indicate that good instruction is taking place, whether traditional or constructivist.

An Eclectic Approach to Learning

A review of the literature on learning theories illustrates many labels being used to describe various models. A categorization of these models provides a spectrum of answers explaining how humans learn. Trying to tie learning to one particular theory is similar to comparing school experiences to the real world. What we learn in a school environment does not always match what we know of the real world. Discovering what works gives some focus to understanding how we learn. A description of each theory suffices in providing enough knowledge for reflecting on the myriad of beliefs described. An eclectic approach to learning makes a great deal of sense seen from this perspective. Most learning models are presented as mental pictures that enable us to understand what we will never see. By modifying our ideas to accommodate for circumstances surrounding learning situations we can decide on appropriate instructional methods. To accomplish this we have to realize that some learning problems require highly prescriptive solutions, whereas others are more suited to learner control of the environment.

From this perspective, the way we teach and learn is viewed as a commonsense process, as are the roles of teachers and students. The eclectic model asks teachers to know what they wish to teach and how they wish to present it. This is the "what" and the "how" of teaching. Without answering these two simple questions, teachers would never be able to facilitate learning. The strategy one decides to employ, whether direct or indirect, should be based on student capabilities and difficulty of content. The choice of method is the teacher's; the learning is the student's. It is not what is taught but what is learned that counts in the end. (See Figures 2.10 and 2.11.)

Figure 2.10 Basic Premises of Eclectic Practice

1. The major assumption is that the teacher can solve managerial problems by applying specific "tried and true" prescriptions.
2. The role of the teacher is to react to various problem situations by following a set of simple remedies.
3. The managerial strategies characteristic of the "cookbook" approach are often drawn from other approaches and are presented as absolutes. Two examples of the typical cookbook remedy go something like: (1) always be consistent in enforcing rules; and (2) never play favorites when rewarding students.

Source: Scarpaci (2007)

Figure 2.11 Behaviors That Determine Effective Eclectic Teaching

1. *Instructional clarity* occurs when you focus lessons on getting students engaged throughout your presentation.
2. *Knowledge of content* enables you to structure and integrate concepts into your subject's curriculum.
3. *Establishment of learning expectations* occurs when you present your lesson objectives before you teach the lesson.
4. *Variation in teaching* is when you plan a variety of strategies that provide for interactive learning rather than simply passive learning.
5. *Utilization of resources* is when many different instructional aids and materials are used.
6. *Knowledge of learning and development principles* occurs when you meet student needs through use of appropriate strategies. Strategies termed traditional, progressive, and constructivist are all brought into play by the effective teacher in implementation.
7. *Communication with students on multiple levels* are the practices you use to clear the lines of communication with a focus on higher order thinking skills.
8. *Enthusiasm* is infectious and a teacher's positive energy is usually returned.

Source: Reinhartz (1997)

1. Students' instructional objectives should be clear and concise. Teachers should *know what they want to teach.*
2. Students' prior knowledge should be ascertained. It is the teacher's responsibility to *know the abilities of those in class.*
3. It is the role of the teacher to *decide on the instructional model* to use.
4. Finally the teacher must *assess student performance* in order to evaluate the effectiveness of instruction.

MINI CASE FROM THE FIELD

The following case from the field presents arguments both for and against behaviorism and constructivism as plausible answers to the question, "How do students learn?" Read the case, then compare and contrast positions presented by Margaret, her friend Jane Hemmings, and Mr. Thompson regarding which approach is best—transmission (traditional) or facilitation (constructivist).

Understanding How Students Learn

Margaret Gomez sat in the teachers' lounge scowling at her friend and colleague Jane Hemmings. She finally said, "I just don't get it! He asked me to explain to him how students learn. Why would Principal Thompson want to know that from me? He's the principal—he should know children learn from good teaching. The better my lessons, the more they learn."

Jane replied, "Are you sure of that? It would seem to me that there is more than one way for children to learn, and the transmission model is so old fashioned."

"You have to be kidding, Jane—the transmission model is the traditional method for instruction, and it's been around since the ancient Greeks. Children need to be taught using a direct instructional approach, an approach that is teacher centered and based on clearly defined objective outcomes, not some fuzzy indirect teaching method that claims to be learner centered."

"Margaret, where did you go to school? Don't you know all learning is based on cognitive operations that assist the learner in creating meaning and reality? It's called constructivism, which is a cognitive learning theory that focuses on mental processes that construct meaning. It's based on learning theories equated with cognitive psychology such as information-processing theory, and scaffolding theory that's linked with the Russian philosopher Lev Vygotsky, and brain-based learning theory connected to the work of neuroscientists."

"So you're implying that a holistic method that emphasizes group work is better than focusing on one method, and the individual child?"

Just then the bell rang, ending the lunch period. Jane left immediately to escort her class from the student cafeteria. Margaret remained for a few moments to reflect on the heated discussion she had just had with Jane. Could she be right? No, it couldn't be. She had

PRACTICE EXERCISE 2.3

Behaviorist, Constructivist, and Eclectic Comparison Chart

Write a brief explanation of each term, then compare and contrast differences. Show how eclectic options can combine both behaviorist and constructivist terms.

Example:

Direct teaching is teacher centered, while indirect teaching is student centered. I would use both direct and indirect teaching strategies based on the abilities and characteristics of my classes. I would plan my lessons in an eclectic fashion based on meeting my students' needs.

Behaviorism	Eclectic	Constructivism
Direct teaching		Indirect teaching
Objectivist		Constructivist
Teacher centered		Learner centered
Behavioral observations		Cognitive operations
Focus on individual		Group work emphasized
Focus on one approach		Holistic in approach

been using a behavior modification program in her class and it had worked like a charm. She had used Skinner's concept of reinforcers to advance student learning. Rewards and punishments were the answer to understanding how children learned. She had implemented this method when Principal Thompson had suggested that she had difficulty in managing her class. She had followed the neo-Skinnerian model in determining the outcomes she wanted and developed a plan that used rules, reinforcers, and consequences to obtain positive results. She had decided to tell Mr. Thompson that children learned by being told what they had to know.

That afternoon Mr. Thompson visited Margaret's classroom and asked if she would meet with him during her administrative period, which was in a few moments. He wanted to discuss the school policy regarding how children learned at the McGraw Elementary School.

Ten minutes later Margaret found herself facing Mr. Thompson across his desk. He was going on about the constructivist learning design process and how it differed from behaviorism and the traditional transmission model. He said it was the school policy to have children actively learning and physically constructing meaning guided by teachers whose role it is to facilitate learning. Teachers were expected to design situations and group children to work in problem-solving situations where they could exhibit their knowledge and reflect with the class on what they had learned. Margaret just bit her tongue.

1. List the points made by Margaret in favor of the traditional behaviorist transmission model. List Jane's counterarguments that advocated a constructivist model for understanding how students learn.
2. Whose arguments were stronger? Justify your reasons.
3. Compare and contrast Mr. Thompson's views with those of Margaret and Jane.
4. Describe and defend your views on how students learn.

So far, we have seen that in order to understand how we learn we must understand two basic approaches to learning: constructivist and behaviorist. The constructivist approach is supported by cognitive, moral, and social developmental theory (Piaget, Maslow, Kohlberg, and Erikson), while behaviorists cling to tradition, common sense, and the works of Skinner and the classicists to support their position. Now we need to look at the engines we as humans use to learn—our brains and our intelligence.

ALTERNATIVE APPROACHES TO UNDERSTANDING

Psychologists have various theories regarding human development and understanding. This section reviews three different approaches that attempt to predict when students are ready to learn, each focusing on a different aspect of learning: needs, morals, and social development. To understand how children learn we have stressed two basic approaches, behaviorist and constructivist, though these are not the only ways to understand learning.

Maslow's Hierarchy of Needs

Abraham Maslow (1890–1970) developed a theory of motivation based on the satisfaction of one to six needs, which has been used to justify both traditional and constructivist approaches. Maslow's theory (1962, 1970) supports student-centered approaches and instructional practices that encourage students to make decisions, such as constructivist methodology advocates. Maslow's focus is on the motivation needed by individuals to accomplish life's tasks. Teaching in this domain is seen as a process of helping children to problem solve and develop a desire to learn for learning's intrinsic worth.

When we look at Maslow we see a traditional psychology of understanding, which can be used by both traditionalists and constructivists. The traditional behaviorist wants to meet the hierarchy of needs by use of stimulus response practices, while the constructivist looks at Maslow as the precursor to constructivist concepts related to needs. When our needs are met we become free to construct meaning for our own reality. The hierarchy starts with the physical needs of safety and security, to the life essential needs of self-fulfillment, and self-actualization. (See Figure 2.12.)

Kohlberg's Theory of Moral Development

Lawrence Kohlberg's theory of moral development is intrinsically related to the theories of Piaget and

Figure 2.12 Hierarchy of Needs

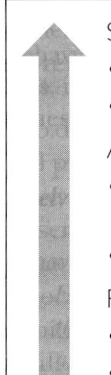

Self-Fulfillment Needs
- Self-actualization
- Aesthetic needs: beauty, order, symmetry

Affective Needs
- Achievement and prestige: approval, recognition
- Belonging and love: acceptance, affection, love

Physical Needs
- Safety and security: freedom from fear, stability
- Life essentials: food, drink, air

Erikson. The degree to which an individual has progressed through the stages of cognitive, personal, and moral development coincides with that person's capacity to reason. Kohlberg based his work on the fact that children develop the capacity for moral reasoning along a similar path used for cognitive and social growth. Piaget (1967) determined that the onset of moral reasoning does not occur until the age of six. He designated two stages of moral development: (1) the heteronomous stage, in which children view rules as unalterable and that breaking them leads to punishment, and (2) the autonomous stage, in which children realize the relative nature of moral thinking. Kohlberg (1981, 1987) determined that moral reasoning develops in an invariable sequence of increasingly complex stages from birth to adulthood. Kohlberg noted that people evolve through three levels for moral development containing two stages at each level. These six consecutive stages occur in a specifically defined order.

Levels of Moral Development

1. *Pre-conventional.* Moral reasoning is concerned with physical punishment and reward. It is entirely self-serving and self-centered.
2. *Conventional.* Moral reasoning is concerned with consideration of others expressed in terms of conformity and loyalty to established patterns.
3. *Post-conventional.* Autonomous or principled level of moral reasoning is concerned with underlying values and principles. It requires sophisticated reasoning and highly developed problem-solving abilities.

Levels	*Stages of Moral Development*
Pre-conventional	*Stage 1:* the punishment and obedience orientation
	Stage 2: the instrumental–relativist orientation
Conventional	*Stage 3:* the interpersonal or "good boy–nice girl" orientation
	Stage 4: the "law and order" orientation
Post-conventional	*Stage 5:* the social contract–legalistic orientation
	Stage 6: the universal ethical principle orientation

Stage 1: **The punishment and obedience orientation** A person in this stage bases moral decisions on the physical exercise of power. Those possessing power should be obeyed to avoid punishment. The right or wrong of an action is measured purely by the physical consequences of the behavior.

Stage 2: **The instrumental–relativist orientation** Moral decisions are based on satisfying personal needs and desires. Acting to meet those desires determines whether the act is right or wrong. A person in this stage is aware of the needs of others, and will work to satisfy those needs when it is to his or her own advantage.

Stage 3: **The interpersonal concordance or good boy–nice girl orientation** At this stage, the person is concerned with pleasing others and receiving their approval. The individual will conform to what the dominant group defines as acceptable thought and action. The intended consequences of an action are judged to be as important as the action itself. A person in this stage thinks in terms of distinct stereotypes, while having a clear idea of right and wrong.

Stage 4: **The "law and order" orientation** In this stage, the solution of moral problems is by legal authority. Laws and legal sanctions are the basis for all legitimate action. The underlying ethic of the individual at this stage is to act within legal guidelines to protect the group.

Stage 5: **The social contract–legalistic orientation** The basic characteristic at this stage is based on the implicit social contract, which exists between the individual and society. Moral dilemmas at this level necessitate ability to reason abstractly and to consider various arguments and consequences in relation to underlying principles.

Stage 6: **The universal ethical principle orientation** At this stage of moral development, reasoning is at its highest level of moral consciousness. Ethical principles that guide one in the solution of moral dilemmas must be logically consistent and broadly applicable. Principles are abstract and not dependent on written formulas, such as legal or moral codes of behavior.

Erikson's Stages of Psychosocial Development

Erik Erikson (1982) views psychosocial development as referring to how we think about, influence, and relate to one another. Social learning theorists such as Erikson seek to combine behavioral and cognitive learning theories with other types of learning. Some believe a great deal of learning can take place through one's modeling the actions of others. Erikson built on Freud's psychoanalytic theories of personality development. Where Freud saw four stages of psychosexual development: oral, anal, phallic, and genital, Erikson saw life divided into eight psychosocial stages, each of which determining the pattern of development for the next (see the list that follows). His reasoning was similar to Piaget's in that he also attempted to categorize behavior in stages related to an individual's age.

Approximate Age and Characteristics	Stage of Psychosocial Development
Infancy (birth–1 year)	*Trust vs. mistrust* If needs are met, infant develops sense of trust. Parents must provide nurturing environment.
Toddler (1 to 2 years)	*Autonomy vs. shame and doubt* Child learns independence/self-confidence and is encouraged to express himself or herself verbally.
Preschool (3 to 5 years)	*Initiative vs. guilt* The child initiates tasks/develops self-discipline and explores sexual identity.
Elementary school (6 years to teen years)	*Competence vs. inferiority* Child learns to be effective or inadequate and explores the world to make social friends.
Adolescence (teen years into 20s)	*Identity vs. role confusion* The child refines its sense of self into a single identity. Physical appearance changes and the use of logic is developed.
Young adulthood (20s to early 40s)	*Intimacy vs. isolation* Young adults develop a capacity for intimate love and caring.
Middle adulthood (mid 40s to early 60s)	*Generativity vs. stagnation* The individual now wants to contribute to the world, work, and family.
Late adulthood (late 60s and older)	*Integrity vs. despair* Reflects on life's success/failure.

THE BRAIN AND LEARNING

We would be remiss if we did not include the brain in our attempt to understand how children learn. Brain-based educators tend to be progressive and opposed to

PRACTICE EXERCISE 2.4

Using Alternative Approaches

Review the three examples of alternative approaches to learning and write a brief description of how you would utilize each basic concept in understanding how your students learn. Be sure to indicate if you think that understanding needs, morals, and social development will make you a more effective teacher.

the factory model of education. They most often favor a constructivist, active learning model. They tend to believe that students should be actively engaged in learning and in guiding their own instruction while teachers should teach for meaning and understanding. This has become a cognitive and constructivist model of learning that is based on psychological research.

Why the sudden interest in brain research? Previously, what most teachers learned about the brain was based largely on behavioral psychology. Today, due to MRIs (magnetic resonance imaging) and PET (positron emission tomography) scans, which now produce three-dimensional maps of the brain in action, a great deal of information can be scientifically proven. These imaging maps reveal which parts of the brain are involved in performing various activities, including learning. The model of how the brain learns is changing, and although some of our teaching strategies are still consistent many are not. As one researcher puts it, "Yesterday's methods worked well for yesterday's students" (Sousa, 1998).

Today's children have become accustomed to rapid sensory and emotional change. They respond more readily to the unique and different. Many schools have changed little, and their teaching approaches are best suited to the turn-of-the century industrial model that used an agrarian calendar for school administration and organization. The new brain-based approach to learning is based on neuroscientific research with a focus on the learning process. The preliminary indications are that when teachers have a thorough understanding of how the brain develops, learns, and organizes itself, they will make better teaching decisions and use programs that include multiple intelligences, learning styles, and cooperative learning more effectively.

Triune Brain Theory

What is the connection between brain functions, learning style, and the most appropriate mode of instruction?

If we understand the theories related to learning, we can seek out the purpose of our brains. As with most things there are a number of views about how the brain makes meaning. The traditional view of the brain is as a computer. Others see the brain as a genetically prewired organ for learning, fully equipped at birth with the basic intelligence and physical attributes needed to survive in our world.

Paul MacLean's **triune brain theory** (1990) states that the brain evolved into three distinct parts: (1) the reptilian brain (brain stem), which houses basic instincts; (2) the limbic system (mammalian brain), which governs all emotions; and (3) the neocortex (thinking brain), which houses higher thought functions. Scientists have assumed that the rational cerebral cortex was in charge of the brain and responded by downshifting to the lower, nonrational regions of the brain (emotional/limbic and survival/brain stem) when confronted by a perceived threat (Hart, 1998). The brain, according to this view, is a biological system not a machine (Rose and Nicholl, 1997). To understand triune brain theory, consider the brain from a top-down or bottom-up perspective as opposed to a left, right perspective. We can use aspects of our hands to understand the brain's three functions. The thumb represents the brain stem, located at the base of the brain and connected to the spinal column. It is responsible for our basic survival instincts. When we wrap our hand's other four fingers around the thumb we create a picture of our limbic system, which governs our emotions. By placing our other hand over the first we create the cerebral cortex, which is located above these survival and emotional areas (Walsh, 2000).

Pat Walsh (2000) developed an intriguing way to explain the functions of the brain. She used her hands as props to help explain the functions of the brain. She claims that by using her two hands she can reach the basic learning styles of most students, visual, auditory, and kinesthetic. She uses four distinct hand motions to explain the functions and basic ideas about the brain.

1. Both hands folded together represent the size of a standard three-pound brain.
2. Hands separated represent the two halves of the brain, left and right.
3. The two thumbs indicate the two frontal lobes that aren't fully developed until much later in life.
4. Interlocked fingers demonstrate that the right and left brains are joined through necessary communication with each other.

Hemisphericity is a debatable theory of how the brain works. It purports to study where mental functions occur in the brain. Imaging techniques allow us to look at brain activity, and identify specific regions where movement is taking place in the brain. Research suggests that the right cerebral hemisphere is involved in visual, nonverbal, spatial, divergent, and intuitive thinking and the left cerebral hemisphere is involved in verbal, logical, categorical, detail-oriented, and convergent thinking. The right hemisphere works with approximations and creativity, whereas the left works with specific analysis.

Teachers tend to focus on the left side of the brain—the cognitive, analytical, and convergent functions—and much less on the right sphere. The theory behind hemisphericity is in much dispute since it has been shown that productive intellectual functioning requires that both sides of the brain be involved. Teachers should concentrate on balancing outcomes and experiences for both sides of the brain.

Downshifting is defined as a psycho-physiological (body/mind) response to threat associated with helplessness or fatigue. When we downshift, we revert to early programmed behavior and to more primitive instinctual responses spoken about by MacLean. Goleman (1995) says our emotional limbic system plays a far greater role in how the brain functions than previously thought. The emotional system was designed, he believes, to have the brain pay attention to a perceived threat before upshifting to any type of reflective activity. The notion of downshifting concludes that challenge enhances learning while threat inhibits it. This concept comes from Hans Selye's theory of stress, which states that "eustress" (from euphoric) is stress that results from positive experiences while "Distress" is stress from negative tension (Selye, 1978). Four conditions reduce downshifting, and if used by teachers enhance student performance, as seen in Figure 2.13. These theories—triune, hemisphericity, and downshifting—are not the only theories of how the brain assists in learning. The literature provides various answers to the question, "How does the brain actually make meaning?" Some of the answers are seemingly vague, others quite specific, and some on the fringe of reality.

Figure 2.13 Methods to Enhance Student Performance

1. Expectations are open ended and provision made for alternative answers. No pre-specified answers.
2. Personal meaning is maximized and students understand why they are learning something.
3. Emphasis is on intrinsic motivation, not on teacher rewards.
4. Tasks are manageable.

Source: Rose and Nicholl (1997)

Theories and Practices

- *Children will learn better if taught about the brain.* Brain research shows that physical activity enhances the learning process, and confirms the idea that the brain must be stimulated in order to learn (Jensen, 1998, 2000).
- *The emotional system drives the attention system, and emotions are the driving force for everything.* Emotions are, according to this view, essential to learning since they drive attention and attention drives learning. Our brain needs a process by which it can focus attention and develop appropriate responses. That process is emotion, which is an "innate, powerful, and principally unconscious process" (Sylwester, 2000).
- *The more you exercise the connections in your brain the stronger they become.* Learning is linked to experiences. Applications lead to student retention when procedures become automatic and memorized through practice. According to this theory memorization is useful for mental exercise, such as creating analogies, metaphors, and similes (Wolfe, 1998).
- *Everything in the mind is the product of the brain, which is a simple organ and not the center of one's being.* Psychology and neurology are needed to understand the relationship between brain and mind. Note, for example, the differences between an auto mechanic and a physicist regarding knowledge of an automobile: The mechanic knows the practical aspect (neurological); the physicist understands the reason (psychological). Brains do not exist in a vacuum; they exist in an ecology where learning becomes a cultural phenomenon (Gardner, 1999).
- Brain research has attempted to demonstrate how it can influence classroom methods in the areas of brain growth, memory, emotions, sensory engagement, timing, biological rhythms, and learning disabilities. *The premise is that brain research can affect pedagogy* (Sousa, 1998).
- A six-step blueprint to learn, called the **accelerated learning method**, effectively uses brain theory to enhance learning. The plan recognizes that each of us has a preferred way of learning, and when instruction matches learning style knowledge is created. When both teacher and student use this method, learning becomes enjoyable, effective, and fast. The plan illustrated in Figure 2.14 is easy to remember since it creates the acronym, MASTER (Rose and Nicholl, 1997).
- The Caines (1990, 1993, 1997) integrated brain research with research from other fields, and developed a *brain-based theory of learning*, which asserts that relaxed alertness, challenging experiences, and reflection lead to technical or conceptual knowledge. A secure loving environment and developmentally

Figure 2.14 Accelerated Learning Method

1. *Motivating your mind.* Establish a mood for learning by creating a relaxed positive environment. Ask, What's in it for me?
2. *Acquiring the information.* To learn we need to acquire and absorb information in a way best suited to our sensory learning preferences (visual, auditory, kinesthetic). Senses are needed to acquire all information.
3. *Searching out the meaning.* Personal meaning is the central element of all learning. This is done through one's intelligence.
4. *Triggering the memory.* Techniques used to memorize materials include categorization, review, association, acronyms, flash cards, storytelling, music, and learning maps.
5. *Exhibiting what you know.* Concretize knowledge by teaching another. Anyone who has tutored can verify that the teacher evidences understanding by exhibiting knowledge.
6. *Reflecting on the process.* The final step is to reflect and review and ask (a) How is the learning task going? (b) How could it have gone better? (c) What's the significance of this for me?

appropriate experiences develop brains. Brain capacity is genetic; it is enhanced by challenge and inhibited by threat. The Caines suggest three approaches to teaching for learning: (1) the traditional chalk and talk; (2) an authentic assessment approach in which the teacher creates more complex experiences; and (3) a partnership approach where learning is aimed at student interests.

Contradictory Views on Brain Theory

Critics claim there is no evidence for the assertions made by brain researchers such as R. and G. Caine regarding many so-called principles of learning. Their assertions come from cognitive and developmental psychology—the behavioral sciences—and not from the biological sciences. They come from our scientific understanding of the *mind*, rather than from scientific understanding of the *brain*, from psychology rather than neuroscience. The mind and the brain have traditionally been studied independently of each other. Cognitive neuroscientists are just beginning to study both the mind and the brain. Brain science appears to give hard biological data and explanations that are more appealing than the soft data from psychological science. Unfortunately, this has led to speculative links between brain science and education. Examples are the links in the literature that claim

PRACTICE EXERCISE 2.5

Classroom Practices

Review and react to the seven brain-based practices listed, and explain how each can become a reality in your classroom. Answers should be shared with classmates for discussion. (See example.)

1. **Brain growth and development.** As a child grows, the brain selectively strengthens connections, based on experiences. This process called *windows of opportunity* continues throughout our lives and is most prevalent between ages two and eleven. Teachers should provide a brain-friendly atmosphere that encourages growth.

   Example:

   I am aware of the concept of age-appropriateness planning. I realize that the brain develops with age and experiences. I would make them a reality by planning my lessons to meet student needs that are developmentally correct.

2. **Memory and recall.** Experiences influence new learning. Brain research indicates that relevancy and retention are based on what we already know. If meaning is lacking by the end of instruction, it is doubtful it will be retained. Lesson planning should focus on paring down and integrating curriculum to assist children in making connections based on their experiences. Making relevant connections will improve student retention and learning.

3. **Emotions in learning.** The amount of student attention is determined by student feelings with regard to instruction. Emotions interact with reason to support or inhibit learning. Students must feel safe and secure before they can focus on curriculum. Teachers must promote emotional security by establishing a positive class climate. Coleman (1995) goes so far as to suggest we teach how to manage moods, motivation, empathy, and self-awareness.

4. **Sensory engagement.** The brain makes new neural connections when it gets involved in challenging situations. Classroom practice should focus on sensory stimulation, and create interactive environments where children are allowed to move about and discuss learning. Task-centered talking is essential to memory process and social interaction.

5. **Timing is crucial.** Shorter learning episodes are more effective. Twenty-minute lesson segments hold student attention better than hour lectures because students are accustomed to quick changes in their environmental stimuli. This is the secret of MTV's success.

6. **Biological rhythms.** Circadian rhythms do affect student performance. Teenagers perform better in problem-solving and memory tasks later in the day rather than earlier. Teachers can adapt scheduling to meet the needs of students.

7. **Learning disabilities.** Scanning technology can reveal which parts of the brain are involved in learning problems such as dyslexia, autism, ADD, speech and language impairment. It may be that some who are called "learning disabled" are merely "schooling disabled." The more we learn, the better we can design schools and the teaching methods that stimulate children's brains and help them learn.

---

brain science supports an assortment of educational theories, such as Bloom's taxonomy, Madeline Hunter's effective teaching, whole language instruction, and Vygotsky's theory of social learning, thematic instruction, portfolio assessment, and cooperative learning. It is difficult to separate the science from speculation (Bruer, 1999).

Right brain versus left brain (brain laterality) is a popular idea that will not die even though it has been criticized and dismissed by both psychologists and brain scientists. It claims that the left side of the brain is more analytical and linear. The right side of the brain's function is considered to be more global and concerned with making patterns. This view of the brain has not been supported by neuroscience (Bruer, May 1999).

The Caines (1997) are also critical of traditional brain "dichotomizers" and warn that the brain does not lend itself to simple explanations. Both hemispheres are involved in all activities. The Caines see the two-brain doctrine as a valuable metaphor that helps educators acknowledge two separate but simultaneous tendencies in the brain for organizing information. Sousa (1998) claims that brain-based literature supports the idea that there is a critical or sensitive period in brain development, lasting until a child is around ten, during which they learn faster and easier. It is called "**windows of opportunity**" (Chugani, 1996). But no other neuroscientist supports this position (Bruer, 1999).

There are problems between neuroscientists and cognitive psychologists regarding understanding the

Figure 2.15 Brain-Based Theory Learning Principles

1. *The brain is a complex adaptive system.* Body, mind, and brain are one dynamic unit. This means that the brain functions on many levels simultaneously and the learner is multifaceted.

2. *The brain is a social brain.* Learning is influenced by our social relationships.

3. *The search for meaning is innate.* Teaching needs to be organized around student purposes and meanings.

4. *The search for meaning occurs through patterning.* Learners must formulate their own patterns of understanding.

5. *Emotions are critical to patterning.* An appropriate emotional climate is indispensable to sound education. The role of emotions is at every level of functioning, including higher-order thinking skills.

6. *Every brain simultaneously perceives and creates parts and wholes.* The two-brain doctrine (left brain/right brain) states that the brain reduces information into parts while perceiving holistically. Therefore, learners should be given global projects.

7. *Learning involves focused attention and peripheral perception.* The brain absorbs information it is aware of and information that is outside its immediate attention.

8. *Learning always involves conscious and unconscious processes.* Much of our learning is unconscious and is best reflected upon through use of metacognitive activities such as creative teaching.

9. *We have at least two ways of organizing memory.* We can classify types of memory as rote-memorization and locale-memories that refer to spatial autobiographical memory, such as what you ate last night.

10. *Learning is developmental.* The brain is plastic; this means its hard wiring is shaped by experiences. In theory there is no limit to the capacities for humans to learn. *Neural plasticity*—The brain is shaped by experience.

11. *Complex learning is enhanced by challenge and inhibited by threat.* (See *downshifting*.)

12. *Every brain is uniquely organized.* We all have the same set of systems, yet we are all different. Learning through multiple intelligences should be characteristic of what it means to be human.

Source: Caine and Caine (1990, 1993, 1997)

brain's functions. Neuroscientists describe the brain as "modular" and believe that its abilities were developed in response to environmental challenges. The brain's capabilities may be genetically predetermined and not created through experience. Neuroscientists say the education establishment is ignorant of evolution and only concerned with experiences. Neuroscientists do not accept the idea that brains learn from experience as espoused in constructivist philosophy. They are convinced that brains accrue specialized systems (adaptations) through natural selection, and they ridicule constructivism (Brandt, 1999).

The *constructivist view of the brain* is that it has a common mechanism that solves the structure of all problems. The controversy is between those who believe that many of the brain's capabilities are built in (neuroscientists) and those who see the brain's ability to change with experience as overriding (cognitive psychologists). Viewing the brain traditionally as an enhanced computer or from a fringe point of view leaves much to be questioned. Views regarding the brain run the gamut of intellectual thought from hemisphericity, brain laterality, downshifting, and windows of opportunity. What it boils down to is the simple adage, "Use it if it works." Most likely, the answer lies somewhere in between both extremes.

INTELLIGENCE AND LEARNING

Intelligence—the other tool we use for understanding and learning—must also be viewed from the perspective of various theories that surround it. Intelligence theory stems from the work of the French psychologist Alfred Binet (1857–1911), who devised a test to identify children with learning problems. The test measured aptitudes that have been historically associated with success in school, memory, vocabulary, spatial thinking, and the ability to draw analogies and solve puzzles. The test was reasonably good at assessing school performance and became known as the IQ test. It predominantly measured an individual's ability with linguistic and logical mathematical challenges as well as some visual and spatial tasks. Twenty-five percent of the test measured general intelligence while 75 percent measured spatial intelligence, aptitude, and social competence. These various mental aptitudes are accepted as aspects of a single underlying trait called *g*, for "general intelligence." William Stern (1912) added the concept of intelligence quotient (Figure 2.16). IQ was defined as one's mental

Figure 2.16 Intelligence Quotient

$$\frac{\text{mental age}}{\text{chronological age}} \times 100 = IQ$$

age (as determined by the test) divided by chronological age. The ratio that resulted was then multiplied by 100 to establish a numerical IQ.

Influenced by the work of Binet and his studies of intelligence in children, Stern reviewed the principal findings in the field and developed the idea of expressing intelligence test results in the form of a single number, the intelligence quotient.

Stern looked at individual test scores as particular mental ages, which could be compared to actual chronological ages to determine a degree of advancement. He took the mental age and divided it by the chronological age, and named this ratio the intelligence quotient. Stern is credited as the inventor of the concept of the intelligence quotient, which was later used by Terman and others in the development of the first IQ tests based on the original work of Alfred Binet. Terman (1916, 1930) is given credit for having standardized the intelligence test by considering population norms; the result was the creation of the Stanford-Binet Test. This has become the traditional approach to measuring intelligence until Howard Gardner developed his theory of multiple intelligences.

Theory of Multiple Intelligences

Howard Gardner contrasts the traditional approach to intelligence when he says intelligence tests measure the ability of people to do well on intelligence tests, and little else of any relevance. Gardner's definition of intelligence claims to explain what intelligence really is. He says intelligence entails the ability to solve problems and fashion end products that are of consequence in a particular cultural setting. Gardner (1983) wonders what people from outer space want to know about our society, certainly not an absolute measurement called IQ. Probably their interest would be related to human performance, not test scores. Intelligence is seen as the development of the cognitive processes involved in performing creative work. Gardner questioned the conventional and asked just how many intelligences there were. He came up with a list that varies from seven to nine. The list has changed the face of educational theory about how we learn. (See Figure 2.17.)

Gardner does not rule out the possibility that an eighth or ninth intelligence such as naturalist or emotional intelligence exists. Progressive educators see multiple intelligences theory as a theoretical rationale for instructional methods such as project-based instruction, thematic instruction, presentations, and team teaching. This strategy was evidenced in a video made by Gardner in 1995 depicting three teachers who taught their classes using the intelligences that were their strengths. Each teacher stressed two intelligences plus linguistics with each of the three classes. This resulted in all three classes

Figure 2.17 Multiple Intelligences

1. *Mathematical.* The ability to follow or build sequential and structured ideas such as those found in math problems, arguments, and scientific experiments. It involves the ability to discover and use patterns.
2. *Verbal-linguistic.* The ability to use words to convey ideas and to use the written symbols of the professional culture. The ability to make an argument, present a case, and fashion a profound concept or articulate an idea.
3. *Visual/spatial.* The ability to use space, understand structure and form, and manipulate the background is fundamental to the work of architects and designers. This intelligence is seldom used in a traditional school setting.
4. *Musical.* The ability to produce and generate musically related products.
5. *Kinesthetic/body.* The ability to move one's body as in sports, acting, and dancing.
6. *Interpersonal.* This intelligence is absolutely fundamental to the success of team learning. It is the ability to share ideas, form relationships, enlist others in common projects, and build interactive structures.
7. *Intrapersonal intelligence.* The ability to reflect.

Source: Gardner (1983)

being exposed to all seven intelligences. This procedure fits nicely into a cooperative learning mode, while also creating a model for learning. It's a model for what good teachers have always done, which is to create environments where all can be accepted and achieved. Gardner's approach provides children an opportunity to learn in their own way because it recognizes each individual child's uniqueness and allows the teacher to teach to his or her strength. Lazear (1991, 1994) goes even further by claiming that if teachers took advantage of the seven intelligences in their teaching and planning, achievement would improve astronomically.

Gardner later acknowledged that there was a ninth intelligence, which he termed *existential* intelligence (1999). He claims this is the intelligence to ponder questions about life, death, and ultimate realities. He now believes that all humans possess at least eight if not nine intelligences, each reflecting the potential to solve problems or fashion products of value. Intelligence is identified by a set of criteria that include representation in specific parts of the brain, susceptibility to encoding in a symbolic system, and the existence of special populations such as prodigies. He states that this set of intelligences helps define our species. His view is different from Chomsky's (1957) and those of other cognitive psychologists who see mental representations as stemming from universal forms. With Chomsky it was the idea of a universal grammar constructed through an inherent language instinct. Chomsky believed that the mind was equipped with rules it constructed to understand sentences created from sets of words. Gardner sees sets of intelligence stemming from universal forms.

Critics of Multiple Intelligence Theory: Gardner has failed to persuade many of his peers, who say his argument boils down to "hunch and opinion," claiming he provides no hard evidence that can be evaluated. He has simply constructed criteria and then run his designated intelligences through these criteria (Traub, 1998). Gardner rebuts this position by arguing, "Why should we accept a definition of intelligence that took a certain skill (what it meant to be a good bureaucrat a hundred years ago) and make that the quintessence of intelligence?" The problem is that intelligence is not a crisp concept, but a term of value. The reason many psychologists don't measure the elements such as "body kinesthetic" intelligence isn't that they doubt it exists—they simply don't think it matters (Gardner, 1991).

Gardner has provided a paradigm that opened up new vistas for the education of children. The heart of the problem with multiple intelligences (MI) is not as a theory, but the way it has been put into practice. It has proved powerful not because it's true but because it allows for the values and presuppositions of school and our democratic culture. Gardner's MI theory legitimizes the fad for "self-esteem," the unwillingness to make even elementary distinctions of value, the excessive regard for diversity, and the decline of diligence. Gardner claims his work represents a paradigm shift by saying, "Socrates defined man as an irrational animal; what MI theory says is that we are the animal that exhibits the eight-and-a-half intelligences."

Some critics claim that most people who study intelligence view MI as rhetoric rather than science. Even colleagues such as Jerome Bruner say they wish Gardner had used a more neutral term like "aptitude" instead of intelligence. If he had done that he would not have appealed to teachers' intuitive sense that children learn in different ways. Bruner claims that the problem with multiple intelligences is not about it as a theory but as a practice. MI theory is powerful not because it's true but because its values and presuppositions of the school world and society are on target. Chester Finn calls MI the cognitive version of the multiculturalist view that school should offer a celebration of diversity.

In his latest book, *The Disciplined Mind: What All Students Should Understand* (1999), Gardner argues for high standards. He is not an apologist for low standards. This book is part of a progressive movement to prove that traditionalists have failed and progressives will lead the way to enduring academic achievement. The text calls for a curriculum based on the ancient Socratic categories of the good, the beautiful, and the true, a course of study that would examine fundamental questions of existence. The concept advocated is that a multiple intelligences perspective allows for better understanding.

Contrasting Models of Intelligence

What is the difference between ability and expertise? According to Sternberg (1985), there is no difference between IQ tests that test ability and achievement tests that test expertise. They test what you know and how well you can use it. What distinguishes ability tests from other kinds of assessments is how they are used, rather than what they measure. There is no qualitative distinction. This conflicts with the conventional model of intelligence, which would lead us to believe that IQ represented some type of intellectual predestination. IQ scores represent the different stages present in developing the expertise measured by IQ tests. In reality, ability and expertise are the same thing. Ability tests were developed to assess young children, while expertise was tested in adults in the form of achievement tests. This historical accident led to two separate types of testing that only differed in the ages of those tested (Sternberg, 1999).

The traditional model claims that intelligence consists of fixed individual differences, and the capabilities that a child inherits which interact with the child's environment to produce, at an early age, a relatively fixed potential for achievement. This idea of fixed genetic inheritance led Francis Galton (1822–1911), who had strong beliefs about the survival of the ethnically fittest, to propose that to improve society the state had to collect detailed mental, physical, and racial information on every citizen. Issue certificates to the superior and pay them for breeding, and encourage inferiors to remain celibate, Galton proposed. In 1883, Galton coined the term *eugenics* from the Greek meaning *well born* to describe this process, as well as the catch phrase, *nature versus nurture*, as a justification for his beliefs (Galton, 1973, 1962). Galton's simplistic theories of intelligence were undermined by a resurgence of the works of Gregor Mendel whose work led to research that showed that most defective genes were carried by outwardly normal parents. Even vegetables didn't follow Galton's simplistic model (Simonton, 2003).

Regardless of reality, Galton's disciples took hold of the academic mainstream, so that by the 1920s and 1930s nearly all geneticists assumed mentally retarded people and other "degenerates" should be actively prevented from breeding. These views made their way into public policy on both sides of the Atlantic, and by 1917, a Harvard geneticist named East was actively promoting the reduction of "defective gene plasma" through segregation and sterilization. Henry Goddard, a pioneer of psychological testing, claimed that feeblemindedness was due to a single defective gene, and enthusiastically volunteered to administer IQ tests to thousands of immigrants arriving at Ellis Island in order to weed out undesirables. Goddard's bizarre finding, that over 80 percent of Italians, Hungarians, Russians, and Jews were mentally retarded, was accepted without question by a wide range of intellectuals and legislators (Goddard, 1917; Zenderland, 1998).

In 1924, the U.S. Congress approved an immigration act curtailing the entry of Southern and Eastern Europeans. The bill was signed into law by President Calvin Coolidge, who declared, "America must be kept American. Biological laws show that Nordics deteriorate when mixed with other races."

Another giant of cognitive psychology, Lewis Terman (1877–1956), developer of the Stanford-Binet IQ test, declared his major goal to be "curtailing the reproduction of feeblemindedness" with a subsequent reduction in "industrial inefficiency." According to Terman, intellectual weakness was "very, very common among Spanish-Indians and Mexican families of the Southwest and also among Negroes. Their dullness seems to be racial . . . children of this group should be segregated in special classes. . . . They cannot master abstractions, but they can often be made efficient workers . . . from a eugenic point of view they constitute a grave problem because of their unusually prolific breeding" (Terman, 1930). This racist swill propagated by Goddard and Terman stems from a dogmatic belief in the infallibility of IQ testing for intelligence.

The new model of intelligence is based on the notion of developing expertise. This means that people are constantly in the process of developing expertise when they work within a given domain. Individuals can differ in rate and time of development. The main constraint is the degree to which students actively engaged in working and being assisted by teachers. The model of developing expertise has five key elements that influence one another at different stages, which accounts for expertise occurring at many levels. (See Figure 2.18.)

Triarchic Theory of Intelligence is predicated on the idea that there are three basic forms of intelligence—practical, analytical, and creative. Intelligence is not a fixed or static reality that can be learned and taught. Intelligence is a multidimensional phenomenon that occurs at multiple levels of our brain, mind, and body system. The problem in our schools is that there is no reward for practical or creative intelligence, but only for

Figure 2.18 Key Elements for Expertise

1. *Metacognitive skills*, which refer to students' understanding and control of their own learning. Metacognition is defined as thinking about thinking. Self-analysis is evidenced in the reflection and metacognition processes.
2. *Learning skills*, which can be divided into explicit (taught) and implicit (picked up) learning.
3. *Thinking skills* are based on practical, analytic, and creative types of thinking that are based on triarchic theory of intelligence.
4. *Knowledge* consists of declarative knowledge (facts, concepts, principles, laws) and procedural knowledge (knowing how, process).
5. *Motivation* consists of practices that engage students.

Source: Sternberg (1999)

Figure 2.19 Three Basic Forms of Intelligence

1. *Practical abilities.* We should stress application, use, and implementation.
2. *Analytical abilities and memory.* We should stress recall, assessment, and analysis.
3. *Creativity abilities.* We should stress creating, inventing, imagination, and design.

analytical. But all intelligences are equally important in teaching and assessment of children. If teaching were directed at basic abilities (see Figure 2.19) and memory, instruction would meet all the criteria needed for learning and teaching (Sternberg, 1997, 1985, 1984).

Emotional Intelligence is a natural outgrowth of the theory of multiple intelligences, and offers a new view on intelligence. It describes a different way of being smart and handling impulse. It adds emotions to Gardner's original seven intelligences. Emotional intelligence amplifies multiple intelligence theory by enhancing the relevance of inter- and intrapersonal intelligences. Emotional intelligence was first defined by saying that you need emotions for a healthy life. Emotions can be viewed as intelligence if we consider their three components—understanding, regulating, and using. Emotions are adaptive and necessary for intelligence (Mayer and Salovey, 1995; Mayer, Salovey, and Caruso, 2000). This concept is in direct contradiction to the traditional western view that emotions interfere with intelligence. Goleman enhanced this idea by adding two components necessary for a definition of emotional intelligence. The five components that make up emotional intelligence are (1) managing mood, (2) motivation, (3) empathy, (4) social skills, and (5) self-awareness (Goleman, 1998, 1995).

Heart Intelligence is based on a scientific approach to creating security within oneself. The concept is that intelligence is the flow of awareness that we experience when emotions are in balance. Heart intelligence transfers intelligence to emotions, and instills the power of emotional management. The heart symbolizes wisdom, love, compassion, courage, and strength. Language is filled with metaphors about the heart—"Speaking from the heart," "With all their heart," and "Thinking with their head, not their heart." There has been more to the word "heart" than a mere metaphor. Many ancient cultures maintained that the primary organ responsible for influencing and directing emotions, morality and decision making was the heart (Childre and Howard, 1999).

Heart intelligence speaks of a phenomenon of nature where systems or organisms come into sync oscillating at the same frequency, such as when two pendulum clocks, set to swing at different paces, eventually come into sync. The goal of heart intelligence is the emotional coming into sync (Childre and Howard, 1999).

Visual Intelligence attempts to understand how we create what we see as illustrated by the following sentence, "If u cn rd ths msg." The theory is based on the work of Hermann von Helmholtz, a nineteenth-century psychologist who described perception as an unconscious inference from sensory stimuli. This is in contrast to behaviorist theory, which holds that perception and behavior are essentially elaborate sets of reflexes developed or conditioned to respond to experience. To Helmholtz, intelligence, reasoning, perception, memory, and language all spring from one's own decision making based on limited sensory evidence. His work can be seen as outside the traditional concepts of intelligence (Hoffman, 1999).

Implications for Classroom Instruction

The understanding of how we learn, and the part the brain and intelligence play, offer some implications for classroom practice. The strategies and classroom practices we pursue should be eclectic, drawing on the best that each theory, concept, or idea has to offer. For learning to occur, the interaction between the method, the brain, and intelligence should be the object of every lesson you plan. As a teacher you should

1. Focus on knowledge by using primary sources and trade books that allow students to construct meanings using mind power and their intelligences.
2. Focus on issues using cognitive terminology such as *synthesize, analyze, create,* and *predict.* This strategy will encourage the development of critical thinking on the part of students, and motivate the mind.
3. Allow for student exploration by promoting student inquiry by using a problem-solving approach to lesson planning.
4. Be eclectic in the selection of the methods you choose to advance instruction. Variety stimulates the mind and one's intelligences.
5. Understand the hierarchy of needs. Relate instruction to address specific student affective needs. By emphasizing strategies appropriate to emotional intelligence, you nurture the whole child, which facilitates learning.
6. Be aware of the appropriate level of your instruction with regard to the psychosocial development of your students.
7. Create a positive climate in your classes. Negative tension causes distress, which hinders learning.
8. Link learning to life experiences because that will assist students in retaining content.
9. Plan instruction and use the accelerated learning method as a guide to student learning. This brain strategy fits nicely with multiple intelligences theory.
10. Recognize that no test is infallible. Attempt to be eclectic in the types of assessments used, while teaching for all three intelligences—the practical, analytic, and creative.
    - Teachers who use ability and achievement tests should stop distinguishing between what the two kinds of tests assess. The measurements are not different in kind but only in the point at which they are being made.
    - Tests measure achieved levels of developing expertise. No test can specify the highest level a student can achieve.
    - Different kinds of assessments (multiple choice, short answer, performance-based, portfolio, and essay) complement one another in assessing multiple aspects of developing expertise. There is no one right kind of assessment.
    - Instruction should be geared not just toward imparting a knowledge base, but toward developing reflective analytical, creative, and practical thinking.

MINI CASE FROM THE FIELD

The following case from the field presents research findings relevant to our understanding of the relationships among understanding how children learn, brain theory, and concepts of intelligence. Read the case and see who is right—Margaret, her friend Jane, or Mr. Thompson.

Are Brain and Intelligence Theories Relevant?

Margaret couldn't believe what she had heard. Mr. Thompson had actually told her that school policy was based on a constructivist philosophy that expected teachers to be facilitators and not traditional instructors who practiced direct teaching techniques. He had further implied that this policy had been arrived at by perusing the relevant studies on brain and intelligence theory. He had claimed that IQs were irrelevant, since they did not measure the whole child. He had expounded upon the theory of multiple intelligences as the key to effective understanding of how children learn. He had never mentioned that most cognitive psychologists didn't accept the theory, but only fuzzy educators. At this juncture Jane Hemmings, Margaret Gomez's lifelong friend and confidante, entered the teacher's cafeteria bubbling over with enthusiasm. She exclaimed excitedly that Mr. Thompson had asked her to present at the monthly staff conference.

Margaret said, "Let me guess—your topic is related to how children learn."

"Oh no, Margaret, he wants me to speak about how we can use the research finding related to brain theory and intelligence to improve our classroom instruction." Jane began outlining the points she hoped to cover in her twenty-minute presentation. She said she would discuss the fact that children learn better in a state of relaxed alertness when expectations are open-ended. Children should be taught about the brain and its functions. Brain theory had principles that could be applied in the classroom. One simple one was that learning is influenced by our social relationships, which indicates that the way we group for instruction is really important. Learning is developmental and shaped by one's experiences, so we have to provide creative exercises that stimulate the brain during these "windows of opportunity."

"Hold on, Jane. You're telling me that the brain is an organ that is governed by genetic principles? I don't accept that. I believe it is ethereal and the center of our mind. I can accept the accelerated learning method because it makes pedagogical sense, not because it's related to brain theory. Besides, Jane, are you aware of all the contradictory views about intelligence and brain theory?"

Jane looked at Margaret and thought to herself that as much as she liked her she was impossible to deal with. But Jane would make her presentation despite Margaret's arguments. Understanding brain theory and intelligence theory was relevant to understanding how children learn.

1. List the arguments made by Jane to support her position. Contrast her arguments with Margaret's argument. Who had the stronger arguments? Why?
2. Was Mr. Thompson justified in establishing school policy without consulting his staff? What should he have done?
3. How has the theory of multiple intelligences helped to justify new and innovative teaching activities?

Chapter Summary

It is easy to see that the study of intelligence has expanded to fringes never considered in the past. From the traditional IQ to visual intelligence, one can readily see we have come full circle from the arguments of the behaviorists and constructivists about how we learn. We have seen how the various explanations of how the brain works can be used to understand learning, from the neuroscientist's view to the psychologist's, both traditional and cognitive. Finally, we have seen the role intelligence plays in understanding learning, from traditional to alternative viewpoints.

The chapter explored the basic concepts that purport to answer the question of how we learn, by focusing on two approaches to learning, behaviorist and constructivist. This organization allows us to build and compare the research-based roots of both traditional and constructivist thought regarding learning. Skinner and the modern neo-Skinnerian theories are contrasted with constructivist philosophy whose roots stem from Piaget, Maslow, Kohlberg, and Erikson to Bruner.

The chapter also examined the role of the brain in the learning process by exploring modern brain theory from various viewpoints, including the *triune brain theory*, the Caines' *brain and mind learning principles*, and Rose and Nicholl's *accelerated learning method's six-step master plan*. Views contradictory to these researchers and their implications for brain-based education's use in the classroom were also noted.

Cases from the Field

CASE ONE

Betty Brown, a student teacher at Harper Elementary School, wondered how to reach her third-grade class, which seemed to reject every approach she attempted. Her cooperating teacher, Mrs. Albert, claimed that children learned by doing, and both physically and theoretically construct knowledge. Betty found that when she attempted lessons designed to achieve this goal the children responded with a total lack of understanding. Betty had asked Mrs. Albert if she could use a more structured approach and possibly a more traditional method such as a developmental lesson. Mrs. Albert just said no.

1. What action, if any, should Betty take now?
2. What advice could the university supervisor give Betty?
3. How could Betty's action affect her success as a student teacher?
4. Should Betty have been content with Mrs. Albert's response?
5. How do your beliefs, with regard to how children learn, affect the type of lesson you will present?

CASE TWO

In his tenth week of student teaching, Ramon Garcia could not understand why his university supervisor insisted upon observing a lesson that had been structured along the lines of the accelerated learning method. When Ramon consulted with his cooperating teacher the response he received wasn't really too helpful. He had just said, "I never heard of that method. What exactly is it?"

1. Was Ramon's action appropriate? Explain.
2. Prepare a lesson in your area of expertise using the accelerated learning method and explain how students should learn if instructed in this fashion.
3. Prepare the same lesson using a constructivist approach.
4. Should a student teacher only use methods he or she is comfortable with?
5. How could Ramon have avoided being caught in this conflict?

CASE THREE

Candice Moran was really disappointed at having received such a poor midyear evaluation by her sponsor teacher. Candice really felt she had been doing a good job in her tenth-grade mathematics class. It wasn't her fault that Mr. Pawl was so upset about her lack of using multiple intelligences theory in her plans. Mr. Pawl had never discussed this issue with her before.

1. How could the sponsor teacher have used different methods of feedback before the midterm assessment?
2. Were Candice's feelings justified?
3. Prepare a lesson in mathematics appropriate for a tenth-grade class using multiple intelligences theory as your guide.
4. How could Candice have used the triarchic theory of intelligence to prepare her lesson?
5. How could Candice have included the multiple intelligences theory in her plans?

CASE FOUR

Anna Chang was a nervous person by disposition. Her treatment as a student teacher in Ms. Klein's ninth-grade science class was driving her blood pressure through the roof. Ms. Klein never gave her feedback as to how effective her lessons had been. All she did was send her generic notes that all ended with the phrase, "Remember behaviorist, constructivist, brain, and intelligence learning theories when teaching your classes."

1. Could Anna have improved relations with Ms. Klein by labeling the theory of learning she was using? Explain your reasoning.
2. How could Anna have given examples of lessons that are eclectic by combining various concepts? Be specific in the examples you select.
3. What approach do you think Ms. Klein favored? Explain your reasoning.
4. What are the underlying issues in this case? Could Anna have personally benefited from an understanding of heart intelligence? Justify your response.
5. If you were advising Anna what would you tell her?

Terms to Remember

Behaviorism
Constructivism
Psychosocial development

Cognitive development
Hemisphericity
Multiple intelligences

Emotional intelligence
Downshifting
Windows of opportunity
Brain laterality

Accelerated learning method
Triune brain theory
Intelligence quotient
Visual intelligence

Discussion Questions

1. Compare the transmission view of teaching and learning to the constructivist view. Which would be more likely appreciated by students? Why?
2. Develop a Behavior Modification Plan based on the neo-Skinnerian model, which includes analysis, planning, and implementation.
3. Constructivist learning design identifies a theoretical process that should be used in preparing classes for learning. Use Figure 2.5 (Design for Learning) as a guide to an essay explaining how these concepts would be used to organize a class for learning.
4. Look at Figure 2.9 (Key Constructivist Assumptions) and decide the practicality of each of the ten assumptions listed. Be sure to give arguments in support or against each assumption.
5. Imagine yourself as a new teacher. Look at Figure 2.8 (Ten Constructivist Teaching Practices). Explain how you could apply each practice in a lesson you expect to teach.
6. Dissect the six-step master plan for accelerated learning found in Figure 2.14, with regard to whether it truly offers a plan focused on how we learn.
7. Why is understanding the various intelligence theories necessary to comprehending how children learn? Justify your response.
8. Write a brief essay titled "How Children Learn." Be sure to include your views on constructivism, behaviorism, intelligence theory, and brain theory.

Field Experience Activities

1. Interview a practicing teacher and ask how he or she believes students learn. Compare and contrast the response to your own beliefs.
2. Visit a classroom and assess whether the teaching learning model is being implemented.
   a. Does the teacher know what he or she wants to teach?
   b. Does he or she know the students' abilities?
   c. Cite evidence of any instructional model being used.
   d. How is student performance being evaluated?

For Further Reading

Airasian, P., and Walsh, M. E. (1997). Constructivist cautions. *Phi Delta Kappan*, 444–449.

Armstrong, T. (1993). *7 kinds of smart: Identifying and developing your many intelligences*. New York: Plume, Penguin Group.

Bandura, A. (1986). *Social foundations of thought and action: A social cognitive theory*. Englewood Cliffs, NJ: Prentice-Hall.

Bloom, B., ed. (1956). *Taxonomy of educational objectives: Handbook I. Cognitive domain*. New York: McKay.

Bruer, J. T. (1993). *Schools of thought: A science of learning in the classroom*. Cambridge, MA: MIT Press.

Chomsky, N. (1967). *Aspects of a theory of syntax*. Cambridge, MA: MIT Press.

Csikszentmihalyi, M. (1990). *Flow*. New York: Harper & Row.

Edmonds, R. E. (1979, March/April). Some schools work and more can. *Social Policy*, 23–32.

Edmonds, R. E. (1981, September/October). Making public schools more effective. *Social Policy*, 56–60.

Fosnot, C. T. (1989). *Inquiring teachers, inquiring learners: A constructivist approach for teaching*. New York: Teachers College Press.

Kohlberg, L. (1963). *Essays on moral development*. San Francisco: Harper & Row.

Lasley, T. J. (1997). *Strategies for teaching in a diverse society*. Belmont, CA: Wadsworth.

MacLean, P. D. (1990). *The triune brain in evolution*. New York: Plenum Press.

Montessori, M. (1967). *The child*. Wheaton, IL: Theosophical Publishing House.

Myers, D. G. (1986). *Psychology*. New York: Worth Publishers.

Penfield, W. (1952). Memory mechanisms. *A.M.A. Archives of Neurology and Psychiatry*, 67, 178–198.

Smith, J. D. (1985). *Minds made feeble: The myth and legacy of the Kallikaks*. Rockville, MD: Aspen.

Sternberg, R. G. (1997). A waste of talent. *Education Week*.

Sylvester, R. (1995). *A celebration of neurons: An educator's guide to the human brain*. Alexandria, VA: ASCD.

Vygotsky, L. S. (1978). *Mind in society: The development of higher psychological processes*. Cambridge, MA: Harvard University Press.

Zenderland, L. (1998). *Measuring minds: Henry Herbert Goddard and the origins of American intelligence testing*. Cambridge: Cambridge University Press.

CHAPTER 3

Planning to Learn

FOCUS POINTS

1. Fail to plan and you plan to fail.
2. Curriculum is the interaction between teacher and learner.
3. Performance objectives are specific, measurable, attainable, results oriented, and achievable within a precise time frame.
4. All lessons have a beginning, middle, and conclusion.
5. Supervisors look for learning.

CHAPTER OVERVIEW

PERSONALITY AND THE ROLE IT PLAYS in becoming an effective teacher was discussed in Chapter 1. In Chapter 2, we attempted to understand how children learn. The objective of these two chapters was to introduce readers to basic approaches to teaching and the theorists who developed these methods. Chapter 3 focuses on how to plan lessons that aid students in acquiring knowledge and self-control. How do we write and plan effective lessons that facilitate learning? How do we get children to master the type of self-discipline that leads to success? Understanding how children learn, and the five keys for effective teaching, provide a platform from which to explore, plan, and create effective lessons. But guidelines are needed for incorporating topics and objectives into plans whose effectiveness can be assessed. Yearly, term, unit, weekly, and daily planning come from a curriculum that provides topics for individual lessons. Topic selection determines the lesson objectives. A plan for instruction, either direct or indirect, and a summary assessment of learning completes the process.

Planning and lesson design has been researched and discussed for many years. This chapter discusses the development of your presentation skills and the inevitable supervisory observation of your performance. Lesson planning does not exist in a vacuum. Before writing, you must understand the curriculum and the standards by which it is measured.

CURRICULUM

The problem with curriculum is that most of us are preoccupied with quantity rather than quality. To address all content at an appropriate level of depth and quality is all but impossible. To accomplish it schooling would have to be extended indefinitely (according to U.S. Department of Education, July 2003). A solution to this dilemma may be found in the concept of intensive and extensive curriculum. The intensive curriculum comprises what students should know in depth, and the extensive curriculum comprises knowledge about which all students should have some grasp (Hirsch, 1987).

One should understand curriculum before beginning to plan lessons. Fortunately, in today's world, curriculum is essentially a given, decided upon by state education departments and school boards, while lesson plans are an individual's creations. Curriculum has been determined long before most are ready to enter their first classroom as a new teacher. Goals and objectives for courses of study will be neatly laid out by respective boards of education, whether in secondary or elementary school. For most of us there truly is no need to worry about goals and objectives; one's only worry is to prepare and present appropriate lessons. The first step in the process is to work on a vision of the activities that students should be engaged in. We know that children, as well as adults, learn primarily by doing. A teacher's role is to look at program standards and see the performance benchmarks that students should achieve, then write a plan based on achieving those benchmarks by using appropriate strategies that facilitate learning. Regardless of approach—expository, discovery teaching, scientific method, or plain discussion—students' learning must be the focus of all instruction. This fact is so whether one is a traditionalist, progressive, constructivist, essentialist, or just plain eclectic. An instructor's philosophy becomes evident upon presentation of a lesson. One plan does not make for a course of study; it must be developed into unit and daily lesson plans. These plans should reflect the details, methods, materials, and resources needed to understand the specific content area and related skills.

Finally, a teacher must assess her work, and either enrich it or re-teach it. The curriculum model for classroom instruction (see Figure 3.1) helps to clarify the process by highlighting four essential components, beginning with (1) vision, (2) benchmarks and performance indicators, (3) assessment, and finally (4) classroom practice (Foriska, 1997, 1998).

Good preparation includes students when making planning decisions. Explain to students how you use the curriculum model for classroom instruction to develop lessons, and encourage students to take an active part in lesson planning. One excellent way to develop students' comprehension is to incorporate them into the planning process by allowing them to assist in making choices about types of activities, instructional approaches, and the amount of independent work, discussions, and assignments. When students are comfortable with the procedures, learning takes place. Of course, one can only go

Figure 3.1 Curriculum Model for Classroom Instruction

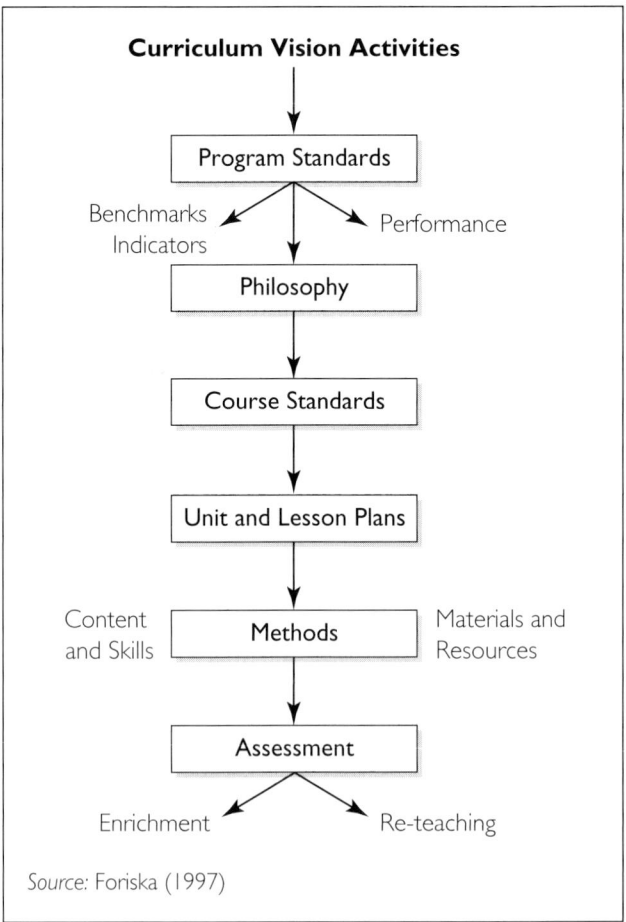

Source: Foriska (1997)

so far with this approach. Nevertheless, it is surprising how often it is successful.

Decision Making

Decision making requires making choices. The choice between action and inaction is not always simple. Classroom teachers must decide on a method of instruction that will result in students learning the instructional standards, and how to raise them. One of the purposes behind any planning is to bring about change in students' understanding of subject matter. The way experienced teachers make decisions and plan is quite different from that of inexperienced teachers. Experienced teachers focus on the content to be taught and the instructional methods necessary to achieve their goals. Inexperienced teachers highlight verbal instructions and keeping students on task rather than focused on content (EGMTL, 2005).

To make a decision one must define the problem, identify and evaluate alternatives, make and implement the decision, and finally assess its effectiveness (Ethics Resource Center, 2005). Decisions made help develop teaching skill competencies intentionally or intuitively. A skill acquisition model defines effective teaching, as when one is able to bring about intended learning outcomes (Hudgins, 1974). Intent and achievement are the two basic dimensions of effective teaching employed by experienced teachers. Effective teachers know: developmental stages of students, current events, course subject matter, philosophy of education and of how we learn, and they understand intelligence theories. They are competent in both theory and practice, while understanding that being effective consists of four essential elements: planning, practice, feedback, and reflection.

The Teacher Decision-Making Model (see Figure 3.2) conceptualizes the instructional role of the teacher into four parts and nine skills. The parts in the model (plan, implement, evaluate, and feedback) appear in most commonsense strategies for problem solving. This is so whether the problem is in class management or in planning a daily or unit lesson. The skills associated with each part of the model must be reflected on to attain mastery, as with the keys to learning. The four areas necessary for teacher competence that allow mastery to be achieved are understanding behavior and learning, positive attitudes, content knowledge, and instructional skills.

Student data also plays a critical role in teacher decision making. It has the power to help teachers understand the planning necessary to increase student learning. With the passage of *No Child Left Behind* (NCLB), teachers must collect and analyze data as well as report it to demonstrate that their efforts are resulting in increased student achievement. At the classroom level, this means that before planning, you must know what your students know and what they do not know.

Topic Aims, Goals, and Objectives Defined

How do we incorporate topic aims, instructional goals, and objectives into our lesson plans? Master teachers exhibit three common traits: They are well organized in their planning; they communicate their instructional objectives effectively to their students; and they have high expectations for their students. They also understand that aims, goals, and objectives answer a key question that teachers focus on, "What will students learn as a result of this experience?" Lesson planning begins by thinking carefully about what the lesson is supposed to accomplish. There is no substitute for this step.

Topic aims are broad statements of very general outcomes. Their planning is based on intentions, variously described as goals, purposes, objectives, and aims. Aims represent broad, general expressions of intention that can be lofty and noble as well as mundane and pragmatic. They provide direction by expressing learning outcomes and providing logical starting points for topic design. Therefore, once we are clear about what we want to achieve we can make decisions about how we will achieve it. Statements of topic aims are general statements formulated in clear language to express the nature and direction of the subject matter. They are broad general statements of educational intent that inform students of the overall purpose of a program or module. Topic aims are:

- Significant and worthwhile
- Clear and unambiguous
- Attainable in terms of available facilities and resources
- Achievable through reasonable effort by all students

Examples of Topic Aims

- To understand the importance of good character.
- To work toward developing self-discipline.
- To develop skills that will allow students to be able to read at grade level or above.

Topic goals are more narrowly defined statements of outcomes that can be used as guides for teaching. They are stated in broad and general terms. They are really statements of intent, the expected outcome of the educational process. A goal is an overall target, while an objective is a short-term end. Long-term objectives or goals are the economic, social, or behavioral targets, which are derived from the educational strategies or policies of a given country. These goals differ universally in many aspects and they are naturally affected by several factors. So, as Humels (1977) stated, "the goals of education are the result of philosophical reflections on man, on human existence, on culture, beliefs on values, on national and individual economic and social needs, and on the system of relationships connecting man to

Figure 3.2 Teacher Decision-Making Model

Parts	Skills
1. Plan	Instructional Planning
	Instructional Objectives
2. Implement	Presentation Skills/Involving Students in Learning
	Questioning Skills
	Concept Learning and Higher-Level Thinking
	Interpersonal Communication/Technology
	Classroom Management
	Cooperative Learning
3. Evaluate	Evaluation/Assessment
4. Feedback	

Areas of Competence

1.	2.	3.	4.
Theoretical knowledge about learning and human behavior	Attitudes that foster learning	Knowledge of subject matter	Repertoire of teaching skills

Source: Cooper (1999)

---

nature, environment and to the society in which he lives."

Examples of Topic Goals

- To help students understand good character by studying moral ethics.
- To develop procedures for students to learn self-discipline.
- To achieve appropriate reading levels through the implementation of a balanced reading program in all grades.

Topic objectives are specific statements of a learner's behavior or outcomes that state the conditions of the behavior and set time limits. To achieve a goal, a series of action steps are needed; these become the objectives. Performance objectives show what is expected, how it will be accomplished, and what the standards are. They should be specific, measurable, attainable, results oriented, and achievable within a specific time frame. Performance objectives indicate what students should be able to do at the end (as an outcome) of the program. They may refer to subject-specific concepts and skills, or abilities and more general attributes. Figure 3.3 provides an acronym that can be used as a guide to understanding topic objectives.

Figure 3.3 SMART Objectives

> **S = Specific:** detailed about particular aspects of expectations and in describing the action and behaviors required for performance to achieve or exceed expectations. They should be clear and understandable.
>
> **M = Measurable, Meaningful:** in language that is understandable to teachers and students as well as measurable for assessment.
>
> **A = Attainable, Appropriate:** reasonable, appropriate to student skill level, and suitable for learners to attain and satisfy standards.
>
> **R = Results oriented, Realistic:** focused on outcomes and not tasks to be achieved within a given practical period.
>
> **T = Time frame, Testable:** some measure of testable progress/achievement made within a specific time frame.

Examples of Topic Objectives

- Studying moral ethics for five periods a week will result in 85 percent of the class passing the ethics examination.

- Motivational exercises employed in daily planning encourage students to improve their weekly quiz scores.
- Direct reading instruction will be delivered in grades three, four, and eight for three hours a day in order to improve achievement on standardized tests.

Objectives in Planning

Ralph Tyler Tyler (1949) suggested that the most useful form for stating objectives is to express them in terms that identify both the kind of behavior to be developed in the student and the content or area of life in which this behavior is to operate. Thus the idea of behavioral objectives was born. Tyler's rationale and his philosophical screening process are followed today by most curriculum makers to some degree, consciously or unconsciously. No human is completely unbiased, and even curricular computer programs are designed by biased humans.

Tyler wrote, "Any device which provides valid evidence regarding the progress of students toward educational objectives is appropriate." "The selection of evaluation techniques should be made in terms of the appropriateness of that technique for the kind of behavior to be appraised" (Pinar et al., 1995). Tyler concluded that there were four basic principles in the development of any curricular project.

1. One has to first define appropriate learning objectives.
2. Useful learning experiences must be provided.
3. Learning experiences must be organized to have a maximum effect.
4. Evaluating the curriculum and revising those aspects that did not prove to be effective must be carried out.

Critics of Tyler's rationale claim, however, that

- Data collected from learners and society is biased and unscientific.
- Selecting behavioral objectives before developing curriculum is a flawed concept.
- Filtering educational objectives through a philosophical screen is vacuous and trivial, with no scientific criteria to choose between objectives.
- Curriculum development is left to a less-qualified group at the local school as opposed to being mandated by state experts (McNeil, 1990, pp. 389–390).

Robert Mager Educators have used instructional or behavioral objectives for at least four decades. With the release of Robert Mager's *Preparing Instructional Objectives* (1962), the use of objectives has become commonplace. His book proposes that the purpose of objectives is to assess student performance, not to direct practice (Mager and Piper, 1997).

The reason the system is called an outcomes approach is that objectives specify student outcomes and/or how students will be evaluated, and not educational intent (see Figure 3.4). An example of the outcomes approach would be, "Given six sentences, fifth graders will identify each that contains a metaphor." Alternatively, "After reading four short stories, fifth graders will be able to identify the different genres."

This approach can be criticized because it does not identify the teacher's intent; its primary emphasis is evaluation statements that specify student outcomes. Critics claim that a better way for describing an objective might be to answer two simple questions.

1. What do I want my students to know?
2. How will I know if my students understand?

Norman Gronlund Gronlund (1991) suggested that objectives should be stated in general terms, beginning with phrases such as *to know, to understand, to apply, to evaluate,* or *to appreciate*. These should be followed by specific behaviors that evidence the objective's attainment. An example of this procedure would be, "To understand the causes of the Civil War by analyzing the economic, social, and political values of the North and the South."

Gronlund said that the planning process consists of four steps:

1. Decide what and how a student should learn.
2. Decide the characteristics of the students in the class in order to meet needs.
3. Have knowledge of the discipline (subject) being taught.
4. Have knowledge of the methods needed to teach the subject.

WRITING A LESSON PLAN

In the planning process, teachers think in terms of daily lesson plans usually confined to twenty- to forty-five–minute periods depending on the grade level. The easiest guide to writing a lesson plan we have found is contained in the mnemonic AMCASH. It summarizes the areas that lesson plans usually address: aim, motivation

Figure 3.4 Outcomes Approach System for Objectives

Good objectives have three parts:
1. an observable behavior
2. the conditions under which the behavior will occur
3. criteria for acceptable performance

PRACTICE EXERCISE 3.1

Writing Objectives

The purpose of this exercise is to develop the skill of writing appropriate objectives for instructional plans. Review what objectives are by looking at Figure 3.3, SMART Objectives, and how objectives have been used in the past. Then write four objectives for a unit of your choice, each to represent a lesson in the unit.

Grade and unit title

Objective

1.
2.
3.
4.

(including materials), content, application (practice or procedure), summary, and homework. These components might be easier to understand if looked at from the standpoint of a theatrical play. In this perspective, aims and motivations would be considered purpose and mood. Content in the terms of the theater would be called the message, while materials would be called props. The applications, procedures, and pivotal questions could be viewed as the script, while the evaluation and summary are the critique or critic's review. (It is interesting to note that actors rarely write their own scripts and plays but teachers always do.) Whatever terms are used for planning, the procedure remains the same. The mnemonic AMCASH provides a simple way to remember how to write lesson plans using research-based theories as a guide to effective lesson design.

AMCASH

Each of the components in AMCASH adds to the substance of a lesson plan. In most cases, a lesson would not be considered complete if one step in the process was discarded. This is not to say that this is the only model for lesson planning, but just one of the most concise. There is no one right way to write a lesson plan.

Aims are the focus for the lesson and should be aligned with specific standards for the course of study. They should act as the guide to direct and focus learning in clear and unambiguous language. The **aim** of the lesson must be achievable within the parameters and available resources at hand. They at times can be considered similar to performance objectives in that they can be achieved and measured within a specific time frame.

Motivation is the explanation or purpose for learning that tells the student "what's in it for me." Students must have a reason for learning that goes beyond a reward or punishment grade. True learning is learning that becomes internalized and part of one's being. Successful **motivation** can be extrinsic or intrinsic. Wondering about the existence of life outside our planet for a lesson on exploration is extrinsic. The lesson becomes intrinsic when we ask how life would be if we could explore and live on another planet without special life supports.

Much of the literature about student motivation looks at what teachers can do to encourage high levels of student performance through extrinsic means, such as rewards and punishments. Rewards come in many forms and can include tokens, such as gold stars and certificates. Punishment usually includes some consequence or loss of privileges. Extrinsic motivators work until the reward or punishment is withdrawn, which usually precipitates the lessening of performance. Students need to own their accomplishments; they need to take pride in their work without fearing failure. They should be motivated to understand that persistence in work tasks will help them to view mistakes as opportunities for positive learning.

Materials are the ingredients, resources, or substances that make up the lesson. A geography lesson would need a map, as an art lesson would need paints. List the technology, handouts, chart paper, text resources, and so on, needed to complete the lesson. Include what you need to do to prepare for your students to complete the lesson.

Content is the body of the lesson. It describes the major ideas and concepts you expect to communicate. It is what you are teaching and what students are expected to learn. Align the content area with the standard number and any key components or benchmarks that are applicable to the lesson.

Application or procedures can best be described as *how to teach* what you expect students to learn. The steps can be seen as a set of directions or instructions that guide the presentation of the lesson. Enumerate the procedure you expect to follow.

Summary is the portion of a lesson in which content presented is summarized and student comprehension is assessed. The most direct way to ascertain what has been learned is to ask, "What have we learned so far?" Students can also be asked to write a statement about what they have learned and share it with their classmates. The teacher might also lead a question-and-answer session based on the lesson's subject matter.

Homework is the cement that seals in learning if prepared and presented properly. The purposes of homework are to reinforce, make concrete, and extend the concepts and ideas presented in class lessons. It can also be used to prepare for sequential lessons. Perspectives vary on the value of homework. Critics claim students receive higher grades with less outside preparation. One researcher found "There was no consistent linear or curvilinear relation between the amount of time spent on homework and the child's level of academic achievement" (Kohn, 2006, p. 15).

Other researchers claim that homework helps students develop responsibility and life skills and the ability to manage tasks and that it provides experiential learning, increased motivation, opportunities to learn to cope with difficulties and distractions, and academic benefits (Corno and Xu, 2004; Coutts, 2004). While many researchers take either a positive or a negative stance on homework, Cooper (2001) takes a more balanced approach, maintaining that "Research on the effects of homework suggests that it is beneficial as long as teachers use their knowledge of developmental levels to guide policies and expectations."

Lesson Presentation Skills

The skills necessary for effective lesson presentation distinguish the professional educator from the college graduate. Both should have content knowledge but only one can effectively facilitate learning. These key skills can be broken down into four general categories.

1. *Set induction* is the way a lesson is introduced. This first step consists of an aim and a motivation. The purposes of set induction (motivation) are to focus student attention, set a framework for the lesson, help understand abstract concepts to come, and stimulate interest. It is best used when you actively relate to student experiences, which will help to clarify goals, begin a smooth transition between topics, and act as a bridge to new content.
2. *Explaining* is the second step and includes the method (direct or indirect instruction) you intend to use. Traditional lecture (direct instruction) consists of clear objectives, appropriate motivation, a summary of main points logically developed, and some form of closure. Cooperative learning (indirect instruction) consists of developing skills that start out as extrinsic and end up as intrinsic; for example, learning to understand others by enhancing social skills.
3. *Providing reinforcement* occurs when we supply support for class work through class applications and homework.
4. *Verbalizing content* is one way to review and recall expected learning. By speaking, teachers and students exercise a final voice in the form of summarizing content.

Lesson Design

Constructivist lesson design is concerned with physical, symbolic, social, and theoretical construction of knowledge. To be able to apply constructivist principles when designing lessons requires a reflective approach to learning. Fortunately, there are five guiding principles that can help you structure constructivist lessons that are applicable at all levels and stages of learning.

1. Problems should be relevant and considered important by students.
2. Learning should be structured around broad principles that affect perception and behavior.
3. Encourage student participation while genuinely valuing students' ideas.
4. Adapt instruction to address student assumptions.
5. The purpose of all instructional endeavors is to add to student learning (Gagnon and Collay, 1996; Brooks and Brooks, 1993).

The three constructivist lesson designs in Figure 3.5 depend on teachers preparing episodes and situations that students need to explain. Teachers are required to assess what students know and what they want them to know. In all three models, teachers are to ask questions and answer, without giving an explanation. The responsibility of the students is to keep a written record of their thoughts and share them with classmates as a final step in the learning process.

In a constructivist teaching style, the individual traditional lesson plan is often inappropriate. Specific objectives and timelines may be included in the unit plan, but lesson plans are more fluid as they cater to student needs and learning styles. As students are asked to engage in problem or inquiry learning, rigid lesson planning with title, behavioral objectives, and specific outcomes within certain time constraints often no longer fit within modern effective pedagogy. Today, formal lesson plans are often not required. Look at Practice Exercise 3.2 and see if you can put together a lesson plan that could be called a constructivist lesson plan.

Backward Design Process The backward design process begins with the end in mind (Figure 3.6). One starts with the end—the desired results (goals or standards)—and then derives the curriculum from the evidence of learning (performances) called for by the standard and the teaching needed to equip students to perform. This design process involves teachers planning in three stages: identifying results, determining valid evidence, and planning instruction that achieves results.

1. ***Identify results.*** In this stage, one asks, What do we really need to understand? The focus is on what you want students to understand, on big ideas, concepts, theories, and principles. The goal is to have

Figure 3.5 Three Constructivist Lesson Designs

1. The *learning cycle instructional model* is a three-step design used as a general framework for many kinds of constructivist activities.
   - The first phase is *discovery and exploration* during which students are encouraged to make hypotheses about various materials displayed by the teacher. The phase centers students' inquiry on a concrete examination of a focusing task. It prompts students' recall and/or assimilation through concrete experiential activities. The instructor acts mainly as observer and supporter of the spontaneous exploration.
   - The second phase consists of *concept introduction and invention.* Here the teacher highlights students' questions and guides them with hypotheses and explains procedures necessary to design experiments. This phase centers students on drawing of generalizations and possibilities from the exploration phase. The goal is having the students construct the relationship(s) for themselves and to test them against others' generalizations. The instructor's role fluctuates between supporting the momentum of students' testing of their generalizations, and encouraging students' expression of different perspectives.
   - The third phase, *concept application,* requires students to reflect and reconsider the concepts studied in the first two steps. This cycle may be repeated many times throughout a lesson or unit. The phase centers students on using their understanding of the concept or skill in new situations. The instructor acts as a facilitator. The goal for this application is to stabilize the constructed principle(s) (Campbell and Fuller, 1981).
2. The *Gagnon and Collay model* (1996) provides steps for the teacher to follow in developing constructivist plans.
   - *Develop* a situation for students to explain.
   - Select a process for *groupings* of materials and students.
   - Build a *bridge* between what students already know and what the teachers want them to learn.
   - Anticipate *questions* to ask and answer without giving away an explanation.
   - Encourage students to *exhibit* a record of their thinking by sharing it with others.
   - Solicit students' *reflections* about their learning.
3. The *information construction (ICON) design model* was developed by McClintock and Black (1995) from several computer technology-supported learning environments at the Dalton School in New York City. It contains seven stages:
   - *Observation.* In the first step, students make observations of primary source materials.
   - *Interpretation construction.* In the second step, students interpret their observations and explain their reasoning.
   - *Contextualization.* Students construct the conditions (contexts) that they use to explain their interpretations.
   - *Cognitive apprenticeship.* Teachers help student apprentices master observation, interpretation, and contextualization.
   - *Collaboration.* Students collaborate in observation, interpretation, and contextualization.
   - *Multiple interpretations.* Students gain cognitive flexibility from multiple interpretations of student and expert examples.
   - *Multiple manifestations.* Students gain transferability by seeing multiple manifestations of the same interpretations.

students obtain enduring understandings such as life, liberty and equality, honesty, truthfulness, brotherhood of man, and so on. Enduring understandings go beyond discrete facts or skills; they should relate to life experiences within or beyond the subject matter being taught.

2. **Determine valid evidence.** How can students demonstrate understanding, and what evidence can they provide? Understanding develops as a result of ongoing inquiry and rethinking; the assessment of understanding should be thought of as a collection of evidence over time instead of a single event (Wiggins, 1998). By continually emphasizing the need to explain, interpret, apply, and discuss, the backward design process determines acceptable evidence.

3. **Plan instruction.** Finally, the learning experiences that will lead to understanding must be implemented. This is accomplished after one has clearly identified results and appropriate demonstrations of understanding. In designing backward, planning for instruction is the last step, rather than the first, as with traditional lesson designs.

Traditional Traditionalists argue that the lesson design emphasis on projects and activities has gone overboard to the degree of making a shambles of education.

PRACTICE EXERCISE 3.2

Preparing a Constructivist Lesson Plan

Use the steps outlined in the constructivist lesson form to develop a lesson in your subject area.

Sample Constructivist Lesson Plan Form

1. **Standards.** (performance, knowledge, and [NETS-S] National Educational Technology Standards for Students)
2. **What concepts do you want students to understand after completing this lesson?**
3. **Essential question.**
4. **Criteria for success.** (How will you know students have gained an understanding of the concepts?)
5. **Resources.** (What resources will you and your students use?)
6. **Management.** (How will students share technology resources? How will you break up the lesson into segments—the number of hours or days?)
7. **Learner Diversity.** (What diverse learner needs should you consider when selecting resources, grouping students, or planning the culminating project? Are there any special considerations such as assistive technologies or second-language learning to take into account?)
8. **Engage.** Capture the students' attention, stimulate their thinking, and help them access prior knowledge.
9. **Explore.** Give students time to think, plan, investigate, and organize collected information.
10. **Explain.** Involve students in an analysis of their explorations. Use reflective activities to clarify and modify their understanding.
11. **Elaborate.** Give students the opportunity to expand and solidify their understanding of the concept and/or apply it to a real-world situation.
12. **Evaluate.** Evaluate throughout the lesson. Present students with a scoring guide at the beginning. Scoring tools developed by teachers (sometimes with student involvement) target what students must know and do. Consistent use of scoring tools can improve learning.

Source: eMINTS (2007). Adapted from materials available at www.mdk12.org/instruction/curriculum/science/5emodel.html.

Figure 3.6 Backward Design Guide

- Where are we headed? Why are we headed there? Make students aware of obligations and assessments up front.
- Hook the student through engaging and provocative entry points. Provide thought-provoking and focusing experiences, issues, oddities, problems, and challenges that point toward essential and unit questions, core ideas, and final performance tasks.
- Explore, enable, and equip by engaging students in learning experiences that allow them to explore big ideas and essential questions. Equip students for final performances through guided instruction and coaching on needed skills and knowledge.
- Reflect and rethink by digging deeper into ideas and issues. Revise, rehearse, and refine as needed to guide students in self-assessment and self-adjustment. Like all planning models, backward design requires revisions and refinements throughout the planning process. "Creating a unit using the backward design planning process is not a neat, tidy, or easy process. It is a recursive one; you will move back and forth across the curriculum map, making revisions and refinements each time you add something to a section of your planning." Retrieved at: www.greece.k12.ny.us/instruction/ela/6-12/BackwardDesign/BDstep5.htm.
- Exhibit and evaluate by revealing what has been understood through performances and products. Involve students in a final self-assessment to identify remaining questions, set future goals, and point toward new units and lessons.

Sewall's view is that the basic problem is learning is hard work, and should not be trivialized. A traditional behaviorist approach is teacher centered and includes prepared lessons, discussions, and frequent interchanges of ideas in class. Appropriate group work is recognized as long as there is a clear sense of direction for the lesson. A lesson should have a beginning and an ending summary that will leave all students with a sense of what has been accomplished. The role of students is to engage in active listening, while taking organized notes and developing the skills necessary for a cumulative aggregation of knowledge and skills for the future. Traditionalists are for passive education. They insist that they want students to evaluate, interpret, compare, extend, apply and analyze, and defend solutions, while communicating clearly (Sewall, 2000).

Traditional planning consists of yearly, unit, weekly, and daily plans directed toward meeting clearly stated objectives aligned to standards and benchmarks. This type of planning usually relies on texts and curriculum guides for content. In effect, unit plans and lesson plans are similar to the scripts in a play. The lesson is one act, and the unit is the entire play. Plans that have clearly

PRACTICE EXERCISE 3.3

Using Backward Design

Read the following blog selection retrieved at http://blogs.edweek.org/teachers/newterrain, and determine the author's position regarding Backward Design. Use the following guide to evaluate the article.

- Was information about the author available?
- What new ideas were explored?
- Is the article too broad or too narrow?
- What is your overall opinion or assessment of this article?

Life . . . in Backward Design

Jessica Shyu

I used to think I was pretty normal. Now I'm beginning to wonder if I, too, am an eduholic. I guess the first tip-off was earlier this summer when I started talking about backward design. I mean *really* talking about backward design. Like most teacher prep programs around the country, Teach for America's teachers are taught to use backward design in their planning. I had first learned about backward design, a.k.a. UbD, in reference to "Understanding by Design" by Wiggins and McTighe, back when I was a first-year teacher. I used it to design my unit plans, but it wasn't until earlier this summer when I was preparing to train our first-year teachers that I really sat down and understood the truth behind backward design. It wasn't until then that I saw the light.

For those unfamiliar with the magic of backward design, it is actually not magic at all. It is the principle that Grant Wiggins and Jay McTighe articulated and popularized in their book that effective planning starts with the end in mind. (For fellow BD aficionados, the following four paragraphs are on the how-to of backward design.)

How to Backward Design

What does backward design look like when planning at a course, unit, or lesson level? Before even starting to brainstorm those really entertaining lessons on longitude and latitude, teachers need to first truly understand the learning goals and enduring understandings they're striving toward. What does standard 9.2(a) really mean, after all? What enduring understandings should the students be really understanding by learning about longitude and latitude? What's the point of learning this?

After that, they need to determine what it will look like when students demonstrate mastery of those learning goals. Will they be able to locate places on a map using coordinates and lines of longitude and latitude? Will they be able to explain the purpose of the imaginary lines? Will they take a paper-pencil test? Will they design their own maps?

Only after completing the two first two steps do backward designers begin planning. What will you need to teach to get your kids to be able to find locations on a map using lines of longitude and latitude? Do they need to first define the terms and identify the lines on a map? How will you teach it?

When working with our new teachers, we kept these three steps of BD on the board:

1. **Identify Desired Results.** Where are we going? What must students know and be able to do at the end of the year/unit/lesson?
2. **Determine Acceptable Evidence.** How will we know that we have gotten there? What assessments will show us that students have achieved our goals?
3. **Plan for Instruction.** How will we get there? Exactly what must I teach and when, in order to lead my students to achieve our goals?

Pitfalls of Not BD'ing

At first blush, this may seem backward (ha ha). If you're trying to plan your unit, doesn't it make sense to think about how you're going to teach it and what activities you'll use, and make the assessment last? Well, yes. It does make sense. We've all done it. But by making the assessment last or by not starting with your standards and enduring understandings, teachers run the dire (and all-too-common) risk of misaligning lessons to the standards, designing tests at a lower level than the standards call for, or not having an assessment that gives you clear evidence of whether your students actually mastered the content.

So that takes me back to where I started. My eduholism. As I work with my teachers on improving their course goals, assessments and plans, my work life revolves around backward design. In a naturally eduholic way, my personal life has taken a turn for BD as well.

Men

Recently, I found myself telling a Friend to use backward design when finding a boyfriend: First, you need to really understand what you want and what your priorities are. Next, if your priority is "nice" and "cute," you need to imagine what "nice" and "cute" would look like when you meet someone. What are some examples of what Potential Boyfriend may do to demonstrate his "niceness" and "cuteness"? Third, start planning for it. If one way Potential Boyfriend could demonstrate "niceness" is by volunteering, then you should start spending your Saturdays around the local animal shelter.

Money

I don't buy $100 shoes, but I'm not particularly budget-savvy either. A month ago, I found myself planning backward to save for the upcoming year. I decided on my goal ($5,000). I figured out how I would "assess" it (I would have $5,000 more in my savings account). Then I worked backward from September 2008 to September 2007 to scratch together a long-term plan for how much I would need to save monthly in order to reach my goal. (It was a good plan. And then I bought a computer. Maybe I'll write another entry on adjusting our long-term plans to deal with unforeseen changes.)

Public Policy

Back in August, I was on a plane reading *The Economist* when I got so giddy by an article on a California city that I yelped a little, marked the page and pulled out a Post-It to jot down a note: "Cerritos, CA uses BACKWARD DESIGN!!!" The piece highlights Cerritos' "superb management and geographical good fortune" and described how the small suburb built beautiful libraries, performing arts centers and parks all while maintaining fiscal success. What I read was that the city managers knew what they wanted from the start (financial stability), they knew what it would look like to get there (lure businesses and investors to set up shop in the city) and had a long-term plan on how to get there, which was directly aligned to their goals (first, establish pipelines and roads, then business parks, policing, and schools).

Opinions expressed in the blog are Jessica's own and do not represent the views of Teach for America or teachermagazine.org. October 9, 2007. With permission.

The author, Jessica Shyu, taught special education for two years at an American Indian reservation school in New Mexico. She has also worked as a program director for Teach for America in the Rio Grande Valley of Texas and in the Washington DC region.

---

defined instructional objects result in better instruction, better outcomes, and better evaluation. Andrew Carnegie once said, "Fail to plan and you plan to fail." It would seem that the industrialist had a clear vision of how to design a lesson without actually knowing the classic elements of lesson design.

In Figure 3.7, nine elements of lesson design are categorized as (1) getting ready to learn (items one to three), (2) giving students information (items four and five), and (3) helping students keep the information they have learned (items six through nine). Upon reflection it can be seen that a good deal of Maas's (1988)

Figure 3.7 Nine Elements of Lesson Design

1. *Anticipatory set* is any activity designed to focus the student on learning, which contains (1) active participation (overt and covert), (2) relevance to student background, and (3) relevance to current learning. For example, "Take a moment, class, to think about what we learned yesterday, and write it down."
2. *Objective of the lesson* will describe what students will be doing during the lesson.
3. *Purpose* is the explanation of what is in the lesson for the student.
4. *Input.* Teacher should only give as much information as students can handle.
5. *Modeling* is when teachers show students how to problem solve, identify what to look for.
6. *Check for understanding* is done by using active participation (overt or covert). The teacher can use finger signals, brief quizzes, flash cards, or monitor students by walking about the room.
7. *Guided practice* is the application portion of the lesson. This is developed and controlled by the teacher.
8. *Independent practice* usually consists of a homework assignment or an independent project done out of the classroom.
9. *Closure* is when the lesson is clinched. Students give a final oral or written summary. It is the opportunity for the student to intellectually absorb what has been learned. The same three principles of an anticipatory set are used for closure, for example, "Think about what we learned today and tell your neighbor. Now write it down." Closure occurs after every meaningful piece of information is given. It helps students check their progress.

Source: Maas (1988)

PRACTICE EXERCISE 3.4

Lesson Design

Design a traditional lesson in your content areas using Maas's Nine Elements of Lesson Design (see Figure 3.7). To further the lesson's effectiveness, incorporate the four practices listed below into your plan.

- *Select* teaching objectives.
- *Monitor* and adjust instruction (validate, evaluate, assessment-turn and talk, questioning).
- *Understand* the Principles of Learning (anticipatory set, motivation, active participation, closure).
- *Teach* to the objective.

Figure 3.8 Seven-Step Model for Learning

1. *Anticipatory set.* Gets the student's attention focused on the lesson. The instructor is developing a state of readiness for instruction. Having a worthwhile anticipatory set will increase motivation, increase retention, and help in making efficient use of class time.

2. *Objective/why.* Enables students to know what they will learn and why it is relevant or important to them. Without an objective, the students, teacher, and lesson have no sense of direction.

3. *Input.* Provides the key information necessary to achieve the objective. The teacher in a simple to complex sequential manner presents information.

4. *Modeling.* Shows students what is expected of them. Not only the modeling itself, but the sequence of events in which modeling occurs, facilitates learning.

5. *Checking for understanding.* A process used to check comprehension. Teachers can ask students questions in a variety of ways, including signaled answers, choral response, or individual responses, to determine if the students truly understand the material. This step prevents teachers from proceeding when students do not understand.

6. *Guided practice.* Allows monitored practice while the teacher is present. The student attempts the new skill while the teacher gives specific feedback about what is being done correctly, what needs to be improved, and how performance can be improved.

7. *Independent practice.* Occurs when the teacher is not present or monitoring student progress. New learning should be performed without major errors, discomfort, or confusion. Homework, a written test, or out-of-school activities are examples of independent practice.

Source: Batesky (1987)

elements of lesson design stem from the classic work of Madeline Hunter (1982), which he expanded upon.

Madeline Hunter's Model for Learning Madeline Hunter considered herself a practitioner who translated research into practice. She developed a seven-step model for learning by watching effective teachers teach (Hunter, 1982, 1984). She claimed the model could increase the probability of successful learning. Its focus is on having the teacher consider what to teach before and while teaching. According to Hunter's model, before planning a lesson a teacher must make three key decisions:

1. What content am I going to teach?
2. What behavior do I want from the learner?
3. What behavior will I as the teacher exhibit?

The seven steps in Hunter's model (see Figure 3.8) do not have to be completed in one lesson or one day and it is not a checklist to be routinely followed. Flexibility and reinforcement are advanced throughout this design. Hunter saw the complexity of teaching, unlike those who think "teaching is just telling kids what to do and maintaining discipline." Hunter compared teaching to surgery where you think fast on your feet and do the best that you can with the information you have. You must be very skilled, very knowledgeable, and exquisitely well trained, because neither a teacher nor a surgeon can say, "Everybody sit still until I figure out what in the heck we're gonna do next." When asked what she wanted to be remembered for most, Hunter replied, "If I could have my wish, I would hope my work would help move teaching from a craft to a profession based on research translated into artistic practice, where the professional is a decision maker and where the professional never stops learning" (Goldberg, 1990).

Jacobsen, Eggen, and Kauchak (1999) claim that there is no "right" format for lesson planning. They present a seven-step model that is quite similar to Hunter's and Maas's yet containing variations. (See Figure 3.9.)

A lesson plan should begin with basic information and embrace all or some of the steps shown in Figure 3.10. Always included should be the *what, how,* and *why* (content, instructional strategy, and purpose). The purpose of a lesson plan is quite simple—it is to communicate. "To whom?" you might ask. The answer is, *you!* The lesson plans you develop are a guide for organizing

Figure 3.9 J. E. K. Model for Planning

1. *Unit topic* is essentially the title for a unit. A unit is made up of lessons that are taught in sequential order. The title reminds us of the relationship between the individual lesson and the unit as a whole.
2. *Objectives* form the heart of a lesson. They give the lesson a purpose, and provide a means of assessment.
3. *Rationale* provides your reason for teaching a particular topic.
4. *Content* is the component that describes the major ideas you plan to teach.
5. *Procedures* are the ways in which you will teach the content.
6. *Materials* should be listed to remind the teacher of materials needed for the lesson.
7. *Assessment* is the component that has a teacher considering how to evaluate what students have learned.

PRACTICE EXERCISE 3.5

Comparison of Traditional Lesson Design Models

Review and compare the three traditional lesson design models presented. Note that there is a commonality in the steps necessary to design a traditional lesson. Write a brief passage defining the terms used and noting similar meanings and differences.

Steps	Maas Model	Hunter Model	J. E. K. Model
1.	Anticipatory set	Anticipatory set	Unit topic
2.	Objective of the lesson	Objective	Objective
3.	Purpose	Input	Rationale
4.	Input	Modeling	Content
5.	Modeling	Check for understanding	Procedures
6.	Check for understanding	Guided practice	Materials
7.	Guided practice	Independent practice	Assessments
8.	Independent practice		
9.	Closure		

material and helping students achieve intended learning outcomes. Whether a lesson plan fits a particular format is not as important as whether it actually describes what you want. A lesson plan that can be interpreted or implemented in different ways is probably not very good. Specificity is key to creating effective lessons. Vague or directionless plans say, "Almost any series of connecting roads will take you from New York City to Houston, eventually." Being specific you would say, "Only one set of connecting roads represents the shortest and best route." A good lesson plan will contain a set of specific and essential directions. (See Figures 3.11 and 3.12.)

MINI CASE FROM THE FIELD

The following case study emphasizes the importance of understanding proper lesson design as necessary to effective teaching skills. Read the case and decide who is making the better argument, Margaret Gomez or her teaching colleague, Ed Child. Assess the principal Mr. Thompson's position related to lesson planning. Decide if Nick Saccone is correct.

Why Write a Lesson Plan?

Margaret was thinking about her discussion with Jane Hemmings on relevant theories that purported to assist in understanding how children learn, when big Ed Child entered the teachers' lounge. Ed was a tall man who weighed over 250 pounds. He had on a fuzzy-looking green tweed jacket, brown twill pants, white shirt with a twisted collar, and string tie with a large misshapen turquoise clasp, which set him off as some misbegotten fashion statement. Margaret offered a cheery hello, while Ed just shrugged and jammed his hands into his pockets. He looked tired, washed out, and worn down by a seemingly endless school year. He finally said, "I feel awful! Mr. Thompson just visited my class and asked to see my lesson plans. When I told him I kept all my plans in my head, he asked if I were some kind of genius. He then went on to lecture me in front of the class on the importance of formal lesson plans." Margaret reminded Ed that the school policy was to keep a set of plans for the week in the middle drawer of your desk. No wonder the principal was mad.

Ed calmly replied that Mr. Thompson was a bully and had unfairly ridiculed him in front of his class. Margaret agreed that it had certainly not been appropriate, but neither was Ed's attitude regarding lesson plans. "A whole school of thought claims that if you do not properly plan you will be an ineffective teacher," Margaret said. "Most lessons have a beginning, middle, and end. What you have to do is have a vision of what you want

Figure 3.10 Essentials for Lesson Planning

Step 1: Heading
Date:
Teacher Name:
Grade Level:
Title of Lesson:
Content Area:

Step 2: Goals/Content
What do you want students to know and do? What knowledge, skills, strategies, and attitudes do you expect children to gain? What important content and concepts will children learn? What local, state, or national standards will be addressed?

Step 3: Guiding Questions
What are the guiding questions for this lesson? Why would students want to know about this topic? What questions will generate discussion about this topic? What questions will be asked to guide the lesson?

Step 4: Assessment
How will you know students have reached the lesson goal? What assessment tool will you use? How will students be involved in ongoing assessment? How will students assess themselves? How can technology support or enhance the lesson?

Step 5: Learning Connections
How does this lesson link to the curriculum and standards? What conceptual difficulties might students have? What curriculum connections will you make in this lesson with other topics you teach?

Step 6: Learning Activities or Tasks
What engaged and worthwhile learning activities and tasks will your students complete? How will they build knowledge and skills; learn independently and with others; demonstrate knowledge, ability, and creativity; manage learning? In what ways is this lesson challenging, authentic, and multidisciplinary? How can the use of technology support student learning?

Step 7: Teaching Strategies
What instructional practices will you use with this lesson? How will your learning environment support these activities? What is your role? What are the students' roles in the lesson? How can the use of technology support your teaching?

Step 8: Management
How and where will your students work—classroom, lab, in groups or independently? How will you provide for students with special needs? How will you modify this lesson for individual learning needs? How will you use additional resources? How can technology support classroom management?

Step 9: Materials and Resources
What other support services and resources will you need? How can technology extend and enhance the lesson in ways that would not be possible without it? Will you need additional people to help with this lesson?

Step 10: Lesson Evaluation and Reflection
This step consists of reflective questions used to evaluate the lesson plan. Was this lesson worth doing? In what ways was it effective? How would I change this lesson the next time I teach it? What did I observe students doing and learning? Did students find the lesson meaningful and purposeful?

Source: Adapted from the North Central Regional Educational Laboratory (NCREL) Lesson Planner (2001)

---

your students to know, and how to get them to understand. Ralph Tyler wrote that more than fifty years ago and it still holds true today. The key to good lesson design is in writing clear objectives. I use an acronym called SMART to guide me in writing performance objectives. You should follow a guide when preparing your lessons. I use a simple one I read about somewhere called AMCASH. Yes, it is another mnemonic device. I find it makes it easier to remember."

"I went to college, too," said Ed. "Why aren't you talking about Madeline Hunter's seven-step model for learning? I was taught that most lesson plans can be related to her model."

"That's true," said Margaret, "but I still like my own simple formulas. They're easier to remember."

Ed said he was still offended by Mr. Thompson's actions, and that he would only write minimalist plans.

Nick Saccone, a science teacher, had been sitting quietly listening. He stood up and said calmly, "You're all a bunch of traditionalists. I use a constructivist format when designing my plans. My goal is not to just instruct. It's for students to learn."

1. Describe Margaret's argument supporting the writing of lesson plans. Should they be written only because of school policy? Explain your reasoning.

Figure 3.11 Sample Lesson Plan Format

Teacher _____   Subject _____
Grade Level _____   Date _____

1. *Content.* This part of your lesson relates to the subject matter, a concept, or a skill. State this as, "I want my students to be able to (name the skill)" or "I want my students to understand (describe the concept)." Usually, content is predetermined by the *curriculum* you are implementing.

2. *Prerequisites.* Indicate what students must know or do to master this lesson. Research indicates that near 70 percent of what a student learns depends upon possessing appropriate prerequisites.

3. *Instructional Objective.* Describe what is to be learned. (Refer to Topic Objectives.)

4. *Instructional Procedures.* Description of instructional strategy you will use, direct or indirect. This to be followed by specific steps you will follow during the lesson. Be sure to include an introduction to the lesson, the actual instructional techniques, and the specific things students are to do, as well as how you will end and summarize the lesson.

5. *Materials and Equipment.* List all materials and equipment to be used.

6. *Assessment/Evaluation.* Describe how you will evaluate if students have attained the instructional objective. Relate your evaluation directly to your instructional objectives.

7. *Follow-up Activities.* Indicate how independent or group activities (homework, problems, and projects) will reinforce and extend the lesson.

8. *Self-Assessment.* Reflect on the completed lesson. Concentrate on the strengths and weaknesses in the lesson. Determine how you will correct any deficiencies and enhance any strong points. Analyze the difference between what you wanted (the objective) and what you got (the results of the assessment).

---

2. Was Principal Thompson justified in criticizing Ed in front of his class? How should the situation have been handled?
3. Compare Margaret's ideas on lesson design with Hunter's model. Explain how they are compatible.
4. Compare and contrast the various lesson designs proposed by Margaret, Ed, and Nick.
5. Which plan would you choose? Justify your answer. ■

Lesson Plan Variety

What is the difference between an exciting class and a boring one? What qualities do you look for in a lesson to make it come alive? The answer is in the variety of activities provided for students. You have to develop devices that gain the attention of students, such as placing a map south side up at the chalkboard during a lesson on geographical direction. Attention-getting devices (see Figure 3.13) are the keys to starting a lesson off in the right direction. The type of device used should arouse curiosity by using thought provoking questions, multimedia presentations, pictures, diagrams, and graphs as well as stories and physical objects that relate to your lesson's objectives.

Personality and enthusiasm are also effective attention-getters. Enthusiasm is infectious and few will learn from a teacher not liked or respected. One cannot always do the same activity; variety is important. Combine rewards and praise with a variety of questions that encourage critical thinking. Be democratic and use ideas your students offer. If they offer no ideas, reflect on the strategies you are using. Always look into yourself when your lessons are not getting the results you expected. The teacher who claims to have taught an excellent lesson, and yet no one learned, has a great deal of reflecting to do. There is no substitute for an engaging personality, and variety helps. (See Figure 3.14.)

Reflective Lesson Planning

John Dewey, one of the most profound thinkers of all time, reflected on thinking by saying:

> We all acknowledge, in words at least, that ability to think is highly important; it is regarded as the distinguishing power that marks man from the lower animals. But since our ordinary notions of how and why thinking is important are vague, it

Figure 3.12 Sample Lesson Plan

Your Name _____

Grade Level _____ (College) _____   Date _____

Aim

1. To teach the five areas of reading instruction.
2. To understand the five areas of reading instruction and the significance of the National Reading Panel's Report.
3. To understand why every teacher is a teacher of reading.

Behavioral Objective: At the conclusion of the session, the student will understand the significance of the National Reading Panel's Report and know the five areas of reading instruction.

Motivation: No Child Left Behind Act of 2001. "Every teacher should be, to a certain extent, a teacher of reading" (Whipple, 1925).

1. How does this Act affect what we as teachers are expected to do in the classroom?
2. Describe your feelings regarding Whipple's statement.

Materials

1. Computer notes
2. Chalkboard
3. Video on lesson design

Procedure

1. Elicit importance of the aim through motivation questions.
2. Display notes and discuss meanings for phonemic awareness, phonics, fluency, vocabulary, and comprehension.
3. Have students complete exercise on word learning tasks for grades 8 and 11.
4. Discuss levels of word knowledge and have students complete exercise.
5. Play demonstration video and have students prepare the teacher lesson plan.
6. Review and discuss student exercises.
7. Discuss text comprehension as the goal of reading instruction.

Summary

1. What have we learned during this session?
2. Why is every teacher a teacher of reading?

Evaluation

1. Have students complete and discuss the behaviors that help text comprehension.

Follow-up

Prepare a lesson plan for "the next time we meet" to be presented in class. The topic should be how to write a lesson plan.

Comments: These reflect your feelings about your lesson's success or failure.

Figure 3.13 Attention-Getting Devices

PRESENTING FOR THE SENSES		
Verbal	Visual	Tactile
Teacher explanation	Charts, graphs, drawings	Touch materials
Questioning	Look at visuals	Use materials
Audiotape	Watch video/film	Construct model
Recitation	See models	Paste, cut, glue
PowerPoint audio	Visualize on screen	Use laptop

is worthwhile to state explicitly the values possessed by reflective thought. In the first place, it emancipates us from merely impulsive and merely routine activity. Put in positive terms, thinking enables us to direct our activities with foresight and to plan according to ends-in-view, or to come into command of what is now distant and lacking. By putting the consequences of different ways and lines of action before the mind, it enables us to know what we are about when we act. It converts action that is merely appetitive, blind and impulsive into intelligent action. (Archambault, 1974)

Dewey's (1997) most basic assumption about reflective teaching was that learning improves to the degree

Figure 3.14 Indicators of Variety

Using Variety	Poor Variety
Effective Teacher	Ineffective Teacher
• Uses attention-gaining devices	Starts lesson without learner attention
• Shows enthusiasm and animation	Speaks in monotone, no emotion or movement
• Varying activities	Doesn't vary modality
• Mixes rewards and reinforcers	Rarely reinforces
• Varies types of questions (see Bloom's taxonomy)	Uses same questions
• Uses students' ideas	Assumes role of sole authority

that it arises out of the process of reflection. **Reflective teaching** clearly contrasts with the direct instructional approach favored by many traditional teachers.

Boyd and Fales (1983) defined reflective thinking by saying it was a process by which one created and understood the meaning of any experience, in their past or present, in terms of "self." In effect, this change in process by using self as a primary determinant of learning is revolutionary. Three types of reflection appear in the literature:

1. *Reflection-on-action,* involves thinking about our actions and thoughts after an action is completed. This is a type of hindsight thinking.
2. *Reflection-in-action* occurs during the action itself (Schon, 1987).
3. *Reflection-for-action* occurs whenever reflective thinking is used to guide future actions (Killion and Todnem, 1991).

There are four stages for reflective lesson planning: describing, informing, confronting, and reconstructing appropriate actions (Smyth, 1989). First, describe the idea you are reflecting on. Second, contemplate communicating the theory associated with the concept. Third, face the environment (social ecology influences the end result). Finally, devise the appropriate instructional strategy. A reflective strategy in planning lessons allows freedom to meet students' needs.

Reflective Thinking

1. **Describing Stage.** Describe the various aspects of the idea or event under reflection.
2. **Informing Stage.** Describe how a theory is associated with the idea or event.
3. **Confronting Stage.** Reflect on how the situation was impacted by the social-cultural milieu.
4. **Reconstructing Stage.** Determine your course of action for future situations.

Reflective Teaching Reflective teaching means looking at what you do in the classroom, thinking about why you do it, and thinking about whether it works. It is a process of self-observation and self-evaluation. By collecting information about what goes on in class, and by analyzing and evaluating this data, we can identify and explore practices and underlying beliefs. The idea behind reflective teaching is to enhance methodology and pedagogical skills. Reflective teaching is an approach to professional development that is done in class. It is a practical application of reflective thinking (Taggart, 2005).

PRACTICE EXERCISE 3.6

A Reflective Activity

Lesson plans should contain all or most of the items listed in the sample below. You are to recreate a lesson you observed or have previously taught. Reflect on the lesson and the decisions made to facilitate instruction.

Sample Lesson Plan

Your Name _____

Grade Level _____ (College) _____ Date _____

Aim (Inform learner of object of the lesson.)

1. To teach . . .
2. To understand . . .
3. Student aim . . .

Behavioral Objective (At the conclusion of the session, what the student will understand.)

Motivation (Gaining attention.)

Materials (Presenting the stimulus materials.)

Procedure (Steps to elicit desired behavior.)

Summary (Stimulating recall of prerequisite learning.)

Evaluation (Assessing behavior.)

Follow-up (Provide feedback exercises and correctives.)

Comments (Your feelings reflecting on the lesson's success or lack of it.)

Teachers and those studying to be teachers can use reflective teaching to refine their classroom presentations. The plan involves preparing a lesson using any instructional strategy. Two or three students should be selected as designated teachers from the class. They then prepare a lesson to run for a limited amount of time (ten to fifteen minutes). The instructor selects the topic for the lesson. The designated teachers then teach a small group of their classmates and conclude by having a discussion on their lesson's effectiveness. The class or group will use the same criteria for judging the effectiveness of instruction (Borich, 1999). A whole-group (class) discussion on shared experiences and teacher effectiveness can be used to end the exercise. A typical topic might be related to persuasion, such as attempting to change fixed attitudes of most people regarding drugs. A sample aim could be stated in the form of a question: "Why should we be tolerant of drug abusers?" The assessment of a reflective teaching exercise can take the form of peer observation, feedback from students, a videotape of a lesson, or simply keeping a diary or journal detailing how lessons taught could be improved upon.

SUPERVISORS AND TEACHER OBSERVATION

Let's stop for a moment and ask, "Who will be looking at my plans?" The answer is, your supervisor. A question you will want answered before you prepare a lesson for observation is what the supervisor is going to look for. There is no simple answer. Supervisors, just like teachers, have a personality and philosophy of education, which determines their views of what an effective lesson is. It is best to ask your supervisor before you prepare your lesson. Generally, they will look for one or more of the fifteen areas described in Figure 3.15.

Figure 3.15 What Is Looked for in a Lesson

1. Supervisors look for *preparation* with regard to lesson plans, materials, organization, and questions. Plans should evidence the amount of work done.

2. *Routines* that have been taught and understood should be demonstrated by the actions of the children. Your supervisor will note whether students raise their hands, move in an orderly fashion, recite in a consistent way, and distribute materials appropriately.

3. Supervisors want to see a *variety of activities*. Clear and concise questions that are logically developed are a focus of observations. Activities must assist students in mastering the objectives of your lesson.

4. Supervisors will want to see that the *motivation* is clearly related to the lesson and arouses student interest. Intrinsic motivations directly related to lesson objectives are usually more effective than extrinsic motivations. For example, when teaching a lesson on opinions about exploration of space, referring to our astronauts' exploration of the moon is better than for instance, saying, "Has anyone ever gotten lost?"

5. Supervisors want to see pivotal *questions* that are distributed to all, thought provoking, graded to individual ability levels, and essentially fault-free. Avoid bad questions such as tugging (he did what?), ambiguous, double questions, questions that elicit one-word answers, and guessing questions (what am I thinking?). Do not allow chorus responses unless called for. Always ask your question first and then call on the student, allowing the student time to answer.

6. Indication that *medial and final summaries* are applicable to the principle, idea, or concept being taught. Where possible, summaries should be authentic, stressing positive values.

7. A supervisor will be waiting to see if your *homework assignment or application* is of appropriate length and difficulty for the students in your class. It should be clear, short, motivating, and individualized if possible.

8. *Grouping* of students should be based on ability levels for various activities. Differentiate your instruction. Supervisors want to see why students have been placed in their respective groups.

9. *Objectives* should indicate the development of values such as character, experience, skills, thinking, knowledge, guidance, exploration, our American heritage, etc.

10. *Drills* when used should be short, motivating, individualized, and based on need.

11. Lessons should use some *review* and draw on previous knowledge.

12. The *timing and tempo* of the lesson should be so constructed that you finish on time without leaving the class feeling rushed.

13. Good feelings and a general harmony should evidence *pupil-teacher rapport*. You like your students and they like you.

14. A supervisor will be attempting to find evidence of *democratic planning* where possible.

15. Teachers should be sympathetic, aware of mental hygiene, use of praise, alert to difficulties, and intellectually alert, as well as demonstrate *caring* and concern.

These fifteen items clearly demonstrate a traditional view of what a supervisor will be looking for in a formal observation. Will you be expected to meet every item? We doubt it. It all depends on the type of lesson you plan and present. It also depends on the most critical component: *Did the students learn?* If student learning was clearly demonstrated during your presentation, then many of the items in Figure 3.15 become extraneous. This would be so especially if you choose to use a constructivist format for a lesson. If learning was effectively demonstrated, you would get an exemplary rating regardless of pedagogical errors contained in the lesson. Learning is not linear but holistic.

Supervisor's Observation Forms

There are two general types of observation forms—narrative and checklist. Of course, both come with many variations and can include a multitude of criteria. A simple checklist form is seen in Figure 3.16; plan your lesson to meet the specific criteria indicated after each objective. The same is true for the pure narrative form in

Figure 3.16 Checklist Form

Evaluation Form (Checklist/Narrative Report)
Teacher _____
Date/Time _____ Class _____ Lesson Type _____
Lesson Title _____

Personal Qualities   Comments
  1. Appearance and bearing _____
  2. Voice _____
  3. Speech _____
  4. Platform manner _____
  5. Teaching personality _____

Instructional Qualities   Comments
  1. Knowledge of subject _____
  2. Preparation and planning _____
  3. Questioning technique _____
  4. Student participation _____
  5. Selection of materials _____
  6. Lesson introduction _____
  7. Lesson development _____
  8. Lesson summary _____
  9. Management _____
 10. Control and discipline _____
 11. Achievement of objectives _____
Codes: 1 = Unsatisfactory
        2 = Below Average
        3 = Average
        4 = Above Average
        5 = Outstanding
I have read and received a copy of this report for my file.
Teacher's signature _____
Supervisor's signature _____

Figure 3.17(a) Narrative Form

> Teacher Evaluation Form (Narrative Report)
> Teacher _____ Date _____
> Class/Subject _____
> This evaluation should be the outgrowth of a collaborative effort and conference held to determine the effectiveness of the observed lesson. The following areas will be highlighted in the evaluation as *Outstanding*, *Satisfactory*, and *Unsatisfactory*. Evaluations will judge your ability to
> 1. Plan and teach effective lessons appropriate to the needs of children while meeting standards;
> 2. Use multiple interactive teaching strategies and develop a positive class environment;
> 3. Achieve objectives that foster the social, cognitive, and creative growth of children.

Figure 3.17(b) Narrative/Checklist Form

> Evaluation Form (Narrative Report)
> Teacher _____
> Subject _____ Date/Time _____
> Aim _____
>
> **Procedure/Application (Description of Lesson)**
> **Comments:** Include the following areas: (1) Room/Environment, (2) Teaching technique/Strategies, (3) Teacher/Pupil relationship, (4) Objective aids/Materials, (5) Questioning, (6) Class management, (7) Individualization, and (8) Achievement of objectives.
>
> **Post-Observation Conference:**
> The following areas in need of attention were discussed. Also discussed were how this lesson meets the standards and specific school goals and missions.
> I have read and received a copy of this report for my file.
> Teacher's signature _____
> Supervisor's signature _____

Figure 3.17(a). This type of narrative report is much more open-ended and allows you more area for creativity, even though it has limited value for focusing lesson planning. Figure 3.17(b) is a combination narrative and checklist form, which shows what the supervisor is looking for, as well as how the report will be discussed. In this type of narrative/checklist report, you have clear objectives and a feedback procedure.

Lesson planning is really an art that can be developed by following your supervisor's guidelines, presented either by an observation form or by direct discussion prior to your observation. No matter what method you use, effective lesson planning will come from who you are and your teaching personality.

 **MINI CASE FROM THE FIELD**

The following case from the field envisions a practice common to teachers—the formal lesson observation. Discussed are its benefits and potential drawbacks. Read the case and determine whether Margaret Gomez or Ed Child has truly understood the importance of prior lesson planning. Look at Jane Hemmings's statements and decide if she's on target.

The Formal Lesson Observation

Ed Child couldn't contain his anger as he stormed into the teacher cafeteria. "I don't believe it, I just don't believe it! How could Principal Thompson pick my birthday for a formal lesson observation?" Ed had been angry with the principal ever since his run-in with Mr. Thompson over his lack of written lesson plans. It was bad enough that he had to write lesson plans, now he was going to be observed! His job was on the line. He doubted that the principal liked him.

Margaret Gomez spotted Ed a few minutes later sitting dejectedly in a corner mumbling to himself. She asked him what his problem was. After Ed finished his diatribe on his bad luck, Margaret asked him how he planned to prepare for the observation. Ed replied that he didn't have to prepare, because he always knew what he was doing. Jane Hemmings, who was seated near Ed, chimed in with, "Oh, just like you didn't need to write lesson plans!"

Margaret said, "Let's all put our heads together and figure out what Mr. Thompson will be looking for." Ed thought he just wanted an orderly classroom, saying that a quiet well-behaved class makes for a happy principal. Jane felt he might be right, and added that probably a lot more goes into an observation, however. "Won't he be looking to see how you prepared for the lesson, like in a lesson plan?" Margaret thought he might take a global view and look at class routines and the type of activities that were done during the class. If Ed's lesson contained a good motivation with some provocative pivotal questions, he would be off to a good start. Jane noted that when she was observed the principal was concerned with the tempo of the lesson. He had told her that most new teachers move too rapidly through a lesson and do not provide enough waiting time for student responses. Margaret said that she believed the principal was concerned about a warm caring environment that fostered democratic planning.

"I think you both have your heads in the clouds," said Ed. "He will only be interested in seeing if I achieve my lesson performance objectives. To put it simply, he will want to see if the kids are learning. You know, I don't think this is going to be tough at all. I always ask my students what they learned at the conclusion of a lesson. Kids will always tell you the truth.

Jane suggested Ed might do some reflective teaching to prepare for his observation. "Why don't you come to my class this afternoon and teach a mini-lesson that Margaret and I can observe and critique? We can all reflect and decide how it could be made better."

"What makes you think that any lesson I teach won't be great?" said Ed.

"Boy, has your attitude changed," said Margaret. "I think you owe us a word of thanks!"

1. List the points made by Margaret, Ed, and Jane.
2. Compare and contrast the suggestions made with regard to relative importance for effective lesson planning.
3. How did Ed demonstrate that he was on the right track?
4. Was he too cocky? Why?
5. If you were Ed, would you follow the plan laid out by your colleagues, or would you use a different approach? Justify your answer.

Chapter Summary

The chapter's title, "Planning to Learn," promised that the chapter would show the importance of writing lesson plans. It emphasizes the practical necessity to create plans that facilitate student learning as an integral part of the teaching process. It discusses planning in relation to curriculum and teacher decision-making models. The use of a mnemonic, AMCASH, is described as an effortless way to understand the basic parts and sequence of a developmental lesson. Constructivist planning is contrasted with various other approaches to lesson design, and three traditional approaches to lesson planning are compared and discussed. The chapter aims to answer three basic questions:

1. Why should I plan lessons?
2. How can direct and indirect lesson planning be used effectively?
3. Why must an effective teacher have command of the curriculum?

Sample lesson plan formats are provided in order to model and assist in the planning process. The chapter stresses the importance of variety and being eclectic, and it offers a reflective teaching exercise to explain an alternative way to prepare plan presentations. The chapter concludes by elaborating on the role of the supervisor in teacher planning.

Cases from the Field

CASE ONE

Celina, a fourth-grade student teacher, wanted to teach a unit on the legislative process. Political science was her favorite subject and she felt she was quite able to teach an effective lesson. Mrs. Kerr, Celina's sponsor teacher, was pleased with Celina's request since it showed Celina's initiative and confidence. Celina told Mrs. Kerr that the unit would take five thirty-minute periods, with a sixth period to be devoted to a unit test. Mrs. Kerr said she would stay out of the room during the entire unit, since it might upset Celina if she were present.

1. Should Celina be left alone with a class for a whole unit at this stage of her career? Explain.
2. How would you describe Mrs. Kerr's reasoning for not staying in the room while Celina was teaching?
3. Can you see any advantage to leaving Celina alone with the class?
4. Can you describe any possible legal issue in this action?
5. What advice would her university supervisor give her?

CASE TWO

Student teacher Andrea seemed born to teach. The children in her eighth-grade language arts class seemed to have really grown fond of her. That was before she was instructed to teach full-period lessons by her cooperating teacher. The problem was planning. Andrea was planning more than what was necessary for a forty-minute lesson, because she was afraid she would run out of material before the lesson was over. Consequently, she always planned to teach more than was reasonable, and this led her to rush through materials by using a lecture format. It also caused students to be overwhelmed by Andrea's lessons.

1. What should Andrea's sponsor teacher have done to assist Andrea in dealing with this problem?
2. Can a lecture format be effectively utilized with eighth-grade students?
3. What type of activities could have been useful for Andrea in her planning?
4. How could this problem be solved and be turned into a benefit for both teacher and student?
5. What advice should Andrea's university supervisor give her?

CASE THREE

José was enjoying his student teaching assignment at Martin High School. His sponsor teacher had shown a great deal of confidence in José by allowing him to teach full time for three of the five classes he had been assigned to teach. But because of his enthusiasm for teaching social studies, José was constantly dismissing students late from the class.

1. What advice should José's sponsor teacher give José?
2. Should José ask for help from his university supervisor?
3. How can José learn to pace his lessons so that they do not run over?
4. Is there any way the students in the class can help José end the class on time?
5. What might the principal of the school say to José?

CASE FOUR

Ileana was very proud of her lesson plans. She had been taught well in her methods course before beginning her student teaching assignment. She was disturbed, however, when she attempted to show her sponsor teacher her plans. Mr. Kravitz said he did not have the time or the desire to review Ileana's plans every time she taught. You learn to teach by trial and error, he told Ileana. You have to learn for yourself what a good plan is, and what a bad plan is. Smiling, he said the children would let her know right away.

1. What should Ileana tell her university supervisor?
2. How do you think her university supervisor will react?
3. Is there any justification for Mr. Kravitz's position that you learn by trial and error?
4. How do you think the principal of the school would have responded to this situation?
5. What would you suggest Ileana do?

Terms to Remember

Curriculum model
AMCASH
Anticipatory set
Constructivist lesson design
Definitions of topic aims, goals, and objectives
Set induction/motivation
Reflective teaching
Narrative and checklist observation forms
SMART

Discussion Questions

1. Describe how the *Curriculum Model for Classroom Instruction* (Figure 3.1) attempts to demonstrate the process necessary for effective lesson plan development.
2. The *Teacher Decision-Making Model* (Figure 3.2) outlines a process and the skills essential to its implementation. What are the most essential components of this model to consider when planning a lesson? Why?
3. Topic aims, goals, and objectives must always be considered before preparing lessons. Using a specific lesson plan as a reference, describe how to incorporate these into a lesson.
4. Write an example of a performance objective using the SMART model as a guide.
5. Prepare a lesson plan in your area of choice using the AMCASH model as a guide. Explain how each item meets the AMCASH criteria.
6. Prepare an argument in support of or against Sewall's (2000) position that the emphasis on projects and activities has gone overboard to the degree of making a shambles of education.
7. Compare and contrast the Nine Elements of Lesson Design (see Figure 3.7) with the Seven-Step Model for Learning (Figure 3.8).
8. In your view, which of the various models presented in this chapter satisfies the criteria for effective planning? Why?

9. Construct a lesson with a variety of instructional activities. Be sure to mention the attention-getting devices related to our senses.

10. Evaluate the relative strengths and weaknesses of reflective teaching.

Field Experience Activities

1. Prepare a lesson to last for fifteen minutes using the AMCASH model as your guide. The lesson is to be presented in class as a reflective teaching exercise. Each member of the class is to evaluate your lesson based on the following criteria:
   a. Was the *aim* of the lesson clearly stated or elicited? Did it focus students on what they would be doing during the lesson?
   b. How did the *motivation* prepare or encourage student response? Was the motivation used appropriate for this lesson?
   c. Was the *content* contained in the lesson developed in a logical and sequential fashion?
   d. How was feedback given during the *application* portion of the lesson? Did the teacher let students know what needed to be improved, and how to achieve improvement?
   e. How was the lesson *summarized*? Specifically how did the teacher check for comprehension?
   f. Was the *homework* a natural outgrowth of the lesson? Did it summarize the lesson while preparing the student for the next logical lesson?

   (If possible, the lesson should be videotaped and reviewed using the same criteria as a live presentation.)

2. Observe a lesson in your area. Evaluate the lesson using a narrative form found in Figure 3.17(a). Use the fifteen areas covering what a supervisor looks for during a formal observation to assist in preparation of your evaluation.

3. Evaluate the same lesson observed in question two using Figure 3.17(b), the Narrative/Checklist Form, and Figure 3.16, the Checklist Form. Which was the most comprehensive?

CHAPTER 4

Methods for the Mainstream

FOCUS POINTS

1. Effective teachers communicate with their students, producing intended results.

2. Effective teachers adhere to basic principles of classroom management by having positive expectations that are realistic, and by designing lessons and assessments that are accurate.

3. Effective teachers understand various methods and approaches to learning.

CHAPTER OVERVIEW

Teachers must determine the tactics, strategies, and methods that they will use to connect with children. The difference between tactics and strategies is that tactics are short term and are used during classroom episodes, while strategies are long-term plans focused on how to deliver a lesson. The methods are the philosophical base from which your strategies and tactics are born. Teachers must accept that learning has nothing to do with what one covers; it has to do with what a student learns. Learning must be the goal of any instructional approach. Putting this understanding into practice places one on the path to implementing methods for the mainstream. The specific approach may vary but the focus on learning is constant in every case.

The various approaches and methods discussed in this chapter should provide a basic arsenal of effective methods and approaches that can be used to advance student learning.

The methods and approaches offered provide choices for teachers to facilitate learning. Methods may differ as to specific instructional strategies, but all depend on teacher input for student success. Learning does not occur in a vacuum; it develops over time within a caring, nurturing ecology, through positive classroom interaction between teacher and learner. Of course, learning can also be passive, but students today seem to prefer interactive involvement. For the most part, they have rejected traditional passivity, opting for interactive communication with peers and teachers as the favored approach to learning.

METHODS FOR LEARNING

Discovery Learning

With discovery learning, knowledge is acquired when students develop, discover, and organize subject matter themselves, rather than having it presented by the teacher. Discovery learning is an active form of learning in which experiences combine to develop new behaviors related to thinking and knowing that allow the learner to discover knowledge. Discovery learning activities cover a wide range of actions, from physical to mental and emotional, engaging students in a whole spectrum of discovery. Discovery can be modulated with regard to the amount of guidance provided by the teacher. The ideal discovery experience or pure discovery occurs without external guidance when the learner forms questions and searches for answers (Driscoll, 2000).

Jerome S. Bruner (1915–), one of the best-known and influential psychologists of the twentieth century, has been a key figure in the cognitive revolution. He developed a theory of instruction that addresses and structures four major aspects of learning:

1. Predisposition toward learning.
2. The ways in which a body of knowledge can be structured so that it can be most readily grasped by the learner.
3. The most effective sequences in which to present material.
4. The nature and pacing of rewards and punishments.
(Bruner, 1966)

Good learning theory allows one to structure knowledge simply and generates proposals, which enable us to understand and manipulate information. The knowledge that results is obtained through one's own intellect. In this process, learning is guided through directed classroom activities that require students to manipulate, investigate, and explore materials. This procedure helps learners discover important principles or relationships (Schunk, 2000).

The discovery approach to learning is based on the premise that to learn is to acquire, manipulate, and evaluate knowledge. Learning begins with problem solving, which in turn leads to the development of necessary skills. The teacher or student poses a question, which is then used as a catalyst to discovery, becoming the motivation for acquiring the necessary skills to solve the problem. Learning is conceived of as an active process that is student centered. Learners are expected to select and transform information, construct hypotheses, and make decisions. This contrasts with many traditional methods that stress memorization (Bruner, 1973).

Any subject can be taught effectively to any child if we understand her stage of development. When we understand the nature and the structure of the academic discipline being taught, our students can learn practically anything. A central conviction to this concept is that intellectual activity anywhere is the same, whether at the frontier of knowledge or in a third-grade classroom (Bruner, 1983). Children should be made to understand the role of structure in learning. They should not simply be focused on mastery of facts and techniques. Once one learns how to focus, later learning becomes easier.

Learning can take place without a teacher present if done in the proper environment and as an independent study. A critical relationship is between how material is presented and how well it is absorbed and applied. Application and use of learning are the keys to learning using this method. Lessons must be organized around a limited set of powerful ideas, called key understandings and principles.

1. We learn by doing.
2. Learning must be authentic.
3. Applications must consist of hands-on activities.

Guided Discovery Learning

In **guided discovery learning** the teacher presents the problem to the learner. Then, through a series of activities, questions, or statements the learner is guided to the answer that is discovered. As for instruction, the instructor should try to encourage students to discover principles by themselves. The instructor and student should engage in an active dialogue (i.e., Socratic learning). The task of the instructor is to translate information to be learned into a format appropriate to the learner's current state of understanding. Curriculum should be organized in a spiral manner so that students continually build on what they have already learned. The **spiral curriculum** revisits the same topics repeatedly, often at different grade levels or stages of development depending on the interest and background of the learner (Le Francois, 2000). The process was conceived of as an ongoing procedure for learning, with curriculum not as a straight line but as a spiral to be continually repeated.

Guided discovery is a process that allows students to practice structuring hypotheses and the solutions while developing problem-solving skills. This hands-on discovery learning approach fits Bruner's description of the *act of learning* as a three-step process (Bruner, 1990).

1. The process of *acquiring* new knowledge
2. The process of *manipulating* knowledge to make it fit new tasks or situations
3. The process of *evaluating* the acquisition and manipulation of knowledge

Benefits of Guided Discovery

1. *Learn how to learn.* Students learn how to problem solve and develop an understanding of their own learning process.
2. *Learning becomes an intrinsic motivation.* The process of learning becomes rewarding and is internalized when the learner comes to his own solutions.
3. *Learning how to problem solve by trial and error aids the learner's memory.* Discovered solutions are better understood than those that are teacher dictated.
4. *Learn through hands-on activities.* Guided discovery engages the student in learning how to develop a problem in such a manner that it can be solved.

Both guided discovery learning and discovery learning allow students "to interact with their environment by exploring and manipulating objects, wrestling with questions and controversies, or performing experiments" (Ormrod, 1995, p. 442). Students are more likely to remember concepts they discover on their own. Both guided and discovery learning are effective when students have prerequisite knowledge and undergo some structured experiences (Roblyer, Edwards, and Havriluk, 1997, p. 68).

Mastery Learning

To understand mastery learning one must be able to justify the statement, "The more time on task a student spends, the more he will comprehend." This method is based on the idea that learning depends largely on the amount of time one spends attempting to understand. The method maintains that all students in a classroom regardless of ability can master a subject when given sufficient time. If you feel this is true, then mastery learning will appeal to you. The method is a systematic way of learning and teaching. The objective of this strategy is to master at least 85 percent of any topic being taught. All coursework is organized into one- or two-week units,

PRACTICE EXERCISE 4.1

Guided Discovery versus Discovery Learning

The purpose of this exercise is to identify and reflect on the similarities and differences between guided discovery and discovery learning. Read the following scenarios and briefly explain which method or methods are reflected.

1. After reading a story, the teacher asks students to write their own ending.
2. The teacher lists potential topics on the chalkboard and asks the class to select one as a unit theme.
3. A student asks the teacher if her answer is correct.
4. Students want to debate the validity of the school's new dress code.
5. Students prepare science projects based on the school district's guidelines.

and comprehension is assessed by testing and retesting materials not mastered. This approach to learning begins with assessing student prior knowledge, followed by teacher-led instruction, which is evaluated by non-graded tests. The process affords the teacher an opportunity to correct errors and guide students to mastery.

There are specific steps a teacher should take before beginning to implement the mastery learning process as an approach to learning. Students should be given a thorough orientation regarding the process. A letter should be sent to parents explaining the program and allaying any fears. The objectives of the curriculum should be discussed with both students and parents, as well as the specific unit being taught. Students should understand that the objective is mastery and not to find fault. This can be demonstrated by explaining the idea of testing until mastery is obtained. Figure 4.1 illustrates the steps to be taken when using the mastery learning method.

Bloom's Taxonomy of Educational Objectives

The taxonomy is appropriate for classifying behaviors in areas that are called domains. These domains are related to a set of beliefs or assumptions about how students learn and behave. They can also be thought of as categories, a classification or hierarchy of learning behaviors. This taxonomy can be seen as the goals of learning in which the learner is expected to acquire new skills, knowledge, and/or attitudes. There are three domains, each having specific goals and objectives. We can explore the nature of these three different domains by ranking and classifying them. Each domain has many

Figure 4.1 Bloom's Mastery Learning Process

- All coursework is organized into one- or two-week units.
- Each student's unit work is first assessed by a diagnostic test and then a retest to correct any errors related to nonmastery of the unit of study.

Basic Components of Mastery Learning

1. Orientation: Goals are clearly stated so that all are aware of the expected outcomes and objectives of the curriculum.
2. A letter to parents explaining the program.
3. Pre-assessment of student's prior knowledge is completed before unit is begun.
4. Subject unit taught: primary instruction is teacher directed.
5. The first test, called a formative assessment, is not graded.
6. Corrective process takes place: Additional instruction is provided to clarify any errors.
7. If a student demonstrates mastery on formative assessment test A or B, she/he can move on to new materials.
8. Summative assessment: Final mastery is reached when 85 percent of material is understood.

Source: Bloom (1971)

Figure 4.2 Bloom's Taxonomy

Bloom's system for classifying educational objectives has also become a standard for determining the effectiveness of questions.

1. *Knowledge questions* are based on the recall of facts. They usually begin with the words *who, what, where, when,* or *list, which,* or *relate.* Basic questions might be "Who signed the Declaration of Independence?" or "What is a verb?"
2. *Comprehension questions* ask you to describe, compare, explain, contrast, classify, demonstrate, or explain something, such as, "Describe your feelings related to abortion," or "Compare and explain the process you would follow to start or resolve an argument."
3. *Application questions* ask you to use previously learned information to solve a problem. They ask you to classify, write an example, model, apply, or use in a new situation. An example might be "Develop a model for good classroom behavior based on your experiences."
4. *Analytical questions* are higher-order questions that require students to think critically, identify causes, support, determine evidence, draw conclusions, dissect, discuss, and analyze. A question in this category might be "What evidence supports the conclusion that time on task results in greater learning?"
5. *Synthesis:* Higher-order thinking questions ask students to perform original and creative thinking. These types of questions usually ask you to predict, imagine, improve, change, create, invent, construct, produce, develop, design, or solve a problem. A question in this category might ask you to "Construct a direct instructional lesson to teach concepts regarding Bloom's Taxonomy."
6. *Evaluation questions* require you to judge an idea, argue, decide, assess, give your opinion, solution, criticize, or prove. An example would be "In your own words, evaluate the effectiveness of Bloom's Taxonomy as it relates to good questioning practices."

Source: Bloom (1984)

levels that offer alternatives and strategies for planning lessons (Bloom, 1956). The three types of learning within these three domains are:

1. cognitive: mental skills (*knowledge*)
2. affective: growth in feelings or emotional areas (*attitude*)
3. psychomotor: manual or physical skills (*skills*)

Cognitive Domain The **cognitive domain** involves knowledge and development of intellectual skills; that includes recall or recognition of facts, procedural patterns, and concepts that serve in the development of intellectual abilities and skills. There are six major categories, which are listed in Figure 4.2, starting from the simplest behavior to the most complex. The categories can be thought of as degrees of difficulties. That is, the first one must be mastered before the next one can take place. The focus of the cognitive domain is on what students will accomplish intellectually—the recall of concepts, generalizations, applying information, synthesizing, and judgments. Knowledge acquisition in the cognitive domain is based on a hierarchy of objectives from simplest to most complex thinking. Cognitive objectives have as their purpose the development of academic knowledge to build intellectual abilities and skills. This taxonomy of objectives is made up of six levels beginning with knowledge and ending with the highest-level evaluation.

Affective Domain The **affective domain** involves one's feelings, emotions, interests, attitudes, and values. It is based on the degree to which you have internalized and organized attitudes and values. Krathwohl, Bloom, and Masia (1964) classified the student's affective domain into five levels of affectivity including receiving, responding, valuing, internalization, and characterization.

This domain includes the manner in which we deal with things emotionally, such as feelings, values, appreciation, enthusiasms, motivations, and attitudes. Five major categories are listed from the simplest behavior to the most complex:

1. *Receiving phenomena* occurs with an awareness and willingness to hear and understand. An example might be the teacher who can recall each student's name after hearing it once.
2. *Responding to phenomena* is considered active participation on the part of the student to react to a particular phenomenon. An example might be the student who questions a new concept presented in class.
3. *Valuing* is the worth one gives to an object, phenomenon, or behavior. This can range from a simple to a complex reaction. Valuing is based on individual beliefs that become internalized. One's values are often expressed in one's behavior. An example would be demonstrating strong beliefs about an issue.
4. *Organization* occurs when one organizes and prioritizes values that create one's own value system. This is done by assessing values and resolving any potential conflicts. The emphasis in organization is on comparing, relating, and synthesizing values. An example would be accepting responsibility for one's actions.
5. *Internalizing values* (characterization) is when one has an established value system that is consistent and predictable in determining behavior. An example would be independently selecting the ethical course of action to resolve a problem.

Psychomotor Domain It emphasizes the development of muscular or motor skill development. It includes physical movement, coordination, and use of the motor-skill areas. Development of these skills requires practice. They are measured in terms of speed, precision, distance, procedures, or techniques in execution. The seven major categories list the simplest behavior to the most complex:

1. *Perception* is the ability to use sensory cues to guide motor activity. This ranges from sensory stimulation, through cue selection, to translation. An example might be hitting a baseball or estimating the length of a dress hem.
2. *Set* is readiness to act. It includes mental, physical, and emotional sets. These three sets are dispositions that predetermine a person's response to different situations (sometimes called mind-sets). An example might be following a sequence in a recipe to make bread.
3. *Guided response* is the early stages in learning; it is a complex skill that includes imitation and trial and error. Adequacy of performance is achieved by practicing. An example could be the signals a catcher gives to a baseball pitcher or the drills performed by a ballet dancer.
4. *Mechanism* is the intermediate stage in learning a complex skill. Learned responses have become habitual and the movements can be performed with some confidence and proficiency. An example would be using a computer keyboard or learning to shift a car.
5. *Complex overt response* involves complex movement patterns that require a quick, accurate, and highly coordinated performance. This includes performing without hesitation, as when a weight lifter utters sounds of satisfaction or expletives upon achieving his goal of lifting heavy weight.
6. *Adaptation* skills are well developed and the individual can modify movement patterns to fit special requirements. An example might be driving a cart and avoiding an accident because of the ability to respond effectively to an unexpected occurrence.
7. *Origination* is creating new movement patterns to fit a particular situation or specific problem. Learning outcomes emphasize creativity based on highly developed skills. An example could be developing a new physical fitness program.

Questioning for Learning

There is a definite relationship between thinking and questioning. Dewey said, "Thinking itself is questioning." When thinking about instructional methods and approaches to learning one must consider strategies that promote thinking. The first step in understanding is thinking. To think one must understand questioning, and the process necessary to promote thinking. It can be said that there are four objectives for teaching and they all include thinking.

1. *Teaching for thinking* occurs when one establishes a safe environment for thinking by modeling risk-taking and acceptance behaviors. This climate can be developed by designing a room that invites interaction and openness. It can arise by a teacher's use of verbal and nonverbal messages that communicate that the teacher is also a learner and listener.
2. *Teaching of thinking* occurs when teachers teach directly and define terms and post aims and objectives while varying instructional presentation.

3. *Teaching with thinking* occurs when students are allowed to process information and interact with material in experimental activities. To accomplish this a teacher has to structure groups flexibly and invite involvement.
4. *Teaching about thinking*, or metacognitive processing, occurs when we get children to think about their thinking. This is accomplished by having students view learning as a process and having students track their own patterns of thinking (Andrade, 1999).

The ancient Greeks believed that to question well was to teach well. Socrates, the chief proponent of this belief, asked, "Why do we ask questions?" He answered his own question by saying we teach to excite interest, arouse attention, and correlate with other knowledge. We must also question if we wish to extend our knowledge and discover new facts. Questions further aid us to organize and fix our knowledge by forcing us to review what we know. Good questioning is really a search for meaning, which is not a search for an abstract body of knowledge. It is a distinctly personal search. The search for meaning is, of course, an ancient search. What we usually learn centers on objective facts rather than personal meanings. Some teachers tell us to look inward for meaning. The crucial test in the search for meaning in education is the "personal implication" of what we learn and teach. We cannot assume that a body of information is in itself meaningful. Much of what we teach is in itself meaningless because we assume that knowledge has value apart from its meaning for the one who acquires it (Jersild, 1955).

Bloom's Taxonomy, when related to questioning, also suggests ways of sequencing questions both inductively and deductively. This is important because when you design a lesson you must decide on the approach you are going to use. Are you going to be Sherlock Holmes and find one solution from many clues, or find many solutions, all stemming from one starting place?

1. **Inductive Reasoning:** specific_____ to _____ general (Specific clues lead to generalization knowledge to evaluation)
2. **Deductive Reasoning:** general_____ to _____ specific (Rule stated; does it fit the rule, evaluation to knowledge)

The lessons you design will fall into one of these two categories.

1. *Inductive lesson design* is based on the concept of inquiry. Specific bits of information are assembled until generalization results. It is like a detective accumulating clues.
2. *Deductive lesson design* is based on a general statement that is outlined and demonstrated. Information is then processed to see if it fits a rule. Doctors use this technique to match symptoms to a specific disease.

The number of questions you ask depends on your purpose. If you are testing for knowledge or attempting to help solve a problem you should ask as many as needed. Questions are essentially classified into two categories: drill and thought. *Drill* (fact) questions can be compared to lower-level questions that ask for knowledge, comprehension, and application. They begin with words such as, *where, when, who, what,* and *which. Thought* questions are considered higher-level questions related to analysis, synthesis, and evaluation. They begin with *why, if, suppose, compare, how, compose, can you contrast,* or *would you.*

Question Design Various factors should be considered when evaluating a question. A good question is direct, concise, simple, clear, and to the point. It is logical and stated in language that all can understand while still being sufficiently difficult to promote critical thinking. The question should also appeal to a majority of the class's interests. The best questions are usually directed toward solving a problem. They consist of pivotal questions that focus students and encourage interactive discussion among students and teacher. In many cases questions are directed to the teacher, while the rest of the class acts as passive listeners. To develop positive social interaction, which is necessary in a democracy, have students direct their responses to their classmates.

There are some specific steps one should take while questioning students. These steps are similar to a lawyer's never asking questions that elicit unwanted responses. You should always know what response you should get. If your question fails to get the desired response, rephrase it until it does. Figure 4.3 provides general steps that will make questioning more effective.

MINI CASE FROM THE FIELD

The following case from the field discusses the importance of understanding specific approaches to learning. Compare and analyze the arguments of Margaret and Ed with those of Principal Thompson. Decide if a teacher should be held responsible for student learning, as well as being judged by student success.

Methodology Counts

Ed Child was really out of sorts after his post-observation interview with Mr. Thompson. Even though Ed was not what anyone would have called an easy person, he could be reasoned with. Ed would have been the first to admit that he was strong-willed, opinionated, extremely self-confident, and very set in his ways. One thing he was not

Figure 4.3 Steps to Effective Questions

> When asking questions, follow these steps:
> 1. Prepare questions before asking.
> 2. Ask your question first, then call on student.
> 3. Give children time to think before they answer.
> 4. Gather questions and move to next item.
>
> The following poor questioning techniques should be avoided:
>
> - Yes or no questions. (Was it good?)
> - Echo questions. (New York is noted for diversity. What is noted for diversity?)
> - Double questions. (Where did Columbus go and why did he go?)
> - Cute guessing questions. (Is the prize behind the door big or small?)
> - Leading questions that give the answer and insult the recipient's intelligence. (Four is the sum of 2 plus 2, right?)
> - Tugging questions, boring for both you and the student. (Four is one-fourth of sixteen, isn't it?)
> - Repeat questions or answers. If necessary, have a student repeat.
> - Inaudible questions. You can't get an answer to a question that is not heard.
> - Vague or poorly phrased questions. These do not deserve an answer. (What about the products of Japan?)
> - Calling on a pupil before you ask the question. First, ask the question, then call on the student by name. This allows time for a thoughtful response.

was clairvoyant. Principal Thompson was just impossible for Ed to understand. Thompson seemed to like his lesson, going by the smile on his face, but the questions he asked just didn't make sense to Ed. Mr. Thompson had asked if Ed was satisfied with the lesson he had just taught. Ed responded positively, yes, he was. Then Mr. Thompson asked why he was satisfied. Ed said the class had behaved and didn't ask foolish questions. "So you judge your effectiveness on student behavior," said Mr. Thompson. "Well I guess so," said Ed.

"Wouldn't it be better to judge your lesson on how much the students had learned?"

"You know Mr. Thompson, there wasn't enough time for a test, even a short quiz."

"Couldn't you have simply asked the students what they had learned or just asked them to turn and tell their neighbor what the lesson was about while you moved about the room?"

Ed flinched at the recollection of that question. He should have responded that he always had students sum up the lesson at its conclusion, rather than look so confused.

Mr. Thompson had asked Ed what qualities he thought were common among effective teachers. Ed had said that good classroom management skills were at the top of his list for effectiveness. "Is that the only quality for effectiveness, Ed?"

"Of course not, Mr. Thompson, you also have to know what you are teaching and how to teach it."

"Really, what would you call knowing how to teach it?"

"I guess it could be called a strategy or an approach."

"What is your approach to learning?"

Ed recalled his answer and laughed. "Mr. Thompson, I don't understand—is this a post-observation conference we are having, or an inquisition? My approach is to talk and use chalk. It is the student's responsibility to do the learning."

When Margaret saw Ed later that day and asked how his observation had gone, he said he didn't know.

"What don't you know?"

"Well, we ended with Mr. Thompson asking me to schedule another meeting when I was able to describe my approach to learning."

"Ed, you mean you don't have an approach to learning? Why didn't you tell Mr. Thompson your beliefs with regard to 'guided discovery' or Bruner's concept of a 'spiral curriculum'?"

"I guess I just froze and couldn't think."

"Come on, Ed, you're a good teacher who is always talking about student mastery. You could have brought up Bloom's 'mastery learning' as an approach to learning. You know what I think? Mr. Thompson was right to put you on the spot."

Ed looked at Margaret and said, "I don't really know what to do, laugh or cry."

"Oh stop it, Ed. All he wanted was for you to acknowledge that methodology counts."

1. List the questions asked by Mr. Thompson and the responses given by Ed. How would you have responded to Mr. Thompson's questions?
2. What was Principal Thompson attempting to achieve by his line of questioning? Was he successful?
3. How could you justify Ed's retorts to Mr. Thompson's questions?
4. Contrast and compare Margaret's answers with those Ed gave. Who had a stronger approach?
5. If you were Ed, what would you do next? Why does methodology count?

Grouping for Instruction

The way you group students for instruction should support your approach to learning. Grouping is fraught with ambiguity. Despite the uncertainty it causes in organizing for instruction, it is essential to any effective educational method. The uncertainty is caused by the confusing variety of terms used in most discussions of theoretical and practical issues surrounding age-grouping practices. The terms ungraded, nongraded, continuous progress, mixed or multiage grouping are usually used interchangeably, causing confusion among many. Figure 4.4 contains a list of definitions that help to clarify the issue of grouping by age.

Grouping by Ability *Student grouping* is a phrase that encompasses several different strategies. The most common of these requires no explanation; it's banding students of similar ages together in the same grade heterogeneously. The second type of grouping is by ability, with its many nuances such as grouping by reading and mathematics scores. Students are assigned to separate classes based on some measure of achievement or ability. This homogeneous grouping is the most common form of tracking, and according to Slavin (1995) the least effective. An alternative is to have students regrouped according to math or reading ability while being kept in heterogeneous classes for other subjects. Slavin favors this approach, as did Albert Shanker, because it reduces the risk of student labeling and recognizes that some students may be weak in reading and strong in math or vice versa. This strategy can be effective if two conditions are met: (1) instructional level and pace are adapted to student performance level, and (2) students are regrouped for only one or two subjects.

Ability grouping is usually defined as the placement of students in classes according to academic ability, which has been demonstrated by achievement on standardized tests with teacher, parent, and counselor recommendations. Another possibility to consider when thinking of ability grouping is *within-class* **ability grouping**. This involves assigning students within a class to homogeneous subgroups that change according to subject. This approach groups students according to specific skills rather than general skills and allows them to remain in a fairly homogeneous setting for most of the day. The management problems that exist with this strategy are easily handled.

In general, research findings on ability grouping have shown that

1. Teachers prefer to teach average- to high-ability groups, with only 3 percent preferring low-ability groups.
2. Socioeconomic and social class differences are increased by grouping and reduced by not grouping.
3. Ability grouping produces conflicting evidence of promoting achievement in superior groups while producing uniformly unfavorable achievement in average and low functioning groups.
4. Self-esteem rises in high achieving groups and is lowered in low achieving groups.
5. Low achievers include many disruptive children who have failed to acquire constructive school attitudes.
6. Ability grouping or achievement grouping in specific academic subjects has proven successful.
7. Ability grouping in all school activities has demonstrated that it stigmatizes lower achievers and reduces achievement for average achievers (Slavin, 1986, 1990b; Kulik, 1997).

A general reading of the literature shows that ability grouping has varying impacts on identifiably different categories of children, rather than a uniform or random

Figure 4.4 *Grouping by Age*

1. *Nongraded or ungraded grouping* refers to placing children of differing ages in classes without grade-level designations. The purpose of this type of grouping is to increase heterogeneity and avoid achievement expectations linked to age. Often, however, children are actually grouped homogeneously based on ability, regardless of age. This results in an increase of homogeneity rather than the heterogeneity intended. The ungraded or nongraded approach acknowledges age as a crude indicator of what children are ready to learn.
2. *Combined grades in bridge classes* include more than one grade level in a classroom. This is usually done for budgetary or programming reasons, such as when classes do not have enough children to make a full register. It normally is not done to facilitate learning or compliment an instructional approach.
3. *Social promotion (continuous progress)* means children remain with their classroom peers in an age-based class regardless of achievement. The term is associated with a strong emphasis on individualizing the curriculum. The goal is to let children progress according to their individual rates of learning and development without being compelled to meet age-related achievement expectations. Social promotion is a developmentally appropriate alternative to a rigid curriculum that denies grade advancement based on test achievement. It also provides a way to sensitize teachers to the variability of child and adolescent development.
4. *Mixed-age or multi-age grouping* refers to grouping children so the age span of the class is greater than one year. The goal is to focus on curriculum practices that maximize the benefits of interaction and cooperation among children of various ages. Mixed-age grouping generates social benefits especially for at-risk children.

impact on all. Thus, the primary concern about ability grouping centers on the idea of its relation to democratic principles. Ability grouping can cause an unequal distribution of students across race and socioeconomic lines that could result in segregation and isolation of minority students. Since grouping is often permanent, children become locked into groups that do not allow for fluidity. This can often cause shame or stigma when a child is associated with the slow or low group. The quality of the curriculum is often unequal between groups, causing further isolation. Most standard groups are based on a narrow view of intelligence that ignores multiple intelligences and talents. This approach is ineffective with the majority of average students (Slavin, 1995).

Grouping Heterogeneously This approach is defined as the placement of students randomly without regard for academic ability or achievement. It is important to remember that homogeneous groups in one area will prove to be heterogeneous in other areas: Children with strengths in language arts may not have strengths in the sciences. Figure 4.5 provides a comparison of ability grouping and heterogeneous grouping.

Cooperative Learning

Other approaches to learning center around **cooperative learning** strategies such as peer tutoring, team teaching, individually programmed instruction, multiple intelligences teaching, and constructivist teaching strategies. These strategies offer alternatives to the traditional ability grouping approach. The cooperative

PRACTICE EXERCISE 4.2

Grouping for Instruction

The way in which you organize and group students in your classes will play a significant role in your effectiveness as a teacher. Identify the grade and subject you (intend to) teach, then react to the following statements and questions. Share responses in class discussion.

- If you were given the authority to group classes, which pattern would you recommend—nongraded, combined grades, social promotion, mixed age, or grouped by age? Support your position and describe how you arrived at your conclusions.
- Forming classes made up of students of similar ages is the traditional way of organizing classes. Describe and compare this traditional organization with any of the proposed alternatives.
- There are various approaches to ability grouping. Select the strategy you favor, and explain why.
- Explain which type of class you would prefer to teach: one grouped by similar ability (homogeneous), or one grouped with children of differing levels of ability (heterogeneous).

learning approach assigns students by ability into heterogeneous, rather than homogeneous, subgroups within a class, usually to perform a specific project or assignment. Effective cooperative learning strategies provide group rewards based on the individual learning of all group members. Cooperative learning is a strategy that is most helpful in many classroom situations.

Slavin (1995) has pointed out that cooperation, not conflict, has been the most valuable form of behavior for humans taken at any stage of their evolutionary history. Like curriculum-based values education, cooperative learning teaches values and academics in a single stroke. Whereas curriculum-based values education does that through the subject matter content, cooperative learning does it through the instructional process. The approach utilizes an interactive method of teaching in which two or more students work together assisted by the teacher. It is a method that requires students to discover information on their own working in groups. Students are set up into teams. Team members are responsible for each other and their own learning. It differs from peer tutoring in that groups are heterogeneous and the teacher offers explanations and teaching. Figure 4.6 outlines the many benefits associated with cooperative learning, including better self-esteem and higher achievement.

Figure 4.5 Ability Grouping versus Heterogeneous Grouping

Ability Grouping	Heterogeneous Grouping
Instruction aimed to ability level	Instruction aimed to center of group
Homogeneous groups easier to work with	Mixed groups more difficult to work with
Students are more comfortable and learn better with peers of similar abilities	Children work in a democratic environment with children of differing abilities
Works well for gifted students	Higher-achieving students positively influence lower-achieving students
Works well for children with special needs	Students show more desirable democratic behaviors

Figure 4.6 Benefits of Cooperative Learning

The cooperative learning method
1. Develops social, problem-solving, and interpersonal skills.
2. Maximizes student involvement in learning.
3. Delivers superior results when more minds work on a problem.
4. Teaches the value of cooperation and pro-social behavior.
5. Builds a learning community in the classroom.
6. Promotes critical thinking and the development of problem-solving skills.
7. Improves academic achievement, self-esteem, and attitude toward school.
8. Offers an alternative to tracking, and can temper the negative aspects of competition.

But how do you set up cooperative groups, and how do they differ from simple small groups? Both small and cooperative groups can be set up by following five easy steps.

1. Teacher *sets goals* for group. The purpose is to focus students on the outcome.
2. Teacher *structures task* and introduces the problem to solve.
3. Teacher *models and demonstrates* how to go about solving the problem using collaboration. (Students must be taught collaborations such as how to communicate respectfully and how to negotiate and share with group members.)
4. Teacher *monitors* each group's work, focusing on the groups that are floundering. The purpose is to encourage and promote group success.
5. Teacher *debriefs and summarizes* the way the group functioned, including both positive and negative views. Students should be encouraged to offer their views and decide how their group will function in the future.

The difference between grouping cooperatively and small groups is accountability. With cooperative groups, both team and individual members are monitored and evaluated. Competition with other teams to achieve objectives is fostered. Student achievement occurs in cooperative groups because when two necessary key elements, *group goals* and *individual accountability*, are used together, the effects on achievement are consistently positive. With traditional small groups, there is limited accountability. Participation is often dominated by the overachievers, leaving the less motivated to just follow along.

Cooperative Learning Activities Numerous cooperative learning projects can be used when planning cooperative lessons. Most of the activities can be described as action orientated. They require students to build something or describe and assess it.

- *Project building* requires teams to construct something using the information and content that they are learning. Examples consist of writing a newspaper, TV script, or a commercial or brochure encouraging people to go to the new world in the 1700s.
- A *describing activity* might require students to analyze, compare, and contrast subject materials, as in a unit on deceptive advertising or propaganda. It could also be used to have students describe how to solve a problem related to the material being studied. A "What if" exercise on women's rights or the Civil War would come under this category.
- Cooperative learning *assessment activities* could consist of exercises that call for students to debate points of view, judge the effectiveness of proposed solutions to problems, or rank and rate as with a list of "The Three Best Presidents." Students would be required to research and decide cooperatively. Another activity might be to predict the outcome of a story being read or a current event. Students should be encouraged to share their personal insights and feelings.

To structure cooperative learning activities, you should adhere to some basic rules that should be modeled for students regardless of grade level. A general outline would consist of teaching students *procedures* you wish them to follow, then *naming teams* and establishing the specific *group size*. Next, discuss the *purpose* of the activity, the necessary *materials*, and the *steps* needed to achieve the team's objectives. Then *teach cooperation* by establishing rules for teamwork that hold all accountable. Explain that developing collaboration is an important classroom skill and goal that builds a classroom learning community. Encourage student reflection on the importance of cooperation for group success. Students should also be taught to evaluate how successfully they worked together. A wonderful culmination to any cooperative learning activity is a debriefing session where both positive and negative outcomes are explored. Cooperative learning activities and groups can be organized in various overlapping ways. Group organization can be either heterogeneous or homogeneous, depending on the teacher's discretion with regard to the social goals of a diverse society.

1. Students can be paired with a learning partner so that each can share the workload of the problem-solving activity they are assigned.

2. Students can be seated in organizations described as cluster groups consisting of four to six students. Smaller groups make it difficult to monitor the teams' work.
3. Students can take tests as a team, as individuals, or both. But team competition should be introduced after the cooperative ethic has been established.

Student team learning begins with the teacher assigning students to four-member teams of mixed ability, sex, and ethnic background. (Teams are changed every five to six weeks.) Then the teacher presents a lesson to the whole class, and teams work on activities provided by the teacher. Children can be tested individually, while team scores are computed by adding up the improvement points earned by each team member. The total is then divided by the number of team members who took the quiz. Team awards are given to all teams that reach a certain average improvement score that has been determined by the teacher (Slavin, 1980).

Jigsaw learning is used with narrative material in grades 3 to 12. Home teams usually consist of five or six students. Each lesson is divided into subtopics with individual team members taking responsibility for a specific topic. A home team is formed for each subtopic, made-up of member experts from each of the teams. Students then meet with members of other groups who have expertise in the same area to pool information. Topic experts then return to their own groups to present their findings and teach their own home team what they learned. Each team member is individually tested and quizzed on all topics (Aronson, 1987).

STAD (Student Teams–Achievement Divisions) is used in grades 2 to 12. Students with varying academic abilities are assigned to four or five-member teams in order to study what has been initially taught by the teacher and to help each reach his or her highest level of achievement. Students can use worksheets as well as other materials to help each other master the presented content. Students are then tested individually. Teams earn certificates or other recognition based on the degree to which all team members have progressed over their past records (Slavin, 1995).

Group investigations are structured to emphasize higher-order thinking skills such as analysis and evaluation. Students work to produce a group project, which they may have a hand in selecting. The structure of the team varies from five to six members. Students may be homogeneously grouped. Projects usually require a written report and some form of oral presentation.

Think-pair-share involves a three-step cooperative structure. During the first step, individuals think silently about a question posed by the instructor. Individuals pair up during the second step and exchange thoughts. In the third step, the pairs share their responses with other pairs, other teams, or the entire group. This form

PRACTICE EXERCISE 4.3

Comparing Cooperative to Small-Group Instruction

This exercise requires that you analyze the arguments for both types of grouping. In a brief paragraph, explain which method would be best for student learning. Then select a cooperative learning activity and prepare an outline of a lesson plan using that method. Explain your plan's strengths.

Cooperative Instruction	Small-Group Instruction
• Group accountability	• No accountability; less pressure
• Individual accountability; each gets graded	• Best students help poor students to get high group grade
• Constant monitoring of collaborative work done	• Group monitors itself
• There is competition among other teams to achieve	• Group work encouraged; no competition necessary

of cooperative learning digresses from the belief that all discussions and recitations must be held in whole-group settings (Lyman, 1981).

Multiple Intelligences Approach to Learning

Howard Gardner, who we spoke about in Chapter 2 with regard to his theory of **multiple intelligences**, claims teachers can incorporate the various intelligences into their lesson plans. Further, instructional approaches such as team teaching, project-based instruction, thematic instruction, presentations/performances, and cooperative learning should be used with MI. Lazear (1994) presents a simple matrix (Figure 4.7, Matrix 1) demonstrating how multiple intelligences teaching can be done. Matrix 2 is the result of Lazear's work.

Differentiated Instruction

Differentiated instruction accepts the proposition that no two students are alike. It affords students various choices with regard to searching out information and constructing meaning to ideas and concepts. This approach meets students' needs by using flexible instructional strategies and adjusting the curriculum to be varied and adaptable.

Planning differentiated instruction requires that you understand student needs with regard to readiness, learning interests, and past experiences. By providing leveling experiences and varying instruction practices,

Figure 4.7 Multiple Intelligences Lesson Ideas

Matrix 1

	History	Language Arts	Science	Mathematics
Verbal Linguistic	Debate key controversial historical decisions.	Write a modern-day sequel to a classical piece of literature.	Model experiment and have students do it.	Write story problems in teams for other teams to solve.
Logical Mathematical	Trace patterns in history.	Predict what will happen next in story.	Use scientific method.	Play math Jeopardy.
Visual Spatial	Create history murals.	Illustrate literature.	Create scientific drawings.	Use math manipulatives.
Body Kinesthetic Musical Rhythmic	Role play minute in musical history.	Role play author's life. Illustrate literature with music, sound.	Build model of project. Make a video demo for math.	Use blocks, play number charades. Write problem-solving raps.
Interpersonal	Children teach each other.	Write with a partner.	Team reports.	Partners teach each other.
Intrapersonal	Imagine past conversations.	Write reflections on literature.	Keep science diary.	Write and think.

Matrix 2

	Global Studies	Practical Arts	Fine Arts
Verbal Linguistic	Conduct a nations of the world spelling bee.	Explain how to make something to a colleague.	Write a critical analysis of a work of art, music, or drama.
Logical Mathematical	Analyze a culture's development chronologically.	Follow a cooking recipe.	Use a graphic organizer to analyze a scene/character/play.
Visual Spatial	Study culture through painting and sculpture.	Create posters that show steps for an exercise.	Have imaginary conversations with art works.
Body Kinesthetic	Learn to play games of different cultures.	Invent something new and teach others how to use it.	Create a living painting/sculpture of an idea or feeling.
Musical Rhythmic	Learn about cultures through music, rhythm.	Use music to improve computer keyboard skills.	Learn math concepts embedded in music and dance.
Interpersonal	Interview people from different cultures.	Teach and play a series of noncompetitive games.	Choreograph a dance about human caring.
Intrapersonal	Brainstorm gifts of different cultures for the individual.	Note your moods when working on a computer.	Write a reflection on your personal taste in music, art, dance.

Source: Adapted from Lazear (1991)

you maximize learning. Research confirms what most experienced teachers have always known:

1. No two children are alike.
2. No two children learn in the identical way.
3. An enriched environment for one student may not necessarily be enriched for another.
4. In the classroom, we should teach children to think for themselves.

Despite the fact that the curriculum is the same for every student, the methodologies we use should still be varied. By focusing on meeting specific student needs we differentiate our instruction and encourage student

PRACTICE EXERCISE 4.4

Multiple Intelligences Test

Take the Multiple Intelligences Test and compare your results with your preconceived ideas. Where does your true intelligence lie? This quiz will tell you where you stand and what to do about it. Read each statement. If it expresses some characteristic of yours and sounds true for the most part, jot down a "T." If it doesn't, mark an "F." If the statement is sometimes true, sometimes false, leave it blank.

1. _____ I'd rather draw a map than give someone verbal directions.
2. _____ I can play (or used to play) a musical instrument.
3. _____ I can associate music with my moods.
4. _____ I can add and multiply in my head.
5. _____ I like to work with calculators and computers.
6. _____ I pick up dance steps fast.
7. _____ It's easy for me to say what I think in an argument or debate.
8. _____ I enjoy a good lecture, speech, or sermon.
9. _____ I always know north from south no matter where I am.
10. _____ Life seems empty without music.
11. _____ I always understand the directions that come with new gadgets or applications.
12. _____ I like to work puzzles and play games.
13. _____ Learning to ride a bike (or skates) was easy.
14. _____ I am irritated when I hear an argument or statement that sounds illogical.
15. _____ My sense of balance and coordination is good.
16. _____ I often see patterns and relationships between numbers faster and easier than others do.
17. _____ I enjoy building models (or sculpting).
18. _____ I'm good at finding the fine points of word meanings.
19. _____ I can look at an object one way and see it sideways or backward just as easily.
20. _____ I often connect a piece of music with some event in my life.
21. _____ I like to work with numbers and figures.
22. _____ Just looking at shapes of buildings and structures is pleasurable to me.
23. _____ I like to hum, whistle, and sing in the shower or when I'm alone.
24. _____ I'm good at athletics.
25. _____ I'd like to study the structure and logic of languages.
26. _____ I'm usually aware of the expression on my face.
27. _____ I'm sensitive to the expressions on other people's faces.
28. _____ I stay "in touch" with my moods. I have no trouble identifying them.
29. _____ I am sensitive to the moods of others.
30. _____ I have a good sense of what others think of me.

Scoring Key

Place a check by each item you marked as "true." Add your totals. A total of four in any of the categories A through E indicates strong ability. In categories F and G a score of one or more means you have abilities as well.

A	B	C	D	E	F	G
Linguistic	Logical Mathematical	Musical	Spatial	Body–Kinesthetic	Intrapersonal	Interpersonal
7 ___	4 ___	2 ___	1 ___	6 ___	26 ___	27 ___
8 ___	5 ___	3 ___	9 ___	13 ___	28 ___	29 ___
14 ___	12 ___	10 ___	11 ___	15 ___		30 ___
18 ___	16 ___	20 ___	19 ___	17 ___		
25 ___	21 ___	23 ___	22 ___	24 ___		

_____ Totals

Source: Statewide Parent Advocacy Network (2000)

ownership of knowledge. Differentiating instruction allows students to construct meaning, while addressing individual needs. The best time to differentiate is during an introduction to a new topic that has various appeals to student interest.

Academically weak students should be given learning activities that offer opportunities for overcoming their challenges by guiding them in developing needed skills. They should also be provided with opportunities to display individual strengths. More advanced students should be encouraged to work on tasks that are inherently at a higher level requiring greater complexity.

Planning Steps for Implementing Differentiated Instruction

1. *Primary assessment of student needs.* The first step for the teacher is to determine student readiness, ability, interests, talents, and the amount of prior knowledge each student has.
2. *Curriculum and specific content.* The second step is aligning state and local standards with the specific content one wishes to teach.
3. *Lesson presentation.* The teacher at this stage must determine how the specific instruction is to be presented (direct or indirect instruction, whole class, groups, pairs, or individually).
4. *Results of instruction.* The fourth and final step is for the teacher to assess the extent of student learning and decide on a formative (ongoing) and summative (final) evaluation.

Four Ways to Differentiate Instruction There are four basic ways to differentiate instruction. You can differentiate content, the way instruction is presented, requirements for student end-products, or simply the environment. Differentiating provides opportunities to enhance instructional methods that can be used in conjunction with each other.

Differentiating content means that we alter the knowledge, skills, and attitudes to best aid in the learning process. It requires pretesting to identify student strengths and weaknesses. Students demonstrating understanding should be allowed to do advanced work. They can skip instruction they have already mastered and proceed to higher-order activities such as project-based problem solving. This strategy, called **curriculum compacting**, expedites the learning process. Another way is to allow advanced students to work independently on some other task while students in need receive direct instruction. Align tasks and objectives to learning goals so that all are able to assess content.

Differentiating presentation means planning and presenting different types of lessons that offer students varied ways to explore and master concepts. Provide alternative paths to develop ideas and concepts. Different activities and materials such as graphic organizers, maps, diagrams, or charts can be used. The complexity of materials should be directly related to the various levels of student abilities. All applications should be organized around different instructional delivery strategies.

Differentiating end-products consists of making allowances for complexity of assignments and requirements used to measure student mastery. Students can be allowed to work at different levels, either reduced for below grade level, or advanced for above grade level. Students should be offered choices for end-products based on their ability levels.

Differentiating environments can be accomplished by enhancing classrooms to accommodate various learning preferences. There has been a great deal of work on various strategies over the last two decades. Dunn (2000) focused on manipulating the school environment, Renzulli (1997) recommended varying teaching strategies, and Howard Gardner (1983) identified individual talents or aptitudes in his multiple intelligences theory. Even though these approaches look at learning styles in different ways, they all have merit. An amalgamation or blending of these concepts is probably more effective than any one approach. The Dunn approach would be most effectively applied in a building designed to accommodate environmental changes, while Renzulli's and Gardner's would be best applied to lesson planning. Varying teaching strategies makes sure that students will occasionally learn in a manner compatible with their own learning preference.

Basic Guidelines for Differentiation

- Clarify key concepts and generalizations to ensure that all learn.
- Use assessment as a teaching tool to extend rather than merely measure instruction. Assessment should occur before, during, and after instruction.
- Emphasize critical and creative thinking as a goal in lesson design.
- Provide a balance between teacher-assigned and student-selected tasks.

We learn 10 percent of what we read, 20 percent of what we hear, 30 percent of what we see, 50 percent of what we both see and hear, 70 percent of what is discussed with others, 80 percent of what we experience personally, and 95 percent of what we teach someone else. (Glasser, 1990)

Each class will contain struggling students and others working at advanced levels. Some learn best alone, others need constant discussion. The objective of differ-

Figure 4.8 Learning Cycle and Decision Factors Used in Planning and Implementing Differentiated Instruction

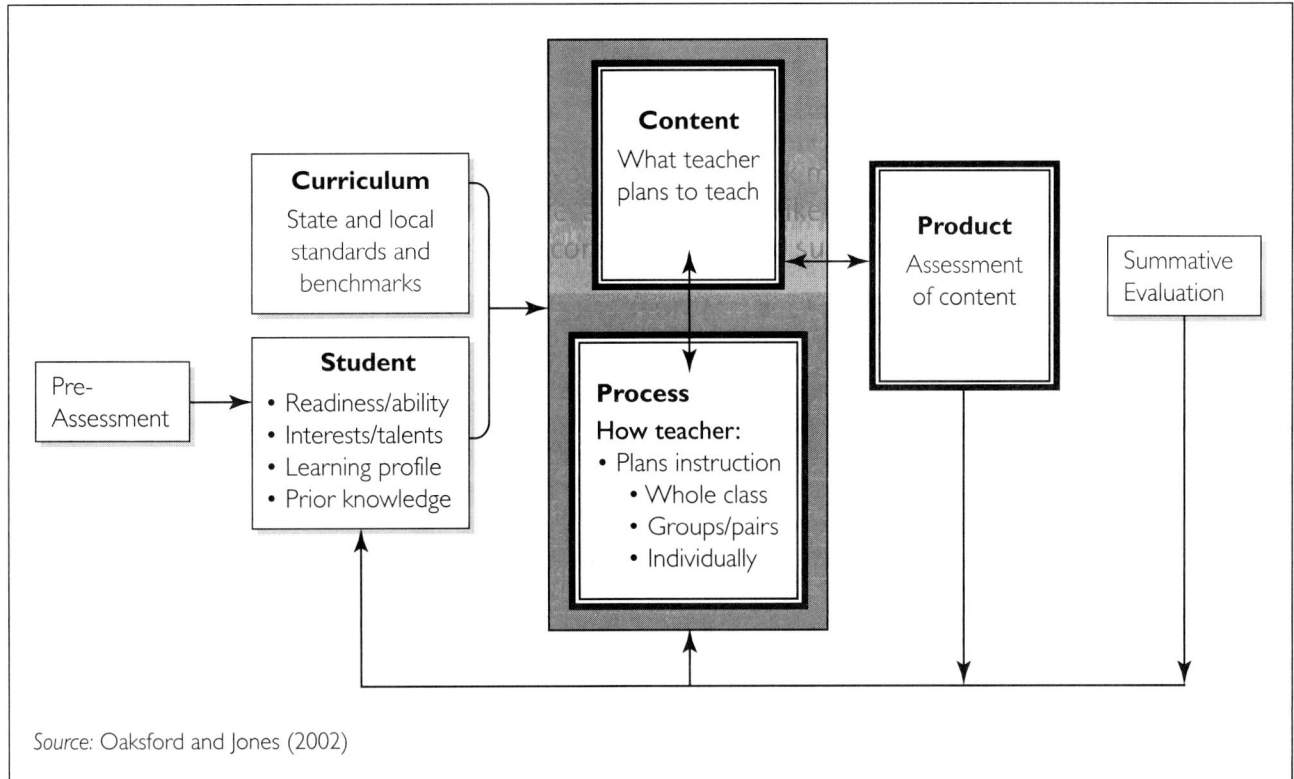

Source: Oaksford and Jones (2002)

entiated instruction is to plan lessons for the entire class while meeting the needs of all. To achieve this:

1. *Know your students.* Have students construct portfolios to record problems and successes. Ask about student preferences regarding best work, and where they have trouble. Ask parents to discuss their child's strengths, weaknesses, and interests.
2. *Center attention on important concepts and skills.* Discover student interests and what is most important for students to learn, and then provide a variety of paths to get there. Always offer students alternatives for demonstrating their mastery.
3. *Develop appropriate classroom environment.* The right environment contains more than flexible seating arrangements, learning centers, and resource areas. Create a classroom culture where all students are respected and supported.
4. *Use flexible grouping.* Group students by needs or interests, and change them often. Group students by ability for one lesson and by interest for another. Vary and mix groups, always allowing students to leave a group they are dissatisfied with.
5. *Remember learning preferences.* Use a variety of instructional strategies, including multiple texts, trade books and supplementary materials, computers, hands-on activities, art, and other creative activities to help each student reach the goal.
6. *Evaluate.* Pretest to find out what students already know and what they need to learn. Assess during the lessons to find out how each student is responding to your strategies. And post-test to see how well your strategies worked.
7. *Ask questions.* Ask higher-level questions for the students who can answer them, and adjust your questions for students with more needs. Also adjust the wait time between the question and calling on a student in order to match that student's speed in processing a response.
8. *Level assignments.* Make sure that assignments are tiered to tasks that are aimed at different ability levels. Each activity should focus on the essential ideas and skills that students need to know. Provide for a level of difference that will keep stronger students engaged while avoiding frustration for weaker students.
9. *Keep a good pace.* Do not differentiate every lesson for every class. Choose different strategies for different classes. Add additional approaches as the opportunities arise. Don't try to achieve all goals in one day. Pace yourself.
10. *Show your personality.* Students are attracted to teaching personalities. They expect teachers to have positive expectations. Challenge and encourage students by expecting them to be the best they can be. Students will rise to the challenge. High expectations,

trust, and honesty are vital if differentiation is going to succeed. Remember that every student is different, and every student learns differently.

School Enrichment Model

The school enrichment model (SEM) focuses on identifying and enriching the talents of all students, not just gifted students. Its goal is to develop the potential found in all students. Its premise is that the factory model of schooling is not appropriate for today's problems. Einstein said, "Problems cannot be solved at the same level of consciousness that created them." One reason for student failure is the top-down pattern of school organization that dominates schools. The model fosters specific classroom strategies that can increase student effort, enjoyment, and performance. The SEM purports to integrate these methods into existing school and classroom structures by using practices found in gifted programs to upgrade performance, and to develop gifted behaviors in all students (Renzulli, 1997).

The SEM model envisions schools and classrooms as places for talent development, where all must play a role in improving society. This vision can become a reality if students are given the necessary opportunities and resources (Renzulli, 1997, 1999). SEM is a systematic approach to authentic learning that identifies individual student ability, interest, and learning style preferences and uses flexible programming and curriculum compacting to modify curriculum and enrich learning. The model advances a common set of goals that advocate flexibility and highlight multiple intelligences to improve student learning.

Enrichment Strategies for All Three essential components must come together if enrichment is to take place.

1. *Learning must be the purpose* for all classroom activity.
2. *Flexible instructional time* must be used as a tool to improve instruction.
3. *Curriculum compacting* is used to provide time for enrichment by modifying the regular curriculum and eliminating repetition. This is accomplished by enlarging flexible grouping and eliminating reteaching. By simply asking students what they have already learned, no time is wasted in reteaching. The process upgrades the level of work while maximizing student capacity.

Quality time is what counts, not increased time on-task. Change should be viewed as an infusion process, not just subject add ons to existing programs. With the SEM approach, instead of looking to remediate, one looks to identify strengths and differentiate instruction based on those strengths. Use flexible grouping and gifted and talented strategies that use innovative methods, such as cooperative learning, peer tutoring, and service learning for all students. The model has children coming together to produce a product or service, working in enrichment clusters of their own choosing. Independent projects and academic competitions are ideal for this type of enhancement. The process functions well across grade levels when students with similar interests are combined. SEM allows youngsters to expand their interests by focusing on application rather than assimilation of knowledge. Authentic learning is achieved because the students' products and services are performed by enjoyable efforts that have been self-selected.

Outcome-Based Education

Outcome-based education (OBE) is a learner-centered method; the principle is that all students can learn. It is designed to produce results that will be retained by students. A results-oriented instructional strategy, OBE clearly identifies what an individual is to learn. Progress is based on demonstrated achievement obtained by accommodating each learner's needs, and allowing time and assistance for all learners to reach their potential through the use of multiple instructional and assessment techniques. OBE highlights setting universal standards, where students are expected to demonstrate both knowledge and application. It differs from traditional methods that focus on what students should be taught (content) and the amount of time necessary for mastery.

PRACTICE EXERCISE 4.5

Enrichment Methods for All

What sets gifted children apart from other students in a classroom? It is primarily the ability to absorb abstract concepts, organize them more effectively, and apply them more appropriately. The SEM model suggests that gifted and talented activities can be used to enrich the classroom environment for all children. Review the list of suggested methods to enrich instruction and write a brief description of how each could be used for the mainstream child.

Independent projects
Academic competition
Peer tutoring
Planning for multiple intelligences
Leveling assignments
Cooperative learning
Bloom's Taxonomy
Service learning
Differentiated instruction

The method proposes four basic elements that can provide for success (Towers, 1996):

1. Clarity of focus, so students know exactly what they are responsible for;
2. Time and resources directed toward the achievement of clearly defined outcomes;
3. All learners must demonstrate achievement by the time they leave school; and
4. High expectations.

Outcome-based education is a philosophy of education that describes what education should achieve and how it should achieve it. OBE allows both students and teachers to become successful learners. With OBE, educators are concerned with what students learn, not when and how they learn it (Spady, 1994). The theory of outcome-based education rests on three assumptions:

1. Every student can be a successful learner.
2. Success, once experienced, leads to more success.
3. School staff must understand they have control over the conditions that make it possible for success to be enjoyed by all students.

These notions were central to the work of Carroll (1963), Bloom (1976), and other writers who helped to develop the concept of mastery learning.

Considering all three assumptions, we see that the OBE model emphasizes achievement, rather than simply measurement. As an instructional method, it prizes individualized mastery learning and promotion based on achievement. It has been claimed that there are similarities between this method and the earlier mastery learning (Glatthorn, 1993; Block and Anderson, 1975).

Figure 4.9 outlines the purposes of OBE and describes the guiding principles to achieve them. The basic premise is that it is not what you learn, but what you do with it that is important in life. The emphasis is on critical-thinking skills, not on content knowledge.

According to W. G. Spady (1994), there are "Five Key Dimensions of Opportunity" and specific practices that enable and determine student advancement.

- *Time.* Considered a flexible resource that is used to meet the needs of teachers and students. The precise timing of activities can be reorganized to allow time to demonstrate mastery.
- *Methods and modalities of instruction.* Methods consist of different learning styles and different teaching modalities that stress multiple intelligences.
- *Operational power principles.* Always be consistent and creative in all classroom operations.
- *Performance standards (indicators).* Use criterion-based standards to demonstrate excellence for all students.

Figure 4.9 The OBE Pyramid

Paradigm:
What students learn is more important than when they learn it.

Purposes:
- Equip all students with knowledge, competencies, and orientations needed for future success.
- Implement programs and conditions that maximize success for all students.

Premises:
- All students can learn and succeed.
- Success breeds success.
- Schools control the conditions of success.

Principles:
- Clarity of focus on culminating outcomes of significance.
- Expanded opportunity and support for learning success.
- High expectations for all to succeed.
- Design down from your ultimate, culminating outcomes.

Practices:
- Define outcomes.
- Design curriculum.
- Deliver instruction.
- Document results.
- Determine advancement.

Source: Spady (1996)

- *Access to essential learning experiences and resources.* Provide students with repeated opportunities for continuous improvement.

Figure 4.10 describes three zones we pass through to achieve success in life. The *traditional zone* is concerned with developing skills in content areas and structured outcomes; most stop at this point. The *transitional zone* is concerned with competency and not specific content, and with application of skills previously taught. The *transformational zone* is concerned with outcomes as demonstrations of higher-order skills that evidence successful project work. This approach fits the standards movement in which states and districts design learning experiences and performances that serve as exit outcomes in preparation for the real world.

Figure 4.10 Spady's Demonstration Mountain

Zones	
Traditional	Structured task performance
	Discrete content skills
Transitional	Complex unstructured task performance
	Higher-order competencies
Transformational	Life role functioning
	Complex role performance

Critics contend OBE does not work, and all that schools need to do is provide students with skills and teach basics. Working in groups is time consuming, and constant retesting, as in mastery learning, provides students with a reason for not studying. Former Secretary of Education William Bennett says its outcomes are nebulous and just social engineering by another name, while another conservative, Chester E. Finn, sees no means for accountability. OBE is not education, they argue, it is a combination of academic control and behavior modification. Social engineering uses behavior modification and values clarification to control the level of knowledge acquired and to change attitudes, behaviors, beliefs, and values (Sykes, 1995). Proponents respond that outcomes are important, not content and performance competencies. They challenge detractors and claim to respond to myths they say surround OBE.

Montessori Method

Maria Montessori (1870–1952) was the first woman to graduate in medicine from the University of Rome. Afterward she worked with mentally retarded children, and then held various university teaching positions. In 1907 she opened the Casa dei Bambini to teach children of normal intelligence with her progressive methods. Most of her remaining years were spent writing, lecturing, and teaching about her methods (Lillard and Jensen, 2003).

The uniqueness of her method was that it assumed children learned by interacting with concrete materials and being respected as individuals. The teacher's role was not to be the fount of all wisdom but a facilitator who organized materials and established a learning environment in the classroom.

The Montessori method is neither direct nor indirect instruction, but is a self-directed instructional approach to learning. Most activities are individual, though the children interact in groups in some activities. Among Montessori's many contributions to education is the idea that children learn through play, which is central in the move toward educational progress (Kramer, 1988). This concept is evident in the wide variety of educational toys available in practically every early childhood program. The idea that children learn through play and that education should begin before kindergarten or first grade put Montessori ahead of her contemporaries. The popularity of preschools and nursery schools for two- and three-year-olds attests to her vision. Montessori's idea that rigidly disciplining young children and restricting activity does more harm than good has become the battle cry of most liberal educators (Lillard, 1996).

Montessori believed that children would use self-discipline when presented with stimulating things to do, and that good instruction leads to good discipline. Age-appropriate learning programs, the concept of reading readiness, and parental involvement all stem from Montessori's early work, as well as her prime goal to develop the whole personality. She developed a rationale that concentrated on the goal rather than the method. The goal of education was defined as the development of a complete human being, oriented to the environment, and adapted to one's time, place, and culture (Lillard, 1996). Figure 4.11 illustrates how, compared to traditional schools, Montessori schools were beacons of enlightenment for the early twentieth century.

Three primary principles are the cornerstone of the Montessori method: (1) observation, (2) individual liberty, and (3) preparation of the environment. Montessori's method adapts education for developmental stages by using materials especially designed for exploration and self-discovery. Children are encouraged to be active rather than passive learners.

Development of personality and social behavior is the most important aspect of the Montessori method. Children develop their personalities through work when given the right materials, a prepared environment, and freedom to explore. The result is that children will exhibit a love for order, concentration, and exactitude. The difference between adult work and children's work is that adults work to change environments, while children use environments to change themselves.

One of the Montessori method's central principles is that human development does not occur in a straight line but in a series of four formative planes divided by age (1 to 6, 6 to 12, 12 to 18, and 18 to 24). Regular schools follow a linear development, which assumes that intelligence increases with age. Another central idea is that complete human development is related to universal actions one commits within one's environment. Humans do not have instincts for survival like animals, but have primary tendencies to obtain basic needs. Their secondary behavioral tendencies—exploration, orientation, order, imagination, manipulation, repetition, precision, control of error leading to perfection, and communication—differentiates humans from other

PRACTICE EXERCISE 4.6

Critics versus Proponents of OBE

Read the following critics' views and proponents' responses. Then write a brief summary of who has the stronger argument based on your own independent research. (Note: Many pro and con arguments can be found on the Internet.)

Critic's View: OBE leads to lower academic achievement because it overemphasizes the teaching of values and attitudes.

Response: OBE raises academic standards for all learners.

Critic's View: OBE is driven by broad, affective learner outcomes that are too vague to be assessed reliably.

Response: OBE establishes reliable assessment of learner outcomes.

Critic's View: OBE replaces academic testing with inaccurate, subjective measurements based on teachers' arbitrary assignment of grades based on subjective criteria.

Response: Educational research contradicts the notion that teachers cannot reliably assess outcome-based performances of students by using scoring scales, surveys, rubrics, and holistic techniques.

Critic's View: OBE is actually a disguised version of "mastery learning" that relies heavily on behaviorist conditioning of learners.

Response: OBE accommodates learner needs through multiple instructional strategies such as cooperative learning, peer coaching, mentoring, small-group instruction and many other student-centered approaches. In addition to traditional paper and pencil tests, OBE's arsenal of assessment techniques includes portfolios, reflective journals, oral interviews, student self-appraisal, and other forms of student-centered activities.

Critic's View: OBE is an attempt by schools to take away parental control over children's education.

Response: OBE is designed to return control of schools to the local community and to the parents. Shared decision making and collaborative planning are cornerstones of outcome-based education. (Baron and Boschee, 1996)

Figure 4.11 Montessori Schools Compared to Traditional Schools

Montessori School	Traditional School
1. Age span (1–6, 6–12, 12–18, 18–24) (Most schools are primary)	1. All ages
2. Children are motivated by need for self-development	2. Motivated by teacher
3. Ungraded	3. Graded
4. Use self-correcting materials	4. Teacher corrects errors
5. Hands-on learning, learn by doing	5. Lecture, discussion, teacher centered
6. Activity cycles are at students' own pace	6. Teacher determines time on task
7. Free movement	7. Teacher determines seating
8. Emphasis on cognitive	8. Emphasis on social development
9. Discipline stems from environment	9. Teacher disciplines
10. Emphasis on teacher as observer	10. Teacher centered
11. Emphasis on concrete, reality, child centered	11. Emphasis on abstract

Source: Lillard (2003)

animals. The final idea is that human's interaction with the environment is most productive when it is self-chosen and founded on one's interest. Montessori teachers don't teach the child in the usual sense; they observe in order to discover needs and interests in order to provide materials or activities to match those developmental needs.

Five major stories and many minor ones introduce children to the universe. The power of imagination is what educates. Stories represent the truths of the universe and appeal to a child's imagination. These stories dramatize known truths. They are broken up into five "great lessons," intended to open doors to general areas of study in which key lessons are taught.

1. The creation of the universe (non-sectarian)—Earth's beginnings
2. Coming of life—Timeline of life
3. Coming of human beings—The coming of life
4. Story of communicating in signs—The history of writing
5. Story of numbers—The history of mathematics (Faust, 2006)

In the Montessori method, education interacts with the environment; this is believed to be the way children learn. The teacher becomes part of the environment and facilitates the instructional process. The final component for children is freedom and acceptance of responsibility. Teachers are expected to record student progress and note completed tasks.

Paideia Program

Mortimer Adler (1982) developed an approach to learning that was essentially a classical method. Its first premise was that "all children can learn." Adler broadened this premise to include the concept of education as a lifelong process where learning is the students' responsibility. The proposal offered a framework for study that consisted of lecture, coaching, and discussion (see Figure 4.11). Adler's Paideia program's clearly stated objective is for learning to make the most of potential. It suggests twelve years of compulsory education with a required curriculum for all, with electives allowed in the upper grades. The program is aimed at providing a liberal arts education for all and excludes vocational training (Adler, 1988). The **Paideia program** is at the opposite end of the spectrum from the Montessori method because its syllabus is focused on a traditional classic education, though it uses progressive methods and concepts. (See Figure 4.12.)

There are four reasons why traditionalists and conservative educators favor the Paideia proposal. (See Figure 4.13.) The first is the basic premise that all children can learn. The second is that it combines the classical rigor of traditional education with progressive teaching and learning practices. Third, it includes effective staff development, which involves the whole community as well as focusing on the teaching and learning relationships of adults and children by instituting, fourth, the Socratic seminar as a learning tool.

Waldorf School Method

Austrian philosopher Rudolf Steiner (1861–1925) started the original **Waldorf School** in 1919. He was concerned with early childhood education and worked with children in preschool, nursery, and kindergarten. His practices were focused on developing methods that allowed children to grow freely within their own world, free from the harmful influences of our age (Seddon, 2005). His approach to learning used the arts as a vehicle for education. His vision of the whole child is rich and full of life, and attentive to the child's healthy growth and development. There are nine skills in his model: (1) planning, (2) instructional objectives, (3) presentational skills, (4) questioning, (5) concept learning, (6) classroom management, (7) interpersonal communication, (8) cooperative learning, and (9) evaluation. Each skill follows in what Steiner considered to a logical order (Prescott, 1999).

PRACTICE EXERCISE 4.7

Design a Montessori Lesson

Select the grade levels and numbers of students to whom you will present a lesson designed in the Montessori method. Be sure to incorporate concepts contained in the OBE pyramid and the primary principles behind the Montessori method. Review the sample lesson outline provided, and then use it as a guide to design your own Montessori lesson in any area of your choosing.

Sample Fifth-Grade Science Lesson Prepared for Twenty-Two Students

My lesson will be about planets found in our universe. I will introduce the topic by explaining that our universe contains planets that move about our sun. Students will formulate research questions of interest regarding planets and universe. I will provide students with reading materials, wooden spheres of various sizes, string, boxes, and pipe cleaners with which they can create dioramas. A class trip to the Planetarium will allow students to observe the planets while encouraging creativity. Completed works will be presented by the class as a demonstration of their understanding. Students will compare and rate projects with standards contained in the state science guide.

Figure 4.12 Framework for Twelve-Year Course of Study in Paideia* Schools

GOALS	Acquisition of Organized Knowledge	Development of Intellectual and Learning Skills	Enlarged Understanding of Ideas and Values
MEANS	Didactic (Lecture)	Coaching	Socratic questioning
	Textbooks	Supervised practice	
AREAS	Language, history	Reading, writing, speaking, listening	Discussion of literature and art
	Literature	Problem solving, estimating, seeing	Involvement in art, music, drama, and visual arts
	Fine arts, math, science, geography		

Source: Adapted from Adler (1984), p. 8

*Paideia from the Greek *pais, paidos,* the upbringing of a child.

Figure 4.13 Basic Paideia Principles

1. All children can learn.
2. All children deserve the same quality of schooling, not just the same quantity.
3. All should be provided the best education.
4. The purpose of schooling is preparation for an educated life.
5. Three goals of schooling are to prepare all students to (a) earn a decent living, (b) be good citizens, and (c) make a good life for oneself.
6. Genuine learning is reflective and aided by teachers.
7. Three kinds of teaching should occur in school: didactic, coaching, and Socratic.
8. The results of these three kinds of teaching should be (a) the acquisition of organized knowledge, (b) the formation of habits of skill in the use of language and mathematics, and (c) the growth of the mind's understanding of basic ideas and issues.
9. Each student's achievement should be evaluated in terms of capacity and not by norm-referenced tests.
10. The principal of a school should never be a mere administrator, but also a teacher who works with faculty in planning and creating a learning community of teachers, students, and parents.

Steiner's approach to the principles for the education of preschool children was opposite from his approach to adults. With adults he presented concepts, aroused interest, and, finally, explained how they should act. With adults he began with concepts and reasons, which he believed a child lacked the experience to understand.

A child, he believed, began by watching an action, then re-enacting the experience, and finally, aiming to understand what has been seen in order to form the concept. For the Waldorf method, the fundamental law of education at this period of childhood is "A child learns through imitation." Steiner described the child as the sense organ wide open to impressions, which pour in for better or for worse (Seddon, 2004).

Within the Waldorf method, activities in nursery school and kindergarten should be arranged to strike a balance between free play and general activities that supplement and stimulate each other. Activities such as painting, working with clay, storytelling, singing, and eurythmy (the art of movement) provide a balance for the children to discover and learn. During free play, toys and equipment become alive in and out of doors. Allow children to freely create and find new applications for what they have learned. Mixed-age groups are better than groups of one age level, especially when the older children learn to assist the younger. Figure 4.14 reflects the diversity of Steiner's views.

The Waldorf method is in every respect an active approach to learning. It strives to become aware of the child's needs and difficulties in order to harmonize them. There are no general rules or procedures. Opportunities that turn up along with ever-changing circumstances of daily life will furnish the material for your work. Every child learns how to paint, sculpt, dance, act, and do "eurythmy" (meditative movements), integrated within the entire program. In effect, children learn through the arts. Textbooks are not used, since children are required to create their own texts based on a systematic prescribed order. An oral tradition of instruction is emphasized based on experiential learning techniques. Steiner used Piaget's developmental theory, breaking it down into three "natural" stages to organize his school.

Figure 4.14 Quotations from Dr. Rudolf Steiner, Founder of the Waldorf Method

1. "We can never repair what we may have neglected to do as educators during the child's first six or seven years."
2. "There are two magic words which indicate how the child enters into relationship with his environment. They are: imitation and example."
3. "The whole life of the child up to his seventh year is a continuous imitation of what takes place in his environment."
4. "It is important to appreciate that you cannot teach a child to be good merely by explanations, but to realize that all you do in his presence is taken directly into his being."
5. "It is immensely important that we do not consciously or unconsciously call upon the child's intellect prematurely, as people are so prone to do."
6. "The child who lives in an atmosphere of love and warmth is living in his right element."
7. "At the age of fourteen or fifteen a child can reason. Before this age we do him harm."
8. "The musical element which lives in the human being from birth onwards and particularly in the child's third and fourth years in the gift of dancing (eurythmy) is essentially an element of the will to learn and express."

Source: Steiner (1996)

The first stage he called the "hands" or the will, the second stage the "heart" or emotional period, and the third stage (high school) he called the "head" or intellect. Steiner also believed in a "spiritual self" or core, which he felt had to be nurtured in each of the three stages, each lasting about seven years. In each stage children were to have the same lead teacher who would act as their mentor (Steiner, 1991).

Opposition to Steiner's Unconventional Views It is easy to see why some of Steiner's views would draw criticism; but remember that each of the approaches discussed in this chapter has critics. Concepts organize one's knowledge structure and keep it from becoming unwieldy. For communication to proceed you need to have mutual concepts and be on the same wavelength. Concepts can be ideas, themes, an all-encompassing statement, or a fundamental element. Steiner's concepts are organized into cognitive structures known as schemata or schemas that should provide the basis for comprehending and learning information.

Steiner's critics attacked his more unorthodox views, in particular his view that matter consists of four elements, earth, air, fire, and water, as well as his mystical language and spiritual ideas. Critics claim Waldorf schools are a missionary arm of a religious sect and that Steiner was a religious dogmatist, whose theories about evolution of human consciousness, a system of belief he called anthroposophy, include belief in reincarnation (Prescott, 1999; Steiner, 1991).

MINI CASE FROM THE FIELD

The following case from the field presents the basic approaches to learning that must be understood if one is to become a successful pedagogue. Read the case and compare Margaret's, Ed's, and Lucille's ideas about what constitutes an effective approach to learning for the mainstream.

Are All Approaches to Learning the Same?

Ed felt his self-esteem could not survive what he was being put through by Mr. Thompson. If Margaret was right, all he wanted was for Ed to clearly explain his approach to learning. Ed recalled him saying something about being able to say in one sentence what you planned to accomplish in a lesson. The problem with most lessons was the lack of clear performance objectives. What did that have to do with a specific approach?

Just then, Lucille Chan entered the teacher's cafeteria carrying some projects her fourth-grade class had prepared for the elementary school science fair. Taking one look at Ed, she said, "I'd better get out of here before you explode." Ed looked at Lucille and said, "What are you talking about?" Lucille told Ed his face was an open book; he was obviously upset about something. Ed told her about the observation conference he

PRACTICE EXERCISE 4.8

The Paideia Program and the Waldorf Method

Compare these two methods with regard to their concepts, principles, and design. Be sure to include both strengths and weaknesses when making your comparison.

had had with Mr. Thompson, and how he was supposed to have another meeting and explain his approach to learning.

Margaret Gomez entered and took her usual seat at the table. Lucille asked her to help Ed out of his dilemma. Margaret couldn't believe that he was still angry over the principal's request. She told him to ask for a postponement to get over his depression. Ed said, "I accept my fate, now come on give me some ideas."

Lucille began by asking Ed to explain how he grouped his high school math classes for instruction. He replied sarcastically that he was lucky to get them all seated. "Oh stop it, Ed, you know what I mean."

"Well, I don't group my classes heterogeneously like you do in the fourth grade. I believe in ability grouping so no student is left behind."

"Have you ever thought about a cooperative learning approach?" Lucille asked.

"In mathematics—you must be kidding. Adolescents need discipline and direction, they don't need to be put in groups where they could fool around."

"But couldn't they be placed in ability groups to cooperatively resolve problems, Ed?"

"I know, Lucille, next you are going to tell me about focusing my lessons on multiple intelligences to motivate my students."

Then Margaret chimed in. Perhaps that wasn't such a bad idea. Variety makes lessons interesting. Ed might even use a combination of approaches based on Renzulli's school enrichment model and Adler's classical Paideia program. Ed could set up cooperative groups based on ability and multiple intelligences preference. His students were old enough to do well with a seminar approach. The question became how to do that and cover the curriculum, Margaret admitted. "That's where Renzulli's idea of curriculum compacting comes in. When it's used properly, time can be created for enhancement."

Then Lucille said, "You know things aren't always black and white the way Margaret is implying, Ed. Your approach to learning should also focus on end results and outcomes. Consider really observing students, as Montessori said, and think about Steiner's affective approach to allow for emotional growth."

"Enough!" Ed cried. "I get it. I am going to be eclectic and use direct instruction based on Bloom [mastery learning] and Adler [Paideia], and indirect instruction by cooperatively grouping my students. Thanks, ladies, I think I have a handle on what my approach to learning is."

1. List the points made by Margaret, Lucille and Ed. Explain where they are similar and where they disagree.
2. What was Lucille attempting to achieve by her line of reasoning? Was she successful in converting Ed? Explain.
3. What was Margaret attempting to achieve by her line of reasoning? Was she successful in converting Ed to her way of thinking? Explain.
4. Contrast and compare Margaret's approach to learning with Lucille's. Who had a stronger approach?
5. Is Ed's approach to learning acceptable? Justify your answer.

Chapter Summary

We have seen in this chapter that there is a wide variety of approaches to learning along with numerous specific methods. Teachers tend to prefer highly structured, goal-directed classrooms with established routines rather than experimental methods. They traditionally use a trial-and-error approach to learning, while emphasizing basic skills and processes through modeling, drill, and practice. Discussed in this chapter were the approaches and methods of Bruner (guided discovery), Bloom (mastery learning), Slavin (cooperative learning), Steiner (Waldorf method), Adler (Paideia program), Spady (outcome-based education), Lazear (seven ways of knowing), the Montessori method, and Renzulli's school enrichment model for learning. Each provides a basis for an individual's approach to instructional practices. In many cases there is a great deal of overlap.

Be aware that one key does not open all doors. No single approach to learning can meet the needs of all. This fact may not seem earth shattering, but it must be understood in order to meet the needs of individual students. In addition, learning styles can also be used to open the doors to learning. Dunn and Griggs (2000) define learning styles as the ways students begin to concentrate, process, internalize, and remember new and difficult information. There are five variables that significantly differentiate the learning styles of individuals and groups—academic achievement level and talent; gender; age; culture; and global or analytic brain processing, all of which have been considered and implied in the various approaches discussed in this chapter.

Stanley Pogrow's (2000) concept, "the cognitive wall," is described as an academic impasse underachieving students may reach. It is a wall that stops progress, which usually occurs after the third grade. This wall limits the benefits gained from high standards and quality instruction. It exists because students have little experience in discussions with adults about ideas. In this chapter we see that wall as justification and rationale for being eclectic in the selection of approaches and instructional methods. Positive interactions between students and teachers produce both ideas about life and academic success. Students need to understand understanding, as we need to understand that a variety of methods and approaches are needed to help students climb over that wall.

Cases from the Field

CASE ONE

Claude had been assigned to a senior high school to student teach. In a meeting with his sponsor teacher, Mrs. Jerome, he was told that he was not meeting the needs of all the students in this tenth-grade, heterogeneously organized, social studies class. Mrs. Jerome said that a direct instructional approach focused on lecture might work for some, but not all, students. She asked Claude to think about cooperative groups for a unit on comparative world governments, and to meet with her at a time convenient for him to discuss his plans for the new unit.

1. Should Claude notify his university supervisor and discuss Mrs. Jerome's request?
2. What do you think will be the university supervisor's response?
3. Is cooperative grouping a viable idea for a tenth-grade social studies class? Why?
4. Does Mrs. Jerome have a right to request instructional approaches that she believes in? Explain.
5. Should students be involved in deciding on how a unit should be taught (a lecture approach or a cooperative approach)?
6. What suggestions for the unit would you make if you were Claude?

CASE TWO

Jack is a student teacher in an elementary school where the focus of the entire school is reading and success on standardized tests. Jack feels that the lack of instruction in the arts is a gross oversight and probably the cause for the school's and his assigned class's poor results. Jack had learned about the Waldorf method approach to learning in one of his methods courses. He felt he should let his sponsor teacher know that he should change the way his class was taught if the children were ever to succeed. Jack's sponsor teacher asks Jack to put his plan for a unit in writing.

1. How do you feel about Jack's approach to improving class achievement?
2. Is the Waldorf approach viable?
3. What steps should Jack have taken before he made his suggestion?
4. How do you think the university supervisor would have reacted to Jack's actions?
5. Prepare a unit outline in any subject area and describe how it relates to the Waldorf method.

CASE THREE

Teresa Blight was upset by her post-observation meeting with her university supervisor, Dr. Jones, and sponsor teacher, Ms. Lippset. Both had told her that her questioning techniques needed a great deal of work and that because of it her lesson was unsatisfactory. She had been told that her questions did not elicit thinking responses from her students. Since most of her questions were focused on the recall of facts they were not thought provoking. Since the class was a regent's honor class this was especially meaningful. Teresa was told that she would be allowed to re-teach her lesson.

1. Was Teresa right to be upset? Explain your position.
2. How could Teresa have taken the criticism and used it in a positive fashion?
3. How could Bloom's taxonomy for questioning have been used to help resolve the problem?
4. What would you have done if you were Teresa?
5. Prepare an outline that describes how Teresa can improve her approach to questions in her next lesson.

CASE FOUR

Mr. Pan was Elsa's third-grade sponsor teacher. He felt that after five weeks it was about time that Elsa taught a full-period lesson. He was tired of seeing all her lessons revolve around a cooperative learning approach in which she taught only for a few moments while the children did all the work. He asked her to use a more traditional approach to learning, in line with Adler's Paideia program.

1. How would you describe Mr. Pan's attitude?
2. Did Mr. Pan have a right to see a different type of lesson? Explain.
3. How could Elsa have explained the potential benefits of cooperative learning?
4. How do you think her university supervisor would have reacted when told of the situation?
5. What would you have done if you were Elsa?

Terms to Remember

Spiral curriculum
Guided discovery learning
Cognitive domain
Psychomotor domain
Ability/Age/Homogeneous grouping
Heterogeneous grouping
Multiple intelligences
Outcome-based education (OBE)
Differentiated instruction
Eurythmy

Mastery learning
Affective domain
Inductive/Deductive reasoning
Cooperative learning
Paideia program
Curriculum compacting
Self-directed instruction
Montessori method
Waldorf school

Discussion Questions

1. How does Jerome Bruner's approach to learning and spiral curriculum differ from the traditional rote memorization model?
2. Explain the statement, *Guided discovery has been considered a hands-on approach that fits into Bruner's description of the Act of Learning.*
3. *Teaching for, of, with, and about thinking can be used as justification for the implementation of a mastery learning program.* Analyze this statement to determine whether it is a valid principle.
4. Use Lazear's "multiple intelligences lesson ideas matrix" to formulate a history or language arts lesson that addresses all seven intelligences.
5. Renzulli's school enrichment model's approach to learning proposes that instead of finding differences and remediating, we should examine abilities and capitalize on student strengths. Predict what would happen if a school adopted this approach.
6. Compare Montessori's methods to traditional school approaches to learning.
7. What solution does Adler's Paideia program's approach to learning offer to those looking to reform education?
8. Why has the uniqueness of the Waldorf approach to learning been attacked by conservatives?

Field Experience Activities

1. Observe three different classes and determine the method being used in each. Identify the method as direct or indirect instruction, guided discovery, lecture, or cooperative learning. If none of these methods is being used, in a brief narrative explain what is happening. Share your observations in class.

For Further Reading

Bloom, B. (1981). *All our children learning.* New York: McGraw-Hill.
Bruner, J. (1996). *The culture of education.* Cambridge, MA: Harvard University Press.
Bruner, J. (1986). *Actual minds, possible worlds.* Cambridge, MA: Harvard University Press.
Bruner, J. (1960). *The process of education.* Cambridge, MA: Harvard University Press.
Dunn, R. (1995). *"Strategies for educating diverse learners."* Fastback 384 (pamphlet) Bloomington, IN: Phi Delta Kappa.
Kramer, R. (1988). *Maria Montessori: A biography.* Radcliffe Biography Series. Chicago: Chicago University Press.

Kramer, R. (1978). *Maria Montessori*. Oxford, U.K.: Blackwell.

Montessori, M. (1912). *The Montessori method*. A. E. George, transl. New York: Frederick A. Stokes Co. (Available at www.infed.org/archives/e-texts/montessori_method_III.htm.)

Oaksford, L., and Jones L. (2002). *Differentiated instruction: Effective classroom practices report*. National Center on Accessing the General Curriculum, U.S. Department of Education, p. 2.

Ornstein, A. C. (1987, May). Questioning the essence of good teaching. *NASSP Bulletin*, 73–74.

Pogrow, S. (1996, June). Reforming the wannabe reformers. *Phi Delta Kappan*, 656–663.

Renzulli, J. S. (1994). *Schools for talent development: A practical plan for total school improvement*. Mansfield Center, CT: Creative Learning Press.

Renzulli, J. S., and Reis, S. M. (1991). The school-wide enrichment model: A comprehensive plan for the development of creative productivity. In N. Colangelo and G. Davis (Eds.), *Handbook of gifted education* (111–141). Boston: Allyn & Bacon.

Renzulli, J. S., and Reis, S. M. (1985). *The school-wide enrichment model: A comprehensive plan for educational excellence*. Mansfield Center, CT: Creative Learning Press.

Renzulli, J. S. (1978). What makes giftedness? Reexamining a definition. *Phi Delta Kappan* 60(3): 180–184, 261.

Slavin, R. E. (1991). Synthesis of research on cooperative learning. *Educational Leadership* 48(5): 71–77.

Slavin, R. E. (1983). *Cooperative learning*. New York: Longman.

Spady, W. G. (2001). *Beyond counterfeit reform*. Lanham, MD: Scarecrow Education.

Spady, W. G. (1998). *Paradigm lost: Reclaiming America's educational future*. Arlington, VA: American Association of School Administrators.

Spady, W. G., and Schwahn, C. (1998). *Total leaders: Applying the best future-focused change strategies to education*. Arlington, VA: American Association of School Administrators.

CHAPTER 5

Methods for the Special Learner

FOCUS POINTS

1. What's special about special education?
2. How does a mainstream teacher prepare for the special learner in her class?
3. Good instructional practices make for effective teaching for all children.
4. All children can learn to the best of their capabilities.

CHAPTER OVERVIEW

THIS CHAPTER WAS WRITTEN because of a concern for the special learner and the problems encountered by mainstream teachers. The purpose is to prepare regular education teachers to work effectively with special children in mainstream environments. The chapter attempts to explain what special education is all about by looking at the federal law that defines it, the Individuals with Disabilities in Education Act. It also aims to be a reference guide to problems that classroom teachers will face, such as inclusion, dealing with learning disabilities, attention deficit disorder, and hyperactivity and dyslexia. The questions of feelings and the hardship of bullying as well as diversity in our changing society are discussed at length. The reader should be aware that this chapter offers an overview of what the mainstream teacher should expect in the inclusion process, and is not intended to be a definitive work for the teacher of special children who are mandated to be in a self-contained class environment.

Just what is special education? There is a great deal of confusion regarding what special education is and is not. Our purpose in this chapter is to attempt to define special education, review its history, and discuss strategies that can be used by the regular education teacher to develop and maintain an effective inclusion program in the regular classroom. Special education has historically been defined as providing an appropriate education in the least restrictive environment, while not ignoring the need for some to have a specialized program. Special education's purpose was to create access to educational alternatives by providing the necessary and appropriate resources. New laws have added a new focus for special education. Access is no longer the primary goal—learning along with inclusion is. Figure 5.1 outlines what special education it is and what it is not.

BRIEF HISTORY OF SPECIAL EDUCATION

Prior to 1972, children were warehoused without hope of redemption in mental hospitals throughout the United States. Hospitals such as Willowbrook State School in New York were exposed on television for their horrific treatment of the mentally delayed. Incidents such as this spurred Congress to pass the Rehabilitation Act of 1973 (Section 504), which attempted to eliminate discrimination against the disabled by decree. In 1975, President Ford signed the Education for All Handicapped Children Act (PL 94-142) into law. It provided benefits in two essential areas.

1. Federal law required that all handicapped children have a free and appropriate public education.
2. It dramatically expanded the role of parents in their children's education.

The Act specifically

- Expanded the federal role in financing special education.
- Created enforcement monitors to assure compliance with the law.
- Required that children be educated in the least restrictive environment.
- Required that children be mainstreamed into regular education whenever possible.
- Established a referral procedure that protected the rights of child and parent.
- Required that each child must have an Individualized Educational Plan (IEP).

The law was designed to move handicapped and disabled children out of institutions and into classrooms. It did not, however, include requirements for academic achievement. Emphasis was on appropriate care of disabilities, rather than on achieving full potential in an academic curriculum. The expectations were low, and children were not prepared to function successfully in the outside world. While the original focus of the special education law of 1975 was to provide access for all special children to public education, a new law written in 1997, the **Individuals with Disabilities in Education Act** (IDEA PL 105-17), focused on improving student learning outcomes, not just providing access. This was a crucial distinction and step forward. No longer was a child to be considered "serviced" by being placed in a special class but was now expected to demonstrate that learning was going on. Significantly, for the first time special education children were expected to function and achieve the same standards as children without disabilities.

On December 3, 2004, President Bush signed the Individuals with Disabilities Improvement Act of 2004 (IDEA), PL 108-446. Closely aligned with the No Child Left Behind Act (2002), it aims to ensure that equity, accountability, and excellence in education is provided for all children with disabilities.

The Special Education Referral Process

The **referral process** for special education involves parents, teachers, social workers, licensed physicians, nurses,

Figure 5.1 What Special Education Is and Is Not

Special Education Is

1. Providing the most appropriate education for each child in the least restrictive environment
2. Looking at the educational needs of children who are mentally handicapped, learning disabled, physically handicapped, hearing impaired, or gifted
3. Creating alternatives that will help general educators serve children with learning or adjustment problems

Special Education Is Not

1. Ignoring the need of some children for a more specialized program that can be provided
2. Allowing children with special needs to be taught in regular classrooms without the support services they need
3. Only available to school districts that can afford it

foster parents, or other agencies requesting an evaluation of a child who has evidenced specific physical or cognitive symptoms that affect his or her ability to learn. Evaluations are conducted by a multidisciplinary team whose goal is to complete a nondiscriminatory evaluation that either does not find a handicap or identifies a specific one, while simultaneously recommending services and class placement options. Provision is then made for an educational plan whose goal in most cases is to correct the deficit and return the child to the mainstream class as quickly as possible. Figure 5.2 defines the general terms pertinent to the referral process.

The first step in seeking appropriate services for a child with special needs is to obtain parental consent for an appropriate evaluation of their child. A school psychologist, an educational specialist, and a social worker then act with parents as a team in the assessment process. Parents are part of the process from the beginning to the final recommendation. Each student is provided an **Individualized Educational Plan (IEP)**, which is a specially prepared program designed to help eliminate or compensate for the obstacles to learning stemming from a child's disability. Before this IEP is prepared, an educational planning conference is held. Parents, special education teachers, a general education teacher (where appropriate), a district representative, and advocates for the parent from outside agencies meet. Whenever appropriate, the student and any individual who can interpret the instructional implications of the evaluation results are also invited to participate. The process is aimed at rendering the best program to meet the individual needs of each child.

There are both positive and negative aspects involved in all programs called Special Education. On the positive side, special education affords the opportunity for all handicapped and disabled children to learn in a classroom setting, rather than being isolated, as in the past. Special children can graduate to the highest level of education that is appropriate for their abilities, as learning problems that were once ignored are now diagnosed and addressed. Advocates for special education claim a child's self-confidence and self-esteem are increased. Critics, on the other hand, believe there are more negative than positive aspects to special education. The stigma of "handicapping" and the low expectations that have traditionally driven achievement down stand out as the two most negative aspects. The problem with special education is that it never was focused on achieving parity in academics for special children, as most parents believed. Four reasons stand out for this lack of academic success: (1) the system was not geared to fundamentals like reading; (2) teachers were not trained in academic curriculum; (3) subjects were watered down or skipped; and (4) tests were modified to help improve grades.

Figure 5.2 Referral Definitions

1. *Referrals:* These can come from pediatricians, parents, or educators who make a request for an evaluation.

2. *Evaluations:* Used to determine if disability impacts the child's learning. Evaluations must be (1) *multidisciplinary*, which means they cannot rely on only one professional or one test. They must also identify the impact on the child's areas of development such as social and emotional behavior, academic and fundamental life skills, and adaptive physical mobility, and (2) *nondiscriminatory*, which means evaluations must look for strengths as well as weaknesses.

3. *Individualized Educational Program (IEP):* Must start with an explanation of the student's strengths and needs. It must include (1) annual goals for the skills the student will master by year's end and (2) short-term objectives or benchmarks by which to assess student progress.

4. *Placement and related services:* Placement is governed by an emphasis on "least restrictive environment." Related services may include speech therapy for the language impaired, the support of a learning consultant, and travel training. The idea is to include special students in regular classes as much as possible and foster interaction among all students.

5. *Placement options:* Can be regular classes, a resource room, self-contained classes, private schools, residential or home placement, and hospital institutions. The Individualized Educational Plan (IEP) is the document used to drive placement decisions.

6. *Transitions:* Are the moves from general education to special education and back to general education or work.

7. *Testing and assessment:* Special education students are to take the same standard tests as regular education students. Under the new law there are to be no exemptions.

8. *Parental involvement:* Must be evident throughout the entire process. Parents have due process rights if they disagree with recommendations. If problems cannot be resolved or mediated they will then go to an impartial mediator for resolution.

INDIVIDUALS WITH DISABILITIES IN EDUCATION ACT (IDEA)

Principles of IDEA

The IDEA of 1997 attempted to correct past errors. It proposed six basic principles, with its primary concern the quality of education, not simply access. These principles were incorporated as essential elements of our national policy toward special children, which was to be focused on ensuring equality of opportunity, full participation, independent living, and economic self-sufficiency and inclusion wherever possible. The principles ensured

1. Free and appropriate public education for all. The new language in IDEA 2004 was designed to ensure that children with disabilities would be taught by highly qualified teachers and receive research-based instruction.
2. Appropriate evaluation
3. Individualized Educational Program (IEP)
4. Least Restrictive Environment (LRE)
5. Parent, teacher, and student participation in decision making
6. Procedural safeguards

Strategy for IDEA

Along with national policy, a strategy had to be developed and implemented in order for the law to work. A practical guideline for improving the academic abilities of all children had to be formulated. The strategy that finally surfaced consisted of seven general dictums.

1. Each IEP should be built based on the general education curriculum.
2. Parents are equal partners in the decision-making process.
3. The general education teacher is to participate at IEP meetings.
4. A general education class placement with supplementary aids and services was to be the first consideration for each student with a disability within the continuum of services.
5. Student progress toward meeting annual goals was to be reported on a regular basis to parents.
6. Minority and non-English-speaking students were appropriately identified and served in general education settings with support services.
7. Students would now be expected to participate in state and district assessments, with modifications where necessary.

Key Sections of the IDEA

Five areas in the new IDEA 2004 stand out when comparing it with the 1997 version. The changes reflect the attempts to have the system meet student needs promptly and appropriately:

Highly Qualified Teachers To be considered highly qualified, a special education teacher must have a state special education certification or license and a bachelor's degree. She must also demonstrate the ability to teach at the appropriate instructional level for students. New special education teachers teaching multiple subjects must meet No Child Left Behind standards in at least one core subject area (language arts, math, or science) in order to be hired.

Opportunities for Professional Development The law requires that 100 percent (compared to 75 percent under IDEA 1997) of all State Improvement Grant money be devoted to professional development. States must use funds to carry out at least one of the following:

1. Offer mentoring, team teaching, reduced class schedules and caseloads, and intensive professional development.
2. Ensure that academic standards are aligned with state content standards as well as professional development.
3. Encourage collaborative and consultative models for early intervention.
4. Encourage and support the training of special education and regular education teachers and administrators to effectively use and integrate technology.
5. Expand professional development activities.
6. Develop and implement initiatives to promote the recruitment and retention of highly qualified special education teachers.
7. Develop programs designed to improve the quality of early intervention personnel, including paraprofessionals and primary referral sources.
8. Train personnel to write effective Individual Education Plans (IEP) and conduct effective and efficient IEP meetings.

Individual Education Plan

- Short-term objectives will only be used for students whose assessment is based on alternative achievement standards; all others will use annual measurable goals.
- For all students, there will be quarterly or periodic reports to parents on their child's progress toward meeting annual IEP goals.

- The law allows fifteen states to design paperwork reduction plans without sacrificing essential civil rights for students.
- The law allows fifteen states to offer voluntary three-year IEPs to all students, provided that there are regular reports to Congress on the effectiveness in reducing paperwork burden on teachers.
- The law requires the U.S. Department of Education to develop model IEP and Individual Family Service Plan (IFSP) forms.
- The law clarifies existing regulations by stating that an IEP team member whose area of the curriculum or related services will not be discussed at an IEP meeting need not attend that meeting.
- A parent and school district can agree to excuse a member of the IEP team from attending an IEP team meeting, as long as that member submits input in writing for their area that is to be discussed prior to meeting.
- The law states that IEP meetings may take place via conference call, video-conference, or other means, rather than in person.
- Substantive school-to-work transition services and planning will begin at age sixteen.

The purpose of both old and new IEPs is to identify the needs of a student with a disability. They identify a number of items ranging from student's progress, to what the student needs to be successful. They specifically define the special education services, along with the goals and objectives of these services. The basic difference between the old IEP's goals and objectives and the new is that the old focused on curriculum content, while the new focuses on the essential skills needed to access the general education curriculum. They provide behavioral intervention strategies for students whose behavior interferes with learning, while also allowing parents to participate in the development of the IEP and annual reviews. The new IEP primarily focuses on two important areas: (1) what the student with disabilities needs to be able to do to access the general education curriculum, and (2) the degree to which the student is able to participate in the general education environment.

Early Intervention for Young Children The law maintains early intervention and preschool special education programs for infants, toddlers, and preschoolers with disabilities and allows states to create a system that gives parents the option to have their child continue early intervention services until the age of five.

Eligibility A child cannot receive services by being labeled a "child with a disability" if the determining factor is (1) lack of appropriate reading instruction, (2) lack of instruction in math, or (3) the student has limited English proficiency. Neither can IQ be the sole determinant of eligibility for learning disabled (LD) students (American Foundation for the Blind, 2005).

INCLUSION

The unspoken word in the law is nevertheless the overriding issue for teachers: **inclusion**. Inclusion has been an ongoing issue at all levels of education. The problem is not simply inclusion versus segregated placement, but rather, who should be included and for how long. Before 1975, many children with disabilities either were excluded from public school or received their educational services in segregated settings. The Individuals with Disabilities in Education Act (IDEA) does not use the term *inclusion*, but instead focuses on the concept of least restrictive environment. This concept contains three basic principles.

1. The individual needs of students are of primary importance.
2. A clear preference is given to integrated placements.
3. Alternative placements must be available to meet student needs.

Those in favor of full inclusion argue for the inclusion of all students regardless of the type or severity of disability. They argue from a social equity perspective that all have the right to be placed with age-appropriate peers who are not disabled. In general, they believe all children have a right to receive their full education in general education classrooms and that inclusion provides a richer educational and social experience for both special and mainstream students (Ferguson, 1995; Lipsky and Gartner, 1996).

Those opposed to inclusion argue that full inclusion is not serving the needs of students with disabilities, especially those with severe disabilities. A handicap is a subjective phenomenon related in limitations of choice and in quality of life. Handicaps are not necessarily disabilities. It is possible to be disabled and not handicapped, as unusual as that might be. Liebermann (2001) defines a candidate for special education as a child with disabilities who is in danger of becoming handicapped if he does not receive special services. These services are provided to prevent handicaps from developing in children with disabilities, as well as to maximize their potential. Any student who cannot succeed in the state-mandated curriculum is not a candidate for special education according to Liebermann's definition. Inherent in the conceptual framework of IDEA, he believes, is its view on academic failure being addressed in the regular classroom through the regular curriculum. A truly disabled child needs an individual life plan, not an individualized educational plan. This view holds that we are compensating and circumventing disabilities and not addressing them through remediation.

Research on Inclusion

Staub and Peck (1994) reviewed studies to see the effects of inclusion on students without disabilities. Lipsky and Gartner (1996) did a parallel study and came up with the same results. Both found:

1. The presence of children with disabilities in the classroom has no effect on the academic progress of children without disabilities.
2. It also had no effect on teacher time and attention.
3. Students without disabilities do not acquire inappropriate behavior through association with their peers with disabilities.
4. Inclusion helped regular students to become more accepting and supportive, reducing prejudice against special children.

Unfortunately this research is contradicted by the horror stories that seem to be emanating everywhere from various field experiences. Most of these stories claim that full inclusion was introduced without support just to save money, since inclusion lowers class size. McLeskey and Waldron (2002, 2000) point out that teachers are opposed to inclusive classes when there is a lack of support, which is not surprising. With proper support from the schools, teacher views of inclusion have been seen to change. The law has made it clear that schools have a responsibility to place students with disabilities in general education classes as often as possible. Research and reports from the field suggest that a high level of inclusion is attainable when there is a strong support system in place (Ruder, 2000). Research also indicates that children with disabilities do well in inclusive settings, while children without disabilities are not harmed. Holloway (2001) found in reviewing the literature that children are best served when efforts by special and mainstream teachers are coordinated in some form of combined model.

Strategies for Inclusion

There are specific strategies that should be used if you are to ensure a successful inclusion program. There also has to be collaboration between regular and special teachers and governmental forces regarding funding for appropriate support services, and parent concerns must be addressed at every step. Good teaching strategies combined with curriculum and environmental adaptations are necessary for inclusion to work. Successful inclusion programs require good teaching practices that cover the spectrum, from direct instruction such as guided discovery, to indirect instruction such as cooperative learning and peer tutoring (McBrien and Brandt, 1997). The key to inclusion strategies is to differentiate your instructional program (Tomlinson, 2006, 1999).

1. *Collaboration among special and regular educators.* Having both sets of educators work creatively together to plan and execute a successful educational program.
2. *Support services.* Providing the necessary direct and indirect support to children and teachers in the regular classroom.
3. *Curriculum adaptation.* Modifying the general classroom curriculum to allow each child to actively participate at his or her own level.
4. *Cooperative learning.* Using a strategy that divides children into small groups of learning and emphasizes cooperative goals.
5. *Peer tutoring.* Providing opportunities for all children to assist each other in learning activities in various ways.
6. *Push-in services.* Integrating related service providers (speech, physical therapy, occupational therapy, counseling, etc.) into the regular classroom to emphasize functionality while maximizing the child's participation in regular education.
7. *Environmental adaptations.* Adapting the classroom so each child participates (e.g., seating a hearing-impaired child closer to the front of the room).
8. *Parent empowerment.* Respecting the rights of parents to enroll their child in a school that reflects their choice of educational philosophy (public, private, or parochial).

Inclusion of the Gifted An area for inclusion that tends to be ignored or looked at with suspicion is how we address the special gifted child in a mainstream class. The NCLB attempts to define *gifted and talented* as students, children, or youth who give evidence of high achievement in areas such as intellectual, creative, artistic, or leadership, or in a specific academic field, who need services or activities not ordinarily provided by the school to fully develop those capabilities (Title IX, Part A, Section 9101(22), p. 544). The question that is left unanswered is how these services are to be provided for gifted youngsters in mainstream classes. Figure 5.3 lists ten suggestions for promoting learning in gifted children. (It should also be noted that these practices are also quite effective with mainstream students.)

Inclusion in a Multicultural, Diverse Society In our society, it is highly unlikely that any form of instruction is culturally neutral. Clearly, our society is becoming increasingly more socially and culturally diverse. Our

Figure 5.3 Inclusion Strategies for the Gifted

> 1. Allow for choice and opinion; choices maximize student interest.
> 2. Follow democratic practices by allowing students to establish learning goals and self-assessment strategies. Gifted students need an environment in which they can develop critical-thinking skills.
> 3. Problem-solving, inquiry, and discovery strategies work best with gifted students.
> 4. Use a variety of questions with each lesson. Questions should be on both a higher and lower order. Ask students to explain where they would find information.
> 5. Use a KWL chart to focus students.
> 6. Always give gifted children credit for understanding concepts.
> 7. Provide challenging activities as practice exercises.
> 8. It is best to direct lessons toward topics that students have previously expressed interest in.
> 9. Peer support is critical. Provide opportunity for gifted students to work with their intellectual peers.
> 10. Avoid drill-and-practice and note-taking activities to highlight project-based learning. They cause boredom and could lead to unacceptable behaviors.
>
> *Source:* Adapted from About (2007)

nation consists of a population divided by race, class, culture, age, gender, ethnicity, religion, sexual identity, and learning and physical abilities. We need to be able to assess achievement in nonprejudicial ways. Multicultural education is a philosophical concept and an educational process. Equality and equity are not the same things; equal access does not guarantee fairness. What needs to be done is to focus on multicultural approaches to teaching rather than teaching the way we were taught. We need to broaden our assumptions about teaching and learning, and deliver instruction in a context familiar to students that builds upon their different learning styles (Grant, 1994).

Diversity and Multicultural Education   There are many misconceptions and myths regarding multicultural education. James Banks (1993) refutes the misconception that multicultural education is an entitlement program and curriculum movement for African Americans, Hispanics, the poor, women, and other victimized groups. He points out that it was designed to restructure educational institutions so all students, including middle-class white males, would acquire the knowledge and skills to work effectively in a diverse society. It is not an ethnic- or gender-specific movement.

Another misconception, according to Banks, is that multicultural education is opposed to Western tradition. In fact, multicultural education grew out of the civil rights movement. Multicultural theorists believe that knowledge relates to one's values and social experiences and is essential to learning. The argument that Western classics are being displaced in our curriculum by ethnocentric works is false, says Banks, arguing that the aim is not to exclude the classics, but to be inclusive to the demands reflected in our nation's diversity.

Albert Shanker once warned that multiculturalism, as it is taught in the United States, is focused on differences instead of commonalities, and that we must teach understanding of shared core values and essential human rights, not foster differences.

Dunn and Griggs (1995) synthesized research by pointing out similarities and differences among the learning styles of culturally diverse populations. They isolated the learning styles of diverse groups and clarified teaching and counseling practices. Multicultural education is a natural for providing instruction in a context focused on learning styles. By designing program learning sequences, contract activity packages, and multisensory instructional packages as alternative ways to meet the needs of our nation's diverse populations, Dunn and Griggs provided learning-style instruction and materials for the major cultural groups in our society.

Critics claim that multicultural education's use of learning-styles techniques leads to divisions in our society. In reality, it seems to assist in transforming our society through a process of social reconstruction into a better world.

America and Multiculturalism   Multiculturalists attempt to explain the changing role of Americans in relation to minorities. Many white Americans, they feel, are uncomfortable with their role transition from dominant status to part of a pluralistic nation. The question they ask is how to create a nation where all cultures are accorded dignity? It is obvious that European Americans all came from somewhere else, and hold varying ideas about ethnic identity. The further ancestors are from the Anglo-Saxon Protestant image of the real American, the greater the pressure to assimilate. Jews, Catholics, Eastern Europeans, Southern Europeans, and minority religious sects have all felt this pressure. These groups were told to forget their native language, change their names to sound more American, and make sure their children spoke only English (Howard, 1993).

White security was based on the economic and political exploitation of others. Tensions remain between the races even though many attempt to deal sensitively with the issue of racism. This is so because it is easier to deny and ignore than to accept or assume collective guilt for the past. The best approach to the past is honesty. Americans must face the fact that they benefited from racism before our nation can move on as one people. One of the greatest contributions we can make to cultural understandings is simply to learn the power of respect and understand that honesty and humility are based on respect. Healing must take place if we are to survive as a pluralistic and just nation.

MINI CASE FROM THE FIELD

A Problem of Inclusion in a Multicultural Classroom

The following case from the field discusses the importance of inclusion and its place in a multicultural, diverse society. The strategies and methods proposed are aimed at meeting the needs of all children and society. Read the case, and compare the ideas presented to your own experience.

Lunch was a time to unwind and relax for Margaret Gomez. She also needed to confide in her friends. Before they met for lunch, Margaret took a moment to reflect on what had transpired over the past few days. It all began Tuesday morning during her sixth-grade homeroom class. Mohammad and five other Islamic youngsters in her class had asked if they could be excused from going to lunch for the next month. Margaret had asked why. Mohammad answered, "It is the time of Ramadan, a time for praying and fasting for Moslems all over the world. We cannot eat during the day until sundown, and going to the lunchroom is a great temptation." Margaret said she had not known that. She asked the boys where they wanted to go during lunch period. They said if they could stay in their homeroom and pray. Then Margaret told the boys that the McGraw Comprehensive School was a public school, and formal prayer was not allowed. The boys responded that they wouldn't be disturbing anyone because everyone else would be having lunch, and besides how would they know what they were doing? Margaret thought about the boys' response and then thought of a perfect solution. The boys could have lunch with her every day for the next month and pray privately by themselves.

Everything went well for the first two days. Then a series of cutting slips were sent to Margaret for the boys' absence from lunch. Margaret had immediately gone to the lunchroom to speak with the teacher who was in charge, explained the situation, and said she felt it was her responsibility to meet the needs of all her students. She believed that diversity should be seen as a strength, and respecting the beliefs of others was a positive message that she wished to send her students.

That afternoon three of her colleagues had approached her after school and said that they thought she was acting unprofessionally and inappropriately, if not illegally. First, by having children excused from lunch; second, by allowing them to practice their religion in a public school. A side remark was also made that no teacher should ever give up a duty-free lunch period, which compromised the rest of the staff. They had said she should return the youngsters to the regular lunch program post haste, tomorrow.

Jane Hemmings and Lucille Chan were the first to enter the faculty lunchroom, followed shortly by Nicholas Saccone and Ed Child. They had all received a brief message from Margaret asking them to meet with her and discuss a serious problem she was facing. When they all sat down, Margaret explained her predicament. Then she asked for each of their opinions on what she should do.

In a booming voice, Ed Child declared, "They had some nerve!" He saw Margaret as on the side of the angels helping the children of color in her class. "There is nothing wrong with your actions," he told Margaret. "They are professional and compassionate and above all, legal. This a free country and you were just helping children exercise their rights as Americans."

"Hold on," Lucille said. "The teachers who approached Margaret did have some very cogent points to make. We cannot allow organized prayer into public schools, and having private lunches with students is at least a questionable practice. I would suggest you return the children to the lunchroom and avoid getting involved any further than you are already."

"But you're taking the coward's way out," Ed told Lucille, "not really taking a stand for anything. What do you think, Jane?"

"I see both sides of this dilemma," Jane replied. "What we need is a reasonable solution, one that is fair and just, and above all, ethical. I think Margaret should go to Principal Thompson and explain what has already transpired. She should also say that in the future she will notify the main office and all appropriate personnel regarding having children removed from a lunch period. As for praying on public property, I think it is quite appropriate as long as it is not done formally or sanctioned by the school. That should put this episode to rest."

"I agree with Jane," Nick Saccone put in. "Margaret's behavior in attempting to resolve this problem of diversity in her multicultural class was ethical and politically correct."

1. Describe the positive actions taken by Margaret with respect to meeting the needs of her students.
2. Explain the merit in the arguments made by Margaret's colleagues with regard to her unprofessional, inappropriate, and possibly illegal behavior.

3. Compare and contrast the positions put forth by Ed and Lucille. Is there any room for compromise?
4. How can Jane's argument be justified as an ethical resolution to a problem dealing with diversity?
5. If you were Margaret, what action would you take?

LEARNING DISABILITIES

We have spoken about the process by which children are placed into special education programs and the laws governing that process. What we have not discussed is just

PRACTICE EXERCISE 5.1

Pros and Cons Regarding Diversity and Multiculturalism

Read the six arguments for and against diversity, pluralism, and multicultural education. After each argument, decide on your position and indicate whether you agree or disagree. Support your decision with your reasons and share them with your classmates.

Argument One: **What is the goal of multicultural education?**

Pro: Its goal is to empower all, and achieve social justice for all. Multiculturalism is a celebration of cultural diversity.

Con: Its goal is divisiveness. Diversity will disunite America and lead to "balkanization" or "tribalism."

Your Position

Argument Two: **All should be welcomed into our society.**

Pro: The United States has been called a melting pot, a mosaic, and a salad bowl because of its diversity. No other country in the world has offered sanctuary to so many.

Con: The United States is not a melting pot for people of color, lesbians, gays, or the poor. We should only welcome groups that can help our society prosper, not deteriorate.

Your Position

Argument Three: **Describe the relationship between political correctness and multicultural education.**

Pro: Multicultural education is the cornerstone on which political correctness is founded. The nonacceptance of political correctness undercuts the acceptance of a shared experience.

Con: Multicultural education is a synonym for political correctness, which is about speech repression, and fear to say what one believes in.

Your Position

Argument Four: **The success of multicultural education will be evidenced by the creation of a common culture.**

Pro: Multicultural education offers an alternative way to achieve a common culture, while preserving traditional American values, and making multiple traditions a reality.

Con: Multicultural education rejects a common American culture. It celebrates the history and cultures of others, while pointing to faults and ignoring the positive aspects of our society.

Your Position

Argument Five: **The problem of racism must be addressed in a diverse society.**

Pro: Race is not a black or brown problem. It is a problem for whites as well as people of color. It is simply not just a minority thing.

Con: Multicultural education is a minority thing. Racism is outdated. Our society needs to address problems such as education and poverty, which cross racial lines.

Your Position

Argument Six: **The relationship between multiculturalism and education is positive.**

Pro: Multiculturalism inoculates tolerance and provides a perspective on our own traditions and values (Hirsh, 1987). The real issue is not whether there will be multiculturalism, but what kind (Ravitch, 2000). Multiculturalism and learning are essential to any quality educational program.

Con: Multicultural education will impede the learning of basic skills. Education is not a social exercise; rather, it is a developmental cognitive experience provided for everyone.

Your Position

>
> ### PRACTICE EXERCISE 5.2
>
> ### *Political Correctness*
>
> Read the following excerpt and write a brief passage regarding the interpretation of political correctness in the print media.
>
> *Brooklyn Cyclones "Bat Persons" Win "Politically Correct" Game*
>
> A minor league team from Brooklyn played Tuesday night in what is being dubbed a "politically correct" baseball game.
>
> The Brooklyn Cyclones, a class A affiliate of the New York Mets, played the Lowell Spinners in Lowell, Mass. The local CBS affiliate, WBZ-TV, reported that, in a bow to political correctness, the first, second, and third basemen were called "base persons." Batboys became "ball persons."
>
> Shortstop was referred to as the "vertically challenged stop," the TV station reported. To spare the feelings of players, errors were not announced to the fans.
>
> The Cyclones won the game, beating Lowell by a score of 9–5.
>
> Source: Durkin (2007)

what a **learning disability** is. Interestingly enough, there is no clear and widely accepted definition of learning disabilities. A perusal of the professional literature indicates at least twelve definitions. There is, however, agreement in some basic areas.

1. Students with learning disabilities have difficulties with academics. What they may actually learn differs from their potential to learn.
2. Students with learning disabilities evidence an uneven pattern of development in the areas of language, academics, or physical growth. These learning problems are not due to environmental disadvantage, mental retardation, or emotional disturbance.

Most definitions of learning disabled say only what it is not: The learning disabled child is not mentally retarded, not emotionally disturbed, not impaired in his or her modalities and has had an opportunity to learn, not hindered by excessive absences, poor teaching, or frequent family moves. The term itself, *LD*, is often referred to as the "hidden handicap," because there is no outward appearance of a disability. This group of children appears no different from their normal peers. Yet it is estimated that 6 percent to 10 percent of school-aged children in the United States are learning disabled. Nearly 40 percent of all children enrolled in special education classes suffer from a learning disability. This is the group that mainstream teachers must address.

Little is really known about the causes of these disabilities aside from some general observations. Some children tend to have a maturation lag, that is, they mature at a slower rate, as demonstrated by their inability to function the same as other children in their age group. They have, for the most part, normal vision and hearing yet misinterpret everyday sights and sounds because of some unexplained disorder of the nervous system. Many have been born prematurely, or have had injuries before birth or in early childhood, which probably accounts for some later learning problem. Interestingly, learning disabilities tend to run in families and are more common in boys than girls.

These children exhibit a wide range of symptoms, which include problems with reading, mathematics, comprehension, writing, spoken language, or reasoning abilities. The primary characteristic of a learning disability is the significant difference between a child's achievement in some areas and his overall intelligence.

Definitions of a Learning Disability

A learning disability is generally defined as a disorder in one or more of the basic psychological processes involved in understanding or in using language, spoken or written. The disorder may manifest itself in an imperfect ability to listen, think, speak, read, write, spell, or do mathematical calculations. Learning disabilities are disorders that affect the ability to understand or use spoken or written language, do mathematical calculations, coordinate movements, or direct attention. A student may have significant problems of learning in school subjects, while other handicapping conditions can be ruled out. The term includes such conditions as perceptual handicaps, brain injury, minimal brain dysfunction, dyslexia, and developmental aphasia. It does not include learning problems that are primarily the result of visual, hearing, or motor handicaps, of mental retardation, of emotional disturbance, or environmental, cultural, or economic disadvantage. Although learning disabilities occur in very young children, the disorders are usually not recognized until the child reaches school age (NINDS, 2006).

According to the National Institutes of Health (NINDS, 2006), one in five Americans is learning disabled. Learning disabilities are neurobiological disorders that affect one's ability to read, write, speak, or compute math. Learning disabilities can also impair social skills. Learning disabilities can be lifelong conditions that, may affect many parts of a person's life. In some children many overlapping learning disabilities may be apparent. Others may have a single, isolated learning problem that has little impact on their lives outside school.

There are three basic types of learning disabilities:

Reading disorders affect accuracy, speed, or comprehension of reading material. In order for a reading disorder to be diagnosed, an individual's reading achievement (as measured by individually administered standardized tests) must be substantially below what would be expected given the individual's age, intelligence, and education.

Mathematics disorders often affect academic achievement and daily functioning involving tasks that require mathematical abilities. People with this type of disorder may have difficulty recognizing or reading numbers, copying numbers correctly, or counting objects. Similar to reading disorders, a mathematics disorder can only be diagnosed if an individual's mathematical abilities are significantly below what would be expected given the individual's age, intelligence, and education.

Written expression disorders interfere with academic achievement and with daily activities that require writing skills. Individuals with this disorder may have extremely poor handwriting, excessive spelling errors, and/or poor grammar and punctuation. Like other types of learning disabilities, these difficulties must be beyond what would be expected given other factors in a person's life. The disorder is not due to a simple lack of education but to the brain's impaired ability to process certain kinds of information. Figure 5.4 describes the common characteristics of several learning disorders.

While any of these characteristics may indicate a learning disability, it is important to keep in mind that no single characteristic is sufficient to warrant being identified as a learning disability. Learning disabilities cannot be cured but can be managed using proper instructional techniques.

How to Teach Children with Learning Disabilities

The most common treatment for learning disabilities is special education. Specially trained educators may perform a diagnostic educational evaluation assessing the child's academic and intellectual potential and level of academic performance. Once the evaluation is complete, the basic approach is to teach learning skills by building on the child's abilities and strengths while correcting and compensating for disabilities and weaknesses. Other professionals, such as speech and language therapists, also may be involved. Some medications may be effective in helping the child learn by enhancing

Figure 5.4 Characteristics of Learning Disabilities

1. *Visual perception disorders* may include confusing letters, misidentifying colors, misspelling sight words, or reading words in reverse, inability to recognize hidden figures in a picture or read partly effaced writing.
2. *Auditory perception disorders* may include confusing sounds, mispronouncing or misspelling multisyllabic words, or having difficulty following auditory directions or sounding out and blending words.
3. *Attention disorders* may include an inability to concentrate, distractibility, impulsivity, hyperactivity, and selective activity and continuing an action beyond normal limits.
4. *Motor function disorders* may include a lack of fine and gross motor skills and directionality, and ability to maintain balance during movements.
5. *Language disorders* may involve articulation, following oral directions (receptive language), grammatically incorrect oral language (expressive language), and written receptive and expressive language.
6. *Thinking disorders* involve memory, concept formation, problem solving, and judgment.

attention and concentration. Psychological therapies may also be used (NINDS, 2006).

The key to teaching the LD child is to remember that good teaching strategies are appropriate for all children. A traditional first step consists of previewing the ideas contained in a lesson while utilizing direct teaching strategies. The idea is to link new learning with previous instruction and experiences. It should not be startling to realize that the same approaches used in regular education classes can be used with children who have learning disabilities.

- Preview concepts to be covered in lesson
- Direct teaching of skills
- Relate new knowledge to previous instruction and experiences
- Use a curriculum-based assessment format
- Summarize the key points
- Correct errors immediately
- Use modeling for special students in regular education classes

These general principles of instruction shown in Figure 5.5 can be broken down into strategies and techniques that are effective in managing a special child. Some of the better-known strategies and techniques are fairly controversial. There has been much controversy

Figure 5.5 Four Principles of Instruction for the Learning Disabled

> 1. *Explicit teaching* is a method employing direct instructional strategies that give students the tools to function in school.
> 2. *Basic language structure* is the exploration of sounds that make language clear and comprehensible.
> 3. *Multisensory approach* directs information to both eyes and ears, and is reinforced by responsive actions of seeing, saying, hearing, writing, and feeling using both small and large muscle movements.
> 4. *Systematic and cumulative approach* means the use of methods that favor review and reinforcement in a structured way, building on past learning.

over the use of medication to treat special children, for example. Nevertheless, for some children medical intervention is an integral part of the solution, though it should never be the sole approach. Behavioral strategies such as behavior modification can also play a part in working with the special child. This approach combined with a cognitive behavioral approach to management, such as the Curwin-Mendler model, has also proven effective.

Emotional Conflict of the Special LD Child

A learning disability occurs when a student manifests significant problems in learning in school. Children with learning disabilities often suffer feelings of anxiety, stress, conflict, and concerns about fairness (Lavoie and Rosen, 1994). The real challenge is to educate others to understand what it means to be learning disabled.

1. *Anxiety.* Affects performance.
2. *Processing.* Learning disabled (LD) children spend time on processing the question while other children have already answered. The inability to process language is the primary problem of the LD child.
3. *Attention span.* The child can be distracted frequently. The teacher must constantly focus the child by using direct instructional techniques.
4. *Risk taking.* Children with learning disabilities may not volunteer because they have experienced failure too often.
5. *Visual perception.* An LD child has difficulty in visual perception. Most teachers blame the child (victim) rather than the cause. Learning disabilities have little to do with motivating a child; it has to do with perceptions.
6. *Reading comprehension.* One's experiences are more influential than vocabulary.
7. *Visual motor coordination.* Try to trace a picture using a mirror image. This will show you how it feels to an LD child.
8. *Oral expression.* Dysnomia is a word-finding problem. The problem exists in the brain's ability to retrieve information.
9. *Associative and cognitive tasks.* Associative tasks can be done in multiples, for example, driving a car and talking. Cognitive tasks require such concentration that you can only do one at a time, for example, drive on an icy road.
10. *Fairness.* Everyone gets what he needs. It doesn't mean everyone gets the same thing.

MINI CASE FROM THE FIELD

The following case from the field discusses the importance of understanding the role of the mainstream teacher with regard to the learning disabled child. Read the case, then compare and analyze Jane's, Ed's, and Lucille's ideas about what constitutes an effective approach for teaching LD children in a regular mainstream class.

How Do I Teach an LD Child?

Lucille was amiable and perpetually restless; she was nothing if not persistent. Her goal was to be the best teacher at McGraw Simpson Elementary and Senior High School. For the past three years, she had worked successfully on three different grade levels—second, third, and now fourth grade. She had always been reasonable and never really complained about teaching different grade levels. Mr. Thompson had encouraged her to view it as a challenge, though she knew better. Because she lacked seniority she was assigned to teach the classes others chose not to teach. That was fine with her. She had always managed to shine under the most difficult circumstances. But now she was being given two learning-disabled children for language arts that she felt totally unqualified to teach. What was she going to do? They might destroy all her prior efforts.

She entered the third floor faculty room that managed to be both spacious and cozy in a modest academic way. McGraw was a well-appointed school. Just then she spotted Jane Hemmings seated by the door. Lucille told Jane about her fears regarding learning disabled children being placed in her class. Jane told Lucille not to worry, she had faced the same situation a few years back. "All you have to do is adapt the curriculum to meet your students' needs. Look at the content and your objectives so that you can develop clear and explicit lessons." Lucille said, "That's what I do now." "Good! Then you should have no problems teaching the LD child," Jane said.

Ed Child had overheard the conversation and just couldn't avoid butting in. "I don't believe it! The great cooperative learning lady is going to be teaching guided lessons." Both Lucille and Jane looked at Ed and said, "That's the way to do it. There is much more than just curriculum to consider—what about materials, presentations, motivations, and reinforcements? You also have to face the reality of inclusion as a democratic attempt to avoid the segregated placements of the past where possible, and I know it's possible for LD kids."

As the discussion progressed Ed made it clear that a direct instructional approach was good for all children, especially those who were learning disabled. That, he insisted, was the best way to teach the skills these youngsters needed. A language art is best taught using a multisensory approach allowing students to see, hear, and write. In this way, you can reinforce past learning.

Lucille said that she appreciated Ed's and Jane's ideas, but still wasn't sure what to do. She claimed that she was a pedagogical agnostic trying to find a path to meet the needs of all her students. As for the children with learning disabilities, she would meet their needs by being the best teacher she could be.

1. List the arguments for how to teach a child with learning disabilities made by Ed, Jane, and Lucille.
2. Who seems to have made the strongest points. Why?
3. Compare and contrast Ed's, Jane's, and Lucille's positions.
4. What do you think Lucille meant by claiming she was a pedagogical agnostic?
5. Prepare a language arts lesson for your grade level, and in a cooperative setting share and discuss strengths and weaknesses.

ATTENTION DEFICIT DISORDER AND ATTENTION DEFICIT HYPERACTIVITY DISORDER

Defining ADD

Attention Deficit Disorder (ADD) is an outdated term and technically should be called **Attention Deficit Hyperactivity Disorder (ADHD)**, but for the purposes of clarity they will be discussed as separate disorders. ADD is a genetic attention disorder that is fashionable to diagnose today. It is distinct from a learning disorder and is genetically predetermined. It is a developmental disorder that runs in families; it affects brain functions causing distractibility and an inability to stay on task. Language disorders, on the other hand, are processing problems, which are constantly misdiagnosed as ADD. Hyperactivity, inattention, and perceptual coordination problems may also be associated with learning disabilities but are not learning disabilities in themselves.

PRACTICE EXERCISE 5.3

Inclusion and the Learning Disabled Child

Read the five statements that follow from the point of view of a mainstream teacher. Write a brief description of how to handle each situation. Then compare and discuss your reflections and strategies with those of your classmates. Determine if any general strategies are apparent, and if not, determine the reasons.

1. Advocates of full inclusion argue that all students, regardless of the type or severity of disability, must be taught in a mainstream classroom.
2. Are children without disabilities emotionally and academically affected by the placement of disabled children in their classes?
3. How would you differentiate your instructional program to meet the needs of all your students?
4. Write your definition for the term *learning disability*. Include types and characteristics usually associated with the LD child.
5. Is it true that the same strategies used in mainstream classes can be used with LD children?

Explain your reasoning in number five based on the following techniques:

- Preview concepts you plan to teach, and summarize key ideas.
- Use direct teaching and modeling for all instruction related to skills.
- Teach new knowledge by speaking about experiences and understood content.
- Relate curriculum to standards while providing a specific assessment format.
- Correct errors immediately.

Determining ADD A cluster of chronic symptoms is used to determine ADD; these include family history, learning characteristics, distractibility, fidgeting, behavior, and ability to pay attention. The American Psychiatric Association's *Diagnostic and Statistical Manual of Mental Disorders* (*DSM-IV*, 1994, 2000) has developed a list of fourteen characteristics for ADD. If eight of the following characteristics are exhibited over a period of six months, a child is considered to have ADD. Formal diagnosis is made by psychologists. The role of the teacher is to refer any child in question to the school psychologist or guidance counselor.

1. Often fidgets with hands or feet or squirms in seat.
2. Has difficulty remaining seated when required to do so.

3. Is easily distracted by extraneous stimuli.
4. Has difficulty waiting his or her turn in games or group activity.
5. Often blurts out answers to questions before they have been completed.
6. Has difficulty following through on instructions from others.
7. Has difficulty sustaining attention to tasks.
8. Often shifts from one uncompleted activity to another.
9. Has difficulty playing quietly.
10. Often talks excessively.
11. Often interrupts or intrudes on others.
12. Often does not seem to listen to what is being said to him or her.
13. Often loses things necessary for tasks or activities at school or home.
14. Often engages in physically dangerous activities without considering the possible consequences.

Feelings of a Child with ADD

The generally accepted view is that there is no physical pain associated with ADD. Most children are unable to see any problem until it is pointed out to them. This usually occurs when they experience failure in school. It is interesting to note that three times as many boys have been diagnosed with ADD than girls. No reason is yet known for this disparity in numbers. It should be noted that ADD is a lifetime condition because it is not acquired but is inherited, or genetic.

Defining ADHD

According to the 2000 *DSM-IV*, ADHD is a disruptive behavior disorder characterized by the presence of a set of chronic and impairing behavior patterns that display abnormal levels of inattention, hyperactivity, or their combination. ADHD has been defined as hyperactivity combined with attention deficit disorder (ADD) caused by noticeable behavior problems in school. ADHD is a highly prevalent disorder estimated to affect 5 to 10 percent of children worldwide (NINDS, 2006).

ADHD is a diagnosis applied to children and adults who consistently display certain characteristic behaviors over a period of time. The most common core features include: distractibility (poor sustained attention to tasks), impulsivity (impaired impulse control and delay of gratification), and hyperactivity (excessive activity and physical restlessness). In order to meet diagnostic criteria, these behaviors must be excessive, long-term, and pervasive. The behaviors must appear before age seven, and continue for at least six months. A crucial consideration is that the behaviors must create a real handicap in at least two areas of a person's life—such as school, home, work, or social settings. These criteria set ADHD apart from the "normal" distractibility and impulsive behavior of childhood, or the effects of the hectic and overstressed lifestyle prevalent in our society.

A child with ADHD has trouble staying focused or concentrating even when working with a tutor. The best way to focus anyone is to have him or her do tasks that they like doing, combined with some type of reward system. Interactive activities such as working on a computer or in cooperative groups provide instructional purpose for these easily distractible students. Fortunately, ADHD can be treated in many cases with drugs that are derivatives of the stimulant methylphenidate under the trade name Ritalin. Concerta (a once-daily tablet) or Metadate (in time-released form) when properly administered and monitored help children maintain emotional health (Khalsa, 2006). Parents and teachers should not abdicate responsibility and believe that pills are the cure, however, or that all problems can be solved with a drug.

Instructional Practices for ADD/ADHD There is yet no cure for ADD/ADHD but this genetic disorder can be managed by using three basic strategies:

1. Focusing on things the child finds easy to focus on, such as playing learning games.
2. Using reward systems to help the child focus.
3. Using interactive activities, technology for instructional purpose such as computers, and multimedia exercises.

To teach a child with ADD, use a program where you continually support instruction in an orderly fashion combined with thematic instructional strategies. Always attempt to be nonjudgmental in all your dealings with this child, as with *all* other children. It is important to model and reinforce instruction. The way to facilitate learning for the child with ADD/ADHD is to turn good strategies into sound instruction. This, combined with proper medical treatment, behavior management techniques, educational intervention, and family involvement, allows us to believe there is hope for a productive life for every child. The American Academy of Pediatrics (2006) and Children and Adults with Attention Deficit/Hyperactivity (CHADD) (Dendy, 2006) recommend several tips for managing instruction during class time shown in Figures 5.6 and 5.7.

Alternative Strategies for ADD/ADHD

The classical view of ADD in children has been that it is an inability to pay attention due to impulsivity and a short attention span. Children and teachers are not responsible since in this medical model, it is really no one's fault. Armstrong (1996a, 1996b) attacks the root causes of a child's ADD problems, rather than what he believes is masking symptoms with medication and behavior modification programs. He advocates a "wellness model" for children.

Figure 5.6 Instructional Strategies for ADD/ADHD

- Use continuous and systematic reinforcement by modeling and reinforcing all instruction.
- Use thematic instructional units to integrate subject areas.
- Focus child by using task analysis of content being studied, and format functions to use for each assignment, as well as giving constant and immediate feedback.
- Work nonjudgmentally and avoid blame.
- Use agenda books for copying assignments.
- Help child by using props and prompts such as a spotlight on homework page.
- Assign a study buddy to keep child focused.
- Turn classroom into a controlled environment by using learning centers for various cooperative and individual activities.

Source: Armstrong (1996a)

Figure 5.7 Instructional Strategies for ADHD

1. Break complex instructions into small parts.
2. Post a daily schedule and homework assignments in the same place each day, or taped to the child's desk.
3. Plan academics for morning hours.
4. Schedule regular and frequent breaks.
5. Establish a secret signal with the child to use as a reminder when he or she is off track.
6. Form small-group settings when possible. Children with ADHD are easily distracted in large groups.
7. Seat the child away from distraction and next to children who will provide positive role modeling.
8. Reward positive behavior continuously and immediately.
9. Deliver negative consequences in a firm, businesslike way without emotion, lectures, or long-winded explanations.
10. Explain to the student what to do to avoid negative consequences.

Source: Armstrong (1996b)

Substantial evidence suggests that children with ADD do not show symptoms when they are having one-on-one interaction with an adult. They are physically indistinguishable from so-called normal children. They perform quite normally when they are paid to do specific activities or when they are involved in activities that interest them. When they reach adulthood approximately 70 percent discover ADD has gone away.

The puzzle is even more mystifying when we consider whether ADHD is a neurological disorder. Why do children with ADD successfully play educational computer games, and struggle with assignments not enjoyed? Children with ADHD can attend very well to tasks they like, but have difficulty with activities disliked. Perhaps

PRACTICE EXERCISE 5.4

Characteristics of ADD and ADHD

1. Compare the characteristics listed for the student with ADHD with those of a student with ADD.* Describe apparent patterns, and write a brief statement about the strategies you would employ to address negative characteristics.

ADHD Characteristics	ADD Characteristics
physically hyperactive	sluggish
show off/egotistical	modest
prone to conduct disorders	docile
rebellious	obedient
impulsive	honors others' boundaries
irritating	overly polite
bossy	underassertive
attracts friends but doesn't easily bond	bond with others but doesn't attract friends
intrusive	shy, socially withdrawn

2. Discuss traditional and alternative strategies for teaching children with ADD and ADHD. Which of those listed in the text appeal to you?
3. ADD/ADHD is not a legally authorized handicapping condition. As a result, others have made recommendations on how to deal with children who evidence the acknowledged characteristics. Discuss the recommendations and share your feelings with your classmates.

- There should be full inclusion for all students.
- Do not label children "special needs."
- Scales for ADD are not reliable, but are only subjective judgments.
- Use multiple intelligences theory to deal with ADD children.
- Medication for child control should be the very last resort.

Source: Baily (2006)

it's more about motivation, and behavior modification, than previously thought. The methods used to determine ADD are suspect since behavior-rating scales such as the *DSM III-R* depend on opinion rather than fact. There are no objective criteria to determine ADD. Suspect also are continuous performance tasks such as the Gordon Diagnostic System used to determine attention to task, done by having a child push a button every time a number 1 is followed by the number 9. The difficulty with standardized assessment for ADD is due to the validity process where two groups of children are formed and compared. The question is how the first ADD group was determined and how correct was the test used. There is no prime mover in charge of tests (Armstrong, 1996a).

The *ADD myth* is essentially a paradigm or worldview that makes assumptions about human beings. It endorses the view that human beings function very much like machines and ADD is a disease. This view holds that disability can be treated as a medical disorder that has no cure. Although this disease claim is made there is no medical proof of genetic factors, biochemical abnormalities, or neurological damage. The U.S. Congress has not officially authorized ADD as a legally handicapping condition, due to lack of evidence. Interaction with learning environment is needed; medication is not. Recommendations for ADD/ADHD are:

1. No labels for children such as "special education." Behavior rating scales used to diagnose ADD are not really reliable, and only call for subjective judgments. Continuous performance tasks measure attention to computer screens and not a child's attention span. (They were originally developed for air traffic controllers.)
2. Use multiple intelligences theory to deal with ADD children. People learn in different ways, and many times kinesthetic learning is ignored. When a child can't sit still, look at it from a growth perspective rather than a deficit perspective and provide more opportunities for movement so the child's energies can be positively channeled.
3. Medication for child control should be the very last resort. Medication to control a social situation may be convenient, but it does not allow one to examine the root causes.

Dyslexia

Another disability in vogue is **dyslexia**, an attention deficit that may occur in as many as 20 percent of school-aged children according to Shaywitz (2005, 1996). Dyslexia is a specific learning disability that is neurological in origin; it is characterized by difficulties with accurate fluent word recognition and poor spelling and decoding abilities. Functional magnetic resonance imaging (MRI) has shown that dyslexia is neurobiologically based (Shaywitz, 2005). It typically results from a deficit in the phonological component of language with secondary problems in reading comprehension and reduced reading experience that impedes vocabulary growth and background knowledge (NICHD, 2006).

Dyslexia is a reading problem that emphasizes defects in language processing rather than the visual system (Armstrong, 1996). Reading ability has been taken as a proxy for intelligence, and subject to educational assessment. In England, bright children were diagnosed as dyslexics over 100 years ago. Early explanations held that dyslexia was related to defects in vision and could be corrected by eye-training exercises. Later research showed that the defect was related to the language system and reflects a deficiency in processing linguistic language units known as *phonemes*. A traditional definition is that learning to read is an unexpected difficulty despite intelligence, motivation, and education. Some of the well-known symptoms of dyslexia are:

- confusion over the direction letters face (*b/d, p/9, p/q*)
- difficulties with left and right
- difficulties with keeping organized
- difficulties with spelling
- difficulties with directions (e.g., East and West)
- missing words when reading

The phonological model for treating dyslexia defines it as an encapsulated deficit often surrounded by significant strengths in reasoning, problem solving, concept formation, critical thinking, and vocabulary (Shaywitz, 1996). The model views language as a hierarchical series of components devoted to particular aspects of language: the upper levels for semantics (vocabulary and meaning), syntax (grammatical structure), and discourse (connected sentences) and the lower levels for processing sound elements that constitute language. To identify a word, it must be understood, stored, or retrieved from memory, and broken down into phonetic units. Processing language is done automatically, and is instinctive for all humans. In processing words, the human speech apparatus automatically compresses and merges phonemes into single sound units.

Reading and speaking rely on phonological processing of phonemes, the smallest segment of language. Only forty-four different phoneme combinations produce every word in the English language. A word like *bat* consists of three phonemes: *buh, aah,* and *tuh*. Speaking is quite natural and automatic; reading is not. Reading is manmade and must be learned. The reader must turn letters (graphemes) into sounds (phonemes) that have meaning. The beginning reader must understand the phonological structure of spoken words represented by the sequence of letters on the page (orthography) that can be comprehended (Shaywitz, 1996).

The Dyslexia Myth

- *Mirror writing is a symptom of dyslexia.* Reversals of letters and words are common for all early learners. Dyslexic children have no problem in copying letters, only in naming them.
- *Eye exercise is an appropriate treatment.* Research has shown that dyslexia is a linguistic deficit and eye-training exercises are of little help.
- *More boys than girls are dyslexic.* This is simply not true.
- *Dyslexia can be outgrown.* This disability is lifelong and cannot be outgrown. Dyslexics can lean to read, but not automatically.
- *Smart people cannot be dyslexic.* Intelligence is not related to phonological processing. (Dyslexia Awareness and Resource Center, 2003)

The dyslexic child has a deficit in language processing that impairs the ability to decode written words. This decoding problem blocks the ability to comprehend, even though that capacity exists. According to phonological theory, a word can only be identified after it has been accessed or decoded. Although dyslexia cannot be outgrown, its effects, with careful planning and hard work, can be overcome (Shaywitz, 2005).

Strategies for the Special and Mainstream Learner The techniques that work best for both special and mainstream learners include motivating lessons, use of technology, guidance approaches, and the use of assessments based on outcomes. The following are effective strategies for all learners.

1. *Stimulate learning activities* such as role playing, painting, sculpting, posters, performing, and many exercises that need imagination.
2. *Find out what interests* students and incorporate their ideas into lessons.
3. *Computers* are good for mainstream and ADD children. They provide short sound and visual feedback, good for writing and spelling instruction.
4. *Physical education.* Hands-on, active movement is helpful.
5. *Organize positive times together.* Include class meetings to solve problems and develop relationships. This can be done using lunch dates when the teacher eats lunch with selected children.
6. *Use alternative assessment models* for evaluation, such as letting children express learning through performances rather than paper and pencil tests. Provide choices to develop responsibility. Allow students to present their own work portfolios to peers, parents, and teachers, which helps develop self-evaluation skills.

MINI CASE FROM THE FIELD

The following case from the field discusses the importance of understanding the role of the mainstream teacher with regard to children who are learning disabled, exhibit ADD/ADHD, or are dyslexic. Read the case and evaluate the procedures and strategies employed by Lucille Chan. Compare and analyze Lucille's views with those of Margaret Gomez and Ed Child. What constitutes an effective approach for teaching children with disabilities in a regular mainstream class?

Teaching the Special Child in a Mainstream Class

Lucille met with her friends Margaret and Ed for coffee at a local diner after school. She was dying to tell them about what she had done to accommodate the two learning disabled children she had been assigned for language arts. First, it was not two but three special children who had been assigned to her class for mathematics, reading, and social studies.

"You got to be kidding," said Ed, "didn't anyone inform you about the change?"

"Yes, Mr. Thompson apologized, said he had no other alternative. He felt confident in my ability to effectively handle the situation."

Ed asked how her direct teaching approach worked with LD kids. Lucille responded by explaining that they

PRACTICE EXERCISE 5.5

Dyslexia

Special needs children come with a wide range of disabilities. Your understanding and recognition of them will benefit your instructional program. Resolve the following problem by reflecting and discussing the issues presented to your classmates and instructor.

Look at the myths surrounding dyslexia described in the text. Develop a plan for working with dyslexic children that demonstrates your understanding of the condition.

weren't all LD. One child was ADHD and the other was dyslexic.

"Well, isn't that the same thing?" "Not really, Ed. Aside from the fact that they are all developmental disorders, they all have specific disabilities."

Lucille went on to explain that she had thought about their discussion last week when she had claimed that she was "a pedagogical agnostic" trying to find a path to meet the needs of all her students. The more she had thought about it the more she had convinced herself to create a differentiated classroom. In that environment she could divide her time and resources and still be effective at facilitating and maximizing student talents. She decided to focus on each child's interests and engage them through their different learning modalities.

"I felt like a distant relative of Sherlock Holmes as I puzzled out my strategy," said Lucille.

Lucille couldn't contain her enthusiasm as she continued to relate her teaching strategy. She knew she had to use a different guide map for each student. To make her task less arduous she thought about Renzulli for enrichment, Lazear and Gardner for multiple intelligences, and Tomlinson for differentiating instruction.

Margaret, who had been attentively listening to the discourse between Lucille and Ed, said, "I thought you were going to follow Jane's suggestion and simply adapt your curriculum content and objectives to develop clear and explicit lessons focused on student needs. When Jane had told me about the strategy she used in her sixth-grade language arts classes I knew she was right."

"Wait one minute, Margaret. Lucille never said she would follow Jane's ideas, she had basically said she was an eclectic and would not teach all her students the same way. I guess she wants to be a diagnostician and prescribe the best possible instruction for each child, including special children."

"Ed's right. I believe that most learners have some similar commonalities and interests, but then again, it's differences that make for individuals," said Lucille.

Lucille went on to say that she felt that no single formula is correct for setting up a differentiated classroom. "Differentiated instruction isn't really an instructional strategy. It's really more like a way of thinking about teaching where you begin with the learner's needs and not a prescribed learning plan."

"How do you assess student progress if everybody is just working on their own needs?" asked Ed.

"Ed, excellence isn't defined by totaling the amount of facts you can retain; it's defined by measuring your students' growth from where they started."

"How do you think Principal Thompson will feel about that?"

1. List the steps taken by Lucille to meet the needs of the special children who were placed in her class.
2. Which points are the strongest and which are the weakest?
3. Compare and contrast Ed's, Margaret's, and Lucille's positions. How do they differ and how are they similar?
4. What do you think Lucille meant by saying that she had combined the thinking of Renzulli, Gardner, Lazear, and Tomlinson in attempting to create a differentiated learning environment?
5. Prepare a lesson in your areas of expertise and grade level that provides for differentiating instruction.
6. Discuss strengths and weaknesses of following a differentiated instructional approach with regular education and special education children.

Chapter Summary

In this chapter, we have seen that special education has a new focus. In the past, the goal was access; today, learning and inclusion through the new Individuals with Disabilities Act has given new meaning to the term *special learner*. We have explored a brief history of special education while reviewing the referral process and seeing how children are classified and placed. Topical areas such as inclusion, ADD, ADHD, and dyslexia have been examined with an eye toward understanding the approaches necessary for successful mainstreaming to occur. Strategies for teaching the special learner were outlined for possible use in regular classrooms. The objective of this chapter was to focus on the realization that good and effective teaching strategies for mainstream children are also effective for special children in an inclusive environment. Teaching is not an easy profession to master. It simply is the most rewarding.

Cases from the Field

CASE ONE

Mrs. Lucille was a mature woman who had entered teaching as a career change. She had worked hard in college to achieve her position as a childhood teacher at Warren Elementary School. In the five years she had been teaching she had received only praise and compliments for her dedication in working with mainstream children as well as those special children who had been placed in her third- and fourth-grade classes. She was shocked when her principal, Mr. Duntz, spoke to her about parent complaints that she was too hard on her special children and that she favored the regular, mainstream children. Parents claimed she expected too much from their special children and this was frustrating them.

1. Was Mr. Duntz acting appropriately by speaking to Mrs. Lucille about the parental complaints? Explain.
2. How do you feel about a teacher having high expectations about their students?
3. Explain the difference between high expectations and inappropriate expectations with regard to student achievement.
4. Why do you think Mrs. Lucille was shocked by Mr. Duntz's comments?
5. If you were Mrs. Lucille what would you have done? What would your reaction be?

CASE TWO

Mr. Juarez could not understand Mrs. Millstone's angry refusal to accept her son Jerold's evaluation of attention deficit disorder (ADD). She claimed the team that had tested her son was prejudiced against minority children; they wanted to keep Jerold in special education forever. Mr. Juarez, as Jerold's fifth-grade mainstream mathematics teacher, tried to explain to Mrs. Millstone that prejudice played no part in the evaluation. Assessment was based on standardize psychological testing that had confirmed her son's inability to function in a regular class environment.

1. What actions could Mr. Juarez have taken before his meeting with Mrs. Millstone?
2. How could the evaluation team have been involved in this conference?
3. Could Mr. Juarez have consoled Mrs. Millstone by explaining the meaning of the ADD diagnosis? Explain.
4. What are the options available to Mrs. Millstone?
5. What would you have done if you were Mrs. Millstone?

CASE THREE

Mr. Howell was asked to speak at his school's PTA meeting and explain the school board's adoption of inclusion for special learners at the Powell Academy prep school. Parents were concerned that their high school was going to have difficulty maintaining their traditionally excellent academic programs.

1. How could Mr. Howell calm parent fears regarding the supposed lowering of standards?
2. Why would inviting parents in to visit an inclusion program help calm fears?
3. Do parents have the right to question mandated programs? Explain.
4. What strategies for inclusion should Mr. Howell explain?
5. How would you handle this situation if you were Mr. Howell?

CASE FOUR

Ms. Burke had been assigned as the replacement for Mrs. Potts's early childhood class. The children were between the ages of six and seven years old, the age range allowed under state regulations. This was Ms. Burke's first job as an early childhood teacher after graduating from Smith College six months ago. She had been licensed as an early childhood teacher but so far had never taught an early childhood class beyond her student teaching experience. Before her first class meeting, the principal informed her that three students who were learning disabled would be mainstreamed in her class for reading. As she prepared to meet her class she thought about how she could best teach learning disabled children with her mainstream children.

1. What direct instructional strategies might Ms. Burke consider?
2. How would you describe a good teaching strategy?
3. Ms. Burke decided that she would follow a precise formula, which included:
   - previewing all the concepts to be covered in each lesson
   - utilizing direct teaching skills
   - relating past experiences and knowledge to the new content she introduced
   - assessing her children based on the curriculum she taught
   - always summarizing key points in each lesson
   - giving feedback immediately
   - providing opportunities to model

   How would you evaluate Ms. Burke's formula? Explain.
4. How should Ms. Burke respond if her principal says she should include a multisensory approach in teaching a special class?
5. How would you compare Ms. Burke's plan to one for a mainstream class without learning disabled children?

Terms to Remember

Individuals with Disabilities in Education ACT (IDEA)
Referral process
Individualized Educational Program (IEP)
Inclusion

Learning disabilities (LD)
Attention deficit disorder (ADD)
Attention deficit hyperactivity disorder (ADHD)
Dyslexia

Discussion Questions

1. Describe in a brief comparative essay what special education is and what special education is not.
2. Prepare an outline that highlights the primary legislative actions that established *special education* as we know it today.
3. Compare and contrast the new Individuals with Disabilities in Education Act with its predecessors.
4. Judge the merit for the recent push for inclusion of special children on all levels of education. Be sure to include in your argument a review of recent research and the most commonly recommended strategies advocated for inclusion.
5. How would you define a learning disability to a concerned parent who has heard only horror stories about how special children are treated?
6. Design a lesson for a special child with a learning disability. Demonstrate in your lesson how each of the approaches you used is also appropriate for mainstream children.
7. What is your opinion regarding the controversy surrounding attention deficit disorder (ADD) and attention deficit hyperactivity disorder (ADHD)?
8. How would you develop an alternative strategy for the special child that focused on the "wellness model"?

Field Experience Activities

1. Interview an experienced mainstream teacher and a special education teacher and ask how they feel education for the special learner has changed in the past few years. Specifically, ask them to focus their responses on:
   - How school policies and procedures regarding special education have changed in the past few years.
   - How their own role in the classroom has changed.
   - Whether education for the special learner has improved or regressed. (If they feel it has regressed, how would they propose to improve education for the special learner?)
2. Observe a regular education class that has special education children. View the class working on an

in-class assignment. As you move about the room focus on the following specific areas:
- The amount of time needed to complete assignments
- The attention span of the students with regard to the assignment
- How the teacher assists students
- If the differences in learning ability are a problem for the teacher
- How the teacher deals with differences in learning ability

For Further Reading

Armstrong, T. (1993). *7 kinds of smart: Identifying and developing your many intelligences.* New York: Plume, Penguin Group.

Barkley, R. A. (1990). *Hyperactive children: A handbook for diagnosis and treatment.* New York: Guilford Press.

Biedermann, J. (2005). ADHD: A selective overview. *Biological Psychiatry* 57: 1215–1220.

Davis, S. (2005). Schools where everyone belongs. Research Press. Available at: http://www.stopbullyingnow.com.

Delpit, L. (1995). *Other people's children: A practical guide for all educators who teach students with disabilities.* New York: New Press.

Ferguson, E. L. (1995). The real challenge of inclusion: Confessions of a "Rabid Inclusionist." *Phi Delta Kappan* 77 (4): 281–287.

Frankel, F. (1996). *Good friends are hard to find.* Glendale, CA: Perspective Publishing.

For Kidsake. (2006). Breaking through the myths. Available at: www.forkidsake.net/bully_myth_answer_sheet.htm.

Liebermann, L. (2001). The death of special education. *Education Week,* 60, 40–41.

Lipson, M. Y., and Wixson, K. K. (1991). *Assessment and instruction of reading disability: An interactive approach.* New York: HarperCollins.

National Research Council Report. (1998). Preventing reading difficulties in young children. *Academy Press,* 61, 80–83.

CHAPTER

Planning for Classroom Management

FOCUS POINTS

1. An effective teacher manages a classroom while an ineffective teacher disciplines a classroom.

2. A management strategy is developed over time through a process of trial and error.

3. The IOSIE method for analyzing student behavior problems is a key to developing a successful strategy.

4. Effective teachers have common characteristics.

5. Most behavior problems are caused because teachers fail to teach students how to follow procedures.

6. The most important person responsible for student achievement is the teacher.

CHAPTER OVERVIEW

THE PURPOSE OF THIS CHAPTER is to assist the reader in planning for effective classroom management. Classroom management is a powerful influence on student achievement, greater than students' general intelligence, home environment, motivation, or socioeconomic status (Wang, Haertel, and Walberg, 1993, 1994). What influence does diversity have on student achievement? We must ask some basic questions: Does diversity require different approaches to classroom management? Is there such a thing as culturally responsive classroom management? Should we examine the kinds of cultural conflicts that can arise in ethnically diverse classrooms? How can we as teachers become multiculturally competent? The IOSIE model (an acronym for Identification, Objectives, Solutions, Implement, Evaluation) is not a total solution to all management problems, but actually a frame of mind, more than a set of strategies or practices that guide management decisions. Teachers should reflect on how their culture influences their expectations for behavior and their interactions with students. Teachers must recognize that the ultimate goal of classroom management is not to achieve compliance or control but to provide all students with equitable opportunities for learning and to guide children in becoming self-disciplined. The goal of classroom management is to create an environment in which students behave appropriately, not out of fear of punishment or desire for reward, but out of a sense of personal responsibility.

CREATING A MANAGEMENT STRATEGY

How do you to develop a strategy for classroom management that will enhance order and discipline while it furthers learning? This question is of prime concern to teachers because there are always behavior problems in schools. The reason is simple enough—we are dealing with human beings, each of whom has a variety of problems. Fortunately, we all share the same psychological

PRACTICE EXERCISE 6.1

Classroom Management and Teacher Retention

Read the following proposal; analyze the arguments made for mandatory training in classroom management.

The Question

Does instruction in effective classroom management practices increase teacher retention and their students' performance?

Approximately one-half of all new teachers leave teaching within their first year of service. The statistics for turnover among new teachers are startling. Some 20 percent of all new hires leave the classroom within three years. In urban districts, the numbers are worse; close to 50 percent of newcomers flee the profession during the first five years of teaching (National Education Association, 2005). In New York City, 40 percent of teachers leave after three years, and 48 percent will be gone after five years, according to the United Federation of Teachers. Teachers say they are overwhelmed by expectations and the scope of the job. This is due in part to their inability to meet the stress of the job and inability to manage classes.

A typical list of why teachers say they leave always includes stress of disruptive students (Dunham, 1977). This is the most commonly cited reason given for leaving teaching. In one study of teachers in urban secondary schools, lack of discipline and motivation was the primary source of teacher stress and most significant predictor of burnout (Gonzalez, 1997). Brownell and colleagues (1995) identified new special education teachers' basic problem as an inability to provide instruction resulting from their inability to handle discipline. This coupled with the fact that their most common coping mechanisms were limited to trying to suppress problems and not resolve them. Abel and Sewell (1999) found that urban teachers attributed greater stress to student discipline and behavior problems than did rural teachers. Constant and increasing pressure on teachers has also made test accountability a primary cause of teacher stress. While it is true that the accountability movement has made teachers more directly accountable for test scores, it, and any reading of the total literature, must inevitably conclude that the preponderance of studies still point to lack of discipline and classroom management as the primary cause of teacher stress and burnout (Darling-Hammond and Sykes, 2003).

Hundreds of thousands of dollars can be saved annually by reducing teacher turnover. A school system with roughly 10,000 teachers and an estimated turnover rate of 20 percent would stand to save approximately $500,000 per year by reducing turnover by 1 percentage point (Benner, 2000).

Recently in Chicago 1,116 nontenured teachers struggling to control their classrooms were let go as of June 2005 (Rossi, 2005). More than half those bumped had problems with classroom management or teacher-pupil relationships, and nearly half struggled with instruction, according to the reasons checked off by principals, obtained by the *Chicago Sun-Times*.

Why Teachers Were Fired

Reasons checked by principals	Percent of fired teachers
Classroom failings (Management, teacher-pupil relationships)	55%
Poor instruction (Planning; methods; knowledge of subject)	46%
Lack of responsibility (Attendance; tardiness; professional judgment)	38%
Other	26%
Poor communication (Parent conferences, staff relations)	24%
Attitude (lack of cooperation, respect for others)	20%

Note: As of June 2006, 1,100 teachers have been dismissed.

Nearly one-half of all new teachers in our inner cities leave teaching within their first five years of service. Preservice and new teachers need well-designed and extensive clinical experience to prepare for the issues and challenges of effective teaching, particularly through their acquisition of classroom management skills (American Productivity and Quality Center, 2003). The nature of teacher preparation has changed tremendously. Fewer new teachers are prepared in traditional undergraduate programs, and more are being prepared in alternative certification and post-baccalaureate programs. To reverse the drain of teacher turnover we must provide professional development and on-site support in effective classroom management practices. Teacher loss causes a negative momentum that needs to be reversed if we as a nation are going to secure our future. This depressing situation can be reversed one teacher, one school, and one district at a time.

A recent article appeared in Education Week entitled "The Looming Teacher Surplus," which could be mistaken for an advertisement in support of this proposal. It stresses the importance of teacher support through professional development, highlighting classroom management and mentoring in effective instructional strategies (Edison Schools, August 8, 2006).

The Looming Teacher Surplus

Why is there a teacher shortage? The answer is because half our public school teachers leave the profession within five years. Nationally, twice as many people are trained to teach as are teaching. We all know what causes talented teachers to quit. And we all know what makes them twice as likely to stay: strong support from the principal and fellow teachers, timely help with classroom management, and thoughtful mentoring in effective teaching techniques.

Is there a way to ensure that teachers receive this kind of support? In a number of schools across the country, including many working in partnership with Edison, teachers have a professional development period each day in addition to planning time. This helps novice teachers to build confidence and master their craft.

If schools routinely built time into the day for professional development our teacher shortage just might become a surplus.

The core philosophy of the proposal is that learning to teach is a career-long, developmental process, and that teacher learning best occurs in collaborative environments. By developing in new teachers a focus on self-assessment and self-prescription with regard to effectively managing behavioral problems, teacher retention rates will increase and their students' academic achievement will improve. A corollary of this program is that teachers who master classroom management skills should raise student achievement by 20 percentile points (Marzano, Marzano, and Pickering, 2003). Seventy-seven percent of teachers in a recent poll claimed that if they could spend more time on instruction and less on dealing with disruptive students, achievement rates would improve (Public Agenda, 2004). This is substantiated by Johnson (2004) who reports that 40 percent of teachers spend more time on keeping order than on teaching.

A learning community created with an agenda such as one that tries to convince teachers they need a particular reading program, or one specific method of classroom management, will not work. If administrators have teachers meet primarily to learn about the mandates they need to follow, then the creation of a learning community will be stillborn. A learning community, such as the one envisioned in the proposal, is based on the assumption that developing faculty is a necessary condition for student, and school, improvement.

1. Why is there a need for instruction in classroom management?
2. Would teachers stay in the field if they were supported in behavioral and instructional management strategies?
3. Does instruction in effective classroom management practices increase teacher retention, and their students' performance? Explain your position.
4. Would merit pay based on student achievement help to retain teachers for more than five years? Explain your position.

needs, which can be addressed through understanding and by effective teaching.

An effective teacher manages her classroom while an ineffective teacher attempts to control a classroom. Control is not the problem; lack of procedures is. The key to good management is the teaching of procedures. Most behavior problems are due to a teacher's failure to instruct students on how to follow procedures. Correlation between good management and teacher effectiveness is evidenced by high student success (Marzano, Marzano, and Pickering, 2003). The only commonality among effective teachers is that they share a teaching personality that encourages student achievement.

The Basics of Behavior

The basics of behavior management can be seen in a research-based rationale that advocates four basic theoretical models of human behavior:

1. Behavioral (stimulus response)
2. Psychodynamic (emotional and guidance approach)
3. Environmental (looks at immediate environment)
4. Constructivist (emphasizes individual choice, which we all construct ourselves)

These models differ in the way they define causes and in the types of intervention they prescribe. To be understood, these models must be explored from the perspective of a general social systems theory in which people are influenced and defined by their surroundings and relationships (Danforth, 2000).

Behavioral Model Behaviorists hold that environmental variables dictate one's behaviors by external stimuli. For a behavior to be modified, interventions must use stimuli such as reinforcers, or rewards. A behavior modification plan based on this model involves

1. Selecting the specific behavior to be changed.
2. Choosing and introducing an appropriate reinforcer.
3. Monitoring the behavior.

Psychodynamic (Guidance) Model This model is a guidance model that looks primarily inside the child. It views behavior as reflective of internal feelings and conflicts and emotions as generated by human behavior. The role of the teacher is to help to develop student self-esteem, personal insight, self-control, and social skills. The model consists of two basic steps, (1) counseling techniques and (2) behavior-influencing techniques.

Environmental Model This model focuses on working with (or helping to develop) the positive aspects of a child's immediate environments (home, school, and neighborhood). The model purports that the way a person lives influences his behavior. The key is to fashion the environment to match the personality and needs of the child. Organization of the environment centers on three points: (1) time, (2) physical space, and (3) patterns of human interaction.

Constructivist Model This model stems from the work of Piaget and others (see Chapter 2). It is based on the assumption that individuals construct their own knowledge based on their schemata of existing beliefs. When viewed from the perspective of classroom management, all of a student's experiences give meaning to his or her actions. The knowledge that has been constructed to cause these actions (behavior) is not fixed and can be modified or changed based on additional experiences. The development of classroom codes of behavior mutually agreed upon is essential to the success of this model. When using this model one has five essential concerns:

1. The qualities of (dis)connectedness, (dis)unity, and (un)caring within the community where the problem occurred
2. How a lack of connectedness, unity, and caring encourages the problem
3. Whether the child feels respected and loved within the community (If not, why?)
4. How power is used within the group
5. Whether connectedness, unity, and caring can be improved

Types and Causes of Misbehavior

Generally speaking, there are approximately five types of misbehavior—moral, personal, legal, safety, and educational. Moral pertains to "sins" such as lying, stealing, cheating, and the like. Personal misbehavior has to do with one's inappropriate actions with others or themselves. Legal and safety issues concern such items as violence, fighting, and endangering one's well-being. These first four types of misbehavior relate best to guidance approaches, while the fifth relates to effective teaching.

The *causes of misbehavior* can be placed in five categories: (1) *Frustration* is in the faces of children unable to comprehend a lesson due to (2) *Ignorance*. (3) *Conflict* results from failure to meet academic or psychological needs. (4) *Displacement*, the most difficult to assess, occurs when a misbehavior is aimed at someone not immediately related to the problem. For example, a child reacts negatively to men who have beards. (5) *Rule breaking* is the cause of many acts of misbehavior.

Analyzing Behavioral Problems: An Overview of the IOSIE Method

The IOSIE method is a five-step rational process for looking at and reflecting upon solutions for behavioral classroom problems. Each letter indicates the steps to follow when analyzing misbehavior in classrooms. The process requires one to *identify* causes of misconduct, determine *objectives*, and propose *solutions*. *Implementation* provides an opportunity to *evaluate* the executed solutions. Its purpose is to assist teachers in resolving classroom management problems. The method draws heavily upon well-known classroom management strategies, while encouraging readers to create a template for one's own management strategy. Figure 6.1 provides a brief outline of the method.

Identifying the Problem Problem behavior analysis is something all teachers have to master. The procedure is unchanging; one cannot fix what is not recognized as broken. The process is not as simple as it might at first seem, however. Do not be deceived by appearances or biases when attempting to identify the cause of a problem (Danforth, 2000). A male child who is arguing with a female student may not be the instigator of misbehavior. Children who are talking loudly are not intentionally being disruptive; and a student who is threatening another student is not necessarily the culprit. Do not jump to conclusions.

In classrooms, a problem only exists if it impinges negatively on learning. The teacher must assess the seriousness and weigh the problem's impact on student learning. Acting-out behaviors, such as threatening, loud talking, arguing, and fighting are problems that must be addressed immediately, while incomplete assignments, absences, sloppy work, and lost books—though readily identifiable problems—can wait to be resolved. Incidents such as cheating, slander, theft, or safety that involve moral codes or physical well-being must also be remedied immediately.

Problems concerning withdrawn behaviors, inattention, depression, drug or alcohol use indicate a desire to flee from reality and must be dealt with expeditiously. It should be understood that most misbehavior is caused by frustration, ignorance, conflict, displacement, or misunderstanding rules and procedures. The reasons for misbehavior can be identified as the desire to achieve one of four immediate goals: attention, power, revenge, or avoiding failure. But above all, the teacher must decide what constitutes a problem (Mager, 1997; Glasser, 1990, 1997).

Objectives Teachers are fortunate when it comes to objectives. In classroom behavioral situations two objectives always remain the same: to facilitate learning and encourage self-discipline. All other objectives relate directly to identifying problems. Objectives describe, in measurable terms, the behaviors needed to attain the desired results within a specific period—for example, Billy will complete all ten incomplete assignments satisfactorily by the end of the semester.

Objectives are specific statements of a learner's behavior. They are the outcomes one wishes to obtain within a specific time limit. They can also be described as statements that answer two questions:

What do I want my students to know?
How will I know if my students understand?

Good objectives show learners what is expected, minimum standards, and how the work will be done. They are explicit, quantifiable, and achievable within a specific time frame.

Solutions One of the keys to the IOSIE process is selection of strategy. The steps though not rigid should be followed in sequence. The method presumes that there are three generic approaches to solutions for classroom misbehavior: a consequence, group guidance, and a guidance approach. A consequence approach such as *assertive discipline* (Canter, 1976) implies consequences for improper actions. A group guidance approach such as *judicious discipline* (Gathercoal, 1993) encourages classes to establish rules to prevent inappropriate actions. Finally, a guidance approach such as *reality therapy* (Glasser, 1999), in which the teacher counsels the offender, encourages students to take ownership of problems. The purpose of each strategy is to help students develop self-discipline and responsibility for their actions. A good strategy must be comprehensive and contain in its design components both a preventive and

Figure 6.1 IOSIE Analysis Method

> *Identification of the problem* enables you to clearly describe the problems in different ways while remaining true to the facts. The "I" represents the first step in the process, to identify and assess the problem.
>
> *Objectives* are reflected upon and determined as a situation evolves. The "O" stands for the objectives that you wish to achieve through your intervention.
>
> *Solutions* are determined based on the theory or theories of management appropriate for the particular case. The "S" stands for the solution, which should be the result of the plan you put into effect to achieve your objectives.
>
> *Implement* a plan of action that clearly describes short- and long-term interventions. The "I" indicates the implementation of your plan and the procedures followed by the people involved.
>
> *Evaluation* of plan involves assessing success of your actions. The acronym concludes with the letter "E" that stands for your evaluation and reflection on results.
>
> *Source:* Scarpaci (2007)

intervention procedure. The ideal is to prevent problems before they occur.

Implementation The most difficult step is the actual implementation. Putting solutions into action is not simply a "just do it" sequence. Basic questions must be addressed before implementation:

1. Who is to implement the solution?
2. How do you get the cooperation and support of everyone involved?
3. How long do you expect it will take before a positive result is accomplished?
4. What happens if your solution does not work?

The answers to the first two questions are easy when the teacher is the implementer. They only become difficult when support and cooperation of parents, staff, and outside professionals need to be elicited. The third question (the amount of time necessary for success) depends on the severity of the problem, the objectives set, and the resistance met. Also to be considered are the personalities of all involved parties. The only way to resolve the final question is to try a different approach to the problem. When these four questions are satisfactorily answered, a guide to evaluation is created.

Evaluation Assessment of results is often forgotten, ignored, or done incorrectly by teachers. The easiest way to evaluate is to look at your objectives. Are they specific, measurable, and attainable within a defined time frame? Outcomes are wishes achieved within an explicit period and should be easily recognizable and readily assessable. The basic premise of any evaluation is to determine if one achieved what one set out to achieve. If the success lasts for only a brief time then the solution was not appropriate. For example, a child who no longer fights at lunchtime now fights after school. Obviously, something is wrong with this picture. If the results are not positive, the whole process must be looked at. Was the problem really identified? Were the objectives attainable in the time span anticipated? Was the proposed solution achievable and appropriate for the objectives? Was the implementation done correctly? Are you sure you did not succeed, even partially?

Sample Case Studies and IOSIE Analysis

Let's look at three case studies, one for each of the basic approaches, beginning with a case study that lends itself to a consequence strategy that might afford positive results if implemented properly.

Consequence Approach Billy Williams, a seventeen-year-old in your twelfth-grade mathematics class, has been accused in an unsigned note of extorting lunch money from his classmates. Billy has a prior record of supposed misdeeds. One specifically, though never proven, was when he was blamed for the recent rash of drug activity outside of the school grounds. Billy's misdeeds have never been proven, since no one has stood up and charged Billy with any specific misbehavior. Essentially, he lives under a cloud of suspicion. There are a few who believe that Billy is innocent of any major wrongdoing. You have spoken to Billy on numerous occasions about his lack of class work, homework, and general deportment during your class, with little or no results. He claims he doesn't know why everyone thinks he's a criminal, since he never did anything wrong. When you ask about his homework, he again changes the subject by confiding to you that even the principal, Mr. Wormock, has threatened him for no reason. He believes people dislike him because he is an African American, and therefore make up false rumors.

His classmates as well as most of the student body at Grover High where you teach are in deathly fear of Billy due to his physical size and menacing presence. There are rumors that he has been in fights after school. A colleague tells you that you also have reason to fear for your own safety. Recently, Ms. Kumar's tires were slashed, and she believes the slashing was retaliation for her failing Billy for the first quarter of the semester. You were also expecting to fail Billy before this morning's incident, when Billy came to you and explained that he had to pass your class in order to graduate. He pleaded with you to give him a break and pass him, saying that if you didn't his parents had would kick him out of their house when he turned eighteen.

IOSIE Analysis Using a Consequence Approach

Identify the Problem What exactly is the problem in this case? Is it the unsigned note claiming that Billy is extorting money? Is it Billy's prior record of misdeeds? Is it Billy's lack of class work, homework, and poor deportment? Is it Billy's charge of racial bias on the part of those who dislike him? Is it the fights after school or Billy's menacing demeanor? Could it be Ms. Kumar's belief that you are in danger because she thinks Billy slashed her tires for failing him the first quarter? Alternatively, could it be the problem Billy presented to you this morning when he said his parents would throw him out of their house if he did not graduate?

Clearly, it is not always easy to determine the problem in any given situation. There are usually a number of problems. Let's look at the potential problems we identified and place them in some type of priority order. A past record of unproven misdeeds and unsigned accusations should go to the bottom of any list of potential problems. Rumors regarding one's behavior outside of school are usually just unconfirmed gossip. Billy's size and someone's unfounded accusation regarding slashed tires is not your problem. Billy's belief that he is the butt of racial prejudice is certainly a concern. It is not necessarily a problem that you face with him, since he has confided in you. Billy's academic performance and poor deportment are the immediate problem that you face. His feelings regarding prejudice should also be addressed as a long-term problem.

Objectives Once the problem has been identified, you have to determine what your objectives should be. What is it exactly that you want Billy to do? In this case, it would appear, based on your identification of the problem, that you would expect Billy to improve his academic performance and his general behavior in your class for the remainder of the school term. With regard to his personal feelings of "racial bias" you should refer Billy to the appropriate support personnel within your school, likely the school guidance counselor or school psychologist. If these personnel are not available, the principal should be notified so that outside assistance might be sought.

Solutions The solution to this problem should go back to how you can most easily achieve your objective. It seems that Billy himself handed the answer to this dilemma to you by telling you of a consequence he did not wish to face, being thrown out of his parent's house. This consequence must be corroborated in order to implement your solution.

Implementation Once you have confirmed with his parents that they have spoken to Billy, you are then ready to implement your solution for your immediate problem of getting Billy to improve academically and behaviorally. Even though the consequence is outside of your control you should offer to assist Billy in avoiding the consequence. Provide tutorial assistance and advise him on exactly the way you expect him to behave in your class. You should also arrange with the guidance counselor for Billy to be counseled with regard to his feelings of prejudice.

Evaluation Your self-assessment of the results in this case study should be easy to recognize. Did you achieve what you set out to do in the time frame you set up? Did Billy's academic performance and behavior improve incrementally by the end of the term as a result of the consequence that he was faced with? It is important to remember that there should be interim evaluations prior to the final assessment. This affords you the opportunity to fine-tune your solution or change direction if it is not working at all. If the answer to the question of his academic success was Yes, congratulations—your solution worked. If the answer was No, then you should go back to your solution and attempt a different approach.

Guidance Approach Sara Ramirez, a thirteen-year-old girl in your eighth-grade social studies class, drops her coat and books wherever she chooses, totally disregarding the comfort of her fellow class members. Students have complained to you but seem to be fearful of addressing Sara directly. Sara comes from a privileged one-parent family in which she has always been the apple of her father's eye. Sara stays with her elderly grandmother when her father is away on business trips, which seems to be most of the time. Sara boasts that she can come and go as she pleases. Sara's mother is fighting for custody but she is having a difficult time due to her past drug and mental hygiene problems.

Sara is an average student with definite adolescent tendencies. She is physically mature for her age, dressing way beyond her years, yet at times she acts like a child. She constantly discards her refuse by placing it on a neighbor's desk when she believes no one is looking or throwing it on the floor when they are. She is the first to push her way into the wardrobe at dismissal to retrieve her coat. She likes to push other students' chairs about the room, creating obstructions so that her classmates have difficulty finding their seats. Sara constantly laughs at the discomfort she creates for her classmates. She teases the boys, and then complains that they are bothering her. During class she is always calling out and gets angry when she is not called on. As a result, her class work has deteriorated. You have spoken to her and warned her that her grade will suffer if she continues being disruptive in class. Sara in true adolescent fashion "yeses you to death," and continues to misbehave.

IOSIE Analysis Using a Guidance Approach

Identify the Problem Is the problem Sara's apparent disregard for her classmates? Is it that she appears to be a physically mature child with less than adequate supervision? Is her grandmother too old and her father too distant? Is she reacting to her mother's attempt to gain custody? Could she just be a mean-spirited child or are there deeper meanings for her antisocial behavior? Is the real problem the deterioration of her grades?

Again, this case study is overburdened with potential problems. Remember, this child's specific actions—throwing papers, pushing, teasing the boys, laughing at others, and calling out—are really not the problem but indications that there *is* a problem. Which problems should you address? The key is to prioritize. Is the first role of a teacher to see that her students are learning? In this case, Sara's grades have fallen so that her academic needs must be considered. Sara's family life seems to be unstable and for an adolescent uncontrollable. Emotional problems are rampant throughout this case description. But her immediate problem is to improve her grades. The question is how you attempt to do that while Sara is facing so many emotional problems at home that are manifesting themselves in her actions at school.

Objectives Your objectives are in two interrelated areas: improvement of academic standing and emotional well-being. Your objective would be to have Sara improve her grades before the end of the marking period. A second and concomitant objective would be to help guide Sara through the emotional upheaval in her young life.

Solution The objectives are easy to establish but the resolution for Sara may be much more difficult. A guidance approach on your part requires a caring, positive relationship with the child. You may want to have a private "heart to heart" in which you encourage Sara to confide in you. You should also explain to Sara that her grades are a major part of her life and must improve. The rationale here is that with guidance Sara could learn to deal with her family environment, which would allow her to work at bettering her studies. Her disruptive behavior and antisocial actions in class should stop of their own accord. Once Sara accepts responsibility for her actions and understands that she cannot necessarily change the actions of others, she will be on the path to understanding her problems. Once she understands that she is responsible for choosing her own behavior, she will be better able to deal with the problems she faces.

Implementation In this case study, the implementation is much more difficult than it was in the previous study. Here, the teacher is expected to assume the role of guide and mentor, roles that not all are suited for. Even if you were suited, the time needed would take away from your primary classroom duties. You would therefore have to seek the assistance of the guidance counselor and involve the family. Most likely, the counselor would suggest family counseling as well as individual sessions with Sara. Your role would remain as guide and mentor but your actual functions would be lessened.

Evaluation When using a guidance approach, assessment of objectives should be ongoing. Emotional problems can be readily inflamed, especially when parents are fighting over custody. Your evaluation of success would be focused on Sara's academic studies and classroom behavior. The counselor should keep you informed about the steps she is taking to service the child and family. The same cooperation and communication must be established with any outside counseling that might occur. In this case, a positive report card would indicate movement in the proper direction.

Group Guidance Approach Third grader Abdul Hussein cries continually during your class. He complains that everyone is picking on him because of his religious beliefs and because he is Arabic. Abdul's behavior has gone from being cooperative and practically docile, to sulking, and at times raging at his classmates. Recently Abdul's classwork has gone from exceptional to abysmal. You have never seen any of the incidents, though they have been graphically described by Abdul and just as vocally denied by his classmates. The incidents described consist of stolen or spoiled lunches, torn textbook pages, missing homework, and obscene drawings in Abdul's notebooks. Abdul further claims that the other children claim he is responsible for 9/11. Abdul cries when he tells you that his uncle was killed in the World Trade Center while working at his job. He implies that the children call him a liar and they blaspheme his faith. Abdul's parents have complained to you and request that you do something to stop the harassment of their son.

The president of the parents' association, whose son is also in your class, claims that her child thinks Abdul is a compulsive liar and is just acting the way he does to get your attention. She also claims that someone had been destroying other children's property in the class and she believes it was Abdul. Other class parents agree with her. The situation comes to a head when you see the children fighting in the schoolyard at lunchtime. The children claim that Abdul attacked them when they said they would not play with him, spitting at them and calling them dirty names.

IOSIE Analysis Using a Group Guidance Approach

Identify the Problem Is the problem Abdul's constant crying and whining during class time? Is it the charges of bias toward Abdul's religion and ethnicity? Is it the multitude of incidents in which Abdul's property has been despoiled? On the other hand, is it Abdul's academic performance? There seems to be a clear link between Abdul's academic performance and the incidents, real or imaginary, that have occurred recently. These incidents appear to have been motivated by group racial bias. In this case study, there are three distinct and interrelated problems that must be addressed: academic performance, racial and religious issues, and physical incidents of misbehavior.

Objectives Your first objective is to have Abdul return to doing his superior academic work, while simultaneously educating the class about racial and religious bias, as well as eliminating incidents of violence and vandalism. If the first two objectives are achieved, the incidents will also end. The physical episodes are a direct result of the apparent racial intolerance that seems to have infected the class.

Solution The solution is based on dealing with the question of group tolerance. Guide the class to solve the problem by using a group guidance exercise. Prepare the class by having them read a children's version of *The Diary of Anne Frank* at home with their parents. Read it aloud to the class during a block of instructional time set aside specifically for this purpose. The project requires dividing the class into two groups by drawing straws out of a hat. The groups comprise those with red circles and those with green circles, which the children must prominently display on their clothing. The children with the red circles are to make all of the class rules, which must be obeyed by all green-circle children. Focus the class by establishing the first three rules:

1. Green-circle children must never line up before a red-circle child at entrance, dismissal, or lunchtime; they must always walk at the back of the line.
2. Green-circle children must keep their heads lower than red-circle children at all times and never look them in the eyes.
3. In any discussion between circle children, the red-circle children will always be considered to be right.

At the end of the experiment (no more than two days) the class will evaluate the impact and the result of creating an intolerant society in which there are rulers and second-class citizens. They will be asked to describe their feelings with regard to injustice and intolerance.

Implementation To implement a scenario as just described takes the cooperation and support of parents, administration, and various mental health providers. The purpose of the exercise should be explained to parents and be supported by the school administration. Mental health providers such as the school guidance counselor, school psychologist, and outside anti-deformation organizations should be involved.

Evaluation Assessments when dealing with mental health problems can only be made by evaluating the end product. What did the children describe as their feelings? Did the class want to continue the project? Have the incidents stopped and has Abdul stopped crying and been allowed to rejoin the class? If the exercise achieves all its objectives, it is a success.

It should be noted that a group guidance approach is fraught with potential for manipulation. It is not necessary to be objective when dealing with a situation as described in this case. One should, however, realize that as human beings we do not see resolutions through the same looking-glass. Children must be given the opportunity to develop their critical thinking abilities if we are to function as a democratic society. A democratic classroom is the single best precursor for a free and democratic nation.

Conclusion The IOSIE management model is essentially a commonsense way for analyzing student behavioral problems. A user-friendly approach provides a framework for teachers to use in resolving the multitude of management problems faced every day. The mnemonic IOSIE applied properly acts as a rubric for guiding teacher actions needed to resolve student behavioral problems. The method provides teachers a strategy to analyze and resolve common, and some not so common, behavioral problems.

Twelve Beliefs That Lead to Effective Management Strategies

Standard teaching practice can be viewed through a prism consisting of twelve beliefs that lead to effective classroom management. These constructs come from a combination of traditional strategies and take the form of an eclectic toolbox approach to management. Three generalized areas offer a foundation for creating an effective management strategy.

1. *Behaviors* are a composite of psychological beliefs, skills, and practices that satisfy student needs, which effective teachers exhibit in common.
2. *Understandings* support the realization that self-discipline is the prime objective for managing students. Teachers who accept responsibility for both student success and shortcomings encourage development of student internal controls and academic success.
3. *Strategies* in the third component area lead to specific management approaches such as the IOSIE method.

These twelve constructs center on qualities that allow the possessor to use specific tactics and methods to manage classrooms. Tactics differ from strategies in that they are short-term and used during classroom episodes, while strategies are long-term plans focused on how to deliver instruction. Methods in this scenario become the fundamental constructs behind how to manage instruction and behavior. They also form the theoretical beliefs used in developing the IOSIE method of behavioral analysis (Scarpaci, 2007). Putting these behaviors, understandings, and strategies into practice establishes the teacher as an effective classroom manager.

Twelve Beliefs of Effective Teachers

Behaviors
1. *Effective classroom teachers have a teaching personality that enables them to bring to their classrooms beliefs, skills, and practices that discourage misbehavior and enhance learning.* They share characteristics that set them apart (Haberman, 2004): persistence, physical and emotional stamina, caring relationships with students,

commitment to acknowledging and appreciating student effort, willingness to admit mistakes, focus on in-depth learning, commitment to inclusion, and organizational skills. They are not judgmental or moralistic. They respond as professionals to situations and listen to what students and parents say to them.

2. *Effective teachers understand the need to master content, the importance of management and pedagogical methods, and the need for high student expectations, as well as having a teaching personality that successfully engages their students.* There are basic areas of competence that effective teachers all master. Each requires a commitment and self-confidence. By reinforcing positive behaviors and highlighting content mastery, teachers make learning possible. By changing focus from coverage of curriculum to the student, a learning paradigm for accomplishment is created. Good management, lessons designed for mastery, effective assignments and accurate assessments are the qualities that fuel success. Teacher competence can be measured qualitatively and quantitatively by student achievement. Competence may be evidenced differently from teacher to teacher but not the end result, student success. Teacher competence results in student learning.
    - Foster learning by encouraging positive attitudes and relationships.
    - Master a knowledge of subject matter until it is part of one's being.
    - Understand developmental stages as the psychological basis for student development.
    - Master presentation skills in order to facilitate student learning.

3. *Effective teachers apply positive, rather than negative, discipline. Effective teachers manage classrooms; ineffective teachers punish students.* The role of the effective teacher is to manage classrooms with care and understanding, while creating an open, warm, nurturing environment that allows less opportunity or incentive for misbehavior to occur (Scarpaci, 2007).

4. *Effective teachers meet students' psychological needs.* These needs include love and acceptance that are created in classrooms with warm and caring environments. They need to feel a part of a learning community with time for fun and laughter. When students' psychological needs for belonging, power, freedom, and fun are met in this way, learning is enhanced and misbehavior discouraged (Glasser, 1986, 1998).

Understandings

5. **Discipline can be positive or negative.** We demonstrate positive discipline by showing interest in our students' well-being. By focusing on remediating social-skill deficits, and by addressing classroom survival skills, we encourage positive discipline in our students (Scarpaci, 2006). This also occurs when teachers are respectful of student feelings, and friendship-making skills (Goldstein and McGinnis, 1997a, b).

6. *The goal of positive discipline is self-discipline (internal control). Teachers should look toward teaching for self-discipline.* Duckworth and Seligman (2006) encourage teachers to model appropriate study practices and priorities for students. Help students develop reasonable schedules for study, as well as explain how to study and where to get help when needed. Teachers are asked to persuade students to defer gratification while celebrating their academic success.

7. *The number-one problem in classrooms is not discipline but lack of procedures and teachers' unwillingness to take responsibility for their students' learning.* Teachers have a sense of responsibility if they accept credit for students' academic success as well as their shortcomings. Responsible teachers do not blame students for failing grades or low test scores. They don't fault students for lack of effort or poor family academic background; responsible teachers attribute most of the poor results to their own efforts and behavior. Their responsibility demonstrates their commitment to facilitate learning (Gossen, 1993).

8. *Students choose their behavior, and teachers choose their management style.* A recent study (Logerfo, 2006) of a nationally representative sample of first graders and their teachers suggests that teachers who have a management style that takes personal responsibility for student learning can improve student achievement; specifically, children with teachers who have a greater sense of responsibility for student outcomes learn more in reading during the first grade.

Strategies

9. *There are three approaches to resolving behavioral issues; a consequence approach, a group-guidance approach, and an individual-guidance approach.* In resolving classroom management problems there is usually more than one specific solution: the idea is to address the immediate problem while furthering a student's movement toward self-discipline. Effective management is both preventive and interventional, and uses one or more of the three generic approaches to resolve behavioral incidents.

10. *To determine causality we must understand the different categories, types, and causes of misbehavior.* There are two categories of misbehavior: acting out and withdrawal. They are fairly easy to recognize. Fighting, swearing, complaining, destroying, stealing, and sexual promiscuity could not be mistaken for

withdrawal behaviors such as not paying attention, threatening suicide, skipping school, being depressed, daydreaming, getting sick, abusing drugs and alcohol. The types of misbehavior teachers deal with can usually be classified among one of five overlapping areas: moral, personal, legal, safety, or educational. The causes of misbehavior can be traced to their frustration, ignorance, conflict, displacement, or rules. Students misbehave to achieve one of four immediate goals; attention, power, revenge, and avoiding failure (Dreikurs and Grey, 1968; Dreikurs et al., 1982).

11. *Individuals are an accumulation of choices and experiences. The IOSIE method allows for an analysis of student behavioral problems based on experiences and trial and error.* Teachers are free to decide on specific strategies. The five steps in the IOSIE process empower teachers by affording them an opportunity to reflect upon the actions needed to rectify any given episode.

12. *A management toolbox consists of generic strategies: (1) authoritarian, (2) tolerant/permissive, (3) instructional/eclectic, (4) group-guidance, (5) socioemotional/guidance, and specific classic management models such as assertive discipline, judicial discipline, and choice theory.* Understanding these generic strategies empowers teachers to deal with practically any behavioral misdeed.

MANAGEMENT STRATEGIES THAT FACILITATE INSTRUCTION

Effective classroom management is essentially a gestalt, made up of a number of interdependent components to be successful. It needs to implement, and provide effective instructional practices with, an engaging curriculum. It also requires a teacher's ability to work with anger, projections, frustration, resistance, conflict, stress, and depression. Further, it must have high expectations while becoming a model for effective classroom management approaches, strategies and practices. If we neglect any of these components, the process is compromised, causing a further need for effective behavior management.

Classroom management has been defined as a four-stage analytic pluralistic process, in which the teacher specifies desirable conditions, analyzes existing conditions, uses management strategies, and assesses effectiveness (Cooper, 1999). This management process leads to a general categorizing of behavioral strategies.

Authoritarian strategies generally rely on enforcing rules to obtain classroom control. Tactics include mild desists, soft reprimands, control through proximity, isolation, or exclusion from class or school. The basic assumption is that the teacher is responsible for controlling the conduct of students (Canter, 1976). An authoritarian strategy is closely related to behavior modification theory, which holds that all behaviors are learned through stimulus and response.

Permissive strategies allow students the freedom to make their own decisions. The teacher encourages students' free expression. Students are assumed responsible for their own conduct.

Eclectic strategies stress a trial-and-error approach to management. Teachers tend to develop remedies that have worked for them in managing classes. The traditional positive reinforcement, rewards, and consequences are examples of eclectic practice (Goodlad, 1994). An eclectic strategy's basic assumption is that teachers can manage by using "tried and true" prescriptions.

Instructional strategies rely on the belief that good lessons prevent management problems. Effective momentum management theory provides rationale for this approach (Kounin, 1977). Good lessons, routines, and clear directions create positive class environments when combined with sensitivity to student needs.

Guidance strategies are rooted in counseling and clinical psychology theory. They advance a belief that positive teacher–student relationships lead to effective management and instruction. Ginott's (1993) ideas regarding effective communication and Dreikurs' (1968) concepts concerning logical consequences and democratic process are the rationale for this practice. The offshoot of individual guidance practice is its natural extension to groups, the idea being that the whole class works toward resolution of problems. One major caution with this strategy is that the teacher must be knowledgeable to group needs and must not use group meetings as trials for student infractions.

MINI CASE FROM THE FIELD

The following case from the field discusses the use of appropriate management strategies when dealing with core values. The strategies and methods proposed focus on meeting the needs of the child and the teacher. Read the case and compare the ideas presented to the reality of everyday classroom life.

Cheating

Margaret was distressed because a boy she had befriended had cheated in her class. Mohammed had plagiarized his midyear research paper. This was the first time she had caught a student cheating. Margaret felt hurt; she had expected better of him. She had been grading his paper when she came across a sentence that surprised her. It just did not fit in with what she had read up to that point. The sentence made proper use of the word "empower," whereas in the previous paragraph the term had been used to describe the embarkation of marginalized people as empowerment.

She had read further and found changes in usage and writing style. Inane ones followed well-written paragraphs. Margaret picked one unusual sentence entered it into an Internet search engine. She found the sentence, word for word, punctuation mark for punctuation mark. It became obvious the entire paper had been plagiarized. This incident greatly disturbed Margaret. She had failed to model a basic core value, honesty.

Margaret told Jane Hemmings about her feelings. Jane was a wonderful listener who usually would empathize. After hearing Margaret retell the episode, Jane responded by saying, "So what? Boys will be boys. Just by you catching him, you taught him a lesson. There is no need to go any further. Just have him reflect on his actions and promise never to plagiarize again. The key to solving behavioral problems is to first identify the problem and use a dab of logic, with a bit of strategy."

"What are you talking about? The boy plagiarized a paper—doesn't he need to be punished? How can I teach him it is wrong to cheat?"

Ed Child and Nicholas Saccone both overheard the discussion. Ed piped in, "You have two choices. Be either authoritarian or permissive. You can punish or let it go, and chalk it up to experience. I would suggest you report him to the principal, as well as inform his parents.

"What kind of a solution is that?" said Nick. "Punishment only creates resentment. The only thing he will learn is not to get caught the next time. Why don't you use the IOSIE method to deal with this problem?" Nick explained that the letters stood for an acronym that identified steps to follow when analyzing behavioral problems. The problem was cheating and the solution was to stop it. The question was, how.

Nick asked everyone what their objectives were for teaching. Margaret replied for all, saying she expected each child to learn and develop self-discipline.

"You realize those words are a teacher's prayer for instructional outcomes, don't you?" said Nick. "Your immediate problem, however, is to eliminate cheating. I would suggest that you provide some type of consequence followed up by some guidance. I would even work on a whole-class lesson on cheating. The decision is yours, Margaret."

1. Describe Margaret's problem. Is it as simple as a child plagiarizing?
2. Explain Jane's arguments made to Margaret. What was Jane trying to say?
3. Compare and contrast the positions put forth by Ed and Jane. Is there any room for compromise?
4. How was Nick's solution different from Jane's or Ed's arguments?
5. If you were Margaret, what action would you take? Would you use a consequence approach, a group-guidance approach, a guidance approach, or a combination of various approaches?

MANAGEMENT MODELS

Management approaches and models can be arranged along a spectrum from least to most teacher control. They can be further categorized in terms of basic focus; that is, whether they fall under a consequences, individual guidance, or group-guidance management approach. When organized in this fashion they comprise a matrix of management strategies that can be fitted to individual situations and individual management styles.

The discussion of management approaches and models rests on the belief that management style reflects one's teaching personality. A practitioner whose style is primarily teacher dominant might choose to use a consequences approach to management, with a strong level of teacher control, while a teacher comfortable sharing control with her students might tend to focus on a group-guidance approach, utilizing a low level of teacher control. Each approach has as its goal the maximization of learning in the classroom as well as the development of self-discipline. Each approach has inherent strengths and weaknesses, which should be understood first. Strategies can be used separately or together as the teacher sees fit. Most teachers will find it beneficial to use a trial-and-error, eclectic approach; if one strategy fails, another takes its place, and the process continues until positive development is recorded (Scarpaci, 2007).

So far, we have discussed approaches for analyzing misbehavior and reviewed basic management practices used in correcting deviant behavior. We understand that management style is related to teaching personality and that management models can be classified into three generic categories: *consequence, group guidance,* and *guidance models*. Many models could have been chosen as examples, but here we have decided to describe two classic models for each category. (Note: For a more developed analysis see Scarpaci, 2007.)

Consequence Models

A consequence approach to classroom management is based on the understanding that teachers must exert strong control over children to create an environment in which learning can occur. All teachers need control within their classrooms. The question is, How much teacher control benefits the classroom, and how is that control to be achieved? The two models used as examples here have a behaviorist, consequences orientation that sees the teacher as facilitating all actions related to classroom management. Students are acted upon, not with. The models are labeled consequences models because they utilize, to varying degrees, teacher-initiated consequences for both negative and positive behavior. There is relatively little, if any, individual guidance advocated. These two classic models can be effectively applied to a variety of classroom situations. *Assertive discipline* and the *Jones model* both reflect the common belief that students need to be controlled by teachers in order to have well managed classrooms.

Assertive Discipline Model Lee and Marlene Canter's (1976, 2001) **assertive discipline** model focuses on training parents and teachers in the use of assertive disciplinary techniques. Teachers insist on proper behavior from students, recognizing and supporting them when they practice such behavior and using well-organized procedures for following through when children do not behave. Assertive discipline is a system in which negative consequences are consistently meted out for rule infractions. Rules are determined by the teacher or other school personnel and must be obeyed; they are nonnegotiable. Consequences increase in severity with repeated incidents of misbehavior. Teachers are encouraged to enlist the help of parents and principal in attempting behavior modification. Teachers use a system of positive reinforcements or rewards, such as praise and extra credit, to encourage good behavior.

The rationale for the model is that teachers insist on decent, responsible behavior from their students because students need this, parents want it, the community expects it. Teachers cannot be effective in an undisciplined classroom. Teachers are ineffective when they fail to maintain adequate classroom discipline and firm control. When maintained correctly control is not inhuman or stifling, contrary to generally held beliefs. Positive behavior results in positive academic performance.

The Canters claim their position centers around student and teacher rights. Teachers' rights include establishing an optimal learning environment and expecting appropriate behavior from students. Teachers also have the right to receive help from administrators and parents when it is needed. Students' rights include a safe and productive learning environment. Students have the right to a full understanding of the teacher's behavioral expectations, and of the consequences that will follow good and bad choices. Critics claim that the approach fosters dependence on the teacher as a determiner of good and bad behavior, and is thus authoritarian, but the Canters counter that carefully defined limits and expectations free children to learn. The teacher is at all times attentive to what is in the best interests of the student, and is expected to take a systemic approach to behavior management based on the beliefs and skills most associated with effectiveness in the classroom. Marzano, Marzano, and Pickering (2003) argue that assertive discipline should "employ a balance of negative and positive consequences as opposed to negative consequences only," which encourages children to choose appropriate behavior. Assertive discipline utilizes five basic procedures:

1. Determine negative consequences for noncompliance and positive consequences for appropriate behavior.
2. Identify your expectations. Draw a clear line between appropriate and inappropriate behavior.
3. Stress why positive behavior is necessary.
4. Persist in reinforcing expectations, using a firm tone of voice and maintaining eye contact. Use nonverbal gestures that clearly convey intention.
5. Be assertive in confrontations with students over behavior, reminding them of expectations, and consequences, without hostility or threats. Make sure the established consequences are consistently enforced.

The Canters advocate the use of teacher assertiveness in setting clear limits and determining consequences. An assertive discipline plan explicitly defines expectations. Nonassertive teachers take a passive approach to teaching in which expectations are unvoiced, and then become hostile when these expectations go unmet. Hostile teachers react to misbehavior in a counterproductive way, often blaming the students when the fault lies in their failure to manage the class. A hostile teacher tends to be abrasive and sarcastic with students, alienating students and further eroding the learning process. The assertive teacher responds to misbehavior in a calm, firm manner. She has a discipline plan with clearly stated rules and consequences that provide positive recognition. Students who comply are positively reinforced, whereas those who disobey rules or directions receive negative reinforcement.

When to Use Assertive discipline can be used at any time the teacher needs to gain control of the classroom. This model appeals most to teachers who believe that the classroom is their domain; students play by the teacher's rules. It supports the inherent beliefs of those who see classroom management as the job of the teacher alone. Uses of the strategy can be both interventionist and preventive.

Strengths The strengths of this model are that it is simple to use and straightforward; the way the classroom is run reflects the beliefs of the teacher. Teachers have the power; this gives them a feeling of security in the classroom and instills in them a measure of confidence in their abilities, which aids their effectiveness in relating to students. They avoid the powerlessness of the nonassertive teacher and the accompanying potential for hostility. The involvement of parents and administrators in the discipline process allows a team effort in directing children to conform to the norms of appropriate behavior. Student security is enhanced because expectations are clear and consequences are consistently applied.

Weaknesses The weaknesses of this model stem from the power inequity it creates in the classroom. Students are not invited into the management process; the teacher sets the rules and the students are punished or rewarded depending on their ability to conform to these rules. The rules are nonnegotiable. Students may resent this approach, feeling disempowered and undervalued. The goal of self-discipline is secondary to the model's aims; control is externally imposed on students. It also fails to deal with the underlying causes of discipline problems, such as emotional distress, parental divorce, poverty, racism, and so on. For extreme misbehavior, the model advocates students' suspension; for some critics, this is an admission of failure. Such punishment stimulates rebellion and promotes the very behavior it is designed to eliminate.

The Jones Model Fredric Jones, a psychologist at UCLA, conducted research (1987) in which he found that teachers needed to use their physical presence in the classroom to ensure that students remained on task and did not disrupt the learning process. According to Jones, classroom management procedures must be positive. They must affirm students while setting limits and promoting cooperation. Discipline procedures must be practical, simple, easily mastered, and not coercive. Jones draws theoretically and conceptually from the knowledge bases of behavior modification, anthropology, and neurobiology on how the brain functions. His basic assumptions are that children need a controlled environment in order to behave properly and that teachers can attain control through nonverbal cues and movements calculated to bring them physically closer to students. Jones views misbehavior as taking time away from learning. Students lose learning time through inattention, and talking and moving about without permission. Jones believes that teachers should offer incentives to prevent time loss. Incentives such as "preferred activity time" keep students on task. Jones (1994) also promotes the involvement of parents and school administration to help gain control of student behavior. He believes that teachers should have procedures to deal with misbehaviors that enable them to get on with the lesson. He is willing to stop instruction to deal with discipline problems. His adage is, do it now because it will only be more difficult later.

Many of the problems teachers experience result from their mismanagement of various routines. Rules must be clarified or students will determine their own limits. The teacher should spend the first two weeks of school reiterating the rules, standards, routines, and expectations of the classroom if needed. Rules must spell out exactly what is expected and how students can comply. They must be revisited periodically throughout the year. They should be enforced through cooperation, not dictatorial means. Students appreciate teachers who systematically organize their classrooms.

The Basic Steps of the Jones Model Jones has specific ideas about classroom organization. He insists that teachers provide for open and quick access to all students. In monitoring what is acceptable and what is not acceptable behavior, teachers are directed to use effective body language and physical proximity. Acts such as placing yourself so that you can monitor the whole room are most effective. (It gives the impression that you have eyes in the back of your head.) Jones says that the following steps can be used as the need dictates.

1. *Address misbehavior.* Discipline comes before instruction because you aren't on task if you're goofing off. Effective procedures can help teachers address misbehavior with minimal loss in teaching time. Always terminate instruction to deal with disciplinary problems. The first step in the procedure consists of excusing yourself, staying calm, and taking two relaxing breaths before you take any action.
2. *Turn, look, name, and wait.* The second step requires you to slowly turn and face the student, making direct eye contact. Then slowly take two breaths and say the names of misbehaving students in a nonthreatening manner.
3. *Walk.* If they do not respond to your initial effort to stop their behavior, move in their direction. Walk slowly in a relaxed manner. Approach the biggest troublemaker first. Stand close to the student's desk and actually brush it with your leg.
4. *Prompt.* Lean in slowly while giving visual prompts such as turning papers, and pointing to redirect them to work. Give a verbal prompt only if necessary. Keep it simple—no more than two declarative sentences. Speak calmly; do not raise your voice.
5. *Palms.* If the response is still insufficient, place your palms flat on the desk while maintaining eye contact. This will discomfort the offender who should cease the objectionable action.
6. *Stand your ground.* Remain near the student until he is back on task.
7. *Move out.* When all is settled, you can move away by quietly thanking the student for getting back to work.

Once this procedure has been undertaken, it is unlikely that you will have to repeat it. A simple look may be all you need. The Jones model is very practical and offers specific procedures for the teacher to take when the situation arises. Many of these practices are easily interchanged with other practices. The key is being eclectic

Figure 6.2 The Jones Positive Discipline Model

Part	Definition	Knowledge Base	Examples
Responsibility training	The use of an incentive system for obtaining new behaviors or increasing existing ones	Behavior modification	Group incentives, preferred activity time (PAT), differential reinforcement
Omission	Getting very difficult student to desist misbehavior	Behavior modification	Differential reinforcement, group incentives
Back-up system	Three levels of intervention from private to public sanctions	Traditional school practice	Office referral, time out, expulsion, suspension, staffing, parent conferencing
Classroom structure	The arrangement of objects and furniture, and the teaching of rules and procedures		Three-step lesson: Say, Show, Do Over Practice
Limit Setting	Actions taken by the teacher to control students	Brain theory	Relaxed breathing, inhibit talking, eye contact, posture

Source: Adapted from Wolfgang (1999)

when dealing with management problems. If it works and helps you to achieve your educational objectives, do it. You can see in Figure 6.2 that Jones is not shy about borrowing from a number of knowledge bases as long as his objective is achieved.

The major strength of the Jones model is that it specifies a set of steps to follow in dealing with discipline problems. The model's major weakness, as with most behaviorist approaches, is that it does not promote autonomy in students. It is also difficult for some teachers to apply techniques because they become uncomfortable getting close to students. The model also tends to encourage teachers to be aggressive and controlling instead of helpful and supportive.

Discipline, according to Jones, is creating time on task in the most unobtrusive fashion. As an example, Jones speaks of pheasant posturing, which is what animals do to put on a great show without anything really happening. In birds, it takes the form of flapping wings and squawking loudly. In humans, it takes the form of body mannerisms such as looking intently at a student without anything really happening. The stakes are only raised if the student continues to misbehave. Jones suggests that classroom discipline be thought of as a card game in which every move you make ups the ante. A commitment to discipline must be shown. In addition, it will take some time. Jones advocates four basic realities of learning, which he claims his model helps achieve.

1. We learn one step at a time.
2. We learn by doing.
3. We learn by teaching.
4. We improve through practice, practice, and practice.

If your objectives are achieved and children are learning, then your choice of this intervention approach to classroom management is the correct one. The Jones model's use of proximity and physical presence to convey nonverbal desists has been described as a strategy of intimidation under the guise of a positive discipline model. But Jones argues that, rather than intimidating students, his program affirms a positive way of setting limits and promoting cooperation.

When to Use The Jones model has practical application to discrete incidents of misbehavior. The quintessential interventionist model, it was developed to be used when your authority as the teacher is challenged. Jones emphasizes that incidents of misbehavior must be dealt with immediately. Infractions don't go away of their own accord. Because its primary tool is body language, the strategy can be implemented at a moment's notice. Jones's strategies can be used in combination with other approaches, or to supplement any preventive management strategy.

Strengths The strength of this model is that it provides the user with a specific, detailed approach to handling discipline problems. It specifies a set of steps to follow in dealing with discipline problems. It tells exactly how far to go in applying discipline techniques and defines the role of the teacher as well as the role of administrators in discipline. Its positive approach avoids the teacher becoming frustrated and resorting to yelling, hostility, or sarcasm.

Weaknesses The weakness of this model is that it does not attempt to understand the underlying causes of misconduct. The model encourages the teacher to be controlling and avoids a helpful, supportive guidance approach. As with most consequences approaches, it does not promote autonomy in students. Some teachers might not be comfortable with its emphasis on physical proximity. Jones's insistence that discipline take precedence over instruction can allow the misbehavior of individual students to penalize the entire class. The strategy may cause some students to become submissive and others to rebel.

Group Guidance Control Models

Most teachers describe themselves as taking a moderate approach to classroom management. Moderate is a relative term, however, and teacher actions that fall in the middle of the management spectrum will still evidence variations in quality of teacher control. The following two models, **Howard's Efficacy Approach** and **Judicious Discipline**, are designed to get students to take responsibility for their actions; this is seen as the best way to attain a positive classroom management environment. In general, strategies of this type are preventative rather than interventionist; they focus on preventing misbehavior before it can take root. Common to moderate control models is their emphasis on group effort as it relates to managerial success.

Howard's Efficacy Model This efficacy in action approach (Howard, 1998) is less a behavior management model than a model for effective learning. It can, however, be viewed as a moderate teacher-control method based on the assumption that when children are motivated to learn they tend not to misbehave. The approach is based on the belief that learners are in control of their success. The model is based on a key question: "Is smart something you just are, or is it something you can get?" What its developer, the psychologist Jeff Howard, is really asking is whether one believes that intelligence is fixed at birth or developed over time. Is it a product of heredity or environment, nature or nurture? According to Howard, the prevailing belief system is based on the conception that some have it and some do not. This conception leads to an operating principal that sorts and selects by ability. The efficacy operating principle is to accelerate all student development. The goal of schooling is to bring all students to the same level of achievement. "Smarts" is not something you're born with, it's something that you get through personal effort.

Howard's maxims are "Learn to think and you can do it" and "Think you can—Work hard—Get smart."

Efficacy concepts recognize that excellence—and by extension, good behavior—can be both taught and learned. This challenges the prevailing belief that talent is inherent, that there are gifted students who are by nature "special." According to this belief, art class will reveal artistic ability or lack thereof. Efficacy models demonstrate that ability is achieved; an individual can learn how to draw well. This parallels understandings of self-discipline, which is achieved through individual student effort. The efficacy model takes an "if at first you don't succeed, try, try again" approach. Howard's "learning zone concept" establishes a practical learning curve. According to this concept, there are three dimensions, or zones, in which learning occurs. The zones distinguish content as too easy, challenging, and too hard with respect to where children are in their learning right now. Children are assessed in terms of where they are now and where they are expected to go. This understanding recalls Lev Vygotsky's (1896–1934) zone of proximal development (ZPD). According to Vygotsky (1930/1978), learning can only occur within the ZPD zone. Teachers must teach neither below nor above a student's learning zone, but in the area of intellectual challenge where learning takes place (see Figure 6.3).

An example of the practical application of efficacy in action would be an activity in which various levels of writing samples are viewed so that a student's present level can be identified and a goal set for improvement. Feedback about where students are now in their writing and what expectations you have for their improvement

Figure 6.3 Efficacy in Action Learning Zones

1. *The Unchallenging Zone* (Too Easy). The goals in this area are too easy, given what the student already knows and can do. Goals set at this level leave the student feeling unchallenged, unsatisfied, and probably bored.

2. *The Learning Zone* (Challenging, Yet Realistic). Goals set in this area involve new challenges. As a student takes on one of these new tasks, he won't always be successful, but will improve and learn something new. Achieving goals in the Learning Zone builds a student's skills and leaves him or her feeling confident and ready to take on the next challenge.

3. *The Unrealistic Zone* (Too Hard for Now). Goals here are too difficult for now, given the student's current level of skills. Goals at this level leave the student feeling disappointed and defeated when he or she fails and simply lucky when successful.

is critical to this process. It's important to understand that feedback is offered to improve performance and not as a punishment. This technique is also applicable to behavior management, which can be utilized in teaching students responsibility for their own actions. Responsibility is inherent in the process because students take responsibility for the level of work. The strength of this model is contained in the spirit generated by the group approach. Children are encouraged to feel that they are part of a team and share in a group effort focused on self-responsibility and self-esteem. The weakness, however, with efficacy in action is that it can be like a cheerleading session that raises self-esteem, which is not really earned. The emotional letdown that follows this could result in misbehavior.

When to Use "Efficacy" implies that the model achieves results in guiding the group and individuals within the group to act appropriately. Group incentives and morale-building exercises are intrinsic to this strategy. Peer acceptance and objectives are focused on moving all members of the group to conform to expected behavior. The assumption is that individuals will bring their behavior in line with group expectations. The class is a team that works together to achieve results

Strengths Efficacy in action, with its group support structure, is a positive model that generally garners an enthusiastic response from children. The group is seen as reinforcing individuals' self-esteem.

Weaknesses The stress on self-esteem may not be realistic. Expectations may be set too high and therefore goals can be unachievable; self-esteem is not earned.

Judicious Discipline Model Judicious discipline (Landau and Gathercoal, 2000) does not aid the teacher in dealing with particular instances of misbehavior, but it does present a model in which the conditions for misbehavior are minimized. It offers a framework (also a legal one) by which teachers can create a climate, attitude, and set of procedures for effectively running a class. It is a comprehensive approach to democratic classroom management based on the constitutional principles of personal rights balanced against societal needs. Judicious discipline is predicated on the understanding that students have individual freedoms. Young children may simply be taught that they have the right to "be themselves." Older children can be taught their individual freedoms under the Bill of Rights. Democratic rights should always be understood as being balanced with responsibilities. The basis for all classroom rules are (1) health and safety of all, (2) protecting individual and school property, (3) facilitating and enhancing the educational experience, and (4) preventing disruption. That is, the classroom should enable students to be safe, be protected, do their best work, and have their needs respected. Students are taught to govern their own behaviors by assessing their actions in terms of time, place, and manner. (Is this the right time for this action? Is this the best manner? Is this the appropriate place?)

Class meetings are key to implementing this strategy. For this group-guidance approach to work there must be a commitment on the part of both students and teacher. The rules governing the process are best served when democratically agreed upon, not imposed by the teacher. If this is done properly it will provide student ownership and hence commitment. Students should participate in deciding how they are to be seated and who can call a meeting. It should also be established at the very start that individuals are not on trial, only issues and procedures. The process can evolve through trial and error. Students learn by their own mistakes. Judicious discipline involves the following procedures:

- Determine who can call a class meeting and when such meetings should be held.
- Seat participants so each can be seen.
- Do not discuss individuals: only issues and procedures.
- Ensure that meetings stay on topic.
- Avoid coercing anyone to participate.
- Have all group members keep a journal of the meeting.

The basic assumptions that support the judicious discipline model are the same as those that support the U.S. Constitution. Schools have traditionally been understood to operate *in loco parentis* (in place of the parent); in this model, students' individual constitutional rights are stressed. Judicious discipline suggests that core constitutional principles should be the basis for establishing school and classroom rules. The assumption is that students who understand and appreciate their constitutional rights will be better prepared and more involved citizens. Thus, all discipline practices or sanctions are established as recognizing the student's due process rights, making this a commonsense approach to the democratic classroom.

Teachers in many instances have difficulty committing to the running of a democratic classroom as well as the teaching of principles associated with individual rights because of the accompanying trade-off in teacher control. Establishing class rules based on three core constitutional amendments—the First (right to free speech), Fourth (protection against unreasonable searches and seizures), and Fourteenth (due process rights)—can easily alleviate the possible management problems that might result from this approach. Teachers should follow some basic procedures in implementing the process.

1. Post and publish the classroom rules.
2. Be sure to establish standards to be used to justify the withdrawal of personal rights. The reason used

should be couched in terms of "compelling state interest."
3. Conduct preliminary lessons that foster a comparison between group rights and individual rights.
4. Conduct lessons that explore judicious consequences for infractions of the laws. These should be explored in depth.

When to Use Judicious discipline is best used as a strategy that helps to develop democratic procedures. By using this group-guidance approach you will be able to develop positive instruction in citizenship while also enhancing respect for the social order necessary to a democratic society. This strategy can effectively supplement other strategies if it is used as a rationale for democratic, not autocratic, action. Teachers earn respect with this approach, rather than demand it as a right of their position, which tends to foster an adversarial climate.

Strengths Judicious discipline provides a historical and cultural (democratic) basis for establishing rules, procedures, and policies that govern the classroom. It teaches civic understanding and instills civic responsibility, educating students about due process and raising their consciousness about right and responsibilities of citizenship.

Weaknesses Judicious discipline does not address teachers' needs to set limits on student behavior, and does not provide remedies to deal with students who misbehave. It can also require a great deal of time to implement. Teachers must reconsider the model of teacher control implied by the traditional legal guideline of *in loco parentis*. The judicious discipline model requires the teacher and school to examine policies and procedures that affect traditional school practices such as absence, lateness, suspension, withholding privileges, dress, corporal punishment, and the like. The model, though logical for a democratic society, goes against time-honored concepts of total adult authority in schools and classrooms.

Guidance Models

Teachers are in general agreement that the purpose of classroom management is to provide a positive learning environment and to assist children in developing a sense of personal responsibility. Individual-guidance models utilize limited teacher control; students are understood to be the primary agents of change. This approach can make implementation difficult for teachers, especially with respect to establishing a time frame in which the desired outcome is achieved. Yet many analysts see a limited control model as most effective, over the long term, in positively influencing student behavior. Teachers see the purposes of good classroom management as providing a positive learning environment and teaching children to learn responsibility. The problem with limited control models is that they are difficult to work with, requiring a certain amount of expertise. Yet most who are asked how they would like to be treated usually say they would prefer a limited control model. The Ginott Model and Reality Therapy are highly regarded guidance models.

The Ginott Model The **Ginott model**, developed by the psychologist Haim Ginott (1993), uses interpersonal communication methods to encourage humanitarian classroom environments. Ginott maintained that discipline results from interaction between student and teacher. Disciplinary "victories" occur when intervention is focused on specific incidents of misbehavior rather than a student's character. The model purports to support positive student self-concepts. This is achieved through quality teacher-student interaction. Ginott advocates positive verbal intercepts. He conceives of the teacher as a role model whose behavior is key to classroom discipline; teachers are seen as modeling the behaviors they wish to see in their students. The role of the teacher is to direct students away from bad behaviors and lead them to socially acceptable behavior that is positive and lasting. Ginott's methods are organized around three basic themes: (1) congruent communication; (2) fostering independence and self-respect; and (3) avoiding the perils of praise.

Practicing Congruent Communication Congruent communication involves conveying acceptance rather than rejection, and avoids blaming and shaming. Teachers are instructed to avoid insults and intimidation and instead demonstrate sensitivity to students' needs and desires. The point is to encourage self-esteem while de-escalating potential conflict.

Fostering Independence and Self-Respect Ginott (1993) believed that, because of their basic understandings about power structures, children are more likely to consider teachers as enemies rather than friends. The reason for this is that children "are dependent on us, and dependency breeds hostility." To lessen dependency and, hence, hostility, teachers should encourage autonomy and facilitate instruction in personal problem solving. Ginott believed that students had to learn to be autonomous and responsible. He further believed that positive communication helped to build student self-respect, which in turn produced better classroom discipline.

Facilitating Responsibility Ginott believed that in order for students to develop self-discipline, teachers must:

- *Facilitate student autonomy.* Children need to make choices about to their behavior; if students become dependent on the teacher to determine appropri-

Figure 6.4 Essential Precepts of Congruent Communication

> 1. *Deliver sane messages.* (messages that are logical and rationally directed, and not influenced by the concept of punishment). *Examples:* If a child forgets his gym clothes, tell him it is impossible for him to participate. If a child fails to turn in homework, remind him to turn it in tomorrow so he can get proper credit. If a child is cheating, tell him he needs to keep his eyes on his own paper, so he can always claim to have done his own work (Edwards, 1997).
>
> 2. *Express anger appropriately.* Anger must be expressed without insult. Teachers should simply describe what they observe and state how they feel using I-messages (statements that begin with "I"). You can attack the problem rather than the person by directing your anger at the behavior, not the individual. Avoid using labels. Ginott claimed that labeling was really "disabling." Avoid criticizing students. Instead, provide help and advice on how a student can improve. Never use hurtful sarcasm. "Verbal spankings do not improve performance or personality. They only ignite hate" (Ginott, 1993, p. 62).
>
> 3. *Show empathy for students' feelings.* It is better to be told that tests are scary than to argue with a child that she has nothing to fear. False assurances should be avoided. Always validate what a student feels.
>
> 4. *Be brief.* Students close their minds to overtalkative teachers.

ate behavior, hostility will inevitably ensue. Start by giving choices about small things (e.g., going to the bathroom by themselves; the number of problems, and type of assignment they are given for homework). Autonomy with respect to day-to-day behavior helps develop in children personal responsibility and autonomy.

- *Guide emotion.* Instead of telling children how they should feel, help them clarify their emotions. This directs them to solve their own problems. Try to withhold your own opinion. Your intervention should focus on acknowledging and respecting student feelings. Act as a sounding board, not a fount of wisdom.

Avoiding the Perils of Praise Ginott believed that teachers have to be very careful in how and when they bestow praise. Praise that promotes dependency trains children to respond to external stimuli rather than their own internal standards. Feelings of self-worth become connected to receiving praise. Appropriate praise tells students what they have accomplished while letting them draw their own conclusions about its value. Teachers should offer interpretations rather than evaluations. Statements should be devoid of value judgments about personalities and only express positive feelings about student work. Ginott also cautions teachers not be condescending or manipulative. For example, instead of saying, "Good job, Bill," say, "I appreciate the way you set up your paper; it makes it easy to read."

Disciplining Students According to Ginott, the most critical aspect of discipline is finding effective alternatives to punishment. Punishment serves to enrage students and make them uneducable. It leads to more misbehavior, which in turn encourages more severe punishments. It does not deter misconduct; it simply makes students more cautious. Ginott believed that attempts to instill values in children through punishment proved fruitless; values cannot be forced on students.

In Ginott's conception, discipline problems are prevented through loving, warm, and patient action on the part of the teacher. A child who spills milk should be treated in the same way as an honored guest who spills a drink. A teacher's actions and intentions are primary in setting the tone of the classroom. Ginott (1993) commented:

> I have come to a frightening conclusion that I am the decisive element in the classroom. It is my personal approach that creates the climate. It is my daily mood that makes the weather. As a teacher, I possess tremendous power to make a child's life miserable or joyous. I can be a tool of torture or an instrument of inspiration. I can humiliate or humor, hurt or heal. In all situations, it is my response that describes whether a crisis will be escalated or de-escalated, and a child humanized or dehumanized.

When to Use Ginott's model conveys empathy and acceptance; it resonates with teachers who believe that results are achieved through kindness rather than punishment. The model is based on commonsense ideas about meeting students' emotional needs. Ginott's model works well in setting an overall positive tone between teacher and student. It can readily be combined with other management methods, even those that are at the other end of the spectrum.

Strengths The model aims at the development of a positive self-concept that leads to self-respect, which is key to avoiding discipline problems. By fostering independence and autonomy in students, teachers avoid circumstances that promote student rebellion and misconduct.

The model encourages positive relationships between teachers and students by advocating sane communications. The approach emphasizes dealing with student feelings, which allows the teacher to assume the role of caring teacher and facilitator.

Weaknesses Critics take issue with the model's long list of do's and don'ts. Many feel that a comprehensive set of principles would be more helpful for teachers. The model has no specific steps for dealing with discipline problems, and insufficient support for teachers who are used to a more traditional role in dealing with students.

Choice Theory and Reality Therapy How can you effectively get students to choose to work and behave appropriately? The psychiatrist William Glasser, the creator of choice theory (1965, 1969, 1986, and 1990), posed this question. The basic premises of **choice theory** revolve around satisfying five basic psychological needs, which Glasser views as genetic: (1) belonging and love, (2) power and achievement, (3) fun and enjoying work (4) freedom and the ability to make choices, and (5) survival (see Figure 6.5). The assumption is that once these five needs are met, children have no reason to misbehave. Disruptive classrooms are defined as environments that interfere with the educational process and infringe on the rights of others. Disruptive behavior is caused when the inner needs of students are not met and children choose to misbehave.

Glasser concludes in his work that individuals are knowingly responsible for their own actions as a result of having free choice. He refers to choice theory as the antithesis of traditional stimulus response theory. In Glasser's view, stimulus response theory simply does not work. According to Glasser, we choose what to do based on what we believe in, not as a reaction to a specific stimulus.

In refuting stimulus-response theory Glasser revisits the Russian physiologist Ivan Pavlov's (1972) classic experiment related to the physiology of salivation. Pavlov saw that a dog salivated when his lab assistant entered the room with a tray of meat. He followed the same feeding procedure but substituted a flashing light before the dog was fed. The dog was observed salivating at the flashing light even though no meat was present. The light stimulus, Pavlov concluded, created a conditioned response that had caused the dog to salivate. But Glasser contends that Pavlov's conclusions were wrong. Had he used cats instead of dogs, his results would have been different. We answer a ringing phone because we choose to, not because it is a stimulus we are conditioned to respond to.

Glasser claims that our needs are satisfied through a process, which depends on learning pictures contained in our mind's eye, not through stimulus response. These pictures are stored in our minds as long as they satisfy us. A student's picture of learning formed in his quality world is based on his perceptions of what he feels creates quality in his learning and life. His picture of a caring teacher who gives easy tests may not be compatible with the teacher's picture of a diligent, self-motivated student. This scenario will certainly cause management problems if the teacher's role in implementing choice theory is not understood.

A quality classroom is a place where student work fosters a sense of personal responsibility. The conditions needed to establish a quality classroom are a warm, caring, and sharing environment that stresses self-evaluation and relevant interaction. When the teacher creates an atmosphere and activities that satisfy student needs, students will choose to behave appropriately. Glasser makes the distinction between an authoritarian teacher and a teacher leader. An authoritarian teacher uses punishments and rewards, drives students, relies on authority, "knows how," and creates confidence. A teacher leader uses persuasion, leads students, relies on cooperation, "shows how," and creates enthusiasm. It is Glasser's contention that the teacher leader is more apt to create the quality classroom.

Figure 6.5 Basic Genetic Psychological Needs

Love/Belonging
- At least one person who cares about me in an unconditional, accepting way
- Groups that accept me as a member
- Self-love, nurturing

Power/Competence
- The ability to create and maintain an impact on the world
- Things I feel capable doing
- Influencing others

Freedom
- Freedom from being manipulated
- Freedom to express myself
- Freedom to make my own decisions
- Availability of options

Fun
- Humor, laughing, jokes
- Activities that give me pleasure
- What I do when I don't have to do anything

Physical/Survival
- Food, shelter, safety

The teacher is viewed by Glasser as a facilitator and modern manager, not a lecturer and controller. Students who won't work and have lost their learning picture need to be guided toward achieving their quality world. Teachers need to change the structure of teaching by using learning teams and ignoring past failures and focus on present achievement. Glasser's learning-team model is an attempt to demonstrate relevance by empowering students through involvement. It does away with individual competition and memorization by using a team-model concept similar to that found in sports, music, and dramatic productions. The team model moves away from a short-term focus on rote learning and looks to long-term assignments based on depth and involvement.

Teachers are urged to see their students as a team. To establish a functioning learning team you must tailor team assignments that demand cooperation structured so students see the benefit of achieving established objectives. The key to this approach is to give students as much responsibility as they can handle. This can be accomplished using a variety of management strategies. Glasser believes that a wide range of approaches, including traditional ones, can be seen as supporting choice theory. (See Figure 6.6 for a comparison of the learning-team and traditional approaches.) Choice theory blends quite smoothly with a constructivist view of education. Children not only have free will and choice but also can construct their own meanings to create their own quality world.

Choice theory is an explanation of how the brain functions as a control system that selects behaviors. It is internally motivated psychology, in which all behavior is understood to initiate from within us, and not as a result of an outside stimulus, as is the case with behaviorist theory. It states that all behavior is chosen except for the odd reflex reactions such as sneezes, itches, or twitches. To make choice theory work, Glasser advocates using a process known as reality therapy.

Reality therapy is a method of educational counseling and human interaction that doesn't infringe on the rights of others and allows individuals to implement personal choice. Glasser believes that when choices are understood, responsibility is developed. Reality therapy is a set of techniques for managing classroom behavior, which leads to meeting a student's basic psychological needs. Reality therapy (also called responsibility training) utilizes four questions intended to lead children toward understanding their actions and taking responsibility for their behavior:

1. What do you want?
2. What are you doing?
3. Is it helping you? (Explanation)
4. What is your plan now?

There is no need to ask the questions in any specific order. Never, however, ask why a student misbehaves—it only leads to excuses. The most difficult aspect of this approach for some is that there is no punishment

Figure 6.6 Comparison of Learning Team Model and Traditional Model

Learning Team Model	Traditional Model
Students gain a sense of belonging by working in heterogeneous teams.	Students work as individuals.
Students achieve success from motivation, see that knowledge is power and want to work harder.	No motivation from belonging, no motivation if student doesn't succeed. Don't see knowledge as power.
Strong students feel fulfilled by helping weak students and feel power and friendship of high-performing team.	Strong and weak students hardly get to interact with and know each other.
When a weak student contributes it helps and is need-fulfilling.	Weak students contribute less and less.
Students depend on themselves and the team, not just the teacher.	Students depend solely on teacher. No incentive to help each other.
Learning teams build a structure for getting past superficial facts to vital knowledge.	Students are bored and don't want to work.
Teams choose how to prove they have learned the material with encouragement from the teacher.	Teacher-designed evaluation encourages little more than studying for a test.
Team members are rotated by the teacher. Sometimes all members get the team score, other times individual score, to create incentive.	Students compete as individuals, winners and losers are evident.

incurred for poor behavior. A student's self-control, rather than enforced control from without, is emphasized. The teacher must accept the fact that he doesn't lose power and authority by giving up control. In reality you gain power by giving it up. A good leader (teacher) gains respect, not power.

When to Use   Reality therapy is most effective when used as an intervention technique immediately after an incident of misbehavior has occurred. Children may have difficulty at first responding to the four questions the model poses. They have been indirectly trained throughout their educational experiences to expect a management approach based on stimulus response and behavior modification rather than one that attempts to meet their needs. Since there is no direct punishment involved, teachers tend to feel that the student has gotten away with misbehavior. If the intervention has worked, the immediate problem has been resolved and the process becomes preventive, since the student has been guided to reflect upon his inappropriate action.

Strengths   Reality therapy, in the context of choice theory, is effective with most students. It is easy to implement, as the questions the model poses are succinct and straightforward. Individual-guidance approaches tend to be the most effective, in the long term, with students who have specific behavioral problems.

Weaknesses   Not all teachers feel comfortable in the role of a guidance counselor. In moving from a more traditional management approach, teachers may feel that reality therapy allows students to "get away with" bad behavior. The program also takes time away from standardized class work.

MANAGING STUDENTS WITH EMOTIONAL PROBLEMS AND PREVENTING BULLYING

One of the most difficult problems facing teachers is dealing with students who may have emotional problems. How can they be identified, and how are they to be dealt with? Recognizing overt emotional behavior is not difficult, but non-acting-out emotional behavior is almost impossible to recognize by the average person. The first thing to do is to be aware of the warning signs of developing emotional problems and, second, to learn how to use strategies to help students overcome these barriers to learning when they are diagnosed.

Early Warning Signs

Some emotional problems you can see, others you cannot. If a student has internalized emotional problems, they may be withdrawn or depressed, which is often difficult to see. If a student has externalized emotional problems on display, they may become disruptive and antagonistic. Non-acting-out behaviors can be identified if we are on the lookout for them. A child who is isolated within his peer group and is never chosen to participate may very well be suffering emotional distress, which could make her or him exhibit moody and apathetic behavior (Henley and Long, 2003).

Students who act out may develop chronic behavior problems if the specific misbehavior is repeated continually. A child who constantly bullies others and acts impulsively while denying responsibility may be on the path to severe emotional problems.

Strategies for Overcoming Emotional Problems

The key is to engage students with meaningful learning while teaching and modeling appropriate behavior. The

Figure 6.7   Internalized Emotional Problems

Students may have internalized emotional problems if they
- Appear isolated from peers
- Seem overly dependent on others
- Are moody
- Exhibit feelings of helplessness
- Show an interest in cults
- Have an inordinate attraction to fantasy
- Are apathetic
- Are victims of bullying
- Are frequently absent because of illness
- Abuse themselves

Figure 6.8   Externalized Emotional Problems

Students may have externalized emotional problems if they
- Become a chronic behavior problem
- Exhibit a lack of empathy or compassion
- Have temper tantrums
- Are often truant
- Experience poor academic performance
- Have conflicts with authority figures
- Bully others
- Damage the property of others
- Become noncompliant
- Become impulsive and/or aggressive

goal to all management strategies is to have children become self-disciplined. The same strategies that succeed with mainstream children will usually be successful with children who have emotional overtones to their behavior. What is needed on your part is understanding and empathy. When children feel that their teachers care they rarely misbehave. When teachers meet the psychological needs of students they limit misconduct. See Figure 6.9 for specific strategies that can be used in dealing with students' emotional problems.

Strategies for Preventing Bullying Bullying among all schoolchildren is hardly a new phenomenon. Every child, including LD, ADD/ADHD and dyslexic children, suffer from bullying at some stage in their school life (Scarpaci, 2006). When this fact is combined with academic difficulties caused by disabilities, bullying has a devastating effect on self-confidence and achievement. Research suggests that reduction of bullying is best accomplished through a comprehensive, school-wide effort that involves everybody within the school environment, especially teachers (Limber, 2003). There are specific teacher behaviors dealing with beliefs, skills, and practices that will limit or prevent bullying for all students. When teachers respect student autonomy and encourage a sense of belonging, as well as teach cause and effect thinking that promotes conscience development, we are likely to deter bullying (Davis, 2005).

Defining Bullying Bullying can be defined as when a more powerful person deliberately hurts, frightens, or intimidates a weaker person on a continual basis. Bullying takes three distinct forms: physical (hitting, shoving, poking, tripping, and slapping); verbal (name calling, insults, putdowns, and racist remarks, teasing); and social (persuading other kids to exclude or reject someone) (Ritter, 2002).

Bullying can also be described as when a student is exposed repeatedly and over time to negative actions on the part of one or more other students (Olweus, 2003). Aside from definition, there are common basic concepts that provide insight and characterize bullies and bullying:

- Bullying takes at least two people: bully and victim.
- Bullies like to feel strong and superior.
- Bullies enjoy having power over others.
- Bullies use their power to hurt other people.

Some view bullying as a normal aspect of childhood. Teachers who prevent bullying know it is not a normal, natural part of childhood; it is a deliberate act that hurts young victims, both emotionally and physically. It also affects people around them by distracting, intimidating, and upsetting them. Basically, bullying in the classroom prevents students from learning and teachers from reaching their students. It does not allow for communication between students and teachers. Research indicates that adopting programs that target antisocial behavior are also likely to boost overall student academic performance (University of Washington, 2005; Glew et al., 2005). The belief that bullying is some sort of childhood disease is false.

Myths about Bullying Olweus (2003) disputes several common assumptions about the causes of bullying. He found that many so-called causes of bullying receive little or no support when confronted with empirical data. Students who wear glasses, are overweight, or speak differently are not more likely to become victims of bullies. Those who are passive or submissive tend to become victims almost 85 percent of the time. This explains why the learning disabled are at such risk. Aggressive victims, those who have a provocative feature to their personality that makes them a target, account for the rest. Several myths about bullying have been exposed online by the U.S. Department of Health and human Services (2006), University of Colorado, Institute of Behavioral Science (2006), School Bully OnLine (2006), and For Kidsake (2005).

1. Bullying is just teasing. How many times have we heard the refrain given by bullies, "I was just kidding around!"?
2. Some people deserve to be bullied.
3. Only boys are bullies.
4. People who complain about bullies are babies.
5. Bullying is a normal part of growing up.
6. Bullies will go away if you ignore them.

Figure 6.9 Strategies for Overcoming Emotional Problems

> *Make learning relevant.* Establish links between curriculum and students' lives.
>
> *Help students establish positive peer relationships.* Help students develop interpersonal skills through peer tutoring and cooperative learning activities (Goldstein, 1988).
>
> *Teach behavior management skills.* Help students practice restraint and conflict resolution.
>
> *Identify and deal with depression.* Understanding and empathy are more effective than reprimands, incentives, or heart to heart talks. Support activities that foster feelings of competence, strengthen social relationships, and bolster self-efficacy. Refer for help.
>
> *Help students cope with stress.* Refer for help so an accurate diagnosis can be made.
>
> *Instill hope.*

7. All bullies have low self-esteem. That's why they pick on others.
8. It's tattling to tell an adult when you're being bullied.
9. The best way to deal with a bully is by fighting or trying to get even.
10. People who are bullied might hurt for a while, but they'll get over it.

Note: Based on a random sampling of university preservice teachers, numbers 6 and 10 may be true sometimes; all the other statements are false. The question, then, is to identify the true indicators of bullying.

Indicators of Bullying   The American Medical Association (AMA) claims bullying can damage a child as much as child abuse (Ritter, 2002). Half of all children in the United States are bullied at some point in their lives, and one in ten is victimized on a regular basis. In order to identify if one of their patients is being bullied the AMA has asked doctors to be vigilant for signs that their young patients might be victims of bullying or be bullies themselves. The AMA suggests that parents and doctors ask the following questions:

- Have you ever been teased at school? How long has this been going on?
- Do you know of other children who have been teased?
- Have you ever told your teacher about the teasing? What happens?
- What kinds of things do children tease you about?
- Do you have nicknames at school?
- Have you ever been teased because of your illness, handicap or disability or for looking different than other kids?
- At recess, do you usually play with other children or by yourself?

Note: This list is also quite appropriate for teachers who suspect that bullying is going on in their classroom. Develop the skill of asking the right questions. It can help deter bullying.

One might conclude from the AMA report that bullying is just as damaging and insidious as early sexual encounters or drug abuse. Bullies often increase violent behavior with age, as well as suffer from depression, suicidal behavior and alcoholism. As they age, victims show signs of low self-esteem, difficulty making or keeping friends, trouble sleeping, unexplained stomach pains, headaches and depression (Ritter, 2002). Frankel (1996) describes the key indicators for a child at-risk:

- A child's grades begins to fall.
- A child shows a decrease of interest in school in general.
- A child feigns illness, complaining frequently of headaches or stomachaches.
- A child chooses alternative routes home.
- A child claims to have lost books, money, or other belongings without a good explanation, or is caught stealing or asking for extra money.
- A child has unexplained injuries, bruises, or torn clothing.
- Bullying may be the cause of any or all of these indicators.

Stopping Bullying—Protecting the Victims   There are two things for a teacher to do when faced with dealing with a bully. First, the teacher must recognize that a student is a victim of a bully, and second, the teacher should know how to neutralize a bully. Children have to be taught to care (Wylie, 2000). The National Education Association (NEA), developed programs that work to neutralize bullies, called "Quit It" and "Bullyproof." They consist of interactive materials highlighting discussions and role playing aimed at educating children about hurtful behaviors and how to deal with them (Froschi et al., 2001).

While violent incidents are relatively uncommon, harassment in various forms is widespread. A National Institute of Child Health and Human Development (NICHD, 2001) study found that 13 percent of children in grades six through ten had taunted, threatened, or been physically aggressive toward classmates, while 11 percent had been the targets of such behavior. Six percent said they bullied others and had been bullied themselves. Boys were more likely to be bullies or victims of bullying than girls, who were more frequently the targets of bullying in the form of malicious rumors, via e-mail bullying, and sexual harassment.

Sexual harassment when viewed as conflict can be described as intentional or inadvertent conduct offensive to a reasonable person. Teachers should investigate all complaints or rumors of sexual harassment. The best tool for the elimination of harassment is prevention, affirmatively raise the subject in class and express strong disapproval for untoward actions, while developing sanctions such as referrals to a higher authority and informing students of their rights to raise the issue of harassment (Scarpaci, 2006).

While the stereotype is that bullies have low self-esteem, they're actually often self-confident, popular, and make friends easily (Posey, 1995). If slighted, however, they may take it out on someone who can't fight back. The reason for this is based somewhere in familiar coping mechanisms that bullies have learned. Many bullies come from homes where they're harassed themselves, they tend to perform poorly at school, and by age twenty-four, 60 percent of former bullies have been convicted of a crime.

To stop bullying, teachers should encourage and practice openness in class. Bullies tend to work in secret; they depend on the silence of their victims. If open communications are practiced, bullies will find it difficult to operate. Hold them accountable for their actions. Use or develop school anti-harassment policies and hold bullies responsible for inappropriate behavior. Four basic principles for the prevention of bullying should be practiced by teachers (Olweus, 2003):

- Providing warm positive interest and involvement from adults.
- Providing consistent application of nonpunitive, nonphysical sanctions for unacceptable behavior or violations of rules.
- Establishing firm limits on unacceptable behavior.
- Acting as authorities and role models.

Olweus has also created a bullying prevention program (1999) that incorporates having regular class meetings with students while establishing and enforcing class rules against bullying.

The way to neutralize a bully is to use the skill of acquiring information about incidents and then enforce consequences if it continues (Frankel, 1996). Victims should be taught how to deal with teasing. Teachers should be educated to be role models who show victims how to make light of teasing by using statements such as: "So what, who cares? Can't you think of anything else to say? I heard that one in kindergarten. That's so old it's from the Stone Age. I fell off my dinosaur when I first heard that. Tell me when you get to the funny part. And your point is . . . ?"

Victims generally have poor social skills and few friends. They may be physically smaller and act or look different. The psychological trauma of recurring harassment puts victims at risk of suffering from depression or low self-esteem as an adult. The younger the child, the more he or she suffers from bullying.

Practice in anger management, impulse control, appreciation of diversity, and mediation and conflict resolution skills can help prevent violence and stop bullying. Bullies are characterized by hypersensitivity toward criticism or being teased, harassed, or being generally picked on by those they were violent toward (Scarpaci, 2007).

Teachers have dual roles: teaching potential bullies social skills while developing capacity to avoid intimidation. Briggs (1996) advocates extending social-emotional learning by viewing incidents of conflict as teachable moments for social learning, and practicing skill streaming, peer mediation, or conflict resolution. Bullying creates conflicts for both the victim and the bully. Conflict should be viewed as normal, and as an opportunity to develop constructive practices to prevent violence. Patricia Phillips (1997) describes how her high school attempted to alleviate and resolve conflicts by establishing a "conflict wall" on which the following list was written.

Steps for Resolving Conflicts

- Cool down. Don't try to resolve a conflict when you are angry.
- Take time out and attempt to resolve the conflict when cooler heads prevail.
- Describe the conflict. Each person should be given the opportunity to explain what happened in his or her own words. (Make no judgments!)
- Describe what caused the conflict. Be specific and insist upon exact chronological order. (Don't place blame!)
- Describe the feelings raised by the conflict.
- Listen carefully and respectfully while the other person is talking.
- Brainstorm solutions to the conflict.
- Try your solutions.
- If it doesn't work, try another solution.

If students cannot resolve a conflict, have them "agree to disagree," which is sometimes the best we can do. Efforts to teach children to resolve conflict constructively have been in vogue since the late 1960s and early 1970s. Unfortunately, such programs as the one just described only address normal conflicts and are not recommended for dealing with bullies. Most bullying prevention programs invite teachers to intervene when children's conflict is about power and control, not negotiation (Craig and Pepler, 1997).

There are specific teacher behaviors that can be learned that will limit or prevent bullying in school. These actions fall into three categories: beliefs, skills, and practices. Understand that the emotional needs of individual students are key to deterring bullying. Reject myths about bullying with basic concepts and beliefs. Believe that student needs should govern decisions that afford opportunities to develop self-discipline. Believe that empowering students strengthens self-esteem. Demonstrate active positive interest in student well-being. Believe the axiom that students choose their behavior and teachers their management style; choose beliefs that aid students. Believe that effective teachers manage classrooms with care and understanding while creating an open, warm, nurturing environment that allows less opportunity or incentive for bullying to occur (Scarpaci, 2007).

Develop the skill of questioning and respectful listening to assess indications of bullying. By learning and teaching conflict resolution skills, teachers create environments that are not conducive to bullying. Employ the skills necessary to address student psychological needs

PRACTICE EXERCISE 6.2

Management Episodes

Analyze the following brief case studies using the IOSIE model. Each of the cases can also be reviewed in class using a role-play format to arrive at appropriate solutions. Solutions should be compared and contrasted.

1. Billy is a second-grader who constantly asks to leave the room to go to the bathroom.
2. Sammy is a fifth-grader who always makes fun of smaller classmates. He calls them derogatory names that incite many to want to fight with Sammy.
3. Mary, a sixth-grader, claims Betty took her pen off her desk and refuses to give it back.
4. Jane, a quiet fourth-grader, is crying in the back of the classroom. When asked what happened, she exclaims, "No one likes me!"
5. Richard, a bright tenth-grader, is always late to class and never has his assignments completed on time.
6. You have just seen students smoking on school grounds in direct violation to school guidelines.
7. John is absent from your class two or three times each week.
8. A child in your kindergarten class cries all the time, not allowing you to complete a lesson.
9. Items are constantly missing from the student wardrobe in your twelfth-grade senior honors class.
10. A child in your second-grade class seems to be excessively slow academically. The parent refuses to have her tested by a psychologist.
11. A child in your sixth-grade class does not want to be promoted to the new junior high school and attempts to fail all tests.
12. A child in your tenth-grade math class begins to fail and acts out in your class. When you speak to her, she claims to be in love with an older man.
13. A student in your third-grade class is very fearful of strange adults.
14. Your fourth-period class is blamed for writing on the classroom desks. The teacher who uses your room the next period claims he can control his students.
15. Jamie never accepts responsibility for his actions. He tells his parents the teacher is wrong or never explained the work to him. His parents say their child never lies.

for belonging, power, freedom, and fun (Glasser, 1998). Focus on remediating students' social skill deficits by addressing classroom survival skills, friendship-making skills, dealing with feelings, and alternatives to aggression as ways to deter bullying.

Teachers must instruct children on how to deal with behaviors that can be hurtful. They should use role playing in class to dramatize how to deal with teasing and threats of physical aggression. Bullying, when understood, can be prevented by doing what we do best—teaching! By combining education about bullying with establishing consequences for continued bullying, we will not only neutralize bullying, we might also prevent it.

Chapter Summary

Parents would prefer that their children choose good behavior rather than being forced to act appropriately. They hope their children develop self-discipline and know the difference between right and wrong. This is the key to discipline: correct choice. No one can tell you what to do. You have to accept responsibility for your own actions. We cannot impose our wills on others and expect them to like it, even when right. What is discipline? How does character affect your class management? How can you practice effective behavior management techniques in your classroom? These questions are related to one's beliefs and one's personality. Effective teaching relies on good planning and a reflective analysis of results. The same is true for effective classroom management.

We have seen in this chapter that classroom management style can be correlated to one's personality. A teacher could either be for firm teacher control or for student autonomy, and possibly both if eclectic. Management styles vary along a spectrum, from most to least teacher control. They all claim the common goal of having students develop responsibility for their actions. Discussed in limited depth were a sampling of classic models that could be used to manage behavioral problems. The basics of behavior include analysis, effective classroom management practices and specific management models that range from limited to moderate to strong teacher control. The key is to be eclectic. The prime concern of classroom teachers is student behavior and how it should be addressed. Everyone shares the same psychological needs, and the role of the teacher is to meet those needs through effective management practices.

An effective teacher manages a classroom and an ineffective teacher disciplines a classroom. Good procedures are the key to good classroom management. Contrary to popular belief, the number one problem in classrooms is not lack of discipline but the lack of procedures. Behavior problems are due to the teacher's failing to teach students how to follow procedures. The most important person responsible for classroom management and student achievement is the teacher. This view relates nicely to the keys for effective teaching discussed in Chapter 1—management, mastery, expectations, methods, and personality. The correlation between management and personality is evidenced by student achievement.

Cases from the Field

Analyze the following brief case studies using the IOSIE method. Reflect on how you as the teacher would react in each situation presented. In completing this exercise, also indicate which of the four basic behavior models described applies to the study.

CASE ONE

John Paladino, a tenth-grade student who has a reputation as a compulsive troublemaker, is constantly disturbing your class presentations. He makes obtrusive sounds by clicking his tongue or tapping on his desk seat. When you tell him to desist, he claims to be innocent and blames another student. His actions cause others to get involved defending themselves. Before you know it, a shouting match takes place among the students. The first thing that comes to your mind is to have John removed from your class. Upon reflection, you decide to analyze this case using the IOSIE method. Describe the steps you would follow.

CASE TWO

Tamara Jones is a very emotional fourth grader. She seems to begin crying without any apparent provocation. You are aware that her parents have recently separated and are presently undergoing a custody battle over Tamara. You have spoken to the parents, who both blame each other for not giving Tamara enough love and affection. When you ask Tamara what the problem is, she claims it is nothing and starts crying all over again. You decide to analyze this case using the IOSIE method and the counseling techniques described in the psychodynamic model to give this child proper guidance. Explain the procedures you would use.

CASE THREE

Billy Marchica, in your seventh-grade English class, doesn't seem to understand anything that you have tried to teach. You have learned that he has been in the country since he was three years old and speaks fluent English. His responses to the questions you ask during class instructional times, though original, are far removed from what you would expect. On one occasion, you were discussing a song about a coal miner's daughter and Billy shouts out, "Anthracite is no longer mined in Wales!" You are flabbergasted. Is Billy just being a wise guy? Is he intentionally disrupting your class by his seemingly outrageous response? Use the IOSIE method to analyze this case, using the constructivist model for a plausible solution. How can constructivist theory be used to resolve this situation?

CASE FOUR

Susan Ramos, a ten-year-old girl in your mainstream fifth-grade class, has rarely received positive academic recognition. She is a sweet child who you believe has a severe learning disability in reading. You assume she is four years delayed in reading, based on the Woodcock Reading Mastery test assessment for reading level that you administered in class. She has never been in any school long enough to be retained or competently assessed, because her mother, a career military person, has been forced to move due to her assignments. She has been in your class for two months, long enough for you to judge her inadequate performance. You wonder if you will be able to help this child become a proficient reader. One of your colleagues claims that you have been too quick to evaluate Susan and that since you had previously taught in a secondary school, your standards were too high. Analyze this case using the IOSIE method.

Terms to Remember

Behavioral model
Psychodynamic model
Environmental model
Constructivist model
Authoritarian
Eclectic
Reality therapy
Classroom management

Management models
Assertive discipline
Jones model
Howard's efficacy in action approach
Judicious discipline
Ginott model
Choice theory

Discussion Questions

1. Describe the five types of misbehavior commonly associated with children and schools.
2. Explain why a social systems theory is needed if one is to truly analyze and understand human behavior.
3. How do you analyze a behavioral classroom management case using the IOSIE model?
4. Write a critical appraisal of the management approaches and practices that facilitate instruction. Which of these approaches do you feel most comfortable with? Why?
5. How can a consequences model such as assertive discipline work to teach student responsibility?
6. How can a group-guidance model such as judicious discipline work to teach student responsibility?
7. How can a guidance model such as reality therapy work to teach student responsibility?
8. Which model do you expect to use? Explain your reasons.

Field Experience Activities

Visit a neighboring school and ask a teacher in your subject area to offer a solution for the management episodes presented in Practice Exercise 6.2. Compare their responses to your own and note similarities and differences.

For Further Reading

Alpert, L. (1996). *Cooperative discipline: How to manage your classroom and promote self-esteem*. Circle Pines, MN: American Guidance Service.

Brissie, J. S., Hover-Dempsey, K. V., and Bassler, O. C. (1988). Individual, situational contributors to teacher burnout. *The Journal of Educational Research* 82: 106–112.

Hasenstab, J. K. (2005). Training the teacher as a champion. Retrieved at www.plsweb.com/.

Jersild, A. T. (1955). *When teachers face themselves*. New York: Teachers College Press, pp. 3, 4, 80.

Kounin, J. (1977). *Discipline and group management in classrooms*. Rev. ed. New York: Rinehart & Winston.

CHAPTER 7

Teaching for Literacy

FOCUS POINTS

1. How to teach for literacy.
2. A balanced approach to literacy is the key to comprehension.
3. There are differences between a traditional classroom and a balanced reading classroom.

CHAPTER OVERVIEW

THERE ARE MANY WAYS TO TEACH READING but not all of them are right for everyone. Do we teach boys differently than girls? Is there such a thing as gender-specific teaching? In this chapter we will see that when teaching reading, what is a good technique for one student may represent serious problems for another. Possibly the most frequent cause of reading difficulty or delay is the level of development in a child's perceptual abilities. Visual, auditory, or kinesthetic perception or any combination of weaknesses in these areas could cause deficits in a child's reading ability. In order to help children overcome these problems, examine their reading style or strengths. This should be done because all too often the remediation of reading disabilities has concentrated on a more intensive repetition of what was unsuccessful in the first place. For example, extensive drilling in phonetic skills to a sight-learner only places emphasis on teaching to the child's weaknesses rather than strengths. This is reflected in reading curricula, reading methods, and standardized tests that stress phonetic decoding at the expense of comprehension.

The same argument could be made in reverse if we were to stress authentic literature and comprehension with reference to word-attack skills. We should be able to conclude at the end of this chapter that a balanced approach will most likely be the best way to approach reading for the majority of our students. We will also observe that many children struggle to learn from content-area textbooks that don't match their reading levels. This problem of mismatched teaching resources is amply summarized by Allington (2002) who claims, "You can't learn too much from books you can't read," especially if the same textbook is used as the main instructional resource for all students. The essence of this chapter is devoted to providing various options for instructional practices that can facilitate teaching for literacy.

TO TEACH FOR LITERACY

To teach for literacy and rectify the inadequacy of an unbalanced approach, we should adopt a balanced whole-language, literature-based approach to reading. An unbalanced approach for the purpose of this argument is one in which a skills (phonics) strategy is accepted over a comprehension (whole language) strategy. What is being proposed is a balanced reading approach that offers an alternative to the extremes of pure phonics or whole language. Whole language should be used to coordinate all of a school's reading programs under one umbrella. It should be understood that whole language is not a program package, or set of materials, a method, a practice, or a technique; rather, it is a perspective on language and learning that leads to the acceptance of certain strategies, methods, materials, and techniques (Watson, 1989). (Please note that throughout this text the term *whole language* has been replaced by the term *balanced language approach*, even though purists might object.) Honig (1996) similarly defines a balanced language approach as "one which combines the language and literature-rich activities associated with whole language with explicit teaching of the skills needed to decode words for all children." According to the California Department of Education (1995, 1996) "the heart of a powerful reading program is the relationship between explicit, systematic skills instruction and literature, language, and comprehension. While skills alone are insufficient to develop good readers, no reader can become proficient without these foundational skills." Researchers and practitioners alike assert that children need training in both phonemic awareness (awareness of individual sounds) and cueing strategies (decoding and comprehending text) (Kelly, 1997). The balanced reading approach should be celebrated for offering an alternative to the extremes of pure phonics or whole language and for providing an effective combination of instructional approaches.

Children of all ages should read good literature in order to become involved in using all modes of communication: speaking, reading, writing, listening, observing, illustrating, experiencing, and doing. All communication skills should be interconnected and integrated into lessons under the umbrella of a whole language balanced reading program. A child should be encouraged to read, write, speak, and listen in response to the literature being experienced. The purpose of language is to communicate with others. Research has shown that children learn to use language by sharing ideas, working cooperatively, and becoming part of a learning community (the class). Reading should never be taught as a separate activity, but in combination with all communication skills. Children learn more effectively when they can see the connections and relationships among ideas and subjects than when they learn in bits and pieces of information presented in isolation. A holistic perspective to literacy is essential for real learning to occur. Each child should be engaged in a full range of reading methods in which both sight and phonic approaches are included. Learning is easiest when it comes from whole to part, in authentic contexts. When children see purpose and meaning, they understand importance. Real-world tasks, such as writing letters and reading for information, are authentic activities that give purpose and meaning to reading.

According to E. D. Hirsch (2001), the latest reading report for the National Assessment of Educational Progress documents no major changes in reading for the past half-century. A consistent reading gap has been shown to exist in fourth grade between rich and poor students, a gap called the "fourth grade slump" by Jeanne Chall (1990; Chall and Jacobs, 1996). A few districts have made inroads toward improving on this gap with programs such as Open Court, Success for All, and Direct Instruction. These traditional skills-based approaches that stress decoding have achieved varied success prior to the fourth grade. Progress has been made in teaching children to decode print (turn print into speech sounds), but the same concomitant improvement in comprehension for all children has not been seen. This gap was always there, but the manner of testing prior to the fourth grade never exposed it. The task of teaching for literacy should focus on creating programs and methods that teach students to comprehend text accurately and fluently. This task is the new frontier in reading research (Hirsch, 2003).

The reading gap can be reduced by combining a reading (decoding) curriculum with a content curriculum that focuses on academic knowledge and oral language in the early grades, rather than the language arts curriculum, which is presently stressed. The key is integrating time spent on reading skills with time spent on subject materials instead of language arts. Critics claim this strategy is simply advocating reading in the content area, which is a perfectly acceptable approach, neither new nor revolutionary.

Some would say that the emphasis on imaginative fiction and lack of emphasis on history and science is a major obstacle to reading improvements. The causes for the reading gap exist because of the differences in children's familiarity with unusual words, standards of pronunciation, and complex syntax. Low-income kindergarten children have only heard half the words and can understand half the meanings and language conventions of high-income children (Hirsch, 2003). Skills programs do not bridge this gap because these programs do not compensate for deficiencies in the limited vocabularies of students. The term *reading gap* is really a language or verbal gap. The question then becomes "How can this gap be reduced?" The Coleman Report of 1966 disclosed that a child's initial family advantage was more important to academic success than the school one attended. The only way to overcome any disadvantage is to enforce strict academic standards for each grade and ensure that every child meets the desired expectations. The basic principle for overcoming the verbal gap is to be explicit, break down what is to be learned into manageable elements, then systematically build on that knowledge with new knowledge. Define the deficit by determining what knowledge and words are lacking, and then teach that knowledge and those words.

Fluency, Vocabulary, and Domain Knowledge

There are three principles that have useful implications for improving students' reading comprehension:

1. *Fluency*, which allows the mind to concentrate on comprehension;
2. *Vocabulary breadth*, which increases comprehension and facilitates further learning; and
3. *Domain knowledge*, the most recently understood principle, increases fluency, broadens vocabulary, and enables deeper comprehension (Hirsch, 2003).

Fluency means "flowing," and in this context, it means "fast." When a child can read rapidly, he has mastered many of the necessary processes involved in reading. If decoding does not happen quickly, the decoded material will be forgotten before it is understood. Try to follow a foreign movie in French. We cannot remember more than seven items that we can hold in our conscious mind at any one time before they are lost, whether the items are simple facts, or numbers, or words representing complex concepts.

Fluency is further enhanced by word and domain knowledge, which creates a strong relationship between fluency and comprehension. It allows the reader to make rapid connections between new and previously learned content. An expert in an area can read a text about that area more fluently than one can in an unfamiliar area. Students can overcome fluency problems by quickly grasping the kind of text and identifying the words.

Vocabulary knowledge correlates strongly with reading and comprehension. A child who starts out with a good vocabulary will comprehend sooner. Students should know up to 80,000 words by grade twelve, starting school with mastery of about 5,000 words. It has even been estimated that by the time a child is six years old she has a 4,000- to 24,000-word speaking and listening vocabulary (Lorge and Chall, 1963).

Domain knowledge is the level of knowledge one possesses about the subject being discussed. **Domain knowledge** enables readers to make sense of word combinations and choose among many possible word meanings. It is also necessary to give meaning to otherwise confusing sentences. Reading requires the reader to make inferences that depend on prior knowledge.

In this view, it is not necessary to spend too much time on teaching formal comprehension skills such as predicting, classifying, and looking for the main idea. After the initial benefit of instruction, further conscious practice of formal skills is a waste of time. There is a plateau or ceiling in the positive effects. If the relevant prior knowledge is lacking, conscious comprehension strategies cannot activate it (Rosenshine and Meister, 1994). Reading comprehension and vocabulary are best served by spending extended time on reading and listening to texts on the same topic and discussing facts and ideas in them. Time spent is determined by time needed to achieve comprehension. An effective language arts program focuses on general knowledge and uses school time effectively. This is the only way to teach for comprehension.

RESEARCH-BASED FINDINGS

This traditional approach to teaching for literacy in the twenty-first century has been advanced in the National Reading Panel report (Adler, 2001). The report supports the research agenda of the National Institute of Child Health and Human Development and the Reading First initiative of the federal *No Child Left Behind Act* of 2001. It is important to note that while Reading First focuses only on grades K to 3, the National Panel report was not limited to research on early literacy but also surveyed the research results on reading throughout grades K to 12. It can be used to provide a foundation to support literacy instruction in the middle school and high school grades just as it did for elementary grades. Promoters of phonics have used the findings to encourage all school reading instruction and all teacher preparation in reading. They want all programs to fall in line with their ideas regarding how reading should be taught. The report itself focuses on five areas of reading instruction: phonemic awareness, phonics, fluency, vocabulary, and text comprehension. Adler summarizes what researchers have discovered about how to teach reading. He describes five steps in this process that can be seen as a guide ladder leading to reading comprehension.

Reading Guide Ladder

- Comprehension   5
- Vocabulary   4
- Fluency   3
- Phonics   2
- Phonemic awareness   1

1. *Phonemic awareness* is the ability to notice, hear, identify, think about, and manipulate the individual sounds (phonemes) in spoken words. The smallest parts of sound in a spoken word must be understood before a child can learn to read print. Phonemic awareness is not phonics. It is the understanding that the sounds of spoken language work together to make words.

   Phonological awareness is a broad term that includes phonemic awareness. In addition to phonemes, phonological awareness activities can involve work rhymes, words, syllables, onsets, and rimes.

   Syllable is a word part that contains a vowel or, in spoken language, a vowel sound. (An example is *e-vent*.)

   Onset and rimes are parts of spoken language that are smaller than syllables but larger than phonemes. An *onset* is the initial consonant sound of a syllable (the onset of bag is *b*; of swim is *sw*). A *rime* is the part of a syllable that contains the vowel and all that follows (the rime of bag is *ag*; of swim is *im*).

2. *Phonics* is the understanding that there is a predictable relationship between phonemes (sounds) and *graphemes* (letters). *Phonics instruction* teaches children the relationships between the letters (graphemes) of written language and the individual sounds (phonemes) of spoken language. These graphophonemic relationships are also known as letter-sound associations. The goal of phonics instruction is to help children learn and use the alphabetic principle: that there are systematic and predictable relationships between written letters and spoken words.

   Programs of phonics instruction are effective when they are systematic and explicit. A systematic plan of instruction includes a carefully selected set of letter-sound relationships that are organized into a logical sequence. Explicit programs provide teachers with precise directions for the teaching of these relationships.

Six Approaches to Phonics Instruction

- **Synthetic phonics**: to convert letters or letter combinations into sounds and then blend sounds to form recognizable words.
- **Analytic phonics**: to analyze letter-sound relationships in previously learned words. Sounds are not pronounced in isolation.
- **Analogy-based phonics**: to use parts of word families that are known to identify words that have similar parts that are not known.
- **Phonics through spelling**: to segment words into phonemes and to make words by using letters for phonemes.
- **Embedded phonics**: to learn letter-sound relationships during the reading of a text.
- **Onset-rime phonics instruction**: to learn to identify the sound of the letter or letters before the first vowel (the onset) in a one-syllable word and the sound of the remaining part of the word (the rime).

3. *Fluency* is the ability to read a text accurately and quickly. Automatic word recognition is necessary, but not sufficient, for fluency. The key to fluency instruction is to provide students with a model of fluent reading, and then to guide them as they read the same passages on their own.

   Student fluency instruction or practice consists of student-adult reading, choral reading, tape-assisted reading, partner reading, and readers' theater (performing before an audience).

4. *Vocabulary* is the collection of words we use to communicate effectively. There are four basic types of oral and reading vocabulary: listening words, speaking words, reading words, and writing words. Children learn the meanings of most words indirectly, through everyday experiences with oral and written language. Traditionally, listening has been regarded, alongside reading, as a passive language skill. But listening requires an active role on the part of the listener. Understanding is not something that happens because of what a speaker says. It happens because of the cognitive process the listener uses to understand what is being said. Effective listeners actively engage in the process of comprehension by constructing their own meanings and interpretations (Anderson and Lynch, 1995). It is believed that for native speakers, listening and oral skills are for the most part mastered during the preschool years, before actual reading and vocabulary instruction begins.

Teachers generally help children with the written forms of language, while assuming that they are effective listeners if they can identify sounds and words and know the syntax of language and meanings of words. Little direct attention is paid in most schools to the development of listening and comprehension skills. The result of research has shown that good listeners are usually good readers and poor listeners are generally poor readers (Neville, 1985).

Listening is both a communicative activity and language learning activity, which involves a multiplicity of skills. The following elements that make up the process of listening must be mastered if vocabulary is to be understood (Anderson and Lynch, 1995):

- Spoken signals have to be identified and discriminated from surrounding sounds.
- Speech has to be partitioned into small units that can be recognized as words.
- Both the speaker's syntax and meaning must be understood.
- Listeners demonstrate comprehension of oral vocabulary by formulating correct and appropriate responses.

Developing student vocabularies is very important. The average first-grader enters school with a listening vocabulary of approximately 5,000 words. This combined with an annual rate of growth of from 3,000 to 4,000 words, leads to a high school graduate's vocabulary of between 40,000 to 80,000 words. Texts used by secondary students contain over 100,000 words. Students might encounter 15 to 55 unknown words in a typical 1,000-word text (Ryder and Graves, 1994, p. 72). The task of learning words is a series of tasks that vary markedly depending on the word being taught, the learner's knowledge of the word and the concepts it represents, and the depth and precision of meaning the student needs to acquire.

Six Word Learning Tasks

- *Learning to read words in student's oral vocabulary.* By the fourth grade, students should be able to read all the words in their oral vocabularies.
- *Learning new labels for known concepts.* An example of this process is the word *patina*. They would know that ornamental metal turns green but they would not know the specific term used.
- *Learning words representing new and difficult concepts.* These are words not in the student's oral or reading vocabulary. An example would be the word *fusion* or *fission*.
- *Clarifying and enriching the meanings of known words.* These words have different meaning in different contexts. An example would be *watershed, morose, trumpet,* and *cornet*.
- *Learning to use words in speaking and writing.* This is the process of moving words from the students' listening and reading vocabularies to their speaking and writing vocabularies. An example would be the word *omnipotent*.
- *Learning new meanings for already known words.* This is learning new meanings for words already known. An example would be *mean* in mathematics, *charter* in history, and *sash* in carpentry. (Ryder and Graves, 1994, p. 73)

There are only *four basic levels of word knowledge* differentiated by maturation. They are the unknown words, words that you must think about before they

---

PRACTICE EXERCISE 7.1

Vocabulary Exercise

Identify word-learning task for eighth graders (answers are *starred)

fling: _____ a new meaning*
_____ a new meaning for a known word

rational number: _____ a new word for a known concept*
_____ a word in students' oral vocabularies

pneumonia: _____ a word in students' oral vocabularies*
_____ a new concept

finite: _____ a new concept*
_____ a new word for a known concept

Identify word-learning task for eleventh graders

fluke _____ a new concept
_____ a new word for a known concept*

languish _____ a word in students' oral vocabularies
_____ a word for a known concept*

fugue _____ a new concept*
_____ a word in students' oral vocabularies

taxonomy _____ a new concept*
_____ a new word for a known concept

Note: Students should create their own examples after reviewing these samples.

are recalled, words easily understood, and words that need to be studied in depth. Some examples are:

1. Unknown words (*iatrogenic, geometric, interconnectedness*)
2. Words acquainted with, which must be thought about to recall meanings (*fiesta, gymnasium, stadium*)
3. Known words (*library, hall, wall*)
4. Words that need to be studied to be understood (*tariff, tangent, mass,* and *sonnet*)

Comprehension of content is the reason for reading. Good readers are purposeful and active. Text comprehension can be improved by instruction that helps readers use specific comprehension strategies.

Six Strategies for Reading Comprehension

- *Monitoring comprehension.* When students recognize what they understand and what they do not understand, they then use fix-up strategies to resolve problems.
- *Use graphic and semantic organizers. Graphic organizers* illustrate concepts and interrelationships among concepts by using a pictorial device. They include maps, webs, graphs, charts, or clusters. *Semantic organizers* (also called semantic maps or semantic webs) are graphic organizers that look like a spider web with lines connected to a central concept from a variety of related ideas and events.
- *Answering questions.*
- *Generating questions.*
- *Recognizing story structure.*
- *Summarizing.*

An effective comprehension strategy for instruction is explicit, or direct. The four steps of explicit instruction include (1) direct explanation, (2) teacher modeling (thinking aloud), (3) guided practice, and (4) application.

APPROACHES TO TEACHING FOR LITERACY

The purpose of content-area reading instruction is to improve students' learning through the integration of instructional strategies in the subject matter curriculum, rather than to present strategies in isolation. It is directed by both the students' academic and sociocultural needs. Whipple (1925) writes, "Every teacher should be, to a certain extent, a teacher of reading" (p. 6).

Guiding Principles of Content-Area Reading Instruction

1. Content-area reading instruction is based on the assumption that students acquire meaning through the application of strategies, skills, and prior knowledge of text material.
2. The classroom is a dynamic social, cultural, and intellectual environment where students acquire information and construct knowledge.
3. Content-area reading allows students to learn from numerous sources of information.
4. Content reading instruction aims to facilitate active learning.
5. Instructional strategies and activities in the content areas are adaptable to the constraints of the classroom. (Ryder and Graves, 1994)

Traditional Approaches

SQ4R is a classic approach for teaching comprehension. (The letters stand for Survey, Question, Read, Recite, Record, and Review. See Figure 7.1.) It has been in use for more than half a century. Developed during World War II to meet the needs of a nation at war, it became the most thoroughly researched strategy in the English language (Caverly et al., 2000; Gunning, 2003). It was ideal for training raw recruits who had limited levels of education to comprehend printed matter such as army manuals.

PRACTICE EXERCISE 7.2

Levels of Word Knowledge

Classify level of word knowledge of the following words for junior high school students.

	(answers)
harmony	2, 3, 4, 1
languid	1, 2, 3, 4
fast food	4, 1, 2, 3
triangle	3, 4, 1, 2

Classify the level of word knowledge of the following words for senior high students.

examinations	4, 1, 2, 3
Pi	3, 4, 1, 2
erstwhile	1, 2, 3, 4
aerobic	2, 1, 3, 4

Figure 7.1 The Six Steps of SQ4R

- **Survey** the chapter by reading it quickly.
- **Question** what you have read.
- **Read** to answer the questions you asked.
- **Recite** your answers to your questions.
- **Record** the important items from the chapter and add to your notes.
- **Review** it all for retention.

SQ4R helps students organize, elaborate, and rehearse information obtained from texts. Many adaptations have occurred over the years, but the essential steps remain the same. Figure 7.2 provides a guide that can be used in practically any content area.

A **directed reading lesson (DRL)** is a basic strategic approach to comprehension that assists teachers in preparing guided and learner-centered lessons. It is a method for guiding students' comprehension of a reading selection where reading becomes the basic source of content knowledge (Roe et al., 2004). There are a number of ways to plan directed reading lessons, but all contain five basic procedures: readiness preparation, motivation, and background; guided reading/silent reading; discussion and oral reading; rereading; and follow-up activities. (See Figure 7.3.)

Five Procedures to Follow in a Direct Reading Lesson

1. *Preparation and readiness concerns:*
   - *Motivation* helps students connect to the topic and focus their attention to the subject of the lesson. It should also arouse curiosity and interest to help students relate to the material.
   - Develop meaningful *background experiences* for the students. Experiences prepare students to understand the reading selection. Comprehension experiences related to previously acquired knowledge assures comprehension of the new information to be learned.
   - Connect *concepts to vocabulary* words that apply in various situations across content areas.
   - To establish *purpose for reading* use text-based questions that require the reader to recognize and record information. The purpose should contain three features: (1) the main topic of the reading, (2) the generic purpose, and (3) the primary thought pattern needed for comprehension.

2. *Silent reading* is a form of guided independent reading used to define the purpose of the reading established during the readiness section of the lesson.
3. *Discussion* and *oral reading* occurs when students read aloud and discuss the text as it relates to the purposes discovered during the silent reading.
4. *Rereading* is to have students extend their understanding of the content and create new purposes.
5. *Follow-up* is used to reinforce the lesson or extend the lesson by enriching information learned through reading and discussion. (Neubert and Wilkins, 2004)

KWL is a strategy used to teach comprehension. The acronym stands for **K**now, **W**ant to Know, and **L**earned. It was developed by Ogle (1986) as a guide for students to use in linking their prior knowledge to what they wanted to learn, and reflecting on what they had learned. The steps used are:

1. List what you already know about the topic.
2. Decide what additional information you want to know about the topic.
3. Read the text and research the areas you want to know about.
4. Make a list of what you have learned. (Nettles, 2006)

Figure 7.2 Sample SQ4R Lesson: Causes for the Civil War (Grade 7)

1. Have students silently **survey** the chapter to get an overview of what it is about. Have them glance at headings to and make a mental guide of how the chapter was organized.
2. Make chapter headings into **questions**. For example, "Economic Causes of the Civil War" rewritten as a question, "What were the causes of the Civil War?" This step provides a purpose for reading.
3. Have class **read** the selection and answer the questions that have been created. This will focus the class on the central issues that need to be addressed.
4. Class will then **recite** the answers they have discovered from reading the text. They will also be encouraged to discuss various interpretations.
5. The class should **record** their answers and any remaining questions. They should also write down and reread points they are not sure of.
6. Finally, **review** text, and reread the sections pertaining to original questions, concepts, or ideas that need to be fully discussed. This process will assist students in retaining material.

Figure 7.3 Sample DRL Literature Lesson (Grade 12)

1. *Readiness preparation:* Motivate students by asking them if they know what a civil war is. Then explain that they will be reading a novel entitled *The Shadow of the Wind* by Carlos Ruiz Zafon. The story takes place in Spain and all of the characters are affected by injustice and violence. This Spanish novel has plots and sub-plots related to horror, politics, and romance. Discuss the setting as Barcelona, 1945: a city slowly healing from its war wounds. Speak about the central character, Daniel, and the mysterious book he finds, and that someone has been destroying all remaining copies.

   Review the vocabulary by having students match a number of words from the story with their definitions.

Words	Definitions
Barcelona	genre of fiction characterized by darkness
prophetic	city in Spain
skeptical	extreme poverty
penury	disbelieving
gothic	predictive

   Discuss the *purpose for reading* as to understand that emotions can determine one's life's direction. Explain that the gothic novel did not die with the nineteenth century.

2. *Silent guided reading:* Have students read the first chapter silently. Have them reflect on purpose questions as they read: What factors in this chapter create an atmosphere of doom and poverty? Why is Daniel so infatuated with a cemetery of forgotten books?

3. *Discussion:* After students have read the chapter, ask the following questions to further discussion. Who is Daniel talking to about his feelings? How does the author's description establish a mysterious setting? What exactly was the cemetery of forgotten books? Why was Daniel plunged into a new world of images and sensations?

4. *Reread:* Have students reread the chapter to resolve any information not clarified during the discussion phase.

5. *Follow-up activities:* Have students write a paragraph visualizing what Daniel looks like. They can also draw a picture of the book jacket of the book he found, as well as describe it in a paragraph.

There are variations of this approach, such as the KWHL, where a step prior to the final step is added. This step is called "How Can I Find Out?" The idea is for students to locate the needed materials using items other than textbooks, such as trade books, newspapers, magazines, encyclopedias, and Internet applications.

Many researchers have been involved in studying the reading process. When all is said and done, however, two models appear to dominate classroom practice: the skills-based *phonics approach* and the psycholinguistic meanings-based *whole language approach.*

Phonics Approach

Gough's Model P. B. Gough (1972) characterized reading as a letter-by-letter progression through text, with letter identification followed by the identification of the sounds of the letters, until words, their syntactic features, and then meanings are finally assessed. Gough's model implies that reading is laborious, and that its teaching should reflect a sequential processing approach. Models of this type focus attention on letter-sound correspondence at the expense of other sources of information (Davies, 1995). The serial processing proposed by Gough imposes a very heavy burden on short-term memory. To teach the 166 different grapho-phonic rules covering the regular spelling-to-sound relationships found in the English language is quite difficult and time consuming.

Gough's description of the reading process is the basis of most phonics approaches, where the sequence of instruction is intended to reflect the assumed sequence of processing: from letters to sounds, to words, to sentences, and finally to meaning and thinking. He begins by looking at the words, then finding and identifying letters that are sounded out. After words are recognized, they are placed into a grammatical class and sentence structure. Meanings are then constructed for sentences that lead to thinking, reflection, and finally, comprehension.

Basal Reading Programs Mainstream publishers of basal reading programs usually market phonics programs. These commonly used programs have been shown to account for 75 to 90 percent of what goes on during reading periods in elementary school classrooms. Basal reading programs are made up of comprehensive packages of instructional reading materials. They normally consist of an entire reading curriculum, which has a teacher-friendly scope and sequence chart for the classroom teacher to follow. These programs also provide instructional strategies for the teaching of reading in scripted user-friendly form. Basal programs usually consist of teachers' manuals, graded anthologies of readings, and practice exercises in the form of worksheets

Figure 7.4 Sample KWL Chart for Current Events Lesson on Immigration (Grade 11)

What I Know	What I Want to Know	What I Learned
• People came to America from different places.	When did my ancestors come?	
• People came for different reasons.	What were my ancestors' reasons?	
• What illegal and legal immigration is.	How do you define *amnesty*?	
	What is the pathway to citizenship?	

and workbooks. An entire basal reading program is organized on a grade-by-grade level, beginning at kindergarten and continuing through grade eight. Phonics in many of these programs is taught as a separate subject with emphasis on drills and rote memorization of phonics rules (Anderson, 1985).

Glass Analysis Glass analysis is a phonics skills-based approach to teaching reading that does not rely on the rote memorization of phonic rules. It focuses on the decoding of entire words. Any method of phonics instruction to be compatible with whole language must foster the integrated teaching of language arts and not be taught as an isolated subject. This approach is an easy way to teach the "non-language" aspect of reading, known as *decoding*. Glass analysis should never be confused with an authentic whole language program. Gerald and Esther Glass (1994) take a position contrary to whole language. They believe reading is not a subject. Reading is a skill (a process) that needs to be practiced. You learn by building blocks. Reading is constructing meaning from symbols. The teaching of reading, they say, can be broken down into four component parts and should not be viewed as holistic. Those parts are

1. *Grapho-phonemic:* Sounds are decoded from symbols. Once one masters this component, it is no longer needed to read; it becomes a natural part of one's approach to reading. Decoding is the only mechanical aspect of reading and should be considered separate from reading.
2. *Semantic system:* The cue system that gives the symbols meaning.
3. *Syntactic system:* The grammar of language.
4. *Prior knowledge:* The accumulated experiences that apply to understanding print.

Glass and Glass claim that two variables are required for decoding: visual and auditory attention. An example of a visual attention task would be to give a child thirty seconds to look at and memorize a list of ten words. An example of an auditory attention task would be to give a child ten familiar words orally and then ask the student to write down as many as he or she could remember.

The Glass program's premise is that visual and auditory attention is not automatic. These two decoding variables, when combined with a third component of sounding out words, must be practiced for the Glass procedure to be learned. Glass analysis includes the shaping of decoding behavior through a continuous process of questioning and immediate reinforcement using whole words. Glass and Glass claim to have found 120 possible cluster sounds for all words by researching various basal readers. The questioning procedure related to each word is for learning the *process of decoding* rather than the particular target word. Each lesson is designed to direct students' attention to the correct auditory and visual responses for the structures within each word.

Glass Procedure for Decoding Words

1. The whole word is exposed and the teacher orally reads the word (for example, *bat*).
2. Questions are asked first from sound to letters, then from letters to sounds, creating visual attention. (For example, What does the *b* sound like? What does the *at* sound like?)
3. Next, take off the letters or sounds and ask for remaining sounds. (For example, take away *b* and ask what sound remains. Take away *at* and ask what sound remains.) This creates auditory attention.
4. Always end by asking the student to say the entire word.

Basic Principles of Glass Analysis

- Decoding is not reading because reading is fundamentally extracting meaning from printed words and utilizing those meanings for personal or academic reasons.

- One can decode without reading but one cannot read without decoding.
- Decoding calls for a narrow set of responses whereas reading taps individual differences of ability and personal qualities.
- Syllabication is not used in reading and should not be part of a decoding program.
- Successful decoders do not consciously apply rules or principles and these should not be part of decoding instruction.
- Words are initially seen as wholes and then as composed of parts. Length of configuration is not related to difficulty in decoding.
- Correct visual and auditory clustering is of crucial importance to the decoding process.
- The correct mental set will cause the decoder to see and respond to the appropriate letter-sound structures within a whole word and then to decode the word correctly.

The central focus of the Glass procedure is to teach decoding using the words and meanings that the learner knows. All effort is applied to learning the decoding with no attempt to discover meaning. Teaching decoding out of context requires learners to focus on sounds and symbols within individual words. The process consists of placing words on flash cards, slides, and chalkboards, and having the learner repeat entire words several times during a lesson to ensure retention.

Whole Language Approach

The distinctive feature of this approach is its emphasis on the central directing role of reader predictions with minimum attention to visual decoding. Prediction precedes confirmation, which precedes correction. This approach is represented as a series of four primary cycles: optical, perceptual, syntactic, and meaning, with meaning in the controlling role (Davies, 1995). The

Figure 7.5 Contrasting Models of Literacy

Traditional Skills-Based Classroom	Comprehensive Meanings-Based Classroom
Basis of Philosophy	
Based on a behaviorist stimulus response model	Based on constructivist developmental psychology
Role of the Teacher	
Teachers transmit and dispense knowledge	Teachers facilitate student learning
Role of the Student	
Success and learning equates to high grades	Success viewed as achieving problem solutions, using critical-thinking skills
Definition of Literacy	
A product of a prescribed curriculum with an emphasis on skill attainment	Outcome is a literate critical thinker who reflects on meaning
Literacy Instruction	
Reading is textual analysis and writings are product centered, all chosen by teachers	Reading and writing are authentic and end products chosen by students
Literacy Strategies	
Lessons focus on sequential skill building from part to whole	Language learning is based on the whole to development part; skills taught in context
Literacy Class Organization	
Students work independently, grouped homogeneously	Students work cooperatively, grouped heterogeneously
Literacy Environment	
Texts are basis of curriculum	Variety of language materials available
Literacy Assessment	
Based on test grades, standardized tests	Based on observation and student demonstration, portfolios

attention of the reader is focused on meaning, whereby each cycle melts into the next and the reader leaps toward meaning. Anticipation and prediction are the driving forces, and the task of processing visual information is reduced merely to the recognition of a graphic display as written language.

Kenneth Goodman (1986) defines whole language as a way of bringing together a view of language, a view of learning, and a view of teachers and students. It represents a leap toward meaning as contrasted with a phonics approach, which can be described as plodding through print. At its core, it places a spotlight on whole-to-part learning, with the center of learning being language. Dorothy Watson (1989) claims that whole language is not a program, package, set of materials, method, practice, or technique; rather, it is a perspective on language and learning that leads to the acceptance of certain strategies, methods, materials, and techniques. It is difficult to establish a firm research base for whole language because of its holistic nature and its susceptibility to a teacher's personal interpretation. Whole language appears to be a perspective on education, containing a philosophy or belief system. It is an educational theory grounded in research and practice, and its practice is grounded in theory and research (Harste, 1989). A way of examining whole language would be to look at its roots, which stem from a constructivist view of learning. Where constructivism is a philosophical explanation about the nature of knowledge, whole language is a view about the development of literacy. There are, however, some commonly accepted principles that can be found in the literature such as:

- Language is learned best when children are immersed in a language-friendly environment, which offers a multitude of opportunities to read, write, speak, and listen. Literature is an integral part of the whole language curriculum. Children learn to read by reading. Classrooms should provide a wide variety of books and related materials. Learning is easiest when the focus is on the whole rather than on parts or on separate skills (Goodman, 1986, 1982).
- When language is integrated and students are actively involved in the process, children learn best. Learning is integrated. Students learn more effectively when they can see the connections and relationships among ideas and subjects than when they learn bits and pieces of information in isolation (Cornett and Blankinship, 1990, p. 19).
- When language is viewed as a way to achieve comprehension, children learn. Whole language tasks are authentic. Authentic activities relate to real-world tasks such as writing letters and reading information. When students can see the purpose and meaning of the work they do, they understand why it is important to do. They engage in fewer different tasks, but larger and more satisfying projects.
- When children are given choices with materials that provide repetitive language patterns, they learn. Learning is social. The purpose of language is to communicate with others. Children learn to use language by sharing ideas, working cooperatively, and becoming part of a community of learners.
- Children who are comfortable taking risks and questioning, and are not fearful of making mistakes, will have success in reading. Whole language classrooms are learner centered. Children feel commitment by being actively involved in the learning process, accepting responsibilities, and making choices and decisions regarding procedures, curriculum, and self-evaluation (Burns, 1996; Cornett and Blankinship, 1990, p. 24).

Whole language represents a holistic perspective toward learning, rather than a traditional building blocks approach. Proponents believe that learning does not occur in pieces, but is an indeterminate, whole process. That all children can learn a language is central to learning. Eight fundamental beliefs make whole language a powerful tool to teach for literacy.

Tenets of Whole Language

1. A holistic perspective toward literacy and learning
2. A positive view of all learners
3. Language as central to learning
4. Learning is easiest when it comes from whole to part, in authentic contexts
5. The empowerment of all learners, including students and teachers
6. Learning as both personal and social, and classrooms as learning communities
7. Acceptance of whole learners, including their languages, cultures, and experiences
8. Learning as both joyous and fulfilling (Watson, 1999)

Whole language is an alternative way of representing the reading process. Figure 7.6 illustrates the differences between whole language and Gough's model.

Balanced Literacy Approach The two basic views regarding reading instruction (the skills-based and meanings-based approaches) have sparked a continuous public debate about how reading should be taught. The term *whole language* means different things to different educators. It can mean simply having printed material readily available to children to use and reading to children to get them excited about reading; or it can denote a belief system used to guide reading instruction. Goodman's psycholinguistic perspective, which asserts that readers rely more on structure and meaning of language, has

Figure 7.6 Whole Language versus the Gough Model

Whole Language	Gough's Model
• Your eyes look at the words. • You think about the words and make predictions about meaning. • You reflectively sample a sentence as a whole to comprehend its meaning. • If you are uncertain about the meaning of the word, study the letters and sounds. • If comprehension is still lacking go back to meanings and predictions. These meanings lead to thinking, reflection, and comprehension.	• Your eyes look at the words. • The letters found are identified and sounded out. • You recognize the words. • You cognitively allocate words to grammatical class and sentence structure. • You construct meaning for sentences.

been placed in opposition to the skills-based phonics approach that stresses graphic information from text. The argument centers on whether or not literacy development parallels language development, or if language development is a sequential process. Both are correct to varying degrees. A common mistake made by many is to view whole language and skills-based instruction as dichotomous. Because the whole language approach claims that when children are immersed in a literacy-rich environment, they can learn to read naturally without direct instruction (Manzo, 1999; Sherman, 1998; Routman, 1996), individual teachers erroneously interpreted this to mean that they should disregard instruction in phonics. This was a mistaken view, since phonics taught in context is a key component of whole language.

It must be remembered that for years the works of skills-based and meanings-based researchers were pitted against each other in a war over which was the best way to teach reading. Snow, Burns, and Griffin (1998) found that teaching reading requires solid skill instruction (including phonics and phonemic awareness) imbedded in enjoyable reading and writing experiences, with whole texts to facilitate the construction of meaning. Their work was a precursor to the National Reading Panel report (2001) that implied that balanced reading instruction should combine the best of phonics instruction with whole language. To meet the reading needs of all children we should teach both skills and meaning as a strategy. It is amazing that the simple direct obviousness of this solution has not been accepted by academia, both researchers and practitioners. A combined approach where children are taught the relationship between letters and sounds in a systematic fashion, and read interesting stories while also writing, is one way to teach for literacy (Diegmueller, 1996).

The revival of the phonics-based, back-to-basics movement is not a cure-all for all reading problems. As noted by the National Association for Education of Young Children (1996), "Phonics should not be taught as a separate subject with an emphasis on drills and rote memorization. The key is a balanced approach and attention to each child's individual needs." Teaching phonics cannot be viewed as teaching reading. We must understand that phonics is merely a tool for the reader to use. Children need to see for themselves the relevance of phonics in their own reading and writing. In effect, we must provide balanced reading instruction for all our children to attain true literacy. Children cannot learn to read without an understanding of phonics. It is a forgone conclusion that children must know their ABCs and the sounds that letters make if they are to communicate verbally. The question is not whether to teach phonics or whole language, but *how* to teach phonics. It should be taught in context rather than isolation, so that children can make the necessary connections between letters, sounds, and meanings. A properly implemented, balanced literacy program can assist all children to become independent readers and writers.

Television and Balanced Literacy A contemporary approach to creating a language-friendly, balanced reading program is to incorporate the use of television. Many people have come to believe that effective comprehensive reading programs must do battle with a child's impetus to watch television. Because of the time spent in front of TVs, many critics lament that "Johnny can't read." The opposite is true. Television, when used correctly by teachers who have knowledge and understanding of the medium, is one of the pedagogue's best instructional tools. There are certainly many ways to teach reading, and all of them are right for someone when included under the blanket of a balanced whole language approach.

No one, to the best of the author's knowledge, has advocated the passive viewing of endless hours of TV programming as an effective reading tool. We need to develop an understanding of how programs are produced in order to generate activities that both develop and reinforce effective and cognitive reading skills. Print and television have many common characteristics that should be explored. Both forms of communication are designed to inform, persuade, or entertain a reader or viewer. To communicate, one must understand language and have the ability to process information. Using TV as a tool enables us to build upon skills already processed. The same cognitive processes one uses to analyze a written paragraph can be used to analyze a segment of a TV program. The same instructional questions apply to media, television, and print: "What was the author's intent?" or "How did the author use details or generalizations to support that intent?" or "How would you describe the main character?" or "What vocabulary was used?" or "What clues were given?" or "How might you predict the ending?" You can readily see the commonalities between print's written word and the visually transmitted spoken word.

The creation of images by television authors is essentially nonverbal, and focuses on actors, props, scenery, lighting, and costuming. Print authors, on the other hand, substitute the usual images found in television with verbal images found in sentences. When children write stories, they begin to understand how images affect interpretations. The cognitive process of analyzing content in print or TV is very similar. What is different is how images are produced. Once children understand this concept, they are ready to develop sophisticated thinking skills. If learning to think and make judgments is necessary for reading comprehension, then the critical-thinking skills employed in analyzing content in TV can help children learn to read with understanding.

A skillful reader develops self-confidence and self-esteem. Stressing the similarities between print and TV with regard to their intent (to inform, persuade, or entertain) and the common characteristics they share (language comprehension, processing information, and imagery) demonstrate the likeness between print and TV. These critical-thinking skills can be integrated within our curricula under the banner of a balanced whole language program. Good literature can be used to make good television. We broaden a child's horizons when we compare and contrast a story presented in both print and video. There are many ways to teach reading, and using TV as a medium does fall under the blanket of a balanced reading program.

Elements of Balanced Literacy Programs The main features of effective primary-grade reading programs are usually identified as skills and strategies that support reading and writing, word identification, fluency, comprehension, writing and spelling, and monitoring for understanding. Effective programs also provide opportunities to read and write. A good literacy curriculum promotes both skills and opportunities to read and write. The purpose of understanding the essential elements of reading is to identify elements of a solid early literacy program to guide schools and teachers in planning programs, instruction, resources, and services to improve reading achievement in the early years. Effective reading instruction is built on the following multiplying factors:

- Use reading to obtain meaning from print.
- Have frequent and intensive opportunities to read.
- Expose children to frequent, regular spelling-sound relationships.
- Have children learn about the alphabetic writing system.
- Provide an environment for understanding the structure of spoken words. (NYS Education Department, 1999)

To be compatible with a balanced program, any method must foster the integrated teaching of language arts in a coherent, meaningful way. It should contain:

1. *Concepts about print.* Teachers help children to learn the overall structure of book reading and conventions of print. This is done through repeated reading of storybooks, and big book activities. Various types of print are used to teach front to back, individual letters, and single words and sentences.
2. *Phonemic awareness.* This is the ability to recognize that our speech can be broken into forty-four small sounds. Knowledge of letter names and phonemic awareness in first grade are predictors of future achievement. Phonemic awareness is developed through frequent interaction with nursery rhymes, jingles, poetry, and books that contain words with rhymes and alliteration.
3. *Alphabetic principle.* Demonstrate the connection of letters and letter patterns into sound. Through phonemic awareness, speech can be segmented into small sounds that can be represented by printed forms.
4. *Word identification.* Teach a variety of processes to identify words. Include decoding or word-attack skills, decoding words by analogy with known words and sight word reading.
5. *Frequency.* Provide practice. Fluency comes from increased experience.
6. *Comprehension.* Teach higher-order thinking processes such as: using prior knowledge to construct meaning, summarizing, sequencing, predicting outcomes, drawing inferences, monitoring for understanding, and asking questions to clarify.
7. *Wide range of language and literacy experiences.* Provide opportunities to read, write, and speak. Use the writing process: prewriting, drafting, revising,

and proofreading in conjunction with instruction in the conventions of grammar, spelling, and punctuation. Also, recognize that oral language is the foundation for reading and writing.

8. *Literature.* Provide a variety of literary genres.
9. *Classroom environment.* It should be print-rich.
10. *Habits and attitudes.* Help students develop a sense of efficacy that evolves from an "I can do" philosophy and positive self-image.
11. *Home-school connections.* Parents should be considered partners in balanced literacy programs. When parents and teachers work together and demonstrate mutual respect, children's learning will be reinforced at home and in the classroom.

Contrasting Models of Literacy Implementing a balanced or eclectic reading program is what good teachers have always done. Eclecticism is not just a little of this and a little of that. It is based on a mix of theoretical perspectives and accomplished through conceptual selectivity. A reading program should be balanced, drawing on multiple theoretical perspectives. A good teacher, however, is more important and has a greater impact on the success of a child's reading than any single fixed reading program, method, or approach. The effective teacher has a personality that does not allow for the failure of students.

When we look at the contrasting models advanced for the teaching of literacy we are forced to see that there is no one solution to achieving literacy. Central to becoming literate is the acquisition of domain knowledge, which in effect is essential for anyone we call educated. The question is not about the end product, but about how we are to arrive at that final destination, literacy. By comparing and contrasting traditional classroom models with whole language classroom models, we hope to come to a middle ground called balanced literacy. This is a task that must be determined by each individual teacher. As long as you understand the contrasting positions, you can use your own best judgment as to which will work for you and the children who come to you eager to learn. It is a task not to be taken lightly. (Refer back to Figure 7.5, page 156.)

Literacy and Gender: Gender-Specific Teaching

This we think we know: American schools favor boys and grind down girls. The truth is the very opposite. By virtually every measure, girls are thriving in school; it is boys who are the second sex. (Sommers, 2000)

For many boys, the trouble starts in kindergarten when they realize they are different from girls physically and mentally. Most five-year-old girls start reading before boys and appear to be more fluent. Boys seem to have better hand-eye coordination, but have less developed fine-motor skills, causing them to have difficulty with pencils and paintbrushes. Boys fidget and act more reckless than girls because they are different from girls, not better or worse. Yet authors such as Mary Pipher (1994) and Carol Gilligan (1982) have claimed that there is a national emergency rooted in "a girl poisoning culture" that kills the preadolescent female spirit, and that our patriarchal society smothers girls' special powers of moral and social understanding.

Differences The difference in abilities stem from the brain's circuitry and the time it takes to develop. There is no way to tell the difference between a male or female brain. Different skills emerge at different ages for boys and girls. Girls develop language skills earlier than boys do, they use more words and tend to be more verbal; boys develop visual and spatial skills earlier than girls. By age two and a half, many girls actively choose not to play with boys, not for any cultural or sociological reason but because boys have not yet grasped the concept of verbal give-and-take (Ryan, 2005).

Boys, with their faster developing spatial skills, are more likely to gravitate to building blocks, train sets, and physical activities that require minimal verbal interaction. Boys are also more likely to find themselves in altercations because they have poor external language to hammer out a solution and poorer internal language to mediate their impulses. Boys' brains have a larger amount of cortical areas dedicated to spatial-mechanical functioning than do girls, who have more in the area of verbal-emotive processing (Blum, 1997).

Thirty years ago, it was girls, not boys, who were lagging. The 1972 federal law, *Title IX*, forced schools to provide equal opportunities for girls in the classroom and on the playing field. Over the next two decades, billions of dollars were funneled into finding new ways to help girls achieve. In 1992, the American Association of University Women issued a report claiming that the work of Title IX was not done—girls still fell behind in math and science; by the mid-1990s, girls had reduced the gap in math and more girls than boys were taking high school–level biology and chemistry. Some scholars, notably Christina Hoff Sommers, a fellow at the American Enterprise Institute, charged that misguided feminism is what has been hurting boys. In the 1990s, she says, girls were making strong, steady progress toward parity in schools, but feminist educators portrayed them as disadvantaged and lavished support and attention them. Boys, meanwhile, whose rates of achievement had begun to falter, were ignored and their problems allowed to increase (Sommers, 2000).

Traditional feminists argue that classic "boy" behaviors are a result of socialization and environmental factors. Today, most scientists believe they are an expression of male brain chemistry. Sometime in the first trimester, a male fetus begins producing male sex hormones that bathe his brain in testosterone for the rest of his gestation. How that exposure wires the male brain is not yet known. New studies show that prenatal exposure to male sex hormones directly affects the way children play. Girls whose mothers have high levels of testosterone during pregnancy are more likely to prefer playing with trucks to playing with dolls.

Do girls and boys really learn differently? There are in fact hard-wired differences in the ways girls and boys learn. There are innate differences in the ability to hear. Baby girls have a more sensitive sense of hearing than baby boys have. Those differences get larger as kids get older. By twelve years old, the average girl has a sense of hearing at least seven times more sensitive than the average boy. We also know that girls are distracted by extraneous noise (another student tapping a pencil, for instance) at sound levels ten times lower than those that distract boys. Most girls learn best in a quiet classroom, free from distractions. That is not true for many boys (Sax, 2005).

Scientists have an understanding of sex differences in brain development. Researchers at Virginia Tech used sophisticated electrophysiologic imaging of the brain to examine brain development of 508 normal children ranging in age from two months to sixteen years. These researchers found that while the areas of the brain involved in language and fine-motor skills such as handwriting mature about four years earlier in girls than in boys, the areas of the brain involved in geometry and spatial relations mature about four years earlier in boys than in girls. When it comes to learning geometry, the brain of the average twelve-year-old girl resembles the brain of the average eight-year-old boy. When it comes to writing poetry, the brain of the average twelve-year-old boy resembles the brain of the average eight-year-old girl (Sax, 2005).

These researchers concluded that various areas of the brain develop in "a different order, time, and rate" in girls, compared with boys. A curriculum that teaches the same subjects in the same sequence to girls and boys runs the risk of giving rise to twelve-year-old girls who think they cannot do geometry, and twelve-year-old boys who do not like to read or write. These cognitive gaps between boys and girls close during high school. Their brains catch up to each other. The problem is that by high school, boys have spent years reinforcing and strengthening their skills in math and science, and girls in language arts. They have formed images of themselves as good in one thing, and bad in the other. Many girls avoid chemistry and calculus in high school, never giving themselves the chance to discover that their visual-spatial capabilities have caught up to the boys. Many boys limit themselves to technical fields, unaware that their verbal aptitude has improved by their mid-teens (Gurian and Stevens, 2005).

Scientists caution that brain research does not tell the whole story—temperament, family background, and environment play big roles, too. Both boys and girls can be scarred by environmental factors such as violence, alcohol, or drug abuse. Nothing is 100 percent. Some boys are just as organized and assertive as the highest-achieving girls.

Key Research Facts

- Girls make higher grades in almost every subject.
- Boys have higher dropout rates, and higher representation in special education classes.
- Boys repeat a grade more often, and create more discipline problems, which gets them more often placed in alternative schools.
- Girls generally outperform boys in tests of verbal skills, while boys score higher in math and science.
- Fewer girls are labeled as gifted than are boys. Girls labeled as gifted are less likely to take rigorous high school math and science, major in either subject in college, or pursue careers in those fields.
- Boys make up 80 percent of those diagnosed with behavioral problems and 70 percent of those diagnosed with learning delays.
- Girls generally multitask better than boys. (Rich, 2000)

By almost every benchmark, boys across the nation and in every demographic group are falling behind. In elementary school, boys are two times more likely than girls to be diagnosed with learning disabilities and twice as likely to be placed in special education classes. High school boys are losing ground to girls on standardized writing tests. The number of boys who said they did not like school rose 71 percent between 1980 and 2001. Nowhere is the shift more evident than on college campuses. Thirty years ago, men represented 58 percent of the undergraduate student body. Now they are a minority at 44 percent. Males and females begin school with similar experiences, although females appear to have an advantage in early literacy. Females outperform males on reading and writing assessments at fourth, eighth, and twelfth grades. Females are less likely than males to repeat grades and seem to have fewer problems that put them at risk (Freeman, 2004). The reasons for these differences are:

- Boys are more often diagnosed with both attention deficit disorders and dyslexia. Frustration from these problems may result in boys acting out in class more often than do girls.
- Girls' hearing is more sensitive. As a result, they are more distracted by small noises. Boys can function in an actively noisy environment much better than can girls.
- The portion of the brain involved in language and handwriting matures about four years earlier in girls

than in boys; the reverse is true for spatial relations. Best practice is not the same in these instances for boys and girls.

Boys have always been boys, but the expectations for how they are supposed to act and learn in school have changed. In the last ten years, school performance has been measured in two simple ways: how many students are enrolled in accelerated courses and whether test scores stay high. Standardized assessments have become commonplace for kids as young as six. Curricula have become more rigid. Instead of allowing teachers to instruct kids in the manner and pace that suits their needs they are told what, when, and how to teach. Student-teacher ratios have risen, physical education and sports programs have been cut, causing new pressures on what psychologists call the "boy brain"—the moving, dynamic, disorganized, and sometimes sparkling erratic behaviors that some scientists believe are hard-wired into the brain, not learned. Michael Thompson (2000, 2005) believes that boys would be better off if they were understood and encouraged to be emotionally literate.

William Pollack (1999) claims that while we may live in a man's world that is not the same as living in a boy's world. His research shows that male infants are more emotionally expressive than female infants, yet as boys age their emotional expressiveness decreases. This is because boys are taught to suppress or cover up their emotions and vulnerability. This results in an inability to show true emotions, which hardens boys until they become emotional eunuchs. There are practical implications:

- Single-sex girls' classes are easier to teach and move at a faster pace.
- Boys prefer three quick activities rather than one longer project. Boys like taking tests, girls enjoy writing stories, and both boys and girls like hands-on activities.
- Teachers report that boys and girls participate more when in a single-sex class.
- Staff development is a key component of successful implementation of gender-specific classes.
- The research on maturation of different areas of the brain suggests that differentiated instruction needs to address these differences in the primary grades to prevent even larger differences by middle school.

King (2006) stresses creating boy-friendly environments that allow for gender differences. This can be accomplished through grouping for gender-specific topics that require physical movement for boys, and quiet areas for girls. Gurian (2005) promotes boy-friendly classrooms that replace lecture time with fast-moving lessons that all kids can enjoy. Curricula would include more multimedia language arts materials and provide individual choice reading, as well as allow the use of laptops for taking notes. Lessons, such as science experiments, could be structured to encourage physical movement. Boys could be grouped to work on boy-friendly projects such as exploring the history of a particular sport. These are essentially easy to do if one is interested in gender-specific teaching. There is nothing revolutionary about the strategies proposed; what is needed is the will to carry them out.

In elementary school classrooms—where teachers increasingly put an emphasis on language and a premium on sitting quietly and speaking in turn—the mismatch between boys and school can become painfully obvious. "Girl behavior becomes the gold standard. . . . Boys are treated like defective girls" (Thompson, 2000).

In middle school, boys are outperformed by girls. Some reasons are that girls reach sexual maturity two years ahead of boys, and their prefrontal cortex—a knobby region of the brain directly behind the forehead that helps humans organize complex thoughts, control impulses, and understand the consequences of their own behavior—develops sooner. In the last five years, brain scans have been used to show that in girls the brain reaches maximum thickness by age eleven and, for the next decade or more, continues to mature, while in boys the process is delayed for eighteen months (Giedd 2005).

The high school years are a critical time for teaching science and math to girls who have become demoralized in junior high school because teaching mathematics was not focused on their learning styles. The same holds true for boys in language arts. This means that we must reintroduce subject matter at various times during a child's development: something that makes no sense this year may make perfect sense the next year. We must spiral our curriculum as Bruner recommended. One of the most reliable predictors of whether a boy will succeed or fail in high school rests on a single question: Does he have a man in his life to look up to? Too often, the answer is no. High rates of divorce and single motherhood have created a generation of fatherless boys. In every kind of neighborhood, rich or poor, an increasing number of boys—now a startling 40 percent—are being raised without their biological fathers. Psychologists say that grandfathers and uncles can help, but emphasize that an adolescent boy without a father figure is like an explorer without a map. That is especially true for poor boys and boys who are struggling in school. Older males model self-restraint and solid work habits for younger ones. And whether they're breathing down their necks about grades or admonishing them to show up for school on time, "an older man reminds a boy in a million different ways that school is crucial to their mission in life" (Gurian, 2005).

We are a long way from having a well-established set of best practices for a gender-specific education. Some believe the answers can be found in *single-sex schools*. One area that needs research is *gender-atypical children*. What about the shy boy who wilts in the noisy, boisterous classroom where most other boys thrive? What about the loud, rambunctious girl who disdains the quiet classroom most girls prefer? Because of the gender-atypical children, single-sex education in public schools must remain voluntary and parents must determine what is right for their child.

It must be understood that the differences between male and female brains are what they are—biological facts devoid of social or political considerations. What we do about those differences between boys and girls is about social and political beliefs. We can espouse an ideology that claims that gender equality means gender sameness and ignore the research that says otherwise. On the other hand, we can choose to utilize new information and focus on achieving real equality, the kind that does not mistake difference for inferiority, but values all those striving toward achievement. No matter what course we take, we will be on the right route if we remain cognizant of the fact that gender-specific teaching is the way to close the achievement gap and its potentially negative implications for our society.

In the last two decades, the education system has become obsessed with a quantifiable and narrowly defined kind of academic success that is harming boys.

PRACTICE EXERCISE 7.3

Literacy and Gender

Read the five selections and determine the author's position regarding literacy and gender. Is the author for (1) single-sex schools, (2) single-sex classes, (3) single-sex grouping, (4) gender-specific teaching, or (5) coeducational classes? Validate your choices by noting the text that supports your position.

- Rebora, A. (2006). Sex education. *Teacher Magazine*.
- Brown, L. M., Lind, M. C., & Stein, N. (2006, June 6). What about the boys? *Commentary* 25(39): 35.
- Viadero, D. (2006, March 15). Concern over gender gaps shifting to boys. *Education Week* 25(27): 1, 16–17.
- Lightfoot, J. (2006). The masculine mystique: Are boys the losers of the ongoing gender wars? *Seattle Weekly Media*.
- Rivers, C., & Barnett, R. C. (2006, October 2). Against single-sex public schools. *Los Angeles Times*.

Boys are biologically, developmentally, and psychologically different from girls—and teachers need to learn how to bring out the best in everyone. They can do this by answering three simple questions that will affect future generations:

1. Should schools consider opportunities for single-sex classes? Why?
2. What issues would you address in developing single-sex classes?
3. Based on available information about different ways that boys and girls learn, what changes should we make in our instructional strategies in any classroom, single-sex or co-ed?

MINI CASE FROM THE FIELD

The following case from the field discusses the importance of understanding the role of the teacher with regard to developing strategies and methods that meet the needs of all children. Read the case, compare, and analyze Nick's, Margaret's, Jane's, Ed's, and Lucille's ideas about what constitutes an effective approach for teaching boys who are failing in a regular mainstream class.

Why Are Boys Failing?

Nicholas Saccone had shown exceptional professional growth since joining the faculty at the McGraw Simpson Elementary and Senior High School. He had overcome his street-smart aggressive attitude and was quickly becoming one of the most effective teachers at school. Principal Thompson said privately that he was a diamond in the rough and he knew how to make him shine. He was uniquely qualified to teach science, being state-certified on all levels with a master's degree in biology. His position was distinctive since it spanned all twelve grades. He taught high school and middle school science, and simultaneously, the science cluster in the elementary school.

Mr. Thompson had asked Nick to lead a faculty discussion group focused on "gender-specific teaching strategies." Nick had accepted the assignment without realizing how difficult it would be to develop consensus on K to 12 schoolwide policies directed at effective instructional practices that were gender specific.

Nick decided he would form a cooperative brainstorming group made up of representatives from the high school, middle school, and elementary school. Margaret Gomez and Jane Hemmings volunteered to represent the social studies and language arts departments from the middle school. Ed Child volunteered to represent the high school math department, and Lucille Chan volunteered to represent the elementary school. Nick would act as the moderator.

Nick began the first meeting by expounding on the difficulty he anticipated in arriving at mutually satisfactory policies and strategies that would address the question of the high rate of male failure throughout the grades. He said it would be similar to squaring a circle, which is not a true problem: it simply aims at what is by definition a contradiction. He went on to say that there are really no contradictions in nature or with this problem of boys failing: contradictions only exist in the mind. It is like the pseudo-problem of what happens when the irresistible force meets the immovable object. Nick assured everyone that something happens when the irresistible force hits the immovable object in nature. We learn if the force is resistible or the object movable. He said he believed that this immovable object, boys failing throughout the grades, could be resolved by the irresistible force that this committee would provide.

Ed Child looked at Nick and exclaimed, "You must be kidding. What exactly are you talking about? I think your question is simply, Why are boys failing and what can we do about it? Don't get so philosophical—it only confuses the issue."

Margaret Gomez chimed in, "I think the real problem is how we teach for literacy with all students. There is no denying that there is a gender gap—which I believe is the result of female success rather than boys failing. The data, if you read it, suggest that boys have made progress or stayed the same, but girls have made improvements faster, especially in mathematics and science. This creates the false appearance that boys are losing ground."

"Hold on a minute," said Ed. "I think you and your data are wrong. Numbers do not lie, and girls have long scored higher than boys in reading at ages nine and seventeen according to the NAEP. I believe the reason is that most female teachers are unknowingly feminizing boys. Simple examples can be seen everywhere. When boys play in a rough-and-tumble fashion at recess it is punished and called aggression. If a first grader hugs a classmate, he is punished for harassment. Women teachers decorate their classrooms with pictures of successful females as role models. The reason boys are failing is that they are not treated as boys!"

Lucille Chan said she took exception to Ed's remarks. His argument would take them nowhere and put them in a zero-sum game where concern for girls would be interpreted as neglect for boys. "It's not girls' or female teachers' fault that boys are not doing well in school," Lucille said, "It is the fault of a society that sends out the message that going to school is not masculine, it's for girls. Being tough is cool. That is where the problem is."

Jane Hemmings said, "If you're looking for a way to reduce failure among boys you're going about it in the wrong manner. As far as I know, accusations are not possible solutions. Why don't we look at making classrooms boy friendly. Research has shown that boys are more aggressive, impulsive, single-task focused, and seem to learn by using spatial kinesthetic strategies. Based on this data, why not increase opportunities for physical movement during class sessions? Let boys select topics that appeal to them like sports. Offer boys support with homework—which seems to be a prime concern at all levels. We could even offer single-gender learning environments by grouping cooperatively for specific boy-friendly topics."

"Wait a minute, Jane," said Lucille. "Just because boys need to be engaged more we can't forget the positive female attributes. They are generally better fit for the verbal-emotive, sit-still, take-notes, listen-carefully, multitasking requirements of traditional and progressive schools. I propose that we provide single-sex classes."

Ed Child looked up and said, "Do you want to create single-gender learning environments?" You know the data identified more than 100 structural differences between the male and female brain. For example, girls' brains generate more cross talk between hemispheres, which leads to better multitasking, while boys tend to lateralize and compartmentalize brain activity, leading to strong single-task focus."

Then Nick stepped in. "My head is spinning from this discussion. I think we need to take some time and reflect on some basic questions that all teachers need to address. Do teachers realize the problems boys face in today's schools? Do teachers understand that there is scientific research that indicates that we need to be developing strategies to meet the specific needs of both girls and boys? How do we develop boy-friendly and girl-friendly learning environments? Do teachers realize that many behaviors of boys or girls are neurologically based? I hope that these questions are challenging, because acting on what we have learned can lead to rewards for both boys and girls."

1. List the points made by Margaret, Lucille, Jane, and Ed. Explain how they are similar and how they disagree.
2. What was Lucille attempting to achieve by her line of reasoning? Was she successful in converting Ed? Explain.
3. What was Margaret attempting to achieve by her line of reasoning? Was she successful in converting Ed to her way of thinking? Explain.
4. Contrast and compare Margaret's approach to resolving the problem of boys failing with Lucille's, Jane's, and Ed's. Whose strategy is the stronger approach?
5. Has Ed the makings of an acceptable approach to learning? Justify your answer.
6. Describe Nick's philosophy. How does his summation give evidence to his beliefs?

PRACTICE EXERCISE 7.4

Guide for Evaluating Articles

Use the following guide to prepare a brief critique on each of the assigned articles in Practice Exercise 7.3.

Preparation

- Skim through the article to get an overall view.
- Carefully read the article, looking for specifics.

Writing the Critique

Introduction

- State the title and the source, use APA style for references.
- Include information about the author if available.

Body

- Write a brief summary of the article.
- Does the article state a problem? Give examples.
- Does the author state a theory? Are there examples to support the theory?
- Does the author explore a new idea?

Data

- Is the article too broad or too narrow? Is there evidence of bias? Is the author objective? Give examples.
- What type of research if any, is used? In what form is the data presented? (e.g., figures, graph)? Do the findings support the author's theory or point of view? Give examples.

Conclusion

- What is your overall opinion or assessment of the article?
- How do you react to the author's conclusion?

PROGRAMS TO IMPROVE LITERACY

There are a number of programs that teachers have used successfully in typical classroom situations. Several of these are offered as a starting point for selecting programs that may be beneficial in the various situations encountered in diverse classrooms. Most of these programs fit in well with a balanced approach to reading (Duffy-Hester, 1999). It is important to note that fewer than one-third of adolescents meet grade-level expectations for reading: among low-income students, the number is closer to one in seven (National Center for Educational Statistics, 2005). With this in mind we should also evaluate elements that that go into making middle and high school students better readers. The *Reading First* feature of the No Child Left Behind Act originally presupposed that if students could master the basics of literacy in the early grades there would be little need to emphasize literacy in the secondary grades. But this has proven not to be the case; students need ongoing support at all grades levels (Torgesen et al., 2007; Biancarosa and Snow, 2004).

The Book Club Program (BCP) answers essential questions related to literacy instruction: Are students engaged in lively, thoughtful discussion? Are they taking responsibility for their own study of literature? Moreover, are they growing to be confident, eager readers? The answers are based on four essential components:

- The class uses the concept of *community share,* whereby a teacher assists children in joining a community of readers by sharing in whole-class read-alouds of new books.
- Reading is taught using a variety of techniques, from reading aloud to silent reading, in no particular order. Children also read independently and possibly share books they have read.
- The writing component consists of children writing stories in their logs and/or other types of writing.
- The Book Club is the heart of the program. Children discuss a common text in small groups. The book club approach provides opportunities for students to work both independently and with others on authentic literacy tasks. At the same time, teachers provide explicit instruction in reading strategies, creating a motivating and supportive literacy environment. (Raphael, 2002)

Concept-Oriented Reading Instruction (CORI) is an integrated approach to teaching reading, writing, and science, and is best implemented in diverse third-grade and fifth-grade classrooms. The CORI program uses real-world events and objects as the basis for instruction, thus creating an authentic purpose for teaching literacy and science strategies. Its stated goals are to increase students' reading comprehension, reading motivation, and science knowledge. It consists of four phases that are focused on (1) reading strategy instruction, (2) science inquiry activities, (3) motivational support, and (4) reading and science integration:

- Observe and personalize occurrences and objects in nature, with students formulating questions from these observations, which are later used in literacy-related activities.

- Search and retrieve information within texts to answer the questions previously formulated. Children learn how to use resources to answer their questions.
- Comprehend and integrate: Children learn comprehension, note taking, and analysis strategies in order to integrate information they are reading to answer their questions.
- Communicate to others: Students present the information they have learned to their peers through communications in order to develop a sense of audience in reading and writing. (Guthrie et al., 2004)

Fluency-Oriented Reading Instruction (FORI) is a program focused on helping children become fluent readers while focusing on text comprehension. Three main components designed to meet the goals of FORI consist of home reading, a free-choice reading period, and a redesigned basal reading lesson. The teacher reads a story aloud, using story maps, questioning, or graphic organizers to assist in discussion. The story is then read again with the whole group/small group or with a partner. Finally, children respond to the text through journals or dramatizations. To achieve this objective five goals were developed:

- Keep the focus of reading lessons on students' comprehension of text.
- Have students read material on their instructional levels.
- Support students in their reading through repeated readings.
- Provide opportunities for children to engage in text-based social interactions through partner reading.
- Expand the amount of time children spend on reading. (Miller, 2005)

Four Blocks Approach (FBA) takes place in the context of "four blocks" of time. The Four-Blocks framework outlines a systematic, multi-level approach to teaching literacy. This model acknowledges that all children learn differently, and provides a framework for teaching with four different blocks: guided reading, self-selected reading, writing, and working with words.

- *Guided reading block.* Children read leveled selections individually, in groups and with a partner. Discussions are held before and after reading. Support groups for struggling readers meet every day.
- *Self-selected reading block.* Teacher reads a book out loud. Children select a text from a variety of genres. While children are reading, teacher is working with individual students. At the end of the block, children share what they read with the class.
- *Writing block.* The teacher models, then students write independently on a topic of their choice using the writing process (prewriting, drafting, revising, editing, or publishing). Children meet with the teacher and then share their writing with others.
- *Working with words block.* Children learn how to read and spell high-frequency words, and to decode and spell other words. A class word wall is used to display five high-frequency words each week. (Cunningham et al., 1999)

Kamehameha Early Child Education Program (KEEP) is a whole literacy curriculum that uses six aspects of literacy as its base for instruction and program design. The program is a language arts program that was designed for underachieving native Hawaiian children. It was developed in the early 1970s to help these children improve their reading skills by emphasizing anthropological knowledge and the importance of cultural compatibility. The children's native culture was used as a basis for instructional practices. The program is grounded in social constructivist thinking and sociocultural perspectives. Its elements consist of:

- Ownership of reading and writing
- Reading comprehension
- The writing process
- Language and vocabulary knowledge
- Word-reading strategies and spelling
- Voluntary reading (Kamehameha Schools, 2003)

Success for All (SFA) is a comprehensive school-restructuring program that includes tutoring, family support services, and instruction in writing/language arts, mathematics, social studies, and science. The reading component consists of three basic programs:

- The Pre-Kindergarten or Early Kindergarten program
- Beginning reading or Reading Roots program
- Beyond reading or Reading Wings program

The Pre-Kindergarten or Early Kindergarten program contains instructional components that are common to other programs because of their reported success. These components consist of a procedure called story telling and retelling (StaR), a process focused on emergent writing and a rhyme with reason strategy. These components combined with shared book experiences, utilizes the Peabody Language Development Kit, with various alphabet activities.

The Reading Roots program usually begins in the second half of kindergarten and continues until students reach primer level. The program consists of a listening comprehension component similar to StaR, a unit similar to the Peabody, and "shared story" lessons. These consist of five parts: a show-time (reading rehearsal and letter formation review); thinking about reading; presenting the story; sound, letter, and word development activities; culminating in story activities.

The Reading Wings program begins with students who are reading on the first-grade level and continues through the elementary years. Children work mainly with cooperative groups or partners. The program has four main components: story-related activities, direct instruction in reading, independent reading, and listening comprehension (Slavin and Madden, 2006).

Program Elements for Successful Middle and High School Literacy   When we look at secondary schools that are achieving, we see that they share a focus on the following program elements. They may not include all of these elements, but enough are present.

- Direct, explicit instruction in reading comprehension
- Reading instruction focused on academic content
- Attention to student motivation and self-directed learning
- Collaborative learning
- Strategic tutoring
- Opportunities for students to read diverse, high-level texts
- Intensive instruction and practice in writing
- A technology component
- Ongoing assessment of students' skills and needs
- Periodic assessment of students' mastery of standards
- Extensive time reserved for literacy learning
- Professional development opportunities for teachers
- Opportunities for teachers to work in teams
- Strong leadership
- Comprehensive coordinated planning. (Biancarosa, 2004; Snow, 2003)

MINI CASE FROM THE FIELD

The following case from the field discusses the importance of understanding and developing strategies that focus on teaching for literacy. Read the case then compare and analyze Nick's, Margaret's, Jane's, Ed's, and Lucille's ideas about what constitutes literacy and how we teach our students to achieve it.

What Exactly Does Teaching for Literacy Mean?

The meeting on gender-specific teaching strategies seemed to have gone on forever. Nick couldn't believe he had to call another meeting based on Margaret's point of order. Margaret had said that she felt it was silly to discuss how to help stop boys from failing when they didn't even have a working definition of literacy, aside from the dictionary's definition "an ability to read and write to a competent level, or have knowledge in a particular subject or area." Nick thought that understanding literacy was more involved than Margaret thought. What about computer literacy, emotional literacy, or media literacy? Should they be considered in any cogent definition of literacy for the twenty-first century, or was it all pseudointellectual philosophizing?

It had been a long time since Nick had done anything spontaneously, let alone react to a proposal that could jeopardize his committee. Finding a solution for the question of why boys were failing had led to a productive discussion on the relationship between gender and literacy. The best way to proceed from this point would be to ask each committee member to define literacy and then jointly develop one inclusive definition. "What does literacy mean in the twenty-first century?" Members were also asked to keep in mind the question of how to promote forward-looking thinking in a changing world. What will it mean to be a literate person?

When Margaret received Nick's survey she thought at least now they were getting somewhere. Literacy to her meant the ability to understand how to learn. She had core beliefs related to learning. She believed that we learn more easily when learning is fun, that everyone is both teacher and learner, and that teachers should use a learner's strengths to overcome deficits. Her definition would be that to be literate one had to be both a learner and a teacher who created a fun-filled learning environment.

Ed thought that to be literate one would have to master content and the truths from which it is constructed. For Ed, mathematics was the central core of all knowledge. The theory of minutiae he had learned in college proposed that there was nothing in life so big that it couldn't be reduced to its component parts, analyzed, and understood. That's what a literate person needed to know in order to understand, he believed.

Lucille Chan responded to Nick's survey by saying that literacy was comprehending what was read and what one wrote. It was as simple as that. Why make a big deal about it?

Jane Hemmings thought the survey was much to do about nothing. It seemed to her that Margaret sometimes acted as an obstructionist. Nick should have ignored her request and just said that a literate person for the twenty-first century must be able to read, write, comprehend, predict, analyze and be a problem solver. That has always been its meaning.

After looking at the responses to his question, Nick said to himself: The key to teaching for literacy is to be a literate critical thinker who is able to understand and use the knowledge he or she has accumulated for further advancing mankind.

1. What part would media, computer, or emotional literacy play in the formulation of any comprehensive definition of literacy for the twenty-first century?
2. Whose definition is the most comprehensive? How would you support it?
3. Compare and contrast Margaret's, Ed's, Jane's, and Lucille's definitions with Nick's final summation.
4. How would you answer Nick's survey questions?

Chapter Summary

In this chapter, we have attempted to gain insights on how to teach for literacy. We began by looking at the purposes of reading and spotlighted the indispensable role of domain knowledge in order to achieve literacy. We briefly reviewed recent research findings that stress the importance of phonemic awareness, phonics, fluency, vocabulary, and comprehension. We spoke about traditional approaches to teaching literacy while providing six sample lesson plans appropriate for adolescents. We then compared and contrasted skills-based traditional phonics approaches to reading with meanings-based, psycholinguistic whole language approaches to reading. Both approaches, if used alone, are open to criticism. A middle ground, called balanced literacy, can resolve these contrasting approaches to literacy. By examining its philosophy, and its teacher and student roles, we have seen how literacy with reading and writing skills in specific class environments has resulted in successful teaching for literacy. In a truly balanced literacy program, *how* you teach is as important as *what* you teach. We have discussed the essential elements of reading along with literacy and gender, though many questions are left unanswered. As always, the selection of what is to be used is left to you, the teacher. The only effective approach is the one that works for you.

Cases from the Field

CASE ONE

Alan has been teaching for five years. In that time, he has depended on a phonics reading program to teach reading to his special sixth-grade class. He believes his program has been effective, based on the teacher-made tests he has used to verify his assumption. His school is moving into a balanced literacy program, which he knows little about. He thinks, "I'm not going to change a program that works. It wouldn't be fair to the children."

1. What steps should Alan take now that his school has decided to change the reading program?
2. How can Alan overcome his natural resistance to change?
3. Should Alan speak to his principal about his reservations regarding the new reading program? What should he say?
4. How can Alan make his point without risking disciplinary action for refusing to follow school policy?
5. If you were Alan, what would you do?

CASE TWO

The Winston Elementary School where Jane teaches has a very influential Parent Teacher Association. The PTA has been able to get the school board to limit the amount of time children are to watch television to no more than twenty minutes an evening. The philosophy they espouse is that you learn to read by reading, not looking at TV. But this goes right to the heart of Jane's communication arts program, which encourages children to study and compare the similarities between the print media and television.

1. What steps can Jane take to keep her program functioning?
2. Jane's school claims to have a balanced reading program. How can Jane show parents that television does fit into a literacy program?
3. How can Jane elicit the principal's and the school board's support?
4. How can Jane demonstrate the efficacy of her position?
5. If you were Jane, how would you handle this situation?

CASE THREE

You're a second-grade teacher in an inner-city elementary school. The school has consistently failed to get more than 30 percent of its fourth-grade students to read on grade level. Because of this deficit, the administration and parents strongly emphasize the use of a skills-based literacy program. Yet you find that your students hate to work in their skills books. Your class's frustration motivates you to abandon the program and to attempt to develop your own literacy program based on reading good books. Your assistant principal visits your class and is shocked at what she terms your inappropriate actions. She then directs you to "get with the program."

1. Why do you suppose the assistant principal acted the way she did?
2. In your opinion, why are the children frustrated by a skills program?
3. How can a compromise be reached to resolve this situation?
4. Which do you think is a better approach, the school's or the teacher's? Why?
5. What would you do in this situation?

CASE FOUR

Carolanetta was a poised and seemingly mature young woman who had just completed college the previous fall. The teaching position at Lane High School was the first she had ever held. As a language arts major she had expected to be teaching the great literary classes, not remedial reading to tenth graders. Her department chairperson Mrs. Kline, asked Carolanetta to review classroom programs that claimed to improve reading growth. She specifically asked her to look for traditional programs. This bothered Carolanetta since she favored a more balanced literacy approach.

1. If you were Carolanetta, how would you go about your task for Mrs. Kline?
2. What type of program would be appropriate for a high school tenth-grade class?
3. Would a book club program be appropriate? Explain.
4. What arguments could Carolanetta make to persuade Mrs. Kline to accept a more balanced approach to literacy?
5. What program or programs would you use? Why?

Terms to Remember

Domain knowledge
SQ4R, DRL, KWL
Gough's model
Basal reading

Glass analysis
Balanced literacy
Gender-specific teaching

Discussion Questions

1. What similarities do you find among balanced language, whole language, and the literature-based approach to reading instruction?
2. Describe the classic approach to reading instruction called SQ4R. Why was it successful in most cases? Compare SQ4R to DRL and KWL. How are they similar, and how do they differ? Why are they appropriate strategies for adolescents?
3. Design a unit plan in which you would use the "guiding principles of whole language" to teach reading to a fifth-grade class.
4. How would you incorporate the essential elements of reading into a structured literacy program for a fourth-grade class?
5. Review the eleven elements that research cites as the foundation of a balanced literacy program and incorporate each into a lesson plan of your choice.
6. Discuss the importance of gender-specific teaching and give examples of how you would provide it in your classroom.
7. Peruse the six classroom programs that claim to improve reading growth. Select one program and explain why you would use this approach in your class.
8. Compare and contrast a traditional classroom with a balanced-reading classroom.

Field Experience Activities

1. Interview two primary school teachers and ask their opinions regarding a traditional basal reading program as compared to a balanced literacy program.
2. Interview two secondary school teachers and ask them to describe the strategies they use to enhance their students' literacy.
3. Compare the responses of both sets of teachers with your own views.
4. Observe two reading lessons and determine whether each is a traditional or a balanced reading program.
5. Observe a reading lesson and determine the following:
   - The basic reading philosophy employed
   - The teacher's role
   - Whether literacy is a product of a prescribed curriculum or is taught in a meaningful context
   - If reading and writing topics are chosen by the teacher or by the student
   - How skills are taught, sequentially or whole to part
   - How the class is organized for literacy instruction
   - The physical environment of the classroom

For Further Reading

Anderson, R. C., Hebert, E. H., Scott, J. A., and Wilkinson, I., preparers. (1985). *Becoming a nation of readers: The report of the Commission on Reading.* Washington, DC: U.S. Department of Education.

Chall, J. S. (2000). *The academic achievement challenge: What really works in the classroom?* New York: Guilford Press.

Ferrara, P. (2004). Single-gender classrooms: Lessons from a New York middle school. *ERS Spectrum,* Summer.

Fountas, I., and Pinnell, G. S. (2001). *Guiding readers and writers.* Portsmouth, NH: Heinemann.

Fountas, I., and Pinnell, G. (1996). *Guided reading: Good first teaching for all children.* Portsmouth, NH: New Zealand Department of Education, Heinemann.

Gersten, R., and Geva, E. (2003, April). Teaching reading to early language learners. *Education Leadership* 60 (7): 44–49.

Gilligan, C. (2002). *The birth of pleasure.* New York: Alfred A. Knopf.

Goodman, K. S. (1992). I didn't found whole language. *The Reading Teacher* 46: 188–199.

Goodman, K. S. (1989). Whole language research: Foundations and development. *Elementary School Journal* 90: 208–221.

Gurian, M. (2002). *Boys and girls learn differently! A guide to teachers and parents.* San Francisco, CA: Jossey-Bass.

Slavin, R. E. (1995). *Cooperative learning: theory, research and practice.* Boston: Allyn & Bacon.

Slavin, R. E. (1990). *Cooperative learning: Theory, research, practice.* Englewood Cliffs, NJ: Prentice-Hall.

Slavin, R. E. (1983). *Cooperative learning.* New York: Longman.

Sommers, C. H. (1994). *Who stole feminism?* New York: Simon & Schuster.

Thompson, M., and Kindlon, D. (2000). *Raising Cain: Protecting the emotional life of boys.* New York: Ballantine Books.

Vacca, R. T., and J. L. Vacca. (2003). *Content area reading: Literacy and learning across the curriculum,* 7th ed. Boston: Allyn & Bacon.

Wolcott, J. (2004). Segregation salvation? *Christian Science Monitor,* May 25.

Yatvin, J. (2002). I told you so! The misinterpretation and misuse of the National Reading Panel report. *Education Week* 56 (April): 44–45.

CHAPTER 8

Thinking for Understanding

FOCUS POINTS

1. All children can learn when exposed to a quality instructional program that encourages critical thinking.

2. All genuine learning is active, not passive.

3. Teaching children to think and not simply to recite or perform is a goal of education.

4. Learning is a student's responsibility, while providing an enriched education for everyone is the role of the school and its teachers.

CHAPTER OVERVIEW

IN THIS CHAPTER, we focus on the relationship between thinking for understanding, and one's philosophy as it affects student learning. We begin by looking at critical thinking and its relationship to effective teaching, and one's personal educational philosophy. Readers can link their own philosophy to historical definitions of educational philosophy. The chapter's purpose is to facilitate the discovery of the philosophy within each of us, and its implications for student learning. By defining our philosophies, we should become better teachers. Most people unfortunately never clearly define their beliefs and philosophies. They may not even be aware that they have a definite and pronounced set of beliefs that everyone else seems to know. There is no escaping one's beliefs and values, since everything we do is predicated on them. Some may denounce theory and philosophy as only of interest to academics. This sends the erroneous message that practitioners need not be concerned with educational philosophy, which of course is ridiculous and at minimum nihilistic. One's philosophy of education does exist and defines everything done in the classroom, while also greatly influencing student learning.

CRITICAL THINKING

The basic concept of critical thinking is, at root, simple. We could define it as the art of taking charge of your mind. Its value is also simple: If we can take charge of our own minds, we can take charge of our own lives; we can improve them, bringing them under our self-command and direction. Of course, this requires that we learn self-discipline and the art of self-examination. This involves becoming interested in how our minds work, and making modifications when necessary. It means examining and reflecting on our accustomed actions in classrooms, and getting into the habit of examining our behaviors and motivations.

Most people rarely scrutinize their behaviors critically to see if they are rationally justified. At times, we act impulsively and buy items we do not really need or cannot afford. As parents and teachers, we often respond to our children impulsively and uncritically, without stopping to determine whether our actions are consistent with how we want to act. Are we contributing to our children's self-esteem and discouraging them from taking responsibility for their own behavior by inappropriate actions? Critical thinking can involve feelings as well as reasons. There is room for emotion when one challenges his or her own beliefs or the beliefs of others. As long as we reflect and understand that critical thinking is a process and not an outcome, we can develop a critical-mindedness with regard to all aspects of life (Kipping, 2000).

As teachers, too often we allow ourselves to teach as we have been taught, uncritically, giving assignments that students can mindlessly do. This practice discourages both initiative and independence, while missing the opportunity to cultivate self-discipline and thoughtfulness.

Critical thinking is an eminently practical goal and value. The ancient Greek ideal of "living an examined life" empowers our students, and us, in quite practical ways and therefore, should be the focus of life. Critical thinking can transform every dimension of school life: how we formulate and promulgate rules; how we relate to our students; how we encourage them to relate to each other; how we cultivate their reading, writing, speaking, and listening; and what we model for them inside and outside the classroom.

To make critical thinking a basic value in school, we have to make it a basic value in our own lives, a part of our philosophy of life. To become adept at teaching to foster critical thinking, we must be committed to thinking critically and reflectively about our own lives and the lives of those around us. We must become active daily practitioners of critical thought for understanding by modeling how to reflectively examine, critically assess, and effectively improve (Paul, 2001).

Definitions

John Dewey introduced the concept of *reflective thinking* in 1910. His basic assumption was that learning improves to the degree that it arises out of the process of reflection. This idea is considered by many synonymous with critical thinking, creative thinking, problem solving, and higher-level thought. Dewey's definition of reflective thinking was "active, persistent, and careful consideration of any belief or supposed form of knowledge in the light of the grounds that support it and the further conclusion to which it tends" (Dewey, 1993).

Creative thinking, on the other hand, involves creating something new or original. It is used to solve problems and think "outside of the box." Its aim is to stimulate curiosity and promote divergence. It is not something you are born with, but something that is learned.

Actually, *critical thinking* is not making decisions or solving problems. It is not the same as reflective thinking, creative thinking, or conceptualization, which is interpreting observations through the prism of a specific concept. These types of thinking have a different purpose than critical thinking, the purpose of which is to create a productive and positive learning activity.

The word *critical* in critical thinking comes from the Greek word for criterion, *kriterion*, which means a benchmark for judging. Critical thinking is judging the reasonableness and truthfulness of statements. The use of critical-thinking skills leads to learning and understanding. It essentially allows us to *think for understanding*. The purpose of critical thinking is essentially to achieve literacy. We need to refocus on critical comprehensive products, advancing reading and writing as tools that will create literate critical thinking young people. A simple definition of critical thinking is to make reasoned judgments (Beyer, 1995).

Literate Critical Thinking

Literate critical thinking is gaining, sharing, and reasoning with information in all its forms. It is a process, not an outcome. It consists of all uses of communication to gain, share, and reason with knowledge. It is the type of thinking needed to succeed in life. To be literate in the age of technology requires learning thinking skills to assist in life's decisions and actions. Literate critical thinking involves the ability to use language and thought combined with the ability to access, analyze, evaluate, and communicate information. It involves feelings as well as reasons. We learn from our experiences, which, by definition, include our senses and feelings.

A basic concept for critical thinking concerns the art of taking charge of your own mind. Reading and writing are but tools to achieve critical comprehensive end products. When we act decisively and take charge of our minds, we also take charge of our lives, which allows for improvement by developing self-command and direction. This presupposes our learning self-discipline and monitoring our actions while reflectively examining any impulsive behaviors we might be accustomed to using (Paul, 2003a, 2003b).

To develop critical thinking is a practical goal with value if one is to be literate. The living an examined life ideal is based on attaining the skills, insights, and values essential to that end. It is a way of going about living and learning that empowers our students, and us, in quite practical ways. It can transform every dimension of school life, from promulgating rules to how we cultivate reading, writing, speaking, and listening. What we model for students inside and outside the classroom should lead them to a rich and literate world existence.

When we make critical thinking a basic value in our lives, it will become a basic value in the lives of our students. To become adept at teaching that fosters critical thinking, we must be committed to thinking critically and reflectively and becoming active practitioners of critical thought by modeling critical thinking. To be literate is to think critically!

Guide to Literate Critical Thinking (SCARPO) There are six essential ingredients for literate critical thinking to take place. The first concerns the ways we behave: we should be *skeptical*, questioning the accuracy, authenticity, and plausibility of what is presented. Always be open-minded and respect evidence and reasoning, which may at times warrant changing your position (Paul, 1991). Second, determine the criteria for making judgments and insist that these *conditions* be met. Use a variety of criteria, based on values, standards, definitions, and rules, to test results. Critical thinking is supporting a proposition with an *argument* that provides evidence based on reasoning. *Reasoning* becomes the cement that binds an argument. While there are no general *procedures* for literate critical thinking, these six elements provide a basis for comprehension. *Opinions* based on experiences should come from different sources to achieve a broader point of view (Lipman, 1991). This approach involves asking questions and making judgments based on specific conditions related to content; literate critical thinking should be considered a way of learning content (Raths et al., 1967). Students should be taught to think logically, analyze and compare, and question and evaluate in all content areas. When skills are taught in isolation, students only learn isolated skills with little relevance. Critical inquiry is an essential outcome of literate critical thinking.

Thinking strategies should be taught in conjunction with subject matter and presented to students in the form of real life problems. Case studies and stories with moral perspectives offer many opportunities for this. Critical-thinking instruction essentially is novel and differs from traditional instruction. Traditional instruction has teachers introduce materials and diversify instructional approaches. It provides students with applications to be completed independently with possible teacher assistance. Critical-thinking instruction, on the other hand, consists of providing a focus question or problem while dividing the class into cooperative groups with specific tasks shared with the class. Each group solves its problem and defends its solution. The teacher provides students with a summary and an opportunity to reflect on various solutions. Critical thinking inevitably leads to the resolution of many controversial issues that are the heart and reason for teaching critically (Gabennesch, 2006).

Thinking for Literacy

Literacy is a word that is open to various interpretations. It can be thought of in terms of command of subject knowledge or ability to read and write a specific language. *Content literacy* is the ability to use reading and writing to learn in a given content area; it is the level of competence needed in reading and writing that determines *functional literacy*, while *cultural literacy* generally refers to what a person should know about one's culture, history, art, and sciences. *Illiteracy* is the inability to read or write a language, whereas *aliteracy* is the lack of a reading habit though one is able to read but chooses not to. To be literate in content area classrooms, one must learn how to use reading and writing to construct meaning through literate critical thinking. No special training is

Figure 8.1 Key Concepts for Critical Thinking Instruction

1. Critical thinking strategies should be taught in conjunction with subject matter.
2. Critical thinking instruction should present students with real-life problems.
3. Critical thinking instruction may be novel (different from traditional instruction).

174 CHAPTER 8 Thinking for Understanding

PRACTICE EXERCISE 8.1

Comparison of Traditional and Critical Thinking Instruction

Compare and contrast the two types of instruction. Give appropriate examples that demonstrate how the characteristics listed can be achieved in your subject area.

Traditional Instruction	Critical Thinking Instruction
Teacher introduces materials and uses various instructional techniques.	Teacher provides focus questions and helps students develop problems to be resolved.
Teacher provides students with specific applications to complete independently.	Class is divided into cooperative groups with a specific task. Each group reports to class on findings for their task.
Teacher assists individual students in completing their tasks.	Teacher provides students with a summary and an opportunity to reflect on various solutions.
Instruction can be direct or indirect, but is most often direct.	Instruction can be direct or indirect.

PRACTICE EXERCISE 8.2

Practices That Encourage Reading and Critical Thinking

To stimulate thinking that encourages poor reading adolescents to read, Ivey and Fisher (2006) suggest four practices that develop students' literacy skills and their higher-order cognitive skills.

- Use texts rich in concepts.
- Use texts that are an appropriate level for student abilities.
- Use read-alouds and think-alouds for difficult materials.
- Use writing as a form of thinking.

View these four practices using the SCARPO Guide to Literate Critical Thinking as your prism. Then read the four statements, and provide judgments as to their truthfulness and reasonableness.

1. By developing a list of textbooks, rich in concepts that connect literacy to critical thinking in your subject area, students will become content literate.
2. After assessing reading levels for students in your classes, and using texts that are at an appropriate level for their abilities, you will increase their content literacy.
3. Student literacy levels will increase when you use read-alouds and think-alouds for assigned materials that are difficult for students to comprehend.
4. Preparing assignments that allow students to write about what they know is not necessarily providing a good instructional strategy for teaching literacy.

needed to assist students' construction of meaning in content areas, only persistence and caring coaching. The student must see reading as thinking with printed symbols, which she must discover, retrieve, and organize in order to understand the ideas and information presented in a text. A text, whether it is literary or informational, demands effective as well as intellectual responses from its readers (Vacca, 2005). The goal for the content-literate student is to know how to learn with texts independently. When a student is unable to achieve this goal, the teacher must provide instructional scaffolding to support the student.

A Literate Critical Thinking Person A culturally literate person is one who possesses basic information needed to thrive and succeed in modern society (Hirsch, 1987). A literate critical thinking person is one who is also culturally literate. Cultural literacy is described as knowing about something yet not necessarily having read it; for example, we know about *Mein Kampf* and *Das Kapital*, but how many have actually read them? The point is that communication, to be intelligible, must take place using shared core knowledge. A literate critical thinking person possesses the skills to make reasoned judgments because he or she is culturally literate.

Rousseau's theories regarding education are the basis of liberal educational thought, which encourages the natural development of young children while delaying adult ideas until appropriate. Education is considered a process of natural development that is content-neutral. A child's intellectual skills develop naturally, without regard to specific content. This position became the developmentally appropriate content-neutral curricula of the elementary school. Education should develop naturally and not be thought of as the mere accumulation of knowledge. Any suitable content advances learning in reading, writing, and thinking skills. Literate critical thinking posits that once relevant knowledge is acquired (cultural literacy), skills follow naturally. The ancient Greeks' *Principle of the Golden Mean* proposed that answers lay somewhere between two extremes, and that one should not rush to judgment.

Literate critical thinking combines uses of communication, including basic language and thought, which allows us to gain and share knowledge as well as reason with it. It is the kind of thinking needed to do well in and out of school. To be literate in our media age requires the acquisition of literate critical thinking skills within a cultural context that guide one to make decisions and take actions. While media literacy consists of communication competencies such as the ability to access, analyze, evaluate, and communicate information in print and other forms, literate critical thinking is gaining, sharing, and reasoning with information in all its forms.

After all is said, critical thinking cannot be divorced from content; in fact, thinking is a way of learning content (Raths et al., 1967). Students should be taught to think logically—analyze and compare, question and evaluate in all content areas. When skills are taught in isolation, students only learn isolated skills with little relevance. Critical inquiry is an essential outcome of critical thinking.

MINI CASE FROM THE FIELD

The following case from the field discusses the importance of critical thinking and understanding the role of the teacher with regard to developing strategies and methods that meet the needs of all children. Read the case, and compare Nick's ideas to those of Mr. Thompson.

A Critical Thinking Program

He was not a stupid man. Nor did he live in a cocoon. There were things that Principal Thompson knew about his staff that at times made him an effective leader. He knew that to get the best out of his people he had to encourage them to think critically because critical thinking is a process, not an outcome. It is about how to think, not what to think. He had made mistakes as a principal—one of his major flaws was that he valued loyalty over experience and competence, which might have been due to his size. He was a small man who carried himself like a big man to earn respect.

Mr. Thompson wanted Nick's Teaching for Literacy Committee to expand its scope and develop a K–12 program combining critical thinking and literacy. He believed that to be a literate critical thinker was to be educated. His basic assumption was that all children could learn when exposed to a quality instructional program that encouraged critical thinking rather than rote instructional practices.

When Mr. Thompson met with Nick, he explained his ideas and asked for cooperation in constructing a school-wide literate critical thinking program. Nick loved the idea, viewing it as the key to an effective education. He believed that his committee could develop a plan to teach respect, responsibility, and ethical values that would encourage good character. Mr. Thompson wanted to know specifically what Nick had in mind. He asked Nick to outline his plan.

"The beauty of my plan," said Nick, "is that we don't have to change anything, just reinforce and enhance what we are already doing. We all use conventional developmental lessons delivered in direct or indirect instructional formats. Every teacher is a born coach and able to tutor and coach students. The end-product of the process I have conceptualized can be evidenced in both classroom and grade seminars age appropriate and relevant for all students."

Mr. Thompson asked Nick to write up a brief description; they could discuss it before he presented it to his committee. The next day Nick presented Mr. Thompson with the diagram shown in Figure 8.2.

1. In a brief paragraph describe and explain the basic assumptions and practices found in this model, the Pantheon Program.
2. How does it propose to foster critical thinking?
3. Explain why you agree or disagree with Nick regarding the feasibility of his plan.
4. Nick believes that good character is the result of teaching responsibility, respect, and ethical values through critical thinking strategies. Mr. Thompson believes that a good quality instructional program focused on critical thinking strategies will lead to literate critical thinkers. How do you feel about each position?

THINKING STRATEGIES FOR UNDERSTANDING

IOSIE Method

The IOSIE method is a five-step process for analyzing student behavioral problems that can also be used in most educational episodes (Scarpaci, 2007). The IOSIE model provides a mnemonic device that can be used in practically every classroom management situation. The model provides an underlying rationale for dealing with and understanding misbehavior, which assists teachers in making decisions, and choices one must make in developing a classroom management style of one's own.

The method is a commonsense way of dealing with analysis that fosters critical thinking. When a problem

Figure 8.2 Pantheon Program Model

Basic Assumption: All children can learn when exposed to a quality instructional program that encourages critical thinking.

Critical Thinking

                Respect + Responsibility + Religion (Ethical Values) = Good Character

                Discipline Code   Guidance   Awards

Teaching Practices

1. Conventional Instruction

Question: How do we acquire knowledge? *Answer:* Knowledge is acquired by means of conventional developmental lessons, textbooks, experience, reason, intuition, authority, and active construction.

2. Coaching Instruction

Question: How do we develop learning skills? *Answer:* They are developed by means of coaching exercises, guided practice, independent study, interest groups, and problem solving.

3. Seminar Instruction

Question: How do we enrich our understanding of ideas and values? *Answer:* By means of Socratic seminar, enrichment activities, and school and community service.

---

occurs, identify the cause and determine objectives needed to be achieved. The solution may utilize the elements of literate critical thinking (SCARPO, which stands for *skeptical, conditions, argument, reasoning, procedures,* and *opinions*). Implement the solution and prepare to assess, and evaluate. This method works best for problem-solving situations because the process is basic to many forms of analysis.

IOSIE Analysis Method

- The **"I"** represent the first step in the process, to **identify** and assess the problem in all its aspects.
- The **"O"** stands for the **objectives** that you wish to achieve through your intervention. Be sure to include both short and long-term objectives that resolve the identified problem.
- The **"S"** stands for the **solution,** which should create a short and long-term solution for the identified problem that achieves your objectives.
- The **"I"** indicates the **implementation** and the personnel; materials and resources needed to implement the strategy.
- The letter **"E"** stands for your **evaluation**. Reflect on the approach taken, assess results, and modify if necessary.

Functional Behavioral Assessment

Regardless of the types of interventions teachers attempt, a small percentage of students will exhibit misbehaviors. As with the IOSIE method, an individualized strategy is called for when all other remedial actions have failed. A **Functional Behavioral Assessment (FBA)** approach (Newcomer and Lewis, 2004) is not simply trial and error as with IOSIE, but a comprehensive assessment that attempts to identify the specific factors that are contributing to the student's misbehavior. It explores environmental, skill, and teacher factors that may have exacerbated the inappropriate behavior. Essentially, it is a five-step process for conducting a functional assessment and developing an individualized behavior plan (Bambara and Kern, 2005).

1. *Prioritize and define the challenging behavior* in a clear and concise fashion.
2. *Conduct a functional assessment* through observation, discussion, and interviews. This can be accomplished by using an ABC Chart of three columns labeled antecedents, the challenging behavior, and consequences.
3. *Develop hypothesis statements* that provide specific theories and suggested actions for solution.
4. *Develop a support plan* that incorporates suggestions for appropriate actions.
5. *Implement, evaluate, and finally modify* your plan as soon as you can evaluate its effect on the behavior in question.

Reasoning Strategies

There are two broad methods of reasoning known as the deductive and inductive approaches. Both can be used effectively if we are able to control our emotions. We all have emotions. Emotions themselves do not compromise the reasoning process. However, our thoughts about emotions will compromise the process if those thoughts are not disciplined. Training controls our thoughts and thoughts control our emotions when we act as literate critical thinkers. Critical thinking involves logical thinking and reasoning, including skills such as comparison, classification, sequencing, cause/effect, patterning, webbing, analogies, **deductive and inductive reasoning**, forecasting, planning, hypothesizing, and analyzing.

Deductive reasoning starts from the general and goes to the specific, a "top-down" approach. It begins with a theory and moves to a specific hypothesis that is tested. The hypothesis is either confirmed or disproved by observation of the test results (theory-hypothesis-observation-confirmation).

1. Formulate a theory from an information base.
2. Develop a hypothesis that tests the theory.
3. Confirm or disprove by observing the results of testing.

Inductive reasoning works the other way, moving from specific to general, a "bottom-up" approach. In inductive reasoning, we begin with specific observations, detect patterns, and create hypotheses that can be tested to develop conclusions or theories (observation-pattern-tentative hypothesis-theory).

1. Search and retrieve facts from an information base.
2. Link two or more facts and form a relationship pattern.
3. Link two or more of these patterns and formulate a hypothesis, theory, or rule.

Inductive reasoning is more open-ended and exploratory, while deductive reasoning is more focused, concerned with testing and confirming hypotheses (Trochim, 2006).

Direct Questioning Activity DQA is an instructional process designed to increase students' self-regulation of critical thinking through active involvement requiring the integration of prior knowledge and text information. It is a type of scaffolded instruction. The process begins with students dependent on the teachers' guidance ending with students acting independently. The process consists of two instructional components: text-explicit and text-implicit instruction (see Figure 8.3).

Seminars and Socratic Questioning *Seminars* are conversations with students, conducted by the teacher who acts as leader or moderator. They are collaborative intellectual discussions propelled by open-ended questions about a text (written document), photograph, work of art, map, math problem, architectural drawing, or anything rich in ideas and ambiguous. They are planned for-

Figure 8.3 Guide to Explicit and Implicit Text Instruction

Text-Explicit Instruction
1. Determine what you want children to learn.
2. Group the content into teachable chunks.
3. Construct a concept map, or other form of graphic organizer, that presents information contained in each chunk of reading.

Text-Implicit Instruction
1. Questions are presented prior to and during a reading rather than at its conclusion.
2. Pre-questions are those presented immediately before reading to establish a purpose for reading.
3. Add-on questions are presented immediately after an assigned portion of a selection has been read to engage students in the critical thinking process. Add-on questions direct students to reread the selection, to reconstruct information acquired in prior questions, then link information to derive a response reflecting a higher level of thinking.
4. Teacher models process to move student toward independent critical thinking. Teacher thinking aloud and structuring overviews of content and critical thinking questions does this.

mal dialogues, actively engaging students with relevant ideas they have read and thought about, or listened to or discussed. The teacher as facilitator designs conditions that provide for optimum student participation. Teaching by questioning (Socratic teaching), is conducting discussions (seminars) whose purpose is to make insights, while increasing student knowledge, comprehension, and reasoning powers. The best seminars occur once or twice a week when issues and questions arise from great books read in advance (Adler, 1983). The task of the seminar leader is to ask questions that define the discussion, and to examine, and to engage students. Figure 8.4 outlines the responsibilities of both teachers and students.

Socratic questioning is a strategy to promote critical thinking through classroom discussion and seminars. It helps students evaluate their own thinking, allows students to compare their own thinking to that of their peers, and promotes consideration of multiple ideas and the interrelationships between those ideas. Socratic questioning seeks to clarify information, identify point of view, discover assumptions, distinguish factual claims from value judgments, and detect flaws in reasoning. It involves:

- Seeking reasons and evidence,
- Looking for implications and consequences,

Figure 8.4 Responsibilities of Seminar Participants

> **Teacher Responsibilities**
> - Selects appropriate text, and prepares open-ended questions for discussion.
> - Coaches students prior to the seminar, and explains that they are to speak and listen to questions.
> - Demonstrates good listening and note-taking skills during a seminar, and poses genuine, provocative follow-up questions.
> - Limits the amount of time she speaks.
> - Develops post-seminar procedures and activities that make activity relevant to children.
>
> **Student Responsibilities**
> - Invests necessary time and energy in reading and studying text.
> - Accepts responsibility for improving questioning, speaking, and listening skills.
> - Consciously contributes to seminar discussion with own ideas while actively listening to others.
> - Agrees and disagrees with others in a thoughtful and respectful manner.
> - Understands that the seminar is a part of the ongoing learning life of their classroom.
> - Practices post-seminar writing as a way of articulating an increased understanding of the values and ideas gained from the text and dialogue.

- Finding and reflecting on assumptions,
- Seeking examples and analogies,
- Looking for objections, and
- Identifying and taking different perspectives.

Socratic questioning distinguishes the known from beliefs, while detecting inconsistencies, overgeneralizations, and vagueness (Paul, 1991). Figure 8.5 describes Socratic questions that teachers can ask to develop student critical thinking.

Guide to Student Thinking Strategies Students have the ability to use words and ideas but may not know how to think ideas through and internalize meanings. By modeling disciplined analysis and assessment, we teach students how to be critical learners. Critical thinking requires both understanding the thought process and how to assess validity. Standards differ with regard to specific disciplines, so we must look for interrelationships in content to make appropriate connections. For example, picture a beautiful tapestry whose inherent unity

Figure 8.5 Socratic Questions That Foster Critical Thinking

> *Origin Question:* Where did you come up with information that helped you answer this question?
>
> *Support Questions:* How do you substantiate this response; do you have proof? Where could you locate evidence to support your response? Is response fact or your opinion?
>
> *Conflict Questions:* What are some counterarguments that people might present to your response? Why would some people have a different point of view? Under what conditions would you consider changing your response to this question? How would you counter an opposing response?
>
> *Implications and Consequences Question:* What are the consequences of your response?

elucidates the path to learning. Learning in mathematics is to think quantitatively, while learning theology is to study spiritual reality. Are there connections? All subjects represent a systematic way of thinking defined by a system of ideas leading to a distinctive and systematic way of questioning. By mastering critical thinking skills, students can learn any subject. These skills that lead to learning any subject are not difficult to master. They can be thought of as keys that open the doors to critical thinking applications for students.

1. Raise questions regarding the content being taught.
2. Gather data and evaluate.
3. Be sure to adopt the point of view of the discipline being studied.
4. Come to well-reasoned conclusions.
5. Communicate and discuss your results.
6. Relate your learning to life.

To understand content as a mode of thinking, we need to recognize that all content has a logic, which is defined by the same eight structures that define the thinking that produced and continue to produce it. When learning any concept, idea, law, theory, or principles, ask to what other concept it is connected. When beginning to learn a subject, it is helpful to formulate an organizational idea to guide your thinking. It is commonly assumed that eight structures define thinking (see Figure 8.6). To become a critical thinker means learning to analyze thinking, which requires practice in identifying these structures and their use. We think for a purpose as if to raise a question or solve a problem. Thinking is based on information, concepts, and ideas. We make inferences and draw conclusions based on

Figure 8.6 Eight Structures That Define Thinking

1. Generate *purpose*. All content/thinking has been generated by organizing goals and purposes. *Example:* The main *purpose* of this article is

    _____ (Author's purpose)

2. Raise *questions*. All content/thinking is defined by the problems it defines and solves through the questions that are asked. *Example:* The key *question* that the author is addressing is

    _____ (Key question in article addressed) Thinking is driven by questions!

3. Use *information*. All content/thinking presupposes the gathering and use of information in performance and problem solving. *Example:* The most important *information* in this article is

    _____ (Information used to support conclusion)

4. Utilize *concepts and ideas*. All content/thinking is structured by concepts (theoretical constructs) that organize, shape, and direct it. *Example:* The key *concepts/ideas* we need to understand are

    _____ (Point out ideas/concepts)

5. Make *inferences and draw conclusions*. All content/thinking requires the making of inferences from relevant data or information to interpretative conclusions. *Example:* The main *inferences/conclusions* in this article are

    _____ (Identify most important conclusions)

6. Make *assumptions*. All content/thinking proceeds from assumptions or presuppositions from which it logically proceeds. *Example:* The main *assumption* underlying the author's thinking is

    _____ (What is the author taking for granted?)

7. Generate *implications*. All content/thinking generates implications and consequences that enable professionals to make predictions and test theories, lines of reasoning, and hypotheses. *Example:* If we take (don't take) this line of reasoning seriously, the *implications* are

    _____ (What is the author implying?)

8. Embody a *point of view*. All content/thinking defines a frame of reference or point of view (which provide practitioners with a logical map of use in considering the professional "moves" they will make). *Example:* The *main points* of view presented in the article are

    _____ (What does the author want you to know?)

Source: Center for Critical Thinking (2007)

assumptions that lead to implications and conclusions. We use ideas and theories to interpret data, facts, and experiences in order to answer questions, solve problems, and resolve issues (Center for Critical Thinking, 2007). To aid students to develop critical thinking skills have them analyze articles, essays, and entire chapters of text using the eight structures that define thinking found in Figure 8.6.

We constantly conceptualize things personally by means of our own unique experiences, often distorting the world to our own perception. The ideas we form are often egocentric in nature—for example, the ideas we inherit from our social indoctrination are typically egocentric. Through critical thinking, we can come to see ignorance, prejudice, stereotypes, illusions, and biases in our own thinking. If you do not think critically, you can confuse very different things: for example, needing and wanting, humility and servility, stubbornness and conviction. Practice Exercise 8.4 explores the content tools that students can use in terms of the manner we think. One way to understand content is to view it as a mode of thinking. Content has a logic that is defined by the same eight structures that define the thinking.

CRITICAL THINKING AND PHILOSOPHY

What is the relationship between a teacher's philosophy of education and student learning? Is it true that a teacher's values with regard to education affect student learning? One of the purposes of this section is to answer these questions and the other is to assist in defining your individual philosophy.

A teacher's philosophy plays a major role in educating, inspiring, and guiding students to become literate critical thinking citizens. Therefore, it is essential that teachers uphold the highest ethical standards to earn the respect, trust, and confidence of students, parents, and the educational community. Before coming to develop your own philosophy, you should look at the classic definition of philosophy. The word *philosophy* comes from the Greek word *philo*, which means love, and *sophos*, which means wisdom. Therefore, we can say that philosophy is the love of wisdom.

MINI CASE FROM THE FIELD

The following case from the field discusses the importance of combining one's educational philosophy with critical thinking. The strategies and methods proposed are aimed at meeting the needs of all children and society. Read the case, and compare Nick's ideas to those of Mr. Thompson.

PRACTICE EXERCISE 8.3

Strategies for Developing Critical-Thinking Skills

For each of these categories, write an additional suggestion for a developmentally appropriate activity for the grade you teach or intend to teach. Be sure to note which of the eight structures that define your thinking. (Do not have eighth graders building piles of blocks by color; have them design an earthquake-proof structure as a science project.)

- *Sorting Items*   Divide a list of foods into high- and low-calorie groups. Select a paragraph in the story you are reading that you consider the best. Find the pairs of synonyms. This activity generates purpose, as defined in structure number one.
- *Classify and Sort*   Children make their own lists and decide on the category. Give children a list of words that they should classify and sort as nouns, verbs, etc. This activity uses information, as defined in structure number three.
- *Difference*   Have children identify and describe the difference between a colon and semicolon. This activity utilizes concepts as defined in structure number four.
- *Similarities*   Have children find similarities in leaders and followers, physical exercise and sleeping. Choose items that are unlike and ask for similarities, such as chocolates and kindness, horses and singing. This activity raises questions and utilizes concepts as defined in structures numbered two and four.
- *Summaries*   Have children identify the main issues in a story in less than thirty words. Have children summarize the main ideas contained in their daily lessons. This activity embodies a point of view as defined in structure number eight.
- *Predictions*   Have children write the ending of a story they are reading, or write a different ending than the author did. This activity makes inferences and draws conclusions as defined in structure number five.
- *Explain Events*   What factors made Harry Potter stories so popular? This activity generates implications, makes assumptions as defined in structures numbered six and seven.
- *Solve a Problem*   Pick a real-life problem to solve, such as pollution, congestion in the city, being late returning library books, etc. This activity utilizes concepts and ideas, and draws conclusions as defined in structures numbered four and five.
- *Brainstorm Alternatives*   Group children and ask them to find alternatives to a homework assignment. This activity raises questions, and draws conclusions as defined in structures numbered two and five.

Combining an Ethical Philosophy with Critical Thinking

Principal Thompson asked Nick Saccone to write up a brief description of a critical thinking program he was using with his science classes. Mr. Thompson had explained that since Nick's students were performing so well he would like to discuss the program and present it to the curriculum committee for possible implementation throughout the entire school. The next day Nick presented Principal Thompson with a diagram entitled "Pantheon Program Model." Nick was shocked at Mr. Thompson's response to his work.

Principal Thompson began by asking Nick why he called his diagram a critical thinking program. Thompson insisted that it obviously was an attempt to create a values-oriented program based on an ethical philosophy.

"Not really," said Nick. "My program addresses both issues, philosophy and critical thinking. I believe you can improve learning with an ethically based critical thinking program. What I am saying is that critical thinking strategies reflect on one's personal philosophy."

"Nick, we share the same goal—to develop literate critical thinkers of good character. But I don't believe we have to adopt such a formal program."

Mr. Thompson made clear his belief that values are inherent in everything we do, and virtues need not be specifically taught. But Nick didn't feel that way. He believed science education needed a particular style of ethical education that was reflected in a teacher's values and assumptions. He said that by teaching we show respect and provide service to our children. Mr. Thompson told Nick that he was highlighting values and moral reasoning without teaching a core set of agreed-upon values.

"But that's the point," said Nick. "We have to help develop a core set of values that will give our students an ethical foundation for life. Don't we all believe in honesty, loving, caring, empathy, respect, responsibility, self-discipline, and virtue?"

Mr. Thompson told Nick that what he was proposing was an autocratic approach that some might claim smacked of brainwashing. Thompson said the model just

PRACTICE EXERCISE 8.4

Modes of Thinking

Reading, writing, speaking, and listening are all modes of thinking. Read each of the brief statements (strategies), and write your view to each of the explanations offered by the author on how to achieve that objective.

1. A truly skilled *reader* can master a subject from a textbook alone, which is how most students learn.

   Author's Explanation How: Read table of contents and introduction sections to get big ideas and perspective on subject.

2. You can *write* to learn.

   Author's Explanation How: Make summaries and determine interconnections.

3. The better you are at *speaking* and explaining materials to others, the better you understand it.

   Author's Explanation How: Highlight, diagram, and explain ideas being studied.

4. The better you *listen*, the better you can express the thoughts of another and the better you will understand them.

   Author's Explanation How: Question those to whom you listen, because thinking is driven by questions.

---

reinforces the development of specific beliefs by behavior modification. The main strength of behavior modification is that it works, but it does not create an ethical program. It is simple to use, and results are immediate. It accommodates most teachers' desire to maintain control while it allows students to feel successful because they obtain rewards. The standards of behavior are uniform, consistent, and clear to all teachers and students. Unfortunately, many tend to mistake good behavior for good student learning. It is not! All that you will achieve is developing an obedient child, not a literate critical thinking child.

1. In a brief paragraph describe and explain the basic assumptions made by Mr. Thompson and Nick regarding the intention of the Pantheon Program.
2. What core values can all agree on?
3. Is an ethical philosophy necessary in order to teach critical thinking skills? Is it ever necessary?
4. Nick believes that students learn as a result of teaching responsibility, respect, and ethical values through critical thinking strategies. How do you feel about his position?
5. Mr. Thompson believes that a good quality instructional program focused on critical thinking strategies will lead to literate critical thinkers, but not necessarily student learning. How do you feel about his position?

Developing a Critical Thinking Educational Philosophy

Educators need to construct a personal educational philosophy based on their individual requirements and experiences. A personal philosophy gives teaching focus and direction. The process consists of reflecting on experiences and established philosophy in order to assess beliefs. From this process a personal philosophy will evolve that will give your teaching a focus and direction. Fortunately, there is no need to reinvent the wheel when you finally put your own philosophy of education to paper. The simplest approach to use is to look at what exists and determine what aspects are appropriate to your beliefs. There are basic educational philosophies that stem from the four listed below. Each of these four have proponents from the past, and each has truths that can help in formulating your own beliefs.

1. *Idealism* is the belief that the ultimate reality is not materialistic but is contained in the world of ideas, eternal truths, and the laws of nature. It is based on Plato's quest for the absolute truth as seen in *The Republic*.
2. *Realism* is based on Aristotle who sought truth in the real world and not in ideas as his teacher, Plato, did. Realism stems from the idea that reality can be known through the senses. Even though one does not experience something, it can still exist. Empirical data is the main source of knowledge.
3. *Pragmatism* emphasizes practicality of knowledge as a way of knowing. If a proposition works then it is true. Values become relative to circumstances, and ends justify the means. The basic question becomes, "what works?" William James (1842–1910) popularized pragmatism by teaching that humans make knowledge and learn by doing.
4. *Humanism* emphasizes the humanness of existence. Humanism was the intellectual core of Renaissance beliefs that basic goodness and free will lead to self-fulfillment. Erasmus believed that children learn in a graded sequence of developmentally appropriate subjects. Literacy was considered essential if you were to read the Bible. Children are at the center of learning for Humanists. "*Teach the whole child.*" Education is a natural process of maturation as taught by Rousseau.

Philosophies of Education

Perennialism is a philosophy based on the belief that the purpose of education is to develop intellectual strength and discipline of mind; it conceptualizes truth as unchanging, and therefore perennial. Philosophers Plato, Aristotle, and St. Thomas Aquinas provide the roots for these beliefs. The pursuit of these unchanging or fixed truths through Western culture has been recorded in its great books that have become its foundation. Perennialism is rooted in idealism. Mortimer Adler (1983), Robert M. Hutchins (1936), and Theodore Sizer (1984, 1992, 1997) have popularized perennialism through their work and writings. A perennialist curriculum proposes a standard that must be adhered to by all. It consists of mathematics, science, humanities, literature (Great Books), history, philosophy, and art. It focuses on preparation for life, not just the now. Lecture, Socratic questioning, and coaching are methods stressed by perennialist teachers. They believe the role of schools is to develop the student's intellect by teaching classical enduring truths, thereby empowering them for life.

Essentialism is a philosophy that views the purpose of education as the transmission of society's heritage and culture. It proposes a back-to-basics, paper-and-pencil curriculum that is academically vigorous, offering traditional courses of study undiluted by the nonessential. The goal for the essentialist, as for the perennialist, is the development of intellect. A teacher-centered classroom, subject-centered curriculum, using ability grouping and testing to achieve standards, spotlights its focus. William Bagley (1874–1946), a prime proponent of essentialism believed that people needed a common body of knowledge for society to function appropriately. School curricula had to be based on essential facts and a common culture to be effective (Bagley, 1941). Essentialists differ from perennialists in that they believe in practical curricula inclusive of vocational training, not only the arts and humanities. Hirsch and colleagues (1993) have popularized this view, holding to the premise that there is a core of knowledge and basic skills for all students. Essentialism has great appeal to those teachers who view their role as transmitters of information and knowledge to students.

Reconstructionism is a philosophy that has a perspective on social justice, and it views schools as the means to change or reconstruct society. Its followers want to build a new social order that advocates a socialist orientation with collectivist ideals. Historically it has been rooted in the radical academic left and student empowerment movements of the 1930s and 1960s. Reconstructionism has at times been linked to pragmatic and progressive movements. It promotes the idea that schools should play a key role in reconstructing society and building a new social order for a new and more effective democratic nation. Dewey's definition of education as "the reconstruction or reorganization of experience which adds to the meaning of experience, and which increases ability to direct the course of subsequent experience" has been used as a justification for social reconstructionism. George Counts (1889–1974), laid out the basic tenets for social change and reconstructionism by suggesting that schools foster a Marxist social agenda (Counts, 1932, 1933).

Neo-Reconstructionist Paulo Freire (1973) wrote *Pedagogy of the Oppressed*, which promoted class conflict in Brazil. His views summarize the most radical aspects of reconstructionism. Freire wanted to know if the knowledge needed to challenge society and the status quo should be taught to all citizens or only to some. He wanted schools to become reform agents and act as catalysts in improving the condition of life for all people. He viewed the role of the teacher as that of a guide who should direct student interest and attention to relevant social issues. Teachers were not simply considered transmitters of knowledge but were to be resurrected as facilitators for social justice.

Constructivism offers an explanation about the nature of knowledge. It claims to be a philosophy and not an instructional approach. It is a theory about how learners come to learn. It claims that knowledge is made up of prior constructions and not absolutes. The constructions are assimilated by using a process of accommodation developed by Piaget. The learner in effect becomes the constructor of his own knowledge. A constructivist curriculum is process based, student centered, holistic, and advocates higher-order thinking skills. It attempts to be idea- and problem centered. Constructivism is a theory of learning that states that learners construct their own knowledge and meaning based on their prior experiences within a social context (Webb et al., 2000). (See Chapter 2 for a full discussion on constructivism.)

Existentialism is a philosophy based on humanism and self-actualization where the individual determines meaning. You decide who you are. You cannot escape responsibility. Soren Kierkegaard (1813–1855) and Jean Paul Sartre (1905–1980) are existentialism's most famous proponents. When applied to education, it focuses on a student's quest for personal meaning or creating knowledge. Education helps students become what they want to become by allowing for choice and individual responsibility. The world is seen as devoid of any universal meaning and it is therefore one's responsibility to create (construct) one's own meanings. It has a root relationship to constructivism while resembling humanism in its emphasis on the uniqueness of each individual and the quest for values and meanings. Living is seen as confrontation concerned with understanding inner experiences to deal with human problems. The basic precepts of existentialism combine existence and essence as outlined in Figure 8.7.

Progressivism is an experiential philosophy that uses a child-centered approach to learning rather than a content-centered one. The teacher is seen as a facilitator who helps students to solve problems. Its core consists of a democratic classroom that utilizes a discovery

Figure 8.7 Tenets of Existentialism

- The *basic theme of existence* is a given; what we make of it becomes our essence.
- Our essence is created by our choices. "I am my choices." We have freedom to choose our essence, and build our own lives. (Jean Paul Sartre)
- The meaning for our lives is based on our values.
- Our obligation is toward each other.
- Socially constructed values and choices give meaning to our lives.

approach and thematic units. Progressivism stressed the process of learning rather than specific content matter. John Dewey (1859–1952) has historically been given credit as the guiding light behind progressivism. Dewey believed that we learn from doing and experimentation. Experimentalism became the philosophical foundation for progressive education. Knowledge was appreciated for its practical value because it could be used to change society through social engineering within a democratic framework. Dewey's problem was how to translate change into social benefits. He opposed the traditional classic approach to education, preferring a pragmatic approach that related education to responsible citizenship (Dewey, 1989).

At the University of Chicago (1896–1904), Dewey established a Laboratory School in an attempt to influence practice by becoming a practitioner. His school was used to test and replicate his theories. It was democratic, with a highly qualified staff that created an atmosphere that abandoned traditional pedagogical practices (drill, recitation, rote memorization, lecturing, and whole-class instruction). It advanced a project problem-solving approach, with open-ended discussion, and field experience. Psychology became the foundation for its educational practice. Critics denigrated psychology as a soft science and education as a craft, not a profession.

At Columbia University in 1905, Dewey ceded the field of educational research to Edward Thorndike (1874–1949) and the administrative progressives, who believed that research should be conducted in universities and that practitioners should not do research. This position is still the accepted view at most universities and a key cause for problems between professors of research and professors of practice (Dewey, 1989).

Dewey's Views

- Students should be empowered through education to work for the good of society.
- Subject matter comes from a child's interest.
- Learning is the reconstruction of experience and knowledge.
- Students must interact with the world.
- Education requires reflection.
- Education is experimental.
- An ounce of experiences is better than a ton of theory. (Dewey, 1993)

Progressive education has developed and branched out over the past one hundred years. It still, however, focuses on individual expression and free activity. Education through experience is considered paramount for learning. The purpose of progressive education is to use skills to obtain social ends. The father of progressive education, Francis W. Parker, advocated child-centered schools, active learning, and cooperative planning related to real life. Figure 8.9 gives a brief list of the various forms that progressive education has adapted.

Conservative critics blame Dewey for the so-called mess that progressive education became. They should have instead attacked William Heard Kilpatrick (*The Project Method*, 1918), who wrote a brief eighteen-page article that claimed children learned when they internalized learning through experience and practiced it in their own lives. Kilpatrick (1871–1965) misconstrued Dewey's ideas, and was in fact responsible for the aimless and content-less curricula many schools followed. He held that we learn through our experiences and that the role of the teacher was not to dictate but guide (Kilpatrick, 1941). His beliefs revolved around the five concepts: (1) have a positive attitude and engage in life-long learning; (2) the source of learning lies within the child; (3) schools have the responsibility to engage students in socially acceptable activities; (4) independent learning; (5) students and teachers should jointly construct curricula.

Traditional education requires children to be receptive, quiet and obedient, and intellectually disciplined. Teachers and textbooks are considered the main sources of standards and rules of conduct, and of factual knowledge. This method has been viewed as the appropriate way for society to pass on its culture to future generations; it is marked by strong content, high standards, and

Figure 8.8 Progressive Model for Thinking

1. Students must have genuine experiences, which they are intrinsically interested in.
2. A genuine problem must develop from the presented situation, which will act as a stimulus for thought.
3. Students must be able to make observations and obtain information to solve problems.
4. Solutions should be developed in an orderly scientific method.
5. Solutions should be tested by application.

Figure 8.9 Branches of Progressive Education

Child-Centered Progressives favored informal, student-centered classrooms, active interdisciplinary learning, and schools with a humane character. They based their ideas on the work of Friedrich Froebal, the inventor of kindergarten, and Johann Pestalozzi, who advocated bringing education into harmony with the natural development of the child. They wanted schools to fit the interests of children, not vice versa.

Social Progressives or Social Reconstructionists believed schools should assume the roles of home, community and work with the purpose being to establish an egalitarian society. This view is still popular with socialists, Bolsheviks, and political idealists today.

Administrative Progressives sought to bring greater efficiency to schools. They led the move to standardized tests, ability grouping, and differentiated curricula. Many of these progressive measures have been adopted by today's conservative standards movement.

Neo-Progressivism advanced tracking by developing a formula for placement of students: 20 percent could do college work, 20 percent should be steered to vocational programs, and the remaining 60 percent needed school to prepare for life's problems. This led to an increase in nonacademic courses, which were low in content, resulting in a call for a standards-based curriculum.

The liberal progressive revival in the 1960s summed up the major premises of the era; the process of learning rather than the knowledge acquired was the goal of education. Open education (1967–1975) was a political agenda aimed at making classrooms responsive to children of all races and income levels. The movement advocated a relaxed style of elementary schooling, which can be seen in the similar physical setup of today's classrooms, with book corners, learning centers, and plenty of materials for exploring.

Sources: Neill (1960), Holt (1964), Kohl (1967), and Silberman (1970)

PRACTICE EXERCISE 8.5

Legacy of the Progressive Movement

The legacy of the progressive movement surprisingly is quite modest. The reason is that schools' traditional organization and structure is almost impossible to change. Every attempt has been met with stiff resistance. It's easier to teach to the test than for skills and process; natural resistance to change has been well documented throughout history. Resistance combined with the commonly held social belief that children need to know content has really limited the impact of progressivism. The legacy is seen in the organization of basic classrooms, use of space, seating and grouping for instruction.

Ideas of progressivism related to problem solving and project-based instruction are used by both progressive and traditionalist alike. The inheritance from progressivism consists of the following practices. Explain how each of these practices has enriched education.

- Provision for social and medical services
- Working with students in small groups and individually
- Integrated curricula
- Project-based learning
- Narrative report cards
- Student involvement in choosing activities
- Movable furniture and flexible use of space
- Working with students in small groups and individually

MINI CASE FROM THE FIELD

The following case from the field discusses the importance of how teachers think about learning and its effect on the students they teach. The premise is that by understanding your own philosophy, your teaching and focus of instruction is enhanced. The question in this case study is whether the way you think improves or detracts from learning. Read the case, and compare Nick's, Ed's, and Jane's ideas to those of Mr. Thompson.

The Effect of Critical Thinking on Student Learning

Ever since Nick Saccone had been authorized by Principal Thompson to form a committee to investigate gender-specific teaching strategies, his quest for solutions had been inflamed. As a science teacher qualified to teach all

schools organized by age and grade. Education is viewed as the art of communicating truth, and its credo is education for intellectual discipline.

Each culture wants its children to master the skills necessary for developing intellectually, morally, socially, emotionally, and civilly, the idea being for society to pass on traditional values. Responsibility for the success of this process lies with parents, peers, teachers, relatives, media, and schools (Gardner, 1999).

grades, he was proud of his understanding and application of the scientific method in his thinking, which he believed was the key to student academic success.

Jane Hemmings, a middle school language arts teacher, had asked Nick if he really believed that because he professed the scientific method he had influenced his students. She said that teachers often fall into the trap of teaching content instead of children. She had quoted from Howard Gardner, who had said, "When students cannot learn the way we teach them, we must teach them the way they learn." Lucille Chan, a fourth-grade teacher overhearing Jane's comment, had said, "That's a powerful statement. But even if we know, in theory, that differentiating our instruction to match the needs of each student is an important key to success, it's still challenging in practice. Many of us have the attitude that 'we will put the information out there, and if they don't get it, it's on them.' We tend to be resistant to the whole idea of differentiation. I believe it starts with the teacher's attitude and expectations. We have to be willing to entertain the idea that not all students will learn the same way or at the same rate, nor will every student respond every time. We've got to be willing to keep trying to reach every student."

Ed Child, a high school math teacher, couldn't resist butting in, and remarking that there is a thought control process that now passes for liberalism in education. "And I'm not talking open-mindedness. In the sciences you live in a political bunker. You constantly measure your words for fear that you might utter some political blasphemy that could end your teaching career. Some students are like the Red Guard: ready to report you to the administration at the first sign of political incorrectness."

Nick turned to Ed and said, "That's not a philosophy of education, it's a philosophy of fear. What ever happened to beliefs regarding academic freedom? The closest you come to a philosophy is existentialism. Your quest for personal meaning creates knowledge—in this case incorrect knowledge."

"Wait one minute, Nick. I'm not preaching fear, all I am saying is that I am a realist who uses empirical data as the main source of knowledge."

"Hold on, Ed, next you're going to tell me that you believe as Mr. Thompson does that the ultimate reality is not materialistic but contained in the world of ideas, eternal truths, and the laws of nature."

Then Jane told both men that they were way off track in describing the influence of their personal philosophies on student learning and that they were both probably essentialists who would like to consider themselves progressives.

1. Describe the basic assumptions that are being made by Nick, Ed and Jane.
2. How does each see the role their thinking plays with regard to student learning?
3. Why do you agree or disagree with each of their positions?
4. Support or refute Jane's closing remarks regarding Ed's and Nick's philosophies.
5. Does teacher thinking affect student learning?
6. Are we in effect the sum total of all the choices we make during our lifetime?

PRACTICE EXERCISE 8.6

Developing a Model Critical Thinking Philosophy

A philosophy of education is a statement of beliefs about the purposes of education. It is about how children learn and how they should be taught. Begin with a declarative statement such as "I believe," and add a principle believed in. For example:

- I believe the purpose of education is (literacy skills, work habits, morals, academic excellence, etc.).
- I believe students learn best when they (study, are motivated, are taught well, etc.).
- I believe students should be taught by use of (fear, love, and structured lessons).

Beliefs, once identified, become a personal philosophy. Questions formulated give that philosophy direction. Describe how you believe children learn and should be taught. Explain why the keys to effective teaching (methods, management, mastery, expectations and personality) are so important. Create a philosophy based on experiences consistent with your beliefs regarding education.

Write a statement that describes your philosophy of education. To get you started, here are a few paragraphs of an educational philosophy that can be used as a model. See if the questions preceding each paragraph are answered to your satisfaction. Write responses to these questions in order to build your model. As a result of this exercise, you should be able to tailor a description of your own personal philosophy.

A Model of a Typical Philosophy

Questions: How do children learn? What is my role as a teacher? What part does personality play in my beliefs?

Sample Response

I'm a pragmatic constructivist who by definition believes every child can learn if taught using an approach that meets the child's individual needs. I want to be in a position where I can help make possible the provision of basic and enriched learning. I view my role as a teacher and decision maker from the perspective of the impact of my decisions on students. My goal as a teacher is to facilitate learning for all children as an affirmation of my effective teaching personality. I further believe that students must be exposed to a multitude of experiences in a safe, secure environment if learning is to flourish.

Question: How would you describe your views relative to discipline and curriculum?

Sample Response

As a teacher, I insist on a safe, warm, caring environment in my class with access to a multitude of learning experiences. I consider myself a traditionalist with regard to discipline and a progressive in relation to curriculum. This I believe is a balanced position to take and one I strongly advocate.

Questions: How would you achieve mastery? What are your expectations?

Sample Response

I believe we are in need of systemic change if we are going to see public education survive in the twenty-first century. It must be a system immersed in the development of cognitive skills and abilities that empower and encourage students to succeed in the technological society of the future.

Questions: How would you manage your class? What methods would you use?

Sample Response

The traditionalist component of my philosophy believes that goals are achieved by delineating responsibilities, defining roles, assigning tasks, pre-planning and following up, through the use of defined monitoring procedures. In implementing this management plan, I would institutionalize these procedures. My success would increase student productivity and create an atmosphere of mutual trust between my students and me. By allowing my students to participate in the decision-making process, I make them responsible for their own behavior as well as the instructional methods we would select. I've found that mutually agreed upon programs afford opportunities for growth in overcoming the natural tendency of many to resist change. By being eclectic and exercising honest leadership and building upon my children's strengths, I will draw from them all the potential that exists.

Chapter Summary

In this chapter we have defined and examined critical thinking. The chapter practice exercises highlighted how we use critical thinking in our instructional practices. We also offered specific thinking strategies focused on practical guides for understanding thinking and the approaches to implementing these strategies in your classes. The final section on critical thinking and philosophy linked them in preparation for developing an ethical educational philosophy. Classic philosophies were used as models and guideposts in this process.

Three major objectives for this chapter were: (1) to understand what critical thinking is; (2) to understand the strategies needed to teach the critical thinking process; and (3) to construct your own critical thinking educational philosophy. The connection among philosophy, critical thinking, and a personal philosophy has been emphasized throughout. We must understand that a philosophy of education exists within each of us; it is a teacher's essence, and it defines our existence. Socrates said it best when he said that the teacher's role is to "know thyself."

Cases from the Field

CASE ONE

Phil Lambert was a man who believed that philosophy and theory overlapped in many ways. He accepted the proposition that theories were groups of principles related to one's observations that could be used to understand one's experiences. He believed that philosophy was in effect a theory about knowledge, truth, reality, and the good. His problem was how to express his beliefs in his teaching. Phil favored essentialism as an educational philosophy and so he became part of the "back to basics" movement. He told his principal that he was going to focus his instruction in his fourth-grade class on basic skills, reading, writing, mathematics, and, to a certain extent, science and geography.

1. How would Phil respond to the principal if he were asked to explain why he was concerned with basic skills at the expense of student-centered curricula and instruction?
2. In responding to his principal, Phil claimed that the essentialist philosophy is found in many teacher education programs. Was Phil correct? Explain.
3. How would Phil explain the differences between perennialism and essentialism if his principal claimed that they were both the same, and if he was wary of educators who placed emphasis on learner-centered education.
4. Why would essentialists most likely be opposed to progressivism?
5. How would Phil feel about reconstructionism and constructivism? Explain.

CASE TWO

As the teacher of a high school American history class, you are concerned that your students are simply becoming passive learners. All they care about is passing the state standardized test. You have tried to develop their critical thinking skills and help them to become problem solvers who can make informed decisions. The students tell you that they are realists and wish you would get real, too. They claim to be pragmatic and see no need for your insistence on constructivist and progressive ideas.

1. Describe the educational philosophy your ideas are most attuned to.
2. Describe the educational philosophy you are least aligned with.
3. How would you explain to the students that their understanding of pragmatism was not correct?
4. Should the teacher have explained his philosophy to the class? What good would that do?
5. How would you deal with this problem if you were the teacher?

CASE THREE

Mr. Osborn has a very bright advanced placement class. He has always been proud of being a progressive who conducted student-centered classes that focused on developing critical thinking skills. He explained his beliefs regarding education to his classes and then assigned an essay for homework. Students were to analyze Mr. Osborn's philosophy and show how he infused it into his teaching. To his surprise, the first essay he read claimed that he was dogmatic and based his instruction on the assumption that truth was absolute and known. The general consensus of the class was that Mr. Osborn was not allowing for freedom of expression. The class believed that truth is tentative and hypothetical, not absolute as implied by Mr. Osborn.

1. How would you rate Mr. Osborn's assignment? Did it foster critical thinking?
2. Would you describe Mr. Osborn's philosophy as progressive or perennialist? Explain.
3. How could his actions be considered constructivist?
4. Is there evidence of democratic education in Mr. Osborn's class? Elaborate.
5. How would you handle this situation if you were the teacher in question?

CASE FOUR

Mrs. Risk asked her senior future teachers class to write an essay that would express their philosophy of education. She provided a guidance outline in which the class was to focus on their beliefs regarding how children learn, discipline, and curriculum, and include instructional practices they liked. Philip, one of her students, asked, "Why was the philosophy of education so important?" Mrs. Risk responded by saying, "Just do the assignment, and hopefully that will answer your own question."

1. Why could the argument be made that Mrs. Risk was a constructivist?
2. How was Mrs. Risk's response to Philip in line with her philosophy?
3. Is being aware of your philosophy important to a prospective teacher? Explain.
4. Would you have responded to Philip as Mrs. Risk did?
5. How would you have handled this situation?

CASE FIVE

Lucille Scarpaci had applied for a position at the McGraw Hill Comprehensive K–12 School. Before her interview with the principal, she was asked to write a brief statement about her educational philosophy. She wrote,

My educational philosophy is influenced by many disciplines, and supported by student needs. I believe all children can learn when a teacher creates an enriched educational climate. My style is eclectic, and has been affected by multiple academic areas. I believe my first responsibility is to create a safe environment, and then earn the trust of my students. I respect students for their individuality; the approaches I use are secondary.

There are five classic philosophies of education: Perennialism, Essentialism, Existentialism, Progressivism, and Reconstructionism. I include a bit of each in my thinking. Perennialism, based on the belief that the purpose of education is to develop intellect and discipline of mind, is my foundation. I believe in structure so I want a standard curriculum for all. My philosophy can be encapsulated in a lesson whose theme is "all people need respect for who they are."

My Essentialist side is tied to realism with a dash of idealism, with emphasis on "academic rigor." It entails a teacher-centered classroom, subject-centered, with a focus on ability grouping and testing standards. I believe in a practical curriculum for all, including vocational training. I see education as constantly changing, while goodness does not.

The Existentialist in me proposes that meaning is determined by the individual—"I am my choices." I see education as a vehicle for constructing knowledge. The Constructivist in me places value on humanism and self-actualization in search of the truth. Teachers should assist students to become what they want to become in life; to that extent I am Existentialist.

I incorporate Progressivism as an instructional manager who has a paramount concern for children. My teaching will be based on democratic ideals, spotlighting child-centered activities, combined with a focus on social justice issues. My philosophy can be summed up in one powerful word, *care!*

1. How does Lucille explain the way children learn?
2. How does she view her role as a teacher?
3. Does her personality play any part in her beliefs?
4. Describe her views relative to discipline and curriculum.
5. What role do her expectations play in relation to her students achieving mastery?
6. How would she manage a class?
7. What methods would you use?

Terms to Remember

Literate critical thinking
IOSIE
Functional behavioral assessment
Deductive and inductive reasoning
Socratic questioning
Child-centered
Modes of thinking

Perennialism
Essentialism
Constructivism
Progressivism
Reconstructionism
Existentialism
Critical thinking

Discussion Questions

1. Describe the importance of literate critical thinking as a teaching objective.
2. Design a scenario in which the elements of the "Socratic Method" are employed.
3. Match the educational philosophy with the classic figure most associated with it.

   - Idealism   A. Plato
   - Realism   B. Socrates
   - Pragmatism   C. Jean Paul Sartre
   - Humanism   D. Søren Kierkegaard
   - Existentialism   E. Rousseau
   -                   F. William James

4. Define the term *progressive education* and analyze its three branches (child, social, and administrative).
5. Show how you would incorporate one of the basic philosophies of education into your class work as a teacher.
6. What are the basic differences between essentialism and progressivism?
7. Reflect upon the various successful teachers you have had. Determine their philosophies and compare the areas of similarity that made them successful in your eyes.
8. What solutions would be offered by a traditionalist to stem the apparent failure of our children?

Field Experience Activities

1. Visit a local school and attempt to determine if the progressive movement has had an impact on the instructional program. Observe to see if the following features are evident:
   - Movable furniture
   - Students working in small groups
   - Availability of medical and social support for students
   - An integrated curriculum
   - Project-based learning
   - Narrative report cards
   - Student involvement in choosing activities
   - Flexible use of space
2. Interview three teachers and ask them to describe their philosophy of education. Ask them the following questions:
   - How do children learn?
   - What is the role of the teacher?
   - What part does personality play in your beliefs?
   - How do you describe your views relative to discipline and curriculum?
   - How would you achieve mastery?
   - What are your expectations for your students?
   - How do you manage your class? What methods do you use?

   Relate and compare each of their statements to one of the basic philosophies of education: Perennialism, Essentialism, Progressivism, Reconstructionism, Constructivism, and Existentialism.
3. Compare and contrast your own personal philosophy to those of the three teachers you interviewed. Explain any changes you would make in your philosophy as a result of this exercise

For Further Reading

Halpern, D. F. (1984). *Thought and knowledge: An introduction to critical thinking*. Mahwah, NJ: Erlbaum.

Kozol, J. (1991). *Savage inequalities: Children in America's schools*. New York: Crown.

Riner, P. S. (2000). *Successful teaching in the elementary classroom*. Upper Saddle River, NJ: Merrill.

Ryder, R. J., and Graves, F. G. (1994). *Reading and learning in content areas*. New York: Macmillan.

Plato. (1998). *The Republic*. Trans. by B. Jowett. New York: Vantage.

CHAPTER

The Standards' Impact

FOCUS POINTS

1. The impact of the standards has affected how and what teachers teach.
2. Standards help us assess learning in relation to clear benchmarks.
3. Standards have positive aspects; they help eliminate redundancy in curricula and they clarify the meaning of high expectations.

CHAPTER OVERVIEW

THE PROPONENTS OF STANDARDS have been largely successful in shaping school policy throughout the United States. Critics maintain that standards based on high-stakes tests narrow the curriculum, devalue teachers' professionalism, and turn off students from learning. This chapter attempts to understand the impact standards have made on teachers, students, and the curriculum. It explores the meaning and impact that the standards movement has made on student achievement. Standards are viewed from the perspective of the teacher's role in lesson planning and assessments. Traditional and progressive schools are compared and discussed in relation to the new expectations for classroom teachers. Methods and procedures to attain these standards are discussed and defined as follows.

1. *Academic/Education standards* describe what students should know and be able to do in the core academic subjects at each grade level.
2. *Content/Grade-level standards* describe basic agreement about the body of education knowledge that all students should have.
3. *Performance standards* describe what level of performance is good enough for students to be described as advanced, proficient, below basic, or by some other performance level.

Standards have become the latest educational fad in our new century. High expectations and, even worse, the testing needed to ensure that these expectations are met is the rage in most academic communities. Educators at times are like the proverbial pilgrim looking for a destination at the end of the journey. The path to that final destination is now aflutter with signs shouting *Standards!* But teachers should question the meaning of national and local standards and the impact they have on effective teaching. Are teachers forced to teach to the test and encourage low-level skill lessons in order to have students pass mindless tests? On the other hand, are standards the best available answer to monitoring student achievement yet devised? The standards are an abstraction that has been reified by high-stakes testing. The answers to these questions are not as simple as they first appear. It's probably best that we lay a foundation before we attempt to draw any conclusions.

STANDARDS AND ASSESSMENT

Standards and assessment go hand in hand. The idea that assessment can affect the curriculum and learning is not new. The power of an examination to shape what is taught and learned was noted as early as the sixteenth century by Philip Melanchthon (1497–1560) in *De Studiis Adolescentum*. He noted that "No academic exercise can be more useful than that of examination. It whets the desire to learn, it enhances the solicitude of study while it animates the attention of whatever is taught" (Melanchthon, 1997).

An assessment in the hands of teachers gives them valuable information about what to teach and how to teach it. It allows the teacher to individualize instruction for students. A fundamental question should be asked: "If standards and testing disappeared tomorrow, what would replace them?" High-stakes testing used as a tool to drive reform and make decisions about policy is another story altogether. The battle lines are drawn: test to improve instruction or test to establish educational policy in order to assess individuals and institutions. Assessments take the form of exhibitions, examinations, or portfolios; all are based on the same basic technology—a sample of student work and inferences about probable performance. Based on this inference, you can classify, describe, or make decisions about individuals or institutions. Minimum competency tests instituted in the 1970s were used to define the minimum performance students should achieve in order to graduate. Today, at least in theory, the traditional standardized multiple-choice test is out and performance assessments, also known as authentic assessments, are in. These authentic assessments are based on the three P's—performance, portfolios, and products. Performance assessment is usually defined as requiring an examinee to construct, supply answers, perform, or produce something for evaluation. Performance assessment has captured the linguistic high ground, just as the term "minimum competency testing" did in the 1970s. Yet it is by no stretch of the imagination a new technology. The history of performance standards and assessment can be divided into three periods: premodern, modern, and present.

History of Performance Standards and Assessment

Premodern Period of Standards and Assessment Until the first decade of the twentieth century, China used a system of assessment that contained two meritocratic examinations, one for civil service and the other for the military. The first was designed to select the most able men for the civil service by placing emphasis on reasoning ability. This approach did not last because government officials worried it was too subjective; they therefore reverted to a system based on rote answers. The second system was for the selection of military officers, testing performance that was considered necessary for an effective soldier. It would be considered job-related testing today.

In Europe during this period, there were also two types of performance standards used, one for artisans and the other for gentlemen. The first devised standards to certify guild members or craftsmen, and the second to assess gentlemen. The first system allowed you to become a master craftsman only when you were able to produce a masterpiece that met a universal standard. The second type assessed gentlemen who studied the seven liberal arts (grammar, logic, music, rhetoric, arithmetic, geometry, and astronomy). The applicant met the content standard through examinations that allowed participants to become priests, knights, lawyers, or scholars. Students were required to memorize a set of answers to given questions about fixed canon and repeat them orally on demand. This approach to assessing who met the standards for gentlemen mirrors the transmission view of learning. Since the domain of knowledge at the time was limited, it was quite easy to assess achievement. This led to so-called Cathedral schools, which practiced the catechetical method of rote instruction, which has lasted to this day.

In the twelveth century the University of Paris and the University of Bologna were first to introduce a modern form of examination and shift from a qualitative appraisal of the individual to a quantitative mark for correct answers that permitted objective ranking. Oral exams were the most popular because of a scarcity of paper and its high cost. In 1845, Horace Mann supplanted the oral exam by introducing the written essay exam. He demonstrated that he could test more students in less time by using written exams rather than oral exams. He also claimed to be able to hold teachers and students accountable for their work.

Boston schools were the first to use print short-answer tests in geography, grammar, history, rhetoric, and philosophy. Citizens were shocked when they discovered that 40 percent of the questions on these uniform examinations were not answered by any of the students. (Sounds like today.) By 1850, Boston reverted to nonstandardized exams that were mostly oral presentations. In 1874 Samuel King, the Portland superintendent, created a uniform curriculum for the city's schools and wrote a test to measure whether students successfully learned it. He published each student's score in the newspaper, which led to his resignation after the community protested. (Will history repeat itself?)

Modern Period of Standards and Assessment (1900–1980) Starting around 1905, when Alfred Binet introduced the intelligence test, the idea of a standard measurement for intelligence was found. With the advent of the psychological testing movement, testing approaches were forever altered. Before this, testing had concentrated on content containing a fixed body of knowledge; now one's aptitude and intelligence could be measured against pre-established standards. The need for rapid testing procedures for large numbers in a short period was lifted to the forefront because of military needs during the World War I. A more efficient, manageable, easily scored, and recorded technology was needed to assess large numbers of men's ability to be soldiers. This need led to the concept of norm-referenced scoring. In 1914, Fredrick Kelly introduced multiple-choice tests as a way to get away from the traditional, inefficient, essay examination. Multiple-choice tests, in all their variety, had supplanted the essay test for most of the twentieth century. When Everett Lindquist introduced the optical scanner in 1955 as a method of rapidly grading, he sealed the eminence of multiple-choice tests for the next forty years.

Present Period of Standards and Assessment (1980) In the late 1980s standardized multiple-choice testing came under criticism and the standards movement for new authentic assessments began. This created a problem from a technical and efficiency point of view. Obviously, authentic assessments are less efficient, more difficult to administer, more time consuming, and more disruptive to a school's organization than are multiple-choice tests, which are administered quite rapidly. Authentic assessments are difficult to standardize due to their subjective nature. They sample a smaller portion of pupil performance and are more costly to administer.

Another problem was inexperience in developing performance assessment instruments linked to performance standards, portfolio measurement approaches, and end-product assessments. Publishers were used to making profits from the sale of answer sheets and scoring services, not on in-service training related to assessing achievement in reaching performance standards. The issues of manageability, standardization, difficulty of administration, subjectivity, unreliability, comparability, and expense must be confronted before we can accurately meet the goals established in performance standards. What is going to happen in the future? The answer will probably be that the publishers will opt for the one that offers the most reliability and profit.

Standards in Traditional and Progressive Schools

Standards are achievable in both traditional and progressive schools. Each type of school chooses a different path to meet the same standards for an educated person. Progressive schools focus on a student's social development, while traditional schools highlight passing on knowledge, skills, and values in society. Progressives view the role of schools as to prepare children for democratic citizenship and to accept their civic duties, while traditionalists view their role as to give children the skills and credentials necessary to get good jobs and ensure their future (Cuban, 1998).

Actually, schools were not established to get students jobs or to replace parents and churches in nurturing social development. They were established to make sure children met the standards for becoming literate educated adults who respected authority, accepted differences of opinion, and fulfilled their civic duties. Society viewed the role of the schools as to instill democratic core values and virtues in each generation. A good school is one that produces graduates who demonstrate and possess democratic behavior, values, and attitudes such as open-mindedness, fairness, and the ability to talk things out. Criteria for good schools are centered on democratic perceptions and actual performance standards.

The *traditional view of education* describes education in terms of the delivery of instruction or transfer of information. This is essentially a transmission model that accepts the empty vessel theory of learning. This view holds that children come to schools as empty vessels and the role of the teacher is to fill these human vessels with knowledge. Teaching usually consists of direct instruction based on behaviorist philosophy. Instruction is didactic, focused on a skill-based approach highlighting sequenced systematic methods. Traditionalists use skill-based tests to measure skills. The traditional behaviorist view of learning sees humans as passive responders to the environment rather than active thinkers and meaning makers.

The *progressive view of education* sees teaching not as performance but as an interactive practice that begins and ends with seeing students in a child-centered milieu. Students cannot be compelled to learn, as behaviorists believe, only invited, encouraged, and helped to learn in a developmentally appropriate way. Instruction is seen as essentially child-centered and cooperative while avoiding scripted approaches. The progressive view advocates a constructivist view of learning that sees learning occurring in a developmental, interactive atmosphere. Students are encouraged to be authentic thinkers and producers. Its credo is better comprehension and reasoning without sacrificing individuality.

Similarities Both progressive and traditional schools have values that stress knowledge, teaching, learning, and the freedom to differ. They share core beliefs such as wanting to foster democratic attitudes, values, and behaviors. Both encourage open-mindedness and a willingness to listen to different opinions while encouraging respect for the values of different people. The American belief for treating all individuals fairly is advanced by developing a commitment to talk problems through various alternatives. Each have similar standards, and would agree that teaching consists of listening, practicing, and learning. Both can have stable committed staffs and core beliefs about what is good for children. Each also stresses the need for parent support.

Differences The contrast is most evident when one looks at the differences between problem project methodology and drill with rote practice. Today that glaring difference has been mostly overcome by understanding and using "best practices." They do, however, differ in their organization, view of learning, and the strategies they believe are needed to teach the curriculum. This can be seen in the physical layout of classrooms. Traditional schools tend to take pride in order and discipline, whereas progressive schools tend to be more concerned with meeting student needs. The stress on instruction in traditional schools as contrasted with the stress on student learning in progressive schools is the essential philosophical difference cited by most researchers.

DEFINING STANDARDS

Most researchers would agree with the premise that master teachers exhibit at least three common traits: (1) they are well organized in their planning; (2) they communicate their instructional objectives effectively to their students; and (3) they have high expectations for their students (Orlich et al., 2001). They would also agree that most effective teachers share the keys to effective teaching. They would, however, be hard-pressed to state specific aims, goals, and objectives that would be shared by all. That is exactly what national and state standards are expected to do. The teacher has been given the responsibility to incorporate these aims, instructional goals, and objectives into her teaching. Recall from Chapter 3 that an *aim* is a broad statement of very general outcomes that lead to goals, which are more narrowly defined statements of outcomes, and finally, to objectives, which are specific statements of a learner's behavior. The curriculum your students are expected to master will be based on the aims, goals, and objectives spelled out in federal, state, and local governmental documents.

The underlying assumption of our standards-based reform is that all students are capable of meeting high expectations. Student achievement data in the United States show long-standing gaps in performance. Expectations in our schools have varied widely, and expectations for economically disadvantaged and minority students have been generally lower than for other students. Many view standards as a foundation on which to build excellence and equity in our nation's public education system.

Goals 2000

The movement began at the federal level in April 1991, when President George H. W. Bush and the nation's governors held an educational summit—strangely, without educators present. They produced a document entitled *America 2000: An Education Strategy* (U. S. Department of Education, 1991), which contained goals for restructuring schools and a strategy for the United States to regain its academic leadership among all other nations. This document was enacted into law on March 31, 1994, as the Goals 2000: Educate America Act. President Clinton said the Act was, in effect, "reinventing education." The goals contained in the act were set up because the nation was led to believe that our educational system was lacking compared to the rest of the world. The answers that were advanced focused on higher standards and new

PRACTICE EXERCISE 9.1

Progressive and Traditional Schools

Reflect on the attributes listed under each type of school. Respond by either supporting the item or disavowing it. Is the implied contrast valid? Be sure to give reasons for your stance. The entire class should discuss and share views.

Progressive Schools	Traditional Schools
1. Freedom to pursue interests of students	1. Orderly schools, honor teachers
2. Multi-age grouping	2. Parent involvement
3. Student-initiated projects	3. High academic standards
4. No numerical or letter grades	4. Drill, practice, and model

forms of assessments. (Figure 9.1 briefly lists the eight main educational goals approved by Congress in 1994.)

It would appear as of this writing that Goals 2000 have not been achieved and may never be achieved for everyone. Because of Goals 2000, each state attempted to adopt laws related to the federal goals that would make them eligible for federal funding.

Compact for Learning

The New Compact for Learning was New York State's plan to achieve the goals set in federal law. The Compact filtered down to the local level and established the strategic objectives shown in Figure 9.2.

Figure 9.1 National Education Goals 2000

1. All children in America will start school ready to learn.
2. The high school graduation rate will increase to at least 90 percent.
3. American students will leave grades 4, 8, and 12 having demonstrated competency in challenging subject matter, including English, mathematics, science, history, and geography; every school in America will ensure that all students learn to use their minds well, so that they may be prepared for responsible citizenship, further learning, and productive employment in our modern economy.
4. The nation's teaching force will have access to programs for professional development.
5. U.S. students will be first in the world in science and mathematics achievement.
6. Every adult American will be literate and will possess the knowledge and skills necessary to compete in a global economy and to exercise the rights and responsibilities of citizenship.
7. Every school in America will be free of drugs and violence and will offer a safe, disciplined environment conducive to learning.
8. Every school will promote parental involvement and participation to promote the social, emotional, and academic growth of children.

Figure 9.2 New Compact for Learning from New York

1. All children will come to school ready to learn.
2. All children will read, write, compute, and use the thinking skills they need to continue learning by the time they are in the fourth grade or its equivalent.
3. At least 90 percent of all young people will earn a high school diploma by age 21.
4. All high school graduates will be prepared for college, work, or both.
5. All high school graduates will demonstrate proficiency in English and another language, mathematics, the natural sciences, and technology; in history and other social sciences; and in the arts and other humanities. (Standards will be developed.)
6. All students will acquire the skills, knowledge, and attitudes needed for employment and effective citizenship.
7. All children will demonstrate commitment to the core values of our democratic society and knowledge of the history and culture of the major groups, which comprise American society and the world.
8. Students of both genders and all socioeconomic and racial/ethnic backgrounds will show similar achievement on state assessment measures.

Curriculum Frameworks

The *Curriculum Frameworks* is an example of a document framed by a local government, in this case by the city of New York, to achieve the goals contained in a state compact and the aims of the federal act. The *Frameworks* is a compilation of strategies within a curriculum, considered necessary to prepare children to be effective citizens. Its purpose was to establish a set of expectations for all, while allowing for flexibility. City districts and schools were allowed latitude to employ different teaching strategies focused on achieving expectations outlined in the *Frameworks*. Figure 9.3 lists six key principles put forth by the NYS Education Department that provided direction.

Standards and Daily Practice

To understand how we use standards in daily practice we must first understand what standards are. An *educational standard* is a statement that depicts what students should know or be able to do because of the teaching and learning they experienced. An example would be a standard expressed in terms of knowledge or performance in a specific content area (e.g., "Children in grades K to 8 must read twenty-five books in various genres each school year").

Developmental standards look at the levels of development exhibited by individual students. These standards are expressed in terms of age appropriateness and attempts to highlight changes in the developing child with regard to personality traits, learning style, and family background. The purpose for understanding developmental standards is to help teachers prepare lessons that are appropriate for a particular age span.

Pierre van Hiele and Dina van Hiele-Geldof described developmental standards when they identified five levels of understanding spatial concepts through which children move on their way to geometric thinking. The levels are sequential, not age dependent, and are influenced by experience. Poor instruction may inhibit learning. Students should move from levels 1 to 3 by the end of the eighth grade. Levels 4 and 5 should be achieved by high school or college. The van Hieles stress that teachers should be aware of these levels. Figure 9.4 contains the van Hieles' developmental standards used by Texas for geometric reasoning.

Grade-level standards are grade-specific standards that identify outcomes expected at a particular grade level or as the result of a particular unit of study. An example can be seen in using the backwards design process (see Chapters 3 and 10). Take the end result, and work backwards (e.g., "Children are expected to read at the conclusion of the third grade. They must complete . . ."). Figure 9.5 shows grade-level standards for kindergarten and first grade in reading.

Content-specific standards identify the expected outcomes for specific subjects with regard to content and conceptual knowledge. These types of standards can act as guideposts for teachers when determining effective lesson strategies. Figure 9.6 depicts content-specific standards for reading.

Figure 9.3 Six Key Principles of the Curriculum Frameworks of New York City

1. All children are capable of learning and contributing to society.
2. Parents and caregivers are the children's first teachers.
3. All students, including those with special needs, should be challenged to fulfill their utmost potential.
4. Limited English proficient (LEP) students must receive parallel instructional programs, and be provided with equal access to quality programs.
5. Schools need to reflect an education that is multicultural.
6. Schools can make a difference in students' lives.

Figure 9.4 Samples of Developmental Standards in Mathematics from Texas

van Hiele Levels of Geometric Reasoning

Level

1. Can name and recognize shapes by appearance, but cannot specifically identify properties.
2. Begins to identify properties of shapes and learns vocabulary related to properties, but cannot make connections between different properties and shapes.
3. Student can recognize relationships between properties and shapes, as well as follow logical arguments using such properties.
4. Can go beyond just identifying characteristics of shapes and be able to construct proofs using postulates or axioms and definitions.
5. Student can work in different geometric or axiomatic systems.

Source: Cognitive and Development Issues. (2007). *van Hiele levels of geometric reasoning.* www.dallassd.com/geometry/DevelopmentalSummary.html

Figure 9.5 Grade-Level Standards from California Department of Education

---

Grade K Reading Comprehension

Students identify the basic facts and ideas in what they have read, heard, or viewed. They use comprehension strategies (e.g., generating and responding to questions, comparing new information to what is already known). The selections in *Recommended Literature, Kindergarten through Grade Twelve* illustrate the quality and complexity of the materials to be read by students.

Structural Features of Informational Materials

2.1 Locate the title, table of contents, name of author, and name of illustrator.

Comprehension and Analysis of Grade-Level-Appropriate Text

2.2 Use pictures and context to make predictions about story content.

2.3 Connect to life experiences the information and events in texts.

2.4 Retell familiar stories.

2.5 Ask and answer questions about essential elements of a text.

3.0 Literary Response and Analysis

Students listen and respond to stories based on well-known characters, themes, plots, and settings. The selections in *Recommended Literature, Kindergarten through Grade Twelve* illustrate the quality and complexity of the materials to be read by students.

Narrative Analysis of Grade-Level-Appropriate Text

3.1 Distinguish fantasy from realistic text.

3.2 Identify types of everyday print materials (e.g., storybooks, poems, newspapers, signs, labels).

3.3 Identify characters, settings, and important events.

Grade One Reading Comprehension

Students read and understand grade-level-appropriate material. They draw on a variety of comprehension strategies as needed (e.g., generating and responding to essential questions, making predictions, comparing information from several sources). The selections in *Recommended Literature, Kindergarten through Grade Twelve* illustrate the quality and complexity of the materials to be read by students. In addition to their regular school reading, by grade four, students read one-half million words annually, including a good representation of grade-level-appropriate narrative and expository text (e.g., classic and contemporary literature, magazines, newspapers, online information). In grade one, students begin to make progress toward this goal.

Structural Features of Informational Materials

2.1 Identify text that uses sequence or other logical order.

Comprehension and Analysis of Grade-Level-Appropriate Text

2.2 Respond to *who, what, when, where,* and *how* questions.

2.3 Follow one-step written instructions.

2.4 Use context to resolve ambiguities about word and sentence meanings.

2.5 Confirm predictions about what will happen next in a text by identifying key words (i.e., signpost words).

2.6 Relate prior knowledge to textual information.

2.7 Retell the central ideas of simple expository or narrative passages.

Source: California Department of Education (2002)

Performance standards make content standards operational by describing how "good" is "good enough." They essentially reflect what children should know and how they can demonstrate that knowledge. Performance standards describe expected outcomes for what students should be able to do. They depict expectations such as the No Child Left Behind Act's **Adequate Yearly Progress (AYP)** feature. The AYP is the performance standard that "All students will experience a year of academic growth for each year of instruction" (Conley, 2005). The AYP is used to track the success of Title I schools and districts in improving student achievement. Schools and districts that exceed their AYP goals for two or more consecutive years are eligible for recognition and are encouraged to share their successful programs. Figure 9.7 provides an example of a statewide AYP plan.

By 2007, there was a semblance of performance standards in most states and school districts throughout our nation. Whether they are all consistent and mesh with each other is another question. Teachers will be given standards regardless of where they teach, and they will be asked to have students achieve at the mandated levels.

Figure 9.6 Content-Specific Standards for Reading Grade Level K–12 from Arizona

Strand 1: Reading Process
Reading Process consists of the five critical components of reading, which are Phonemic Awareness, Phonics, Fluency, Vocabulary, and Comprehension of connected text. These elements support each other and are woven together to build a solid foundation of linguistic understanding for the reader.

Concept 1: Print Concepts	Demonstrate understanding of print concepts.
Concept 2: Phonemic Awareness	Identify and manipulate the sounds of speech.
Concept 3: Phonics	Decode words, using knowledge of phonics, syllabication, and word parts.
Concept 4: Vocabulary	Acquire and use new vocabulary in relevant contexts.
Concept 5: Fluency	Read fluently.
Concept 6: Comprehension	Employ strategies to comprehend text.

Strand 2: Comprehending Literary Text
Comprehending Literary Text identifies the comprehension strategies that are specific in the study of a variety of literature.

Concept 1: Elements of Literature	Identify, analyze, and apply knowledge of the structure and elements of literature.
Concept 2: Historical and Cultural Aspects of Literature	Recognize and apply knowledge of the historical and cultural aspects of American, British, and world literature.

Strand 3: Comprehending Informational Text
Comprehending Informational Text delineates specific and unique skills that are required to understand the wide array of informational text that is a part of our day-to-day experiences.

Concept 1: Expository Text	Identify, analyze, and apply knowledge of the purpose, structures, and elements of expository text.
Concept 2: Functional Text	Identify, analyze, and apply knowledge of the purpose, structures, clarity, and relevancy of functional text.
Concept 3: Persuasive Text	Explain basic elements of argument in text and their relationship to the author's purpose and use of persuasive strategies.

Source: Arizona Department of Education

The war over developing standards appears to be over, and now the battle to implement them has been engaged. Our cities and states have decided after a decade that fixed academic-content standards and performance standards are here to stay. No longer will norm reference tests be the sole indicator of student performance. The achievement of students will no longer be measured against their peers but against specific mandated content. Standards will also likely be used to increase the quality of our nation's teachers.

NATIONAL STANDARDS FOR TEACHERS

In 1987, the **National Board of Professional Teaching Standards (NBPTS)** was established with the assistance

Figure 9.7 Plans for Adequate Yearly Progress (AYP) from Michigan

Adequate Yearly Progress (AYP)

In Michigan, the AYP is a measure of year-to-year student achievement on the Michigan Education Assessment Program (MEAP) test. According to NCLB, states must develop target-starting goals for AYP and the state must raise the bar in gradual increments so 100 percent of the students in the state are proficient on state assessments by the 2013–2014 school year. AYP applies to each district and school in the state; however, NCLB sanctions for schools that do not make AYP for two or more years in a row only apply to those districts and schools that receive Title I funds.

Corrective Actions

Schools and districts that fail to make AYP for two consecutive years are identified for improvement and required to implement improvement plans. They are also required to use a portion of their Title I funds for professional development to support their plans.

The No Child Left Behind Act of 2001 also established new educational options for students who attend Title I schools that are identified for improvement. School districts must offer these students the option to transfer to another school in the district that is not identified for improvement and must provide or pay for transportation. If the district does not have space to accommodate all transfer requests, it must give priority to low-achieving students from low-income families.

If the district does not have any other school to which students can transfer, it is required to attempt to make arrangements with neighboring districts and is expected to make additional efforts to improve the services in the identified schools.

Schools that fail to make AYP for a third consecutive year are also subject to new requirements for "supplemental educational services," which are instructional services provided outside of the school day by an educational service provider selected by the parents from a state-approved list. These services are available only to low-income students, with priority given to low-achieving students.

If schools fail to make AYP for a fourth or fifth year, the district must continue to offer the transfer option and supplemental educational services. It must also take one or more specific actions to make major changes in the school, such as providing a new curriculum and appropriate professional development, decreasing the school's decision-making authority, appointing an outside expert to advise the school, or changing the structure of the school.

If districts that have been identified for improvement continue to fail to make AYP, the Michigan Department of Education is required to take one or more corrective actions with respect to the district. These actions are similar to those required for individual schools.

Source: Michigan Department of Education

PRACTICE EXERCISE 9.2

Translating State Standards

Go online and take a look at your state's standards. Select one standard in each content area and translate it into normal everyday language. Adolescent majors should choose four specific standards and restate their meanings into normal everyday language. Share your translations with the rest of your colleagues. (The example shown here was taken from the New Jersey Core Curriculum Content Standards.)

Original State Standard	Translation and Restatement
All students will demonstrate knowledge of United States and New Jersey *history* in order to understand life and events in the past and how they relate to the present and future.	Teach chronologically using themes such as political and religious freedom from the colonial period to the present. Stress that to understand the present and prepare for the future we must understand the past.
(Listening) All students will listen actively to information from a variety of sources in a variety of situations.	Students will learn to actively listen, and develop critical-thinking skills to evaluate what they are listening to.

of the Carnegie Corporation. The premise was that great schools begin with great teachers; quality teaching is the key to improved student achievement. NBPTS today is recognized for developing professional standards that define what accomplished teachers should know and be able to do. NBPTS also administers National Board

Certification, which is a voluntary assessment program that certifies educators who meet those standards. Nearly 7,800 teachers achieved National Board Certification in 2006, bringing the total to more than 55,000.

There are five core propositions that form the foundation for the NBPT standards. These standards create a vision for what the accomplished teacher should know. Figure 9.8 lists the propositions that form the framework for the twenty-four certificate areas offered.

The INTASC Standards and Indicators for Achievement

What teachers know and can do makes the most difference in what children learn. (Anon.)

An integral component of the new performance-based process is the use of the Interstate New Teacher Assessment and Support Consortium (INTASC) standards. These standards reflect the requisite knowledge, skills, and attitudes necessary for teachers starting their careers (see Figure 9.9 on page 202).

Benchmarking is a process developed in 1956 by the Xerox Corporation and the U.K.'s Rank Organization. It is used in business organizations to evaluate various aspects of operations in relation to established best practices. The strategy allows organizations to develop plans on how to adopt practices that work.

Benchmarking can be used to overcome educational paradigm blindness, a type of thinking that claims there is no need for change since we have always done it this way, and it is therefore the best way. Benchmarking focuses on new methods, ideas, and tools to improve effectiveness.

MINI CASE FROM THE FIELD

The following case from the field discusses the use of appropriate strategies when dealing with assessing student and teacher performance. The strategies and methods proposed focus on meeting the needs of child and teacher. Read the case, and compare the ideas presented to the reality of everyday classroom life.

Are Standards Good for Education?

"Please give me a break. How can anyone consider himself or herself to be an effective teacher if they have no standards?"

"Margaret, do you know what you are saying?"

"Yes, I do, Ed! Without standards and benchmarks, we would have no way of determining what our students have learned."

"Couldn't you just ask them?"

"Ed, do you realize how much time that would take? We might as well return to the Middle Ages when all testing was oral."

"Margaret, you sound more like the mathematician than I do. I know that to obtain quantifiable data with regard to achieving standards implies comparing test results on standardized tests. My question is, So what? I don't teach for reference-based examinations, I teach for children to learn."

A schoolwide memo from Principal Chandler Thompson had precipitated the argument between Margaret Gomez and Ed Child. Thompson had written that all student grades would conform to national and state standards. If grades did not conform, students were to receive a failing grade. An addendum to this memo stated that teacher salaries would be based on the success of their students in achieving the standards.

Nicholas Saccone, a K–12 science teacher and teacher advocate, exclaimed that Thompson's memo sounded like a police warning: "You are not obliged to say anything, but anything you say will be taken down and may be used against you." Lucille Chan, a veteran fourth-grade teacher, piped up and told Nick to stop being silly, that this was a serious professional problem. Lucille explained that she also thought that standards for both teachers and students were necessary if the quality of education were to improve. She expressed the view that she shared Mr. Thompson's views but did not approve of his authoritarian method for implementation. Nick looked at Lucille and finally said, "You know, I think you are right. We should form a committee and ask to speak with the principal so that we can come to mutually acceptable standards for both teachers and students."

"That sounds fine," said Ed. "But just whose standards would we use? For teachers we could use the INTASC standards and for students our state standards. "Well, Mr. Compromise, what do you think the principal had in mind? Why don't we just develop our own teacher and student standards?" asked Nick. "That would be like re-inventing the wheel," Lucille said.

Ed took out a piece of paper on which he claimed to have copied a summary of standards for teachers that they could all agree upon. "Well, what do you think?"

Standard Number	Standard Narrative
1	The teacher (candidate) promotes the well-being of all students and helps them learn to their highest levels of achievement and independence, demonstrating an ability to form productive connections with students with diverse characteristics and backgrounds, students for whom English is a new language, students with varying abilities and disabilities, and students of both sexes.

Figure 9.8 NBPTS Propositions

Proposition 1: Teachers Are Committed to Students and Learning

1. NBCTs are dedicated to making knowledge accessible to all students. They believe all students can learn.
2. They treat students equitably. They recognize the individual differences that distinguish their students from one another and they take account for these differences in their practice.
3. NBCTs understand how students develop and learn.
4. They respect the cultural and family differences students bring to their classroom.
5. They are concerned with their students' self-concept, their motivation, and the effects of learning on peer relationships.
6. NBCTs are also concerned with the development of character and civic responsibility.

Proposition 2: Teachers Know the Subjects They Teach and How to Teach Those Subjects to Students

1. NBCTs have mastery over the subject(s) they teach. They have a deep understanding of the history, structure, and real-world applications of the subject.
2. They have skill and experience in teaching it, and they are very familiar with the skills gaps and preconceptions students may bring to the subject.
3. They are able to use diverse instructional strategies to teach for understanding.

Proposition 3: Teachers Are Responsible for Managing and Monitoring Student Learning

1. NBCTs deliver effective instruction.
2. They move fluently through a range of instructional techniques, keeping students motivated, engaged, and focused.
3. They know how to engage students to ensure a disciplined learning environment, and how to organize instruction to meet instructional goals.
4. NBCTs know how to assess the progress of individual students as well as the class as a whole.
5. They use multiple methods for measuring student growth and understanding, and they can clearly explain student performance to parents.

Proposition 4: Teachers Think Systematically about Their Practice and Learn from Experience

1. NBCTs model what it means to be an educated person—they read, they question, they create, and they are willing to try new things.
2. They are familiar with learning theories and instructional strategies and stay abreast of current issues in American education.
3. They critically examine their practice on a regular basis to deepen knowledge, expand their repertoire of skills, and incorporate new findings into their practice.

Proposition 5: Teachers Are Members of Learning Communities

1. NBCTs collaborate with others to improve student learning.
2. They are leaders and actively know how to seek and build partnerships with community groups and businesses.
3. They work with other professionals on instructional policy, curriculum development, and staff development.
4. They can evaluate school progress and the allocation of resources in order to meet state and local education objectives.
5. They know how to work collaboratively with parents to engage them productively in the work of the school.

Source: National Board for Professional Teaching Standards (2006)

---

2. The teacher (candidate) has solid foundations in the arts and sciences, breadth and depth of knowledge of subject to be taught, and understanding of subject matter pedagogy and curriculum development.
3. The teacher (candidate) understands how students learn and develop.
4. The teacher (candidate) effectively manages classrooms that are structured in a variety of ways, using a variety of instructional methods, including education technology.
5. The teacher (candidate) uses various types of assessment to analyze teaching and student learning and to plan curriculum and instruction to meet the needs of individual students.

(continues on page 204)

Figure 9.9 INTASC Standards

Standards

1. Content Pedagogy

The teacher understands the central concepts, tools of inquiry, and structures of the discipline he or she teaches and can create learning experiences that make these aspects of subject matter meaningful for students.

Candidate Indicators

- Demonstrates an understanding of the central concepts of his or her discipline
- Uses explanations and representations that link curriculum to prior learning
- Evaluates resources and curriculum materials for appropriateness to the curriculum and instructional delivery
- Engages students in interpreting ideas from a variety of perspectives
- Uses interdisciplinary approaches to teaching and learning
- Uses methods of inquiry that are central to the discipline

2. Student Development

The teacher understands how children learn and develop, and can provide learning opportunities that support a child's intellectual, social, and personal development.

Candidate Indicators

- Evaluates student performance to design instruction appropriate for social, cognitive, and emotional development
- Creates relevance for students by linking with their prior experiences
- Provides opportunities for students to assume responsibility for and be actively engaged in their learning
- Encourages student reflection on prior knowledge and its connection to new information
- Accesses student thinking as a basis for instructional activities through group/individual interaction and written work (listening, encouraging discussion, eliciting samples of student thinking orally and in writing)

3. Diverse Learners

The teacher understands how students differ in their approaches to learning and creates instructional opportunities that are adapted to diverse learners.

Candidate Indicators

- Designs instruction appropriate to students' stages of development, learning styles, strengths, and needs
- Selects approaches that provide opportunities for different performance modes
- Accesses appropriate services or resources to meet exceptional learning needs when needed
- Adjusts instruction to accommodate the learning differences or needs of students (time and circumstances of work, tasks assigned, communication, and response modes)
- Uses knowledge of different cultural contexts within the community (socioeconomic, ethnic, cultural) and connects with the learner through types of interaction and assignments
- Creates a learning community that respects individual differences

4. Multiple Instructional Strategies

The teacher understands and uses a variety of instructional strategies to encourage student development of critical thinking, problem solving, and performance skills.

Candidate Indicators

- Selects and uses multiple teaching and learning strategies (a variety of presentations/explanations) to encourage students in critical thinking and problem solving
- Encourages students to assume responsibility for identifying and using learning resources
- Assures different roles in the instructional process (instructor, facilitator, coach, audience) to accommodate content, purpose, and learner needs

5. Motivation and Management

The teacher uses an understanding of individual and group motivation and behavior to create a learning environment that encourages positive social interaction, active engagement in learning, and self-motivation.

Candidate Indicators

- Encourages clear procedures and expectations that ensure students assume responsibility for themselves and others, work collaboratively and independently, and engage in purposeful learning activities
- Engages students by relating lessons to students' personal interests, allowing students to have choices in their learning, and leads students to ask questions and solve problems that are meaningful to them
- Organizes, allocates, and manages time, space, and activities in a way that is conducive to learning
- Organizes, prepares students, and monitors independent and group work that allows for full and varied participation of all individuals
- Analyzes classroom environment and interactions and makes adjustments to enhance social relationships, student motivation/engagement, and productive work

Figure 9.9 *(Continued)*

6. Communications and Technology

The teacher uses knowledge of effective verbal, nonverbal, and media communication techniques to foster active inquiry, collaboration, and supportive interaction in the classroom.

Candidate Indicators

- Models effective communication strategies in conveying ideas and information and when asking questions (e.g., monitoring the effects of messages, restating ideas and drawing connection, using visual, aural, and kinesthetic cues, being sensitive to nonverbal cues both given and received)
- Provides support for learner expression in speaking, writing, and other media
- Demonstrates that communication is sensitive to gender and cultural differences (e.g., appropriate use of eye contact, interpretation of body language and verbal statements, acknowledgment of and responsiveness to different modes of communication and participation
- Uses a variety of media communication tools to enrich learning opportunities

7. Planning

The teacher plans instruction based upon knowledge of subject matter, students, the community, and curriculum goals.

Candidate Indicators

- Plans lessons and activities to address variation in learning styles and performance modes, multiple development levels of diverse learners, and problem solving and exploration
- Develops plans that are appropriate for curriculum goals and are based on effective instruction
- Adjusts plans to respond to unanticipated sources of input and/or student needs
- Develops short and long-range plans

8. Assessment

The teacher understands and uses formal and informal assessment strategies to evaluate and ensure the continuous intellectual, social, and physical development of the learner.

Candidate Indicators

- Selects, constructs, and uses assessment strategies appropriate to the learning outcomes
- Uses a variety of informal and formal strategies to inform choices about student progress and to adjust instruction (e.g., standardized test data; peer and student self-assessment; informal assessments, such as observation, surveys, interviews, student work, performance tasks, portfolio, and teacher-made tests)
- Uses assessment strategies to involve learners in self-assessment activities to help them become aware of their strengths and needs and to encourage them to set personal goals for learning
- Evaluates the effects of class activities on individuals and on groups through observation of classroom interaction, questioning, and analysis of student work
- Maintains useful records of student work and performance and can communicate student progress knowledgeably and responsibly
- Solicits information about students' experiences, learning behavior, needs, and progress from parents, other colleagues, and students

9. Reflective Practice and Professional Development

The teacher is a reflective practitioner who continually evaluates the effects of his or her choices and actions on others. The teacher also actively seeks out opportunities to grow professionally.

Candidate Indicators

- Uses classroom observation, information about students, and research as sources for evaluating the outcomes of teaching and learning and as a basis for experimenting with, reflecting on, and revising practice
- Uses professional literature, colleagues, and other resources to support self-development as a learner and as a teacher
- Consults with professional colleagues within the school and other professional arenas as support for reflection, problem solving and new ideas, actively sharing experiences and seeking and giving feedback

10. School and Community Involvement

The teacher fosters relationships with school colleagues, parents, and agencies in the larger community to support students' learning and well-being.

Candidate Indicators

- Participates in collegial activities designed to make the entire school a productive learning environment
- Links with counselors, teachers of other classes and activities within the school, professionals in community agencies, and others in the community to support students' learning and well-being
- Seeks to establish cooperative partnerships with parents/guardians to support student learning
- Advocates for students

Source: North Carolina Department of Public Instruction (2006)

6. The teacher (candidate) promotes parental involvement and collaborates effectively with other staff, the community, higher education, other agencies, and cultural institutions, as well as parents and other caregivers, for the benefit of students.
7. The teacher (candidate) maintains up-to-date knowledge and skills in the subject taught and in methods of instructions and assessment.
8. The teacher (candidate) is of good moral character.

1. List the arguments made by Margaret to support her position. Contrast her arguments with Ed Child's argument. Who had the stronger arguments? Why? Whose side was Lucille on?
2. Was Mr. Thompson justified in establishing school policy without consulting his staff? What should he have done?
3. How has the standards movement affected the lives of teachers and students alike?
4. Describe your feelings about Ed's list of appropriate standards for teachers.
5. Is there a need for teacher and student standards? How would you use them to better educate students and attract qualified and competent teachers?

STUDENT PERFORMANCE STANDARDS

The true test for the success of teacher standards lies in recognizing its link to student performance standards. A teacher succeeds when her students achieve. Performance standards are essentially outgrowths of content standards found in textbooks, state curriculum guides, and the like. They have always existed in a haphazard way. The University of Pittsburgh prepared New York City's performance standards, called the New Standards. These performance standards were linked to the content standards of various national councils of teachers. The process contained benchmarks as guides in assessment, and was enhanced by comparing our national standards with world standards. These performance standards specified what students should know and be able to do at each grade level in all academic areas. The performance standards make content standards operational. They specify how good is good enough. They provide a description of performance needed to meet a content objective. This can be clearly seen when one visualizes judges rating Olympic high dives. Each judge knows what the standard is and what surpasses it. This is what standards are attempting to do for education (specifically reading and math).

New Standards and National Performance Standards

The New Standards based on our National Performance Standards describe the performances necessary to demonstrate student knowledge in four areas—English language arts, mathematics, science, and applied learning (to apply knowledge to analyze and solve problems). These New Standards are assessed by (1) reference examinations, (2) use of a portfolio system, and (3) teacher assessment of student achievement.

To work properly this approach must be uniform and standard-driven. It must contain both content and performance standards. It should have a comprehensive planning component for both school districts and individual schools. Curriculum instruction and professional development is assessed and all are accountable. This process is usually reinforced by a public reporting of all test results.

The expectations focus on clarity in describing performance standards. The requirement to read twenty-five books of quality and complexity is an example of such clarity. To make the standards clearer in all areas, work samples and commentaries to illustrate meaning were included. Figure 9.10 provides an overview taken from the New York City standards.

The completion of standards leads to the question, "How do we make them a reality in the classroom?" Standards are easy to accept but implementation is another matter. Teachers should follow the suggestions outlined in their state's education department guides. Most states have provided assessments aligned to test their performance standards. Teachers must implement standards-based instruction for students to thrive. This requires teachers to engage in staff development and self-training. For instruction to put standards into practice and become an integral part of school and each classroom, district comprehensive plans and school comprehensive plans should be linked to the classroom teacher's comprehensive plan. For performance standards to be realized they must be reflected in demonstrations of student learning. The goal is to bring standards-based planning directly related to state and national standards into the classroom.

STANDARDS-BASED LESSON PLANNING

The problem with **standards-based lesson** planning is that there are no explicit directions for how this is to be accomplished. The *Standards-Based Classroom Operator's Manual* (2002) for teachers attempts to develop directions. The manual contains a set of tools designed to

PRACTICE EXERCISE 9.3

Examining National Standards for Teachers

The purpose of this exercise is to reflect and become familiar with the national standards for teachers as advanced in the NBCT propositions and INTASC standards.

- *Reflect* on and review each of the five NBCT propositions and the ten INTASC standards.
- *Match* each of the NBCT propositions to one or two of the INTASC standards.
- *Strategize* by writing a brief description of how you would hope to achieve each item listed.

Class or Small-Group Activity: Compare and discuss your reflections, matches, and strategies with those of your classmates. Determine if any general strategies are apparent, and if not, determine the reasons.

NBCT Propositions

1. Teachers are committed to students and learning.
2. Teachers know the subjects they teach and how to teach those subjects to students.
3. Teachers are responsible for managing and monitoring student learning.
4. Teachers think systematically about their practice and learn from experience.
5. Teachers are members of learning communities.

INTASC Standards

1. Content Pedagogy
2. Student Development
3. Diverse Learners
4. Multiple Instructional Strategies
5. Motivation and Management
6. Communications and Technology
7. Planning
8. Assessment
9. Reflective Practice and Professional Development
10. School and Community Involvement

PRACTICE EXERCISE 9.4

Benchmarking Standards for Teachers

The purpose of this exercise is to understand and reflect on how to achieve the standards (NBCT propositions and INTASC) through an approach called *benchmarking*. There are four basic steps to follow when using benchmarking. For each step, indicate how you could implement the process to help you achieve high standards for yourself and your students.

1. Identify your problem.
2. Identify others (determine if their approaches are worthy of replication and study).
3. Survey practices (as identified by colleagues to share best practices).
4. Implement the "best practice."

---

1. Identify content standards
2. Design assessment task
3. Determine performance levels
4. Design curriculum
5. Plan instruction strategies
6. Implement instruction
7. Assess students
8. Evaluate and refine whole process

The Standards Achievement Planning Cycle

Another approach is the **Standards Achievement Planning Cycle (SAPC)**, which offers a first step in developing strategies for effective standards-based planning. SAPC is a synthesis of ideas associated with outcome-based education, Japanese Lesson Study, functional standards, and the use of state standards as instructional targets. In SAPC, learning outcomes are written from standards and frameworks that form instructional targets of standards-based lesson plans. The lesson objectives consist of observable skills or products that are demonstrable and can be evaluated by teachers (O'Shea, 2005). Figure 9.11 defines ideas contained in SAPC.

SAPC Five-Step Process for Writing Lessons to Achieve Standards

1. *Identify standards.* This can be accomplished by perusing your state standards and state resources guides. Textbooks and authentic resource materials should be used to motivate lessons, not to identify appropriate standards. Once identified, standards provide focus for lesson objectives.
2. *Analyze standards.* Once you have identified the standards deemed essential they must be analyzed

---

answer the questions, "What do standards look like in my planning and in my classroom?" and "How do we achieve them?" when designing learning experiences. The activities move from the theoretical to actual implementation of standards. The approach consists of eight sequential steps in a standards-based design process that includes planning, delivery, and evaluation of instruction.

Figure 9.10 Sample of Performance Standards in English Language Arts

1. *Reading*
    a. Read twenty-five books of quality and complexity.
    b. Read and comprehend four books on the same subject, or by the same author, or in the same genre.
    c. Read and comprehend informational materials.
    d. Read aloud fluently.
2. *Writing*
    a. Produce a report of information.
    b. Produce a response to literature.
    c. Produce a narrative account (fictional or autobiographical).
    d. Produce a narrative procedure.
3. *Speaking, Listening, and Viewing*
    a. Participate in one-to-one conferences.
    b. Participate in group meetings.
    c. Prepare and deliver an individual presentation.
    d. Make informal judgments about TV, radio, and film.
4. *Conventions, Grammar, and English Language Usage*
    a. Demonstrate a basic understanding of the rules of the of the English language in written and oral work.
    b. Analyze and subsequently revise work to improve its clarity and effectiveness.
5. *Literature*
    a. Respond to nonfiction, fiction, poetry, and drama using interpretive and critical processes.
    b. Produce work in at least one genre that follows the conventions of the genre.

Figure 9.11 Japanese Lesson Study/Functional Standards/Outcome-Based Education

Lesson study is a century-old idea imported from Japan where it provides the underpinning for that country's student-centered focus for schooling. It is rapidly attracting interest as a long-term school improvement strategy because of the hope it offers for sustained changes in teaching. Lesson study is far more complex than simply having teachers write lessons together. It is neither lesson planning nor curriculum design in the traditional sense. It can be compared to quality circles that establish long-term goals, by measuring work against goals, and then making changes. It's not about producing lots of different lessons, it's about learning how children learn (www.NSDC.org).

Functional standards are documents that define and differentiate the skill requirements for functional skills qualification currently being developed. The term should be considered in the broad sense of providing learners with the skills and abilities necessary to take active roles in school and society (www.qca.org.uk/15895.html).

Outcome-based education (OBE) is an educational reform model for K–12 schools. It measures student achievement based on a student's demonstrated performance. There is no single, authoritative model for outcome-based education. Frameworks for OBE share an emphasis on systems-level change, observable, measurable outcomes, and the belief that all students can learn. William Spady's model for OBE urges schools to generate "exit outcomes" based on the challenges and opportunities that students will face after graduation, and then to "design down" from the outcomes for all other aspects of educational delivery.

as to the content knowledge students are expected to master. Student outcomes have to be transformed into student performances that can be measured.

3. ***Describe student performances.*** Paint a picture of what students have to accomplish in order to master the content standards you have selected. The guide for this step is to imagine the activities necessary to master the knowledge and skills appropriate to achieve mastery.
4. ***Select learning activities.*** After identifying the standards, and analyzing the content to be learned, as well as the necessary student performances, you must then select specific learning activities. Activities must translate into coherent developmental experiences that result in achievement of lesson objectives.
5. ***Evaluate students' work.*** Student achievement is evidenced by the quality of work produced as a result of the standards-based lesson. Student work must demonstrate comprehension of the standard as described in your vision of mastery in student performances. It should be noted that performance descriptions are the key to providing a rubric and should serve as the prime assessment tool in evaluation of student success.

O'Shea (2005) cautions that SAPC is really not a formula for translating state standards, but is essentially a guide for preparation. It only works well, he claims, when teachers share curriculum expertise to plan standards-based lessons.

It is obvious that these strategies are essentially commonsense approaches to instructional planning. To be successful, teachers have to plan effective lessons that link to state-mandated specific curriculum objectives (see Chapter 3). In addition, good planning should include selection of activities that address four basic genetic psychological needs: love/belonging, power/competence, freedom, and fun (Glasser, 1998).

Skills for Effective Lessons

After addressing psychological needs our concern should focus on four basic skills categories needed for effective teaching: reasoning, reorganization, remembering, and relating. Any instructional model used for lesson planning will by necessity incorporate one or more of these skills. Each lesson must highlight at least one skill category as a purpose for instruction.

- *Reasoning skills* consist of critical thinking, concept attainment, and problem solving skills stemming from the work of Jerome Bruner (1996). These skills stress comparison, contrast, differentiation, and interpretation. They also focus on inquiry, which is designed to teach students to form questions, create hypotheses, and test theories (Suchman, 1962).
- *Reorganizing skills* are those that re-examine what was learned. Concept formation helps to make connections, comparing, contrasting, grouping data, and testing hypotheses (Taba, 1973). The process of *synectics* (connecting ideas, use of graphic organizers) was created to use analogies, metaphors, and the power of personal imagination as tools for problem solving. This reorganization skill helps to develop creativity (Gordon, 1961).
- *Remembering skills* are those that stress practice, drills, and memorization with an emphasis on retention. Mnemonics is used to assist memory in both low-level and complex concepts. Direct instruction (Adams and Engelmann, 1996) was specifically designed to help students learn basic skills. It is effective in reading and mathematics instruction. It utilizes a systematic sequence of teaching to help students recall and recognize facts and data.
- *Relating skills* are those that allow students to understand others and to develop interpersonal communication skills, while improving their group process approaches. Cooperative learning develops team-building skills and group-working skills (Slavin, 1995). Oral discussion, also known as the Socratic method, is a process that uses teacher questions to check student comprehension. It develops positive class interactions and enhances higher-order thinking skills.

PRACTICE EXERCISE 9.5

Making Standards a Reality in the Classroom

The purpose of this exercise is to review and analyze the six following suggestions for making standards a reality in the classroom. Its intent is to assist in development of student self-training.

The class should be divided into six groups each to research the validity of the suggestion topic. Discuss each group's findings. *Note:* Preservice and practicing teachers may approach assignment from their own perspective.

1. Standards are easy to accept but "How do we get there?" Examine pieces of student work and focus on how the criteria for the standards are reflected in the work. For practicing teachers, view your students' work related to your state's content and performance standards. For preservice teachers, review your own coursework using your course syllabus as the standard.
2. Standards are for all grades, all children, and all teachers. Compare the elementary, middle, and high school standards in order to see the logical sequence that has been devised.
3. The focus of standards should be reflected in a district comprehensive plan, a school's comprehensive plan, and a classroom teacher's comprehensive plan. Visit a school, obtain each plan, evaluate, and describe how standards are reflected.
4. Standards should be ongoing and an integral part of the fabric of the school and each classroom. Visit a school and ask teachers how they are attempting to meet the standards.
5. Classroom instruction puts standards into practice. Observe various lessons and describe how standards are achieved.
6. Performance standards are reflected in the student demonstrations of their learning. Review student portfolios and evaluate their success in demonstrating mastery of particular standards.

Best Practices for Planning

The effect of standards on classroom performance is immense. Critics say teachers feel coerced into teaching for the high stakes test, and students fear the shame of being labeled a failure. Critics feel that too much creative instructional time is wasted by preparing students

PRACTICE EXERCISE 9.6

Meeting the Standards

Select a standard from your state's list of standards or a professional organization's list. Based on that standard, answer the following five questions. The questions were developed by Deborah Meier (2002, 1995) to assist teachers in creating a variety of strategies when constructing a standards-based lesson. (Note that no student should be expected to meet an academic requirement that a cross-section of society cannot.)

1. How do we know what we know? (Evidence)
2. Whose perspective does this represent? (Point of view)
3. How is this related to that? (Connection)
4. How might things have been done otherwise? (Supposition)
5. Why is it important? Who cares? (Relevance)

5. *Utilization of resources* is to use many different instructional aides and materials.
6. *Knowledge of learning and development principles* occurs when you meet student needs through use of appropriate strategies (traditional to progressive to constructivist approaches).
7. *Communication with students on multiple levels* is the practice you use to clear the lines of communication with a focus on higher-order thinking skills.
8. *Enthusiasm* is infectious and a teacher's positive energy is usually returned.

Practice Exercises 9.6, 9.7, and 9.8 on standards move from the how (meeting), to the critical (need), and finally to the evaluative.

MINI CASE FROM THE FIELD

The following case from the field presents the standards as an objective that is achievable through quantifiable results. The quandary posed is whether standards reflect success if achieved. Should the standard bar always be raised when success is near? Read the case and compare Jane's, Lucille's, Nick's, Ed's, Margaret's, and Mr. Thompson's ideas about what constitutes an effective approach to attaining instructional standards.

to pass standardized tests rather than enhancing learning experiences. Contrasting this view is the belief advanced by proponents that standards-driven instructional practice provides an environment where learning can best take place and quality can be maintained. Both proponents and critics can achieve their dissimilar objectives by following behaviors that make for effective teaching regardless of pedagogical philosophy. These behaviors can easily be considered **best practices** to achieve educational success. Whether the focus is on teaching to meet standards or augment students' knowledge bases, good quality methods apply for all.

Teaching Standards: Methods for All The way to incorporate targeted standards into lessons is simply to teach good lessons. Eight items come to mind when one reflects on the instructional quality found in first-rate lessons. Teachers who embody these qualities practice strategies that produce student mastery. Good methods allow standards achievement to become a reality.

1. *Instructional clarity* occurs when you focus lessons on engaging students throughout your presentation.
2. *Content knowledgeability* is when you are able to structure and integrate concepts into your subject's curriculum.
3. *Establishment of learning expectations* occurs when you present your lesson objectives before you teach the lesson.
4. *Variation in teaching* is when you plan a variety of strategies that provide for interactive learning rather than simply passive learning.

When Can We Consider Standards High Enough?

Margaret faced two complex yet related problems—the numbers of students being placed on the honor roll and school standards. To reach the honor roll a student had to achieve a 90 percent academic and an 85 percent nonacademic average. Students had to evidence good school citizenship with a passing grade in social behavior. Because of this policy, 50 percent the students at the McGraw Comprehensive K–12 School made the list every year, while 80 percent of Margaret Gomez's students did. This precipitated a complaint that too many of her students made the list. Margaret surmised that if the problem was the number of students making the list, she and her colleagues could ask Principal Thompson to raise the criteria to lower the numbers. If the problem was a perception of watered-down instruction and inflated grades, she had another problem altogether.

Mr. Thompson told Margaret said that he appreciated her interest in the school honor roll. He suggested that she survey a random sampling of teachers to see if they thought the school policy on standards for the honor roll needed to be addressed.

Lucille Chan thought that raising the criteria for inclusion and including other sources of data such as a portfolio would do the trick. Unfortunately, Lucille reminded Margaret that portfolios require a rubric or

PRACTICE EXERCISE 9.7

Needs and Purposes for Standards

The purpose of this exercise is to clarify the need and use of standards. Sergiovanni (2000) indicates that standards and tests aligned with them have always tended to change with the political persuasion of the elite in power. He poses questions that he feels makes clear the issue of standards and assessment. Read each question and respond in a brief succinct paragraph. This exercise can be done in small groups that can then share their ideas and perceptions with the rest of the class. (Note if there is any evidence of philosophical bias in Sergiovanni's questions.)

1. Is a school that commits itself to teacher learning as the focus of its change strategy successful if it changes from a "let's help our students learn to use their minds well" kind of place to a "let's go for the high test scores by narrowing the curriculum, learning how to implement alignment strategies, and emphasizing test-taking skills" kind of place?

2. Is a school successful in change if it restructures by requiring all teachers to adopt a particular school design, even though 20 percent of the teachers oppose the change, and parents and students have had no say in the decision?

3. Is a school that motivates teachers with cash incentives or coerces them by posting the scores of the children they teach in the local newspaper successful if teachers are now involved in their work for calculated reasons, rather than professional or moral reasons?

4. Is a school that changes from a thinking curriculum in math and science successful because students achieve higher scores on aligned assessments, even if they understand less?

PRACTICE EXERCISE 9.8

Standards—Good or Bad

Read the following passage and react to the author's statement. Share opinions in class.

The danger with standards is not in the standard but in the preparation. To prepare students for the necessary assessment that goes hand in hand with standards requires teachers to exchange a rigorous curriculum for repetition and drill on timed practice tests. Given up are exercises in which students write analytic essays, thoughtful research papers, original science experiments, and advanced math applications. As these tests become part of our schools, students will only be asked to focus on skills necessary to pass. The rigorous instruction and high standards of the original reform movement will be replaced by test-driven lower standards. Of course, a contrary argument could be made that claims this argument is based on assumption and faith that if standards were eliminated every classroom would offer expectations that were clear, rigorous, and objective. It also assumes that testing conducted by teachers would be inherently fair because it would be based on the achievement of an objective result rather than comparison of one student to the other.

---

some other standard to judge their merits. She went on to say that she had already raised the idea of revisiting the grading system in courses within her department, and that perhaps they should all reconsider their expectations for student standards.

Jane Hemmings thought all of the changes were great, but asked, "Just for clarification here . . . as it stands, are students automatically placed on the honors list if they have a 90 average? With these new suggested requirements and higher average, would students have to apply to get on the list? If this is so, I think we would need to form a committee to review portfolios and other materials."

Nick Saccone chimed in. "I agree with the others that the average needs to be raised and a portfolio of written work submitted. I would also recommend an interview in which the candidates have the opportunity to highlight some of the work in their portfolio. This would allow assessment of students to include grades, written work samples, and oral communication skills."

Margaret finally asked Ed Child what he thought. "I don't know if the percentage of people reaching the honor roll makes a difference," he said. "Would changing the standard from 90 to 95 significantly affect the number of recipients on the list? I doubt that would solve the problem. I would prefer to use a percentage as the cutoff rather than a fixed inflated grade as the standard. How many students should make the honor roll? Five percent, 10 percent, or what? If we allow the top 5 percent or 15 percent to get on the list, would that influence the quality of instruction? I believe that the problem is with perception, not reality and numbers. Are too many people on the list? Is that a bad thing? I vote for the top 25 percent to be on the list! It would eliminate the disappointment of being in the darkened depths of the lowest performing students. I am not sure that my suggestion is a strong predictor of a quality graduate who can deal with the exigencies of life. But maybe it is!"

Margaret wondered if everyone was really talking about raising instructional quality to realize standards. If that was the case, shouldn't they first discover who taught well? Who would do that? How do we make quality quantifiable? Who gives those inflated higher grades, and how can you fix the problem? This really was getting sticky. Margaret felt the answer was for everyone to reflect upon his or her teaching to improve practice. She hoped it could be done.

1. List the arguments made for increasing the average for the honor roll list.
2. Contrast Lucille's, Jane's, and Nick's arguments with Ed's. Who had the stronger arguments? Why?
3. Whose side do you think Mr. Thompson would be on, if anyone's?
4. Discuss your views of the intended policy to raise the standards because too many students have achieved them. When are standards good enough?
5. If given the opportunity, how would you resolve this issue?

Chapter Summary

Reforms in education have always tended to follow a pattern that consists of blown-up identification of problems, overpromised reforms, and unimplemented reforms. Many reform efforts are driven by ideology, not educational practicality. It is hardly surprising that most reforms have little impact on schools, teachers, or students. The reason is that many reforms were implemented by states for political rather than educational purposes. Of course, when they inevitably fail to produce the desired outcomes, teachers and students are blamed. We have discovered in this chapter that if standards are to improve schools and student achievement they must not punish teachers, schools, and children for political advantage. Standards must be appropriate, tests fair, and implementation reasonable.

Standards have two primary purposes. The first is economic. Students must be prepared to join the workforce of the twenty-first century. The second purpose is to address the disparity between high- and low-achieving students, in effect, a social goal to achieve equality for all our citizens. In the past, these two purposes led to a movement for child-centered schools, rather than the test-centered schools that we are leaning toward today. What is needed is agreement about the content and the performance for standards with the understanding that standards are about ends, not means. Teachers should be left to implement standards that are considered world-class and meet with public approval. With this responsibility, it is easy to see why standards will have an impact on everything future teachers do.

It is very difficult to question the value of standards in today's educational climate. One who does is put in the position of being thought a fool. Everyone recognizes the importance of improving student performance and achievement, so what could be wrong with the standards? Standards have many positive aspects—they help us eliminate curriculum redundancy, clarify what we mean by high expectations, and assess student learning in relation to clear benchmarks. The problem is not with the standards but with their top-down implementation. Change never occurs in any meaningful or enduring way if teachers do not recognize the need for the change. Teachers will always find subversive ways to circumvent changes they see no reason for. The impact that standards have on teachers' performance is considerable. The question is how to make that impact positive so that our students can achieve world-class standards. Standards will work when teachers use proven methods that assist them in delivering quality standards-based lessons.

Cases from the Field

CASE ONE

Abdul Kali never realized how difficult it would be to teach his fourth-grade class and have them all meet the state-mandated standards. His children were all reading two to three years below grade level and were similarly delayed in mathematics. When he had been offered the position, the principal, Mr. Palace, had impressed upon Abdul that no child was to be left behind. Mr. Palace said he expected all lessons to be related to the English language arts standards and that they should be labeled accordingly.

1. Were Mr. Palace's expectations unrealizable? Explain.
2. How could Mr. Kali have his class meet a requirement to read twenty-five books of quality and complexity?
3. What is the relationship between standards and performance?
4. How can standards be used for instructional improvement?

5. What type of plan would you develop if you were Mr. Kali?

CASE TWO

Mrs. Chang was aware that standards and assessment had traditionally gone hand in hand. She was aware that examinations had the power to determine what is taught in the classroom. This was exactly what she was opposed to. She and her colleagues at the Evans Middle School felt it was an academic sin "to just teach to a test." It deprived students of the opportunity for an enriched education, one that included the arts, music, and theater.

1. Are standards necessary for a formal assessment program to be effective? Why?
2. Must teachers always teach to the test if standards are to be maintained? Explain your reasoning.
3. How can one have an enriched curriculum and still achieve standards?
4. How can performance assessment be used to assure parents that standards are being met?
5. If you were Mrs. Chang, what would you tell your colleagues?

CASE THREE

Mr. Morse was asked by his principal Mr. Nasser to prepare different types of tests for the ninth-grade social studies department midyear examinations at Morley Junior High School. The tests were to be linked to the state standards for social studies. Morse decided that he had better speak with the other five ninth-grade teachers to get their input on the type of tests they felt could meet the standards. The responses he received ran the gamut from written essay question to oral questioning of students to having each member of the department teach the same standards-based test every day. Rather than clarify his approach, his survey had muddied the waters.

1. How could Mr. Morse get all five teachers to agree on the type of midterm examination to administer that would reflect a link to the standards? How could benchmarking have been used?
2. Were Mr. Morse's actions appropriate for the development of an accurate performance assessment tool for a standards-based curriculum? Explain.
3. How could a research paper or portfolio have been used to determine achievement in a standards-based curriculum?
4. Was the principal, Mr. Nasser, correct in asking for different types of tests to judge mastery of standards? What do you think his reasoning was?
5. What would you have done if you were confronted with Mr. Morse's problem?

CASE FOUR

Carl Pincus was a new teacher at Public School 102. He felt he had been fortunate in being assigned to such an innovative school where his professionalism would be appreciated. The school had a reputation as one of the best in the district. The principal, Mrs. Scraps, was a fair-minded administrator and, everyone said, a pleasure to work for. She had even introduced standardized testing because she claimed it removed the subjectivity of individual teachers' grading methods and helped to maintain academic standards. Carl's dilemma was, if things were so wonderful, why was he having such a difficult time adjusting?

1. Carl's job satisfaction seems to depend on professional growth and not financial considerations. How could Mrs. Scrap's policy regarding standardized tests have been perceived as limiting to professionalism?
2. Is pay an important factor to be considered in the selection of your first teaching position? Could other things besides money influence you?
3. Is an innovative school necessarily a successful one? Explain.
4. Do you think a traditional approach would appeal to Carl? Why?
5. How would you feel if you were in a school such as the one described in the case study?

Terms to Remember

Interstate New Teacher Assessment and Support Consortium (INTASC)
National Board of Professional Teaching Standards (NBPTS)
Standards
Benchmarking
Performance standards
Progressive schools
Traditional schools
Best Practices
Standards-based lesson
Adequate Yearly Progress (AYP)
Standards Achievement Planning Cycle (SAPC)

Discussion Questions

1. Describe three common traits exhibited by master teachers.
2. Compare and contrast the New Compact for Learning, the Curriculum Frameworks, and Goals 2000.
3. Define and contrast content standards and performance standards.
4. How can standards be made a reality in the classroom?
5. Describe how you would prepare a standards-based lesson plan.
6. Explain how you would prepare a standards-based lesson using each of the skill categories for effective lessons.
7. Discuss arguments for and against standards.
8. Contrast the INTASC and NBPTS descriptions of what qualities are inherent in effective teachers.

Field Experience Activities

1. Analyze the standards that are being used in the course in which you are using this book. Comment on the following areas:
   - The performance standards expected
   - The content-specific standards expected
   - The practices employed to achieve the standards

   Use the same approach and analyze the standards evidenced in your local elementary school.
2. Interview two teachers and ask them how standards have affected how they teach. Ask them how they would improve upon the present system they operate under. Ask if they favor or oppose standards, and the reasons for their response.

For Further Reading

Kohn, A. (1999). *The schools our children deserve, moving beyond traditional classrooms and tougher standards.* Boston: Houghton Mifflin.

Meier, D. (2002). *The power of their ideas.* Boston: Beacon Press.

Ravitch, D. (2000). Contemporary school ills trace roots to progressive movement. *Education Week* (Sept. 13): 6–7.

Ravitch, D. (2000). *Left back: A century of failed school reforms.* New York: Simon & Schuster.

CHAPTER 10

Assessment Practices for Achievement

FOCUS POINTS

1. Assessment practices have two purposes: to measure learning and to provide tools for instructional management.

2. Assessment is either subjective or objective, quantifiable or qualitative.

3. The term *authentic assessment* refers to evaluation procedures that allow students to demonstrate abilities in real life settings. It uses portfolios and projects including action research, ethnography, and case studies.

4. Reflection that includes careful analytical thought leads to effective behavioral and instructional management.

CHAPTER OVERVIEW

IN THIS CHAPTER, we attempt to describe assessment practices we can use to foster student achievement, and evaluate effectiveness in dealing with instruction. To understand the importance of assessment we need to understand its purposes, meanings, and uses. Assessment has two purposes: (1) to assist in measuring student learning and (2) to provide tools to evaluate and resolve instructional management problems. Assessment is an integral part of a teacher's management style and personal attributes. Likes and dislikes are evident in the tools selected to assess students and situations. In many instances, the tools are similar. Poor academic performance and poor behavior are improved by delivery of lessons and preparation of examinations. If the purpose of instruction is to facilitate learning and comprehension, we can assume a need to assess, or evaluate. Knowledge of assessment practices is essential to understanding the effectiveness of teaching upon learning. To measure success one must have reliable and valid assessment procedures.

The use of action research within an IOSIE framework demonstrates an authentic assessment of learning. The method provides a logical framework in which the theory used as your solution is essentially what is evaluated. An example of this process can be understood if we visualize an underachieving, inattentive child during an instructional session. The identified problems are underachievement and inattentiveness; the objective is to have the child improve academically. The solution will correspond to the practice used to achieve the objective. The question is how to evaluate the solution and its effectiveness.

This chapter outlines the basics of assessment in order to understand the use of theory-based evaluation, in which you measure a solution against claims and tacit assumptions of specific programs. Theory-based evaluation uses a form of logical analysis to identify what "should" happen as a project develops. This type of evaluation simply checks to see if the project unfolded as expected, and identifies any unexpected difficulties and the "learning" that occurred (Weiss, 2004).

Some authors distinguish between the terms *assessment* (the process of collecting or discovering what students are learning in order to make instructional decisions, an ongoing daily process) and **evaluation** (making judgment or assigning value to a program or student work, after the completion of instruction). For our purposes here we will consider the terms synonymous (as does Kellough, 2004).

BRIEF HISTORY OF ASSESSMENT IN AMERICA

One word can sum up the difference between assessments and testing—purpose. Teachers' assessment is concerned with the judgment they make with regard to student ability. The purpose of this assessment is for the teacher to provide appropriate instruction. Testing today unfortunately has come to be associated with negative consequences that result from poor performance. This difference in purpose between judgment for instruction and testing for consequences sadly has been a major drawback to the standards movement. David Hoff (1999) concluded that traditional psychological testing in addition to being used as justification for negative consequences for poor performance has also inflamed racial prejudice by reaching erroneous conclusions. Three of the greats of modern psychological testing, beginning with Thorndike, have developed procedures that have revolutionized how we view student achievement, while simultaneously causing psychological damage that we are still attempting to overcome today. We can see that each stride forward somehow seems to have resulted in two steps backward. Figure 10.1 describes the founders of psychological testing.

Oral examinations were used as early as 1845 as the first form of uniform testing. Refer back to Chapter 9, where we discussed how Boston was the first to use print short-answer tests in geography, grammar, history, rhetoric, and philosophy and the results.

At the start of the twentieth century, standardized testing used to determine content knowledge was the province of urban school districts. Its purpose was to measure how well students were learning. Scores usually remained under wraps to all but a few administrators. These standardized tests had great appeal because they removed the subjectivity of individual teachers' grading methods. With an objective test, the experts said, a student's score could be confidently compared with those of classmates. The purpose of these tests was to see how well a student performed against a prescribed curriculum. Unfortunately, psychologists designed tests to measure innate ability and predict future performance, instead of evaluating whether students had mastered the material in a curriculum.

Alfred Binet (1857–1911) designed a test to identify students who would be unable to benefit from instruction for the Paris school system in 1904. He devised a scale that predicted how well a child would learn and estimated his or her "mental age." Lewis Terman and others adapted his work in 1912 to create the Intelligence Quotient (IQ), which was calculated by dividing a person's "mental age" by his chronological age. This was said to yield students' innate intelligence. Binet further claimed in 1922 that a student's score would be constant over time, which led to the test being used as the sole criterion in child placement. This was a blatant misuse of the test, but it was common practice, leading to tracking and reflecting the consensus of social scientists that intelligence was a hereditary trait.

Figure 10.1 Greats of Psychological Testing

Edward L. Thorndike (1874–1949), a psychologist who taught at Teachers College, Columbia University, was the originator of a scale of achievement in a wide variety of subjects. His work allowed educators to compare their students' performance against the average achievement, commonly called the norm. The norm consists of a representative sample of children. Thorndike's work established various norms for arithmetic, reading, handwriting, and other subjects. He focused on handwriting because he believed that its style, beauty, and uniformity revealed as much about test-takers' intelligence and character as did content knowledge in other subjects. Today all major standardized tests compare individual test-takers and groups of students against such norms. His work during World War I led after the war to the development of the National Intelligence Tests. Various school officials used these tests across the nation when assigning students to academic tracks. The emphasis on tracking students based on intelligence tests has been interpreted by academics as a prime cause for the racial unrest that has been experienced throughout our history.

Lewis M. Terman (1877–1956), of Stanford University, is best known for his longitudinal research in intelligence tests and achievement tests of gifted children. He found that gifted children had the kinds of well-rounded personalities and skills that prepared them for leadership roles in society. He coined the term *meritocratic society* to explain his vision of the perfect society. Terman used IQ tests to investigate the link between intelligence and heredity. In 1929, one of his students completed a dissertation suggesting that children's intelligence was not influenced by environment but by heredity. Even though it was disputed by simultaneous research conducted at the University of Chicago, Terman continued to believe there was a genetic link to intelligence. He was also active in the racially charged eugenics movement, which advocated the propagation of individuals who were deemed genetically superior. Segregationists clung to his conclusions to justify their erroneous claims to racial superiority. It should be noted that even the best-intentioned efforts could be subverted, as was Terman's.

Robert M. Yerkes (1876–1956), a psychologist at Johns Hopkins University, created the Alpha-Bets Test that was used in World War I to gauge the intelligence of soldiers. The Alpha assessed the literate recruits; the Beta tested the illiterate. His results indicated that black men as well as Southern and Eastern Europeans scored the worst. Even though Yerkes called for a cautious interpretation of the results, policymakers used them in 1921 and 1924 as reason for restricting immigration from such countries as Russia, Italy, and Poland. The seeds of prejudice were deeply embedded in American culture and the new psychological testing was used to support erroneous conclusions. It was not until the 1930s that other research disputed Yerkes. Critics claimed that few immigrants knew English when they took the test, and the average African-American in the South attended schools only about half the amount of time that white students did. Such disadvantages were shown by later research to evidence lower scores on these supposedly unbiased tests.

The Stanford Achievement Test developed by Lewis Terman (1877–1956) measured student achievement in specific subjects across several grades in order to predict future success. The Iowa Tests of Basic Skills followed it in 1929. The Iowa was based on textbooks commonly used throughout the state. To speed scoring, the authors relied on multiple-choice, matching, and fill-in-the-blank questions.

The Scholastic Aptitude Test's (SAT) objective was to predict a student's future performance for colleges and universities. Admissions testing was spurred after World War II. Critics have held that it is not a fair measure because its social bias reinforces existing hierarchies of race and class. The College Board maintains that the SAT is the second-best predictor of how well a student will perform in college. The best, they claim, is high school grades.

The Coleman Report (1965) found that students' family backgrounds and the socioeconomic makeup of their schools were more meaningful factors in student achievement than the quality of their schools.

Minimum competency tests were instituted in the 1970s to define the minimum students should know in order to graduate. (They also raised questions of racial fairness.) Since that time, the policy of "high-stakes" testing has been advanced in most states. With the 2001 No Child Left Behind Act, standardized tests have been used to align content standards with measurements.

The Backward Design Process

The most recent approach to assessment and planning is called the **backward design** process, which begins with the end in mind. The idea is to decide on expected understandings, and then present questions that provide a path to those understandings. In short, one begins by identifying results and proceeds backward to determine acceptable evidence and appropriate learning experiences. The process has changed our ideas thinking about assessment and planning. As Wiggins and McTighe (2001) describe it, "One starts with the end—the desired results (goals or standards)—and then derives the curriculum from the evidence of learning (performances) called for by the standard and the teaching needed to equip students to perform" (p. 8).

Backward design is a three-stage planning process, each with a focusing question:

Stage	Focus Question
1. End result	What must we understand?
2. Acceptable proof	What type of evidence will lead to this understanding?
3. Type of instruction	What instructional approach will lead to the desired understandings?

Backward design's focus is on enduring understandings and essential guiding questions. Enduring understandings go beyond facts and skills and highlight larger concepts, principles, or processes. Examples might include:

- What do we mean by "protecting national security"?
- What does it mean to care for the environment?
- Civil liberties must be protected at all costs.
- What does it mean to say, "The more things change, the more they remain the same"?

These worthwhile understandings should represent a big idea that has lasting value throughout life. The big idea should be at the core of a topic being studied. An enduring understanding is in effect defined by a big idea, which indicates student understanding. Civil rights would be a big idea when studying slavery. Big ideas with enduring values go beyond plain facts or skills. They lie at the heart of any subject being taught. Jerome Bruner said, "For any subject taught in a primary school, we might ask, Is it worth an adult's knowing, and whether having known it as a child makes a person a better adult?"

Six Essentials of Understanding Evidence Comprehension

- can explain   (Explanation)
- can interpret   (Interpretation)
- can apply   (Application)
- has perspective   (Perspective)
- can empathize   (Empathy)
- has self-knowledge (Self-knowledge)

(Wiggins and McTighe, 2001)

Planning with Backward Design To plan using backward design, provide learning experiences and instruction that clearly identify results (enduring understanding). Planning should start with a big idea. Next, plan how students are to understand the big idea. To do this, certain key questions should be considered.

- What enabling knowledge (fact, concept, and principles) and skills (procedures) will students need to perform effectively to achieve desired results?
- What will need to be taught and coached, and how should it best be taught, in light of performance goals?
- What materials and resources are best suited to accomplish these goals?
- Is the overall design coherent and effective?

In the last stage of the backward design process, teachers design the sequence of learning experiences that students will undertake to develop understanding. After students master a topic, they must continue to reinforce the obtained knowledge by using real-life applications (Wiggins and McTighe, 2001, p. 99).

Use the acronym WHERE as a backward design guide:

- **W**here are we headed? Why are we headed there? Make students aware of obligations and assessments up front.
- **H**ook the student through engaging and provocative entry points. Provide thought-provoking and focusing experiences, issues, oddities, problems, and challenges that point toward essential and end unit questions, core ideas, and final performance tasks.
- **E**xplore, enable, and equip by engaging students in learning experiences that allow them to explore big ideas and essential questions. Equip students for final performances through guided instruction and coaching on needed skills and knowledge.
- **R**eflect and rethink by digging deeper into ideas and issues. Revise, rehearse, and refine as needed to guide students in self-assessment and self-adjustment. Like all planning models, backward design requires revision and refinements throughout the planning process.
- **E**xhibit and evaluate by revealing what has been understood through performances and products. Involve students in a final self-assessment to identify remaining questions, set future goals, and point toward new units and lessons. (Greece Central School District, 2006)

BASIC ASSESSMENT PRACTICES

The reasons for assessment are both diagnostic and evaluative. The reasons can be seen as diagnostic for the purpose of ongoing instructional effectiveness (formative), and the purpose of final evaluations (summative). The final evaluation is precisely the reason you must understand basic assessment practices and their relationship to resolving classroom instructional problems. Unresolved problems do not just go away—they fester until they erupt into worse situations. As teachers we are part of the standardized test movement. We are given the responsibility of administering diagnostic tests at the behest of state and local governments. These standardized tests have little to do with the everyday conduct of classrooms. They do, however, play a primary role in determining student final scores and class placements. The managerial decisions made are based on the diagnostic tests that are either norm-referenced or criterion-referenced tests.

The impact of standardized testing on instructional practices is apparent in that it determines how a course of instruction is developed, and how that instruction is managed. The content stressed reflects the content in the standardized test. Lessons are focused on meeting mandated standards and local curricula. The problem of maintaining the intellectual integrity of the instructional process is ongoing.

Understanding Assessment

Terms used for assessment help interpret both objective and subjective evaluations of classroom episodes. On the other hand, classroom tests constructed by teachers are the method used to evaluate daily student achievement. Finally, teachers' summative evaluation consists of test results from instruction combined with results from standardized instruments. The question arises as to what can be done when students are not achieving as expected. The answer will come upon reflection of one's effectiveness as a pedagogue, and by reviewing one's assessment practices for achievement.

Student assessment is aimed at answering three basic questions: What do we want to know if the tests we use are reliable? How do they compare to standardized tests? and finally, Can they be improved?

What Does It Mean for a Test to Be Reliable? **Reliability** means that a test yields similar results even when an equivalent form of the test is used. A reliable test can be viewed as consistent, dependable, and stable. Reliability is usually expressed numerically in terms of coefficients with 1.00 being perfect reliability, .99 to .80 high reliability, .79 to .40 fair reliability, and .39 to 0 low reliability. There are three ways to measure reliability: test and retest, equivalent forms of the test, and splitting a test into two equivalent halves. An example would be to give the same test to the same group twice. To have reliability, similar results should be obtained in both instances.

Validity means that a test measures what it claims to measure. If a test is expected to measure geographic knowledge, it will not have questions focused on historical accuracy. The three basic areas measured for validity are content validity, curricular validity, and predictive validity, which are the same areas used by the nationally administered college admissions examinations, the SATs.

Usability is a criterion for selecting a test. It answers questions such as, Is it easy for the student to understand? Easy to administer and score? Appropriate in degree of difficulty? If the questions on any test are too difficult, we can question its validity. A reliable test is one that is valid and usable.

Comparing Standardized Tests and Teacher-Prepared Classroom Tests **Norm-referenced tests** (standardized tests) allow us to compare one individual with other individuals. Scores are reported in the form of percentiles. The test measures a student's level of achievement compared to students elsewhere. An example would be if the highest number of correct responses on a 100-item test were 70, the raw score of 70 would be reported as the 100th percentile.

Criterion-referenced tests (teacher-prepared classroom tests) measure an individual's ability concerning specific criteria. Scores do not represent a relative level of achievement. Criterion-referenced tests are scored based on specific recall of course information. This means that in the example just given, the raw score of 70 would be worth 70 percent.

The difference between these two types of tests is that the norm-referenced is based on the median scores of students, while criterion-referenced tests are focused on a predetermined level of performance to be given a grade. Simply stated, *a criterion-referenced test is based on content, whereas a norm-referenced test is based on judgments of how individual scores compare to others.*

Improving Assessment

How Can Classroom Tests Be Improved? In general, testing can be improved by limiting test anxiety and feedback time. Tests can be open book or home examination. This, of course, presupposes that the test is one that is testing higher-order thinking skills such as analysis, evaluation, synthesis, and the use of one's judgment. When constructing tests, be clear as to their purpose. If you want to measure written expression or critical thinking, use an essay. If you want to measure broad knowledge of the subject or results of learning, use short-answer items. This affords you a rapid way to assess your effectiveness by measuring student comprehension. If you wish to compare a group to children in the same age

Figure 10.2 Comparing Norm-Referenced and Criterion-Referenced Tests

Characteristic	Norm-Referenced (Standardized) Test	Criterion-Referenced Test
1. Major emphasis	Measures individual's achievement in relation to similar group at a specific time.	Measures change over an extended period of time.
2. Reliability	High reliability: .90 or better	Mastery/performance test
3. Validity	Content, construct, predictive validity usually high	Content, curricular usually high
4. Usability	Diagnose student difficulty	Diagnose difficulty
	Estimates performance in a broad area; large group testing	Estimates performance in a specific area
		Small and individual testing
5. Content covered	Not related to coursework	Related to coursework
6. Test items	Usually short answer	Both essay and short answer
7. Item selection	General content area	Specific content tested
8. Student prep	No need to study	Study helps get better grade
9. Standards	Norms used to classify students	Measure performance and standards

group, use a standardized test. Most teachers are more than satisfied to prepare their own tests because for the most part they are less concerned with non-criterion-referenced tests. They expect children to understand and apply what has been taught in class.

Without standards and expectations, we would be relegated to a return to the Bell curve where content knowledge does not matter, but only your place in relation to your fellow student. To improve testing practices one might follow Diez's (2000) suggestions in Figure 10.3.

TESTING PRACTICES

There are essentially four ways to assess student performance: essays, multiple-choice questions, portfolios, and authentic performances. The spectrum of testing ranges from subjective written responses to objective short answers, to evidence of student work, to actual live performance and demonstration. The most common test construction tools used by teachers are the short-answer question and the question that requires an essay for a response. These two basic test forms combined with oral questioning constitute the basic types of tests administered by teachers. Teachers, however, rarely consider oral questioning as part of objective testing. Teachers should understand that good oral questioning can generate incisive responses that are, in many cases, superior to written responses. Figure 10.4 outlines basic strategies used in developing classroom tests and their purposes.

Forms of Testing: Subjective, Objective, and Authentic

Student measurement can take many forms, from objective to subjective, from rational to whimsical. The practices you follow should allow you to be as accurate as possible in your assessment of students. Your assessments are really measurements of content knowledge, the students' ability to take the test, and their ability to read and understand the questions. This means that you should supplement written tests with discussion and observation if you expect to plan for successful lessons.

A decision-making model for planning and evaluation focuses on simple questions:

- What do I want the students to understand?
- How will I know if they understand?
- At what level of recognition or production do we expect students to learn? (Jacobsen et al., 2002)

The process of measuring students' understanding of abstractions consists of looking at product versus recognition items. There is probably no process more central to teaching than assessment, the process that involves the making of decisions. Decisions are based on data gathered formally or informally. Teachers feel more confident in the use of their own judgment while testing because grading is a painful process to master (Lazar-Morris et al., 1984). In most cases, testing strategies are usually learned from college textbooks, course instruction, and discussion with peers, by intuition and through trial and error—more commonly known as expe-

Figure 10.3 Elements Found in Assessment That Can Improve Testing

1. *Performance.* Assessment of student performance allows the teacher to have a sense of what students know and what they can do with that knowledge. It provides a guide when preparing lessons.
2. *Public, explicit outcomes and criteria.* This is accomplished by standards with clear expectations of students' knowledge and student performance. The standards guide curriculum development by linking them to students' tasks.
3. *Feedback.* Provides the learner with the criteria they need to complete activities and gain comprehension.
4. *Self-assessment.* When this skill is developed, the students become their own coach and critic. This is a long-term objective in line with teaching and encouraging self-discipline.
5. *Multiplicity.* The use of multiple forms of assessment. Variety enhances the classroom environment.
6. *Externality.* The process by which students see the relevance of their work outside the classroom. The key is practical applications for conceptual knowledge.
7. *Cumulative in nature.* The standards that guide instruction are always larger than any one assessment or set of assessments. Learning is essentially cumulative.
8. *Expansive in nature.* Demonstration and performance eventually result in assessment as learning. Students should also learn from assessment.

PRACTICE EXERCISE 10.1

Assessment Beliefs

The purpose of this exercise is to understand oneself in relation to one's beliefs regarding assessment. Your teaching personality is evidenced by your beliefs and the educational philosophy you espouse. Reflect on your responses to the following questions. Share your conclusions with classmates.

1. Is assessment about sorting students into those who can and those who cannot?
2. (Alternative View) Or is assessment about diagnosing where each student is so that the teacher and student can together set goals and identify learning experiences to lead to those goals?
3. Is assessment a series of marks that even though not equivalent in size and scope are averaged into a "final grade"?
4. (Alternative View) Or is assessment the development of a rich and full picture of the learner's growth over time, with a cumulative sense of what the student knows and can do?

rience. The form of assessment should make use of both subjective and objective types of tests. Most teachers use these types of paper-and-pencil tests in order to evaluate achievement and learning.

Subjective tests take the form of essay questions that focus on the higher-order thinking skills by requiring children to analyze, describe, synthesize, and compare. You as the constructor of an essay must keep in mind what you wish your students to understand and how their end product should be expressed. Wilen and colleagues (2000) provide six helpful suggestions you can use in grading essays fairly, quickly, effectively, and with minimum mental fatigue (Figure 10.5). You should find this list to be exceptionally helpful since it parallels the traditional commonsense approach to subjective assessment.

Figure 10.6 on page 221 describes the areas contained in a rubric for grading a general content–type essay. To apply this rubric to essay writing, note that each text is evaluated in five categories on a scale of 1 to 5. In each category, check the appropriate score. Maximum total points in all five areas would be 25.

Objective tests take the form of short-answer tests. These types of tests have usually taken the appearance of measurement at the lower thinking levels of knowledge and comprehension—who, what, where, and when. They are most useful when covering a large body of material in a quick, easy-to-score format. A test requiring one-word answers usually means assessing student memory and recall. The most effective objective form is the multiple-choice question. The best approach to writing this type of question is to write a statement of fact such as, "_____ was the first president of the United States of America," and then decide on distracters, or other plausible answers.

Short-Answer Test Constructions

Short-answer tests assume various forms of objective testing, including multiple-choice, matching, true/false, short-answer fill-ins, and one-minute essay-type exercises.

Question Preparation   Your questions should focus on the topic and follow a clear set of consistent rules for formulation.

Figure 10.4 Basic Testing Practices

1. You can use oral or written answers to a series of questions (e.g., essay questions, short-answer questions, and oral disputations).
2. You can have a product-centered assessment (e.g., a portfolio, a research paper, a piece of work).
3. Require a person to perform an act to be evaluated against certain criteria and assess using a rubric such as: Excellent = 5, Very good = 4, Satisfactory = 3, Less than satisfactory = 2, Unsatisfactory = 1. Be sure to make clear to students by concise description what excellent means to what unsatisfactory means.
4. Select an answer to a question from among several options (e.g., multiple-choice or true/false items).

Short-Answer Tests	Essay Tests	Oral Tests
1. Provides good item pool	Calls for higher levels of thinking	If phrased properly, call for higher-level thinking skills
2. Samples objectives and broad content	Measures ability to select and organize	Measures students grasp of both objective and subjective conceptual ideas
3. No writing ability needed	Tests writing ability	Tests ability to speak and think on your feet
4. Specific answers required	Measures problem-solving skills	Requires both specific and problem-solving skills
5. Objective, easy to score	Subjective scoring	Scoring is subjective

Figure 10.5 Grading Essays

1. Write the essay question or the statement of the essay assignment incisively.
2. Inform the students clearly about your expectations for their essays; a rubric for this purpose is recommended. (Rubrics are outlines of the criteria the teachers uses to evaluate a student's work.)
3. Determine test components and the value of each: for example, comprehensiveness (60%), expressive quality (20%), insight and creativity (20%).
4. Make a list of points that the essay should address to ensure focus and consistency in your grading.
5. Read several selected papers before marking to get a feel for the manner in which students have responded.
6. Respond to students' papers with praise where deserved and with constructive corrective feedback that will be helpful. Keep in mind that essays are most useful when accompanied by immediate feedback.

Question topics: In developing the types of assessment questions you wish to write, be sure to relate questions to your course objectives. Questions should be purposeful and relate to class activities. Always attempt to avoid questions on trivial or inconsequential details, or those that can be answered solely because of intelligence or general knowledge.

Question-writing rules: When formulating your questions, be clear, concise, and precise with the language you use. Each item (question) should test only one idea, and only contain material relevant to its solution. Avoid using acronyms in the questions unless they are defined or you are asking for a definition of the acronym. After your own review and editing, ask someone else to review for clarity and grammar.

Multiple-Choice Questions This type of question consists of two parts. The first is a question or incomplete statement called the stem, and the second consists of choices or options that complete the statement.

Characteristics: Multiple-choice questions can present problems involving reasoning and judgment, as well as recall and recognition of facts. Scoring is objective rather than subjective.

Sample

Which type of test would you use to test for critical-thinking skills?

a. essay
b. true or false
c. matching
d. none of the following

(Answer is a)

Advantages: They are easy to score and can provide diagnostic information through item analysis. They

Figure 10.6 Grading Essay Rubric

A. Command of Topic

5—Essay addresses the assignment, demonstrating both familiarity with pertinent critical issues and independent thought.

4—Essay addresses the assignment, both topic and strategies.

3—Subject is clear—although essay misses some element of assigned topic and/or strategies.

2—Subject is generally clear but not in keeping with assigned topic and/or strategies.

1—Essay is not in keeping with assigned topic and/or strategies.

B. Argumentative Development

5—Essay shows especially careful development of related ideas in coherent, sequential paragraphs.

4—Essay shows careful development of related ideas in coherent, sequential paragraphs.

3—Sequence of ideas is traceable—although paragraphing and structure are faulty.

2—Essay relies on unrelated generalizations, vague argument, uncertain information.

1—Essay is not coherent, showing little development of or relationship among ideas.

C. Organization

5—Student has edited the essay, ensuring that sentences are forceful, clear, and logical.

4—While the student has edited the essay, some tangential ideas, unassimilated quotations, needless summary, and organizational flaws remain.

3—Incomplete editing is evident in excess (summary, unassimilated ideas, and accessory information) and absence (support, transitions, flow).

2—Faulty editing shows in flawed sequence of ideas.

1—Student has neglected to edit the paper for content or paragraph construction.

D. Syntactic Variety and Language

5—Student has edited the essay, ensuring that sentences are forceful and clear and logical, avoiding gratuitous abstraction, tortuously convoluted sentences, and purple passages.

4—While the student has edited the language of the essay, moderate stylistic and formal flaws and inappropriate usages remain.

3—Incomplete editing is evident in moderate stylistic weaknesses.

2—Faulty editing shows in serious stylistic weaknesses.

1—The essay is stylistically inappropriate.

E. Control of Mechanics

5—Essay is generally free from errors in word choice and mechanics.

4—Essay may have a few errors in word choice and mechanics.

3—Essay has an accumulation of errors in word choice and mechanics.

2—Essay is marred by numerous errors in word choice and mechanics.

1—Essay has serious and persistent errors in word choice and mechanics.

Source: Wardell and Haro (2000)

---

can assist your planning by allowing the teacher to see which learning objectives have been achieved.

Disadvantages: Multiple-choice questions are difficult to create if you wish to develop critical-thinking, higher-order type questions. They also do not provide a venue to test student ability to organize and present knowledge.

Matching Questions Questions consist of two lists of related items such as words, phrases, pictures, or symbols. Each item is paired with at least one or more items in the other list.

Characteristics: Matching questions are used to recognize relationships and make associations. They can be used with a wide range of subject matter by matching terms, procedures with operations, causes with effects, definitions, and symbols. Matching items that are well constructed can be easily converted to multiple-choice items.

Sample

Column A contains a list of characteristics. Column B contains terms that match these characteristic. Each response in Column B may be used once, more than once, or not at all.

Column A	Column B
1. Least useful for educational diagnosis	a. Multiple-choice
2. Measures greatest variety of learning outcomes	b. True/false
3. Most difficult to score objectively	c. Short answer
4. Provides the highest score by guessing	

(Answers: 1 = b, 2 = a, 3 = c, 4 = b)

Advantages: Matching questions are easy to write and score. They are space efficient and afford a compact method to assess learning.

Disadvantages: Matching questions do not measure any type of interpretation, judgment, or application. Students tend to guess and use rote memorization rather than higher-order cognitive reasoning.

True/False Questions Students answer simple statements as either true or false.

Characteristics: True/false questions are primarily used to measure the students' ability to identify the veracity of statements, facts, principles, and generalizations. They can be used to poll an entire class to evaluate levels of understanding.

Sample

The true/false item is also called an alternative-response item.
a. True
b. False

(Answer: false)

Advantages: True/false questions are easy to write and score; they are objective by design.

Disadvantages: Students have a 50 percent chance of being correct on any item. They encourage guessing since there are only two alternatives.

Short-Answer Questions Teachers use this type of question to check recall or ability to provide names of items in graphics or pictures or specific parts, tools, words defined, and so forth. Short-answer questions may be referred to as "fill-in-the-blank" or "completion" questions.

Characteristics: Short-answer questions can be used for recall rather than recognition. They allow for constructing higher-level type questions that require specific, definite, and exact information that needs no interpretation.

Sample

Another term used to describe a short-answer test is called _____.

(Answers: fill-in-the-blank test, or completion test)

Advantages: Short-answer questions are easy to write and they reduce guessing. They do demonstrate student learning.

Disadvantages: Short-answer questions measure ability to memorize content, not comprehension. Grading can be subjective, and exact answers are not always given. They also, unfortunately, may be open to interpretation with regard to the number of correct responses.

One-Minute Essay Questions These questions are focused and have a specific goal that can be answered within a minute or two. A one-minute essay question can be used to check understanding, provide feedback, and promote reflection.

Characteristics: One-minute essay questions are short, clear, concise questions that require students to demonstrate comprehension quickly. They can be used to determine areas of a lesson that are not understood. They can be written with a sentence or one or more complete paragraphs.

Sample

In one to three minutes, describe what was most confusing in today's discussion about short-answer tests (today's homework, reading, etc.). Why was this concept confusing?

Advantages: One-minute essay questions promote reflection and critical-thinking skills. Teachers can assess their own effectiveness in the delivery of lessons, as well as reveal student misconceptions and background knowledge. They are easy to construct and do not require formal grading aside from traditional requirements associated with class participation.

Disadvantages: They do not measure in-depth understanding, and students may not take them seriously if they are not graded (Pennsylvania State University, 2003).

Authentic assessment takes the appearance of evidence tests such as portfolios, projects, and performance outcomes. These forms of demonstrations are used as evidence of student learning, and have come into vogue whenever discussing methods of assessment. Portfolios have become the prime alternative means of assessment for the majority of teachers. It consists of original products produced by the student, which provide a continuous means of monitoring student progress prepared and

Figure 10.7 Preparing Student Portfolios

- A table of contents divided into the major aspects of the work you have completed with an explanation of each item's worth.
- Samples selected by the student that demonstrate the work accomplished. A written description of each specific project should be included.
- A portfolio could also include any multimedia demonstrations that could be presented in the form of photographs, computer disks, video, and audiotapes.

selected by the student (Grady, 1992). Portfolio entries should include a wide variety of original products that demonstrate the work a student has achieved. Figure 10.7 describes items that should be included in most student portfolios, but it is not all-inclusive. It should be noted that portfolios can provide a rich variety of information about students, which can be useful in making sound decisions regarding individual performance. The importance of portfolios should not be underestimated; to be effective they must be more than just a collection of items. They must provide evidence that bears a direct relationship to the highlighted learning outcome.

Assessment practices for learning and classroom management necessitates using not only basic assessment concepts but also interpersonal intelligence skills, as defined by Gardner (1983). Before we begin to evaluate we must determine a procedure for our assessment to follow. This starts with our understanding both what we wish our students to learn and what specific management problem we are evaluating. To evaluate whether learning has taken place we must determine if our students have understood our aims, goals, and the objectives of our instruction. To determine student comprehension we must relate our tests to the specific content we have provided in our lesson plans. Once that is clear we are obliged to develop methods to collect the data through the use of specific types of tests, while developing forms for the appropriate reporting of test scores. Procedures for assessing student learning are basically concerned with

1. What is to be assessed?
2. How will the material be collected?
3. How do we report and reflect on the results of our testing?

To evaluate management practices we must determine if the solution we have attempted to implement has succeeded. This is often not as simple as it may first appear. We are dealing with human beings who are developing and maturing at varying rates. All children do not respond the same way to the implementation of similar solutions. To say it succinctly, "one key does not unlock all doors." Procedures for assessing student instructional and behavioral management problems are basically concerned with the questions

1. What was the identified problem?
2. What are the objectives you wish to achieve?
3. Was your solution successful in achieving those objectives?

To determine effectiveness as a teacher, focus and reflect on the end result of instruction—learning. A spotlight aimed at higher level learning can create a paradigm shift. A paradigm shift is a shift from providing instruction to producing learning, from a teaching paradigm to a learning paradigm. Bloom's taxonomy needs updating to identify significant kinds of learning; it is not important how people learn but what they learn. This concept leads to a higher level of learning that can be used at all educational levels. It essentially revolves about two basic questions: What are students learning about with regard to phenomena, ideas, self, and others? and What kinds of changes occur in learners related to knowing, thinking, connecting, acting, and caring? This idea does not offer a systematic solution but a potential rubric from which to judge instructional effectiveness through student assessment (Fink, 2000).

MINI CASE FROM THE FIELD

The following case from the field suggests ways to align planning with assessment. The purpose for connecting lesson planning to assessment within your daily practice is that it should result in greater student learning. A backward design–based approach to planning offers opportunities for teaching about complex systems in a coherent accessible manner.

Review the assessment glossary and basic assessment practices and relate them to the backward design process. Then read the study in which Nick Saccone attempts to design lessons that will align his practice with the forms of assessment he uses. Compare Nick's strategies and methods with those proposed by his colleagues. Decide if Nick's focus on aligning lesson preparation to assessment is necessary for effective teaching. Read the case, and compare the ideas presented to the reality of everyday classroom life.

Design and Assessment

Nick Saccone, a K–12 science teacher at McGraw Comprehensive School, had difficulty explaining his views on

PRACTICE EXERCISE 10.2

Basic Assessment Glossary

The purpose of this exercise is to develop a working knowledge of basic assessment terms. After reading and discussing each item write a brief, specific example of how each can be used to drive instruction.

Basic Assessment Glossary

Achievement Test: A standardized test designed to measure the amount of knowledge and/or skill a person has acquired, usually as a result of classroom instruction. Such testing produces a statistical profile used as a measurement to evaluate student learning in comparison with a standard or norm.

Action Research: School- and classroom-based studies initiated and conducted by teachers and other school staff. Action research involves teachers, aides, principals, and other school staff as researchers who systematically reflect on their teaching or other work and collect data that will answer their questions.

Alternative Assessment: Alternatives to traditional, standardized, norm- or criterion-referenced traditional paper and pencil testing.

Aptitude Test: A test intended to measure the test-taker's innate ability to learn, given before receiving instruction.

Authentic Assessment: Evaluation is based on assessing the behavior the learning is intended to produce. The goal of authentic assessment is to gather evidence that students can use knowledge effectively and be able to analyze their own efforts.

Benchmark: Student performance level(s) of student competence in a content area. A benchmark defines the stages along the road toward achieving the standard.

Competency Test: A test intended to establish that a student has met established minimum skills and knowledge standards necessary to achieve.

Criterion-Referenced Tests: Performance is compared to an expected level of mastery in a specific content area rather than to other students' scores. Tests question what the student was taught and measure the student's mastery. The "criterion" is the standard of performance established as the passing score for the test.

Essay Test: A test that requires students to answer questions by writing brief or extensive responses.

Evaluation: Either qualitative or quantitative, its purpose is to assess pupil behavior or instructional achievement.

Formative Assessment: Teacher observations that determine on a daily or regular basis if students are learning the topic being taught. Teachers prepare their plans for future lessons based on these assessments. (See Summative Assessment.)

Mean: The average score is arrived at by adding the total and dividing by the number of samples. (Four tests: 90 + 95 + 100 + 50 = 335 ÷ 4 = 83.3%)

Median: The point on a scale that divides a group into two equal subgroups.

Multiple-Choice Tests: Tests that expect students to choose the correct or best answer from a menu of alternatives.

Norm: The midpoint (or median) score for a group's performance. The results will always have 50 percent above and 50 percent below the norm score.

Norm-Referenced Tests: A test in which a student's performance is compared to that of a norm group. The student's score is compared to the group and not specific content responses.

Objective Test: This type of test provides only one correct answer for any item.

Performance Criteria: Performance criteria are used to assess and maintain objectivity and provide students with information about expectations.

Portfolio: Student-organized collections of work. They should exhibit evidence of effort, achievement, and progress over a prolonged period. They should also include information about performance criteria, and evidence of student self-reflection. Portfolios can be assessed by evaluating each item or holistically using a consensus with regard to standards.

Reliability: The term used to describe a testing instrument's consistency. An instrument should yield similar results over time with similar populations in similar circumstances.

Rubric: A scoring guide used in subjective assessments.

Sampling: Examining a random selection of group members in order to obtain information about a large group.

Self-Assessment: A process in which one engages in a systematic review of performance, focused on future improvement.

Standardized Test: An objective test that provides a uniform method for scoring. Scores are often norm-referenced.

Subjective Test: A test whose score is determined by the evaluator's opinion.

Summative Assessment: An evaluation by a teacher at the conclusion of a unit of study.

Validity: A term applied when a testing instrument's assessment accurately reflects what it was designed to measure.

designing effective lesson to his colleague Ed Child. Nick believed that all true learning stemmed from problem- or project-based planning designs. Designing good lessons in all their forms were just variants of a constructivist learning model that emphasized guided student engagement in discovery learning. Every lesson had to be designed to present students with problems or projects that challenged, requiring them to identify and use the appropriate knowledge and skills to address and solve the problem. This meant that students had to be taught how to use the scientific process of discovery (observation, theory building, experimentation, data analysis, and drawing conclusions) to solve problems. Nick felt this was a better and more effective way to learn than a traditional lecture or presentation in which students were simply given solutions.

The ecosystem of the McGraw School had the ability to seduce and destroy initiative. Nick had long faced the conclusion that his own self-image depended on the conceit that he was too smart and too ambitious to fail. His design-based assessment idea had to work. Nick believed that he could accurately assess student achievement by having them demonstrate that they understood through performances and products. He wanted to involve students in final self-assessments. Students could help to identify any remaining questions not understood, set future goals, and point toward new units and lessons.

After listening to Nick, Ed said, "Are you talking about using the backward design process for developing plans as an assessment format?"

"Something like that," answered Nick.

Overhearing, Lucy Chan could not help but say that what Nick was proposing was not quantifiable. It was way too subjective for both elementary and high school kids. Lucy understood the three stages of backward design, beginning with the end-result, and then determining what type of evidence would indicate learning, and finally the specific instructional method that should be used. What she proposed was to use one-minute essay questions because they check understanding, provide feedback, and promote reflection. These, combined with multiple-choice questions, would assess for reasoning and judgment, as well as recall and recognition of facts. The most important point, she claimed, was scoring, which in this case was objective and quantifiable rather than subjective.

Then Margaret Gomez interjected, "I think Nick has a point; he's just using the wrong terminology." Nick was really talking about authentic assessment. Nick could use student portfolios to assess learning. Portfolios containing examples of student work allowed teachers to calculate the rate at which students were achieving. Rubrics aligned to content exhibit evidence of effort, achievement, and progress over a prolonged period, Margaret insisted. And specific performance criteria, and evidence of student self-reflection, should be included in any assessment design plan. "Portfolios can easily be assessed by evaluating each item that has been requested in your original criteria," she told Nick.

Lucy told Margaret that her suggestions certainly had merit, but where would anyone ever get the time to do what she suggested? It was probably easier, more valid, usable, and reliable to use short-answer questions.

"I know what to do," said Nick.

1. List the arguments made by Nick for wanting to develop a design-based assessment plan.
2. If you were Nick, how would you respond to Ed Childs's interpretation of your position on assessment?
3. Contrast Lucille's arguments with Nick's. Who had the stronger position? Why?
4. Discuss your views regarding design-based assessment. Would it be effective in accurately assessing student achievement?
5. How do you think Nick planned to resolve the issue of assessment? How would you?

REFLECTING ON EFFECTIVENESS

Teacher effectiveness is directly related to student performance. Without effective teaching, student achievement is diminished. Teachers need to reflect on appropriate uses of assessment for student achievement and classroom management. Understanding suitable assessment practices improves both student performance and teacher effectiveness.

Assessment and evaluation can be considered a two-step process—formative and summative. The first step, **formative assessment** (observational judgments), consists of daily teacher assessments about student performance. These assessments influence a teacher's daily plans with regard to determining pace, preparation, diagnosing student needs, and content. The second step, **summative evaluation**, is used to report a summary of student progress periodically (Cangelosi, 1990). Effective teachers use this traditional approach to student assessment by making both types of judgments. They also reflect on the practical meaning of these assessments. To this simple process a unique proviso can be added. Before assessing others, reflect on and evaluate your own strengths and weaknesses. Do they correlate to student-demonstrated strengths and weaknesses? Such reflection allows you to evaluate students' performances more comprehensively.

Though we can control our own actions, we are never sure if we can control others'. Rather than looking to control others, we should look to control our own actions. If you are to manage a classroom that is to be a model for academic success and deportment, you must begin with what is achievable—your own behavior.

Reflection and Self-Evaluation

Teaching offers many opportunities for self-evaluation and reflection. When a teacher is effective and knows it, he or she gets indescribable satisfaction seeing students develop into young confident adults. Reflection is part of any teacher's successful approach to self-evaluation. Professional development that leads to professional growth is amplified when teachers take an active part in a continual appraisal of their own goals and effectiveness. Self-evaluation is the first step one should take to improve one's teaching and instructional practices. Self-evaluation can be performed objectively with written instruments, while reflection is both an inner dialogue and other-oriented open discussion among colleagues focused on self-improvement. Reflection occurs when one learns to analyze and interpret events in ways that guide one's development and improve day-to-day practice (Ornstein, 2000).

Reasons for Reflection

Reflection requires an ability to be honest with yourself and with colleagues or peers, and to listen to them as they help you analyze your own teaching. There are good reasons for teachers to reflect on their effectiveness as pedagogues. One reason is to evaluate instruction by measuring effectiveness in communicating content. Another reason is the pride experienced when students exhibit learning as a direct result of that instruction.

Reflecting on Effective Instruction

One way to improve your effectiveness is through periodic reflection and assessment of your teaching performance. Monitoring professional growth through student achievement defines the concept of the learning paradigm, where it is not what is taught but what is learned that truly matters. Teacher effectiveness is clearly related to student learning. Teachers can judge their performance by the feedback they receive from colleagues. They can also monitor and assess themselves by forms, charts, and checklists, combined with the personal observations of peers.

Pupils need to be evaluated for achievement and teachers for effectiveness. A supervisor who evaluates performance by observing a teacher- or student-teacher–presented lesson has made a teacher assessment in a traditional way. Teacher assessment can also be made by a technique called *micro peer teaching* (Kellough, 2004) or simulated classroom lessons (Orlich, 2004). Both of these procedures consist of presenting a mini-demonstration lesson to peers. It allows an opportunity for the preservice or practicing teacher to develop and rehearse specific teaching skills in a school environment before actually facing a real classroom situation. A practicing teacher can use this technique with his or her own class, using a video camera whose tape can be reflected upon privately. These types of experiences basically contain two essential components:

1. Preparation and implementation of a demonstration lesson of 5 to 10 minutes in duration or longer if deemed appropriate.
2. Completion of an analysis of a summative peer assessment and self-assessment, with statements of how you would change the lesson and your teaching of it if you were to repeat the lesson.

For your demonstration lesson, you should identify one concept and develop your lesson around the understanding of that concept. Review various types of lesson-planning strategies and consult with your professor or supervisor before you prepare a micro lesson. Use a simple technique for writing a developmental lesson, such as AMCASH described in Chapter 4. Each of the letters in this model represents an essential ingredient found in a developmental lesson. In this acronym, the *A* stands for aims or objectives, the *M* for motivation, the *C* for content, the *A* for application, the *S* for summary, and the *H* for homework. This lesson-planning model will allow you to concentrate on creating a typical outline for a developmental lesson in brief.

When you have completed the initial planning of your lesson, you should prepare a copy or full plan for your classmates and/or colleagues. Your peers should be asked to evaluate your lesson based on objectives agreed on before the presentation. After your lesson, collect your peer evaluations and prepare a self-analysis based on analysis of your classmates' evaluations. Finally, prepare a summary analysis that includes weaknesses and strengths, as well as how you would improve the lesson if you were to redo it. Include in your summary:

Figure 10.8 Guides to Self-Evaluation and Reflection

> 1. Self-evaluations may be used as part of the contract or formal evaluation process.
> 2. Self-ratings should be compared with student ratings if the same items are included in the forms. Discrepancies between the ratings should be interpreted or analyzed.
> 3. Self-evaluations can be used as a starting point for formal evaluation of the teachers.
> 4. Reflection takes place when teachers volunteer to participate and exchange ideas among colleagues.
> 5. Reflection allows teachers to better understand themselves and confront their strengths and weaknesses.

1. Analysis of peer evaluations
2. A self-evaluation
3. A summary analysis

The aim of assessing your own effectiveness through reflection is self-evident. Your ability to reflect on your approach to instruction will make you that much more effective as a teacher. Reflection will also make you more effective as a classroom instructional manager.

Reflecting on Effective Management

How can you measure your effectiveness as a classroom manager of behavior? The simplest approach would be to evaluate your success in resolving classroom problems. This can be done by keeping a basic score card or management journal of incidents that occur in your class that utilizes an IOSIE format. Next to each recorded incident *identified*, allocate a column for immediate actions taken. A column for *objectives* and one describing long-term *solutions* or plans of action to resolve the identified problem should make up the rest of the page. *Evaluation* will be based on your self-evaluation with regard to attaining objectives. Self-evaluation in this process is reflective. The ability to reflect allows for assessment of managerial effectiveness (Scarpaci, 2007).

PRACTICE EXERCISE 10.3

Peer Assessment for Microteaching

Rate student micro-lessons using the following items. Assign points to each item (5 = superior; 3 = average; and 1 = one needs more work):

　　　　　　　　　　　　　　　　　　　　　Rating

1. Introduction was appropriate and motivating. _____
2. Purpose of lesson was clear. _____
3. Lesson was logically organized. _____
4. Explanation was clear. _____
5. Evaluation indicated student understanding. _____
6. Teacher and/or students summarized main points of lesson. _____
7. Teacher used pauses to allow time for students to think. _____
8. Lesson plan quality: _____

　　　　　　　　　　　Points Scored _____
　　　　　　　　　　　(Maximum is 40)

Add your comments at the end.

The two questions posed earlier in this chapter can now be addressed with a certain amount of finality.

1. How do you evaluate your success in classroom management?
2. Is instructional effectiveness linked to student success?

The answer to the first question, how we evaluate the success of classroom management, is contained in the previous paragraph. Evaluate success by using the IOSIE method by preparing a management journal. The second question is not as easily answered since it is difficult to assign causality to correlations and say effectiveness is linked to student success. Recent research has, however, indicated that teachers are the single most important influence on student progress.

To attribute student gains to individual teachers is difficult to assess. It means testing students in each grade and subject every year. It also means accounting for student mobility, as well as teacher practices. Some say this can be done by using a statistical model known as a *mixed-model methodology*. The model weighs results based on the amount of information obtained. The magic performed is called *shrinkage estimation*, and what it yields is termed a *Best Linear Unbiased Predictor*, or BLUP (Archer, 1999). This **value-added assessment** model allows us to measure individual teachers' effectiveness, based on how well students perform over a period of years.

Researchers who have measured learning growth assume that teachers are the single most important influence on student progress, even greater than socioeconomic status. Therefore, the effects of good and bad teachers can remain with children for years. The value-added concept focuses on gains instead of raw scores, and each student's performance is compared against their own past performance, not against other similar students'. This is different from other researchers who struggle to control for differences in students' backgrounds, income, family education or other social factors. In value-added assessment, each student acts as his or her own control. The idea is that schools and teachers should at least be adding value to each student's performance every year (Sanders and Horn, 1994).

Supporters of this growth model approach (measuring individual student growth over time) argue that it is a positive alternative to the single end-of-the-year tests often used to satisfy the accountability requirements of the No Child Left Behind Act, and a way to determine teacher effectiveness. Critics retort that the idea may not work in urban schools, where the student turnover rate is often high. A way to address this problem is to have schools align their curricula and tests, measuring the growth of students who move between schools. This will be hard to do since the neediest, most vulnerable, and lowest-scoring students tend to move most often.

MINI CASE FROM THE FIELD

The following case from the field discusses connecting standards to assessment within your daily practice. Look at the standards discussed in Chapter 9 or look on the Internet for your state's department of education to locate your state's standards for a guide to expectations. Then read the study in which Nick Saccone attempts to use strategies that will align his state's standards with the forms of assessment he uses. Compare Nick's strategies and methods with those proposed by his colleagues. Decide if Nick's focus on children is in line with local standards. Read the case, and compare the ideas presented to the reality of everyday classroom life.

Aligning Assessments to Standards

Nick Saccone, a K–12 science teacher at the McGraw Comprehensive School, found himself in a quandary. He had just received a note from Principal Thompson directing him to connect his science plans to the state's standards. Nick liked the suggestion; he just did not know how to accomplish the task. Lucille Chan suggested that Nick go to the state's education Web site to see what he could find out. He found the following:

Mathematics, Science, and Technology Standards

Standard 1: Analysis, Inquiry, and Design Students will use mathematical analysis, scientific inquiry, and engineering designs, as appropriate, to pose questions, seek answers, and develop solutions.

Standard 2: Information Systems Students will access, generate, process, and transfer information using appropriate technologies.

Standard 3: Mathematics Students will understand mathematics and become mathematically confident by communicating and reasoning mathematically, by applying mathematics in real-world settings, and by solving problems through the integrated study of number systems, geometry, algebra, data analysis, probability, and trigonometry.

Standard 4: Science Students will understand and apply scientific concepts, principles, and theories pertaining to the physical setting and living environment and recognize the historical development of ideas in science.

Standard 5: Technology Students will apply technological knowledge and skills to design, construct, use, and evaluate products and systems to satisfy human and environmental needs.

Standard 6: Interconnectedness: Common Themes Students will understand the relationships and common themes that connect mathematics, science, and technology and apply the themes to these and other areas of learning.

Standard 7: Interdisciplinary Problem Solving Students will apply the knowledge and thinking skills of mathematics, science, and technology to address real-life problems and make informed decisions.

Nick's immediate response was, "Now what do I do?" Nick's buddy, Ed Child, said, "You write your plans—what else do you think you do?"

"Do I have to include every standard in every lesson for each of the grades I teach?"

"I doubt you could do that," said Ed. "Even if you could, the amount of time would be excessive. Why don't you do what I do, and select one standard for every lesson? It's not so difficult." Ed explained that he used the same standards for mathematics. He simply wrote his lesson and then found the standard that it came closest to achieving.

"Isn't that like putting the cart before the horse?" said Lucille. "Why don't you just select the standards you wish to achieve and write your lessons accordingly?"

Nick looked at Ed and Lucille and asked, "Could both approaches work? Even if they did that wouldn't explain how I could align my assessments to the standard." Ed and Lucille said, practically in unison, that any form of assessment could work as a formative assessment, as long as it was valid and reliable. You could assess standard seven by simply asking how what was taught could be applied to real life.

Nick added that he was concerned that all this attention to standards and assessments would stop him from focusing on his students. He said he did not want to be one of those teachers who just taught to the test. Lucille said by teaching to the standards and using appropriate assessments Nick would be focusing on the welfare of his students.

1. Compare Ed's and Lucille's suggestions with regard to writing lessons that reflect the standards. Which approach would you favor? Why?
2. Describe your reaction to Nick's statement that either approach could work for aligning standards to lessons.
3. Why did Nick feel assessments were not aligned simply by writing lessons focused on achieving a particular standard?
4. How would you respond to Ed's and Lucille's suggestion?
5. What is your reaction to Nick's and Lucille's arguments regarding concern for children?

Chapter Summary

This chapter has described assessment practices that foster student achievement and evaluate teacher effectiveness. For assessment to be valuable it must have a clear purpose, which is to provide the basic tools necessary to measure student learning and teacher effectiveness. We have briefly discussed the history of standardized testing and the pioneers who established modern psychological testing, along with the backward design process, stressing how the process has refocused our ideas about assessment and planning.

We reviewed basic assessment practices and highlighted a practical assessment glossary. We looked at terms basic to any understanding of assessment and testing practices. The next portion of the chapter dealt with reflection and its importance to assessment for evaluation and effectiveness. The argument that teacher effectiveness is directly related to student performance was bolstered by discussion of value-added assessment using a mixed-model methodology strategy. The value-added, or growth model, approach's strengths and weaknesses were mentioned as a possible solution to effective student assessment. Finally, we looked at a case study about aligning assessment to standards

Cases from the Field

CASE ONE

Don Randazzo worried that his fifth-grade class, located in an economically depressed area, had not improved in reading. The state's standardized test was to be given within two months. Mr. Randazzo had worked hard to implement the school's traditional reading program, and he had selected books that he knew were appropriate for his students. He believed in a balanced approach to literacy, but why couldn't he tell if it was working? Analyze the situation using the IOSIE method and then answer the following five questions.

1. What forms of assessment would you suggest Mr. Randazzo use?
2. How do you feel about his intuitive approach to assessment?
3. What procedures should Mr. Randazzo have used to prepare for student assessment?
4. Mr. Randazzo was assessing his own effectiveness through self-reflection. Is this what is really meant by self-reflection? Explain.
5. What would you do if you were Mr. Randazzo?

CASE TWO

Mary Kelly was a very serious student who had always had a great desire to teach young children. Her coursework had focused on theories regarding learning, intelligence, methods, and management. She had not actually taught a lesson until she took Professor Burke's class on effective teaching methods. He required her to prepare and present a micro-lesson for ten minutes. Mary just panicked. Analyze her situation using the IOSIE method and then answer the following five questions.

1. How should Mary go about preparing a micro-lesson?
2. How can her peers be involved in the process?
3. How could Mary's classmates utilize a checklist form?
4. Could a practicing teacher also use this procedure to evaluate effectiveness? Explain.
5. If you were Mary, what type of lesson would you consider presenting?

CASE THREE

Carol Terwilliger had been asked to speak at her school's parents association meeting on the topic of "Homework Used as an Assessment Tool." Carol was flattered that she had been asked to speak but she was not so sure if she had a positive or negative view to express regarding the topic. Analyze her situation using the IOSIE method and then answer the following five questions.

1. What advice would you give Carol about the correct position to take?
2. Since homework is a primary source for determining whether children are learning what is being taught, how would you design a homework assignment to reflect what a child has learned?
3. How could you expand your assignments to require students to apply what was learned in class?
4. Could you expand your homework to include assignments that allowed for creativity? Explain.
5. How would you respond to these terms with regard to homework: *time for assignment, parent's role,* and *feedback?*

CASE FOUR

Pat Gingerich was aware of the importance of assessment to a middle grades teacher. She understood that the assessment process consisted of evaluation and measurement. She understood tests but was unclear about how formal and informal approaches should be used in assessing her students. How much weight should each carry? She decided to make a list of the various assessment procedures she was aware of. Her list included teacher-made tests, standardized tests, portfolios, observation, performance assessment, interviews and questionnaires, and sociometric devices. Even after constructing the list Pat still was unsure of the worth of the various approaches to evaluation. Analyze her situation using the IOSIE method and then answer the following five questions.

1. Which items on Pat's list of assessment procedures are formal and which are informal?
2. How would you use a sociometric device to understand the interpersonal relationships between the students in your class?
3. How could you combine the idea of performance assessment with a teacher-made test?
4. Why are your observations important in assessing student understandings?
5. Teacher-made tests are usually constructed as true/false, completion, multiple-choice, or matching tests. Also included in this traditional taxonomy are essay tests. Which type of test do you consider the most effective, and why?

Terms to Remember

Assessment (evaluation)
Reliability
Validity
Usability
Norm- and criterion-referenced tests
Testing practices

Case studies
Subjective, objective, and authentic assessments
Reflection
Value-added assessment or growth model approach
Backward design

Discussion Questions

1. Why is it important to know yourself before you attempt to evaluate others?
2. Identify the advantages and disadvantages of each of the following types of assessment:
   - Essay questions
   - Short-answer questions
   - Multiple-choice questions
   - True/false questions
   - One-minute essay questions
3. Describe the type of assessment form you would want someone evaluating you to use—a narrative, checklist, or combination of both. How could you use the same methods with your own students?
4. Why is reflection so important to good assessment practices?
5. How can authentic assessment be used effectively to evaluate students? Give examples of how you would use this approach in your class.

Field Experience Activities

1. Visit a class when the teacher is giving a test or quiz. Describe how the teacher deals with the following issues:
   - Directions to students, oral or written
   - Proctoring the test
   - Grading procedures
2. Present a mini-demonstration lesson of ten minutes to your classmates. Identify one concept and prepare your lesson around the understanding of that concept. (*Example:* Global warming is a spurious and flawed issue.) After the simulated lesson is presented, discuss how it could be improved. This process could also take place using a video recording for your lesson presentation.
3. Observe two classroom teachers with regard to their task orientation. Compare their performances using the following rubric:
   - Is the lesson related to a specific standard?
   - Are clerical tasks handled efficiently?
   - Has the teacher developed an appropriate discipline plan?
   - Are children motivated because of the instructional strategy used by the teacher?

For Further Reading

American Productivity and Quality Center. (2003). Teacher education and preparation. Northeast Ohio Council of Higher Education. Retrieved April 15, 2005, at www.Noche.org/pdfs/tep_report.pdf.

Anderson, G. L., Herr, K., & Nihlen, A. S. (1994). *Studying your own school: An educator's guide to qualitative practitioner research*. Thousand Oaks, CA: Corwin Press.

Hubbard, R. S., and Power, B. M. (1993). *The art of classroom inquiry*. Portsmouth, NH: Heinemann.

Peterson, P. L. (1979). *Direct instruction reconsidered*. In P. L. Peterson and H. J. Walburg (eds.), *Research on teaching: Concepts, findings, and implications*, 57–69. Berkeley, CA: McCutchen.

Popham, W. J. (2000). The mismeasurement of educational quality. *The School Administrator* 57 (11): 12–15.

Ravitch, D. (2000). *Left back: A century of failed school reforms*. New York: Simon & Schuster.

Reed, C. (2000). *Teaching with power: Shared decision making and classroom practice*. New York: Teachers College Press.

Roschewski, P. (2003). Nebraska STARS line up. *Phi Delta Kappan* (March): 517–520.

CHAPTER 11

Becoming an Effective Teacher

FOCUS POINTS

1. Teacher empowerment translates into teacher effectiveness.
2. An effective teacher is a validated change agent who positively affects student achievement.
3. The learning paradigm must be embraced.
4. The plan is to empower teachers through funding and staff development in order to promote student learning.

CHAPTER OVERVIEW

IN THIS CONCLUDING CHAPTER, educational effectiveness is correlated to teacher empowerment, which results in student achievement. Its premise, supported by ethnographic case studies and a call for action research, demonstrates the relationship between effectiveness and improved learning outcomes. The goal of effective teachers is to facilitate learning and develop self-discipline for all students. An effective teacher is seen as a validated change agent who gauges success based on student achievement. The question is how best to achieve the goal.

The chapter begins by analyzing change that empowers and validates teachers to become effective educators. Basic change leads to teacher empowerment, with student achievement as the product. Effective teachers are created through experience, staff development, teacher assessment practices, and special funding.

Personality is a key concept and a major variable in becoming an effective teacher, as viewed through actual case studies. Personality describes that intangible quality teachers use to facilitate learning. It is embraced when we understand the paradigm that what students learn, not what is taught, is what really counts. When teaching is professionalized, teachers become empowered to act as validated change agents who influence student achievement.

The final section of the chapter deals with the reality of interviewing for a teaching position. This is essential since the best plan is useless unless one is in a position to implement it.

BECOMING A VALIDATED CHANGE AGENT

In education, two types of change can occur—systemic, or organizational, and individual. Organizational change is usually described in terms of systemic change. The *systemic change model* approach concentrates on the use of charter schools, privatization, and choice plans. This model's actions do not directly change classroom practices such as standards, assessments, accountability, and governance. But it has brought about some significant changes such as performance-driven budgeting, assessment strategies, and accountability. Unfortunately, top-down changes do not have a sufficiently strong effect on student achievement unless they are coupled with reforms that target classroom practices. Teachers need methods and techniques that are effective, well tested, and replicable in the classroom.

The *change agent model* for effective class change takes place at the school level when teachers design and carry out their own innovations. It occurs on a school-by-school, class-by-class basis. Permanent change is rarely achieved by outside agencies. This model is still believed to be the only way to achieve lasting change. Teachers have historically demonstrated difficulty in implementing externally developed programs. They tend to resist change or engage in token compliance because they have not taken ownership of a program. However, when teachers are involved in identifying and modifying a program to meet their specific needs, ownership and commitment do occur. It is not necessary for teachers to invent a program in order for them to be committed to making it a success. It is also not true that teachers only give commitment to programs they themselves design. This would be like saying that actors can only give great performances with material they write. Educators are no different from other professionals; they need to feel validated and empowered to become successful. When teachers have mastered the methods of instruction and are able to manage their classrooms and subject content, they become validated change agents that influence student achievement.

For teachers to become change agents depends on how they envision their classrooms. Are classrooms static, or evolving daily? Should one's teaching practice be eclectic and include the use of technology? Does the educational process enhanced by technology really revolutionize education? Is the role of teachers to expose students to ideas that encourage intellectual growth? Should teachers provide the tools and strategies that

PRACTICE EXERCISE 11.1

Classroom Change Problems

Prepare a brief response to each of the four following problems. Share your thoughts with your colleagues and try to arrive at a consensus about each.

1. In an elementary school, time drips away in all the extras like fundraising, holiday celebrations, and so on. At the high school, sports and clubs eat into the school day, with players and members leaving early and disrupting classes. Academic learning has become a small part of what schools provide. How do we change that culture so that we see schools as sacred places where learning is at the core, rather than as community centers where PTA sales compete with math instruction, and parents demand to have their children's birthday parties during instructional time? Develop a plan to increase instructional time without destroying school and community school spirit.

2. The trend in professional development is for a school's teachers to collaborate in order to learn whatever is necessary to increase student achievement. Prepare an action research project outline aimed at increasing instructional time in your classes.

3. There has been much dispute over the use of block scheduling. Is it better for students to learn a little every day on each subject, or to have more time, 80 to 90 minutes, on alternative days?

4. Research shows that the adolescent brain requires neural rest states during the day. Single Photon Emission Computed Tomography (SPECT) scans have enabled us to understand these brain rest states (Gurian and Stevens, 2005). Boys attempt to avoid being bored or sleepy by being physically active, while girls can retain academic ability during these periods. How can we schedule learning that is based on this existing research?

encourage student learning? A validated teacher is one who has achieved self-actualization and feels empowered. Teachers feel empowered when they master their pedagogical practice. Change seen from this perspective becomes the sum total of all applications used to facilitate learning.

A teacher who is a validated change agent demonstrates a vision for structural classroom change that requires classroom cultural change. The effective teacher considers rules, roles, and relationships, and beliefs, values, and learning process. To be effective, a classroom culture must be democratically established, which all understand. Students must voluntarily be willing to participate and work in the created environment. This is accomplished by the validated teacher bringing teaching personality to the classroom in the sense of integrity, an articulated vision, and an ability to inspire children and parents to share a vision. Educational achievement is easiest to accomplish at the individual class level when teachers are empowered. A teacher who is a validated change agent has a model for success similar to a self-fulfilling prophecy.

To expect teachers to educate is to expect what is reasonable.

MINI CASE FROM THE FIELD

The following case from the field discusses the relationship of school organization to student success. Read the study and decide which of the organizational strategies discussed will improve student success, and assist teacher effectiveness. Compare Dr. Conley's plan to the strategies and methods proposed by the faculty. View the ideas presented from the perspective of everyday classroom life.

Systemic or Individual Change: A New Look at an Old Alternative, K–8

Dr. Conley gave an address at the McGraw Comprehensive K–12 School. He exclaimed that change does not necessarily mean new, it can also mean a return to old ideas such as the K–8 school organization model. Studies have shown some seemingly startling results. A University of Michigan project followed 3,000 students in twelve school districts as they moved from sixth grade to seventh. The research showed that children who were given less control over their lives in the middle school developed a lower self-concept of ability. The study also found a change in the relationship between teachers and students. Students tended to characterize middle school teachers as less caring, less warm, less friendly, and less supportive than their elementary school teach-

PRACTICE EXERCISE 11.2

Components for Change

Reflect on each of the five statements that follow. Write an argument for or against each while keeping in mind how each relates to the keys for effective teaching (mastery of content, methods, management expectations, personality). Responses should be shared with the class.

1. *Professional development.* Ongoing staff development is essential to be effective and current with regard to educational pedagogy. Schools that support classroom success with funding and democratic governance empower teachers. Classroom methodology and mastery of content is a lifelong obligation. When teachers are empowered to succeed, students achieve.

2. *Objective-based budgeting.* Classroom discipline and behavior problems are not the only areas that concern good classroom management. Managerial skill in providing innovative classroom funding can be inspired by teachers. By getting money into the classroom where it is needed, instructional programs are strengthened. Teachers must learn how best to identify and link classroom goals with allocated monies to enhance student achievement.

3. *Master curriculum and standards.* To improve achievement in congruence with performance standards, remedy failure and reward success. An effective teacher focuses on content, performance, and caring.

4. *Technology.* Use technology as a tool to gain knowledge while preparing children to succeed in our global society. It gives children a unique opportunity for success by engaging them in interactive learning experiences. The beauty of technology is that it allows for equity for all children. The use of technology is as relevant today as the use of pencils once was.

5. *Parental involvement.* It is essential to one's success as a teacher. Parents must have an active role in the classroom decision-making process. The goal is to provide meaningful parent input for the benefit of all children. Meet on a regular basis with parents and be sure not to limit involvement simply to consultation. Involvement should include sharing programs and practices that work in class. Be prepared to implement workshops in areas of parent interest.

ers. Such attitudes could have a negative impact on emerging adolescents who are in need of positive adult relationships during their development.

Dr. Conley further stated that the present K–12 comprehensive grouping at the McGraw School was too overpowering for most students because of the mandatory transitions. The school was organized by pre-kindergarten to fifth grade, with children moving to the adjacent middle school building for grades six to nine, followed by movement to the high school for grades ten to twelve.

Standardized test results indicated a general academic decline from fifth to sixth grade in middle school. Dr. Conley felt there was substantive evidence that children were "turning off" in mathematics during the transition to middle school, citing researchers who found that middle school teachers were "less caring, less sympathetic, and less friendly." He concluded his remarks by hypothesizing that the increased impersonalization might be a consequence of the departmentalized nature of secondary schools and lack of student maturity. He had come to believe, he said, that "adolescent students in K–8 schools are better off because the traditional middle school environment isn't appropriate for this age group."

Nick Saccone turned to his colleague Ed Child and said, "What is Dr. Conley talking about? How can you reorganize a school when children are in different buildings? I think this type of movement would only cause more disruption for students and teachers." "I couldn't agree more," said Ed.

Lucille Chan, overhearing the conversation, piped in saying she had read a study from Johns Hopkins University that supported Dr. Conley's views. It found that regardless of their socioeconomic status children tended to do better on sixth-grade mathematics, English, and reading tests. This was true especially if they had only a single teacher in self-contained classrooms. That study also found that middle school teachers were less accommodating to the special needs of preadolescents. Lucille felt that some primary school empathy would make a big difference in how students related to middle school. As a fourth-grade teacher she believed that the movement from a child-centered elementary school to an impersonal middle school created many emotional difficulties for children.

Margaret Gomez, a middle school teacher, said, "Sending preadolescent children in grade five to a middle school is both educationally and emotionally unsound. I think we should explore the reestablishment of K to 8 schools wherever feasible. It would give parents of preadolescents the option of sending their children to a child-centered school or a traditional middle school. It's obvious that there is no one single answer, so why not opt for a combination of both child-centered and subject-centered approaches to revitalize our schools?

No single school organization design is best. Educational choice by parents is an essential determining factor. But children must come first if we're going to provide good education in a sound emotional environment."

1. Compare Nick's and Ed's suggestions with regard to viability with those made by Dr. Conley. Which approach would you favor? Why?
2. Describe your reaction to Lucille's statement that implied that a child-centered approach could work in the middle school.
3. Analyze Margaret Gomez's position. Is her assessment viable? Is offering a choice to parents realistic?
4. How would you organize a school to meet the needs of students, and teachers?
5. React to the following statement. "Positive systemic or organizational change is impossible without individual change taking place."

Problems with School Change

Comprehensive school and classroom change faces a problem that may very well be its undoing. The problem concerns two distinct schools of thought; one proposes that change can only come about by instituting a standards-based agenda that defines in detail what every student should do, and the other wants to decentralize and democratize our public schools. Today the standards-based agenda as reflected in the plethora of national and state performance standards appears to be the chosen approach. Government and private foundations support the standards agenda because it advances the establishment of world-class academic standards, which have become the clarion call of our purported national education agenda advocates.

The standards approach to change and restructuring is a return to traditional top-down, highly centralized, bureaucratic school systems that we have always had. Critics might claim that this is not systemic change, but simply a return to the scientific industrial management model. Frederick Taylor introduced an efficiency model for businesses around the turn of the nineteenth century. This industrial model for public school efficiency views our schools as social factories in which children are the products. Everyone in this approach has to be standardized in order for it to succeed. Teachers are supposed to teach the same content using the same methods. Traditionally this model has produced a maze of authoritarian, bureaucratic rules and regulations that ensure that no school or teacher deviates from imposed standards. Goals 2000 was based on an updated form of this old industrial model, which can be termed a global corporation model, which is sleek, modern, complex and technologically advanced. The language has become more sophisticated and up-to-date since Taylor's time, but the autocratic, antidemocratic, dehumanizing ideology of corporate domination and control is essentially the same.

The second group of school reformers can be termed modern-day "progressives" whose roots can be traced back to John Dewey. They want a democratic, progressive, decentralized school system, one that will lead to semiautonomous charter schools, which stem from the magnet schools movement of the 1960s and '70s. Their basic educational assumption is that due to the diversity of our population it is educationally unwise and counterproductive to insist that all children undergo a single predetermined highly academic educational process. They also believe there is a wide array of differing philosophical and pedagogical beliefs, from the traditional perennialist to the progressive constructionist. They therefore conclude that due to our society's diversity we should provide different types of schools to address these differing needs. They wish to create schools to which parents can choose to send their children, and in which teachers can choose to practice the methodologies they wish to practice.

These two groups share a deep and honest desire to see dramatic improvement in our present system of public education. However, these movements start from quite different philosophical and educational assumptions. "How can we make these two change movements compatible?" This dichotomy, between the *back to basics standards-driven conservatives* and the *child-centered, developmentally appropriate progressives*, may yet lead to the unraveling of present initiatives to the detriment of all children.

School change remains at the center of the public agenda after many years of discussion, legislation, and state and local action. Achievement is improving but still remains below acceptable levels. Multitudes of efforts are in progress to set high standards for student learning. Governmental incentives and sanctions have been put in place. A number of school reform models are beginning to demonstrate the ability to transform entire schools into high-performing learning centers. It is critical for schools and districts to be aware of both the range of widely available schoolwide models and the evidence that exists to support them. The Obey-Porter legislation established the criteria for researching models that we live under today (Obey and Porter, 2002). The nine primary conditions that are a part of the qualifying factors of CSRD Act are described in Figure 11.1.

Teachers acting as validated change agents can assist in making decisions about selecting improvement models by creating plans, with their administration's leadership teams, that assess and review. They can also select programs that enhance their school and classroom programs. They should:

1. Assess their school needs for instructional improvement.

Figure 11.1 Components of Comprehensive School Change

1. *Effective, research-based, replicable methods and strategies.* A comprehensive school reform program employs innovative strategies and proven methods for student learning, teaching, and school management that are based on reliable research and effective practices, and have been replicated successfully in schools with diverse characteristics.

2. *Comprehensive design with aligned components.* The program has a comprehensive design for effective school functioning, including instruction, assessment, classroom management, professional development, parental involvement, and school management. The program must align the school's curriculum, technology, and professional development into a schoolwide reform plan. The plan must be designed to enable all students to meet challenging state-mandated content and performance standards. It also must address needs identified through a school needs survey.

3. *Professional development.* The program provides high-quality, continuous staff development.

4. *Measurable goals and benchmarks.* A comprehensive school change program has measurable goals for student performance tied to the state's content and performance standards.

5. *Support within the school.* School faculty, administrators, and staff support and collaborate on programs.

6. *Parental and community involvement.* The program provides for the meaningful involvement of parents and local community in planning and implementing school improvement activities.

7. *External technical support and assistance.* The program utilizes high-quality external support and assistance from a comprehensive school reform entity (which may be a university) with experience or expertise in schoolwide change and improvement.

8. *Evaluation strategies.* The program includes a plan for the evaluation of the implementation of school changes and the student results achieved.

9. *Coordination of resources.* The program identifies how other resources (federal, state, local, and private) available to the school will be used to coordinate services to support and sustain the school change.

Source: University of Alabama at Birmingham (2007)

2. Review various models.
3. Select models that match school needs.

Unless school change moves in a collaborative fashion, it is unlikely to be any more successful than past attempts.

TEACHER EMPOWERMENT MODEL

Substantive reform requires intellectual sophistication and unity of purpose seldom attained under existing models of school governance. For change to be successful an environment must be established in which all understand the prevailing factors (leadership theory, governance, organizational theory, change theory), and are willing to integrate this knowledge into a coherent change effort. A model demonstrating this type of reform is outlined in Figure 11.2. Chiefly important is that effective teacher empowerment, combined with innovative funding and egalitarian governance, result in improving instructional and curriculum practices that affect student outcomes positively.

In an unpublished study conducted over a three-year period (1996–1999) at a Brooklyn, New York, public school, findings led to the development of the *Teacher Empowerment Model to Improve Learning Outcomes* (see Figure 11.2). The suppositions made by the model that teacher empowerment would lead to innovative instructional practices and enhance student outcomes were substantiated. A procedure titled **alternative teacher assessment** focused funding on improving student achievement through creative teaching. During the 1990s the idea of using a teacher empowerment model to improve learning outcomes was taking root in New York City. The model's concept is that teacher empowerment, innovative funding, and governance created improved instructional and curriculum practices that would result in enhanced student outcomes. The research occurred at the Bayview School P.S. 102, located in the historic southeast corner of Bay Ridge, Brooklyn. Its two well-kept hundred-year-old buildings housed almost 1,500 children. The population of the school community changed dramatically prior to the turn of the twenty-first century. New arrivals from fifty-six nations speaking eighteen different languages, including Arabic, Chinese, Russian, and Spanish, gave the school a multicultural and international flavor.

In 1990, the school organized itself under a governance plan called *School-Based Management/Shared Decision Making (SBM/SDM)*. Its mission was to establish a childhood program that improved student outcomes. The chancellor selected the school and the local school district to participate in a "performance-driven budgeting initiative," which allowed the school-based management team to put funds to work supporting school goals. These funds were combined with funds accrued from savings based on good teacher attendance. This meant that money was directly allocated, at the point of service, into classrooms. As a result, the school moved boldly in its attempt to improve student literacy.

With great enthusiasm and confidence, the school attempted to create a professional empowerment model that would lead to creative curriculum development, enhance student outcomes, and afford systemic change. This represented a change in the way money was allocated and how teachers viewed their professional roles. The core belief was that if one of the variables (funding, professional empowerment, or curriculum) was changed schools would also change. The question was, "Would teacher empowerment through funding and governance ensure classroom practices that would result in improved academic outcomes?" Figure 11.2 provides a visual overview of this model.

The program was put in motion in 1995 when the school successfully petitioned to keep and allocate any school accrual monies that resulted from good teacher attendance. Previously, all monies were returned to the local district. The program allowed the school to retain its own accruals, which were to be used at the school level to implement new curriculum development projects. The school-based management team dispensed money through a granting procedure in which teachers presented innovative curriculum projects to a committee of their peers.

To enhance the program, a **teacher empowerment** program entitled **Alternative Teacher Assessment (ATA)** allowed teachers to develop year-long curriculum projects in lieu of formal supervisory observations. The theory was that teachers, because of this empowerment and this newfound source of revenue, would positively influence student learning. The pilot program was successful in every class where teachers acting as validated change agents chose to participate.

The process allowed teachers to be creative in developing programs to achieve academic goals and offered them the opportunity to change the traditional ways in which schools and classes operate. A paradigm had been created in which teachers were in control of what they do best: teach. The supervisor's role also changed to that of facilitator in support of teacher curriculum initiatives. Specifically, the process involved the teacher selecting objectives in support of democratically arrived-at school goals and then voluntarily taking part in the ATA program by completing a form indicating their plans, activities, and strategies. Teachers assessed and evaluated their own work in consultation with facilitators. Funding could be obtained through an in-school accrual granting program administered by the SBM team made up of teachers, administrators, and parents.

Programs were cost effective because all monies were expended at the school site and directly influenced classroom instructional programs. The cost to the school district remained the same. The only difference was

Figure 11.2 Teacher Empowerment Model

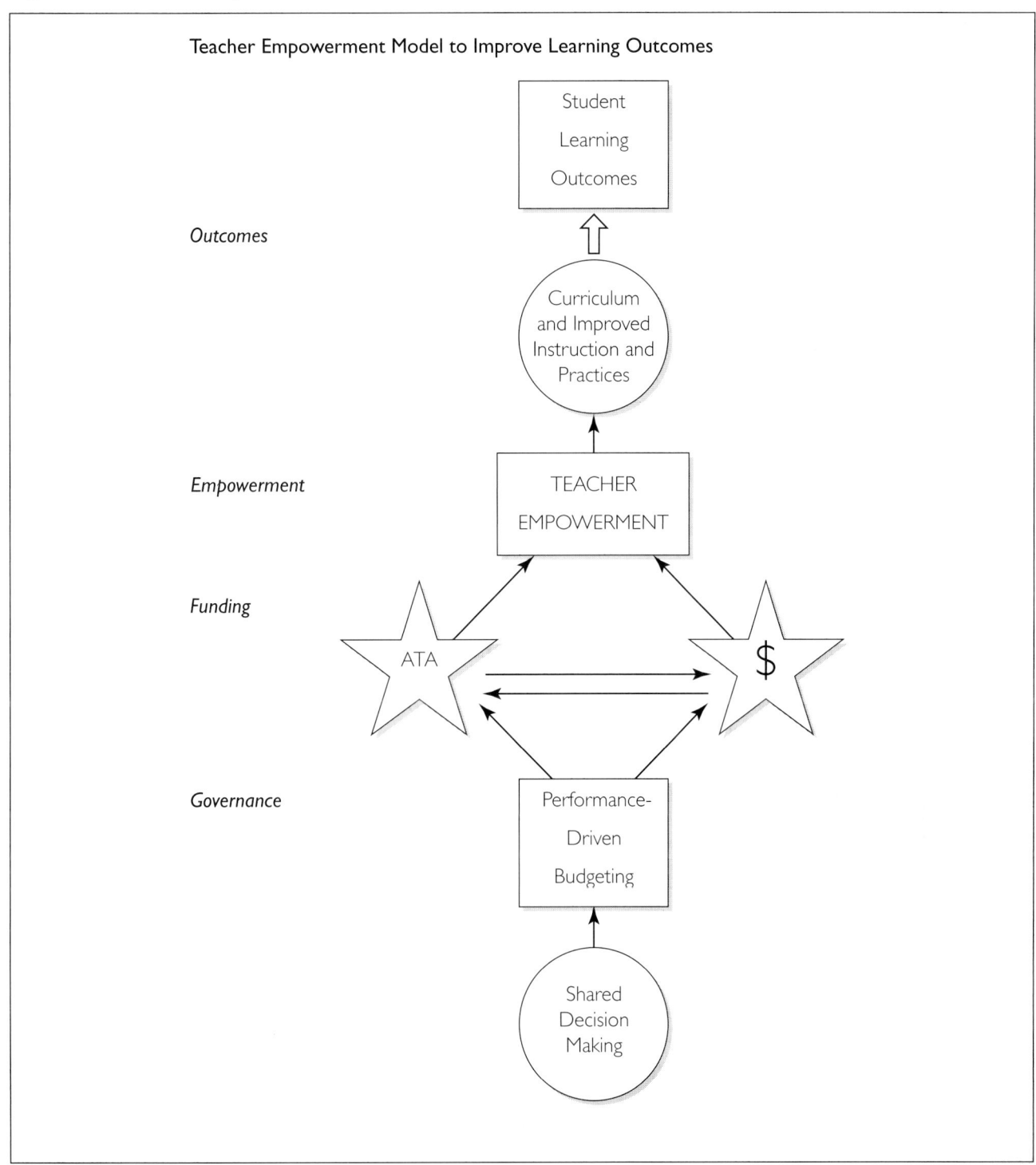

where monies were allocated. The original plan called for a school-specific fund budgeted but not spent for substitute teachers to cover teacher absences. A three-year trial period provided the following results shown in Figure 11.3.

During the *first year* of the project, twenty-five teachers applied for $57,870 and received $12,999 because that was all that had been allocated. In the *second year,* thirty-four teachers applied for $7,988 and thirty-three teachers received $6,415. In the *third year,* ten teachers applied for and received all of the accrued funds, $12,737.

In the last year of the project fewer teachers applied for funds. This seeming failure to get teachers involved really was misleading. Fewer teachers applied because fewer teachers needed additional funds. This is an

Figure 11.3 Accrual Money Dispensed

Years	Amount Allocated	Amount Teachers Received	Number of Teacher Applications/Number Receiving Funds
1995–96	$12,999	$12,999	25/25
1996–97	$ 7,988	$ 6,415	34/33
1997–98	$12,732	$12,732	10/10

astounding fact when one considers what usually happens with school budget requests. When asked why so few had applied, the teachers commented that they were still spending and working on their previous project and required less money.

During the *first year* thirty-five teachers out of sixty-three elected to participate in the pilot. In the *second year*, fifty of sixty-three elected to participate, an increase of 24.3 percent. This demonstrated significant movement toward voluntary staff involvement and empowerment. In the *third year*, forty-nine teachers out of sixty-five chose to participate. This represented an insignificant decline from the previous year's high of fifty participating teachers. The following case studies reflect the types of projects developed by teachers that changed and positively affected student academic growth.

Studies of Teacher Empowerment Leading to Student Improvement

1. Curriculum enhancement was achieved in the work of Mr. John Volpe (1995–1998) in the form of a project entitled *The Development of an Aeronautics Curriculum in the Classroom*. He used the ATA process to allow for his involvement with NASA and Cislunar. He won a federal grant to work on a three-year project to evaluate and create curricula geared to the elementary school in the form of a *K–8 Aeronautics Internet Textbook*. Because of this project, he changed both his instructional approach and created curricula heretofore not included in grade four. He also changed the instructional methods he employed by including computer technology as a basic tool for instruction. Improvement in writing became an outgrowth as well as the focus of his efforts.

2. Ms. Maryann Jarema initiated *An Enhanced Lighting Program for Delayed Readers*. Working with a consultant (Mr. Robin Mumford, Director of the Mumford Institute) Ms. Jarema led her corrective reading students in a project focused on assessing the value of enhanced lighting and its relationship to remediating delayed readers. The project attempted to test the variables of student speed and accuracy under different lighting conditions. The results indicated that time on task was increased under the project lighting when compared to natural and fluorescent lighting. The implications inherent in this project led to the NYC Board of Education's request for a pilot study in 1996. A preliminary study in 1997–98 revealed a 10 percent increase in reading and math standardized test scores for the thirty children in the pilot sample.

3. The ATA and accrual funding project evolved as a flexible process that allowed for ongoing revisions as need indicated. A case in point was that of Ms. Susan Mawdsley and the school library cluster. Her original goal in 1995 was to develop an author studies program for the school library. This turned into an ATA project, *Developing a Power Library P.S. 102 Style*. Ms. Mawdsley used the services of a consultant from Brooklyn College to assist in redesigning the school library for the twenty-first century. Accrual funds in 1996, 1997, and 1998 paid for this project.

4. A case study that demonstrates a zenith in curriculum enhancement is that of Mrs. Ann Ortega. Her ATA, *A Trip around the World* in 1995–96, integrated fifth-grade curricula and technology to develop a core experience within a thematic approach to social studies. Her constructivist approach to social studies had children using the Internet, developing portfolios, writing a newspaper, and filming videos. She

Figure 11.4 Alternative Teacher Assessment Pilot Project Participation

Year	Total Eligible	Teachers Applying	Percentage Participating
1995–96	63	35	55.0%
1996–97	63	50	79.3%
1997–98	65	49	75.3%

combined technology, art, literature, and music, while garnering parental support. Her class constructed virtual core experiences in order to learn about people around the world. She used the ATA process and accruals to enhance curriculum, develop innovative practices, and improve student outcomes without additional costs to taxpayers. In the following years the project's name was changed to "Who Am I?" The program was replicated by the entire fifth grade as a celebration of diversity.

5. Mrs. Cynthia Willies's project, *Career Awareness and Business Development* (1995–1998), promoted activities that enhanced career awareness and culminated in the establishment of a class book-binding business, Buy the Book Corporation. Children started a business and made a profit, which was used to purchase materials for future years. This ATA project helped to establish an instructional strategy that could be replicated and ensured career awareness learning.

6. Mrs. Rena Goudelias's ATA in 1996 was entitled *Using Technology and Whole Language Practices to Enhance Reading*. The Internet was used to access information to create "Big Books" to be read to kindergarten children by fifth graders. To avoid scheduling problems children videotaped all presentations. This innovative instructional strategy combined technology and the whole language philosophy. Added in 1997 was an author study component. In 1998 a new project entitled *Wonderfully Exciting Books (W.E.B): The Link Between Home and School* was added to her list of successful projects, demonstrating that success appears to breed more success.

7. Mrs. Grace Susino and Mr. Joseph Grant collaborated on an ATA project entitled *Improved School Services for Limited English Proficient Students and Parents* that demonstrated the flexibility of the ATA process. Their unique approach combined accrual funding with a state grant. The program focused on helping parents of limited-English-speaking children improve their literacy skills so that they could eventually assist in their own child's education. This project allowed the school to provide needed services to those newly arrived to our country by stressing literacy and parent involvement. The following year, the team of Susino and Grant collaborated on creating an at-risk program for ESL children, using videotaping of students for individual teacher and student assessment. The success of these programs was evidenced by a 50 percent increase in the number of students testing out of ESL classes.

8. Mrs. Fran Betron and Mr. Georgio Lantieri also worked collaboratively on an ATA project (1995–1998), *A Global Electronic School Newspaper*. Their goal was to develop a school newspaper that supported the whole language approach to learning. The paper, *What's up at Bayview?*, gave all students access to having their work published every month. Children and faculty alike were able to demonstrate their powers with the written word. An outgrowth of this ATA has been a fifteen-session staff development course entitled *The Internet: An Introduction to Classroom Use*. Teacher empowerment supported by governance and necessary accrual funding led to enhanced curriculum and innovative instructional practices that show evidence of improved student academic outcomes.

9. Mrs. Patricia Harner's ATA, *Establishing a Record Resources Library for Kindergarten Classes*, enhanced an existing curriculum through purchases that directly influenced the fine arts instructional program for eight kindergarten classes. Through the infusion of a few hundred dollars in accrual funds, 200 kindergartners were exposed to the arts on regular basis. Teacher empowerment and innovative funding did lead to enhanced educational outcomes. In 1998, Mrs. Harner developed a program entitled *Using Puppets to Develop Language*, which was added to the school's curriculum as an enhancement to the kindergarten program.

The problem with understanding the causal relationships between teacher empowerment and improved student outcomes is how to reconcile powerful intuition with studies that fail to support this contention. One can

PRACTICE EXERCISE 11.3

Teacher Empowerment Equals Student Achievement

Review and reflect on the previously discussed studies. Answer the following questions.

1. Analyze each of the studies described and briefly explain which, if any, are true examples of teacher empowerment.

2. In your judgment, which, if any, of the nine cases described reveal positive student outcomes? Explain the reasons for your decisions.

3. From the nine cases presented, select the strongest example and the weakest example of teacher empowerment's effect on student outcomes. Explain your reasoning.

4. Discuss your reaction to the following statement, "Teacher empowerment equals student achievement."

5. How would you define teacher empowerment?

only turn to the ancient Greeks who understood the nature of knowledge. In their study of epistemology, they came to believe that we learn through our experiences, the authority of others, reason, intuition, and the active construction of our minds. To paraphrase Plato's "Allegory of the Cave," educating children into the light, out of the world of belief (cave), into the realm of knowledge (light), brings one to true knowledge and goodness (sun). On most subjects, the Greeks said it first and said it well. Based on faith, experience, and intuition, one sees that these studies present a convincing case for an educational model that enhances student outcomes and leads to improved student performance.

The ATA process offers teachers an opportunity to view their roles proactively. Positive results were achieved because of the natural incentive empowerment offers for instructional advances. These mini case studies out of approximately 150 viewed over three years are examples that support the basic contention that when teachers are empowered and funding provided, innovative instructional practices follow. They also show that individual and systemic change took place at this school. Teachers saw themselves as proactive educators, and supervisors viewed themselves as facilitators. The accrual funding (now called performance-driven budgeting) addressed the challenge for reformers—financing implementation. We should note that finances are needed to fund good ideas. The plethora of available good ideas needs money to finance them. Teacher empowerment gained through innovative funding (such as accrual funds), governance (such as SBM/SDM) does affect classroom instructional practices and curriculum, resulting in improved academic performance in the classrooms where it is attempted. This can be seen through the case studies presented and from one's intuitive faith in one's prior experiences. The question of whether enhancing teacher empowerment through innovative funding and governance strategies affect classroom instructional and curriculum practices resulting in improved student academic outcomes has been answered. *Yes!*

Improving Classroom Performance through Action Research: A Strategy for Instructional Improvement

One strategy to improve the quality of your classroom performance is to become a student of your own teaching. This approach is commonly referred to as action research. The tactic allows teachers to become reflective using a form of critical inquiry applied to their practice. It provides tools and strategies to work on teaching dilemmas and resolve classroom problems. This is accomplished by focusing on four steps that consist of (1) identifying problems and immediate questions, (2) collecting data, defining objectives and terms, (3) analyzing data and proposing solutions, and (4) implementing an action plan, which is then evaluated. The strategy follows an unbiased mixed methodology process that yields valid and reliable results. The findings become immediately applicable to their individual classroom or school situation, whether behavioral, organizational, or curricular problems.

Example One: Behavioral Problem   Mary is a disruptive second grader who often erupts into loud boisterous displays of uncontrolled anger after returning from lunch. Mrs. Hardtack, her teacher, usually attempts to rectify the situation by removing Mary and placing her in a colleague's class. Mary is kept out of her class until she regains control of her emotions. It takes the class nearly an hour to settle down and get back on task, despite the efficient way the problem is handled. Mrs. Hardtack does not want to refer Mary to special education because of the inordinate amount of time necessary to complete all the referrals. She decides to make Mary the object of an Action Research project that her supervisor had suggested.

Action Research Procedure

1. Mrs. Hardtack's first step was to *identify the problem* and ask the question, What triggers Mary's disruptive behavior?
2. The second step was to *collect data* and define *objectives* and terms. What data should be collected to answer her question? Should parents and children be consulted? Would it help the psychologist to look into Mary's psychological make-up? Mrs. Hardtack decided to keep a journal and note what happened immediately before and after each disruption.
3. The *solution* was arrived at after the data were *analyzed*. Mrs. Hardtack's notes discerned a pattern in Mary's misbehavior. She consulted with her colleagues, who offered varying opinions. It was agreed that Mary erupted every time she felt she was going to be called upon. When confronted, Mary appeared frustrated and fearful of being seen as ignorant by her classmates.
4. A *plan of action* was *implemented* and *evaluated*. The plan called for Mrs. Hardtack to speak privately with Mary. Mary was told that she would only be called upon when Mrs. Hardtack stood in front of Mary and placed her hand on her desk. Questions would be appropriate to Mary's skill level. Mrs. Hardtack also proposed further in-depth analysis into Mary's psychological make-up.

Example Two: Organizational Problem   The process works equally well on all levels and with all grades, including schoolwide organizational problems. For example, why are grades of students so poor during a transitional year from elementary school to middle school, or middle school to high school? Why does that happen? What can we do about it? How could an action research plan be implemented?

Action Research Procedure

1. The first step is to *identify the problem* and pose a *question* that we can attempt to answer. How can school and teachers make transition from elementary to middle school "user friendly"?
2. Clarify terms and *objectives,* and collect data. This could be done by developing a simple random sample survey of transitional students. The sample should consist of two groups of average and at-risk students, matched by gender and ethnicity.
3. The *solution* should come from the *data analysis.* Responses from the survey will form a pattern that leads to possible solutions. In this case, regarding transition, students in both groups could feel overwhelmed by the social challenges of moving into the anonymous setting of a large school as opposed to a more nurturing setting of a small school.
4. An *action plan* would then have to be *implemented* and *evaluated* to address the issue of student transition. A possible plan involving conscious efforts to welcome new students could be adopted. Special classes offered by counselors could be offered as well as developing a freshmen center that deals directly with incoming students' needs.

Example Three: Curriculum Problem The action research process using an IOSIE framework works as well for curriculum issues. For example, if we address the fact that boys seem to be failing in English at higher rates than girls, we might ask, "Why are girls doing better?" Should we determine the time on task necessary to master specific skills for boys and girls when taught using the standard approach and curriculum? Can we compare the performance of three different classes grouped into underachiever, average, and advanced according to gender? The process is as follows:

Action Research Procedure

1. The first step is to *identify the problem* and pose a question that we can attempt to answer. "Why are boys failing in greater number than girls?"
2. Clarify terms and *objectives,* and collect data. This could be done by comparing the standardized test results in the language arts examinations. We could also survey a random sample of boys and ask them why they are failing. We could compare the performance of three different classes grouped into underachiever, average, and advanced according to gender.
3. The *solution* should come from the data analysis. Responses from the survey will form a pattern that leads to possible solutions. In this case, regarding curriculum, boys might feel deprived of choice in reading matter. It could be that gender-specific instruction might be appropriate to get the boys back on track. Some form of experimentation would appear to be called for.
4. An action plan would then have to be *implemented* and *evaluated* to address the issue of male student failure. The option of single-sex classes might be considered. Based on available information about the different ways boys and girls learn could determine instructional strategies and gender-appropriate curricula. (See Chapter 7, Teaching for Literacy.)

In each of the three descriptions presented, teachers identified the problem, chose the question, defined objectives, and proposed solutions based on the analysis of collected data. The implementation of action plans was based on findings that allowed teachers to solve their own problems and evaluate their teaching practices. That is what action research is supposed to do—allow teachers to resolve their own behavioral and instructional problems (Reed, 2005). Teachers who use action research are well on the way to becoming validated change agents and effective teachers.

MINI CASE FROM THE FIELD

The following case from the field discusses the importance of retaining effective teachers. It shows how solutions to organizational problems can be addressed using action research procedures. Read the case, and compare and analyze the proposal made by Principal Thompson. Evaluate the proposal from the perspective of its possible success by using action research within an IOSIE framework.

The Proposal: An Action Research Model to Save Effective Teachers

Chandler Thompson had been principal of the McGraw Comprehensive K–12 School for the past ten years. In all that time he had never faced a problem such as Superintendent Conley had placed before him. The superintendent was concerned with the faculty turnover rate at Thompson's school. He had gone into a long soliloquy about the reasons.

"Thompson, you must be aware of the fact that approximately one-half of all new teachers leave teaching within their first five years of service. The statistics for turnover among new teachers at McGraw are startling. Some 20 percent of all new hires leave the classroom within three years. In urban districts, the numbers are worse; close to 50 percent flee the profession during the first five years (National Education Association, 2005).

In New York City, 40 percent of teachers leave after three years, and 48 percent are gone after five years, according to the United Federation of Teachers. Teachers say they are overwhelmed by expectations and the scope of the job. This, Chandler, I believe is due in part to new teachers' inability to meet job stress and manage classes. This problem needs to be resolved here at McGraw and throughout the rest of district."

Dr. Conley explained that his research found that that a typical list shows that the most common reason given for leaving teaching always includes stress from disruptive students (Dunham, 1977). In one study done in urban secondary schools, lack of discipline and motivation was the primary source of teacher stress and most significant predictor of burnout (Gonzalez, 1997). Brownell and colleagues (1995) identified new special education teachers' basic problem as an inability to provide instruction and handle discipline. Able and Sewell (1999) found that urban teachers attributed greater stress to student discipline and behavior problems than did rural teachers.

Constant and increasing pressure on teachers has also made assessment and test accountability a primary cause of teacher stress. Still, any reading of the total literature inevitably leads to the conclusion that lack of discipline and classroom management are a major cause of teacher stress and burnout (Darling-Hammond and Sykes, 2003).

Dr. Conley felt that he could save hundreds of thousands of dollars annually by reducing teacher turnover. A school system with roughly 10,000 teachers could save approximately $500,000 per year by reducing turnover by 1 percentage point (Benner, 2000). "If you look at the chart, you can see the reasons given for dismissing teachers in Chicago" (Rossi, 2005.) "1,116 nontenured teachers struggling to control their classrooms were let go as of June 2005. More than half those bumped had problems with classroom management or teacher-pupil relationships, and nearly half struggled with instruction, according to the reasons checked off by principals obtained by the *Chicago Sun-Times*." (See Figure 11.5.)

Superintendent Conley asked Mr. Thompson to develop a plan to reverse the potential disaster of losing faculty facing the McGraw School and the rest of the district. Mr. Thompson promised to think about what he had said and come up with a proposal by the end of the week.

Mr. Thompson started by checking Dr. Conley's assertions, and found that they were true. Nearly one-half of all new teachers leave teaching within their first five years of service. Pre-service and new teachers need well-designed clinical experiences to prepare them for the challenges of effective teaching (American Productivity and Quality Center, 2003). The nature of teacher preparation has changed tremendously. Fewer are prepared in traditional undergraduate programs, and more are prepared in alternative programs. Mr. Thompson found his staff at McGraw mirrored the national attrition averages.

Figure 11.5 Why Teachers Were Fired

Reasons checked by principals	Percentage of fired teachers in trouble for each reason
Classroom failings (Management, teacher-pupil relationships)	55%
Poor instruction (Planning, methods, knowledge of subject)	46%
Lack of responsibility (Attendance, tardiness, professional judgment)	38%
Other	26%
Poor communication (Parent conferences, staff relations)	24%
Attitude (Lack of cooperation, respect for others)	20%

Note: As of June 2006 1,100 teachers had been dismissed.

Based on his perusal of the data, Mr. Thompson decided his proposal would attempt to reverse teacher turnover at the McGraw. He would provide on-site support in effective instructional and behavioral classroom management. His proposal would be focused on turning around this depressing situation one teacher and one school at a time.

The core philosophy of his proposal was that "learning to teach is a career-long, developmental process, and that teacher learning best occurs in collaborative environments." By developing in new teachers a focus on self-assessment and self-prescription teacher retention rates would increase along with student achievement.

On Monday morning, Mr. Thompson delivered the following proposal outline to Dr. Conley.

Proposal

1. The first step is to *identify the problem* and pose a question that we can attempt to answer.
   Proposal Title: "Relationship between Effective Classroom Management, Teacher Retention, and Student Achievement."

The Question: Does instruction in effective classroom management practices increase teacher retention and students' performance?

The *first stage* is to provide new teachers the necessary tools to develop effective classroom management skills, such as the IOSIE Method (Scarpaci, 2007). The study group participants will consist of newly hired teachers who volunteer for the project; those who choose not to volunteer will make up the control group. Participants are to complete ten hours of staff development, and two follow-up workshops. A hotline phone number for ongoing assistance, follow-up consultations, observations, and analysis of student records will be made available.

2. The second step is to clarify terms and *objectives,* and collect data. New teachers will be identified, and student standardized achievement results will be compared for the sample and control group.

The *second stage* has participants doing action research on classroom management problems they perceive in their own educational practice. This is done by collecting data, analyzing, and reflecting on what was done, and why. The results of these action research projects will be presented at follow-up workshops.

3. The *solution* should come from the data analysis. Data should form a pattern that leads to possible solutions.

The *third stage* will be a five-year longitudinal study of the collected data with regard to effective management training's relationship to teacher retention rates, participants' perceptions of teaching, and trained participants' relationships to student achievement.

4. An action plan would then have to be *implemented* and *evaluated* to address the issue of teacher effectiveness, retention, and student achievement.

The *fourth stage* of the research is designed to test two hypotheses: that effective management training positively influences teacher retention rates, and students of teachers who perceive themselves as strong managers demonstrate academic achievement. This research will also validate the IOSIE method.

It is expected that teachers who receive training will remain in teaching longer, and their students will score better than students of teachers who have not received training,

1. List the arguments made by Dr. Conley to support his position that steps had to be taken to address the problem of teacher retention. Give your reasons for support or disapproval of his position.
2. Is Mr. Thompson's proposal a justified action research project using IOSIE as a framework? Write a brief statement defending your position.
3. How will this proposal affect the lives of teachers and students alike?
4. Describe your feelings with regard to the issue of the relationship between teacher effectiveness, retention, and student achievement.
5. How would you resolve the problem of losing effective teachers?

BECOMING AN EFFECTIVE TEACHER

Behaviors of Effective Teachers

The key to all instructional methods is the teacher, whose concerns, strivings, satisfactions, hopes, and heartaches pervade their everyday lives. Jersild (1955) said many years ago, "Self-understanding requires something quite different from the methods, study plans, and skills of a "know-how" sort that are usually emphasized in education . . ." Approaches to teaching depend on who and what one is, not on what someone tells you. Effective teachers share common qualities. They are good managers and instructors who design lessons to achieve mastery, while preparing effective assignments and appropriate student assessments. Assignments are designed to reflect what students need to accomplish and know. They are written in simple, clear, concise language. Effective teachers have positive expectations of students. They believe students are capable of achieving. They tend to be good instructors and administrators who prepare and deliver lessons that meet students' needs. They construct tests that measure what they are

PRACTICE EXERCISE 11.4

Action Research Project

Action research allows teachers to solve their own problems and evaluate the effect of their own teaching practices. Teachers are required to

- *Identify* the problem and pose a question.
- Define *objectives* and define terms.
- Propose *solutions* based on analysis of collected data.
- *Implement* an action plan based on findings.
- *Evaluate* and assess results.

Use the five-step IOSIE outline described, and prepare an action research project based on any problem(s) you are facing in your classroom. (If you are not currently teaching, be creative and develop a situation you can research using the action research outline.)

purported to measure—what the children should learn, and the criteria to measure it.

Effective teachers emanate an aura of interest, humor, and enthusiasm that motivates and involves. Their behaviors reflect empathy and sensitivity to student needs and interests. Classrooms organized to facilitate learning involve students in planning, and accommodate different learning styles are common among successful teachers. They also teach in a logical sequential fashion and ask thought-provoking questions. They never lose poise and direction because they have mastered the management strategies necessary to deal with deviant student behavior (Hasenstab, 2005).

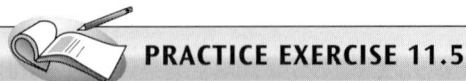

PRACTICE EXERCISE 11.5

Behaviors and Common Qualities

The purpose of this exercise is for you to reflect on the qualities that lead to effective teaching. Think back to your former teachers and write a few lines explaining how they achieved the bulleted criteria.

- Good instructors
- Good classroom-management skills
- Teach for mastery
- Positive expectations for student success
- Assess students for mastery

Figure 11.6 Effective Behaviors

- Emanate an aura of interest and enthusiasm.
- Use humor and storytelling to motivate and involve.
- Evidence empathy and sensitivity to student needs and interests.
- Master questioning techniques that allow for clearly stated questions and statements.
- Organize classrooms to encourage learning.
- Teach in a logical sequential fashion, asking thought-provoking questions.
- Vary lesson formats to accommodate and illustrate concrete and abstract concepts.
- Involve students in planning and achieving group goals.
- Master classroom management strategies to deal with deviant behavior while never losing poise and direction.

Source: Hasenstab (2005)

Effective teachers become professional educators who share common qualities and a vision of learning. They emanate enthusiasm that encourages high student collaboration and productivity. Because effective teachers are internally motivated learners themselves, they are able to share and model the joys of learning with students. Modeling lifelong learning is a hollow concept unless teachers create learning communities that engage in meaningful activities. Students in such environments model behaviors of respected teachers. Teachers should model behaviors that call for

- *Practical applications.* Teachers should share ideas and display the practices that guided their own learning and development.
- *Collaboration.* Teachers should encourage collaborative activities for students.
- *High productivity.* Teachers should continually call for increased output from students.
- *Community.* Teachers should promote positive peer relationships that create a sound learning environment.

Assessing Teacher Competence

There are basic areas of competence that effective teachers all master. Each requires a commitment and self-confidence. By reinforcing positive behaviors and highlighting content mastery, teachers make learning possible. By changing our focus from coverage of curriculum to student learning, we create a paradigm for true student accomplishment. Good management, lessons designed for mastery, effective assignments, and accurate assessments are the qualities that fuel success. Teacher competence can be measured qualitatively and quantitatively by student achievement. Competence may be evidenced differently from teacher to teacher, but student success, the result, cannot. Teacher competence results in student learning. Competent teachers

- Foster learning by encouraging *positive attitudes and relationships.*
- *Master a knowledge of subject matter* until it is part of their being.
- *Understand developmental stages* as the psychological basis for student development.
- *Master presentation skills* in order to facilitate student learning.

Characteristics of the Professional Educator

The goal of teaching is to facilitate learning. The goal of the teacher is to become a professional educator, effective teacher, and validated change agent. These terms—professional, effective, and validated—in this context are used synonymously. This goal can be achieved by aggres-

PRACTICE EXERCISE 11.6

Identifying Effective Teacher Behaviors

Review the preceding sections on qualities and behaviors of effective teachers. Then read the following list of student episodes and identify the actions an effective teacher would take. Give an example that supports your position.

1. Students are seated in rows, and are constantly turning around to speak to their neighbors. This causes a great deal of disruption during teacher instructional time.
2. Students are often not on task. They tend to be distracted by minor noises during class discussions.
3. During a classroom sharing session a strange noise sounding like flatulence is heard, which disrupts the class learning.
4. Students claim they do not understand your assignments.
5. Students complain that your marking procedures are unfair and causing them to fail.

---

sive professional development that focuses on improving teacher performance. One generally becomes a professional when one secures a position that offers good pay, decision-making authority, and a respected status. Teaching, though called a profession, has rarely been considered a well-paid position, even though it offers opportunities for decision making and status. Four criteria shape the traditional view of a profession: remuneration, social status, autonomous or authoritative power, and service (Pratte and Rury, 1991). It should be noted that there is a clear distinction between professionalization and professionalism.

- *Professionalization* is the process by which an occupation becomes a profession.
- *Professionalism* describes the quality of practice expected in that profession. Effective teaching needs both professionalism and professionalization.

A professional educator has a personality that leaves no doubt about his or her effectiveness in the classroom. There are four basic characteristics shared by all professionals.

1. **Learning.** Professional educators are lifetime learners, who read the professional journals and keep current on the latest techniques and strategies, while expanding on their content mastery at every opportunity. They are constantly learning and mastering content, while being open to new and creative teaching methods.

2. *Acquires information.* They look to all sources—books, technology, professional dialogues—to improve upon their understanding of effective management and methodology.
3. *Wants to improve.* Professional educators want to improve, and also want others to improve. They are empathetic to student needs. They want to share their knowledge, and they have high expectations that their students will be successful and surpass them.
4. *Takes responsibility.* Professional educators are, most of all, sincere, and they have personalities that allow them to take complete responsibility for their actions. They do not look to find fault, but solutions.

Design Principles of Professional Development

A path has been designed for becoming an effective teacher; it is acquired through experience and reinforced by professional development. Quality teaching

PRACTICE EXERCISE 11.7

Keys to Becoming an Effective Teacher

Review the characteristics essential to becoming an effective teacher. Look at the keys to effective teaching discussed in Chapter 1.

1. Write a brief paragraph explaining how a truly effective teacher integrates practice (the characteristics) with the theory (the keys).
2. Read the three following statements about professionalism. Review the research base and discuss whether these comments are relevant today.

   - Since there is no codified knowledge base for teaching, some would find it difficult to call it a profession. A major characteristic missing is the presence of a *collegium*, a governing group in which each member has approximately equal power (Goodlad, 1990).
   - What is needed is an agreed-upon set of standards of professional practice shaped by practitioners. Until teaching is viewed as closer to parenting than to debating in a courtroom, selection of standards will remain an open question (Hammond, 2005).
   - Like other professionals, teachers cannot become effective by following scripts; they need to create knowledge in the classroom. Teaching is not a set of teacher guides but interaction between student and teacher. From this interaction, learning evolves (Sergiovanni, 1997).

emanates from validated teachers and is the most powerful influence on student learning. Good professional development is used to support quality teaching by aligning it with the content and skills needed for student achievement. Figure 11.7 describes nine design principles for learner-centered professional development.

Professional Development Models

Professional development proponents believe development occurs best in professional development schools (PDS) formed through collaborations between school districts, colleges, and teachers' unions. The idea is that practitioners, researchers, and clinical faculty working together will expand the knowledge base of teaching while preparing for future teachers. Those who support this view rely on the medical model of professionalism. They expect schools to provide practical experience for beginning teachers in much the same way as teaching hospitals provide it for beginning physicians.

Five basic staff development models that can be used by entire staffs or by individuals are outlined here. At the core of each model is the idea of parity in collaboration.

1. The *Coursework model* is developed at the university level to support specific education plans or programs. This model is similar to one in which a teacher develops a plan and imposes it on a class. The coursework model focuses on behavioral principles and relies on data-based decision making. The model is as good as the instructor.
2. The *Half-Day Professional Development* model creates programs in which small groups are released periodically during the school day for half-day group meetings. The actual materials can be developed by the group itself or by outside consultants. Teachers could utilize the same concept with lunchtime meeting with their classes or groups to decide on personal or academic objectives to be reached within a specific period.
3. The *Institute model* offers participants intensive learning experiences joining theory and practice to achieve effective instructional practices. These models are provided by organizations and focus on meeting the needs of individual teachers, schools, and school districts. Support is given both on site and off. The key is to decide on the types of outside assistance necessary to help improve classroom instruction. The model is basically a diagnostic prescriptive clinical approach that uses consultants to diagnose problems and provide solutions.
4. The *Collaborative Mentor/Coaching model* provides participants with ongoing feedback and consultation on mutually identified areas in need of enhancement. The strategy can be included in any model that focuses on individual support. Coaching is an effective tool that offers immediate results. Consultation is usually described as a voluntary process in which one person assists another in addressing an identified problem related to the other or a third party. The advisor designs the services to be rendered in conjunction with the consulted.
5. *Participatory school-based inquiry projects* provide a model of research conducted by school practitioners in collaboration with outside researchers. School-based research means that the staff or a significant group of teachers has identified questions that they want to explore. This concept can include project-based learning within the classroom. School-based research is uniquely suited to practitioners because it allows teachers, not outside experts, to ask and answer questions about what is happening in their classrooms and schools (Barnes, 2000). This school team model is an effective way to achieve col-

Figure 11.7 Principles of Professional Development

1. The content of professional development should focus on what students are to learn and how to address the problems students may have in learning that material.
2. Professional development should be driven by analyses of the differences between (a) goals and standards for student learning and (b) student performance.
3. Teachers should identify what they need to learn and how they wish to learn it for professional development to work.
4. Professional development should be primarily school based.
5. It should provide learning opportunities that relate to individual needs.
6. It should be continuous and ongoing, involving follow-up and support from sources external to the school that can provide necessary resources and outside perspectives.
7. It should incorporate evaluation of multiple sources of information on outcomes for students and processes that are involved in implementing the lesson learned through professional development.
8. It should provide opportunities to engage in developing a theoretical understanding of the knowledge and skills to be learned.
9. Professional development should be integrated with a comprehensive change process that addresses impediments to student learning.

Source: Hawley and Valli (2000)

Figure 11.8 Stages of Team Development

1. *Forming.* Members of a team form and examine the task to be completed.
2. *Storming.* Members resolve leadership issues, procedures, and goals.
3. *Norming.* Teams establish and define role relationships and procedures for completing the task.
4. *Performing.* Work toward completing tasks.
5. *Adjourning.* Completed task allows teams to disband.

Source: Truckman and Jensen (1977)

laboration. Teams can engage in a myriad of decision-making activities, such as addressing questions of curriculum, school image, governance, professional development, and resource management. Teams can also function with individual grades or classes. A school team is defined as a group of individuals from different disciplines who contribute their unique skills in pursuit of their common goal of cooperatively solving a problem (Pfeiffer, 1981). Figure 11.8 outlines specific stages involved in school team formation.

Professional development models in education have traditionally focused on top-down solutions to problems ignoring collaboration. A synthesis of these models indicates that collaboration offers the most hope for professional development. It is not a synonym for consultation but an entirely different entity. True collaboration is a direct interaction between coequal parties, who voluntarily share in making decisions regarding a common goal (Friend and Cook, 2000). These five basic models stem from business applications as well as education. With various modifications, these development strategies are applicable for classroom use. They essentially are guides to professional development that leads to an effective, validated, professional teacher.

MINI CASE FROM THE FIELD

The following case from the field reflects the relationship between student teaching and becoming an effective teacher. Read the study and decide which of the organizational strategies discussed will better prepare preservice teachers to become effective teachers. Compare Dr. Conley's plan to the strategies and methods proposed by the faculty. View the ideas presented from the perspective of everyday classroom life.

A Professional Student Teaching Model

Dr. Conley was delivering his keynote address at the annual summer district retreat. Present were the entire district staff. Dr. Conley was discussing the establishment of Professional Development Schools (PDSs) that could provide for effective professional training. He evidenced its need by citing a survey that found preservice teachers had little subject matter or pedagogical preparation. There seemed to be a disconnect between theory and practice. Preservice teachers, he found, had inadequate opportunities for classroom experience, an overwhelming obstacle to developing effective teachers. He reasoned that low college admission standards and eight weeks of field experience were inadequate preparation. He felt that the push for certified teachers led to a lowering of standards for the profession. He asked, "Who in this audience believes that two hundred hours of instruction over a summer prepares one for the classroom?" (Koppich, 1999).

"I want to change our district's factory model approach that leads to state prescriptions and standardization. I want students to make a lifelong commitment to learning. We need to develop a turnkey model in which tenured teachers become leaders in preparing new teachers. Teacher education should be a shared responsibility between teachers, schools, and universities. I propose a program in which everyone works collaboratively—schools, mentor teachers, and clinical faculty. Each shares the responsibility for developing effective teachers." Dr. Conley had distributed copies of his plan to the faculty, outlining the specific steps. The specific steps are as follows:

Schools

1. Our school district designates the McGraw Comprehensive K–12 School as a Professional Development School to partner with our local university.
2. The University will provide student teachers prepared to go into classrooms. It will also provide in-school staff development to nontenured teachers, as well as provide assistance in grant writing to fund the program.
3. Our Professional Development School will assume responsibility with the University for the preparation of new teachers. It will also provide master teachers as mentors.

Mentors

1. Classroom teachers are asked to volunteer to be mentors. The University will appoint the mentors as unpaid adjuncts who will receive compensation from the district.
2. All courses will be in the hands of school mentors. All methods courses will be taught on the school site

by mentors. Courses such as Teaching Elementary Mathematics or Social Studies will be taught as part of our student teaching program.

Clinical Faculty

University-based teacher education supervisors (clinical faculty) will be required to spend half of their time actively supervising in schools. The rest will be spent teaching, writing, and researching. Tenured clinical faculty will

1. Provide workshops for student teachers and non-tenured staff.
2. Write and assist in grant writing for school-based reform efforts.
3. Grade all student practicums.

"The University and Principal Thompson have already agreed to participate in the program, and have made binding commitments. I am asking for a final commitment from you, our faculty members. That commitment should be in the form of your applying to be a mentor teacher for next term."

Nick Saccone turned to Ed Child and said, "I like the idea of being a mentor." Ed agreed, saying the superintendent's plan seemed simple enough. "All that's needed is a committee of teachers with their union representative to iron out the actual compensation." Nick added that a period of training is necessary if the program is to be successful. Ed said, "Couldn't that be done by the clinical faculty?"

"Both of you are on the wrong track," said Jane Hemmings. "This could never work. Who would cover our classes while we helped the student teachers? Would we get free preparation time? We should keep the program the way it has been in our district. A sink or swim strategy has always been the most effective way to train new teachers."

Then Lucille Chan said, "I can't believe what I'm hearing. Don't you feel an obligation to help new teachers succeed? Haven't we been talking all year about the problems we face? I don't recall anyone refusing to help. I, for one, will support the program because it really is needed."

Margaret Gomez said quietly, "Lucille's right. If it weren't for you guys helping me this year, I don't know how I would have survived."

1. What questions have to be addressed for Dr. Conley's plan to work?
2. Describe your reaction to Lucille's statement that she had an obligation to help new teachers.
3. Analyze Jane Hemmings's position. Is her belief that the best way to learn to teach is to *do it unsupervised* realistic?
4. Prepare two lists that address the following:
    - As a perspective teacher, what type of help would you expect?
    - As a teacher mentor, what type of assistance will you provide?
5. Review Dr. Conley's plan and develop an outline for an action research project to address the topic of an effective student teaching and professional development program.

PREPARATION FOR A JOB INTERVIEW

The final focus of this book will be preparation for employment. One cannot become an effective teacher without a position. First, let's address a myth that has been perpetuated over the years that there are more applicants than available teaching positions. That statement is not necessarily true. The pendulum for positions swings from year to year, and community to community. Rest assured, parents and communities will always seek the best teachers for their children. Presenting oneself in the best light during a short interview is vital to securing any position. Certain characteristics set apart a teacher interview from a general business interview. A teacher interviewer is looking for diplomacy, poise, and most of all, teaching personality. Interviewers will also be concerned with mastery of content, classroom management, instructional methods, and one's expectations for children.

Preparing for tough interview questions takes some anticipation on your part. A candidate who prepares for questions in advance will present something tangible for the interviewer to evaluate. Keep in mind that whatever you prepare must convey a positive image and illustration of the strengths you possess.

Typical Interview Format

Each interview is a unique event; because interviewers are different, so are the types of interviews they conduct. Some interviewers are skilled at interviewing; others are not. Some are talkative; others let you do most of the talking. Most interviews, however, will range from open-ended, in which the interviewer asks questions and lets you do most of the talking, to the highly structured, in which the interviewer asks many specific questions following a planned format. Many interviews fall between these extremes; you should be prepared for any style. Four basic stages occur in a typical interview:

1. ***Introductory stage.*** The interviewer establishes rapport and attempts to create a relaxed businesslike atmosphere. A first impression is created at this stage.

2. ***Background and interests stage.*** The questions asked at this stage establish your qualifications for the position sought. Questions will be based on the four "W's"—*what, why, where,* and *when.* What special skills do you have, and what have you accomplished? Why do you want to teach here? Where did you go to school? When are you able to start? One of the interviewer's objectives is to see if your qualifications match your work interests. Give concise but thorough responses to questions.
3. ***Qualifications and matching stage.*** The interviewer wants to match your qualifications and interests to the available opening. If there seems to be a match, the interviewer will probably explain job details to see how interested you are in the position.
4. ***Conclusion.*** The final step for the interviewer is to explain the specific hiring process. You will be given an opportunity to make a final statement supporting your candidacy. Convey a positive image by replying promptly with any appropriate additional information. The interviewer may ask if you have any questions. If you have little experience, inquire about the availability of a master or mentor teacher. This demonstrates that you're seeking guidance and you are interested in developing as a professional. End on a positive note and thank the interviewer for her time.

Preparation Guide

1. Spend at least three hours preparing for each interview.
2. Wear suitable interview clothes.
3. Take copies of your resumé. Your answer to the initial opening statements—the "ice breakers"—in the job interview are important.
4. Arrive on time. Have a firm handshake.
5. Look alert and interested. Scan the room once and keep your eyes on the interviewer.
6. Wait until offered a chair before you sit down.
7. Stress your achievements.
8. Always conduct yourself professionally and if something beyond your control occurs, show a sense of humor.
9. Be enthusiastic and show it in your replies and body language.
10. Answer questions with more than a simple yes or no, but try not to go over one minute.

Common Questions

- *Why should we hire you?* Briefly and succinctly, lay out your strengths and qualifications. Set yourself apart by telling the interviewer about your unique qualities.
- *Why do you want to work at our school?* This is one tool interviewers use to see if you have done your homework. Never attend an interview unless you know about the school, its direction and goals.
- *What are your greatest weaknesses?* Be honest about your weaknesses, but explain how you have turned it (them) into strengths. If you had a problem with organization explain the steps, you took to improve your skills.
- *Describe a problem situation that you solved.* Sometimes it is hard to come up with a response to this request. Interviewers want to see that you can think critically and develop solutions, regardless of experience.
- *Of what accomplishment are you most proud?* Be specific and select an accomplishment that relates to the position. Think of the needs the school is looking to fulfill and demonstrate how you meet those needs.
- *Tell me about yourself.* This query is difficult to answer because it is so broad. Answer from a professional perspective. Pick professional experiences and your career goals: Stick to those points. Wrap up your answer by bringing up your desire to be a part of the school.

PRACTICE EXERCISE 11.8

Sample Interview Questions

Reflect on each of the following questions and prepare a brief response that you can share for evaluation with your classmates.

1. What is your approach to handling behavior problems? (For example, a child who does not meet a deadline.)
2. How would you analyze your own teaching performance?
3. How would you implement an equal opportunities policy with regard to boys and girls?
4. If a student said she thought you were the worst teacher she ever had, what would you say?
5. What is the last book you read?
6. How do you handle a child who seems gifted but is a discipline problem?
7. What is your student teaching experience?
8. How do you handle noise in the classroom?
9. What is your educational philosophy?
10. It is the first day of class, you are writing something on the board, and a paper wad hits you in the back. What would you do?

PRACTICE EXERCISE 11.9

Preparing for a Job Interview

Before your interview you should prepare a general list of talking points that you use to structure your presentation. The typical format for an interview consists of four parts—an introduction, a background check of qualifications, reasons for seeking the position, and finally, a question from the interviewer that requires you to explain why you should be hired. Following is an application form for a position as elementary, middle school, and high school teacher in your specific subject area. Complete the application form and prepare for your interview. Students can role-play using the assessment scale to provide feedback.

Application Form

Name _____

Address _____

Applicant for position of _____

Qualifications:

- License _____
- Colleges attended and dates of degrees _____
- Prior experience _____

Why are you seeking a position at the McGraw K–12 Comprehensive School?

- How would you rate your *mastery of content* for the position you seek?
- How would you handle *classroom management* when it's related to poor behavior?
- What type of *instructional methods* can we expect you to employ at our school?
- Describe your *expectations* for your students.
- What do you bring to the McGraw School that makes you stand out?

Assessment Scale for Job Interview

Volunteers will be asked to role-play a mock job interview. Each member of the class will evaluate the interview based on the assessment scale. The actual interviewer (class instructor or guest) will rate the interview on the following items (5 = Superior, 4 = Above Average, 3 = Satisfactory, 1 = unsatisfactory). At the conclusion of the interview, the class led by the instructor will discuss positive and negative aspects of the role-play.

	Rating
1. Applicant introduced self appropriately.	_____
2. Position sought was clear.	_____
3. Presentation was logically organized.	_____
4. Explanation of qualifications for position was clear.	_____
5. Applicant indicated understanding and enthusiasm.	_____
6. Applicant's educational philosophy was clear and concise.	_____
7. Applicant stressed achievement.	_____
8. Applicant used pauses and proper body language.	_____
9. Applicant was professional.	_____
10. Applicant concluded interview on a positive note.	_____

Points Scored _____
(Maximum is 50)

Interviewer's Comments

Interview Assessment

Various indicators can assist in evaluating your performance and chances for selection for the position. Following are clues to help you decode the interview.

1. *How did you interact with the interviewer?* A give-and-take dialogue indicates a solid performance. If the interviewer is just reading questions automatically, you may not be making a solid impression.
2. *Listen for positive verbal clues, while watching for physical clues.* A good indication is when the interviewer asks for further elaboration. A bad indicator is if the interviewer looks bored. To get back on track ask if you are answering the question. Subtle clues are in a person's body language. If an interviewer has a positive impression, she may nod her head or lean toward you, or smile. An encouraging indication is noted in a posture as that conveys interest in what you have to say. The reverse is true if an interviewer rushes the interview and is not taking notes.
3. *Time your responses.* Keep all your answers to less than one minute. Long-winded responses turn off interviewers. Be yourself. When interviewers give you the opportunity to ask questions, this is your cue to ask questions that establish a rapport by demonstrating that you have done your homework with regard to the school.
4. *Availability and position match.* If asked how soon you can start, be honest and give the soonest date available. If the interviewer asks how you will fit in, answer enthusiastically that you are very excited about working at such a wonderful school with such a professional staff. If you know someone at the school be sure to mention it.
5. *Length of the interview.* Interviewers normally decide within the first few minutes if they are interested in your candidacy. The rest of the time is spent validating their initial opinions. If an interview takes less than a half hour, you have not engaged the interviewer. If your conversation is flowing and the enthusiasm is evenly shared between you and the interviewer, you may have scored a touchdown and be on the road to becoming an effective teacher.

Chapter Summary

In this chapter, we began with an analysis of what is a validated change agent, and concluded with preparation for a job interview. A model for educational change through teacher empowerment was discussed as a focal point for effective teaching. A new basic change model was proposed as a way to meet the instructional needs of all children. Teachers were encouraged to look at the model based on five key elements—methods, management of behavior and budgets, mastery of content, expectations, and teaching personality.

Personality and handling social situations are crucial to the effective professional teacher. Personality is the key that unlocks the door, opening the vista of academic excellence for students. An effective teacher must demonstrate a sense of efficacy, doing a job, no matter how difficult or demanding. Professional competence and self-determination leads to self-actualization and fulfillment. Rarely has personality been considered an essential element of effective teaching, let alone the key determinant. Yet it is a clear determinant to success. Different personality types can be effective teachers because they share common core characteristics—caring and hard work.

Who we are matters as much as what we know, and how we teach it (Banner, 1997). Teaching is made up of more than just knowledge, pedagogy, and method. Character and personality, qualities inherent in all of us, is the paint that makes teaching an art rather than a science. The implements of the artist—paint, brush, and canvas—do not alone make a picture, and knowledge of content and method do not make a teacher; personality and hard work does. Your personal characteristics and values combined with the knowledge and method of teaching make for effectiveness. The keys to effective teaching (management methods, mastery, expectations, and personality) are your passport to becoming a successful and effective teacher.

Cases from the Field

CASE ONE

Mr. Gades, the principal of the Midtown Elementary School, had come to an impasse with the faculty steering committee. Thomas Gades had been a proponent of teacher empowerment as a tool to educational change and improved student learning. The program had worked well for the first three years when enthusiasm was high and objectives were being developed. Now teachers just saw the term teacher empowerment as a way to get more for teachers with regard to pay increases, vacation time, and less time on staff development. Mr. Gades was on the verge of dropping the empowerment program and going back to a top-down type of organization.

1. How could the teacher's arguments regarding, pay, time, and professional staff development be resolved?
2. Could any school or school district ever agree to resolve those issues?
3. What would happen if those issues were resolved?
4. Are there any other issues that could stop teacher empowerment from succeeding? Include your definition of empowerment in your response.
5. Do you think there is a causal relationship between teacher empowerment and improved student outcomes?

CASE TWO

Caroline Kelly believed strongly that personality and reaction to the social situations determined teacher effectiveness. Her colleagues told her and she must be kidding. The only thing that mattered, they claimed, was whether you could teach an effective lesson and whether your students learned. Caroline said she had never negated practice or outcomes, but insisted that neither would be improved in a class where the instructor did not have a teaching personality.

1. Why do you think Caroline's colleagues did not see personality as a factor?
2. Was Caroline's retort effective in carrying her argument?
3. How could Caroline have expanded upon the keys to effective teaching?
4. Which of the five keys do you consider the most important? Why?
5. Do you feel that an effective teaching personality is the prime factor to be considered when evaluating whether a teacher is effective or not? Why?

CASE THREE

Jiana was a student teacher in Mrs. Holland's mathematics class. As a student Jiana was very reflective and a keen observer. She noticed that the students in Mrs. Holland's classes ran the gamut from highly motivated to those with a total lack of interest in mathematics. Jiana discussed her observations with Mrs. Holland and asked her permission to talk to a sample group of students to hear their views regarding mathematics. The students met as a focus group with Jiana and were very anxious to discuss their feelings. They all said they hated learning mathematics. Their reasons included, "I hate math," "I hate this class because the teacher stinks," "Mrs. Holland tries but I don't understand anything she says," "She has a terrible personality."

1. How should Jiana handle the information she has accumulated?
2. How do you think Mrs. Holland would react if she knew how the students felt?
3. Describe some suggestions that Jiana could make.
4. Should Jiana tell Mrs. Holland that the students did not respond to her personality?
5. Could Mrs. Holland do anything to make herself a more effective teacher?

CASE FOUR

Nicoletta was a sweet young woman with a pleasant disposition. She wanted to be a good teacher, one who was loved and respected by her students. She realized that as a new teacher she could not please everyone. Nicoletta was doing fine until Amos was placed in her fourth-grade class. Amos did not fit into the traditional class structure that Nicoletta had established. Nicoletta spoke to her colleagues who suggested she give thought to differentiating or individualizing instruction. They also felt she did not make enough use of technology.

1. Were the suggestions made to Nicoletta realistic? Why?
2. How could one student cause so much turmoil in Nicoletta's class?
3. Should Amos be directed to fit into the class or should a special program be constructed for Amos?
4. How could the class become part of the solution?
5. What would you do if you were Nicoletta?

Terms to Remember

Effective teacher
Components of comprehensive school reform
Teacher empowerment
Alternative teacher assessment
Professional educator
Professional development models

Discussion Questions

1. Would the agenda for change described in this chapter be effective? Ineffective? Give reasons to support your arguments.
2. Is a return to the traditional K–8 a viable alternative? Why?
3. Reflect and discuss your opinion with regard to the following concept. "Teacher empowerment leads to improved student learning outcome." Support your position using facts, reasons, and examples from your experience.
4. Which would you prefer, an observation by a supervisor or an alternative teacher assessment as described in this chapter. Why?
5. Review the nine case studies on empowerment and categorize them into three categories: easy to replicate, difficult to replicate, could not be replicated. Give your reasons for each of your choices.
6. Explain the idea of a validated change agent. Is it realistic?
7. What do preservice teachers need to master before they can function effectively in a classroom?
8. List the characteristics of the ideal teaching position.

Field Experience Activities

1. Visit a school or district's central office. Interview an official and ask the following questions:
   - What is the vision or mission of this school or district?
   - How is the school/district's curricula organized with regard to core subjects and assessments?
   - Ask the official to evaluate the climate for learning. What are class sizes, types of teaching schedules, and available support services?
   - How are core values taught? Is there is a specific character education program?

   After obtaining this information, compare and contrast it to your own views.
2. Interview two teachers and ask them whether they would prefer a formal supervisory observation or an alternative type of assessment based on an evaluation of their work output. Compare and contrast their responses to your responses given to discussion question number four.

For Further Reading

American Educational Research Association. (2005). Teaching teachers: Professional development to improve student achievement. *Research Points, Essential Information for Educational Policy* 3(1): 1–4.

Boyer, E. (1995). *The basic school: A community for learning.* New York: Carnegie Foundation.

Brophy, J. E., and Good, T. L. (1986). Teacher behavior and student achievement. In *Handbook of Research on Teaching,* 3rd ed., ed. M. C. Wittrock, 328–375. New York: Macmillan.

Chall, J. (2000). *The academic achievement challenge.* New York: Guilford Press.

Coalition of Essential Schools. Publisher, 564 Eddy St., Suite 248, Oakland, CA.

Darling-Hammond, L. (1992). Teaching and knowledge: Policy issues posed by alternative certification for teachers. *Peabody Journal of Education* 67(3): 123–154.

Glanz, J. (2003). *Action research: An educational leader's guide to school improvement,* 2nd ed. Norwood, MA: Christopher-Gordon.

Moore, D. W. (1983). Reading achievement, attitude toward school, self-esteem, perception of teachers, pupil control behavior, and school attendance of seventh and eighth-grade students in K–8 and junior high school. Ed.D dissertation, St. John's University.

National Staff Development Council. (2001). *Standards for staff development,* rev. ed. Oxford, OH: Author.

Pearson Achievement Solutions. (2007). Transforming the culture of teaching. Retrieved at www.personachievementsolutions.com/abouttransforming.cfm.

Sergiovanni, T. J., and Moore, J. (1990). *Target 2000: A compact for excellence in Texas schools.* San Antonio, TX: Watercress Press.

GLOSSARY

Accelerated learning A method that advocates the use of brain theory to enhance learning.

Adequate yearly progress (AYP) Used to track the success of Title I schools and districts in improving student achievement. The promise is that each student will experience one year's growth for each year of instruction.

Affective domain Involves a person's feelings, interests, and attitudes, while being also concerned for values that allow for the classification of objectives with regard to emotional responses.

Aims Broad statements for specific topics that suggest very general outcomes.

Anticipatory set A strategy used at the beginning of a lesson that prepares and engages students for learning. The best strategies link prior knowledge with new information. This technique is also known as set induction.

Assertive discipline A management model developed by Lee Conter. It uses consequences as a control to eliminate misbehavior.

Assessment The process of collecting data about students, classes, schools, and districts for making immediate or long-term instructional decisions. Its purpose is to evaluate ongoing student performance by using various means of measurement, teacher-made tests, standardized tests, observations, portfolios, and student performances.

Assertive discipline A discipline model that focuses on assertive disciplinary techniques that provide consequences for misbehavior.

Attention Deficit Disorder (ADD) A genetic attention disorder that should be called ADHD.

Attention Deficit Hyperactivity Disorder (ADHD) A diagnosis applied to children and adults who show signs of distractibility, impulsivity, and hyperactivity. Must meet the criteria behaviors as measured according to the *Diagnostic and Statistical Manual of Mental Disorders*.

Authentic assessments Practices that allow students to demonstrate their abilities by performance, portfolio, or project related to a genuine life experience.

Backward design An approach to assessment and planning in which the expected understanding or outcome is first determined, then a strategy is designed to lead to it.

Balanced literacy A combination of skills-based and meaning-based approaches to reading. Children are taught the relationship between letters and sounds in a systematic fashion while reading and writing interesting stories.

Basal reading A reading program made up of comprehensive instructional materials that stress phonics to varying degrees. Basal programs contain stories scripted to deal with specific skills.

Behavioral model A basic theoretical behavior management theory that proposes that one's behavior can be influenced by external stimuli.

Behaviorism This view of teaching advocates a transmission model where students respond to stimuli presented by the teacher. It equates learning with changes in the student's behavior.

Benchmarking A process used to evaluate performance in relationship to established best practices. It also assists in establishing measuring points on the road to achievement.

Best practices A term used to refer to educational methods that have been found to deliver the best results determined by research.

Brain laterality A supposition that one side of the human brain dominates over the other; for example, the right for creativity and the left for linear analysis.

Child-centered Classroom environments that focus on student needs, in which students participate in planning and decision making.

Choice theory A management model by William Glasser; the theory claims that we are genetically programmed for specific psychological needs, such as love, belonging, fun, and freedom. It claims that no misbehavior will occur when a student's genetic psychological needs are met.

Classroom management skills The organizational skills that teachers must develop in order to manage, and understand, student behavioral and instructional problems so that learning and positive social interaction can occur.

Cognitive domain The area of learning that involves knowledge and development of intellectual skills, such as information processing, thinking, and memorization.

Constructivism A view of teaching that advances the belief that knowledge occurs in a social and cultural context that requires an inquiry approach or problem-solving approach to learning. The learner constructs meaning from experience while interacting with others.

Constructivist lesson design Concerned with physical, symbolic, social, and theoretical construction of knowledge, it applies the principles of constructivism to creating learning lessons.

Constructivist model A basic theoretical rationale for behavior management that stems from the work of Piaget. It assumes that each person constructs knowledge. It also maintains that behavior can be influenced by mutually agreed upon codes of conduct.

Cooperative learning A small group instructional approach that holds students accountable for group and individual products.

Criterion-referenced test A test that assesses a student's performance against a preset standard.

Critical thinking The art of taking charge of one's mind by identifying problems, proposing solutions based on available data, and then assessing results.

Curriculum Refers to what is planned by teachers for students to learn and what is actually being taught. It is essentially the interaction between student and teacher.

Curriculum compacting A technique used to provide time for enrichment by modifying the regular curriculum by eliminating repetition.

Curriculum spiraling/spiral curriculum A curriculum that revisits the same topics to reinforce and build on what has already been learned.

Deductive reasoning The type of reasoning that starts with general principles as premises that lead to particular information. It is used in planning lessons when learning proceeds from specific to general concepts.

Direct instruction A teacher-centered approach focusing on structured, goal-oriented lessons delivered sequentially.

Direct Reading Lesson (DRL) An approach to reading comprehension that consists of five basic procedures: preparation for reading, silent reading, discussion, rereading, and follow-up.

Discovery method An approach to teaching that encourages student problem solving in order to comprehend concepts and principles. When it is teacher-centered, it is called *guided discovery*.

Discussion A teaching approach that is based on verbal interactions between teacher and student.

Diversity Referring to people of different ethnic, religious, and cultural backgrounds that exist in society and schools.

Domain knowledge A learner constructs new knowledge based on past experiences. This is from Piaget and has been expounded on by Hursch.

Downshifting A psychological–physiological response to threat associated with helplessness or fatigue. It is a return to prior behaviors.

Dyslexia A learning disorder that is characterized by the failure to attain adequate reading skills; neurological in origin.

Effective teacher A teacher whose students learn curriculum, content, skills, and develop wholesome democratic attitudes; can usually be defined by their students' success.

Emotional intelligence An outgrowth of multiple intelligences theory, it is the ability to be empathetic and understand others' personal needs. It enhances the relevance of inter- and intrapersonal intelligences.

Environmental model A basic theoretical behavior management theory that claims the way one lives one's life and the environment in which one lives influences behavior.

Essentialism A philosophy of education that views its purpose as the transmission of society's heritage and culture. It advances a strenuous basic paper-and-pencil curriculum.

Eurythmy The art of movement associated with the Waldorf School Method.

Existentialism A philosophy based on humanism and self-actualization in which the individual determines meaning. It has a root relationship to constructivism.

Expository A teacher-centered direct instructional approach, also known as didactic, or traditional teaching.

Functional behavioral assessment A comprehensive assessment process that attempts to identify the specific factors that are contributing to a student's misbehavior.

Gender-specific teaching The teaching of literacy focused on a specific gender; usually associated with single-sex education.

Ginott model A discipline model that uses individual guidance techniques to improve behavior and instruction. It utilizes interpersonal communication methods to encourage humanitarian classroom environments.

Glass analysis A skill-based phonics strategy for teaching reading that does not rely on rote memorization of phonic rules. Developed by Gerald G. and Esther Glass in 1970.

Goal A broad instructional outcome that stems from a particular learning experience. It can be related to a specific course or teacher expectation.

Gough's model A sequential processing approach to reading characterized as a letter-by-letter progression through text, with letter-sound identification that forms words, and finally meaning. The model is the basis of most phonics approaches to reading.

Grouping *Ability grouping* is the placement of students in classes according to their academic ability. *Homogeneous grouping* places children in classes based on intelligence, ability, or achievement. *Heterogeneous grouping* is the placement of children in classes without regard to academic ability or achievement.

Growth model approach An assessment procedure that measures individual student growth over time.

Guided discovery Also known as guided practice, children are given problems and encouraged to resolve them with the assistance of the teacher.

Hemisphericity A highly controversial theory, similar to brain laterality. It presupposes where mental functions occur in the brain. Humans rely on a mode of cognitive processing linked to their left or right cerebral hemisphere.

Inclusion The placement of children with physical and learning disabilities into mainstream classrooms (also known as *mainstreaming*).

Indirect instruction A student-centered instructional approach focusing on student inquiry and problem-solving skills.

Individualized educational program (IEP) An individual prescription identifying the needs of a student with disabilities, which specifically defines special education services and their goals and objectives.

Individuals with Disabilities in Education ACT (IDEA) A law enacted in 2004 that attempts to align regulations for special education children with those of the 2002 No Child Left Behind Act.

Inductive reasoning When planning a lesson, the learning moves from specific ideas or data to general concepts, rules, and principles.

Inquiry-based education An approach to teaching that encourages students' independent inquiry by asking questions based on conclusions drawn from data.

Intelligence Quotient (IQ) One's mental age (as determined by test), divided by chronological age and multiplied by 100 to arrive at a numerical IQ.

Interstate New Teacher Assessment and Support Consortium (INTASC) A consortium of state education agencies and national educational organizations created in 1987, dedicated to the reform of the preparation of teachers. Its standards reflect the requisite knowledge, skills, and attitudes necessary for beginning teachers.

IOSIE An acronym representing a five-step process for analyzing student behavior—identify, objectives, solution, implementation, and evaluation—that can be used in most education environments.

Jones model A discipline model that focuses on physical presence as a technique to improve behavior and instruction.

Judicious discipline A discipline model that uses group guidance techniques to improve behavior and instruction.

KWL An acronym used to describe a teaching strategy for reading comprehension: listing what you Know, listing what you Want to know, and describing what you Learned.

Learning disabilities (LD) A generic term referring to a group of learning disorders presumed to be caused by central nervous disorder. They are also defined as a disorder in the psychological processes involved in understanding or in using language, spoken or written.

Literate critical thinking A process by which we gain, share, and reason with information in all its forms.

Mastery learning An approach to instruction based on the idea that learning depends on the amount of time one spends on comprehension. All are capable of learning given the right amount of time for instruction. Content must be mastered before moving on to new material.

Motivation When students are told the purpose for learning a specific lesson and what they will gain by the particular learning activity, it creates motivation, a desire to learn.

Modes of thinking Various types of thinking, for example, random thoughts, reasoning, recollection, remembrance, conceptualization, critical, reflective, and creative.

Multiple intelligences A theory that claims that intelligence is the ability to solve problems and fashion products that are of consequence in a particular cultural setting. The theory advances the belief that there are seven to nine different intelligences—verbal/linguistic, body/kinesthetic, musical, logical/mathematical, naturalist, visual/spatial, interpersonal, and intrapersonal.

National Board of Professional Teaching Standards (NBPTS) Develops professional standards that teachers should know and administers the National Board Certification Test that certifies teachers as meeting standards and becoming board certified.

Norm-reference test Standardized text that allows one individual performance to be compared with others in the overall group.

Objectives Specific statements of a learner's behavior or outcomes, which state conditions of behavior, set time limits, and specify steps necessary to achieve a broader goal.

Outcome-based education A results-oriented method designed for students to retain knowledge that can be demonstrated in final outcomes.

Paideia program A classical approach to learning that claims that all can learn if provided a proper course of study for all. It stems from the work of Mortimer Adler.

Pedagogy The methods and approaches to teaching that are contained in the study of teaching.

Perennialism An educational philosophy based on the belief that the purpose of education is to develop intellectual strength and discipline of mind through a classical liberal arts education.

Performance standards Standards that describe the outcomes of what students are expected to achieve.

Progressive schools Schools that highlight a student's social development. They view their role as to prepare students for democratic citizenship and civic duties. They are child centered and advance a constructivist approach to learning.

Progressivism An experimental philosophy espousing a child-centered, rather than a content-centered, approach to learning.

Psychodynamic model A basic theoretical behavior management theory that looks inside the child and uses a guidance approach to manage behavior.

Psychomotor domain The area of learning related to physical movement, gross and fine motor skills, found in Bloom's taxonomy.

Reality therapy A method of behavior management that relies on educational counseling. It is a guidance approach, also known as responsibility training.

Reconstructionism A philosophy with a social justice perspective, which views schools as a means to change or reconstruct society.

Referral process The procedures that must be followed before any child can receive special services.

Reflection Analytical thought , in the case of teacher self-evaluation, about how your practices influence learning.

Reflective teaching Thinking about what you do and why you do it and its effects on a lesson. It is self-analytic, and allows for assessing data as well as identifying lesson strengths and weaknesses.

Reliability The degree to which a test gets consistent results over several administrations in measuring a given item.

Scientific method An approach to teaching that fosters a self-directed inquiry process that begins with identifying a problem, hypothesizing, gathering and analyzing data, and forming conclusions.

Smart classrooms Classrooms that are designed to make use of modern technology.

Socratic method Also known as a *seminar model,* the Socratic method consists of conversations with students conducted by teachers who act as leaders or moderators in collaborative, intellectual discussions regarding specific problems.

SQ4R A classic approach of six steps for teaching reading comprehension—survey, question, read, recite, record, and review.

Standards The criteria used for determining the content knowledge, skills, attitudes, and learning strategies students are to be taught in any given subject area. They usually consist of statements that explain what students should know, and should be able to do.

Standards achievement planning cycle (SAPC) An approach to developing effective standards-based planning. It consists of a synthesis of ideas associated with outcome-based education and Japanese Lesson Study. It highlights a five-step process for writing lessons to achieve standards.

Standards-based lesson A lesson aligned with standards. Included in the process is the planning, delivery, and evaluation of instruction.

Teacher empowerment Giving teachers the right to participate in developing school goals and policies, and allowing teachers to exercise their professional judgment with regard to curriculum and teaching methods. Some believe that when teachers are empowered to make educational decisions, student creativity and achievement will increase.

Teaching paradigms Referring to the purpose of teaching. The *instructional* paradigm defines the purpose of teaching as good instruction rather than student learning. The *learning* paradigm sees the purpose of teaching as student learning.

Traditional schools Teacher-centered, traditional schools are concerned with the transfer and delivery of instruction, passing on knowledge, skills, and social values.

Triune brain theory A theory developed by Paul MacLean that the brain has evolved into three distinct parts: the reptilian, the limbic, and the neocortex.

Usability A method of measuring the ease of use of testing materials. It denotes criteria for selecting types of tests, for example, to test for word comprehension as a multiple-choice vocabulary test.

Validity When a test measures what it claims to measure.

Value-added assessment A way to measure teaching and learning. It identifies student progress and determines the extent to which individual teachers and schools have contributed. It is a procedure that measures individual teachers' effectiveness, based on how well students perform over a period of time.

Visual intelligence A theory that attempts to explain how we create what we see. Intelligence according to this theory comes from one's own decision making based on sensory evidence.

Windows of opportunity Times when children are ready to learn.

REFERENCES

Able, M. H., and Sewell, J. (1999). *Stress and burnout in rural and urban secondary school teachers.* Journal of Educational Research 92 (5): 23–35.

About. (2007). About Inc., *New York Times.* Retrieved at: http://specialed.about.com/od/giftedness/a/giftedsteps.htm.

Adams, G. L., and Engelmann, S. (1996). *Research on direct instruction: 25 years beyond DISTAR.* Seattle, WA: Educational Achievement Systems.

Adler, M. J. (1982). *The Paideia proposal: An educational manifesto.* New York: Collier Books.

Adler, M. J. (1984). *The Paideia program: An educational syllabus.* New York: Macmillan.

Adler, M. J. (1988). *Reforming education.* New York: Macmillan.

Adler, R. C., ed. (2001, September). *Put reading first: The research building blocks for teaching children to read.* National Institute for Literacy, U.S. Department of Education. Partnership for Reading.

Allington, R. (2002). You can't learn much from books you can't read. *Educational Leadership* 60 (3): 16–19.

American Academy of Pediatrics. (2006). Children's health topics: ADHD. Retrieved at: www.org/helthtopics/adhd.cfm.

American Foundation for the Blind. (2005). Summary of key sections of the Individuals with Disabilities Education Improvement Act (IDEA) of 2004, Public Law 108–446. *Josephine L. Taylor Leadership Institute National Education Program.* Retrieved at: www.afb.org.

American Productivity and Quality Center. (2003). *Teacher education and preparation.* Ohio: Northeast Ohio Council of Higher Education. Retrieved April 15, 2005 at: www.Noche.org/pdfs/tep_report.pdf.

American Psychiatric Association. (1994). *Diagnostic and Statistical Manual.* 4th ed. DSM-IV. Washington, DC: American Psychiatric Press.

American Psychiatric Association. (2000). *Diagnostic and Statistical Manual.* 4th ed. Text Revision. DSM-IV-TR. Washington, DC: American Psychiatric Press.

Anderson, A., and Lynch, T. (1995). *Listening.* Hong Kong: Oxford University Press.

Andrade, A. (1999). The thinking classroom. Harvard Zero Project. Retrieved at: http://learnweb.harvard.edu/alps/thinking/ways.cfm.

Archambault, R. D. (1974). *John Dewey on education: Selected writings.* Chicago: University of Chicago Press.

Archer, J. (1999, May). Tennessee value added assessment system. *Education Week.*

Armstrong, T. (1996a, February). ADD—Does it really exist? *Phi Delta Kappan.*

Armstrong, T. (1996b). *Beyond the ADD myth: Classroom strategies and techniques.* Port Chester, NY: Professional Resources, Inc.

Aronson, E. (1987). *The jigsaw classroom.* Beverly Hills, CA: Sage Publications.

Ausubel, D. P. (1962). A subsumption theory of meaningful verbal learning and retention. *Journal of General Psychology* 66: 213–244.

Bagley, W. (1941). The case for essentialism in education. *National Education Association Journal* 30 (7): 202–220.

Bailey, E. (2006). Your guide to attention deficit disorder. *About.* Retrieved at: http://add.about.com.

Bambara, L. M., and Kern, L. (2005). *Individualization supports for students with problem behaviors.* New York: The Guilford Press.

Banks, J. (1993). Approaches to multicultural curriculum reform. In J. A. Banks and C. A. McGhee Banks (Eds.), *Multicultural education: Issues and perspectives,* 195–214. Boston: Allyn & Bacon.

Banks, J. (1993, September). Multicultural education: Development, dimensions, and challenges. *Phi Delta Kappan* 75 (1): 22–28.

Banks, J. (1997). *Teaching strategies for ethnic studies.* 6th ed. Boston: Allyn & Bacon.

Banner, J. M., Jr., and Cannon, H. (1997). *The elements of teaching.* New Haven: Yale University Press.

Banner, J. M., Jr., and Cannon, H. (1997, April 16). The who of teaching. *Education Week.*

Bar, R. B., and Tagg, J. (1995). From teaching to learning: A new paradigm for undergraduate education. *Change* 27: 6.

Barnes, N. (2000, January 19). *Teachers teaching teachers. Education Week* 38–42.

Baron, M., and Boshchee, F. (1996, April). Dispelling the myths surrounding OBE. *Phi Delta Kappan* 77 (8): 574–576.

Batesky, J. (1987, September). In-service education: Increasing teacher effectiveness using the Hunter lesson design. *Journal of Physical Education, Recreation, and Dance* 88–93.

Belkin, G. S., and Gray, J. L. (1977). *Educational psychology: An introduction.* Dubuque, IA: William C. Brown Publishers.

Benner, A. D. (2000). The cost of teacher turnover. Austin: Texas Center for Educational Research. Retrieved April 15, 2005, at: www.sbec.state.tx.us/SBEConline/ttxbess/turnoverrpt.pdf.

Beyer, B. (1995). *Critical thinking.* Bloomington, IN: Phi Delta Kappa Educational Foundation.

Biancarosa, G., and Snow, C. (2004). *Reading next: A vision for action and research in middle and high school literacy. A report to Carnegie Corporation of New York.* Washington, DC: Alliance for Excellent Education. Retrieved at: www.all4ed.org.

Block, J., and Anderson, L. (1975). *Mastery learning in classroom instruction.* New York: Macmillan.

Bloom, B. (1971). *Mastery learning and its implications for curriculum development.* In E. W. Eisner (ed.), *Confronting curriculum reform.* Boston: Little, Brown.

Bloom, B. (1976). *Human characteristics and school learning.* New York: McGraw-Hill.

Bloom, B., ed. (1956). *Taxonomy of educational objectives. Handbook I: Cognitive domain.* New York: McKay.

Bloom, B., et al. (1984). *Taxonomy of educational objectives. Handbook I: Cognitive domain*. White Plains, NY: Allyn & Bacon/Longman.

Blum, D. (1997). *Sex on the brain: The biological differences between men and women*. New York: Viking.

Borich, G. D. (1999). *Observation skills for teaching*. 3rd ed. Upper Saddle River, NJ: Prentice-Hall.

Boyd, E., and Fales, A. W. (1983). Reflective learning: Key to learning from experience. *Journal of Humanistic Psychology* 23 (2): 99–117.

Brandt, R. (1999, November). Educators need to know about the human brain. *Phi Delta Kappan* 81 (3): 235–238.

Briggs, D. (1996). Turning conflicts into learning experiences. *Educational Leadership* 54 (1): 60–63.

Brooks, J. G., and Brooks, M. G. (1993). In search of understanding: The case for constructivist classrooms. Alexandria, VA: Association of Supervision and Curriculum Development.

Brownell, M., Smith, S., McNelles, J., and Lenk, L. (1995). Career decisions in special education: Current and former teachers' personal views. *Exceptionality* 5 (2): 83–102.

Bruer, J. T. (1998). Let's put brain science on the back burner. *NASSP Bulletin* 82 (598): 9–19.

Bruer, J. T. (1999, May). In search of . . . brain-based education. *Phi Delta Kappan* 80 (9): 648–657.

Bruer, J. T. (1999). *Myth of the first three years*. New York: The Free Press.

Bruner, J. S. (1960). *The process of education*. Cambridge, MA: Harvard University Press.

Bruner, J. S. (1966). *Toward a theory of instruction*. Cambridge, MA: Harvard University Press.

Bruner, J. S. (1973). *Going beyond the information given*. New York: W.W. Norton.

Bruner, J. S. (1983). *Child's talk: Learning to use language*. New York: Norton.

Bruner, J. S. (1990). *Acts of meaning*. Cambridge, MA: Harvard University Press.

Bruner, J. S. (1996). *The culture of education*. Cambridge, MA: Harvard University Press.

Burns, P. C., Roe, B. D., and Ross, E. P. (1996). *Teaching reading in today's elementary schools*. Boston: Houghton Mifflin.

Caine, R., and Caine, G. (1990, October). Understanding a brain-based approach to learning and teaching. *Educational Leadership* 48: 66–70.

Caine, R., and Caine, G. (1993). The critical need for a mental model of meaningful learning. *California Catalyst* 118.

Caine, R., and Caine, G. (1997). *Teaching and the human brain*. Tucson, AZ: Zephyr Press.

California Department of Education. (1995). *Every child a reader: The Report of the California Task Forces*. Sacramento: Author.

California Department of Education. (1996). *A balanced comprehensive approach to teaching reading in pre-kindergarten through grade twelve*. Sacramento: Author.

Campbell, T. C., and Fuller, R. G. (1981). A teacher's guide to the learning cycle. In R. G. Fuller (Ed.), *Piagetian programs in higher education*, 27–30. Lincoln: University of Nebraska Press.

Cangelosi, J. S. (1990). *Designing tests for evaluating student achievement*. New York: Longman.

Canter, L., and Canter, M. (1976). *Assertive discipline: A take charge approach for today's educator*. Seal Beach, CA: Canter and Associates.

Carroll, J. (1963). A model of school learning. *Teachers College Record* 64: 723–733.

Caverly, D. C., Orlando, V. P., and Mullen, J. L. (2000). Textbook study reading. In R. F. Flippo and D. C. Caverly (Eds.), *Handbook of college reading and study research*, 105–147. Mahwah, NJ: Erlbaum Associates.

Center for Critical Thinking. (2007). *The elements of thought*. Retrieved at: www.criticalthinking.org.

Chall, J. S., and Jacobs, V. A. (1996). The reading, writing, and language connection. In J. Shimron (ed.), *Literacy and education: Essays on the memory of Dina Feitelson*, 33–48. Cresskill, NJ: Hampton Press.

Chall, J. S., Jacobs, V. A., and Baldwin, L. E. (1990). *The reading crisis: Why poor children fall behind*. Cambridge, MA: Harvard University Press.

Childre, D., and Howard, M. (1999). *The HearthMath Solution*. San Francisco: Harper & Row.

Chomsky, N. (1957). *Syntactic structures*. The Hague: Mouton.

Chugani, H. T. (1996). *Neuroimaging of developmental nonlinearity and developmental pathologies*. In R. W. Thatcher et al. (eds.), *Developmental Neuroimaging*, 187–195. San Diego: Academic Press.

Cognitive and Development Issues. (2007). *Van Hiele Levels of Geometric Reasoning*. Retrieved at: www.dallassd.com/geometry/DevelopmentalSummary.html.

Conley, M. W. (2005). *Connecting standards and assessment through literacy*. New York: Pearson.

Cooper, H. (2001). Homework for all—in moderation. *Educational Leadership* 58: 34–38.

Cooper, J. M., ed. (1999). *Classroom teaching skills*. 6th ed. Boston: Houghton Mifflin.

Cornett, C., and Blankinship, L. (1990). Whole language = whole learning. Bloomington IN: Phi Delta Kappa.

Corno, L., and Xu, J. (2004). Homework as the job of childhood. *Theory into Practice* 43: 227–233.

Costa, P. T., Jr., and McCrae, R. R. (1992). Normal personality assessment in clinical practice: The NEO Personality Inventory. *Psychological Assessment* 4: 5–13.

Counts, G. S. (1932). *Dare the schools build a new social order?* New York: John Day.

Counts, G. S. (1933). *A call to the teachers of America*. New York: John Day.

Coutts, P. M. (2004). Meanings of homework and implications for practice. *Theory into Practice* 43: 182–188.

Craig, W., and Pepler, D. J. (1997). Observations of bullying and victimization on the schoolyard. *Canadian Journal of School Psychology* 2: 41–60.

Cuban, L. (1998). *A tale of two cities. Phi Delta Kappan* archives.

Cunningham, P. M., Hall, D. P., and Sigmon, C. M. (1999). *The teacher's guide to the four blocks*. Greensboro, NC: Carson-Dellosa Publishing.

Danforth, S., and Boyle, J. R. (2000). *Cases in behavior management*. Upper Saddle River, NJ: Merrill/Prentice-Hall.

Darling-Hammond, L. (2005). Preparing tomorrow's teachers. The case for a national teacher test. *Northwest Education*. Retrieved at: www.nwrel.org.

Darling-Hammond, L., and Sykes, G. (2003, September 17). *Wanted: A national teacher supply policy for education. Education Policy Analysis Archives.* 11 (3). Retrieved at: http://epaa.asu.edu/epaa/vlln33.

Davies, F. (1995). *Introducing reading.* London: Penguin Books Ltd.

Day, C. W. (2003). Smarter classrooms. *KeepMedia.* Retrieved June 3, 2004 at: www.keepmedia.com.

Dendy, C. A. Zeigler, et al. (2006). *CHADD educator's manual on AD/HD.* Landoner, MD: CHADD.

Dewey, J. (1902). *The child and the curriculum.* Chicago: University of Chicago Press.

Dewey, J. (1906). *Democracy and education.* New York: The Free Press.

Dewey, J. (1910). *How we think.* Boston: D.C. Heath.

Dewey, J. (1916). *Democracy and education.* New York: Macmillan.

Dewey, J. (1933). *How we think.* Boston: D.C. Heath.

Dewey, J. (1938). *Experience and education.* New York: Macmillan.

Dewey, J. (1989). *My pedagogic creed. Early Works,* 5. Edited by J. A. Boydston. Carbondale IL: Southern Illinois University Press.

Dewey, J. (1993). *How we think: A restatement of the relation of reflective thinking to the educative process.* Boston: Houghton Mifflin.

Dewey, J. (1997). *How we think.* Mineola, NY: Dover Publications.

Diegmueller, K. (1996, March 20). The best of both worlds. *Education Week.*

Diez, M. E. (2000, May 3). Teachers, assessment, and the standards movement. *Education Week.*

Dreikurs, R., and Grey, L. (1968). *A new approach to discipline: Logical consequences.* New York: Hawthorne.

Dreikurs, R., Grunwald, B. B., and Pepper, F. C. (1982). *Maintaining sanity in the classroom: Classroom management techniques.* 2nd ed. New York: Harper & Row.

Driscoll, M. P. (2000). *Psychology of learning for instruction.* 2nd ed. Boston: Allyn & Bacon.

Duckworth, A., and Seligman, M. (2006). Self-discipline is a better predictor of academic success than IQ. Retrieved at: www.pdkinti.org. "Teaching Self-Discipline."

Duffy-Hester, A. M. (1999, February). Teaching struggling readers in elementary school classrooms: A review of classroom reading programs and principles for instruction. *The Reading Teacher* 52 (5).

Dunham, J. (1977). The effects of disruptive behavior on teachers. *Educational Review* 19 (3): 181–187.

Dunn, R., and Griggs, S. (1995). *Multiculturalism and learning style: Teaching and counseling adolescents.* Westport, CT: Praeger.

Dunn, R., and Griggs, S.A., eds. (2000). *Practical approaches to using learning styles in higher education.* Westport, CT: Bergin & Garvey.

Durkin, E. (2007, August 2). Brooklyn Cyclones "bat persons" win "politically correct" game. *New York Sun,* p. 3.

Dyslexia Awareness and Resource Center. (2003). Myths about dyslexia. Retrieved at: www.dyslexiacenter.org.

Edison Schools. (2006, August 8). The looming teacher surplus. *Education Week* 25 (44): 2.

Elementary General Music Teaching and Learning Center (EGMTL). (2005). Teacher planning and decision making. Retrieved July 26, 2005 at: www2.potsdam.edu.

eMINTS (Enhancing Missouri's Instructional Networked Teaching Strategies National Center, *University of Missouri*). (2007). Constructivist lesson plan form. Retrieved at: www.emints.org/tools/constructivistlesson-form.pdf.

Erikson, E. (1968). *Identity: Youth and crisis.* New York: W.W. Norton.

Erikson, E. (1982). *The life cycle completed.* New York: W.W. Norton.

Farris, P. J. (1999). *Teaching bearing the torch.* 2nd ed. New York: McGraw-Hill.

Faust, F. (2006). Ms. Faust's class. Retrieved at: www.faustclass.com?montessori_education.htm.

Ferguson, E. L. (1995). The real challenge of inclusion: Confessions of a "rabid inclusionist." *Phi Delta Kappan* 77 (4): 281–287.

Fink, D. L. (1999/2000). Higher level learning: Taxonomy for identifying different kinds of significant learning. *Teaching Excellence* 11: 2.

Foriska, T. J. (1997). *A toolkit for developing curriculum and assessment.* Mankato, MN: Ten Sigma.

Foriska, T. J. (1998). *Restructuring around standards: A practitioner's guide to design and implementation.* Thousand Oaks, CA: Corwin Press.

Fosnot, C. T., ed. (1996). *Constructivism: Theory, perspectives, and practice.* New York: Teachers College Press.

Freeman, C. E. (2004). Trends in educational equity of girls and women: 2004. *The Statistics Quarterly* 6 (4).

Freire, P. (1973). *Pedagogy of the oppressed.* New York: Seabury Press.

Friend, M., and Cook, L. (2000). *Interaction: Collaboration skills for school professionals.* New York: Longman.

Froschi, M., Sprung, B., and Mullin-Rindler, N. (2001). *Quit it! A teacher's guide on teasing and bullying for use with students in grades K–3.* Wellesley, MA: Educational Equity Concepts.

Gabennesch, H. (2006, March/April). Critical thinking: What is it good for? *Skeptical Inquirer* 302: 36–41.

Gagnon, G. W., and Collay, M. (1996). Constructivist learning design. Paper presented on the Internet. Retrieved at: www.prainbow.com/cld/cldp.html.

Galton, F. (1962). *Hereditary genius: An inquiry into its laws and consequences.* New York: Macmillan.

Galton, F. (1973). *Inquiries into faculty and its development.* New York: AMS Press.

Gardner, H. (1983). *Frames of mind.* New York: Basic Books.

Gardner, H. (1991). *The unschooled mind: How children think and how schools should teach.* New York: Basic Books.

Gardner, H. (1999). *The disciplined mind: What all students should understand.* New York: Simon & Schuster.

Gathercoal, P. (1993). *Judicious discipline.* 3rd ed. San Francisco: Caddo Gap Press.

Gay, G. (2000). *Culturally responsive teaching: Theory, research, and practice.* New York: Teachers College Press.

Giedd, J. (2005). Child in adolescent psychiatry: New view from brain imaging. Paper delivered January 2005 at the Alliance for Research progress, National Institute of Mental Health. Retrieved at: www.nimh.nih.gov/outreach/alliancereport24jano5.pdf.

Gilligan, C. (1982). *In a different voice: Psychological theory and women's development.* Cambridge, MA: Harvard University Press.

Ginott, H. (1993). *Teacher and child: A book for parents and teachers.* New York: Colliers.

Glass, G., and Glass, E. (1994). *Glass analysis for decoding only.* Garden City, NY: Easier to Learn, Inc.

Glasser, W. (1965). *Reality therapy.* New York: Harper & Row.

Glasser, W. (1969). *Schools without failure.* New York: Harper & Row.

Glasser, W. (1986). *Control therapy in the classroom.* New York: Harper & Row.

Glasser, W. (1990). *The quality school.* New York: Harper & Row.

Glasser, W. (1997). A new look at school failure and school success. *Phi Delta Kappan* 78: 596–602.

Glasser, W. (1998). *Choice theory: A new psychology of personal freedom.* New York: Harper Collins.

Glatthorn, A. (1993). Outcome-based education: Reform and the curriculum process. *Journal of Curriculum and Supervision* 8 (4): 354–363.

Glew, G. M., et al. (2005). Bullying, psychosocial adjustment, and academic performance in elementary school. *Archives of Pediatrics and Adolescent Medicine* 159 (11): 1026–1031.

Goddard, H. H. (1917). Mental tests and the immigrant. *Journal of Delinquency* 2: 243–277.

Goldberg, L. R. (1990). An alternative "description of personality": The big-five factor structure. *Journal of Personality and Social Psychology* 59: 1216–1229.

Goldberg, L. R. (1993). The structure of phenotypic personality traits. *American Psychologist* 48: 26–34.

Goldberg, M. F. (1990). Portrait of Madeline Hunter. *Educational Leadership* 47 (5): 141–43.

Goldstein, A. P., and McGinnis, E. (1997a). *Skillstreaming for adolescents.* Champaign, IL: Research Press.

Goldstein, A. P., and McGinnis, E. (1997b). *Skillstreaming for the elementary school child.* Champaign, IL: Research Press.

Goleman, D. (1995). *Emotional intelligence: Why it can matter more than IQ.* New York: Bantam Books.

Goleman, D. (1998a). *Emotional intelligence.* New York: Bantam Books.

Goleman, D. (1998b). *Working with Emotional intelligence.* New York: Bantam Books.

Gonzalez, M. A. (1997). Study of the relationship of stress, burnout, hardiness, and social support in urban secondary school teachers. Unpublished Ph.D. dissertation. Philadelphia: Temple University.

Goodlad, J. (1983). *A place called school.* New York: McGraw-Hill.

Goodlad, J. I. (1990). *Teachers for our nation's schools.* New York: McGraw-Hill.

Goodlad, J. I. (2004). *Romance with schools: A life in education.* New York: McGraw-Hill.

Goodman, K. S. (1982). *Language and literacy: The selected writings of Kenneth S. Goodman. Vol. I: Process, theory, research.* Edited by F. V. Gollasch. Boston: Routledge & Kegan Paul.

Goodman, K. S. (1986). *What's whole in whole language.* Portsmouth, NH: Heinemann.

Gordon, W. J. J. (1961). *Synectics.* New York: Harper & Row.

Gossen, D. C. (1993). *Restitution: Restructuring school discipline.* Chapel Hill, NC: New View Publications.

Gough, P. B. (1972). One second of reading. In J. F. Kavanagh and I. G. Mattingly (eds.), *Language by ear and by eye.* Cambridge, MA: MIT Press.

Grady, E. (1992). *The portfolio approach to assessment.* Bloomington, IN: Phi Delta Kappa Educational Foundation.

Grant, C. A. (1994). Challenging the myths about multiculturalism. *Multicultural Education* 2 (2): 4–9.

Grant, C. A., ed. (1995). *Educating for diversity: An anthology of multicultural voices.* Boston: Allyn & Bacon.

Greece Central School District (2006). Backward Design. (North Greece, New York.) Retrieved at: www.greece.k12.NewYork.us/instruction/ela/6-2/BackwardDesign/BDstep5.htm.

Gronlund, N. (1991). *How to write and use instructional objectives.* 5th ed. Upper Saddle River, NJ: Merrill/Prentice-Hall.

Gunning, G. T. (2003). *Building literacy in content areas.* Boston: Pearson Education.

Gurian, M., and Stevens, K. (2005). *The minds of boys: Saving our sons from falling behind in school and life.* San Francisco: Jossey-Bass.

Guthrie, J. T., Wigfield, A., and Perencevich, K. C., eds. (2004). *Motivating reading comprehension: Concept-oriented reading instruction.* Mahwah, NJ: Erlbaum Associates.

Haberman, M. (1995, 2004). *Star teachers of children in poverty.* Houston: *Haberman Educational Foundation.*

Haberman, M. (2004, May). Can star teachers create learning communities? *Educational Leadership* 61 (8): 52–56.

Harste, J. C. (1989). *New policy guidelines for reading: Connecting research and practice.* Urbana, IL: National Council of Teachers of English.

Hart, L. (1998). *Human brain and human learning.* (Rev. ed.) Kent, WA: Books for Educators.

Hasenstab, J. K. (2005). Training the teacher as a champion. Retrieved at: www.plsweb.com/.

Hawley, W. D., and Valli, L. (1999). The essentials of professional development: A new consensus. In L. D. Hammond and G. Sykes (eds.), *Teaching as the learning profession: Handbook of policy and practice,* 127–150. San Francisco: Jossey-Bass.

Henley, M., and Long, N. (2003, November). Helping students with emotional problems succeed. *Classroom Leadership* 7 (3): 1–4.

Hirsch, E. D. (2001, May 2). The latest NAEP scores: Can we narrow the fourth-grade reading gap? *Education Week* 60: 41.

Hirsch E. D. (2003, Spring). Reading comprehension requires knowledge of the words and the world. *American Educator* 10–13, 16–22, 28–29.

Hirsch, E. D., Jr. (1987). *Cultural literacy: What every American needs to know.* Boston: Houghton Mifflin.

Hirsch, E. D., Jr., Kett, J. F., and Trefil, J. C. (1993). *The dictionary of cultural literacy.* Boston: Houghton Mifflin.

Hoff, D. J. (1999, June 16). Pioneers of modern testing. *Education Week.*

Hoffman, D. (1999). *Visual intelligence: How we create what we see.* New York: W.W. Norton.

Holloway, J. H. (2001, March). Research link: Inclusion and students with learning disabilities. *Educational Leadership* 58 (6): 86–88.

Holt, J. (1964). *How children fail.* New York: Delta.

Honig, B. (1996). *Teaching our children to read: The role of skills in a comprehensive reading program.* Thousand Oaks, CA: Corwin Press.

Howard, G. R. (1993, September). Whites in multicultural education. *Phi Delta Kappan.*

Howard, J. (1998). *Efficacy in action: Working to get smart* (co-produced video). Bloomington, IN: Efficacy Institute and Phi Delta Kappa International.

Hudgins, B. B. (1974). *Self-contained training materials for teacher education: A derivation from research on the learning of complex skills. Report 5, National Center for the Development of Training Materials in Teacher Education.* Bloomington: University of Indiana.

Humel, C. (1977). *Education today for the world of tomorrow.* Paris: UNESCO.

Hunter, M. (1982). *Mastery teaching.* El Segundo, CA: TIP Publications.

Hunter, M. (1994). *Enhancing teaching.* New York: Macmillan.

Hutchins, R. M. (1936). *The higher learning in America.* New Haven, CT: Yale University Press.

Hutchins, R. M. (1952). *Great books of the western world:* Vol. 1, 1–131. Chicago: Encyclopedia Britannica.

Ingvarsson, E. T., and Morris, E. (2004, Fall). Post-Skinnerian, Post-Skinner, or neo-Skinnerian? *Psychological Record* 54: 97.

Institute of Education Services. (2005, July). Connecting ideas a strategy for extending the curriculum. U.S. Department of Education. Washington, DC. Retrieved July 23, 2005 at: www.mcre.org.

Jacobsen, D. A., Eggen, P., and Kauchak, D. (2002). *Methods for teaching.* 6th ed. Upper Saddle River, NJ: Prentice-Hall.

Jensen, E. (1998). *Teaching with the brain in mind.* Alexandria, VA: Association for Supervision and Curriculum Development (ASCD).

Jensen, E. (2000). *Different brains, different learners.* San Diego: Brain Store.

Jersild, A. T. (1955). *When teachers face themselves.* New York: Teachers College Press.

Johnson, J. (2004, June 23). Why is school discipline considered a trivial issue? *Education Week* 23 (41): 4, 8.

Jones, F. (1987). *Positive classroom discipline.* New York: McGraw-Hill.

Jones, F. (1994). *Positive classroom discipline: A video course of study.* Santa Cruz, CA: Fredric H. Jones.

Kamehameha Schools. (2003). Kamehameha schools' philosophy of education. Retrieved at: http://oahu.ksbe.edu.

Kellough, R. (2004). *A resource guide for teaching K–12.* Upper Saddle River, NJ: Merrill/Prentice-Hall

Kelly, H. (1997). How children learn to derive meaning from text. ERIC Clearinghouse: [ED416459].

Khalsa, K. P., and Willard, T. (2006, August). Help for ADHD. *Herbs for Health.* 7–10.

Killion, J. P., and Todnem, G. R. (1991). A process for personal theory building. *Educational Leadership* 48 (6): 14–16.

Kilpatrick, W. H. (1941). The case for progressivism in education. *Today's Education: Journal of the National Education Association* 30 (8): 231–232.

King, K., and Gurian, M. (2006, September). With boys in mind: Teaching to the minds of boys. *Educational Leadership* 64 (1): 56–61.

Kipping, P. (2000). Think TV: A guide to managing TV in the home. *Nova Scotia Department of Education,* iv–vii.

Kohl, H. R. (1967). *36 children.* New York: Plume.

Kohlberg, L. (1981). *Essays on moral development. Vol. 1: The philosophy of moral development.* New York: Harper & Row.

Kohlberg, L. (1987). *The measurement of moral judgment. Vol.1: Theoretical foundations and research validation.* London: Cambridge University.

Kohn, A. (1999). *The schools our children deserve.* Boston: Houghton Mifflin.

Kohn, A. (2006, September). Abusing research: The study of homework and other examples. *Phi Delta Kappan* 8–22.

Koppich, J. E. (1999). Teacher education at Trinity University. *American Education* 24–25, 45.

Kozol, J. (1967). *Death at an early age.* New York: Penguin Books.

Krathwohl, D. R., Bloom, B. S., and Marsia, B. B. (1964). *A taxonomy of educational objectives: The classification of educational goals. Handbook II: Affective domain.* New York: McKay.

Kulik, J. A., and Kulik, C. (1997). *The handbook of gifted education.* 2nd ed. Boston: Allyn & Bacon.

Landau, B., and Gathercoal, P. (2000). Creating peaceful classrooms: Judicious discipline and class meetings. *Phi Delta Kappan* 81: 450–454.

Lavoie, R. D., and Rosen, P. (1994). *Understanding learning disabilities: Frustration, Anxiety, Tension: The F.A.T. city workshop* (Videotape). Peter Rosen Productions in conjunction with Koppel Films, Inc., for PBS.

Lazar-Morris, C., Polin, L., May, R., and Burry, J. (1984). *A review of the literature in test use.* Rep. No. 144. Center for the Study of Evaluation, University of California.

Lazear, D. (1991). *Seven ways of knowing: Teaching for multiple intelligences.* 2nd ed. Arlington Heights, IL: Skylight Training and Publishing.

Lazear, D. (1991). *Seven ways of teaching: The artistry of teaching with multiple intelligences.* Palatine, IL: Skylight Training and Publishing.

Lazear, D. (1994). *Multiple intelligence approaches to assessment: Solving the assessment conundrum.* Tucson, AZ: Zephyr Press.

Lazear, D. (1994). *Seven pathways of learning: Teaching students and parents about multiple intelligences.* Tucson, AZ: Zephyr Press.

LeFrancois, G. R. (2000). *Psychology for teaching.* University of Alberta: Wadsworth Thomson Learning.

Lillard, P. P. (1996). *Montessori today.* New York: Random House.

Lillard, P. P., and Jessen, L. L. (2003). *Montessori from the start.* New York: Random House.

Limber, S. P. (2003). Efforts to address bullying in U.S. schools. *Journal of Health Education* 34: S-23–S-29.

Lipman, M. (1991). *Thinking in education.* Cambridge, UK: Cambridge University Press.

Lipsky, D. K., and Gartner, A. (1996). Inclusion, school restructuring, and the remaking of American society. *Harvard Educational Review* 66 (4): 762–796.

Logerfo, L. (2006). Climb every mountain. Hoover Institution, Washington, DC. Retrieved at: www.educationnext,org/20063/68.html.

Lorge, I., and Chall, J. (1963). Estimating the size of vocabularies of children and adults: Analysis of methodological issues. *Journal of Experimental Education* 32: 147–157.

Lyman, F. (1981). Think-pair-share. University of Maryland. Howard County Public Schools. Retrieved August, 2007 at: http://mywebpages.comcast.net/millere10/web.MAACIE/article22.html.

Maas, D. Lecturer. (1988). *Maintaining Teacher Effectiveness*. [Videotape]. Indiana: OMNI Productions, Phi Delta Kappa.

MacLean, P. D. (1990). The triune brain in evolution. New York: Plenum Press.

Mager F. R., and Piper, P. (1997). *Analyzing performance problems: Or you really oughta wanna*. 3rd ed. Atlanta, GA: The Center for Effective Performance.

Mager F. R., and Piper, P. (1997). *Preparing instructional objectives*. 3rd ed. Atlanta, GA: The Center for Effective Performance.

Manzo, K. K. (1999, March 17). Whole-language model survives despite swing back to basics. *Education Week* 18 (27).

Marzano, R., Marzano, J., and Pickering, D. (2003). *Classroom management that works: Research-based strategies for every teacher*. Alexandria, VA: Association for Supervision and Curriculum Development (ASCD).

Maslow, A. H. (1962). *Toward a psychology of being*. New York: Van Nostrand Reinhold.

Maslow, A. H. (1970). *Motivation and personality*. 2nd ed. New York: Harper & Row.

Mayer, J. D., Salovey, P., and Caruso, D. R. (2000). Models of emotional intelligence. In R. J. Sternberg (Ed.), *Handbook of intelligence*, 396–420. Cambridge, UK: Cambridge University Press.

Mayer, J., and Salovey, P. (1995). Emotional intelligence. *Applied and Preventive Psychology* 43: 197–198.

McClintock, R. O., and Black, J. B. (1995). *An interpretation of construction approach to constructivist design found in constructivist learning environments*. Edited by B. Wilson. Englewood Cliffs, NJ: Educational Technology Publications. Retrieved at: http://ilt.columbia.edu/publications/papers/ICON.html.

McBrien, J. L., and Brandt, R. S. (1997). *The Language of learning: A guide to education terms*. Alexandria, VA: Association for Supervision and Curriculum Development (ASCD).

McIntosh, H. (2005). The Peace Rug: Its effectiveness and value as a conflict resolution tool. Retrieved at: www.peacerug.com.

McLeskey, J., and Waldron, N. (2002). School change and inclusive schools: Lessons learned from practice. *Phi Delta Kappan* 8 (4): 65–72.

McLeskey, J., and Waldron, N. (2000). *Developing inclusive schools: Lessons learned*. Alexandria, VA: Association for Supervision and Curriculum Development (ASCD).

McNeil, J. D. (1990). *Curriculum: A comprehensive introduction*. 4th ed. Glenview, IL: Scott Foresman.

Melanchthon, P. (1997). *Melanchthon year 1997 in Germany. The Philip Melanchthon Quinquennial*. Retrieved at: www.melanchthon.de/e/lehrer.

Miller, C. P. (2005). Addressing the forgotten element: Improving fluency in struggling readers. Retrieved at: www.education-world.com.

National Association for the Education of Young Children. (1996). Phonics and whole language learning: A balanced approach to beginning reading. Washington, DC: Author.

National Board for Professional Teaching Standards. (2006). Retrieved at: www.nbpts.org.

National Center for Educational Statistics. (2004). *Indicators of crime and safety*. Retrieved at: http://nces.ed.gov/pubsearch/pubsinfo.asp?Pubid=20050002.

National Center for Educational Statistics. (2005). *National Assessment of Educational Progress*. Washington, DC: U.S. Department of Education.

National Commission on Excellence in Education. (1983). *A nation at risk: The imperative for education reform*. Washington, DC: U.S. Department of Education.

NAEP Questionnaire (1998). *National Reading Assessments, Data Almanac* 451, 471, 501.

National Education Association. (2005). Attracting and keeping quality teachers. Retrieved April 16, 2005, at: www.nea.org/teachershortage/index.html.

National Institute of Health. (2001). Bullying widespread in U.S. schools. Retrieved at: www.nichd.nih.gov/bullying.

National Institute of Neurological Disorders and Stroke. (2006). NINDS learning disabilities information page. *National Institutes of Health*. Retrieved at: www.NINDS.NIH.gov.

National Research Council. (1998). Preventing reading difficulties in young children. *Academy Press* 61: 80–83.

Neill, A. S. (1960). *Summerhill: A radical approach to child rearing*. New York: Hart.

Nettles, D. H. (2006). *Comprehensive literacy instruction in today's classrooms: The whole, the parts, and the heart*. Boston: Allyn & Bacon.

Neubert, G. A., and Wilkins, E. A. (2004). *Putting it all together: The directed reading lesson in the secondary content classroom*. New York: Pearson Education.

Neville, M. (1985). *English language in Scottish schools*. Scottish Education Department Report.

New York, The State Education Department. (1999). Essential Elements of Reading. Retrieved at: www.emsc.nysed.gov/c.a.

Newcomer, L. L., and Lewis, T. J. (2004). Functional behavioral assessment: An investigation of reliability and effectiveness of function based interventions. *Journal of Emotional and Behavioral Disorders* 12: 168–181.

North Carolina Department of Public Instruction. (2006). *The INTASC standards*. North Carolina Public Schools.

North Central Regional Educational Laboratory (NCREL). (2001). Lesson planner. Retrieved July 27, 2005, at: www.ncrtec.org.

O'Shea, M. (2005). *From standards to success*. Alexandria, VA: Association for Supervision and Curriculum Development.

Oaksford, L., and Jones, L. (2002). *Differentiated instruction: Effective classroom practices report*. National Center on Accessing the General Curriculum, U.S. Department of Education 2.

Obey, D., and Porter, J. (2002). Researched based reform gets boost from Obey-Porter. *The Comprehensive School Reform Demonstration Program*. Retrieved at: www.ed.gov/bulletin/fall1998/resbsdscl.html.

Ogle, D. (1986). K-W-L: A teaching model that develops active reading of expository text. *The Reading Teacher* 39 (6): 564–570.

Olweus, D. (2003). A profile of bullying at school. *Educational Leadership* 60 (6): 12–17.

Orlich, D., et al. (2001). *Teaching strategies: A guide to better instruction*. Boston: Houghton Mifflin.

Orlich, D., et al. (2004). *Teaching strategies: A guide to effective instruction.* 7th ed. Boston: Houghton Mifflin.

Ormrod, J. (1995). *Educational psychology: Principles and applications.* Englewood Cliffs, NJ: Prentice-Hall.

Ornstein, A. C., and Lasley, T. J. (2000). *Strategies for effective teaching.* 3rd ed. New York: McGraw-Hill.

Ornstein, A. C., and Hunkins, F. P. (1998). *Foundations, principles, and issues.* 3rd ed. Boston: Allyn & Bacon.

Paul, R. W. (1991). Dialogical and dialectical thinking. In A. L. Costa (Ed.), *Developing minds: A resource book for teaching thinking.* VA: Association for Supervision and Curriculum Development (ASCD).

Paul, R. W., and Elder, L. (2003). *Critical thinking: Tools for taking charge of your learning and your life.* 2nd ed. New York: Prentice-Hall.

Paul, R. W., and Elder, L. (2003). *The thinker's guide for students on how to study and learn a discipline using critical thinking concepts and tools.* 2nd ed. Sonoma, CA: Foundation for Critical Thinking.

Pennsylvania State University (2003). Guidelines for question writing. Retrieved at: http://tlt.its.psu.edu/questionwriting/rules.shtml.

Pfeiffer, R. N. (1981). The school based interpersonal team: Recurring problems and some possible solutions. *Journal of School Psychology* 18: 330–333.

Philips, P. (1997). The conflict wall. *Educational Leadership* 54 (8): 43–44.

Piaget, J. (1952). *The origins of intelligence.* New York: International Universities Press.

Piaget, J. (1967). *The moral judgment of the children.* New York: Free Press.

Pinar, W., et al., eds. (1995). *Understanding curriculum.* New York: Peter Lang.

Pipher, M. (1994). *Reviving Ophelia.* New York: Random House.

Pogrow, S. (2000, April 19). Beyond the good star mentality. *Education Week.*

Pollock, W. (1999). *Real boys: Rescuing our sons from the myths of boyhood.* New York: Random House.

Posey, K. C. (1995). *How to handle bullies, teasers, and other meanies.* Chicago: Rainbow Books.

Powell, A. G. (1996). *Lessons from privilege: The American prep school tradition.* Cambridge, MA: Harvard University Press.

Pratte, R., and Rury, J. L. (1991). Teachers' professionalism and craft. *Teachers College Record* 93: 59–72.

Prescott, J. O. (1999, Nov./Dec.). A day in the Rudolf Steiner School. *Instructor* 109: 2, 21–25.

Public Agenda. (2004). *Teaching interrupted: Do discipline polices in today's public schools foster the common good?* Retrieved at: www.publicagenda.org.

Raphael, T. E. (2002). *Book club: A literature-based curriculum.* Small Planet Communications.

Raths, L. E., et al. (1967). *Teaching for thinking, theory, and application.* Columbus, OH: Merrill.

Reaves, J. (2001). Why he's in the headlines. Retrieved at: www.warroom.com?school/%20shooting/charleswilliams.htms.

Reed, C. (2005). *Action research: A strategy for instructional improvement.* Retrieved May 2, 2005, at: www.newhorizons.org.

Reed, C. (2000). *Teaching with power: Shared decision-making and classroom practice.* New York: Teachers College Press.

Reinhartz, J., and Beach, D. M. (1997). *Teaching and learning in the elementary school: Focus on curriculum.* Columbus, OH: Merrill.

Renzulli, J., Enrichment Model. (1997, October). A rising tide lifts all ships, developing the gifts and talents of all students. *Phi Delta Kappan* 104–110.

Renzulli, J. (1999). *Developing the Gifts and Talents of All Students* (Videotape). Port Chester, NY: National Professional Resources.

Rich, B., ed. (2000). *The Dana brain daybook.* New York: Charles A. Dana Foundation.

Ritter, J. (2002, June 20). *AMA puts doctors on lookout for bullying. Chicago Sun Times* 1.

Roblyer, M. D., Edwards, J., and Havriluk, M. (1997). *Integrating educational technology into teaching.* 4th ed. Columbus, OH: Prentice-Hall.

Roe, B. D., Stooddt-Hill, B. D., and Burns, P. C. (2004). *Secondary school literacy instruction: The content areas.* 8th ed. Boston: Houghton Mifflin.

Rose, C., and Nicholl, M. (1997). *Accelerated learning for the 21st century.* New York: Dell Publishing.

Rose, C. (1985). *Accelerated learning.* New York: Dell Publishing.

Rosenshine, B., and Meister, C. (1994, Winter). Reciprocal teaching: A review of the research. *Review of Educational Research* 64: 479–530.

Rossi, R. (2005, April 15). 1,116 City teachers flunk out. *Chicago Sun Times.* Retrieved April 21, 2005 at: www.lib.usm.edu/~instruct/guides/apa.html.

Routman, R. (1996). *Transitions.* Portsmouth, NH: Heinemann.

Ruder, S. (2000, September). We teach all: How to differentiate instruction. *Educational Leader* 58 (1): 49–51.

Ryan, J. (2005, March 3). *Brains of men and women only part of story in science.* Retrieved at: www.sfgate.com/cgi-in/article.cgi?f=/c/a/2005/03/03/BAGSKBJI981.DTL.

Ryder, R. J., and Graves, M. F. (1994). *Reading and learning in content areas.* New York: Macmillan.

Sanders, W. L., and Horn, S. (1994). The Tennessee Value-Added Assessment System TVAAS: Mixed-model methodology in educational assessment. *Journal of Personal Evaluation in Education* 8: 299–311. (www.epi_center.org/sanders.htm for further information on Sanders's work.)

Sax, L. (2005). *Why gender matters: What parents and teachers need to know about the emerging science of sex differences.* New York: Doubleday.

Sax, L. (2005, March 2). The promise and peril of single sex public education. *Education Week.*

Scarpaci, R. T. (2006, Summer). Bullying: Effective strategies for its prevention. *Kappa Delta Pi Record* 42 (4): 170–174.

Scarpaci, R. T. (2007). *Case study approach to classroom management.* Boston: Allyn & Bacon.

Scarpaci, R. T. (2007, January/February). IOSIE: A method for analyzing student behavioral problems. *The Clearing House* 80 (3): 111–116.

Schon, D. A. (1987). *Educating the reflective practitioner.* San Francisco, CA: Jossey-Bass.

School Bully OnLine. (2005). *Myths and misconceptions about school bullying.* Retrieved at: www.bullyonline.org/schoolbully/myths.htm.

Schunk, D. (2000). *Learning theories: An educational perspective.* 3rd ed. Upper Saddle River, NJ: Prentice-Hall.

Seddon, R. (2004). *Rudolf Steiner.* Berkley, CA: North Atlantic Books.

Seddon, R. (2005). *Philosophy as an approach to the spirit: An introduction to the fundamental works of Rudolf Steiner.* East Sussex, UK: Temple Lodge Publishing.

Selye, H. (1974). *Stress without distress.* New York: McGraw-Hill.

Selye, H. (1978). *The stress of life.* 2nd ed. New York: McGraw-Hill.

Sergiovanni, T. J. (1997). *Moral leadership: Getting to the heart of school improvement.* New York: Jossey-Bass.

Sergiovanni, T. J. (2000, February 3). Changing educational change, substance, not process is what matters. *Education Week* 27, 31.

Sewall, G. T. (2000, Summer). Lost in action. *American Educator.* 4–9, 42–43.

Shaywitz, S. (1996, November). Dyslexia. *Science American Magazine* 98–104.

Shaywitz, S. (2005). *Overcoming dyslexia: A new complete science-based program for overcoming reading problems.* New York: Random House.

Shaywitz, S., and Shaywitz, B. (1991). Introduction to the special series on attention deficit disorder. *Journal of Learning Disabilities* 24 (2): 68–71.

Sherman, L. (1998, Fall). Seeking common ground. *Northwest Education Magazine.*

Silberman, C. (1970). *Crisis in the classroom.* New York: Random House.

Simonton, D. D. (2003). Francis Galton's hereditary genius: Its place in the history and psychology of science. In R. J. Steinberg (Ed.), *The anatomy of impact: What makes the great works of psychology great.* Washington, DC: American Psychological Association, 3–18.

Sizer, T. R. (1984). *Horace's compromise.* Boston: Houghton Mifflin.

Sizer, T. R. (1992). *Horace's school.* Boston: Houghton Mifflin.

Sizer, T. R. (1997). *Horace's hope.* Boston: Houghton Mifflin.

Skinner, B. F. (1948). *Walden two.* Upper Saddle River, NJ: Prentice-Hall.

Skinner, B. F. (1968). *The technology of teaching.* New York: Appleton, Century, Crofts.

Slavin, R. E. (1980). *Using student team learning.* Baltimore: Johns Hopkins Learning Project.

Slavin, R. E. (1986). Ability grouping and student achievement in elementary schools. *A best-evidence synthesis.* Rep. No. 1. Baltimore: Johns Hopkins University Center for Research on Elementary and Middle Schools.

Slavin, R. E. (1990a). *Cooperative learning: Theory, research, and practice.* Englewood Cliffs, NJ: Prentice-Hall.

Slavin, R. E. (1990b). Cooperative learning and the gifted: Who benefits? *Journal for the Education of the Gifted* 14: 28–30.

Slavin, R. E. (1994). Student teams assessment divisions. In S. Sharon (Ed.), *Handbook of cooperative learning methods* 2–19. Westport, CT: Greenwood.

Slavin, R. E. (1995). *Cooperative learning: Theory, research, and practice.* Boston: Allyn & Bacon.

Slavin, R. E., and Madden, N. A. (2006). Success for all/Roots and wings: 2006 summary of research on achievement outcomes. Baltimore: Johns Hopkins University, Center for Research and Reform in Education. Retrieved at: www.sucessforall.net.

Smyth, J. (1989). Developing and sustaining critical reflection in teacher education. *Journal of Teacher Education* 40 (2): 2–14.

Snow, C. E., and Biancarosa, G. (2003). *Adolescent literacy and the achievement gap: What do we know and where do we go from here?* New York: Carnegie Corporation.

Snow, C. E., Burns, M. S., and Griffin, P., eds. (1998). *Preventing reading difficulties in young children.* Washington, DC: National Academy Press.

Sommers, C. H. (2000). *The war against boys.* New York: Simon & Schuster.

Sommers, C. H. (2000, May). *The war against boys. The Atlantic Monthly* 285 (5): 59–74. Retrieved at: http://theatlantic.com/prem/200005/war-againstboys.

Sousa, D. A. (1998, December). Is the fuss about brain research justified? *Education Week* 16: 35.

Sousa, D. A. (1995). *How the brain learns: A classroom teacher's guide.* Alexandria, VA: National Association of Secondary School Principals.

Spady, W. G. (1994). Choosing outcomes of significance. *Educational Leadership* 51 (6): 18–22.

Spady, W. G. (1994). *Outcome-based education: Critical issues and answers.* Arlington, VA: American Association of School Administrators.

Spady, W. G. (1996). OBE Pyramid *Free World Research.* Retrieved at: www.Wccta.netgallery/fwr/oubaobpy,htm.

Standards-Based Classroom Operators Manual. (2002). Just Ask Publications and Professional Development. Alexandra, VA.

Statewide Parent Advocacy Network. (2000). Appendix B multiple intelligences work sheet. Retrieved July 11, 2006 at: www.spannj.org/BasicRights/appendix_b.htm.

Staub, D., and Peck, C. A. (1994). What are the outcomes for non-disabled students? *Educational Leadership* 52 (4): 36–40.

Steiner, R. (1991). *The spiritual guidance of the individual and humanity.* Translated by S. Desch from lectures given in 1911. Herndon, VA: Anthroposophic Press/Steiner Books.

Steiner, R. (1996). *The education of the child: An early lecture on education.* Herndon, VA: Waldorf Education/Steiner Books.

Stern, W. (1916). *The psychological methods of intelligence.* Translated by G.Whipple. Baltimore: Warwick & York.

Sternberg, R. G. (1984, September). How can we teach intelligence? *Educational Leadership* 38–48.

Sternberg, R. G. (1985). *Beyond IQ: A triarchic theory of human intelligence.* New York: Cambridge University Press.

Sternberg, R. G. (1997). *Successful intelligence.* New York: Plume.

Sternberg, R. G. (1999, Spring). Ability and expertise: It's time to replace the current model of intelligence. *American Educator* 10–13, 50–51.

Strauss, H. (2002). New learning spaces: Smart learners, not smart classrooms. *Syllabus.* Retrieved June 3, 2004 at: www.syllabus.com.

Suchman, R. (1962). *The elementary school training program in scientific inquiry.* Report to the U.S. Office of Education. Urbana: University of Illinois.

Sykes, C. J. (1995). *Dumbing down of kids.* New York: St. Martin's Press.

Sylwester, R. (2000). *A biological brain in a cultural classroom: Applying biological research to classroom management.* Thousand Oaks, CA: Corwin Press.

Taba, H. (1973). *Curriculum development: Theory and practice.* New York: Harcourt, Brace, and World.

Tagg, J., and Ewell, P. T. (2003). *The learning paradigm college.* New York: Jossey-Bass.

Tapscott, P. (1998). *Growing up digital: The rise of the net generation.* New York: McGraw-Hill.

Taqqart, L. G., and Wilson, A. P. (2005). *Promoting reflective thinking in teachers.* Thousand Oaks, CA: Corwin Press.

Terman, L. M. (1916). The uses of intelligence tests. (From *The measurement of intelligences,* Chap. 1). Boston: Houghton Mifflin.

Terman, L. M. (1930). *Autobiography of Lewis M. Terman.* In C. Murchison (Ed.), *History of psychology in autobiography.* Vol. 2, 297–331. Worcester, MA: Clark University Press. Retrieved July 17, 2005 at: http://psychclassics.yorku.ca/Terman/Murchison.htm.

Thompson, M., and Kindlon, D. (2000). *Raising Cain: Protecting the emotional life of boys.* New York: Balantine Books.

Tomlinson, C. A. (1999). *Differentiated classroom: Responding to the needs of all learners.* Alexandria, VA: Association for Supervision and Curriculum Development (ASCD).

Tomlinson, C. A., and McTighe, J. (2006). *Integrating differentiated instruction and understanding by design.* Alexandria, VA: Association for Supervision and Curriculum Development (ASCD).

Torgesen, J., et al. (2007). *Academic literacy instruction for adolescents: A guidance document from the Center on Instruction.* Portsmouth, NH: RMC Corporation, Center on Instruction.

Towers, J. M. (1996). An elementary school principal's experience with implementing an outcome-based curriculum. *Catalyst for Change* 19–23.

Traub, J. (1998, October 26). Multiple intelligences disorders. *The New Republic* 20–23.

Truckman, B. W., and Jensen, M. A. C. (1977). Stages of small group development revisited. *Group and Organizational Studies* 2: 419–427.

Tyler, R. (1949). *Basic principles of curriculum and instruction.* Chicago: University of Chicago Press.

U.S. Department of Education. (1991). *America 2000: An education strategy.* Washington, DC: U.S. Government Printing Office.

U.S. Department of Health and Human Services. (2006). Bullying is not a fact of life. Retrieved at: www.mentalhealth.samhsa.gov/publications/allpubs/SVP-0052/.

University of Alabama at Birmingham. (2007). *Obey-Porter Comprehensive School Reform Demonstration Act.* Reading Recovery Council of North America. Retrieved at: http://ed.uab.edu/soeweb/readrec/reform.htm.

University of Washington. (2005). School programs targeting antisocial behavior can boost test scores, grades. Retrieved at: www.newswise.com.

Vacca, R., and Vacca, J. (2005). *Content area reading: Literacy and learning across the curriculum.* 8th ed. Boston: Allyn & Bacon/Longman.

Vossekuil, B., et al. (2000). U.S.S.S. Safe School Initiative: An interim report of the prevention of targeted violence in schools. Washington, DC: U.S. Secret Service, National Threat Assessment Center.

Walsh, P. (2000). A hands-on approach to understanding the brain. *Association for Supervision and Curriculum Development* 58 (3): 76–78.

Wang, M. C., Haertel, G. D., and Walberg, H. J. (1993). Toward a knowledge base for school learning. *Review of Educational Research* 63 (3): 249–294.

Wang, M. C., Haertel, G. D., and Walberg, H. J. (1994). What helps students learn? *Educational Leadership* 51 (4): 74–79.

Wardell, M., and Haro, S. (2000). Essay rubric. Adapted from California State, San Marcos, English Placement Test. Retrieved at: http://csusm.edu/lwap/lessessayrubric.html.

Watson, D. (1989). Defining and describing whole language. *The Elementary School Journal* 90: 130–141.

Watson, D. (1999). Whole language: Why bother? *The Reading Teacher* 147 (8): 602.

Webb, D. L., Metha, A., and Jordan, F. K. (2000). *Foundations of American education.* Upper Saddle River, NJ: Prentice-Hall.

Whipple, G. M., ed. (1925). Report on the national committee on reading: 24th *Yearbook of the National Society for the Study of Education.* Bloomington, IL: Public School Publishing.

Wiess, C. H. (2004). *Evaluation.* 2nd ed. Upper Saddle River, NJ: Prentice-Hall.

Wiggins, G., and Tighe, J. (2001). *Understanding by design.* Upper Saddle River, NJ: Prentice-Hall.

Wilen, W., Ishler, M., Hutchison, J., and Kindsvatter, R. (2000). *Dynamics of effective teaching.* 4th ed. New York: Allyn & Bacon/Longman.

Wolfe, P., and Brandt, R. (1998). What do we know from brain research? *Educational Leadership* 56 (3): 8–13.

Wolfgang, C. H. (1999). *Solving discipline problems.* 4th ed. Boston: Allyn & Bacon.

Wong, H., and Wong, R. (1997). *The first days of school: How to be an effective teacher.* Mountain View, CA: Harry K. Wong Publications.

Wylie, M. S. (2000, September/October). Teaching kids to care. *Family Therapy Networker.* 24 (5): 26–35. Retrieved at: www.cary-memorial.lib.me.us/bullyweb/networker.htm.

Yero, J. L. (2002). *Teaching in mind: How thinking shapes education.* Hamilton, MT: Mind Flight Publishing.

Zenderland, L. (1998). *Measuring minds: Henry Herbert Goddard and the origins of American intelligence testing.* Cambridge, MA: Cambridge Press.

INDEX

Ability, grouping by, 78, 79
Abstract operations, 26
Academic standards, defined, 192
Accelerated learning method, 35
Accountability, 49
Achievement test, defined, 224
Action research, 214
    case studies of, 243–245
    in the classroom, 242–243
    and effective teaching, 224, 242
Activities, in lesson, 64
Activity reinforcers, 24
Adaptation, model of, 27
Adaptation skills, 75
Adequate Yearly Progress (AYP), 197, 199
Adler, Mortimer, 90, 182
Administrative progressives, 184
Advanced organizers, 8
Affective domain, 74–75
Age, grouping by, 78
Aims, in lesson plan, 52
    topic, 49, 50
Aliteracy, 173
Alpha-Beta test, 215
Alternative teacher assessment, 238, 240
AMCASH technique, 51, 52–54, 226
America 2000: An Education Strategy, 194
Analogy-based phonics, 150
Analytic phonics, 150
Analytical intelligence, 40
Analytical questions, 74
Anticipatory set, 57, 58
Application, of teaching, 52
Application questions, 74
Aptitude test, defined, 224
Aristotle, 22, 181, 182
Assertive discipline, 123
Assertive discipline model, 131–132
Assessment
   alternative, 224
   authentic, 193, 213, 222–223, 224
   beliefs of, 219
   case studies of, 223, 224, 228, 229–230
   characteristics of, 219
   of cooperative groups, 80
   history of, 192–193, 214–215
   improvement of, 217–218
   in J.E.K. model, 59
   in lesson plan, 60
   norm-referenced vs. criterion-referenced, 217, 218
   practices in, 217–218
   for special education, 99
   standardized vs. teacher-prepared, 217
   summative, 224
   of teacher competency, 246
   traditional view of, 214
   understanding, 217–218
Attention Deficit Disorder (ADD), 109
Attention Deficit Hyperactivity Disorder (ADHD), 109
Attention disorders, 107
Attention-getting devices, 62
Auditory perception disorders, 107
Ausubel, David, 8
Authoritarian strategies, 129
Autonomy vs. shame and doubt, Eriksonian stage, 33

Backward design, 53–54
   of assessment, 215–216
   benefits of, 56
   planning using, 216
   procedures for, 55
   for real life, 56–57
Bagley, William, 182
Balanced language approach, 148
Balanced literacy approach, 157–158
   elements of, 159–160
   television and, 158–159
Banks, James, 103
Basal reading programs, 154–155
Bay View School, Brooklyn, New York, 238–240
Behavior
   beliefs about, 127–128
   described, 127
   misbehavior, 122–127
   models of, 122
Behavior modification, 23
   planning for, 24
   strengths and weaknesses of, 23
Behavior shaping, 23
Behavioral objectives, 51
Behaviorist approach, 3, 22–23
   to behavior, 122
   neo-Skinnerian, 23–24
Behaviorist learning theory, 24–25
   contrasted with constructivist approach, 27, 30–31
Benchmark, defined, 224
Benchmarking, 200
   for teachers, 205
Bennett, William, 88

Best Linear Unbiased Predictor (BLUP), 227
Best practices, 208
Binet, Alfred, 38, 193, 214–215
Block scheduling, 234
Bloom's taxonomy, 36, 73, 74
   related to thinking, 76
Book Club Program (BCP), 165
Brain
   characteristics of, 37
   development of, 36
   exercising, 35
   hemisphericity of, 34
   imaging techniques for, 33, 234
   in learning, 41–42
   teaching about, 35
   triune theory of, 34–35
Brain laterality, 36
Brainstem, 34
Brainstorming, group, 14
Bridge classes, 78
Bruner, Jerome, 8, 22, 25, 39, 72, 207
Budgeting, objective based, 235
Bullying
   defined, 141
   e-mail, 142
   indicators of, 142
   myths about, 141–142
   preventing, 141, 143–144
   protecting victims of, 142

Caine, R. and G., 35
Canter, Lee and Marlene, 131
Caring and concern, in lesson, 64
Carnegie, Andrew, 57
Case studies, 213
   in indirect instruction, 14
Chall, Jeanne, 148
Change agent model, 234–235
Characterization, 75
Cheating, 129–130
Checking for understanding, 58
   in lesson design, 57
Chicago, University of, Lab School, 9
Child-centered progressives, 184
Children
   concerns of, 4
   love of learning of, 4
Choice theory, 138–139
Circadian rhythms, 36
Classroom
   design of, 7
   smart, 7, 8
   technology in, 7

Classroom management, 119–120
  behavior and, 122
  case studies of, 124–127, 129–130, 144, 145–146
  consequence models of, 130–134
  to facilitate instruction, 129
  group guidance control models of, 134–136
  guidance models of, 136–140
  philosophical underpinnings of, 127–130
  reflection for, 227–228
  strategy for, 120, 122
  and teacher retention, 120–121
Closure, in lesson design, 57
Cognitive development, stages of, 26
Cognitive domain, 74
Cognitive process, 27
Cognitive psychologist's approach, 22
Coleman Report, 149, 215
Collaborative mentor/coaching model of professional development, 248
College Board, 215
Combining grades, 78
Communication, between teacher and student, 5, 208
Compact for Learning, 195–196
Competence vs. inferiority, Eriksonian stage, 33
Competency test, defined, 224
Competency testing. *See* Assessment
Complex overt response, 75
Comprehension
  in expository approach, 8
  strategies for, 152
Comprehension questions, 74
Computer-assisted instruction, 23
Concept formation, 207
Concept introduction, in learning cycle, 54
Concept-Oriented Reading Instruction (CORI), 165–166
Concrete knowledge, 26
Concrete operational stage, 26
Conditioned reinforcers, 24
Conflict resolution, 143–144
Confronting stage, in reflective thinking, 63
Congruent communication, 136–137
Connections, in lesson plan, 60
Consequence approach, 124
  and IOSIE method, 124–125
Consequence models, 130–132
Constructivist approach, 22
  assumptions of, 28
  basis of, 25
  to behavior, 122
  contrasted with behaviorist approach, 27, 30–31
  and learning design, 25–26, 53, 55
  neuroscience and, 37

  philosophy behind, 182
  teaching practices influenced by, 28–29
  varieties of, 26–28
Content, 52
  in J.E.K. model, 59
  in lesson plan, 60
Content application, in learning cycle, 54
Content knowledge, importance of, 5
Content knowledgeability, 208
Content literacy, 173
Content standards, defined, 192
Content validity, 217
Content-area reading instruction, 152
Content-specific standards, 196
Contingencies of reinforcement, 23
Continuous progress, 78
Conventional moral reasoning, 32
Cooperative learning, 13–14, 79, 102, 207
  activities in, 80
  assessment in, 80
  benefits of, 80
  setting up, 80
  small-group instruction contrasted with, 81
Copernicus, Nicolaus, 22
Counts, George, 182
Coursework model of professional development, 248
Creative intelligence, 40
Creative thinking, 172
Criterion-referenced testing, 217, 218, 224
Critical thinking, 172
  case studies in, 175, 179, 180–181, 184, 186, 187
  concepts for, 173
  described, 172, 174–175
  etymology of, 172
  instruction in, 174
  literate, 172–173
  strategies for, 173, 174, 175–176
  strategies for developing, 180
  structures in, 179
  student strategies for, 178–179
Critical thinking educational philosophy, 179
  case studies of, 180–181, 187–188
  development of, 181–182, 185
Curricular validity, 217
Curriculum
  and change, 235
  compacting of, 86
  as fait accompli, 48
  intensive vs. extensive, 48
  model for, 48
  special education, 102
  spiral, 72
Curriculum Frameworks, 196

Darwin, Charles, 22
Decision making, 49
  model for, 49, 50
Decoding, of words, 155
Deductive lesson design, 76
Deductive reasoning, 76, 176, 177
Democratic planning, of lesson, 64
Demonstration mountain, 88
Descartes, René, 22
Describing activities, 80
Describing stage, in reflective thinking, 63
Developmental constructivism, 27
Developmental process, 27
Developmental standards, 196
Developmental theory of cognition, 26
Dewey, John, 9, 25, 61, 62, 172, 182, 183, 237
Differentiated instruction, 81–82
  flow chart for, 85
  guidelines for, 84–86
  implementation of, 84
  types of, 84
Direct instruction, 207
Direct instruction practices, 10–11
  benefits and drawbacks of, 12–13
  exercise on, 16
  indications for, 11
  types of, 12–13
Direct Questioning Activity (DQA), 177
Directed Reading Lessons (DRL), 153
  sample, 154
Discipline, 128
  types of, 123
Discourse, 112
Discovery, in learning cycle, 54
Discovery approach, 8–9
Discovery learning, 72
  distinguished from guided discovery learning, 73
Discussion
  benefits and drawbacks of, 12–13
  small group, 13
Discussion approach, 10
Distress, defined, 34
Diversity, 7
  exercise on, 8
  and inclusion, 102
  and multicultural education, 103
Domain knowledge, 149
Drill questions, 76
Drills, in lesson, 64
Dyslexia, 112
  myths about, 113
  treatment of, 112–113

Eclectic model, 22
  commonsense aspects of, 29–30
  premises of, 29
  teaching behaviors in, 29
  variations on, 32–34

Eclectic strategies, 129
Edible reinforcers, 24
Education for All Handicapped Children Act, 98
Educational standards, 196
 defined, 192
Effective teaching, 4
 assessment and evaluation and, 225
 behaviors in, 5, 245–246, 247
 beliefs in, 127–129
 case studies about, 6, 243–245, 254–255
 cases from the field about, 17–18
 and change, 234
 characteristics of, 5
 classroom design and, 7
 cultural awareness and, 7
 discovery approach to, 8–9
 discussion approach to, 10
 and diversity, 7
 exercise on, 3, 5
 expository approach to, 8
 inquiry approach to, 9–10
 keys to, 247
 methodology and, 76–77
 personality and, 234
 reflection and self-evaluation in, 226–227
 teacher empowerment and, 238
 teacher personality and, 4, 5
Efficacy in action model, 134–135
Embedded phonics, 150
Emotional intelligence, 40
Emotional problems, 140
 strategies for overcoming, 140–141
 warning signs of, 140
Emotions
 in learning, 35, 36
 and patterning, 37
Enrichment
 essentials of, 86
 exercise for, 86
 SEM model, 86–87
Enthusiasm, of teacher, 5, 208
Environmental adaptations, in special education, 102
Environmental model of behavior, 122
Environmental process, 27
Environmental theory, 27
Erikson, Erik, 25, 32–33
Essay tests, 220
 defined, 224
 one-minute, 222
 rubric for grading, 221
Essentialism, 182
Eugenics, 39
Eurythmy, 91
Eustress, 34
Evaluation
 defined, 224
 in lesson plan, 60
 of lesson plan, 65–66
 questions for, 74
 special education, 99
 See also Assessment; Testing
Examinations, history of, 193
Existential intelligence, 38
Existentialism, 182
 tenets of, 183
Expectations, 2
 establishing, 208
 importance of, 5
Experience, and learning, 35
Explaining, in lesson, 53
Explicit text instruction, 177
Exploration, in learning cycle, 54
Expository approach, 8
Extensive curriculum, 48
Extinction, 24
Extrinsic motivation, 52

Fact questions, 76
Fantasy stage of teaching, 4
Finn, Chester, 88
Five Factor model, 2
Fluency, defined, 149, 150
Fluency-Oriented Reading Instruction (FORI), 166
Formal operational stage, 26
Formative assessment, 225
 defined, 224
Four Blocks Approach (FBA), 166
Fourth grade slump, 148
Freire, Paulo, 182
Freud, Sigmund, 32
Functional Behavioral Assessment (FBA), 176–177
Functional literacy, 173
Functional standards, 296

Gagnon and Collay model, 54
Galton, Francis, 39
Gardner, Howard, 25, 38, 39, 81, 84
Gender
 case study of, 163–164
 and learning style, 161
 as literacy issue, 160–161
 readings in, 163
 research on, 161–162
Gender-specific teaching, 160–161
Generativity vs. stagnation, Eriksonian stage, 33
Geometric reasoning, levels of, 196
Gifted, inclusion of, 102, 103
Gilligan, Carol, 160
Ginott, Haim, 136
Ginott model, 136–138
Glass, Gerald and Esther, 155
Glass method, 155
 for decoding words, 155
 principles of, 156
Glasser, William, 138

Goals
 in lesson plan, 60
 topic, 49, 50
Goals 2000: Educate America Act, 194, 195, 236
Goddard, Henry, 40
Goleman, Daniel, 28
Good boy–nice girl orientation, 32
Gough method, 154
 distinguished from whole-language approach, 158
Grade-level standards, 196
 defined, 192
Graphemes, 150
Great Books, 182
Gronlund, Norman, 51
Group brainstorming, 14
Group guidance approach, 126
 and IOSIE method, 126–127
Group guidance control models, 134–136
Group investigations, 81
Grouping, 64, 77
 by ability, 78, 79
 by ability within class, 78
 by age, 78
 exercise on, 79
 heterogeneous, 79
 nongraded, 78
Growth model approach, 227
Guest speakers, 13
Guidance approach, 125
 and IOSIE method, 125–126
Guidance models, 136–140
Guidance strategies, 129
Guided discovery, 8
Guided discovery learning, 72–73
 benefits of, 73
 distinguished from discovery learning, 73
Guided practice, 57, 58
Guided response, 75
Guiding questions, in lesson plan, 60

Half-day model of professional development, 248
Heart intelligence, 40–41
 keys to, 41
Helmholtz, Hermann von, 41
Hemisphericity, 34, 36
Heterogeneous grouping, 79
Hierarchy of needs, 31, 41
Highly effective teachers. *See* Effective teaching
Hirsch, E. D., 148
Hoff, David, 214
Homework, 52
 for lesson, 64
 pros and cons of, 53
Howard's efficacy model, 134–135
Humanism, 181

Hunter, Madeline, 58, 59, 60
Hutchins, Robert, 182

Idealism, 181
Identity vs. role confusion, Eriksonian stage, 33
Illiteracy, 173
Implicit text instruction, 177
Inclusion, 101
  case studies of, 115–116
  diversity and, 102–103
  of the gifted, 102, 103
  of LD students, 109
  research on, 102
  strategies for, 102
Independent practice, 57, 58
Indirect instruction practices, 11–12
  benefits and drawbacks of, 13–15
  exercise on, 16
  types of, 13–15
Individualized Educational Plan (IEP), 98, 99
  under IDEA, 100–101
Individuals with Disabilities Education Act (IDEA PL 105-17), 97, 98
  function of, 100
Individuals with Disabilities Improvement Act (IDEA), 97, 98
  early intervention in, 101
  eligibility for services under, 101
  principles of, 100
  provisions of, 100–101
  strategy for, 100
Inductive lesson design, 76
Inductive reasoning, 76, 176, 177
Initiative vs. guilt, Eriksonian stage, 33
Input, 58
  in lesson design, 57
Inquiry approach, 9–10
Instructional clarity, 208
Instructional paradigm, 2–3
Instructional strategies, 129
Instrumental-relativist orientation, 32
Integrity vs. despair, Eriksonian stage, 33
Intelligence(s)
  case studies about, 43–44
  and learning, 37–38
  multiple, 25, 38, 42, 43
  testing of, 37, 40, 193, 214–215
  traditional models of, 39–40
  triarchic theory of, 40
Intelligence Quotient (IQ), 37, 214–215
  Stanford-Binet, 40
Intensive curriculum, 48
Internalizing values, 75
Interpersonal concordance orientation, 32
Interpersonal intelligence, 38
Interpretations, in ICON model, 54

Interstate New Teacher Assessment and Support Consortium (INTASC), 202
  case study about, 200–201
  standards of, 202–203
Intimacy vs. isolation, Eriksonian stage, 33
Intrapersonal intelligence, 38
Intrinsic motivation, 52
Invention, in learning cycle, 54
IOSIE method, 122–123
  action research in, 214
  case studies of, 124–127, 144, 145–146
  components of, 123–124
  and consequence approach, 124–125
  and critical thinking, 175–176
  and group guidance approach, 126–127
  and guidance approach, 125–126
Iowa Test of Basic Skills, 215

J.E.K. model, 59
James, William, 181
Japanese Lesson Study, 206
Jigsaw learning, 81
Job interviews, 250
  assessment scale for, 252
  common questions for, 251
  format for, 250–251
  preparation for, 251, 252
  self-assessment for, 253
Jones, Fredric, 132
Jones model, 132–134
Journal articles, evaluating, 165
Judicious discipline, 123
Judicious discipline model, 135–136

Kamehameha Early Child Education Program (KEEP), 166
Kelly, Fredrick, 193
Kierkegaard, Soren, 182
Kilpatrick, William Heard, 183
Kinesthetic intelligence, 38
King, Samuel, 193, 214
Knowledge, 40
  concretizing, 35
  constructivist vs. traditional view of, 27
  of learning and development principles, 5
Knowledge questions, 74
Kohlberg, Lawrence, 25, 31–32
KWHL method, 154
KWL method, 153–154, 155

Language, aspects of, 112
Language arts, sample standards for, 206
Language disorders, 107

Law and order orientation, 32
Learning
  accelerating, 35–36
  behaviorist approach to, 22, 23–25
  brain role in, 33–37, 41–42
  case studies about, 43–44
  constructivist approach to, 22, 25–29
  contrasts among approaches to, 30–31
  cooperative learning, 79–81
  discovery, 72, 73
  eclectic approach to, 22, 29–34
  enhancing, 34, 36
  guided discovery, 72–73
  intelligence and, 37–38
  mastery, 73, 74
  multiple intelligences and, 81, 82
  questioning and, 75–76
  and search for meaning, 37
  seven-step model of, 58
Learning cycle instructional model, 54
Learning disabilities, 36, 105–106
  case studies of, 108–109, 113–116
  characteristics of, 107
  defined, 106
  emotional aspect of, 108
  inclusion and, 109
  teaching in the face of, 107–108
  types of, 107
Learning paradigm, 2–3
Learning skills, 40
Learning team model, 139
Least Restrictive Environment, 100
Lecture, benefits and drawbacks of, 12
Lecture and discussion, benefits and drawbacks of, 12
Lesson design
  backward, 53–54, 55, 56–57
  case study in, 59–60
  components of, 57
  constructivist, 53, 55
  deductive, 76
  desired results of, 53–54
  exercise for, 58
  inductive, 76
  traditional, 54–56, 59
Lesson evaluation, 64
Lesson planning, 48
  best practices for, 207–208
  elements of, 60
  importance of, 59
  reflective, 61–62
  sample format for, 61
  sample plan, 62
  standards and, 204–208
  student role in, 48
  variety in, 61
Lesson presentation, 53
Lesson study, 206
Limbic system, 34
Lindquist, Everett, 193

Literacy
    case studies in, 163–165, 167–168, 168–169
    components of, 149
    future research in, 162–163
    and gender, 160
    models of, 156, 160
    program elements for, 167
    programs to improve, 165–166
    research in, 149–152
    socioeconomic issues in, 148–149
    teaching approaches for, 148, 152–163
    types of, 173
Literate critical thinking, 172–173
    guide to, 173

Maas model, 57, 59
MacLean, Paul, 34
Mager, Robert, 51
Mainstreaming, 101
    case studies of, 115–116
Mammalian brain, 34
Mann, Horace, 193
Maslow, Abraham, 25, 31
Mastery, 2
    as stage of teaching, 4
Mastery learning, 73
    components of, 74
Matching questions, 221–222
Material reinforcers, 24
Mathematical disorders, 107
Mathematical intelligence, 38
McTighe, Jay, 56
Mean, defined, 224
Meaning, search for, 37
Meaningful reception, 8
Measurement. *See* Assessment; Testing
Mechanism, defined, 75
Median, defined, 224
Meier, Deborah, 208
Melanchthon, Philip, 192
Memory
    organization of, 37
    triggering, 35
Meritocratic society, 215
Metacognitive skills, 40
Metadate, 110
Methods
    case studies in, 92–94
    in teaching, 2, 5
    types of, 71–92
Methylphenidate, 110
Micro peer teaching, 226, 227
Misbehavior, 122
    causes of, 122, 123
        IOSIE method and, 122–127
Mixed-age grouping, 78
Mixed-model methodology, 227
Mnemonics, 207
Modeling, 58

in lesson design, 57
Montessori, Maria, 25, 88
Montessori method
    contrasted with traditional methods, 89
    exercise for, 90
    history of, 88
    principles of, 88, 90
Moral development, 32
Motivation, 40, 52
    in lesson, 64
Motor function disorders, 107
Multi-age grouping, 78
Multicultural education, 103
    aspects of, 103–104
    case study of, 104–105
    and culture building, 105
    goals of, 105
    political correctness and, 105
    views on, 105
Multimedia, in indirect instruction, 14
Multiple intelligences theory, 25
    case study in, 42, 43
    components of, 38–39
    criticisms of, 39
    learning based on, 81, 82
    self-test on, 83
Multiple-choice tests, 193, 224
    question preparation for, 220
Musical intelligence, 38

National Board of Professional Teaching Standards (NBPTS), 198–201
    certification by, 200
    propositions of, 201
National Performance Standards, 204
Neo-reconstructionism, 182
Neocortex, 34
Neoprogressives, 184
New Standards, 204
No Child Left Behind Act (NCLB), 49, 62, 98, 149, 165, 215, 227
Nongraded grouping, 78
Norm, defined, 224
Norm-referenced testing, 217, 218, 224

Objective testing, 219, 224
Objective-based budgeting, 235
Objectives, 58
    behavioral, 51
    exercise in writing, 52
    in J.E.K. model, 59
    of lesson, 64
    in lesson design, 57
    for planning, 51
    taxonomy of, 74
    topic, 50–51
Observation
    case studies of, 66–67, 67
    evaluation form for, 65–66

in ICON model, 54
of lesson, 64
narrative report for, 66
narrative/checklist form for, 66
Onset, defined, 150
Onset-rime phonics instruction, 150
Open Education, 184
Operant conditioning, 23
    refutation of, 138
Organization, defined, 75
Origination, 75
Outcome-based education (OBE), 86–87, 205, 206

Paideia program, 90
    framework of, 91
    principles of, 91
Pantheon Program, 175, 176
Parents
    and change, 235
    role of, in special education, 99, 102
Parker, Francis, 183
Participatory school-based inquiry projects, 248–249
Pavlov, Ivan, 22, 25, 138
Peabody Language Development Kit, 166
Pedagogy, 8
Peer tutoring, 102
Perception
    learning, 37
    defined, 75
Perennialism, 181–182
Performance criteria, defined, 224
Performance standards, 196, 204
    defined, 192
    history of, 192
    for students, 201–202
Permissive strategies, 129
Personality, in teaching, 1–2, 4, 5, 234
    case studies of, 254
Phonemes, 112, 150
Phonemic awareness, 150
Phonics
    defined, 150
    perspectives on, 158
    and reading instruction, 154–155
Phonological awareness, 150
Piaget, Jean, 8, 25, 26, 27, 32, 33, 91, 182
Pipher, Mary, 160
Pivotal questions, in lesson, 64
Placement, for special education, 99
Political correctness, 105, 106
Pollack, William, 162
Portfolios, 193
    defined, 224
    preparing, 223
Positron emission tomography (PET), 33
Post-conventional moral reasoning, 32

Practical intelligence, 40
Pragmatism, 181
Pre-conventional moral reasoning, 32
Predictive validity, 217
Prelogical knowledge, 26
Preoperational stage, 26
Preparation, of lesson, 64
Preparing Instructional Objectives, 51
Presentation, of lesson, 53
Professionalization, 247
Progressive view of education, 194, 195
Progressivism, 182–183
    branches of, 184
    legacy of, 184
Project building, 80
Psychodynamic model of behavior, 122
Psychomotor domain, 75
Psychosexual development, Freudian view of, 32
Psychosocial development, Eriksonian view of, 33
Punishment, 23, 24
    as motivation, 52
Punishment-obedience orientation, 32
Purpose, in lesson design, 57
Push-in services, 102

Questions
    design of, 76, 77
    drill (fact), 76
    guiding, 60
    pivotal, 64
    and thinking, 75–76
    types of, 74

Racism, 104, 105
Rapport, in lesson, 64
Rationale, in J.E.K. model, 59
Reading comprehension, standards for, 197, 198
Reading disorders, 107
Reading First, 165
Reading gap, 148–149
Reading guide ladder, 150
Reading Roots, 166
Reading Wings, 166
Realism, 181
Reality therapy, 123, 139–140
Reasoning skills, 207
Recall, in expository approach, 8
Receiving phenomena, 75
Reconstructing stage, in reflective thinking, 63
Reconstructionism, 182
Reflection-for-action, 63
Reflection-in-action, 63
Reflection-on-action, 63
Reflective teaching, 63
Reflective thinking, 63, 172
Rehabilitation Act of 1973, 98
Reinforcement, 24
    contingencies of, 23
    in lesson, 53
Reinforcers, types of, 24
Relating skills, 207
Reliability, 217, 224
Remembering skills, 207
Reorganizing skills, 207
Reptilian brain, 34
Research surveys, 15
Resource utilization, 5, 208
Resources, in lesson plan, 60
Responding to phenomena, 75
Response-cost procedures, 24
Review, in lesson, 64
Rewards, as motivation, 52
Rime, defined, 150
Ritalin, 110
Role playing, in indirect instruction, 14
Rousseau, J. J., 181
Routines, in lesson, 64
Rubric, defined, 224

Sampling, defined, 224
Sartre, Jean-Paul, 182
SCARPO, 173, 176
Schemas, 27
Scholastic Aptitude Test (SAT), 215
School change
    components of, 237
    issues in, 236–238
School Enrichment Model (SEM), 86–87
School-Based Management/Shared Decision Making (SBM/SDM), 238
Self-assessment, 226
    defined, 224
    tips for, 226
Self-directed instruction, Montessori method as, 88
Selye, Hans, 34
Semantics, 112
Seminar model, 10
Seminars, 177
    roles and tasks in, 178
Senses, in learning, 36
Sensorimotor stage, 26
Set, defined, 75
Set induction, 53
Seven-step model of learning, 58, 60
Sexual harassment, 142
Shanker, Albert, 79, 103
Short-answer tests, 193
    question preparation for, 219–220
Shyu, Jessica, 56–57
Single Photon Emission Computed Tomography (SPECT), 234
Single-sex schools, 162
Sizer, Theodore, 182
Skill acquisition model, 49
Skinner, Burrhus Frederic, 22–23, 25
Small-group discussion, 13, 15
Small-group instruction, contrasted with cooperative learning, 80
Smart classroom, 7, 8
SMART objectives, 50
Social constructivists, 27, 28
Social contract–legalistic orientation, 32
Social progressives, 184
Social promotion, 78
Social reconstructionists, 184
Sociocultural theory of cognition, 27
Socrates, 76
Socratic method, 10, 72, 177–178, 207
    sample questions for, 178
Sommers, Christina Hoff, 160
Spady, W. G., 87, 206
Special education
    case studies of, 113–116
    defined, 98
    history of, 98
    inclusion in, 101–103
    legal mandate for, 98
    positives and negatives of, 99
    referral for, 98–99
    strategies for, 113
Spelling, phonics instruction based on, 150
Spiral curriculum, 72, 162
SQ4R approach, 152–153
STAD (student teams–achievement divisions), 81
Staff development models, 248–249
Stage theory, 26
Standardized testing
    defined, 224
    See also Assessment
Standards
    analyzing, 205–206
    and assessment, 192–194
    benefits and drawbacks of, 209
    case studies of, 200–204, 208 210–211, 228, 229–230
    and change, 235
    in the classroom, 207
    defining, 194–196
    and daily practice, 196–197
    functional, 206
    history of, 192–193
    identifying, 205
    and lesson planning, 204–208
    meeting, 207
    need for and purposes of, 209
    state, 199
    student performance, 192, 204
    for teachers, 198–200
    in traditional vs. progressive schools, 193–194, 195
    types of, 192, 196–197
Standards Achievement Planning Cycle (SAPC), 205–206

Standards-Based Classroom Operator's Manual, 204
Stanford Achievement Test, 215
Stanford-Binet IQ test, 40
StaR procedure, 166
Steiner, Rudolf, 90, 91, 92
Stern, William, 37
Sternberg, R. G., 39
Stimulus-response theory, 23
   refutation of, 138
Student teaching, case study of, 249–250
Student team learning, 81
Students
   basic needs of, 138
   role in lesson planning, 48
Subjective testing, 219, 224
Success for All (SFA), 166–167
Summaries, in lesson, 52, 64
Summative assessment, 225
   defined, 224
Supervision, of teaching, 65–67
Support services, for special education, 102
Survival stage of teaching, 4
Syllable, defined, 150
Synectics, 207
Syntax, 112
Synthesis, 74
Synthetic phonics, 150
Systemic change model, 234

Taylor, Frederick, 236
Teacher Empowerment Model to Improve Learning Outcomes, 238–240
   diagram of, 239
   studies of, 240–243
Teachers
   assessment of, 246
   characteristics of, 246–247
   empowerment of, 242, 254
   inexperienced, 4
   master, 4
   personality of, 1–2, 4, 127–128
   shortages and surpluses of, 121
   standards for, 198–200, 205
   supervision and observation of, 64–66
   termination of, 121
   traits affecting teaching, 5
Teaching
   accountability in, 49
   decision making about, 49–50
   differentiated instruction, 81–82, 84–85
   effective. *See* Effective teaching
   keys to effectiveness of, 2
   for literacy, 147–170
   mastery of, 4
   paradigms for, 2–3
   about thinking, 76
   for thinking, 75
   of thinking, 75
   with thinking, 76
   variations in, 5, 208
Teaching strategies, in lesson plan, 60
Team building, 249
Technology
   and change, 235
   in classroom, 7
   in indirect instruction, 14
The Technology of Teaching, 23
Terman, Lewis, 40, 214, 215
Testing
   essay, 220
   forms of, 218–219
   improvement of, 219
   matching questions, 221–222
   multiple-choice, 193, 220, 224
   one-minute essay, 222
   practices in, 218–220
   short-answer, 193, 219–220
   for special education, 99
   subjective vs. objective, 219
   true/false, 222
   See also Assessment
Think-pair-share, 81
Thinking, modes of, 181
Thinking brain, 34
Thinking disorders, 107
Thinking skills, 40
   deductive vs. inductive, 76
   questioning and, 75–76
Thomas Aquinas, 182
Thompson, Michael, 162
Thorndike, Edward, 183, 214, 215
Time out, 24
Timing
   case study of, 68
   in lesson, 64
Topic aims, 49
   examples of, 49, 50
Topic goals, 49
   examples of, 49, 50
Topic objectives, 50
   examples of, 50–51
Traditional view of education, 194, 195
Transitions, to special education, 99
Transmission approach, 22
Transmission models, 27
Triarchic theory of intelligence, 40
Triune brain theory, 34–35
True/false questions, 222
Trust vs. mistrust, Eriksonian stage, 33
Tyler, Ralph, 51, 60

Understanding
   beliefs about, 128
   described, 127
   fostering, 2
Ungraded grouping, 78
Unit topic, in J.E.K. model, 59
Universal ethical principles orientation, 32
Usability, 217

Validity, 217, 224
Value-added assessment model, 227
Values, internalizing, 75
Values and character education, 15
Valuing, 75
van Hiele, Pierre, 196
van Hiele-Geldorf, Diana, 196
Verbal-linguistic intelligence, 38
Verbalizing, of content, 53
Visual intelligence, 41
Visual perception disorders, 107
Visual/spatial intelligence, 38
Vocabulary
   breadth of, 149 [ed: breath on 149]
   defined, 150
   development of, 151
   exercise in, 151
   tasks in, 151–152
Vygotsky, Lev, 25, 134

Waldorf School method, 90–91
   criticisms of, 92
Walsh, Pat, 34
Watson, John B., 22, 25
WHERE paradigm, 216
Whole-language approach, 148
   and balanced literacy, 157–160
   described, 156–157
   tenets of, 157
Wiggins, Grant, 56
Windows of opportunity, 36, 37
Written expression disorders, 107
Yerkes, David, 215

Zone of proximal development (ZPD), 134